Contributions to Management Science

The series *Contributions to Management Science* contains research publications in all fields of business and management science. These publications are primarily monographs and multiple author works containing new research results, and also feature selected conference-based publications are also considered. The focus of the series lies in presenting the development of latest theoretical and empirical research across different viewpoints.

This book series is indexed in Scopus.

José Duarte Santos · Paulo Botelho Pires ·
Joaquim Pratas
Editors

Artificial Intelligence Transforming Marketing

Renewed Theoretical Bases and New Paradigms

Springer

Editors
José Duarte Santos
CEOS.PP, ISCAP, Polytechnic of Porto
São Mamede de Infesta, Portugal

Paulo Botelho Pires
CEOS.PP, ISCAP, Polytechnic of Porto
São Mamede de Infesta, Portugal

Joaquim Pratas
CEOS.PP, ISCAP, Polytechnic of Porto
São Mamede de Infesta, Portugal

ISSN 1431-1941 ISSN 2197-716X (electronic)
Contributions to Management Science
ISBN 978-3-032-22359-3 ISBN 978-3-032-22360-9 (eBook)
https://doi.org/10.1007/978-3-032-22360-9

This Springer imprint is published by the registered company Springer Nature Switzerland AG
The registered company address is: Gewerbestrasse 11, 6330 Cham, Switzerland

Preface

Artificial Intelligence (AI) is profoundly transforming the world and redefining how organizations operate. Strategies, business models, decision-making processes, and day-to-day operations are being transformed at an unprecedented pace.

This transformation is particularly evident in the field of marketing, where increasingly personalized, data-driven, automated, and increasingly efficient practices are redefining how organizations and brands connect with people. At the same time, AI is unlocking new opportunities for organizations, boosting sales, enhancing customer satisfaction, streamlining processes, and ultimately increasing organizational profitability.

As a cornerstone of the ongoing digital transformation, AI can be seen as the engine powering deep structural change. It's not just about a technological shift. It's about a profound transformation in processes, internal culture, and how data is collected, interpreted, and used to generate value.

In marketing, AI signals a decisive shift from a predominantly communicational paradigm to one that is analytical, automated, responsive, and integrated across all organizational layers. With the evolution of digital marketing, this shift becomes even more pronounced. Strategies are now executed through digital platforms, real-time data flows, intelligent automation, advanced segmentation, and levels of personalization that were unimaginable just a few years ago.

Within this context, the application of AI to marketing activities (its impacts, opportunities, challenges, and the new skills it demands), has become one of the most relevant and widely discussed topics of recent years.

It was from this observation, that an initial idea developed by researchers from the Digital Marketing subgroup of the Communication and Technologies research group at the Center for Organizational and Social Studies of the Polytechnic Institute of Porto (CEOS.PP), evolved into this book. The work brings together contributions from these researchers as well as from professors and specialists from various institutions who joined the project. Across twenty chapters, the book "Artificial Intelligence Transforming Marketing: Renewed Theoretical Bases and New Paradigms" explores the many intersections between AI and Marketing.

The chapters address, among other themes, the transformations AI is driving in management and marketing, including:

- Market research and consumer behavior analysis.
- Challenges, opportunities, and ethical considerations in AI adoption.
- Decision-making processes within organizations.
- Customer relationships and the development of the marketing mix (including loyalty and personalization, environmental sustainability, content generation, sales force management, advertising communication, public relations and crisis management, customer service, and neuromarketing topics).
- Data usage, analytical approaches, and optimization of marketing activities through AI, including real-time value propositions and point-of-sale optimization.
- AI applications in business-to-business (B2B) markets.
- Digital influencers, chatbots, and new AI-mediated consumer experiences.
- The evolution of training and teaching practices in marketing management in this new era shaped by Digital Transformation and AI.

The diversity and depth of the topics presented reflect not only the scale of the transformations underway, but also the urgency of critically understanding AI's role in the present and future of organizations. This book aims to offer an integrated, multidisciplinary perspective capable of supporting research, professional practice, and skill development in a rapidly evolving landscape.

Our hope is that this book serves as a solid guide for interpreting the changes AI brings to marketing and management, while inspiring new approaches, strategies, and research paths.

We thank everyone who contributed to this work, especially the authors of each chapter, whose dedication and scientific rigor made this collective project possible, and the publisher who believed in its relevance.

We hope that teachers, researchers, students, and professionals in administration, marketing, and related fields will find in these pages a valuable resource for consultation, reflection, and deepening their understanding of AI, enabling them to apply this knowledge in their daily practice and contribute to more innovative, efficient, and future-ready organizations.

Porto, Portugal

José Duarte Santos
Paulo Botelho Pires
Joaquim Pratas

Contents

The Impact of Artificial Intelligence on Marketing Research

Andreia Ribeiro, Bruno Sousa, and Luzia Arantes

Abstract In the new era of Artificial Intelligence, all areas of marketing research are undergoing transition, with AI reshaping data collection, analysis, and decision-making. This chapter reviews how Artificial Intelligence is transforming research by enhancing data collection, analysis, and decision-making, while addressing ethical challenges and proposing a conceptual framework for responsible AI adoption. Through a conceptual methodology, this study aims to investigate how AI has influenced marketing research, identifying the principal changes that it generated, as well as the challenges and opportunities that arise. A literature review is conducted that presents the development of marketing research over the years and its synergy with technological advances, covering a study on critical AI capabilities such as machine learning and big data. This chapter describes the possibilities opened by AI, such as hyper-targeted personalisation in real time or data-driven decisions, with potential ethical and privacy issues, as well as algorithmic bias or transparency. In addressing these tensions, a conceptual model for the responsible adoption of AI in marketing research is proposed, bringing together technological, strategic/business development-oriented, and ethical aspects, as well as sustainability. The need for AI applications to be user-centred, ethical, and sustainable is highlighted, driving company advances to achieve a positive social impact beyond business growth. This study seeks to provoke critical thinking and suggest avenues for future research, together with practical implementation in the emerging field of AI use in marketing. The study supports SDG 9 (Industry, Innovation and Infrastructure) and SDG 12

A. Ribeiro · B. Sousa · L. Arantes (✉)
Polytechnic University of Cávado and Ave, Barcelos, Portugal
e-mail: lamorim@ua.pt

A. Ribeiro
e-mail: a20946@alunos.ipca.pt

B. Sousa
e-mail: bsousa@ipca.pt

L. Arantes
University of Aveiro, Águeda, Portugal

Sustainable Development Research Group, EKA, Riga, Latvia

J. D. Santos et al. (eds.), *Artificial Intelligence Transforming Marketing*, Contributions to Management Science, https://doi.org/10.1007/978-3-032-22360-9_1

(Responsible Consumption and Production) by promoting ethical and sustainable AI practices in marketing research.

1 Introduction

Over the past few decades, Artificial Intelligence (AI) has been one of many technologies and disciplines that have evolved rapidly across different areas, including management and marketing. AI has become central to both academic research and business practice, profoundly reshaping marketing research.

Recent contributions substantiate this trend, illustrating the transformation of predictive modelling, consumer analytics, and decision-making in marketing research through AI (Davenport et al., 2020; De Luca et al., 2021; Syam & Sharma, 2018).

This topic is also very relevant in the context of marketing research. AI-driven workflows are making huge breakthroughs, converting immense data into real-time examination and extracting concealed patterns yielding high presentiment accuracy; ultimately replacing traditional methodologies that were specifically developed to observe standalone activity. This redefinition changes the state of play not only for market research methods but also concerning some urgent ethical and social questions about privacy, algorithmic bias, or transparency.

Despite the growing number of studies, existing literature remains fragmented, often focusing on specific applications of AI rather than offering an integrative perspective. Few works attempt to consolidate the technological, ethical, and strategic implications of AI for marketing research into a comprehensive framework. This chapter seeks to address that gap.

Given the evolving nature of this field and the limited availability of consolidated empirical evidence, this chapter adopts a conceptual methodology. By integrating insights from the existing literature and theoretical perspectives, it aims to investigate how AI has influenced marketing research, identifying the principal changes that it generated, as well as the challenges and opportunities that arise. The objectives of this chapter are therefore threefold: To analyse how AI has transformed the methods, scope, and practices of marketing research; to develop a conceptual framework that integrates technological, strategic, and ethical dimensions of AI in this context; to highlight the challenges and opportunities that emerge, paving the way for more responsible and valuable AI methodologies in marketing.

To meet these goals, this chapter looks at the following research questions (RQ):

RQ1: How has AI altered the essence and execution of marketing research?
RQ2: What conceptual framework can encompass both the opportunities and the threats of AI in this field?
RQ3: What ethical, strategic, and social factors should be included in marketing research that uses AI?

This chapter is divided into several interconnected parts. Following this introduction, a literature review will be presented that contextualises the development of marketing research and AI. Next, a review of the main effects that AI has on gaining customer insights, personalisation, and strategy decoding will be presented. Next, the ethical, privacy, and bias challenges that arise as AI is introduced into this domain are presented. To conclude, a framework is developed that brings together the insights offered and provides avenues for future academic and practical research in AI within marketing.

2 Literature Review

2.1 The Evolution of Marketing Research

Marketing research has undergone a profound transformation since its inception, keeping pace with changes in economic, social, and technological paradigms. The first systematic manifestations of marketing research emerged in the early twentieth century, with companies recognising the need to better understand markets and consumers to make more informed business decisions (Berghoff et al., 2012). From the 1930s to the 1950s, traditional methods predominated, strongly anchored in quantitative and qualitative techniques such as interview surveys, opinion polls, and focus groups (Berghoff et al., 2012). These instruments allowed for the collection of primary data in a structured manner, albeit limited by the available technology and the need for physical contact with participants.

During the second half of the twentieth century, the growth of behavioural sciences and the development of more robust statistical models brought greater sophistication to marketing research (Williams, 1981). Market segmentation, multivariate analysis, and consumer behaviour theory became central pillars, underpinning strategic decisions based on empirical data (Wayne-Mitchell & Walsh, 2001). However, these methodologies remained largely linear, static, and dependent on samples limited in time and space, which restricted their ability to capture dynamics in increasingly volatile markets (Cui et al., 2025; Zhang et al., 2025).

The digital revolution of the last three decades has changed the face of marketing research into a new paradigm. Internet penetration across the globe, digitalisation of social and commercial exchanges with mobile devices, has fundamentally changed how data collection is done at scale (Abdoul Aziz et al., 2024). Big data has become a key part of this time. It gives us access to both structured and unstructured information from a wide range of sources, including social media, online transactions, and IoT devices. This kind of diversity makes it possible to get more insights, but it also makes it harder to compare and trust (Căuniac et al., 2025). At the same time, the constant collection of data in real time makes it possible to make behaviour profiles, which are used by AI-based decision support systems and predictive algorithms.

However, this potential is accompanied by ethical discussions regarding privacy and surveillance (Madanchian, 2024; Oğuz, 2024).

Another aspect of this evolution is social media analytics. Revolutionised digital marketing, social media are not only new channels for brands to communicate, advertise or sell products, but they also provide vast amounts of customer data on preferences, behaviours and interactions (Oğuz, 2024; Walsh & Feigh, 2022). Sentiment analysis, mention monitoring, and influencer mapping are no longer the stuff of fiction, as brands generate much more advanced insights through these processes than was ever possible with traditional methodologies (Lee et al., 2024; Xu et al., 2024). Mobile research also offers the added dimension of closeness and in-the-moment spontaneity, meaning we can even capture people directly after, during or right before their experience occurs without any retrospective mediation (or bias), recycling experiences from memory (Stocchi et al., 2022; Vercammen et al., 2023).

Yet at the same time, it is not easy or always possible to move wholly into digital. Conventional methods, even when deemed antiquated, still provide substantial benefits like analytical depth, variable control, and methodological strictness. They allow for richer, more qualitative, reflective, and situation-specific types of social and cultural explanation, which should form the basis of our understanding of consumer behaviour (Patel et al., 2023; Rokka, 2021). At the same time, digital approaches have come under considerable scrutiny for concerns around data accuracy and generalisability associated with some practices (Hair & Sarstedt, 2021); lack of informed consent in certain contexts (Hanlon & Jones, 2023); as well as challenges of deriving insights from voluminous unstructured sources (Hewett & Lehmann, 2021).

Further maturation of methodologies is for integrating traditional and digital research sources, especially in data triangulation, metric comparability, and ethical approaches to handling information (Ahmad Al Serhan & Zhang, 2025). Further, the increasing reliance on algorithms and automated models may result in biases being propagated as well as distortions that can have significant ethical and social consequences (Akter et al., 2022).

Even with these improvements, there are still tensions between traditional and digital methods. Digital approaches offer unprecedented scale and speed, while traditional methods continue to provide contextual depth, interpretative richness, and methodological rigour. This coexistence highlights both complementarities and contradictions, particularly regarding validity, interpretability, and ethical safeguards. As markets become increasingly dynamic, AI has emerged as a key technological enabler for addressing these challenges, supporting more integrated, adaptive, and data-driven forms of marketing research.

2.2 *Artificial Intelligence: Concepts and Capabilities*

The intelligence is generally conceived as the ability to process information and adjust to the environment, despite the limited amount of knowledge or resources (C. X. Wang et al., 2020). It may be defined as an ongoing act of studying and representation of actual or abstract phenomena (Shevchenko & Sosnitsky, 2020) which can be either natural or artificial (Havlík, 2019). Even though dictionaries disagree on which definition of AI to provide (Russell & Norvig, 2020), it is not an exception when it comes to developing concepts because, as Wang (2019) notes, this is typical of such concepts.

The initial views placed AI as an attempt to model human intelligent activity using computational systems (Simon, 1995), which allowed the machines to execute the tasks that are traditionally performed by intelligent agents (McCarthy, 2007; Prentice et al., 2020). AI has thus been defined as the behaviour of machines and software who can serve as assistants to individuals or businesses (Prentice et al., 2020) or the simulation of human cognition by a computer (Wang et al., 2020). According to other authors, AI is a general category of technologies that can identify, interpret, teach, and exhibit higher levels of cognition (McCartney & McCartney, 2020). Such behaviour can be enclosed in systems of software or hardware like robots (European Commission, 2018). Limna et al. (2021) point out the symbolic union of intelligeness and artificially to refer to a man-made type of thinking capacity.

The concept of AI is closely associated with the idea that machines are expected to imitate the human mental processes, by means of algorithms and computational models (Pantano & Scarpi, 2022). An intelligent system has shared two key attributes, which include perception of the surrounding environment and learning through actions to optimise performance (Gretzel, 2011). According to Russell and Norvig (2020), AI views fall into the category of human thinking, human behaviour, rational thinking, and rational behaviour. Pennachin and Goertzel (2007) also include that AI systems should possess specialised knowledge and demonstrate analytical and emotional intelligence.

There are three essential components to the development of AI, namely algorithms, big data, and processing power (Bulchand-Gidumal, 2022; Knani et al., 2022). The following elements have progressed greatly with the improvements in data accessibility, algorithm complexity, and computational power (Bulchand-Gidumal, 2022).

Several typologies exist. Kaplan and Haenlein (2019) make a distinction between Artificial General Intelligence (AGI) and Artificial Narrow Intelligence (ANI), whereas Huang & Rust (2018) differentiate between mechanical, analytical, intuitive and empathetic AI. According to Pantano and Scarpi (2022), there are types that are based on logical-mathematical, social, visual-spatial, linguistic, and processing intelligence. Moreover, there are seven further subfields of AI, such as knowledge representation, reasoning, planning, decision-making, optimisation, machine learning, and algorithms (Latah & Toker, 2019). Philosophically, AI can be considered weak or strong based on its flexibility, autonomy, and resemblance to the human reasoning (Bariah & Debbah, 2024; Wirth, 2018). It has even been suggested to employ hybrid forms which are combinations of the two extremes (Bulchand-Gidumal, 2022; Russell & Norvig, 2020).

This notwithstanding diversity, most typologies boil down to identifying patterns, learning through data, and acting out of information. To relate AI concepts to marketing research, a general differentiation between narrow and general capabilities, task-focused, and consumer-facing applications is a wide enough concept to have in this chapter (Kong et al., 2023).

In the context of AI, there are a few technologies that should be mentioned robotics, machine learning, deep learning, big data, natural language processing, and chatbots (Aldoseri et al., 2023) in a nutshell which are presented in Table 1.

These AI typologies have big effects on marketing research because they make it possible to do things like advanced segmentation, personalisation, and predictive insights that weren't possible with older methods.

Table 1 Concepts of artificial intelligence

Concept	Definition	Author
Robotics	An interdisciplinary field that integrates computer science and the technology of designing, building, operating, and using automated machines capable of performing tasks autonomously or semi-autonomously. Robotics is used to maximise process efficiency	Wewerka and Reichert (2023)
Machine learning	A subfield of AI that focuses on developing algorithms and statistical models that enable computers to learn and perform tasks without being programmed to do so. They identify patterns in data and make predictions or decisions based on those patterns. Machine learning is found in virtual assistants and self-driving cars	Abdel-Jaber et al. (2022)
Deep learning	A subfield of machine learning that uses multi-layered artificial neural networks to model data representations at hierarchical levels. It is capable of automatically learning complex data characteristics, enabling tasks such as speech recognition and natural language processing	Khosravani et al. (2023)
Big data	A set of data characterised by its high volume, velocity, variety, and veracity, which requires special analytical methods and software technologies. The analysis of unemployment and prices are example of aspects that can be analysed by big data	Sharda (2021)
Natural language processing	A subfield of AI that enables computers to understand, interpret, and generate human language in a meaningful way. It involves the analysis and manipulation of text and speech to perform tasks such as machine translation and chatbots	Chandrakala et al. (2024)
Chatbots	Software systems are designed to simulate human conversations, enabling automated interactions between humans and machines. They use natural language processing and machine learning to understand and respond to users.	Lin et al. (2023)

Source Authors

These ideas and abilities help us understand what AI can do, but the most important question for this chapter is how they change marketing research. The next subsection addresses this issue directly.

3 Method

This chapter adopts a conceptual approach, appropriate for a field that is still emerging and fragmented, such as Artificial Intelligence applied to marketing research. The existing literature reveals scattered contributions, focused mainly on specific applications, which reinforces the need for a synthesis that articulates technological, strategic, ethical, and social dimensions in an integrative framework.

To this end, a narrative review of the literature was conducted on an academic reference database (Web of Science), bringing together recent contributions on AI, marketing research, ethics, and sustainability. The comparative analysis of these works allowed us to identify convergences and gaps, from which we developed a conceptual framework that organises the impact of AI into four main dimensions. Although no empirical validation was conducted, this proposal paves the way for future studies that could test the model in different contexts and sectors.

4 Qualitative Analysis

This part is a synthesis of the qualitative findings of the available literature, critically evaluating the role of Artificial Intelligence in reinventing marketing research in four critical dimensions, including redefined methodology, consumer insight, personalisation, and strategic decision-making. All these developments are fundamentally associated with the issues of ethics, privacy, and sustainability, as they outline what opportunities and threats the field may entail. This analysis is refined with the subsections that follow and proceed to the specific thematic areas and define the conceptual framework that is proposed.

4.1 Consumer Insights and Predictive Analytics

The application of AI in marketing research has enabled significant advances in how organisations understand, segment, and interact with consumers (He & Zhang, 2023). Its aptitude for managing a large amount of data and recognising intricate patterns can drive exceptional segmentation at scale, as well as mass customisation in communication/product/experience (He & Zhang, 2023; Wang, 2022).

The capacity of AI to gather and process vast amounts of data revolutionises market segmentation for organisations. Unlike traditional demographic or geo criteria, AI tools let you establish dynamic and behavioural segments that are nimble enough to send targeted micro-segments (Wang, 2022).

This opens the door for hyper-contextualised personalisation, where messages, offers, and recommendations can be adapted live not only to consumers' profiles but current behaviour (both online and offline), location, device used at any time-point in a session, and even their mood (Oğuz, 2024; Teepapal, 2025). This way, the AI enables real-time, hyper-personalised marketing (Gao & Liu, 2023), as seen in leading digital platforms that continuously adapt messages and recommendations based on live user behaviour.

In addition, AI-based predictive analytics allows companies to predict future consumer behaviours and preferences with unprecedented accuracy (Oğuz, 2024). In practice, businesses use machine learning algorithms and modern data modelling to predict purchase intention, probability of churn behaviour, length of service, or volumes of emotional engagement (Zhao et al., 2023). Not only do these insights support better marketing strategies, but they also serve to intervene proactively, developing campaigns that increase customer engagement and therefore decrease churn (Wu et al., 2021).

It is particularly effective when predictive models are used to customise real-time recommendations in applications such as e-commerce sites, content delivery, or for online digital advertising (Oğuz, 2024). And these systems are learning, so marketers can recommend products or services informed by both individual and aggregated behavioural patterns, which better align with the current (and future) needs of consumers (Geetha & Karthika Renuka, 2024; Oğuz, 2024). This dynamic ability leads to a greater conversion rate, increased customer satisfaction, and loyalty over time (Sahne & Daronkola, 2025).

AI-powered recommendation and decision systems enable real-time personalisation on a large scale, converting individual signals into customised offers and experiences. In marketing research, this links measurement with activation, enabling researchers to assess the uplift and heterogeneity of treatment effects while overseeing privacy and fairness risks (Gao & Liu, 2023; Teepapal, 2025).

At the same time, AI enables the processing and consolidation of various data streams, from transactional records to click records, biometric sensors, and sentiment analysis, to compile a holistic consumer profile (Xing et al., 2023). It thus enables organisations to create much more detailed campaigns, so that the impact of their work exploits both reason and emotion, with a higher perceived value (Vrtana & Krizanova, 2023).

The ongoing learning undertaken by AI implies that this segmentation and personalisation are not set in stone; it develops over time to keep pace with consumer behaviour, which is fluid given how the digital landscape has evolved (Alijoyo et al., 2025). That evolution supports the made-to-measure consumer journeys that can be predicted to help consumers self-navigate down one of those pathways towards conversion, engagement, or advocacy (Gao & Liu, 2023).

And yet, despite the clear and unprecedented AI benefits in more advanced segmentation technology and predictive analysis capabilities, there exist ethical concerns regarding privacy of data use as well as transparency/reliability issues

Table 2 Impacts of AI on marketing research

Impact	Description	Real-world example
Consumer segmentation	Enables dynamic, behaviour-based segmentation beyond traditional demographic models	Netflix content recommendations based on viewing patterns
Real-time personalisation	Delivers hyper-personalised content, offers and messages adapted instantly to consumer behaviour and content	Amazon product suggestions during live browsing
Predictive analytics	Anticipates future consumer behaviours such as churn, engagement, or purchasing intent, allowing proactive marketing actions	Starbucks is tailoring campaigns using predictive insights
Automated recommendations	Provides personalised product, content, or service suggestions based on machine learning	Spotify generation based on listening history
Sentiment analysis	Extracts emotions and opinions from text or social media to inform marketing actions and brand positioning	Companies are monitoring twitter sentiment for brand feedback

Source Authors

surrounding factor-based bias inevitable at any algorithmic base layer (Akter et al., 2021; Al Haj Eid et al., 2024). This is why responsible AI practices are crucial to make personalisation efforts work towards consumer trust and not against it (Al Haj Eid et al., 2024).

The main impacts of AI on marketing research are summarised in Table 2.

The combination of these AI capabilities is fundamentally altering how organisations design marketing strategies, craft consumer journeys, and maintain ongoing engagement. The ability to process and act upon real-time insights allows for more adaptive, responsive, and human-centred marketing approaches.

At the same time, these innovations bring forth new challenges, particularly regarding ethical considerations, transparency, and consumer privacy, which are further explored in the following sections.

4.2 Decision-Making and Strategic Planning

As a core domain of impacts, as marketing research has become more data-driven over the years, strategic decision-making and long-term planning have started to rely on real-time analysis of high-volume datasets. The advent of AI as an important managerial enabling tool to assist the managers in opportunity identification, trend anticipation, and formulating more informed and adaptable strategies.

Russell and Norvig (2020) mention in their study that AI integrates machines equipped with intelligence and certain behaviours like those of humans, with applicability in businesses and companies to improve their operational efficiency. AI facilitates predictive and prescriptive analysis of data that, in turn, helps deliver better, quicker, and smarter insights (Lepenioti et al., 2021). It enables an evidence-based management model grounded on the identification of hidden patterns in the day-to-day uses and provides intuition or a limited historical perspective with a potential course of action (Besiri, 2024). The adoption of AI has led to the creation of innovative products/services, processes, business models, and social innovation (Mariani et al., 2023). In general, AI is a factor of change that will transform the production and consumption of goods and services and revise best practices (Kim et al., 2025).

The analysis of AI algorithms enables the identification of future trends from the consumer's perspective, allowing the hotel industry to optimise prices, stock management, and marketing strategies (Naqvi et al., 2023). Access to Big Data sources in the industry helps to expand the information network so that increasingly accurate forecasts of demand can be made, consumer profiles defined, and consumer needs identified (Buhalis, 2020; Nannelli et al., 2023). Using Big Data, it is also possible to ensure good marketing management, analyse financial and environmental performance, and understand consumer satisfaction (Lv et al., 2022).

For marketing research, these capabilities are not only about timely and improved accuracy in data collection/analysis, but also about how strategic decisions are continuously informed by insights (He & Zhang, 2023; Kumar et al., 2024). Thus, AI becomes fundamental in supporting the formation of market strategies, positioning, and consumer relations, with a direct impact on competitiveness and organisational innovation (El Fawal et al., 2024).

4.2.1 Ethical, Privacy, and Bias Concerns

As AI is increasingly adopted as part of market research, the ethical, bias, and privacy issues that come from using it cannot be ignored. These concerns become increasingly pressing as consumer data collection intensifies, often without explicit consent or understanding (Al Haj Eid et al., 2024; Oğuz, 2024).

Through this collection, many organisations can build extensive profiles of consumers by combining behavioural data with transactional data derived from credit card purchases or online transactions and even supplementing these with biometric data (Madanchian, 2024; Oğuz, 2024). At times, the line between personalisation and invasiveness is drawn in a shallow stream and companies that engage without transparency risk breaching consumer trust (Teepapal, 2025).

A key issue is the risk of biased algorithms. AI models are based on the dataset with which they were trained, and since this dataset is often biased due to historical social, cultural or organisational practices, these biases can go unnoticed or even be exacerbated by automated systems, which can then make biased decisions that affect different groups in unique ways (Akter et al., 2022; van Giffen et al., 2022). For example, algorithms for market segmentation may treat one group more favourably than another, ultimately departing from the principles of equity and inclusion.

Furthermore, many of these AI systems are too complex or lack transparency to fully explain algorithmic decisions, a problem known as the 'black box' (Von Eschenbach, 2021). This lack of transparency makes it difficult for organisations to explain their actions to the public and means that companies cannot easily identify errors or biases (Von Eschenbach, 2021).

Accountability also becomes a primary concern: if an AI decision harms someone, who is responsible? This legal and ethical uncertainty requires the establishment of robust AI governance structures, which should be guided by values such as fairness, accountability, transparency in decision-making processes, and respect for individual rights (Dokumacı, 2024; Kulaklıoğlu, 2024).

In general terms, legislation such as the General Data Protection Regulation and legality only takes you so far when it comes to ethical marketing research with AI (Meszaros & Ho, 2021). This implies a proactive, human-centred approach that aims to ensure that technologies are used to promote value, trust, and social well-being, rather than just maximising profits or operational efficiency (Sigfrids et al., 2023).

It is in this area that researchers and marketers need to be accountable for clear policies and procedures that protect safe and ethical frameworks, from system design to development and ongoing monitoring (Khan et al., 2023). To drive a more ethical, transparent, and sustainable marketing research ecosystem, adherence to the principles of 'responsible AI' (including technical systems) will be necessary, as well as collaboration between various stakeholders, such as technologists/marketers/legislators/civil society (Al Haj Eid et al., 2024; Ferrell & Ferrell, 2024; Habibipour, 2024).

These effects together led to the integrative framework in Sect. 5, which shows how technological capabilities, strategic use, ethics, and sustainability work together to create value for consumers in marketing research.

5 Proposed Conceptual Framework: The AI-Driven Marketing Research Model

The conceptual framework presented in Fig. 1 aims to facilitate understanding and summarise the main dimensions that represent the implications of AI in Marketing Research. It portrays a holistic perspective of AI, focusing beyond its technological advances and on its strategic, ethical, and social impacts, both in research and in marketing practice.

While the framework is an original contribution of this chapter, its construction was informed by previous perspectives on AI and marketing research (e.g., Wedel & Kannan, 2016; Davenport et al., 2020; De Luca et al., 2021), which provided the

Fig. 1 Conceptual framework on the impact of Artificial Intelligence on Marketing Research (proposed by the authors, conceptually inspired by Wedel & Kannan, 2016; Davenport et al., 2020; De Luca et al., 2021). *Source* Authors

conceptual foundation for integrating technological, strategic, ethical, and consumer-centric dimensions.

The construction of this framework directly mirrors the insights derived from the literature review. The historical progression of marketing research underscored the necessity for methodological innovation, whereas the examination of AI concepts illustrated its ability to manage complexity and scale. These insights guided the selection and organisation of the framework's components, guaranteeing that it is both theoretically sound and practically applicable.

The framework also makes it clear that segmentation and personalisation are two of the most important ways that AI can be used in marketing research. Segmentation is the ability to find smaller groups of customers by using advanced data clustering. Personalisation, on the other hand, is the ability to turn these insights into personalised interactions with each customer. Both blocks are connected to technology (like machine learning, natural language processing, and computer vision) and to making things that are valuable to consumers. The ethical and sustainability aspects were also broadened, emphasising not only concerns of privacy and bias but also the necessity of upholding fairness, transparency, and enduring social responsibility. The model shows how AI affects marketing research in a big way by giving a detailed explanation of how each block works and interacts with the others.

At the centre of this figure is Marketing Research, conceived as a disciplinary space in which all these dimensions meet. Artificial Intelligence has made a difference in how this field works, not only in methods and tools, but also in data collection (different types), data analysis, and application to convert that data into value.

AI capabilities, which are the basic definitions, concepts, and techniques that drive the evolution and development of future trends for interacting with marketing research, are the first step. Here, we can see how good the different components of AI can be, for example, if the algorithms are now highly condensed, but to optimally exploit their potential, it is worth adding machine learning or deep learning. These are the capabilities behind AI applications and their implications for marketing. For example, Walmart uses big data analytics to forecast consumer demand and manage inventory efficiently, reducing waste, and improving responsiveness.

The practical materialisation of these capabilities for use across various marketing research processes is called AI applications. It fits into the block on providing more meaningful insights, to drive data-based decision-making and mass personalisation using AI. These use-cases allow organisations to gain levels of segmentation, behaviour prediction and the creation of a personalised experience never seen before, becoming core pillars in competitive differentiation. For example, Netflix uses AI to recommend content based on viewing patterns, while Amazon dynamically personalises product suggestions during shopping sessions.

However, the increased use of AI in marketing research also raises several ethical issues that cannot be ignored. Still, these challenges raise valid concerns about consumer privacy, the unfair amplification of algorithmic bias, and black boxes in automated decision-making processes. How these ethical issues are addressed affects the effectiveness of AI-supported marketing, promoting consumer trust rather than generating scepticism or creating additional social divides. LinkedIn provides an example by auditing its algorithms to avoid discrimination in job recommendations, fostering inclusion and trust.

Sustainability is a strategic part of AI-driven marketing research. In addition to being a normative principle, it influences how data collection processes are set up (for example, by reducing the environmental impact of storage and computation), how long-term value creation is measured, and how social responsibility metrics are used in research.

Consumer-centric value it isn't just about personalisation; it can also be linked to things that can be measured, like customer satisfaction scores, retention rates, and how willing customers are to work with brands to make something new. These indicators make it possible to test how AI affects meaningful consumer experiences in real life.

The AI typologies block then presents the various practical ways of doing this, from mechanical and repetitive systems at one end of the spectrum to more analytical, curious, or perhaps empathetic approaches, together with a wide range of potential marketing applications. This typology helps us understand that different levels of AI sophistication and transformation are needed; we need the ability to select a standard tool and then adjust it as necessary, application by application. Each typology supports specific marketing needs, from automation to emotional engagement.

The arrows spreading across each block demonstrate how interrelated and fluid these dimensions are. The ecosystem is a complex and interactive system in which all elements are connected, so that technological capabilities affect applications, giving rise to ethical issues along the way, sustainability requirements define the behaviour of applications, and these dimensions must achieve an efficient balance to produce value for consumers. At this convergence between technology, ethical strategy, and society lies marketing research, as a discipline in constant reinvention.

Therefore, this conceptual framework aims to offer an integrated and holistic analytical lens for the advancement of future works in Artificial Intelligence and Marketing Research. Not only as a theoretical tool that wants to foster critical thinking, but also to support the establishment of some less problematic, ethically charged, and consumer-oriented practices when it comes to AI use in marketing.

Our model introduces two key innovations that set it apart from earlier frameworks in AI and marketing research (e.g., Davenport et al., 2020; Wedel & Kannan, 2016) that focus on either technological typologies or business applications. First, it makes ethical and sustainability factors operational drivers instead of things that are not very important. Second, it links AI-enabled processes directly to outcomes that are good for customers. This creates a link between what technology can do and what marketing can measure. These new ideas make the framework both new in theory and useful in practice.

6 Conclusions

This chapter will claim that artificial intelligence is not just an extension of the existing technological innovation but is a disruptive factor that alters the magnitude, approaches, and tactical importance of marketing research. AI not only makes it possible to produce highly granular and real time and predictive data, but also further intensifies the issue of privacy, transparency, and algorithmic fairness. The opportunities and threats of AI, in turn, require a cautious and ethically responsible implementation that will be based on human-centred and sustainability-focused principles.

One of the major contributions of the work is the conceptual framework that we suggest, and which incorporates the technological, strategic, ethical, and social dimensions into a single construct. Instead of treating AI as a collection of isolated tools, the framework makes it a part of a larger organisational and societal ecosystem, thus proposing responsible, context-aware, and value-oriented research practices.

This integrative approach adds novelty to the model because it takes the traditional fields of study that have been traditionally studied independently and provides an analytically consistent prism through which to comprehend how AI transforms marketing research. In addition, the framework highlights its practical applicability, which describes how a moderate and sensible implementation of AI could both enhance the scholarship and guide managerial decision-making simultaneously.

The discussed transformations are correlated with the desires of the Sustainable Development Goals, specifically SDG (Industry, Innovation and Infrastructure) 9 and SDG (Responsible Consumption and Production) 12. Ethical, inclusive, and sustainable marketing ecosystems could be created through responsible application of AI. Finally, informed, equitable decisions, reduce manipulation, and support sustainable value creation to the individual, organisations, and the society in general must be underpinned by AI-enabled research.

6.1 Theoretical Implications

The offered framework contributes to the theoretical knowledge in several ways. To begin with, it often integrates various sources of literature, AI abilities, marketing analytics, ethics, and sustainability, into a single conceptual framework, overcoming the problem of fragmentation that was discovered in the literature.

Second, it explains the redefinition of the fundamental elements of marketing research, especially segmentation, personalisation, and strategic decision-making by using AI, which presents an organised basis of future theoretical progress.

Lastly, the framework also allows considering ethical and sustainability concerns in the analytical model as a part of it and not as a limiting factor, which helps to create a more complete conceptualisation of responsible AI in marketing research.

6.2 Practical Implications

To practitioners, this chapter offers insights on how AI can be tactfully and ethically embraced within marketing research procedures. The model depicts how organisations can use AI to achieve better consumer knowledge, real-time personalisation, and decision-making based on evidence while mindful of such concerns as data protection, transparency, and equitability.

The framework also emphasises the significance of governance systems and cross-functional cooperation and provides a practical roadmap on implementing AI systems that develop trust, foster sustainable practices and meaningful value creation to consumers.

6.3 Future Research and Limitations

There are two limitations of this study. To begin with, the conceptual framework has not been empirically proved. Second, which is also connected to the fast development of AI technologies, some of the insights are going to become outdated as new methods will arise. Future studies thus ought to experiment the structure in various industries, study consumer attitudes towards AI-based research, and investigate the way ethical and sustainability values can be implemented in the real world.

References

Abdel-Jaber, H., Devassy, D., Al Salam, A., Hidaytallah, L., & El-Amir, M. (2022). A review of deep learning algorithms and their applications in healthcare. *Algorithms, 15*(2), 1–55. https://doi.org/10.3390/A15020071

Abdoul Aziz, H., Abba Ari, A. A., Ndam Njoya, A., Djedouboum, A. C., Mohamadou, A., & Thiare, O. (2024). A collaborative WSN-IoT-animal for large-scale data collection. *IET Smart Cities, 6*(4), 372–386. https://doi.org/10.1049/SMC2.12089

Ahmad Al Serhan, T. F., & Zhang, S. (2025). The paradox of digital marketing: Sustainable framework for effective strategies and regulatory challenges. *Information Development, 41*(2), 529–545. https://doi.org/10.1177/02666669241303451

Akter, S., Dwivedi, Y. K., Biswas, K., Michael, K., Bandara, R. J., & Sajib, S. (2021). Addressing algorithmic bias in AI-driven customer management. *Journal of Global Information Management (JGIM), 29*(6), 1–27. https://doi.org/10.4018/JGIM.20211101.OA3

Akter, S., Dwivedi, Y. K., Sajib, S., Biswas, K., Bandara, R. J., & Michael, K. (2022). Algorithmic bias in machine learning-based marketing models. *Journal of Business Research, 144*, 201–216. https://doi.org/10.1016/J.JBUSRES.2022.01.083

Al Haj Eid, M., Abu Hashesh, M., Ahmad Sharabati, A. A., Khraiwish, A., AL-Haddad, S., & Abusaimeh, H. (2024). International journal of data and network science conceptualizing ethical AI-enabled marketing: Current state and agenda for future research. *International Journal of Data and Network Science, 8*, 2291–2306. https://doi.org/10.5267/j.ijdns.2024.6.002

Aldoseri, A., Al-Khalifa, K. N., & Magid Hamouda, A. (2023). Re-thinking data strategy and integration for artificial intelligence: Concepts, opportunities, and challenges. *Applied Sciences, 13*(12), 1–33. https://doi.org/10.3390/APP13127082

Alijoyo, F. A., Aziz, T. S. A., Omer, N., Yusuf, N., Kumar, M. D., Ramesh, A. V. N., Ulmas, Z., & Baker El-Ebiary, Y. A. (2025). Personalized marketing: Leveraging AI for culturally aware segmentation and targeting. *Alexandria Engineering Journal, 119*, 8–21. https://doi.org/10.1016/J.AEJ.2025.01.074

Bariah, L., & Debbah, M. (2024). AI embodiment through 6G: Shaping the future of AGI. *IEEE Wireless Communications, 31*(5), 174–181. https://doi.org/10.1109/MWC.015.2300521

Berghoff, H., Scranton, P., & Spiekermann, U. (2012). The origins of marketing and market research: Information, institutions, and markets. In H. Berghoff, P. Scranton, & U. Spiekermann (Eds.), *The rise of marketing and market research* (pp. 1–26). Palgrave Macmillan. https://doi.org/10.1057/9781137071286_1

Besiri, D. (2024). AI-driven predictive analytics: Transforming decision-making in business. *Human Computer Interaction, 8*(1), 163–163. https://doi.org/10.62802/8NY1WW06

Buhalis, D. (2020). Technology in tourism-from information communication technologies to eTourism and smart tourism towards ambient intelligence tourism: A perspective article. *Tourism Review, 75*(1), 267–272. https://doi.org/10.1108/TR-06-2019-0258/FULL/XML

Bulchand-Gidumal, J. (2022). *Impact of artificial intelligence in travel, tourism, and hospitality* (pp. 1943–1962). Springer Books. https://doi.org/10.1007/978-3-030-48652-5_110

Chandrakala, C. B., Bhardwaj, R., & Pujari, C. (2024). An intent recognition pipeline for conversational AI. *International Journal of Information Technology (Singapore), 16*(2), 731–743. https://doi.org/10.1007/S41870-023-01642-8/FIGURES/20

Cui, Y., Sun, Z., Xiao, Y., Sha, Z., Koskinen, J., Contractor, N., & Chen, W. (2025). Network analysis of two-stage customer decisions with preference-guided market segmentation. *Journal of Computing and Information Science in Engineering, 25*(6), 1–15. https://doi.org/10.1115/1.4066420

Davenport, T., Guha, A., Grewal, D., & Bressgott, T. (2020). How artificial intelligence will change the future of marketing. *Journal of the Academy of Marketing Science, 48*(1), 24–42. https://doi.org/10.1007/S11747-019-00696-0/FIGURES/2

De Luca, L. M., Herhausen, D., Troilo, G., & Rossi, A. (2021). How and when do big data investments pay off? The role of marketing affordances and service innovation. *Journal of the Academy of Marketing Science, 49*(4), 790–810. https://doi.org/10.1007/S11747-020-00739-X/TABLES/7

Dokumacı, M. (2024). Legal frameworks for AI regulations. *Human Computer Interaction, 8*(1), 133–133. https://doi.org/10.62802/YTST2927

El Fawal, A., Mawlawi, A., Zakhem, N. B., Baydoun, H., Yassine, D., & Kassably, C. (2024). The impact of AI marketing activities on consumer-based brand equity: The mediating role of brand experience. *Journal of Infrastructure, Policy and Development, 8*(7). https://doi.org/10.24294/JIPD.V8I7.3851

Ferrell, O. C., & Ferrell, L. (2024). Building a better world: The role of AI ethics and social responsibility. *Journal of Macromarketing, 44*(4), 928–935. https://doi.org/10.1177/02761467241285793

Gao, Y., & Liu, H. (2023). Artificial intelligence-enabled personalization in interactive marketing: A customer journey perspective. *Journal of Research in Interactive Marketing, 17*(5), 663–680. https://doi.org/10.1108/JRIM-01-2022-0023/FULL/XML

Geetha, M. P., & Karthika Renuka, D. (2024). Deep learning architecture towards consumer buying behaviour prediction using multitask learning paradigm. *Journal of Intelligent and Fuzzy Systems, 46*(1), 1341–1357. https://doi.org/10.3233/JIFS-231116/ASSET/86E70F39-AA51-4A5E-B29B-37F637179FC0/ASSETS/GRAPHIC/10.3233_JIFS-231116-FIG 11.JPG0

Gretzel, U. (2011). Intelligent systems in tourism: A social science perspective. *Annals of Tourism Research, 38*(3), 757–779. https://doi.org/10.1016/J.ANNALS.2011.04.014

Habibipour, A. (2024). Responsible living labs: what can go wrong? *Journal of Information, Communication and Ethics in Society, 22*(2), 205–218. https://doi.org/10.1108/JICES-11-2023-0137/FULL/PDF

Hair, J. F., & Sarstedt, M. (2021). Data, measurement, and causal inferences in machine learning: Opportunities and challenges for marketing. *Journal of Marketing Theory and Practice, 29*(1), 65–77. https://doi.org/10.1080/10696679.2020.1860683

Hanlon, A., & Jones, K. (2023). Ethical concerns about social media privacy policies: Do users have the ability to comprehend their consent actions? Journal of Strategic Marketing. *34*(1), 41–58. https://doi.org/10.1080/0965254X.2023.2232817.

Havlík, V. (2019). The naturalness of artificial intelligence from the evolutionary perspective. *AI and Society, 34*(4), 889–898. https://doi.org/10.1007/S00146-018-0829-5/METRICS

He, A. Z., & Zhang, Y. (2023). AI-powered touch points in the customer journey: A systematic literature review and research agenda. *Journal of Research in Interactive Marketing, 17*(4), 620–639. https://doi.org/10.1108/JRIM-03-2022-0082/FULL/XML

Hewett, K., & Lehmann, D. R. (2021). Introduction to the special issue on data and methodological issues for new insights in international marketing. *Journal of International Marketing, 29*(3), 1–2. https://doi.org/10.1177/1069031X211031507

Huang, M. H., & Rust, R. T. (2018). Artificial intelligence in service. *Journal of Service Research, 21*(2), 155–172. https://doi.org/10.1177/1094670517752459/ASSET/634322AD-F9FE-4B67-B3B9-78A57357C567/ASSETS/IMAGES/LARGE/10.1177_1094670517752459-FIG 4.JPG

Kaplan, A., & Haenlein, M. (2019). Siri, Siri, in my hand: Who's the fairest in the land? On the interpretations, illustrations, and implications of artificial intelligence. *Business Horizons, 62*(1), 15–25. https://doi.org/10.1016/J.BUSHOR.2018.08.004

Khan, A. A., Akbar, M. A., Fahmideh, M., Liang, P., Waseem, M., Ahmad, A., Niazi, M., & Abrahamsson, P. (2023). AI ethics: An empirical study on the views of practitioners and lawmakers. *IEEE Transactions on Computational Social Systems, 10*(6), 2971–2984. https://doi.org/10.1109/TCSS.2023.3251729

Khosravani Pour, L., & Farrokhi, A. (2023). Language recognition by convolutional neural networks. *Scientia Iranica, 30*(1), 116–123. https://doi.org/10.24200/SCI.2022.59110.6064

Kim, H., So, K. K. F., Shin, S., & Li, J. (2025). Artificial intelligence in hospitality and tourism: Insights from industry practices, research literature, and expert opinions. *Journal of Hospitality and Tourism Research, 49*(2), 366–385. https://doi.org/10.1177/10963480241229235

Knani, M., Echchakoui, S., & Ladhari, R. (2022). Artificial intelligence in tourism and hospitality: Bibliometric analysis and research agenda. *International Journal of Hospitality Management, 107*, 103317. https://doi.org/10.1016/J.IJHM.2022.103317

Kong, H., Wang, K., Qiu, X., Cheung, C., & Bu, N. (2023). 30 years of artificial intelligence (AI) research relating to the hospitality and tourism industry. *International Journal of Contemporary Hospitality Management, 35*(6), 2157–2177. https://doi.org/10.1108/IJCHM-03-2022-0354/FULL/XML

Kulaklıoğlu, D. (2024). Ethical AI in autonomous systems and decision-making. *Human Computer Interaction, 8*(1), 87–87. https://doi.org/10.62802/JB2PTT89

Kumar, V., Ashraf, A. R., & Nadeem, W. (2024). AI-powered marketing: What, where, and how? *International Journal of Information Management, 77*, 1–24. https://doi.org/10.1016/J.IJINFOMGT.2024.102783

Latah, M., & Toker, L. (2019). Artificial intelligence enabled software-defined networking: A comprehensive overview. *IET Networks, 8*(2), 79–99. https://doi.org/10.1049/IET-NET.2018.5082

Lee, S. J., Paas, L., & Ahn, H. S. (2024). The power of specific emotion analysis in predicting donations: A comparative empirical study between sentiment and specific emotion analysis in social media. *International Journal of Market Research, 66*(5), 610–630. 10.1177/14707853241261248/ASSET/8DFD19BC-40F5-4959-9D7F-5B58FF2A0074/ASSETS/IMAGES/LARGE/10.1177_14707853241261248-FIG 2.JPG

Lepenioti, K., Bousdekis, A., Apostolou, D., & Mentzas, G. (2021). Human-augmented prescriptive analytics with interactive multi-objective reinforcement learning. *IEEE Access, 9*, 100677–100693. https://doi.org/10.1109/ACCESS.2021.3096662

Limna, P., Siripipatthanakul, S., & Phayaphrom, B. (2021). The role of big data analytics in influencing artificial intelligence (AI) adoption for coffee shops in Krabi, Thailand. *In International Journal of Behavioral Analytics, 1*(2), 1–17. https://papers.ssrn.com/abstract=3944075

Lin, C.-C., Huang, A. Y. Q., & Yang, S. J. H. A. (2023). A review of AI-driven conversational Chatbots implementation methodologies and challenges (1999–2022). *Sustainability, 15*(5), 1–13. https://doi.org/10.3390/SU15054012

Lv, H., Shi, S., & Gursoy, D. (2022). A look back and a leap forward: A review and synthesis of big data and artificial intelligence literature in hospitality and tourism. *Journal of Hospitality Marketing & Management, 31*(2), 145–175. https://doi.org/10.1080/19368623.2021.1937434

Madanchian, M. (2024). Generative AI for consumer behavior prediction: Techniques and applications. *Sustainability, 16*(22), 1–21. https://doi.org/10.3390/SU16229963

Mariani, M. M., Machado, I., & Nambisan, S. (2023). Types of innovation and artificial intelligence: A systematic quantitative literature review and research agenda. *Journal of Business Research, 155*, 1–14. https://doi.org/10.1016/J.JBUSRES.2022.113364

Mccarthy, J. (2007). *What is Artificial Intelligence?* Stanford University. http://www-formal.stanford.edu/jmc/

McCartney, G., & McCartney, A. (2020). Rise of the machines: Towards a conceptual service-robot research framework for the hospitality and tourism industry. *International Journal of Contemporary Hospitality Management, 13*(12), 3835–3851. https://doi.org/10.1108/IJCHM-05-2020-0450/FULL/XML

Meszaros, J., & Ho, C. H.. (2021). AI research and data protection: Can the same rules apply for commercial and academic research under the GDPR? *Computer Law & Security Review, 41*. https://doi.org/10.1016/J.CLSR.2021.105532

Nannelli, M., Capone, F., & Lazzeretti, L. (2023). Artificial intelligence in hospitality and tourism. State of the art and future research avenues. *European Planning Studies, 31*(7), 1325–1344. https://doi.org/10.1080/09654313.2023.2180321

Naqvi, G., Saddique, M. H., Sarim, M., & Riyan, S. U. (2023). Application of AI in hotel management and its benefits. *Journal of Statistics, Computing and Interdisciplinary Research, 5*(1), 1–13. https://doi.org/10.52700/SCIR.V3I2.141

Oğuz, A. (2024). Consumer behavior in the era of AI-driven marketing. *Human Computer Interaction, 8*(1), 147–147. https://doi.org/10.62802/H9FRXH42

Pantano, E., & Scarpi, D. (2022). I, robot, you, consumer: Measuring artificial intelligence types and their effect on consumers emotions in service. *Journal of Service Research, 25*(4), 583–600. https://doi.org/10.1177/10946705221103538/ASSET/167E895C-140E-47D6-B0AE-9625D288DD05/ASSETS/IMAGES/LARGE/10.1177_10946705221103538-FIG 2.JPG

Patel, J., Sharma, A., Shukla, Y., & Das, K. (2023). Role of culture in consumer marketing: Thematic trajectories and theoretical roots. *Journal of Creative Communications*. https://doi.org/10.1177/09732586231205069

Pennachin, C., & Goertzel, B. (2007). Contemporary approaches to artificial general intelligence. *Cognitive Technologies, 8*, 1–30. https://doi.org/10.1007/978-3-540-68677-4_1

Prentice, C., Dominique Lopes, S., & Wang, X. (2020). Emotional intelligence or artificial intelligence–an employee perspective. *Journal of Hospitality Marketing & Management, 29*(4), 377–403. https://doi.org/10.1080/19368623.2019.1647124

Rokka, J. (2021). Consumer culture theory's future in marketing. *Journal of Marketing Theory and Practice, 29*(1), 114–124. https://doi.org/10.1080/10696679.2020.1860685

Russell, S., & Norvig, P. (2020). *Artificial Intelligence: A morden approach* (4ª ed). Pearson. https://www.bertrand.pt/livro/artificial-intelligence-a-modern-approach-global-edition-peter-norvig/25382906?srsltid=AfmBOoqCoLoYRaFYixWIqCteLmjO_JKdiBFrgOPM5EdUdEVs5H2vQsln

Sahne, S. S. K., & Daronkola, H. K. (2025). Enhancing loyalty in luxury fashion with AI: The mediation role of customer relationships. *Asia-Pacific Journal of Business Administration, ahead-of-print* (ahead-of-print). https://doi.org/10.1108/APJBA-08-2024-0456/FULL/XML

Sharda, M. (2021). Incorporating big data tools for social media analytics in a business analytics course. *Journal of Information Systems Education, 32*(3), 176–198.

Shevchenko, A. I., & Sosnitsky, A. V. (2020). *Universal Meta-Definition of Intelligence*. The 11th IEEE International Conference on Dependable Systems, Services and Technologies, DESSERT'2020, 1–7.

Sigfrids, A., Leikas, J., Salo-Pöntinen, H., & Koskimies, E. (2023). Human-centricity in AI governance: A systemic approach. *Frontiers in Artificial Intelligence, 6*. https://doi.org/10.3389/FRAI.2023.976887/BIBTEX

Simon, H. A. (1995). Artificial intelligence: An empirical science. *Artificial Intelligence, 77*(1), 95–127. https://doi.org/10.1016/0004-3702(95)00039-H

Stocchi, L., Pourazad, N., Michaelidou, N., Tanusondjaja, A., & Harrigan, P. (2022). Marketing research on Mobile apps: Past, present and future. *Journal of the Academy of Marketing Science, 50*(2), 195–225. https://doi.org/10.1007/S11747-021-00815-W/METRICS

Syam, N., & Sharma, A. (2018). Waiting for a sales renaissance in the fourth industrial revolution: Machine learning and artificial intelligence in sales research and practice. *Industrial Marketing Management, 69*, 135–146. https://doi.org/10.1016/J.INDMARMAN.2017.12.019

Teepapal, T. (2025). AI-driven personalization: Unraveling consumer perceptions in social media engagement. *Computers in Human Behavior, 165*. https://doi.org/10.1016/J.CHB.2024.108549

van Giffen, B., Herhausen, D., & Fahse, T. (2022). Overcoming the pitfalls and perils of algorithms: A classification of machine learning biases and mitigation methods. *Journal of Business Research, 144*, 93–106. https://doi.org/10.1016/J.JBUSRES.2022.01.076

Vercammen, C., Oosthuizen, I., Manchaiah, V., Ratinaud, P., Launer, S., & Swanepoel, D. W. (2023). Real-life and real-time hearing aid experiences: Insights from self-initiated ecological momentary assessments and natural language analysis. *Frontiers in Digital Health, 5*, 1104308. https://doi.org/10.3389/FDGTH.2023.1104308/BIBTEX

Von Eschenbach, W. J. (2021). Transparency and the black box problem: Why we do not trust AI. *Philosophy and Technology, 34*(4), 1607–1622. https://doi.org/10.1007/S13347-021-00477-0/METRICS

Vrtana, D., & Krizanova, A. (2023). The Power of Emotional Advertising Appeals: Examining Their Influence on Consumer Purchasing Behavior and Brand–Customer Relationship. Sustainability, 15(18), 1–18. https://doi.org/10.3390/SU151813337.

Walsh, S. E., & Feigh, K. M. (2022). Understanding human decision processes: Inferring decision strategies from behavioral data. *Journal of Cognitive Engineering and Decision Making, 16*(4), 301–325. https://doi.org/10.1177/15553434221122899

Wang, C. (2022). Efficient customer segmentation in digital marketing using deep learning with swarm intelligence approach. *Information Processing & Management, 59*(6), 103085. https://doi.org/10.1016/J.IPM.2022.103085

Wang, C. X., Di Renzo, M., Stańczak, S., Wang, S., & Larsson, E. G. (2020). Artificial intelligence enabled wireless networking for 5G and beyond: Recent advances and future challenges. *IEEE Wireless Communications, 27*(1), 16–23. https://doi.org/10.1109/MWC.001.1900292

Wang, P. (2019). On defining artificial intelligence. *Journal of Artificial General Intelligence, 10*(2), 1–37. https://doi.org/10.2478/JAGI-2019-0002

Wayne-Mitchell, V., & Walsh, G. (2001). Consumers' decision-making style as a basis for market segmentation Thorsten Hennig-Thurau. *Journal of Targeting, Measurement and Analysis for Marketing, 10*, 117–131.

Wedel, M., & Kannan, P. K. (2016). Marketing analytics for data-rich environments. *Journal of Marketing, 80*(6), 97–121. https://doi.org/10.1509/JM.15.0413

Wewerka, J., & Reichert, M. (2023). Robotic process automation-a systematic mapping study and classification framework. *Enterprise Information Systems, 17*(2). https://doi.org/10.1080/17517575.2021.1986862

Williams, K. C. (1981). *Behavioural aspects of marketing*. Butterworth-Heinemann. https://books.google.com/books/about/Behavioural_Aspects_of_Marketing.html?id=4-YbAQAAMAAJ

Wirth, N. (2018). Hello marketing, what can artificial intelligence help you with? *International Journal of Market Research, 60*(5), 435–438. https://doi.org/10.1177/1470785318776841

Wu, S., Yau, W. C., Ong, T. S., & Chong, S. C. (2021). Integrated churn prediction and customer segmentation framework for telco business. *IEEE Access, 9*, 62118–62136. https://doi.org/10.1109/ACCESS.2021.3073776

Xing, X., Huang, H., & Hedenstierna, C. P. T. (2023). Selling through online marketplaces with consumer profiling. *Journal of Business Research, 164*. https://doi.org/10.1016/J.JBUSRES.2023.114022

Xu, Q. A., Jayne, C., & Chang, V. (2024). An emoji feature-incorporated multi-view deep learning for explainable sentiment classification of social media reviews. *Technological Forecasting and Social Change, 202*, 1–23. https://doi.org/10.1016/J.TECHFORE.2024.123326

Zhang, Q., Shi, Q., Alatas, B., & Yuan, Y. H. (2025). Optimization of dynamic pricing models for consumer segmentation markets and analysis of big data-driven marketing strategies. *Journal of Organizational and End User Computing (JOEUC), 37*(1), 1–33. https://doi.org/10.4018/JOEUC.368840

Zhao, S., Wu, R., Tao, J., Qu, M., Zhao, M., Fan, C., & Zhao, H. (2023). Percltv: A general system for personalized customer lifetime value prediction in online games. *ACM Transactions on Information Systems, 41*(1). https://doi.org/10.1145/3530012

Behavioural Customers Analysis with Artificial Intelligence: Challenges and Pitfalls of Un(Biased) Decision-Making

Ana Torres and Sandra Filipe

Abstract This chapter examines the evolution of Artificial Intelligence (AI) in consumer behaviour, highlighting the transition from predictive to generative systems, and aims to answer the following two research questions: (i) How are predictive AI systems evolving with generative AI to open new possibilities for understanding and influencing customer behaviour? (ii) Which AI approaches offer not only predictive accuracy but also fairness, interpretability, and ethical soundness in customer behaviour analysis? A narrative review approach was adopted, drawing on peer-reviewed literature published in the last 10 years, between 2016 and 2025, across marketing, consumer behaviour, and AI research. The review systematically synthesizes applications of predictive and generative AI, critically discussing their empirical boundaries, contradictions, and emerging gaps. By clarifying the coexistence, replacement, and hybridization of AI approaches, we advance theoretical understanding of consumer–AI interactions. This chapter contributes by proposing a refined research agenda derived directly from the identified gaps, focusing on multimodal analysis, trust and delegation in AI-assisted decisions, and governance of consumer-facing AI applications.

1 Introduction

In the rapidly evolving digital landscape, understanding and predicting consumer behaviour has become a cornerstone of strategic business decision-making. The growing complexity and dynamism of consumer preferences, driven by increased

A. Torres
INESC TEC, Porto, Portugal

A. Torres (✉) · S. Filipe
Higher Institute of Accounting and Administration of the University of Aveiro, Aveiro, Portugal
e-mail: ana.torres@ua.pt

S. Filipe
GOVCOPP Research Unit, Aveiro, Portugal
e-mail: sandrafilipe@ua.pt

J. D. Santos et al. (eds.), *Artificial Intelligence Transforming Marketing*, Contributions to Management Science, https://doi.org/10.1007/978-3-032-22360-9_2

digital interaction and data generation, have challenged traditional analytical tools. In response, Artificial Intelligence (AI) has emerged as a transformative solution, offering advanced capabilities to extract meaningful patterns, detect trends, and generate actionable insights from massive, heterogeneous datasets (Babu et al., 2023). AI's potential to revolutionize consumer behaviour analysis lies in its ability to not only predict future actions but also generate hyper-personalization content and experiences, fundamentally reshaping the marketing and customer relationship paradigms (Sheta, 2021).

As AI techniques continue to mature, businesses are increasingly leveraging Machine Learning (ML), natural language processing (NLP), and deep learning (DL) models to anticipate purchasing behaviours, improve customer satisfaction, and enhance user engagement. These models enable the analysis of consumer sentiment, social media behaviour, and purchasing history at an unprecedented scale and accuracy (Chaudhary et al., 2021). Simultaneously, the proliferation of Internet of Things (IoT) devices and the rise of the Internet of Behaviour (IoB) have expanded the data ecosystem, offering new dimensions for behavioural inference and intervention (Bobin et al., 2023).

AI-powered behavioural customer analysis is revolutionizing how businesses approach customer segmentation, personalization marketing, and retention strategies. By harnessing ML and data mining techniques, companies extract detailed behavioural insights to predict consumer actions and enhance engagement. AI-powered behavioural customer analysis enables precise segmentation, personalization marketing, and improved retention by leveraging advanced ML and data mining techniques. ML algorithms, driven by advancements in computational power and data processing capabilities, have revolutionized how businesses gain insights into consumer preferences and purchasing patterns. These algorithms can process vast amounts of data, identifying subtle patterns, and generating highly accurate predictions. For example, a recent Statista study reported that companies applying machine learning to customer segmentation achieved an average revenue growth of 23% (Yixuan, 2024).

However, ML models are frequently considered 'black boxes' due to their lack of interpretability, which limits transparency and trust (Adadi & Berrada, 2018; Miller, 2019). Moreover, biases embedded in historical training datasets—such as under-representation of demographic groups—can lead to systematically unfair outcomes (Shneiderman, 2016; Birhane, 2022). These vulnerabilities have sparked increasing concern about the ethical implications of AI in marketing, especially when decisions are automated and lack human oversight (Du & Xie, 2021).

Despite these capabilities bring significant business value, yet also introduce critical concerns related to privacy, equity, explainability, and algorithmic accountability (Faria et al., 2023; Zhang & Liu, 2024). In fact, the integration of AI into consumer analytics is not without challenges. Issues such as data privacy, algorithmic bias, and ethical concerns have sparked significant debate regarding the responsible deployment of AI systems (Schwartz et al., 2022; Varsha, 2023). Therefore, the shift from predictive to generative AI introduces new opportunities and risks, requiring a re-evaluation of existing models, strategies, and regulations.

While offering significant business benefits, AI-powered behavioural customer analysis also presents challenges ensuring customers' data privacy, trustiness (Faria et al., 2023), addressing equity and ethical concerns, and interpreting complex AI models for actionable business use (Babu et al., 2023; Yixuan, 2024). However, further research is still in need to better understanding new opportunities and risks, vulnerabilities, and the ethical implications of AI in marketing consumer behaviour decision-making.

By addressing this research gap this chapter examines the evolution of AI models in consumer behaviour, highlighting the transition from predictive to generative systems, aiming to answer the following two research questions (RQ):

RQ1. How are predictive AI systems evolving with generative AI to open new possibilities for understanding and influencing customer behaviour?
RQ2. Which AI approaches offer not only predictive accuracy but also fairness, interpretability, and ethical soundness in customer behaviour analysis?

AI has rapidly become a defining force in marketing and consumer behaviour research. While predictive models have long supported segmentation, targeting, and personalized recommendations, generative AI introduces qualitatively new dynamics by producing creative outputs and enabling novel forms of consumer interaction. Previous reviews have tended to describe applications or focus narrowly on technological aspects. In contrast, this chapter makes a theoretical contribution by explicitly articulating how the predictive–generative distinction reframes consumer behaviour theories: predictive AI as optimization of known patterns, and generative AI as expansion of choice architectures and meaning-making.

This chapter has a total of six sections. After this introduction, the methodology is presented. This chapter follows with the theoretical background. Section 4 is dedicated to AI applications in consumer behaviour. Section 5 highlights several pitfalls and challenges associated with AI. Section 6 presents the future research avenues and Sect. 7 is the conclusion.

2 Methodology

This chapter follows a narrative review approach, integrating conceptual and empirical findings to answer the research questions posed. The scope included peer-reviewed journal articles, book chapters, and conference proceedings published in the last 10 years, between 2016 and 2025 in the fields of marketing, consumer behaviour, and AI. Literature was identified using academic databases (Scopus, Web of Science, Google Scholar) with keywords such as 'consumer behaviour', 'predictive AI', 'generative AI', 'trust in AI', and 'human–AI interaction'. Priority was given to studies offering conceptual frameworks, empirical findings with theoretical implications, and reviews addressing consumer-facing AI applications. While not systematic, this narrative review is rigorous in scope, aiming to synthesize current knowledge and identify research gaps.

3 Theoretical Background

3.1 The Role of AI in Consumer Behaviour Prediction

AI plays a pivotal role in transforming how businesses understand and forecast consumer behaviour. Traditional models based on demographic and historical data are being replaced or augmented by AI-driven systems capable of real-time processing and dynamic adaptation. These systems employ ML algorithms to identify hidden patterns in large datasets, enabling marketers to predict purchasing behaviour, churn risk, and consumer engagement with high precision (Afolabi et al., 2016; Rosário et al., 2024).

Social media platforms, e-commerce environments, and IoT-enabled devices continuously generate vast amounts of structured and unstructured data. Predictive models built using this data can capture nuanced insights into consumer preferences, motivations, and decision-making processes (Chaudhary et al., 2021). AI models can detect sentiment shifts, forecast demand fluctuations, or personalize user interfaces based on behavioural analysis (Sheta, 2021).

Furthermore, the Internet of Behaviour (IoB), an extension of IoT, enhances AI's predictive capabilities by linking digital behaviour patterns to psychological and emotional states (Bobin et al., 2023). By integrating sensor data from smart devices with behavioural analytics, businesses can refine targeting strategies and deepen customer engagement.

The extensive body of literature reviewed highlights the rapidly growing intersection between AI and consumer behaviour prediction (e.g., Gkikas & Theodoridis, 2022; Prasad & Ghosal, 2022; Prakash et al., 2023). Across diverse domains, ranging from e-commerce and digital lending to building energy management and telecom (e.g., Gochhait et al., 2020; Olu-Ajayi et al., 2022; Khrais, 2020; Talukdar et al., 2023), AI models have demonstrated strong potential to enhance the accuracy and efficiency of behavioural forecasting. Techniques such as Artificial Neural Networks (ANN), Support Vector Machines (SVM), Gradient Boosting, and Deep Neural Networks (DNN) frequently outperform traditional statistical models in classification tasks related to customer preferences, churn prediction, and fraud detection.

A recurring theme across the academic literature on the topic is the versatility of AI in capturing implicit consumer signals through both structured (e.g., transaction data) and unstructured (e.g., social media) inputs (e.g., Afolabi et al., 2016; Chaudha et al. 2021; Perez-Vega et al., 2021; Safara, 2022). Particularly notable is the application of NLP and sentiment analysis in understanding consumer attitudes, a critical component of adaptive marketing strategies. In several instances, hybrid and ensemble models—such as Bagging combined with decision trees or

XGBoost—yielded superior predictive performance, highlighting the importance of model integration and optimization (Lalwani et al., 2022).

Despite these technological advancements, the literature consistently underscores several persistent challenges. First, ethical considerations—including data privacy, algorithmic bias, and transparency—remain underexplored in operational contexts. The implementation of Explainable AI (XAI) is advocated as a necessary step towards improving model interpretability and building trust among both consumers and stakeholders (Prakash et al., 2023). Second, there is a notable gap in research focused on real-time personalization and customer engagement, areas that are increasingly relevant with the rise of generative AI (e.g., Gochhait et al., 2020; Perez et al., 2021).

Finally, much of the existing research concentrates on narrow use cases or industry-specific applications, suggesting a need for broader, cross-sectoral frameworks.

Future studies on the field of AI-driven systems predicting consumer behaviour should adopt interdisciplinary approaches that integrate technical, ethical, and consumer behaviour perspectives to develop holistic, and more effective human-centred AI analysis. These directions will be critical in transitioning from purely predictive models to intelligent systems that not only forecast behaviour but also interact with consumers in ethical, transparent, and responsive ways.

3.2 The Transition from Predictive to Generative AI

AI is revolutionizing marketing through two main paradigms: predictive AI and generative AI (GAI). Each offers unique capabilities, and understanding their differences is crucial for effective marketing strategy. Table 1 presents the main distinctions, applications, and implications of both techniques.

While predictive AI focuses on identifying future consumer actions based on past behaviour, GAI represents a paradigm shift. Generative models such as Generative Adversarial Networks (GANs) and large language models (LLMs) go beyond forecasting—they can create new content, simulate user responses, and dynamically design customer interactions. These systems allow businesses to generate personalization of product descriptions, marketing copy, and even virtual influencers tailored to individual consumer profiles (Verma et al., 2021).

Overall, both approaches provide several benefits for marketing strategy: Predictive AI (Analytical AI) powers large-scale operational decisions, such as targeting, pricing, and customer retention, by analysing historical data to forecast future behaviours (Grewal et al., 2025; Hermann & Puntoni, 2024).

Generative AI enables rapid, personalized content creation, campaign design, and real-time customer engagement, often leading to higher conversion rates and improved customer experiences (Đaković & Rikalović, 2025; Grewal et al., 2025; Madanchian, 2024a). While predictive AI excels at forecasting and optimizing marketing operations, generative AI transforms content creation and personalization.

Table 1 Comparison of predictive and generative AI in marketing

Issue	Predictive AI	Generative AI	Author(s)
Core function	Analyses past data to forecast future outcomes	Creates new content (e.g. text, images, video) from data	Grewal et al. (2025) Hermann and Puntoni (2024) Madanchian (2024a)
Typical algorithms	Regression Supervised learning: Neural networks, Decisions trees, random forests	GANs, VAEs, transformers, LLMs	Grewal et al. (2025) Madanchian (2024a) Reed et al. (2025).
Data type	Structured numerical	Structured and unstructured (e.g. text, images, audio)	Grewal et al. (2025) Madanchian (2024a)
Output	Clustering Predictions (e.g., next purchase, churn risk)	Original content (e.g. ads, product descriptions, images)	Đaković and Rikalović (2025) Grewal et al. (2025) Madanchian (2024a)
Use cases	Customer segmentation Targeting Pricing Churn prediction	Content creation Campaign design personalization	Đaković and Rikalović (2025) Grewal et al. (2025) Madanchian (2024a)
Human involvement	Often requires human oversight for interpretation	Varies: Can automate creative tasks, but oversight needed.	Đaković and Rikalović (2025) Grewal et al. (2025) Reed et al. (2025).

Source Authors

The transition to generative AI introduces significant advantages in creativity, scalability, and adaptability. It empowers firms to deliver hyper-personalization experiences at scale, transforming digital marketing and customer service landscapes. However, it also introduces challenges, such as hallucinated outputs, transparency issues, and unintended reinforcement of biases (Schwartz et al., 2022; Varsha, 2023). Thus, managing the interplay between creativity and control becomes a key theoretical and practical concern in consumer AI applications.

AI applications in customer behaviour analysis are rapidly shifting from traditional predictive models to generative systems capable of simulating consumer interactions and generating novel content (Hermann & Puntoni, 2024). Predictive AI, often reliant on supervised learning, focuses on identifying patterns and forecasting future behaviours, such as purchase likelihood or churn risk. In contrast, generative AI—powered by diffusion models and LLMs—can synthesize new data points, simulate human-like conversations, and create personalization content, enabling hyper-adaptive customer engagement (Puntoni et al., 2021; Zhang & Liu, 2024).

This shift enhances marketing innovation but also magnifies concerns around model explainability, misuse, and the ethical boundaries of synthetic personalization (Davenport et al., 2020; De Bruyn et al., 2020).

Researchers view the integration of GAI in customer behaviour analysis as a process of augmentation, coexistence, or deliberate combination, rather than replacement of predictive AI. Grewal et al. (2025) argue that GAI should be used to enhance and extend traditional predictive and analytical methods, not to supplant them entirely. Their work highlights that AI is most effective when it augments human managers and existing systems, leveraging generative capabilities to provide new insights, while maintaining the strengths of established predictive models.

The augmentation and deliberate combination of GAI with existing approaches in customer behaviour analysis bring new insights and challenges for marketing. Grewal et al. (2025) and Akter et al. (2021) support the augmentation over replacement, suggesting that GAI can automate routine tasks and generate new content or insights, but human oversight and traditional analytics remain crucial for context, empathy, and decision-making.

Cillo & Rubera (2024) advocate for a deliberate combination of generative and predictive AI, where generative models synthesize new data or simulate scenarios, and predictive models validate and interpret these outputs for actionable marketing strategies.

Therefore, the integration of generative and predictive AI in customer analysis raises some considerations. Predictive AI is valued for its interpretability and reliability but may miss nuanced or creative opportunities (Grewal et al., 2025; Hermann & Puntoni, 2024). GAI offers creativity and efficiency but raises concerns about transparency, authenticity, bias, data privacy and ethical use, requiring responsible implementation and human oversight (Đaković & Rikalović, 2025; Grewal et al., 2025; Madanchian, 2024a).

The field continues to evolve, with generative AI opening new possibilities for understanding and influencing customer behaviour. XAI techniques aim to make ML models more transparent and interpretable. Also, they help businesses understand why a model makes specific predictions, which is crucial for building trust and addressing regulatory requirements (Yixuan, 2024).

3.3 Predictive Methods in AI-Based Customer Analysis

The methods underpinning AI-based customer analysis are diverse, spanning supervised and unsupervised learning, optimization algorithms, and hybrid systems. Supervised models, including decision trees, random forests, and neural networks, are commonly used to classify and predict consumer behaviour (Van Thiel & Van Raaij, 2019). Among these, artificial neural networks have emerged as a dominant technique due to their capacity to learn complex nonlinear relationships from vast datasets (Afolabi et al., 2016).

Optimization algorithms such as Adam, RMSProp, and Gradient Descent are integral to fine-tuning AI models and improving prediction accuracy (Gaddam et al., 2022). These algorithms enable efficient training of models on high-dimensional data, often resulting in improved scalability and performance. Additionally, NLP is employed for sentiment analysis and opinion mining, while clustering techniques assist in market segmentation and behavioural profiling (Babu et al., 2023; Sheta, 2021).

Big data platforms further enhance the scalability of AI-driven analytics. Cloud-based ML environments, such as Microsoft Azure or Google Cloud AI, facilitate real-time deployment and testing of customer behaviour models across business functions (Shapi et al., 2021). Moreover, the integration of behavioural economics principles into AI systems enhances the interpretability of outcomes, enabling decision-makers to align machine outputs with real-world marketing objectives (Stubseid & Arandjelovic, 2018).

AI techniques for analysing customer behaviour include:

1. Clustering and Segmentation: Algorithms like K-means, Self-Organizing Maps (SOMs), and deep clustering methods segment customers based on behavioural patterns such as preferences, transaction or purchase history, and engagement patterns. Wang (2022) proposes combining deep learning with swarm intelligence to optimize segmentation performance, boosting customer engagement, product recommendations, and sales.
2. Supervised and Unsupervised Learning: Models such as decision trees, deep neural networks (DNN), and enhanced Long Short-Term Memory (LSTM) architectures support the prediction of consumer actions, such as purchases. Malik et al. (2024) illustrate a three-step process involving Z-score normalization, Recursive Feature Elimination (RFE), and LSTM to improve classification accuracy and personalization in CRM systems.
3. Feature Engineering: Feature selection remains key to increasing model robustness. Methods like Swarm Optimization and RFE help reduce dimensionality and avoid overfitting, while retaining key behavioural indicators (Malik et al., 2024; Wang, 2022).

These models empower businesses to decode complex behavioural data, enabling predictive insights and actionable marketing strategies.

4 AI Applications in Consumer Behaviour

4.1 Personalization Marketing

One of the most impactful applications of AI in consumer behaviour analysis is personalization marketing. AI enables businesses to tailor messages, product recommendations, and promotional offers based on individual user profiles, past interactions, and inferred preferences. Recommendation engines powered by collaborative filtering, deep learning, and reinforcement learning are extensively used to drive engagement and conversion across digital platforms (Rosário et al., 2024).

Companies use AI to dynamically adjust website content, recommend complementary products, or send targeted email campaigns—actions that significantly enhance user experience and brand loyalty. The granularity of personalization achieved through AI not only increases return on marketing investment but also shifts the strategic focus from market segments to 'segments of one' (Verma et al., 2021).

AI technologies significantly enhance personalization marketing by leveraging real-time data and predictive analytics to tailor offers and content to individual consumers. Bhagat et al. (2023) propose an integrated AI model that captures consumers' consciousness, faith, and subjective norms, showing a direct link between AI integration and increased purchase intention in e-retailing. Similarly, Yeo et al. (2022) highlight the effectiveness of AI-powered technologies in the fashion and apparel industry, particularly on Instagram, where emotional value, perceived quality, and electronic word-of-mouth (eWOM) significantly influence purchase decisions.

AI-driven behavioural segmentation facilitates hyper-targeted marketing, increasing engagement and conversion rates (Aneja, 2023; Malik et al., 2024). Malik et al. (2024) emphasize that accurate behaviour prediction is achieved through advanced LSTM models that capture subtle patterns in consumer behaviour, enhancing personalization strategies and CRM.

The integration of GAI technologies with advanced predictive models has significantly enhanced the potential for hyper-personalization in marketing (Pires et al., 2025). The fusion of GAI with predictive analytics that forecast customer behaviours and preferences enables the synthesis of realistic consumer data and the design of highly personalized marketing content. This synergy advances campaign individualization beyond traditional segment-based approaches and fosters unprecedented opportunities for marketing innovation (Davenport et al., 2020).

Furthermore, beyond its application in content generation, GAI enhances the sophistication of customer engagement through conversational interfaces and virtual assistants. These systems support natural language interactions capable of adapting to individual communication styles and preferences, thereby fostering more engaging, immersive, and effective customer experiences (Huang & Rust, 2021).

In addition, reinforcement learning is increasingly being used to optimize marketing and advertising strategies in real time. By learning from user interactions, reinforcement learning models can make personalization's recommendations and decisions to maximize engagement and conversions (Yixuan, 2024).

4.2 Customer Relationship Management

Customer Relationship Management (CRM) systems have been transformed by AI technologies that provide real-time, predictive insights into customer behaviour. AI enhances CRM platforms by automating customer profiling, scoring leads, and suggesting retention strategies based on lifetime value or churn probability Afolabi et al., 2016). Chatbots and virtual assistants—powered by NLP—handle routine queries and improve service responsiveness, while ML models forecast customer satisfaction and recommend proactive interventions.

Moreover, AI allows CRM systems to integrate emotional and behavioural data sourced from IoT devices and digital footprints, thereby building a 360-degree view of the customer (Bobin et al., 2023). This fusion of behavioural and transactional data results in more intelligent decision-making and more personalization customer journeys. Nonetheless, CRM applications require careful handling of sensitive personal data, raising concerns related to data governance and algorithmic fairness.

AI provides CRM systems with dynamic, data-driven capabilities, enabling real-time response to customer needs and preferences. Predictive analytics help firms prioritize high-value customers and recommend optimal service actions (Huy et al., 2023; Zhang & Liu, 2024). Malik et al. (2024) contribute to the advancement of AI applications in CRM, by following the LSTM rigorous process, providing inputs to help companies to improve their strategy, offer more customized experiences, improve customer satisfaction and boost the possibility of consumers completing a purchase by delivering relevant insights.

Conversational AI interfaces can foster deeper consumer–brand relationships by mimicking human-like communication patterns. Bergner et al. (2023) develop a conceptual model based on three properties of human dialogue—turn-taking, turn initiation, and grounding—to show how verbal embodiment in AI enhances perceived humanness and consumer intimacy. This leads to improved brand loyalty, advocacy, and willingness to pay premium prices. AI thus becomes a critical component in relationship marketing strategies, creating more empathetic and dynamic interactions.

4.3 Market Trend Forecasting and Strategic Insights

AI is increasingly used to forecast market trends and anticipate shifts in consumer demand. Predictive models process data from diverse sources—social media, transactional logs, economic indicators, and sensor networks—to detect emerging preferences, sentiment fluctuations, or macroeconomic changes (Babu et al., 2023; Chaudhary et al., 2021). These insights support strategic decisions in pricing, inventory management, and product development.

For example, businesses can identify upcoming product categories with high growth potential or anticipate downturns in customer engagement well before they materialize. AI also helps firms simulate multiple market scenarios using generative models, thereby enhancing their agility and resilience in volatile environments (Stoycheva & Vitliemov, 2024). The ability to detect weak signals early enables firms to lead rather than follow market movements.

AI's predictive capabilities offer robust tools for forecasting consumer trends and informing strategic decision-making. Dwivedi et al. (2021) present a comprehensive review of AI's transformative potential across various industries, including retail and supply chain, emphasizing its role in enabling dynamic responses to changing consumer preferences. By incorporating ML and autonomous decision-making, businesses can proactively address market shifts and optimize operations.

Through unsupervised learning and behavioural clustering, AI systems can detect emerging preferences and respond to shifting consumer demands—an increasingly critical capability in fast-evolving markets (Aneja, 2023; Volkmar et al., 2022).

By analysing behavioural patterns, AI models identify in real time at-risk customers and suggest retention strategies, which is crucial in highly competitive markets (Huy et al., 2023). Gochhait et al. (2020) point out that in e-commerce, AI combined with predictive analytics was proven to be successful in analysing and forecasting customer behaviour pattern s.

The integration of GAI technologies transcends the technical dimension of model selection, encompassing the strategic orchestration of multimodal data—including textual, visual, and behavioural inputs—within advanced analytical frameworks. This integration demonstrates how real-time adaptive feedback can be leveraged to co-create value through personalized customer experiences, thereby enhancing advertisement relevance and fostering deeper, more sustained engagement (Madanchian, 2024a). Therefore, multimodal analysis holds immense promise to gain insights from consumer behaviour data, which combines multiple modalities, (such as text, images, and video), enable a deeper understanding of consumer behaviour and preferences (Yixuan, 2024).

4.4 AI-Enabled Consumer Engagement and Autonomous Decision-Making

AI systems improve consumer engagement by enriching the user experience, especially through social media platforms. Bilal et al. (2024) apply social support theory to demonstrate that AI positively impacts consumer engagement and purchase intention by enhancing the consumer experience on social media. Affective attachment plays a moderating role, amplifying satisfaction and brand loyalty. This confirms the vital role of emotional engagement in consumer decision-making. Therefore, the interaction with AI agents is also affecting consumers' moral and emotional responses.

Giroux et al. (2022) investigated how consumers' moral and emotional responses differ when interacting with AI agents, or self-service machines versus human cashiers in retail settings. Their research revealed that consumers tend to display lower moral intention, such as a reduced likelihood of reporting errors or unethical outcomes, when engaging with AI agents rather than human employees. The reduced moral intention with AI means that consumers are less likely to act ethically (e.g., report being undercharged) when the agent is a machine rather than a person. Additionally, the decline in moral behaviour is primarily driven by a reduced feeling of guilt during interactions with non-human agents. The less human-like the machine is perceived, the less guilt consumers feel, which in turn lowers their likelihood of acting morally.

This attenuation of moral responsibility stems partly from the perceived absence of social reciprocity and emotional accountability in human–AI exchanges. Interestingly, Giroux et al. (2022) also find that this reduced moral intention can coexist with strong affective attachment to AI interfaces or brands employing them, suggesting that emotional response may persist even when consumers experience weaker moral engagement. Such affective attachment can enhance brand loyalty and repeated usage, yet it also raises concerns about ethical complacency and asymmetrical accountability within AI-mediated relationships. While this attachment may enhance loyalty and repeated usage, it simultaneously increases the risk of ethical complacency and uncritical dependence on AI intermediaries.

Automatic recommendation systems enabled by generative AI are progressively being used by consumers to make daily purchase decisions, affecting human involvement in the decision-making process.

Within the marketing decision literature, the extent of human involvement is a central dimension for distinguishing among AI-enabled systems. *GAI-based recommendation* tools exemplify a low-autonomy configuration, where the technology functions as a collaborative assistant that generates personalized content or product suggestions while preserving human decision over the final choice (Huang & Rust, 2021). An illustrative example is Netflix using GAI to recommend and describe shows based on a user's viewing patterns and inferred preferences. *Decision support systems* (DSS) similarly operate under bounded autonomy, providing analytical insights and predictive models that augment, rather than supplant, managerial judgement and the final decision (Davenport et al., 2020).

Conversely, autonomous decision-making systems reflect higher levels of algorithmic agency, as they independently analyse data and implement actions within predefined strategic or ethical parameters, minimizing real-time human oversight, (e.g., self-driving cars deciding optimal routes and driving actions in real time) (Haenlein & Kaplan, 2023). At the furthest end of this autonomy continuum, *AI-driven purchasing agents* (e.g. an AI procurement bot automatically placing orders based on market conditions and inventory data) demonstrate full operational autonomy, conducting transactions and adapting to market dynamics without human intervention once governance rules are established (Madanchian, 2024b). Figure 1 illustrates this continuum shift from *AI-augmented decision-making*, where human oversight predominates, towards *AI-delegated autonomy*, where the AI assumes primary decision authority. Collectively, these configurations show the progression from high human involvement to full AI autonomy, raising critical implications for accountability, control, and trust in marketing practice (Rust, 2023).

Recent advancements in AI have facilitated the emergence of autonomous decision-making systems, wherein consumers increasingly delegate routine purchasing decisions to algorithmic agents. Sharma et al. (2024) demonstrate that perceived ease of use, performance expectancy, and social influence are key determinants in the adoption of such autonomous AI systems.

This evolution fundamentally challenges traditional models of consumer decision-making, which have historically assumed active, rational, and conscious engagement in information processing and choice. As AI systems increasingly act as proxies for

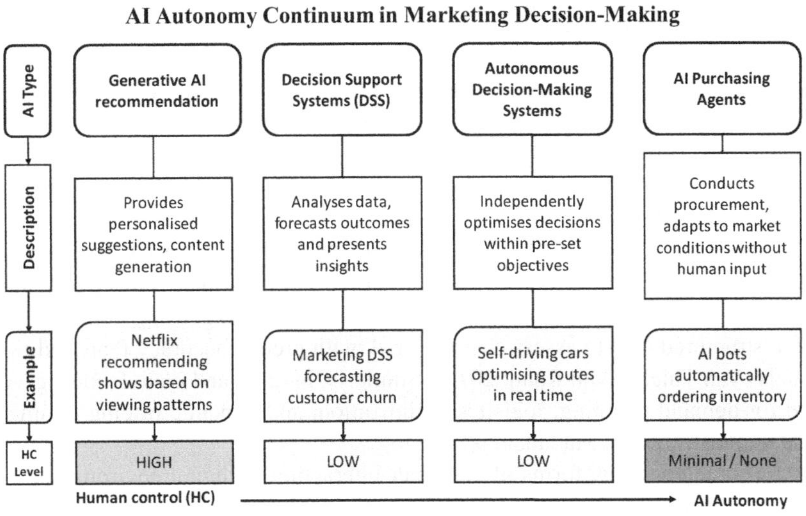

Fig. 1 AI Autonomy versus human control in marketing decision-making. *Source* Authors

consumers—filtering options, evaluating alternatives, and executing decisions—the locus of decision authority shifts from human cognition to algorithmic processes.

This shift carries substantial implications for marketing strategies concerning branding, advertising, and consumer trust, particularly in the context of low-involvement purchases. Klaus and Zaichkowsky (2022) advance this understanding through the AI-influenced decision-making (AIDM) model, which demonstrates that consumers increasingly delegate purchasing tasks to voice-based or algorithmic assistants. Such delegation reconfigures the traditional consumer–brand dynamic, as AI intermediaries determine exposure and preference formation, thereby reducing direct consumer engagement with brands. In low-involvement contexts, where habitual and convenience-driven behaviours dominate, AI mediation heightens the need for brands to sustain trust and recognition through consistent messaging, transparency, and algorithmic visibility. Accordingly, marketers must develop strategies that target not only human perceptions, but also the decision criteria encoded within AI systems that increasingly shape consumer choice.

These findings underscore the necessity for marketers and system designers to embed transparency, fairness, and moral reinforcement mechanisms within AI systems to sustain both consumer trust and ethical integrity in AI-mediated marketplaces.

Together, these developments suggest a paradigm shift in consumer autonomy and marketing practice, calling for new theoretical frameworks that integrate emotional, ethical, and algorithmic dimensions of decision-making in an era increasingly defined by human–AI symbiosis.

4.5 A Brief of the AI Benefits

The strategic use of AI in marketing brings measurable benefits, including enhanced customer experiences, reduced churn, and improved ROI (Syam & Sharma, 2018; Zulaikha et al., 2020). AI supports both short-term gains—via personalization offers and dynamic pricing—and long-term strategic insights, such as trend forecasting and lifetime value estimation.

AI applications extend beyond traditional marketing and CRM into domains such as financial risk prediction, fraud detection, and operational optimization. In financial services, AI models are employed for real-time credit scoring, using both structured and unstructured data to assess customer risk with greater accuracy than traditional models (Van Thiel & Van Raaij, 2019). Similarly, in retail and manufacturing, AI is used for demand planning, logistics optimization, and dynamic pricing (Kumar & Sundaramurthy, 2023; Madanchian, 2024b).

AI also enables new forms of customer interaction in digital environments. For instance, virtual showrooms or digital avatars driven by generative AI can offer immersive shopping experiences, while behavioural analytics can help design more intuitive digital interfaces (Sheta, 2021). These applications exemplify the versatility and scalability of AI as a tool for enhancing business intelligence and customer-centric innovation.

5 Pitfalls and Challenges

5.1 Lack of Transparency and Explainability

Many of the most accurate AI models—especially deep neural networks—are inherently opaque, making it difficult for business users and regulators to understand how decisions are made. This lack of interpretability undermines accountability and poses challenges in sensitive domains such as credit scoring, insurance, and medical recommendations (Stoycheva & Vitliemov, 2024; Van Thiel & Van Raaij, 2019).

Despite their predictive power, many AI models lack interpretability, because of algorithms' opacity, making it difficult to explain how they arrive at certain predictions or suggestions. This 'black-box' nature undermines decision-making and trust (Adadi & Berrada, 2018; Miller, 2019). Therefore, XAI frameworks are essential to bridge this gap, yet their integration into business systems remains limited.

Model interpretability also deals with model overfitting and noisy data drawbacks. Overfitting occurs when a model learns to perform well on the training data but fails to generalize to new, unseen data. This is a common challenge in consumer behaviour analysis, especially when dealing with noisy or incomplete data (Yixuan, 2024).

XAI was proposed to make AI systems more interpretable and transparent in decision-making processes. More importantly, facing the increase of the digital economy, the incorporation of ethical and models in e-commerce are crucial (Khrais, 2020). Understanding how and why a model makes a specific prediction is essential, particularly in applications where transparency is required (Yixuan, 2024).

Efforts to improve model transparency include the development of XAI methods, which aim to provide human-understandable justifications for algorithmic outputs. However, the trade-off between accuracy and interpretability remains a key limitation, particularly in high-stakes business applications.

5.2 Built-in Bias and Discrimination

AI models are susceptible to biases embedded in training data, algorithm design, or deployment contexts. These biases can manifest as unfair treatment, stereotyping, or exclusion of certain consumer groups—particularly marginalized populations (Schwartz et al., 2022; Varsha, 2023). For example, biased data may lead to discriminatory marketing offers or reduced access to financial services.

Biased datasets can result in unfair algorithmic outcomes—such as discriminatory pricing, exclusion of underrepresented groups, or gendered stereotypes in digital assistants (Anica-Popa et al., 2021; Spencer et al., 2018). Birhane (2022) argues that AI systems often automate structural injustices when built on flawed epistemologies and uncritical data practices.

ML models may also be seen as 'black boxes' due to stereotyped data and misrepresentation of the data used to train the model which causes a built-in bias, a vulnerability usually imputed to AI (Shneiderman, 2016).

Therefore, if the data used to train a model is biased, the model's predictions may also be biased. Thus, the issue of underrepresentation within the datasets used to train ML algorithms is a critical factor contributing to embedded bias within these systems. This systemic bias, often attributed to AI, stems from imbalanced or non-representative training data, which can skew algorithmic outcomes (Shneiderman, 2016). As a result, the reliability and fairness of AI systems are called into question, particularly in contexts where decisions significantly impact individuals or communities.

Moreover, the development of trustworthy AI must account for the tendency of ML algorithms to reflect the implicit biases of their human creators. These inherited biases can lead to discriminatory behaviours, such as the emergence of racist or sexist outputs in AI applications, including chatbots (Anica-Popa et al., 2021). A notable illustration of this phenomenon is the widespread depiction of digital assistants as young caucasian women, a design choice that perpetuates stereotypical associations of women with subservient or administrative roles (Spencer et al., 2018).

Another drawback in training data is using past consumer behaviours, as a base for sales forecasting, which may carry on a bias because it is no longer relevant to a customer's current buying need or preference (Anica-Popa et al., 2021). Thus, the development and training of AI algorithms must be responsible and accurate to avoid costly mistakes. In addition, as consumer behaviour is dynamic and subject to change, it requires continuous model adaptation.

Given that, there is a considerable risk that AI-enabled marketing strategies can generate biased decision-making processes. This highlights the need of ML models to adapt to evolving consumer preferences and market trends, which requires continuous training and updating of models (Yixuan, 2024).

Bias in AI is not only a technical flaw but a societal risk, as it may reinforce existing inequalities and erode public trust. Responsible AI practices require systematic auditing, inclusive dataset curation, and explainability tools to identify and mitigate harmful patterns. However, implementing these safeguards remains a significant operational and methodological challenge for many firms.

5.3 *Ethical and Legal Risks*

Unregulated AI use in marketing can violate privacy norms and ethical boundaries. As AI systems customize offers based on personal data, they may cross the line from personalization to manipulation (Gerlick & Liozu, 2020). Fariza et al. (2020)

warn that while marketing automation drives efficiency, it also introduces risks of malicious activity, data misuse, and consumer distrust.

Du and Xie (2021) highlight ethical paradoxes—where AI offers functional benefits but undermines autonomy or wellbeing. Companies must actively mitigate these tensions through responsible governance and transparent AI practices.

AI implementation intrinsically depends on the amount and quality of personal information organizations gather from their customers. Yet, companies must have ethical considerations and choose the right balance between personalization advantages and privacy risks (Inman & Nikolova, 2017). Noticeably, to take advantage of an AI-powered shopping experience, customers are being increasingly pressured to share private information, which can easily make them mistrust AI, raising privacy issues.

In addition, ethical principles need to be implemented when deploying algorithms to foster pricing and promotions, since retailers could use AI to socially discriminate against customers by using different messages and prices, based on customers' specific profiles (Gerlick & Liozu, 2020).

Another example of ethical issues concerning the use of sensitive personal data of customers involve digital services. Hospitality is one of the pioneer sectors that has adopted AI technology to create novel services such as smart hotel rooms, personalization services (Nair, 2020). While digital data enable organizations access to huge volumes of information that can have strategic implications, its rapid evolution and adoption at large has prompted researchers to raise questions on the ethicality involved in the sharing and usage of big data (Goldsteen et al., 2021).

5.4 Trust and Privacy Concerns

Several methodologies and AI techniques are employed in predicting consumer behaviour (e.g., ML algorithms, NLP, and deep learning models), but several challenges are faced, namely data privacy concerns and ethical considerations (Babu et al., 2023; Cheng et al., 2022).

In fact, one of the most pressing concerns is the protection of consumer privacy. AI systems rely on vast amounts of personal and behavioural data, often collected passively through IoT devices, social media, and e-commerce platforms. While this data fuels predictive and generative models, it also raises critical questions regarding informed consent, data ownership, and the right to be forgotten (Bobin et al., 2023; Rosário et al., 2024). In many cases, consumers are unaware of the extent to which their data is collected, analysed, and monetized.

Privacy concerns regarding the collection and use of personal information for marketing purposes already exist. However, AI broad use is boosting those concerns, as users' data is being collected and processed by machines and algorithms. Therefore, guaranteeing that data has consistently high quality, since the sources and volume (e.g. web, social media, mobile devices, sensors, and IoT) have increased considerably, it is a critical AI implementation challenge (Anica-Popa et al., 2021).

Addressing regulatory requirements is critical. The EU General Data Protection Regulation (GDPR) mandates the principle of data minimization, which requires that only data necessary to fulfil a certain purpose be collected (Hissou et al., 2023). The implementation of AI systems must therefore comply with privacy regulations such as the GDPR and CCPA, and organizations must establish transparent policies for data handling. Privacy-preserving ML techniques, such as federated learning and differential privacy, are gaining prominence as means to balance innovation with user rights (Ojha et al., 2023).

To overcome data privacy concerns, emerging federated learning allows multiple parties to collaboratively train a ML model without sharing sensitive data. This approach is particularly valuable in consumer behaviour analysis, where data privacy is a paramount concern.

Customer mistrust in AI systems is often linked to poor communication, unclear data usage policies, or past breaches (Hengstler et al., 2016; Inman & Nikolova, 2017). Hengstler et al. (2016) state that AI technology must be trusted for applied AI to work, the company's role is essential in the process of delivering trusted communication as well. As a result, businesses need to start developing trust as technology develops.

As AI becomes embedded in customer service, transparency and human oversight become essential to maintaining brand loyalty. Faria et al. (2023) argue that AI-powered customer experiences must align with consumer expectations regarding privacy, otherwise companies risk reputational damage and disengagement. Significant challenges that emerge from the trustworthiness of AI are personal or organizational privacy and security concerns, the use of biased systems, and even the role that AI can take in decision-making processes.

5.5 Cautions Regarding the Integration of AI into Marketing Strategies

The growing integration of AI into marketing strategies raises important questions about the role of these systems in mediating consumer choices. On the one hand, AI promises gains in efficiency, convenience, and personalization (Dwivedi et al., 2021; Jain et al., 2024). However, as personalization deepens, the importance of ethical data usage and consumer trust becomes paramount. On the other hand, concerns arise regarding consumer privacy (Cheng et al., 2022) and even less ethical behaviour on the part of consumers, since the non-human nature of the technology reduces feelings of guilt and, consequently, the intention to act ethically (Giroux et al., 2022). Therefore, when adopting these technologies, brands need to balance the benefits of automation with building relationships of trust and respect for users' rights (Jain et al., 2024).

The integration of AI into consumer behaviour analysis also faces internal barriers within organizations. These include a lack of skilled personnel, resistance to change, insufficient data infrastructure, and misalignment between AI capabilities and business goals (Witek-Hajduk et al., 2025). Organizations may adopt AI without fully understanding its requirements, leading to suboptimal implementation or failure to realize value. Additionally, firms operating in global markets must navigate diverse legal frameworks, cultural expectations, and digital maturity levels, all of which complicate the deployment of AI systems (Kumar & Sundaramurthy, 2023). These complexities require a strategic, cross-functional approach to AI adoption that incorporates legal, technical, and human-centred perspectives.

6 Theoretical Integration and Future Research Avenues

Overall, AI applications in marketing, customer engagement, and business strategy have opened new frontiers for personalization experiences and data-driven decision-making. However, these advancements also raise questions about ethics, trust, and consumer autonomy. As AI continues to evolve, both scholars and practitioners must navigate the balance between innovation and responsibility. However, most evidence supporting the effectiveness of generative AI in hyper-personalized marketing stems from simulations, case studies, and offline benchmarks, rather than from large-scale field experiments (Madanchian, 2024a; Wang, 2022). This underscores a significant gap in the literature: while systematic reviews and new empirical studies shed light on the technical and organizational pathways for implementing generative AI in marketing, there is a collective call for more rigorous, theory-driven frameworks and robust evaluation metrics to guide future advancements in this rapidly evolving field (Kshetri et al., 2024; Madanchian, 2024a).

Future research should emerge from the identified gaps rather than broad themes. Key directions include (Fig. 2):

- Multimodal consumer analytics: Empirical testing of cross-modal integration, accuracy, and cultural variations.
- Trust and delegation in AI-assisted decisions: Investigating psychological and contextual drivers of consumer willingness to delegate.
- Hybrid AI models: Examining coexistence of predictive and generative approaches, particularly in personalization marketing.
- Governance and ethical frameworks: Developing models for transparency, accountability, and fairness in consumer-facing AI.

7 Conclusion

AI has emerged as a transformative force in the field of consumer behaviour prediction, enabling businesses to move from reactive decision-making to proactive and even generative strategies. By harnessing vast and diverse datasets, AI systems offer

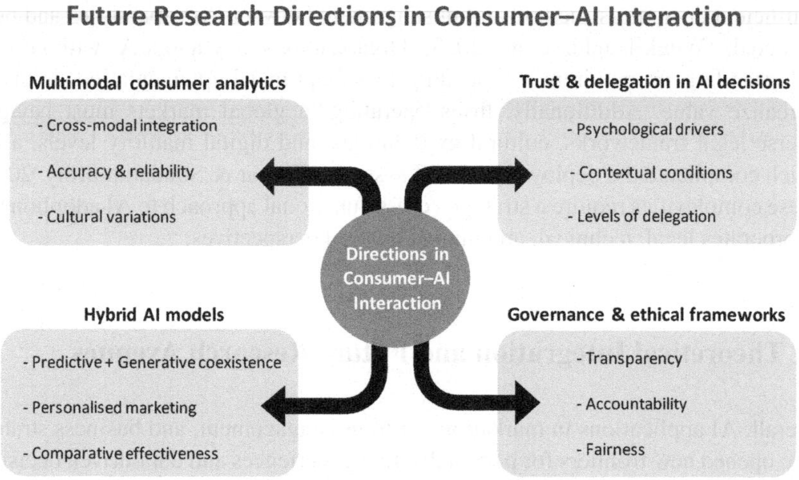

Fig. 2 Future research directions in consumer–AI interaction. *Source* Authors

unprecedented accuracy in forecasting purchasing patterns, personalizing user experiences, and optimizing customer engagement. Techniques such as ML, NLP, and generative models have empowered marketers to operate with a level of precision and scalability that was previously unattainable (Babu et al., 2023; Sheta, 2021).

However, this transformation is not without significant challenges. The increasing reliance on consumer data raises critical concerns about privacy, informed consent, and data protection (Bobin et al., 2023). In parallel, issues of algorithmic bias and model opacity continue to threaten the fairness and transparency of AI applications (Schwartz et al., 2022; Varsha, 2023). Moreover, the organizational readiness to integrate AI effectively varies widely across sectors and geographies, often limiting the full realization of its potential (Witek-Hajduk et al., 2025).

This chapter provided a comprehensive analysis of how AI is transforming behavioural customer analysis, with a particular focus on the fusion of predictive with generative models. By reviewing key AI techniques—such as clustering, supervised learning, and deep neural networks—it became clear that AI is reshaping customer segmentation, personalization, and retention strategies. However, alongside these advances come substantial ethical and technical challenges, including model opacity, embedded bias, and privacy concerns.

In response to RQ1, the findings indicate that GAI significantly enhances traditional model capabilities. It enables the simulation of consumer interactions, generation of hyper-personalization content, and adaptive engagement in real time, still requiring human choice and final decision, marking a major step forward in behavioural modelling and marketing innovation. The most effective marketing strategies increasingly combine both, leveraging predictive insights to inform generative outputs, while addressing ethical and operational challenges for sustainable success.

Regarding RQ2, the study concludes that while advanced models like LSTM and clustering techniques offer high predictive power, they often fall short in terms of transparency and fairness. The integration of XAI frameworks and ethical design principles remains essential to bridge this gap.

Despite complex AI models approaches offer enhanced predictive accuracy, however it also can lack model fairness, interpretability, and ethical soundness in customer behaviour analysis. To overcome these gaps there are several actions that experts and businesses can tackle. Namely, addressing algorithm bias is a critical ethical consideration in consumer behaviour analysis. These biases often stem from the data used to train AI systems, which may reflect individual inequalities or unbalanced representations of consumer groups, and potentially can lead to discriminatory practices and poor customer experience.

The consumer reliance on AI-mediated decision-making amplifies the importance of maintaining consistent brand recognition, data-driven personalization, and transparent ethical practices to sustain consumer trust. This paradigm shift from human-to-AI autonomy in decision-making demands that marketing strategies evolve from targeting individual perceptions to influencing algorithmic gatekeepers that now shape purchasing pathways.

Consequently, marketers are compelled to reconceptualize their strategic approaches (e.g. algorithmic rather than human intermediaries), optimizing brand visibility within AI ecosystems, and ensuring ethical transparency in AI-enabled interactions. This transformation underscores the need for new theoretical and practical frameworks capable of addressing marketing dynamics in an AI-dominated environment.

Retailers are also encouraged to design AI agents that evoke more human-like qualities (e.g. anthropomorphism), to help maintain ethical consumer behaviour and moral intentions, during interactions with non-human agents.

From this comprehensive study, we also conclude that AI emerges as an effective marketing tool, as well as a powerful manipulation tool. There is a considerable reputational risk that AI-enabled aggressive strategies, such as dynamic price discrimination or biased communication strategies, can generate customer defection that could provoke major financial and operational problems.

On the other hand, the dependency on AI can raise a significant risk for organizations and customers. Organizations use AI to maintain good customer service and optimize costs in delivering automated services. This way, the customer service is less personalization, might lack transparency, and can raise concerns about privacy and security issues, resulting in unsatisfied customers.

Finally, we need to know how customers interact with these AI applications, as they are becoming a big part of any company's service infrastructure. Understanding customer trustworthiness, privacy and security perceptions, and moral and emotional responses around the different AI applications in various fields is vital.

References

Adadi, A., & Berrada, M. (2018). Peeking inside the black-box: A survey on explainable artificial intelligence (XAI). *IEEE Access, 6*, 52138–52160. https://doi.org/10.1109/ACCESS.2018.2870052

Afolabi, I. T., Oladipupo, O., Worlu, R. E., & Akinyemi, I. O. (2016). A systematic review of consumer behaviour prediction studies. *Covenant Journal of Business and Social Sciences, 7*(1).

Akter, S., Dwivedi, Y., Biswas, K., Michael, K., Bandara, R., & Sajib, S. (2021). Addressing algorithmic bias in AI-driven customer management. *Journal of Global Information Management, 29*, 1–27. https://doi.org/10.4018/JGIM.20211101.OA3

Aneja, A. (2023). Artificial Intelligence-Based Customer Behavioural Analysis: Techniques, Applications, and Business Insights. *2023 International Conference on Innovative Computing, Intelligent Communication and Smart Electrical Systems (ICSES)*, 1–5. https://doi.org/10.1109/ICSES60034.2023.10465316

Anica-Popa, I., Anica-Popa, L., Rădulescu, C., & Vrîncianu, M. (2021). The integration of artificial intelligence in retail: Benefits, challenges and a dedicated conceptual framework. *Amfiteatru Economic, 23*(56), 122–122. https://doi.org/10.24818/EA/2021/56/120

Babu, S. M., Kumar, P. P., Devi, S., Reddy, K. P., & Satish, M. (2023). Predicting consumer behaviour with artificial intelligence. *2023 IEEE 5th International Conference on Cybernetics, Cognition and Machine Learning Applications (ICCCMLA)*, 698–703. https://doi.org/10.1109/ICCCMLA58983.2023.10346660

Bergner, A. S., Hildebrand, C., & Häubl, G. (2023). Machine Talk: How Verbal Embodiment in Conversational AI Shapes Consumer–Brand Relationships. Journal of Consumer Research, 50(4), 742–764. https://doi.org/10.1093/jcr/ucad014.

Bhagat, R., Chauhan, V., & Bhagat, P. (2023). Investigating the impact of artificial intelligence on consumer's purchase intention in e-retailing. *Foresight, 25*(2), 249–263. https://doi.org/10.1108/FS-10-2021-0218

Bilal, M., Zhang, Y., Cai, S., Akram, U., & Halibas, A. (2024). Artificial intelligence is the magic wand making customer- centric a reality! An investigation into the relationship between consumer purchase intention and consumer engagement through affective attachment. *Journal of Retailing and Consumer Services, 77*, 103674. https://doi.org/10.1016/j.jretconser.2023.103674

Birhane, A. (2022). Automating ambiguity: Challenges and pitfalls of artificial intelligence.. http://arxiv.org/abs/2206.04179.

Bobin, C. B., Mariyappan, M. S. R., & Sanal, A. (2023). Benefits and pitfalls of internet of behaviour. In *Internet of Behaviours (IoB)* (pp. 1–13). CRC Press.

Chaudhary, K., Alam, M., Al-Rakhami, M. S., & Gumaei, A. (2021). Machine learning-based mathematical modelling for prediction of social media consumer behaviour using big data analytics. *Journal of Big Data, 8*(1). https://doi.org/10.1186/s40537-021-00466-2

Cheng, X., Lin, X., Shen, X. L., Zarifis, A., & Mou, J. (2022). The dark sides of AI. *Electronic Markets, 32*, 11–15. https://doi.org/10.1007/s12525-022-00531-5

Cillo, P., & Rubera, G. (2024). Generative AI in innovation and marketing processes: A roadmap of research opportunities. *Journal of the Academy of Marketing Science, 53*(3), 684–701. https://doi.org/10.1007/s11747-024-01044-7

Đaković, M., & Rikalović, A. (2025). The future of generative AI in digital marketing: challenges and opportunities. *International Conference on Business, Management, and Economics Engineering Future-BME*. https://doi.org/10.24867/future-bme-2024-101

Davenport, T., Guha, A., Grewal, D., & Bressgott, T. (2020). How artificial intelligence will change the future of marketing. *Journal of the Academy of Marketing Science, 48*(1), 24–42. https://doi.org/10.1007/s11747-019-00696-0

De Bruyn, A., Viswanathan, V., Beh, Y. S., Brock, J. K. U., & von Wangenheim, F. (2020). Artificial intelligence and marketing: Pitfalls and opportunities. *Journal of Interactive Marketing, 51*, 91–105. https://doi.org/10.1016/j.intmar.2020.04.007

Du, S., & Xie, C. (2021). Paradoxes of artificial intelligence in consumer markets: Ethical challenges and opportunities. *Journal of Business Research, 129*, 961–974. https://doi.org/10.1016/j.jbusres.2020.08.024

Dwivedi, Y. K., Hughes, L., Ismagilova, E., Aarts, G., Coombs, C., Crick, T., & Williams, M. D. (2021). Artificial intelligence (AI): Multidisciplinary perspectives on emerging challenges, opportunities, and agenda for research, practice and policy. *International Journal of Information Management, 57*, 101994. https://doi.org/10.1016/j.ijinfomgt.2019.08.002

Faria, R., Torres, A., & Beirão, G. (2023). Trustworthy artificial intelligence and machine learning: Implications on users' security and privacy perceptions. In P. Pires, J. Santos, I. Veiga, & Torres (Eds.), *Confronting security and privacy challenges in digital marketing* (pp. 330–352). https://doi.org/.4018/978-1-6684-8958-1

Fariza, W., Rahman, W. A., Azila, A., Fauzi, C., Salfarina, W., Husain, W., Hasrinafasya, S., Hassan, C., Nahdiya, N., Kamaruzaman, N., Hanis, W. A., & Aziz, W. (2020). The usage of artificial intelligence in marketing automation: Potentials and pitfalls. *Journal of Mathematics and Computing Science, 6*(2), 1–8.

Gaddam, D. K. R., Ansari, M. D., Vuppala, S., Gunjan, V. K., & Sati, M. M. (2022). A performance comparison of optimization algorithms on a generated dataset. *Lecture Notes in Electrical Engineering, 783*, 1407–1415. https://doi.org/10.1007/978-981-16-3690-5_135

Gerlick, J. A., & Liozu, S. M. (2020). Ethical and legal considerations of artificial intelligence and algorithmic decision-making in personalised pricing. *Journal of Revenue and Pricing Management, 19*(2), 85–98. https://doi.org/10.1057/s41272-019-00225-2

Giroux, M., Kim, J., Lee, J. C., & Park, J. (2022). Artificial intelligence and declined guilt: Retailing morality comparison between human and AI. *Journal of Business Ethics, 178*(4), 1027–1041. https://doi.org/10.1007/s10551-022-05056-7

Gkikas, D. C., & Theodoridis, P. K. (2022). AI in consumer behaviour. In *Learning and analytics in intelligent systems* (Vol. 22, pp. 147–176). Springer Nature. https://doi.org/10.1007/978-3-030-80571-5_10

Gochhait, S., Mazumdar, O., Chahal, S., Kanwat, P., Gupta, S., Sharma, R., Pandit, V., Brahma, R., & Sachan, R. (2020). Role of artificial intelligence (AI) in understanding the behaviour pattern: a study on e-commerce. *ICDSMLA 2019: Proceedings of the 1st International Conference on Data Science, Machine Learning and Applications*, 1600–1606.

Goldsteen, A., Ezov, G., Shmelkin, R., Moffie, M., & Farkash, A. (2021). Data minimization for GDPR compliance in machine learning models. *AI and Ethics, 2*(3), 1–15.

Grewal, D., Satornino, C. B., Davenport, T., & Guha, A. (2025). How generative AI is shaping the future of marketing. *Journal of the Academy of Marketing Science, 53*(3), 702–722. https://doi.org/10.1007/s11747-024-01064-3

Haenlein, M., & Kaplan, A. (2023). Artificial intelligence and robotics: Shaking up the business world and society at large. *Journal of Business Research, 124*, 405–407. https://doi.org/10.1016/j.jbusres.2020.10.042

Hengstler, M., Enkel, E., & Duelli, S. (2016). Applied artificial intelligence and trust-the case of autonomous vehicles and medical assistance devices. *Technological Forecasting and Social Change, 105*, 105–120. https://doi.org/10.1016/j.techfore.2015.12.014

Hermann, E., & Puntoni, S. (2024). Artificial intelligence and consumer behavior: From predictive to generative AI. *Journal of Business Research, 180*, 114720. https://doi.org/10.1016/j.jbusres.2024.114720

Hissou, H., Benkirane, S., Guezzaz, A., Guezzaz, A., Azrour, M., Azrour, M., & Beni-Hssane, A. (2023). A novel machine learning approach for solar radiation estimation. *Sustainability, 15*(13), 10609.

Huang, M. H., & Rust, R. T. (2021). A strategic framework for artificial intelligence in marketing. *Journal of the Academy of Marketing Science, 49*(2), 30–50.

Huy, P., Shavkatovich, S., Abdul-Samad, Z., Agrawal, D., Ashifa, K., & Arumugam, M. (2023). Resource management projects in entrepreneurship and retain customer based on big data analysis and artificial intelligence. *The Journal of High Technology Management Research, 34*(2), 100471. https://doi.org/10.1016/j.hitech.2023.100471

Inman, J. J., & Nikolova, H. (2017). Shopper-facing retail technology: A retailer adoption decision framework incorporating shopper attitudes and privacy concerns. *Journal of Retailing, 93*(1), 7–28. https://doi.org/10.1016/j.jretai.2016.12.006

Jain, V., Wadhwani, K., & Eastman, J. K. (2024). Artificial intelligence consumer behaviour: A hybrid review and research agenda. *Journal of Consumer Behaviour, 23*(2), 676–697. https://doi.org/10.1002/cb.2233

Khrais, L. T. (2020). Role of artificial intelligence in shaping consumer demand in e-commerce. *Future Internet, 12*(12), 1–14. https://doi.org/10.3390/fi12120226

Klaus, P., & Zaichkowsky, J. L. (2022). The convenience of shopping via voice AI: Introducing AIDM. *Journal of Retailing and Consumer Services, 65*. https://doi.org/10.1016/j.jretconser.2021.102490

Kshetri, N., Dwivedi, Y. K., Davenport, T. H., & Panteli, N. (2024). Generative artificial intelligence in marketing: Applications, opportunities, challenges, and research agenda. *International Journal of Information Management, 75*, 102716.

Kumar, R., & Sundaramurthy, S. (2023). Ai and iot in manufacturing and related security perspectives for industry 4.0. In *Artificial intelligence and cyber security in industry 4.0* (pp. 47–70). Springer.

Lalwani, P., Mishra, M. K., Chadha, J. S., & Sethi, P. (2022). Customer churn prediction system: A machine learning approach. *Computing, 104*(2), 271–294.

Madanchian, M. (2024a). Generative AI for consumer behavior prediction: Techniques and applications. *Sustainability, 16*(22). https://doi.org/10.3390/su16229963

Madanchian, M. (2024b). The impact of artificial intelligence marketing on e-commerce sales. *Systems, 12*(10), 429. https://doi.org/10.3390/systems12100429

Malik, V., Mittal, R., Chaudhry, R., & Yadav, S. (2024). *Predicting Purchases and Personalizing the Customer Journey with Artificial Intelligence.* 2024 11th International Conference on Reliability, Infocom Technologies and Optimization (Trends and Future Directions) (ICRITO), 1–5. https://doi.org/10.1109/ICRITO61523.2024.10522362

Miller, T. (2019). Explanation in artificial intelligence: Insights from the social sciences. In *Artificial Intelligence* (Vol. 267, pp. 1–38). Elsevier B.V. https://doi.org/10.1016/j.artint.2018.07.007

Nair, S. R. (2020). A review on ethical concerns in big data management. *International Journal of Big Data Management, 1*(1), 8–25.

Ojha, N., Kumar, A., Tyagi, N., Ranjan, P., & Vaish, A. (2023). Use of machine learning in forensics and computer security. In *Artificial intelligence and cyber security in industry 4.0* (pp. 211–236). Springer.

Olu-Ajayi, R., Alaka, H., Sulaimon, I., Sunmola, F., & Ajayi, S. (2022). Building energy consumption prediction for residential buildings using deep learning and other machine learning techniques. *Journal of Building Engineering, 45*. https://doi.org/10.1016/j.jobe.2021.103406

Perez-Vega, R., Kaartemo, V., Lages, C. R., Borghei Razavi, N., & Männistö, J. (2021). Reshaping the contexts of online customer engagement behaviour via artificial intelligence: A conceptual framework. *Journal of Business Research, 129*, 902–910. https://doi.org/10.1016/j.jbusres.2020.11.002

Pires, P. B., Santos, J. D., & Torres, A. I. (2025). Hyper-personalised marketing with generative AI and predictive models: A systematic review. In A. Rosário & A. C. Boechat (Eds.), *Adapting global communication and marketing strategies to generative AI* (pp. 79–112). IGI Global. https://doi.org/10.4018/10.4018/979-8-3373-2502-6.ch004

Prakash Babu S. M., Kumar, P. P., Devi, S., Reddy, K. P., & Satish, M. (2023). *Predicting Consumer Behaviour with Artificial Intelligence.* 5th IEEE International Conference on Cybernetics, Cognition and Machine Learning Applications, ICCCMLA *2023*, 698–703. https://doi.org/10.1109/ICCCMLA58983.2023.10346660

Prasad, B., & Ghosal, I. (2022). Forecasting buying intention through artificial neural network: An algorithmic solution on direct-to-consumer brands. *FIIB Business Review, 11*(4), 405–421. https://doi.org/10.1177/23197145211046126

Puntoni, S., Reczek, R. W., Giesler, M., & Botti, S. (2021). Consumers and artificial intelligence: An experiential perspective. *Journal of Marketing, 85*(1), 131–151. https://doi.org/10.1177/0022242920953847

Reed, C., Wynn, M., & Bown, R. (2025). Artificial intelligence in digital marketing: Towards an analytical framework for revealing and mitigating bias. *Big Data and Cognitive Computing, 9*(2). https://doi.org/10.3390/bdcc9020040

Rosário, A. T., Cruz, R., Moniz, L. B., & Casaca, J. A. (2024). Predictive analytics for customer behaviour. In *Data-driven Marketing for Strategic Success* (pp. 37–72). IGI Global.

Rust, R. T. (2023). The future of marketing. *International Journal of Research in Marketing, 40*(1), 15–26. https://doi.org/10.1016/j.ijresmar.2022.11.001

Safara, F. (2022). A computational model to predict consumer behaviour during COVID-19 pandemic. *Computational Economics, 59*(4), 1525–1538. https://doi.org/10.1007/s10614-020-10069-3

Schwartz, R., Vassilev, A., Greene, K., Perine, L., Burt, A., & Hall, P. (2022). *Towards a standard for identifying and managing bias in artificial intelligence.* US Department of Commerce, National Institute of Standards and Technology. https://doi.org/10.6028/NIST.SP.1270

Shapi, M. K. M., Ramli, N. A., & Awalin, L. J. (2021). Energy consumption prediction by using machine learning for smart building: Case study in Malaysia. *Developments in the Built Environment, 5*. https://doi.org/10.1016/j.dibe.2020.100037

Sharma, S., Islam, N., Singh, G., & Dhir, A. (2024). Why Do Retail Customers Adopt Artificial Intelligence (AI) Based Autonomous Decision-Making Systems? *IEEE Transactions on Engineering Management, 71*, 1846–1861. https://doi.org/10.1109/TEM.2022.3157976

Sheta, S. V. (2021). Artificial intelligence applications in Behavioural analysis for advancing user experience design. *International Journal of Artificial Intelligence (ISCSITR-IJAI, 2*(1), 1–16.

Shneiderman, B. (2016). The dangers of faulty, biased, or malicious algorithms requires independent oversight. In *Proceedings of the National Academy of Sciences of the United States of America* (Vol. 113, Issue (48), pp. 13538–13540). National Academy of Sciences. https://doi.org/10.1073/pnas.1618211113

Spencer, D. J., Poggi, J., & Gheerawo, R. (2018). Designing out stereotypes in artificial intelligence: Involving users in the personality design of a digital assistant. *ACM International Conference Proceeding Series*, 130–135. https://doi.org/10.1145/3284869.3284897

Stoycheva, B., & Vitliemov, P. (2024). Challanges of using artificial intelligence in management decision making. *Strategies for Policy in Science and Education-Strategii Na Obrazovatelnata i Nauchnata Politika, 32*(3s), 42–51. https://doi.org/10.53656/str2024-3s-4-cha

Stubseid, S., & Arandjelovic, O. (2018). Machine Learning Based Prediction of Consumer Purchasing Decisions: The Evidence and Its Significance. *The Workshops of the Thirty-Second AAAI Conference on Artificial Intelligence*, 100–106. http://www.aaai.org

Syam, N., & Sharma, A. (2018). Waiting for a sales renaissance in the fourth industrial revolution: Machine learning and artificial intelligence in sales research and practice. *Industrial Marketing Management, 69*, 135–146. https://doi.org/10.1016/j.indmarman.2017.12.019

Talukdar, J., Singh, T. P., & Barman, B. (2023). Knowledge representation and reasoning. In *Artificial intelligence in healthcare industry* (pp. 17–40). Springer.

Van Thiel, D., & Van Raaij, W. F. F. (2019). Artificial intelligence credit risk prediction: An empirical study of analytical artificial intelligence tools for credit risk prediction in a digital era. *Journal of Risk Management in Financial Institutions, 12*(3), 268–286.

Varsha, P. S. (2023). How can we manage biases in artificial intelligence systems—A systematic literature review. *International Journal of Information Management Data Insights, 3*(1), 100165. https://doi.org/10.1016/j.jjimei.2023.100165

Verma, S., Sharma, R., Deb, S., & Maitra, D. (2021). Artificial intelligence in marketing: Systematic review and future research direction. *International Journal of Information Management Data Insights, 1*(1), 100002. https://doi.org/10.1016/j.jjimei.2020.100002

Volkmar, G., Fischer, P. M., & Reinecke, S. (2022). Artificial intelligence and machine learning: Exploring drivers, barriers, and future developments in marketing management. *Journal of Business Research, 149*, 599–614. https://doi.org/10.1016/j.jbusres.2022.04.007

Wang, C. (2022). Efficient customer segmentation in digital marketing using deep learning with swarm intelligence approach. *Information Processing and Management, 59*(6). https://doi.org/10.1016/j.ipm.2022.103085

Witek-Hajduk, M. K., Grginović, M. G., & Targański, B. (2025). *Digital internationalisation of firms: Strategies, challenges, and legal aspects*. Routledge.

Yeo, S. F., Tan, C. L., Kumar, A., Tan, K. H., & Wong, J. K. (2022). Investigating the impact of AI-powered technologies on Instagrammers' purchase decisions in digitalization era–a study of the fashion and apparel industry. *Technological Forecasting and Social Change, 177*, 121551. https://doi.org/10.1016/j.techfore.2022.121551

Yixuan, Z. (2024). Utilizing machine learning algorithms for consumer behaviour analysis. *Applied and Computational Engineering, 49*, 213–219.

Zhang, Y., & Liu, C. (2024). Unlocking the potential of artificial intelligence in fashion design and E-commerce applications: The case of Midjourney. *Journal of Theoretical and Applied Electronic Commerce Research, 19*(1), 654–670. https://doi.org/10.3390/jtaer19010035

Zulaikha, S., Mohamed, H., Kurniawati, M., Rusgianto, S., & Rusmita, S. (2020). Customer predictive analytics using artificial intelligence. *The Singapore Economic Review, 70*(4). https://doi.org/10.1142/s0217590820480021

Artificial Intelligence in Marketing Education: Shaping the Future of Learning

Ana Estima and Rúben Pinhal

Abstract The growing integration of Artificial Intelligence (AI) into higher education is reshaping pedagogical models, learning experiences, and the role of educators, particularly in dynamic and practice-oriented fields such as marketing. This chapter explores the evolution of marketing education, tracing methodological shifts from traditional didactic approaches to the emerging wave of AI-enhanced learning. We begin by outlining the historical development of marketing pedagogy and the initial adoption of educational technologies. We then examine how the recent democratisation of generative AI tools—such as ChatGPT and image-generation platforms—has opened new opportunities and raised significant challenges for marketing educators and students. Drawing on recent literature, practical examples, and critical perspectives, this chapter examines the implications of AI for curriculum design, student engagement, assessment practices, and academic integrity. The research concludes with a forward-looking research agenda that addresses AI literacy, educator preparedness, and the development of ethical frameworks to ensure the responsible use of AI in marketing education. By combining retrospective analysis with prospective insights, this chapter contributes to an informed debate on how AI shapes the future of learning in marketing.

A. Estima (✉) · R. Pinhal
GOVCOPP, Aveiro, Portugal
e-mail: aestima@ua.pt

R. Pinhal
e-mail: rubensilvapinhal@ua.pt

A. Estima
CIDTFF, Aveiro, Portugal

A. Estima · R. Pinhal
ISCA, Aveiro, Portugal

University of Aveiro, Aveiro, Portugal

J. D. Santos et al. (eds.), *Artificial Intelligence Transforming Marketing*, Contributions to Management Science, https://doi.org/10.1007/978-3-032-22360-9_3

1 Introduction

The rapid advancement and diffusion of Artificial Intelligence (AI) have introduced profound changes across various sectors of society, including healthcare, communication, management, and, increasingly, education. In the context of marketing education, a field marked by its responsiveness to innovation and its close ties to professional practice (Pinheiro et al., 2018), AI is not simply a technological novelty but a disruptive force that challenges foundational assumptions about what it means to teach, learn, and prepare students for a digitally mediated marketplace (Crittenden, 2024; Sihi & Ryan, 2025).

As AI systems become more powerful and accessible, their use in content creation, predictive analysis, simulation, and human–machine interaction is becoming commonplace. Tools such as ChatGPT, DALL·E, Gemini, and MidJourney are now integrated into daily learning routines, enabling students to generate texts, personas, visual content, and marketing strategies through prompt-based interaction (Guha et al., 2024; McAlister et al., 2024). These tools extend what can be done in the classroom and how knowledge is constructed and negotiated, reshaping learning experiences, teaching roles, and academic expectations (Kim & Koo, 2024).

However, this technological evolution also raises urgent pedagogical and ethical questions. As educators and researchers in marketing, we are compelled to reflect critically on how AI should be integrated into curricula in pedagogically meaningful and socially responsible ways. These pedagogical and ethical questions also intersect with broader policy and regulatory frameworks. The OECD AI Principles (OECD, 2019), for instance, emphasise human-centred values, transparency, and accountability, while the forthcoming EU AI Act seeks to classify and regulate AI systems according to risk levels, including potential applications in education.

This involves navigating tensions between efficiency and depth, automation and creativity, institutional innovation and ethical deliberation (Chew & Gilani, 2024; Mutongi et al., 2025). The growing reliance on AI-mediated outputs—whether in writing, image generation, analysis, or feedback—demands a reevaluation of academic integrity, authorship, and the role of human judgment in the educational process. These concerns are especially salient in marketing, a discipline that increasingly relies on data, algorithms, and automation but also requires cultural sensitivity, ethical reasoning, and critical thinking (Grewal et al., 2025; McAlister et al., 2024).

This chapter explores how AI is reshaping marketing education by examining its historical trajectory, recent innovations, and future directions. It begins by revisiting the dominant pedagogical models that have historically structured marketing education, including lectures, case studies, and project-based learning, followed by an analysis of how the digital turn—through platforms like learning management systems and marketing simulations—set the stage for more radical technological shifts (Cadwallader et al., 2013; Von der Heidt & Quazi, 2013).

We then trace the emergence of AI in education, distinguishing between early applications such as intelligent tutoring systems and the recent democratisation of generative AI tools, now available to students and educators at an unprecedented scale (Zawacki-Richter et al., 2019). Building on this, we analyse current trends in integrating AI into marketing pedagogy, focusing on its impact on curriculum design, active learning methodologies, and assessment practices. Drawing on examples from recent literature and classroom implementations, we examine how AI is redefining the role of the educator, raising new challenges around transparency, feedback, and student agency (Kim & Koo, 2024; Richter et al., 2024; Sihi & Ryan, 2025).

Finally, the chapter proposes a forward-looking research agenda, identifying key areas for empirical investigation, such as AI literacy, educator readiness, algorithmic feedback, and ethical governance. As marketing educators, we argue that a reflective, strategic, and ethically grounded approach to AI is necessary and urgent. By anticipating technological shifts and cultivating a critical awareness of their implications, we can help ensure that AI is integrated into marketing education in innovative and human-centred ways.

2 Historical and Methodological Evolution in Marketing Education

2.1 Traditional Approaches

Marketing education has traditionally been anchored in well-established pedagogical models such as lectures, case study analysis, and project-based learning. These approaches have long served to provide foundational knowledge and foster analytical thinking in students preparing for careers in marketing. However, over time, scholars have begun to question the limitations of these teacher-centred models in equipping learners with the competencies required in an increasingly complex, digital, and global marketing landscape.

In response, a growing body of literature has advocated for curriculum innovation and a rethinking of pedagogical strategies. Authors such as Beggs, (2011), Borin & Metcalf, (2010), and Cadwallader et al., (2013) call for the inclusion of new thematic domains—ranging from sustainability (Borin & Metcalf, 2010; Bridges & Wilhelm, 2008; Markley Rountree & Koernig, 2015; Weber, 2013) and ethics (Ferrell & Keig, 2013) to information management ((Burger & Schmidt, 1987), Geographical Information Systems (GIS) (Miller et al., 2007, 2014), and database marketing (Teer et al., 2007).

Beyond content, pedagogical reform has focused on methodological transformation. Influenced by constructivist principles, several authors (e.g. Kennedy et al., 2001; Marshall et al., 1996; Von der Heidt & Quazi, 2013) advocate a shift from transmissive to experiential and student-centred models. Strategies such as service learning (Cadwallader et al., 2013), experiential learning (Kolb & Kolb, 2017; Li et al., 2007; Maher & Hughner, 2005; Roy, 2006; Spanjaard et al., 2018; Wiese & Sherman, 2011), situated learning (Bay, 2021), simulations (Kirpalani, 2009; Vos, 2015), and creative problem-solving (Čančer, 2014; Wee et al., 2003) have gained traction for their capacity to foster active engagement, critical reflection, and transferable skills.

Some educators have also explored more unorthodox methods to enhance emotional and cognitive resonance with learners. These include music-based metaphors (Weinrauch, 2005), reflective exercises such as designing one's own funeral (Butler, 2007; Schiller et al., 2013), and the use of virtual platforms like Second Life to increase immersion and retention (Schiller et al., 2013).

This gradual pedagogical shift occurred parallel with the growing use of digital technologies in the classroom. Within this evolving context, the digital transformation of marketing education began to accelerate. The following section explores this digital turn in greater depth, examining how the proliferation of technology—before the advent of generative AI—reshaped the structure and dynamics of marketing pedagogy.

2.2 *The Digital Turn*

The transition from traditional, instructor-led approaches to more interactive and technology-supported forms of teaching marked a pivotal moment in the evolution of marketing education. This digital turn, accelerated in the early 2000s and further reinforced by the proliferation of online platforms in the 2010s, reflected both the pedagogical desire for more student-centred learning and the increasing availability of digital infrastructure in higher education.

The first wave of this transformation centred on adopting Learning Management Systems (LMS) such as Moodle, Blackboard, and Canvas. These platforms offered educators new ways to structure content, monitor student progress, and facilitate communication. LMS tools introduced greater flexibility and accessibility, enabling asynchronous learning and multimedia integration, thereby reshaping the pace and format of learning experiences (Means et al., 2014).

In parallel, the development of marketing simulations provided powerful new avenues for experiential learning (Kolb & Kolb, 2017; Roy, 2006). Tools like Markstrat or Mimic Pro allowed students to practice strategic decision-making in competitive, risk-free environments. Cadwallader et al. (2013) and Pollack and Lilly (2008) highlight that simulation-based learning fosters deeper engagement by connecting theoretical concepts to practical, real-time scenarios. These methods aligned well with marketing's applied nature, encouraging active participation and the development of transferable skills.

A significant innovation during this period was the emergence of Massive Open Online Courses (MOOCs). Platforms like Coursera, edX, and FutureLearn offered open-access marketing courses from leading institutions, extending educational reach and providing modular, self-paced content. While MOOCs were initially praised for democratising knowledge, they also posed pedagogical challenges related to retention, motivation, and limited interaction (Hollands & Tirthali, 2014).

Marketing educators began experimenting with multimedia content, flipped classrooms, collaborative tools such as blogs (Kaplan et al., 2010; Muncy, 2014), wikis (Muñoz, 2012), and cloud-based platforms. These digital resources supported more constructivist learning environments, where students co-created content, engaged in peer-to-peer learning, and worked on problem-based projects. As Brennan et al. (2018) and Von der Heidt and Quazi (2013) argue, this transition required a shift from content transmission to learning facilitation, placing the student at the centre of the educational process.

However, as promising as these innovations were, their adoption was not uniform. Some institutions enthusiastically embraced digital tools, while others implemented them superficially or resisted significant pedagogical change. Cadwallader et al. (2013) and Kennedy et al. (2001) stress that technology alone does not guarantee transformation; its effectiveness depends on integrating appropriate methodologies and developing new competencies among educators.

Crucially, this pre-AI digital phase prepared the ground for what would follow: a more radical integration of intelligent technologies into the classroom. The digital turn was a bridge between traditional methods and the forthcoming wave of AI-driven education by familiarising educators and students with hybrid learning environments and embedding digital literacy into curricula.

In the next section, we turn to the emergence of Artificial Intelligence itself, beginning with its early applications in education before the rise of generative AI.

3 The Emergence of Artificial Intelligence in Education

3.1 Early Applications of AI in Education

Although the popularisation of AI in education is a relatively recent phenomenon, early applications of AI in learning environments date back several decades. Well before the rise of generative tools such as ChatGPT, researchers and developers were exploring how machine learning, rule-based systems, and natural language processing could be used to enhance educational practices.

One of the earliest domains of AI application was the development of Intelligent Tutoring Systems (ITS)—computer-based programs designed to simulate one-to-one tutoring by adapting feedback to individual learners' needs. Systems such as AutoTutor (Graesser et al., 2005) and ELM-ART (Weber & Brusilovsky, 2001) represented important steps in personalised education. These platforms could analyse student input, provide real-time guidance, and adjust instructional content accordingly, often based on cognitive modelling.

Parallel efforts focused on automated assessment, particularly in grading short-answer or essay-type questions. Natural Language Processing (NLP) models were developed to assess syntax, coherence, and relevance to prompt questions (Shermis &

Burstein, 2013). While these tools offered scalability in assessment, their reliability and fairness were often questioned, particularly when dealing with nuanced or creative responses.

In the context of marketing education, however, the adoption of early AI applications has remained limited. Most institutions focused on broader digital tools such as Learning Management Systems. At the same time, AI-based systems were more often embedded in STEM disciplines or language learning platforms (e.g. Duolingo's early adaptive algorithms). Nevertheless, some isolated studies explored how data mining techniques could be applied to analyse student behaviour in marketing courses, or how chatbots could support frequently asked questions related to course content or logistics (Luckin et al., 2016).

A major constraint during this period was the accessibility and cost of AI technologies. Implementing ITS or developing AI-powered feedback systems typically requires substantial technical infrastructure and expertise, often limiting their deployment to research-intensive institutions or commercial educational platforms.

Moreover, the pedagogical frameworks for integrating AI were still underdeveloped. As Selwyn (2019) noted, early discussions on AI in education were largely speculative, lacking empirical grounding and often driven by technological determinism rather than educational theory. The field was characterised by a technocentric optimism that AI could enhance efficiency and personalisation, but with limited attention to ethical or equity-related concerns.

Despite these limitations, this early phase laid foundational concepts that would be revisited and significantly expanded with the emergence of generative AI. Key themes such as adaptive feedback, learner modelling, and data-informed instruction remain central in today's debates, now enhanced by the computational power and accessibility of large-scale AI systems.

As we explore in the next section, democratising AI tools post-2020 radically altered the educational landscape, making AI not just a backend system but a front-facing co-creator in the learning experience.

3.2 Democratisation of AI Tools

Since late 2022, ChatGPT's public release has widely recognised its potential in marketing education, particularly in empowering students to explore advanced concepts such as segmentation, market analysis, and brand creation through prompts (Hadi Mogavi et al., 2024).

The rapid adoption of ChatGPT in academic environments altered traditional dynamics, as students began generating case studies, persona designs, and SWOT analyses directly with algorithmic support (Ding et al., 2024).

In many institutions, this use led to reforming lecture-based sessions into interactive formats, where students would first produce content with AI and subsequently compare the results with human-based approaches (Tafesse & Wood, 2024). These pedagogical sequences foster reflective learning grounded in comparative evaluation between human and artificial intelligence (McAlister et al., 2024).

In early 2023, the DALL·E platform became accessible in numerous educational contexts related to marketing and branding, enabling students to generate images of personas and consumer environments using simple prompts. This democratisation allowed for creating multiple visual materials at no cost, stimulating visual literacy and discussions around symbolic meaning in digital marketing (Ding et al., 2024).

Lecturers began comparing these graphic outputs with hand-drawn assignments, encouraging critical reflection on visual bias and aesthetic choices (Nassif et al., 2024). Democratic access to a tool previously confined to the visual industry transformed the process of real-time image creation within the classroom (Tsidylo & Chele, 2023).

Also in 2023, sophisticated multimodal models such as Gemini and Midjourney emerged and were used to generate visual narratives for marketing campaigns (Yin et al., 2023). Students combined textual and visual generation, using Gemini to write slogans and DALL·E or Midjourney to produce corresponding images, thereby promoting an integrated approach to design and linguistics (Nassif et al., 2024). This media integration enhanced students' ability to think holistically about multimodal campaigns, prompting them to simultaneously consider aesthetic, cultural, and communicative dimensions (Tsidylo & Chele, 2023).

Copilot was introduced as a writing assistant in the field of persuasive writing in 2024, providing suggestions for headlines, calls to action, and product descriptions (Barry & Kohtamäki, 2025). Students would submit drafts to Copilot and refine them based on algorithmic feedback, which contributed to improved textual clarity, linguistic economy, and enhanced support for strategic persuasion (Wiboolyasarin et al., 2024). The alternation between manual production, automated revision, and classroom discussion fostered iterative learning in technical marketing writing (Roy, 2024).

In parallel, lecturers began introducing modules on prompt engineering, teaching students how to formulate effective prompts and critically evaluate the generated outputs (Walter, 2024). Students learned to distinguish between vague prompts and those yielding strategic insights, engaging in reflections on structure, lexical clarity, and alignment with communicational objectives (Nazari & Saadi, 2024). These exercises underscore the need for advanced algorithmic literacy skills, now essential in both educational and professional marketing contexts (Pötzsch & Pereira, 2022).

To ensure transparency and promote academic integrity, assessment rubrics began to require disclosure of the platforms used and the prompts applied (Yusuf et al., 2024). These rubrics asked students to justify their choices, analyse potential biases, and reflect on the intersection between human and AI authorship (Kim & Koo, 2024). This initiative marked a shift in assessment practices, which started to value metacognition, source awareness, and reflexive processes (Yusuf et al., 2024).

Significant innovations emerged in continuous assessment, including implementing adaptive quizzes using AI in 2024 via Gemini for Education, integrated into Google Classroom (Sun et al., 2025). These quizzes automatically adjusted to each student's performance, offering tailored reviews and differentiated questions to address specific misunderstandings, so the democratisation of such platforms enabled automated personalisation and equitable learning opportunities. It freed educators' time for more targeted pedagogical interventions (Mustafa et al., 2024).

Within project-based learning (PBL), Han et al. (2023) documented how AI tools began generating dynamic market scenarios for problem-solving activities, enriching assignments with variables previously unavailable. The ability to simulate markets, provide feedback on pricing or positioning changes, and allow students to revise strategies accordingly represented a profound democratisation of didactic possibilities (Farrell, 2020).

While these advances are promising, Zawacki-Richter et al. (2019) warn that the mere availability of such tools does not ensure deep learning, especially in the absence of pedagogical mediation. In response, educators developed dedicated sessions to discuss the algorithmic nature of these platforms, underlying datasets, limitations of creativity, and the risks of bias or AI hallucinations (Qian, 2025). For example, in international marketing classes, debates on the use of AI in global campaigns underscored the importance of contextualising cultural values and data parameters (Prabhakaran et al., 2022).

The process of democratising AI has imposed new demands on teacher professional development, evidenced by the emergence of synchronous classes focused on AI in marketing, teacher training workshops on algorithmic literacy, and practical guides for integrating AI with pedagogical intent (Romero, 2024). These efforts have ensured educators do not relinquish critical mediation to algorithms but instead retain epistemological control over the learning process (Qian, 2025).

Several authors have proposed frameworks to alternate between AI-supported and AI-free activities to maximise pedagogical impact to foster critical discernment (Yatani et al., 2024). Awadallah Alkouk & Khlaif (2024) suggest iterative assessments to monitor students' evolving ability to design prompts and analyse outputs. The democratisation of tools such as ChatGPT, DALL·E, Gemini, and Copilot can only be fully pedagogically effective if accompanied by reflective practices, critical result management, and epistemological transparency (Yuan & Hu, 2024).

The democratisation of AI in marketing education has enabled students and educators to access advanced tools for creation, analysis, and experimentation, significantly lowering previous technological and cognitive barriers (Costa et al., 2024). Nevertheless, this accessibility alone does not guarantee educational value. These tools fulfil their pedagogical potential through mediated, ethically grounded, and critically reflective integration. When used within structured learning environments, guided by educators who remain epistemologically engaged, AI-driven platforms can transform classrooms into spaces of co-creation, interpretative dialogue, and iterative knowledge construction (Costa et al., 2024; Roll & Wylie, 2016).

4 AI in Marketing Education: Current Trends and Examples

4.1 Curriculum Integration

AI is beginning to enter the curricula of marketing and business education programmes with increasing consistency, mirroring developments across other academic disciplines. This trend suggests that existing, well-established pedagogical methodologies—many of which have demonstrated long-term effectiveness—are now being enriched through the progressive introduction of AI as a complementary tool to support teaching and learning processes.

However, the extensive presence of AI across virtually all dimensions of contemporary life—including education, professional environments, and private spheres—necessitates a more critical and comprehensive curricular response. In fields such as marketing and management, where the professional application of AI is rapidly becoming widespread, this transformation appears particularly urgent. While there is a growing interest in embedding AI more fully into educational programmes, the academic literature remains relatively scarce in mapping the specifics of this integration—namely, where it is occurring, how it is being operationalised, and under what institutional or national conditions.

Many higher education institutions are only now taking initial steps towards developing formal policies to guide the use of generative AI tools in academic settings. These policies vary significantly depending on geographical and institutional contexts, reflecting broader sociocultural and regulatory differences. Nevertheless, a shared concern is evident in institutions' objectives, which often centre on "emphasising academic integrity, enhancing teaching and learning practices, and promoting equity" (Jin et al., 2025, p. 1). While some institutions adopt restrictive approaches, including outright prohibitions or stringent rules regarding AI use, others demonstrate more openness, provided that ethical safeguards are clearly defined and consistently applied.

A fundamental question thus arises: how should AI be introduced into the curriculum, and through what strategies can this be achieved responsibly and effectively? Although, as noted, the current literature remains scarce, existing contributions emphasise specific areas such as personalised learning environments, data analytics, simulations, and machine learning (Thontirawong & Chinchanachokchai, 2021). These applications are frequently positioned as mechanisms to enhance the quality of teaching and learning and the development of skills increasingly demanded by the digital economy. In this regard, AI is framed less as a discrete content area to be taught in isolation and more as an enabler that reshapes existing pedagogical processes and learning outcomes.

Notably, the examples reported in the literature focus more on how AI tools can be harnessed to address traditional marketing concepts and activities, rather than on developing entirely new curricular content. For instance, case-based learning, market analysis, customer segmentation, and campaign design are being reimagined through the affordances of AI technologies, thereby offering students enhanced opportunities to experiment, iterate, and make data-informed decisions (Nnanna-Ohuonu, 2025). This pedagogical shift signals a gradual but significant movement towards a curriculum in which AI is not merely an external tool but becomes embedded as both a subject of study and a medium of instruction.

Consequently, integrating AI into marketing education cannot be approached as a simple matter of technical adoption. It calls for thoughtful curricular redesign, interdisciplinary collaboration, and the establishment of robust ethical frameworks to support equitable access and responsible use. In doing so, educational institutions can begin bridging the gap between technological innovation and pedagogical tradition, ensuring that the next generation of marketing professionals is equipped with digital fluency and the critical judgement required to navigate and shape the evolving landscape of AI-enhanced business practice.

In the next section, we will examine in greater detail how this methodological transformation is unfolding within the context of marketing education. Rather than replacing established pedagogical foundations, AI technologies are reshaping how those foundations are operationalised—introducing new dynamics in how knowledge is delivered, how students engage with content, and how educators design, monitor, and adapt learning processes. This includes using generative AI to create learning materials, integrating intelligent systems into assessment and feedback mechanisms, and the growing reliance on data-driven insights to personalise instruction. Special attention will be paid to how AI reconfigures active learning strategies—such as Problem-Based Learning, Case-Based Learning, and Team-Based Learning—and how these shifts redefine the role of the educator from knowledge transmitter to facilitator of complex human–machine interactions. Through this analysis, we aim to uncover the pedagogical logic behind AI adoption and its implications for teaching practice in marketing programmes.

4.2 Pedagogical Applications

The introduction of AI into higher education has catalysed structural transformations in marketing education. It is reshaping the role of educators, pedagogical methods, and the way students construct and acquire knowledge (Elhajjar et al., 2021).

AI has emerged as a disruptive force that challenges traditional instructional paradigms, typically centred on the unidirectional transmission of content, while simultaneously expanding the scope for personalisation and technological mediation in learning processes (Chew & Gilani, 2024).

This transition requires a curricular and methodological renewal by educators, who are now integrating AI-based tools into teaching, assessment, and monitoring student performance (Kim & Koo, 2024). In marketing education in particular, a field where adaptability to innovation is crucial, AI allows instructors to design data-driven learning experiences, predictive simulations, and intelligent adaptive tutoring systems (Sihi & Ryan, 2025).

Initially, AI was treated merely as content to be taught, especially in data analysis and digital transformation courses, where instructors retained their traditional role as knowledge transmitters, incorporating AI only as an object of study (Daldıran, 2024). However, with the rise of generative models such as ChatGPT and MidJourney, AI has shifted from being just content to becoming an active mediator in the pedagogical process (Kim & Koo, 2024).

These systems now generate syllabi, lesson plans, assessment rubrics, and even adaptive feedback tasks that were once the exclusive domain of educators (Sihi & Ryan, 2025) Yet, despite the efficiency of such outputs, research shows that students tend to perceive content as less credible when they learn it was AI-generated, highlighting the need for pedagogical transparency (Kim & Koo, 2024).

These shifts directly impact active learning methodologies such as Problem-Based Learning (PBL), Case-Based Learning (CBL), Team-Based Learning (TBL), the Flipped Classroom, and Experiential Learning, all of which had already emerged as alternatives to traditional lecturing (Zawacki-Richter et al., 2019).

In PBL, for example, AI enables the creation of problem ecosystems grounded in real-world data, simulating multiple outcomes and providing real-time feedback as students engage in problem-solving (Sihi & Ryan, 2025). In this model, the educator transitions from being the designer of problems to the curator of AI-mediated scenarios (Kim & Koo, 2024).

In CBL, static cases are now dynamic. AI can adjust contextual variables based on student input, requiring educators to make real-time pedagogical decisions (Mutongi et al., 2025).

TBL is also reconfigured by AI, which can automatically form heterogeneous groups, monitor participation, and generate reports on collaborative performance (Peres et al., 2023). The instructor's role evolves from that of facilitator to architect of human–machine interactions that maintain the cognitive rigour of teamwork (Baltà-Salvador et al., 2025). For example, in a Digital Marketing course at the University of Aveiro, students used ChatGPT, DALL·E, and MidJourney to create consumer personas and prototype campaign imagery based on short descriptive prompts. The instructor then facilitated a critique session in which students analysed aesthetic biases, cultural assumptions, and representational limitations emerging from the generated visuals. With this, the students engaged in reflective discussion on visual literacy and the ethical dimensions of automated creative work. This activity demonstrated how AI can enrich experiential learning without diminishing the role of critical interpretation.

In the Flipped Classroom model, AI makes it possible to deliver adaptive pre-class materials and predictive dashboards that alert educators to students' difficulties before in-person sessions begin (Kim & Koo, 2024). This enables instructors to intervene more strategically during class, focusing on critical learning points based on real-time data (Sihi & Ryan, 2025).

In Experiential Learning, AI simulates complex market environments where students can test marketing strategies and see the algorithmic impact of their decisions with immediate feedback (Baltà-Salvador et al., 2025). Such personalisation would be impossible without technological support. However, it also demands careful attention to ethics, diversity, and authorship to prevent learning processes from being colonised by homogenising Western algorithmic standards (Mutongi et al., 2025).

Table 1 summarises these pedagogical shifts, showing how AI expands traditional active learning methods and redefines the role of the educator.

Figure 1 provides a visual synthesis of the pedagogical transformation described in this section, mapping how AI reshapes curriculum design, teaching methodologies, and the evolving role of the educator. This visual summary supports the reader's understanding of the transition from traditional models to digitally mediated and AI-enhanced learning environments.

This evolution has led authors to view AI not merely as a tool, but as a standalone educational methodology. A recent systematic review found that AI-driven systems now fulfil core active-learning criteria, such as student-centredness, adaptability, real-time feedback, and authentic problem-solving contexts (Wang et al., 2024). AI systems that plan, monitor, adapt, and evaluate learning experiences meet the

Table 1 AI integration on traditional active learning and the redefinition of the role of the educator

Methodology	Traditional focus	Effects of AI integration	Change in educator role
Problem-based learning (PBL)	Collaborative problem-solving based on real cases	AI co-creates scenarios and allows iterative simulations	From problem designer to curator of AI-mediated environments
Case-based learning (CBL)	Analysis of predefined cases	Cases become dynamic, generated and modified in real time	From case selector to orchestrator of interactive systems
Team-based learning (TBL)	Team tasks with shared responsibility	AI assigns tasks and simulates group dynamics based on performance	From team assessor to facilitator of AI-mediated collaboration

Source Authors

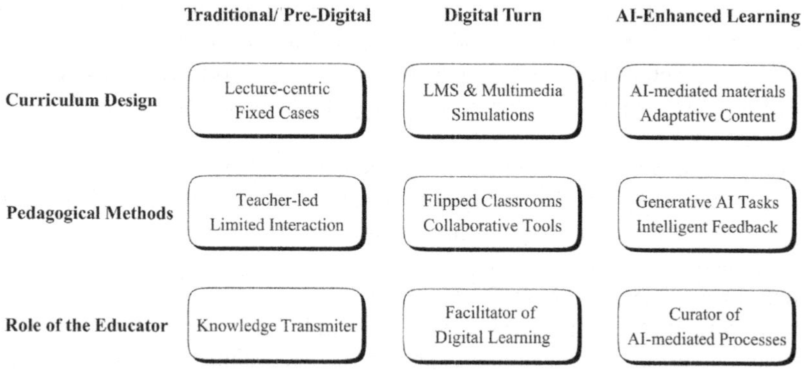

Fig. 1 Visual synthesis of AI integration in marketing education. *Source* Authors

core criteria of active methodologies: student-centredness, adaptability, real-time feedback, and engagement with real-world problems (Guha et al., 2024).

This evolution requires educators to acquire new competencies, technical, ethical, and epistemological, to act as critical curators of AI-mediated processes (Baltà-Salvador et al., 2025). Ultimately, it is the educator's responsibility to ensure that learning environments are not only effective but also fair, culturally sensitive, and pedagogically meaningful (Mutongi et al., 2025).

Hence, while the integration of AI into marketing curricula has begun to transform both course content and instructional design, it is crucial to complement this structural perspective with an exploration of how such changes are perceived and experienced by those most directly involved in the educational process—namely, students and educators. Their expectations, concerns, practical engagement, and varying levels of preparedness play a decisive role in shaping the implementation and pedagogical impact of AI in the classroom. Although the existing literature on these perspectives remains limited, the following section brings together emerging insights from both groups, highlighting points of convergence as well as areas of tension in the reception and appropriation of AI within marketing education.

4.3 Students and Educators Perspectives

The integration of AI into the pedagogical landscape of marketing education necessitates an examination of the perceptions and adaptive behaviours exhibited by both students and educators. This section delineates their emergent perspectives, critically assessing the affordances and constraints inherent in this transformative paradigm shift.

4.3.1 Student Perspectives

Business students articulate considerable apprehension regarding the perceived misalignment between the evolving demands of AI-driven labour markets and the preparedness afforded by HEIs. A survey involving 95 students across 27 HEIs in the Netherlands (Elhajjar et al., 2021) revealed a prevalent sentiment that their respective institutions are inadequately equipped or have not fully leveraged their extant resources to effectively cultivate competencies requisite for AI-augmented professional environments. This empirical finding underscores a critical imperative for curricular recalibration and infrastructural enhancements within educational frameworks, aimed at fostering congruence with contemporary AI-enabled vocational ecosystems.

Beyond these macro-level concerns, the micro-level dynamics of student engagement with AI tools represent a burgeoning area of scholarly inquiry. While the literature frequently emphasises educators' roles or institutional strategic blueprints, there is a pronounced lacuna in understanding the intricate cognitive, affective, and social dimensions characterising student-AI interactions (Lookadoo et al., 2025; Sihi & Ryan, 2025).

4.3.2 Educator Perspectives

Marketing educators universally acknowledge AI as a disruptive force that fundamentally reconfigures global industries, including the educational sector. Their engagement extends to a nuanced exploration of diverse AI applications spanning instructional design, scholarly research, and administrative efficiencies. This includes a critical appraisal of AI's potential to augment productivity, enhance instructional efficacy, and catalyse pedagogical innovation, while simultaneously recognising its inherent limitations (Rogers et al., 2024a).

A pivotal challenge for educators lies in transcending mere content delivery about AI to actively integrating AI as a mediational tool within the learning process itself. This encompasses leveraging sophisticated generative models for the automated synthesis of syllabi, detailed lesson plans, comprehensive assessment rubrics, and adaptive feedback mechanisms. Nevertheless, the principle of transparency is predominant, as empirical evidence suggests that students tend to ascribe lower credibility to content explicitly known to be AI-generated. Consequently, educators are strategically implementing dedicated instructional modules focused on deconstructing the algorithmic underpinnings of these platforms, scrutinising underlying datasets, acknowledging inherent limitations in creative autonomy, and mitigating risks associated with algorithmic bias or AI hallucinations. Concurrently, the pedagogical emphasis is shifting towards equipping students with advanced prompt engineering competencies, thereby empowering them to formulate optimised queries and critically appraise the veracity and utility of AI-generated outputs (Grewal et al., 2025).

The widespread accessibility of AI tools has instigated new demands for robust teacher professional development initiatives. This has manifested in the proliferation of synchronous instructional sessions, specialised training workshops focused on algorithmic literacy, and the development of practical pedagogical guides for the judicious integration of AI with deliberate instructional intent (Peña et al., 2025). Such endeavours are critical to ensuring that educators maintain epistemological autonomy over the learning process, thereby preventing an uncritical abdication of crucial mediational roles to algorithmic agents (Sihi & Ryan, 2025).

5 A Research Agenda for AI in Marketing Education

Building on the emerging literature and current practices, it is possible to outline several key areas that warrant focused academic inquiry in the short to medium term. Although the intersection between artificial intelligence and marketing education remains relatively underexplored, its transformative potential demands structured and sustained investigation. Given the rapid and exponential evolution of technology, particularly generative AI, marketing education operates within an increasingly dynamic and unstable environment. A forward-looking research agenda must therefore be both adaptive and anticipatory.

One of the first dimensions that deserves deeper exploration concerns how marketing students engage with AI tools in authentic learning contexts. Existing research tends to focus on educators' perspectives or institutional strategies, but little is known about students' perceptions, behaviours, and critical reflections when interacting with AI systems. Future studies should examine the cognitive, emotional, and social dynamics of student–AI interaction, addressing questions such as trust in AI-generated outputs, over-reliance, and the development of critical literacy in evaluating AI content (Abdelwahab et al., 2023; Lookadoo et al., 2025; Selvaratnam et al., 2025).

Another major axis for research involves assessment reform considering AI. Traditional assessment models are being disrupted by the availability of generative tools that can produce text, visuals, and even analytical insights. This raises important questions about the validity of existing evaluative practices and calls for the design of new assessment formats that emphasise process over product, originality over replication, and ethical judgement over mechanistic output (Oc et al., 2024). Empirical research is needed to test innovative forms of evaluation that integrate or respond to AI-generated content, particularly in fields like marketing or business, where creativity and strategic thinking are dominant.

Closely linked to this is the need to define what constitutes AI literacy for marketing graduates. Unlike technical disciplines, marketing requires a nuanced understanding of how AI shapes consumer behaviour, data interpretation, branding, and ethical communication. Therefore, future research should attempt to map the competencies required by marketing professionals in an AI-mediated world. Comparative studies across educational contexts could reveal best practices for fostering these competencies through curricula and co-curricular activities.

Equally important is the question of educator readiness. While students are often early adopters of new technologies, educators may struggle to keep pace due to institutional constraints, lack of training, or resistance to change (Baltà-Salvador et al., 2025). Research is needed to assess current levels of AI literacy among marketing educators, identify their professional development needs, and evaluate the effectiveness of institutional support mechanisms (Siu & White, 2025).

Curriculum transformation remains a central concern. Beyond integrating AI as a topic of study, there is a growing need to embed AI as a pedagogical method. This involves rethinking the structure and content of marketing courses to reflect the realities of an AI-rich environment. Future studies could investigate how AI tools can be used not just as supplements but as structuring elements of the curriculum, affecting learning objectives, teaching strategies, and student assessment (Richter et al., 2024).

Cultural and contextual differences also merit investigation. AI's adoption and impact in marketing education will likely vary across regions and institutional types. National policy, digital infrastructure, pedagogical culture, and socioeconomic context may shape how AI is integrated into teaching and learning practices. Comparative studies could illuminate how these variables influence the speed and nature of AI adoption and help develop culturally sensitive implementation strategies (Pan & Yang, 2021).

Longitudinal research is also needed to trace the impact of AI tools over time. While many studies offer snapshots of usage or perception, few explore how sustained interaction with AI affects learning outcomes, academic identity, or professional preparedness. Long-term studies, following marketing student cohorts across their educational journey, could provide invaluable insights into the developmental implications of AI-enhanced education.

Another promising but underexplored area concerns the use of AI in providing feedback. Generative tools such as ChatGPT or AI-based writing assistants can offer students immediate, personalised responses on their assignments, an aspect traditionally limited by educator availability. This development introduces new pedagogical possibilities and raises questions about quality, interpretation, and trust. Future research should explore how students perceive and act upon AI-generated feedback, whether it improves learning outcomes, and how it can be ethically and effectively combined with human input. The role of feedback in shaping students' critical thinking, self-regulation, and motivation in AI-supported environments warrants particular attention (Addison et al., 2024).

Finally, no research agenda would be complete without addressing the ethical dimensions of AI integration. Issues such as academic integrity, algorithmic bias, data privacy, and the transparency of AI decision-making processes should form a core strand of future inquiry. Research should establish ethical frameworks and institutional policies that ensure responsible use of AI while promoting inclusivity, fairness, and academic rigour in marketing education (Dwivedi et al., 2023; Means et al., 2014; Rogers et al., 2024). Future research should also engage more explicitly with international regulatory and ethical frameworks. The OECD AI Principles provide a global benchmark for trustworthy AI; the EU AI Act establishes binding obligations within the European context. Together, these frameworks offer a foundation for developing robust governance structures in marketing education.

The proposed research directions highlight not only conceptual gaps in current scholarship but also practical imperatives for educators and institutions. As AI continues to shape marketing practice, these agenda points provide a roadmap for designing pedagogical strategies that cultivate analytical literacy, ethical awareness, and critical engagement with intelligent systems. By aligning future empirical work with the evolving demands of AI-mediated learning environments, researchers and educators can ensure that curriculum development, assessment innovation, and instructional design remain coherent and responsive. This perspective naturally sets the stage for the concluding reflections on the broader implications of AI for the future of marketing education.

6 Conclusion

As the integration of AI continues to accelerate, marketing education stands at a decisive crossroads. This chapter has examined how AI is reshaping pedagogical paradigms, the role of educators, and the structure of active learning methodologies. Far from introducing new tools, AI is catalysing a profound reconfiguration of the educational ecosystem, requiring institutions to rethink how knowledge is transmitted, how learning is personalised, and how students are prepared for a rapidly evolving professional landscape.

The predictions articulated by Shabbir (2020), as cited in Crittenden, (2024), provide a valuable roadmap for envisioning the next decade of marketing education. Among these, the continued growth of online learning, the normalisation of personalised learning, the revolutionising effect of AI, and the increasing globalisation of education are particularly salient. These trends not only echo the transformations already underway but underscore the urgency of proactive and informed engagement with AI's pedagogical and ethical dimensions.

This chapter has illustrated how AI tools—such as ChatGPT, MidJourney, and Google Gemini—are being incorporated into curriculum design, assessment practices, and active learning models. These technologies enable greater efficiency, dynamic interactivity, and deeper levels of feedback. At the same time, they compel a redefinition of the educator's role: no longer a mere transmitter of knowledge, but a facilitator of complex human–machine interactions and a guardian of academic integrity, inclusivity, and ethical literacy (Kim & Koo, 2024; Sihi & Ryan, 2025).

However, the integration of AI also introduces significant challenges. These include concerns about privacy and data protection, algorithmic bias, the authorship and provenance of AI-generated outputs, and the risk of over-reliance on automated systems (McAlister et al., 2024). Addressing these requires not only robust institutional policies and professional development strategies but also a pedagogical culture rooted in critical thinking, ethical reflection, and transparency (Baltà-Salvador et al., 2025).

Preparing marketing graduates for an AI-augmented economy demands a holistic approach. It is insufficient to equip students with technical skills alone; they must also develop meta-competencies such as strategic thinking, creativity, and ethical judgement (Grewal et al., 2025). Future research must therefore explore emerging constructs such as trust calibration in AI-generated outputs, the risk of cognitive dependence, and the development of critical and algorithmic literacy. In parallel, empirical investigations into AI literacy among marketing educators and the efficacy of institutional governance frameworks will be vital (Guha et al., 2024; Richter et al., 2024).

In short, marketing education is entering a period of profound transformation. Generative AI is not merely an object of study but a pedagogical agent in its own right. Its integration into the learning environment requires both visionary planning and careful stewardship. As educators and researchers, we are called upon to ensure that AI is an enabler of human potential, enhancing rather than replacing the creative and critical capacities that define the very essence of education. As such, the integration of AI into marketing education must not only be technologically innovative but also aligned with existing regulatory frameworks such as the EU AI Act and the OECD AI Principles. These frameworks provide valuable guidance to ensure that AI adoption supports human-centred, transparent, and ethically responsible education.

This approach advocates for active student engagement and learning development through direct interaction with AI technologies, bridging the gap between theoretical knowledge and practical application (Richter et al., 2024).

References

Abdelwahab, H. R., Rauf, A., & Chen, D. (2023). Business students' perceptions of Dutch higher educational institutions in preparing them for artificial intelligence work environments. *Industry and Higher Education, 37*(1), 22–34. https://doi.org/10.1177/09504222221087614

Addison, L., Ramdial, P. T., & Hosein, P. (2024). An Investigation Into the Use of Large Language Models for Adaptive Grading of Course Projects. *2024 IEEE International Conference on Technology Management, Operations and Decisions (ICTMOD)*, 1–6. https://doi.org/10.1109/ICTMOD63116.2024.10878239

Awadallah Alkouk, W., & Khlaif, Z. N. (2024). AI-resistant assessments in higher education: Practical insights from faculty training workshops. *Frontiers in Education, 9*, 1499495. https://doi.org/10.3389/FEDUC.2024.1499495/BIBTEX

Baltà-Salvador, R., El-Madafri, I., Brasó-Vives, E., & Peña, M. (2025). Empowering engineering students through artificial intelligence (AI): Blended human–AI creative ideation processes with ChatGPT. *Computer Applications in Engineering Education, 33*(1). https://doi.org/10.1002/CAE.22817

Barry, N., & Kohtamäki, M. (2025). *The role of artificial intelligence in the future of work*: Insights from the Marketing Field. https://osuva.uwasa.fi/handle/10024/19178

Bay, J. L. (2021). Beyond situated learning: Rethinking internship theory and practice in the distributed workplace. In *Effective teaching of technical communication: Theory, practice, and application* (pp. 13–27). The WAC Clearinghouse, University Press of Colorado. https://doi.org/10.37514/tpc-b.2020.1121.2.01

Beggs, J. M. (2011). Seamless integration of ethics. *Marketing Education Review, 21*(1), 49–56. https://doi.org/10.2753/mer1052-8008210107

Borin, N., & Metcalf, L. (2010). Integrating sustainability into the marketing curriculum: Learning activities that facilitate sustainable marketing practices. *Journal of Marketing Education, 32*(2), 140–154. https://doi.org/10.1177/0273475309360156

Brennan, L., Lu, V. N., & von der Heidt, T. (2018). Transforming marketing education: Historical, contemporary and future perspectives. In *Australasian Marketing Journal* (Vol. 26, Issue 2, pp. 65–69). Elsevier Australia. https://doi.org/10.1016/j.ausmj.2018.05.011

Bridges, C. M., & Wilhelm, W. B. (2008). Going beyond green: The "why and how" of integrating sustainability into the marketing curriculum. *Journal of Marketing Education, 30*(1), 33–46. https://doi.org/10.1177/0273475307312196

Burger, K. J., & Schmidt, S. L. (1987). Integrating information management skills into the marketing curriculum: An example using the marketing research course. *Journal of Marketing Education, 9*(1), 12–18. https://doi.org/10.1177/027347538700900103

Butler, D. D. (2007). Planning your funeral: A helpful pedagogical tool. *Marketing Education Review, 17*(1), 95–100. https://doi.org/10.1080/10528008.2007.11488993

Cadwallader, S., Atwong, C., & Lebard, A. (2013). Proposing community-based learning in the marketing curriculum. *Marketing Education Review, 23*(2), 137–150. https://doi.org/10.2753/mer1052-8008230203

Čančer, V. (2014). Teaching creative problem solving methods to undergraduate economics and business students. *Journal of Further and Higher Education, 38*(4), 485–500. https://doi.org/10.1080/0309877X.2012.726968

Chew, P., & Gilani, H. (2024). Artificial intelligence in marketing education. In *Decolonizing marketing theory and practice: Beyond inclusivity and sustainability debates* (pp. 218–236). Routledge, 10.4324/9781032698083-15.

Costa, C. J., Aparicio, M., Aparicio, S., & Aparicio, J. T. (2024). The democratization of artificial intelligence: Theoretical Framework. *Applied Sciences 2024, Vol. 14, Page 8236, 14* (18), 8236. https://doi.org/10.3390/APP14188236

Crittenden, V. L. (2024). What is the future of marketing education? *Journal of Marketing Education, 46*(1), 3–5. https://doi.org/10.1177/02734753231220115

Daldıran, K. (2024). Integrating AI into entrepreneurial marketing strategies. *Journal of Entrepreneurship and Innovation Management, 13*(2), 78–100. https://doi.org/10.15659/jeim.12.2.004

Ding, M., Dong, S., & Grewal, R. (2024). Generative AI and usage in marketing classroom. *Customer Needs and Solutions, 11*(1), 1–25. https://doi.org/10.1007/S40547-024-00145-2

Dwivedi, Y. K., Kshetri, N., Hughes, L., Slade, E. L., Jeyaraj, A., Kar, A. K., Baabdullah, A. M., Koohang, A., Raghavan, V., Ahuja, M., Albanna, H., Albashrawi, M. A., Al-Busaidi, A. S., Balakrishnan, J., Barlette, Y., Basu, S., Bose, I., Brooks, L., Buhalis, D., & Wright, R. (2023). So what if ChatGPT wrote it? Multidisciplinary perspectives on opportunities, challenges and implications of generative conversational AI for research, practice and policy. *International Journal of Information Management, 71*, 102642. https://doi.org/10.1016/j.ijinfomgt.2023.102642

Elhajjar, S., Karam, S., & Borna, S. (2021). Artificial intelligence in marketing education programs. *Marketing Education Review, 31*(1), 2–13. https://doi.org/10.1080/10528008.2020.1835492

Farrell, C. (2020). Do international marketing simulations provide an authentic assessment of learning? A student perspective. *The International Journal of Management Education, 18*(1), 100362. https://doi.org/10.1016/J.IJME.2020.100362

Ferrell, O. C., & Keig, D. L. (2013). The marketing ethics course: Current state and future directions. *Journal of Marketing Education, 35*(2), 119–128. https://doi.org/10.1177/0273475313491498

Graesser, A. C., Chipman, P., Haynes, B. C., & Olney, A. (2005). AutoTutor: An intelligent tutoring system with mixed-initiative dialogue. *IEEE Transactions on Education, 48*(4), 612–618.

Grewal, D., Guha, A., Beccacece Satornino, C., & Becker, M. (2025). The future of marketing and marketing education. *Journal of Marketing Education, 47*(1), 61–77. https://doi.org/10.1177/02734753241269838

Guha, A., Grewal, D., & Atlas, S. (2024). Generative AI and marketing education: What the future holds. *Journal of Marketing Education, 46*(1), 6–17. https://doi.org/10.1177/02734753231215436

Hadi Mogavi, R., Deng, C., Juho Kim, J., Zhou, P. D., Kwon, Y., Hosny Saleh Metwally, A., Tlili, A., Bassanelli, S., Bucchiarone, A., Gujar, S., Nacke, L. E., & Hui, P. (2024). ChatGPT in education: A blessing or a curse? A qualitative study exploring early adopters' utilization and perceptions. *Computers in Human Behavior: Artificial Humans, 2*(1), 100027. https://doi.org/10.1016/J.CHBAH.2023.100027

Han, F., Ellis, R. A., & Guan, E. (2023). Patterns of students' collaborations by variations in their learning orientations in blended course designs: How is it associated with academic achievement? *Journal of Computer Assisted Learning, 39*(1), 286–299. https://doi.org/10.1111/JCAL.12747

Hollands, F. M., & Tirthali, D. (2014). Resource requirements and costs of developing and delivering MOOCs. *The International Review of Research in Open and Distributed Learning, 15*(5). https://doi.org/10.19173/irrodl.v15i5.1901

Jin, Y., Yan, L., Echeverria, V., Gašević, D., & Martinez-Maldonado, R. (2025). Generative AI in higher education: A global perspective of institutional adoption policies and guidelines. *Computers and Education: Artificial Intelligence, 8*, 100348.

Kaplan, M. D., Piskin, B., & Bol, B. (2010). Educational blogging: Integrating technology into marketing experience. *Journal of Marketing Education, 32*(1), 50–63. https://doi.org/10.1177/0273475309335652

Kennedy, E. J., Lawton, L., & Walker, E. (2001). The case for using live cases: Shifting the paradigm in marketing education. *Journal of Marketing Education, 23*(2), 145–151. https://doi.org/10.1177/0273475301232008

Kim, H., & Koo, T. K. B. (2024). The impact of generative AI on syllabus design and learning. *Journal of Marketing Education.* https://doi.org/10.1177/02734753241299024

Kirpalani, N. (2009). Developing entrepreneurial self-efficacy in marketing students by using simulation-based pedagogy. *Society for Marketing Advances Proceedings*, 194–196.

Kolb, A. Y., & Kolb, D. A. (2017). Experiential learning theory as a guide for experiential educators in higher education. *Experiential Learning & Teaching in Higher Education, 1*(1), 7–44.

Li, T., Greenberg, B. A., & Nicholls, J. A. F. (2007). Teaching experiential learning: Adoption of an innovative course in an MBA marketing curriculum. *Journal of Marketing Education, 29*(1), 25–33. https://doi.org/10.1177/0273475306297380

Lookadoo, K., Moore, S., Wright, C., Hemby, V., & McCool, L. B. (2025). AI-based writing assistants in business education: A Cross-Institutional Study on Student Perspectives. *Business and Professional Communication Quarterly.* https://doi.org/10.1177/23294906241310415

Luckin, R., Holmes, W., Griffiths, M., & Forcier, L. B. (2016). Intelligence unleashed. An argument for AI in Education, 18. Pearson.

Maher, J. K., & Hughner, R. S. (2005). Experiential marketing projects: Student perceptions of live case and simulation methods. *Journal for Advancement of Marketing Education, 7*(Hamer 2000), 1–10. http://www.mmaglobal.org/publications/JAME/JAME-Issues/JAME-2005-Vol07-Issue1/JAME-2005-Vol07-Issue1-Maher-Hughner-pp1-10.pdf

Markley Rountree, M., & Koernig, S. K. (2015). Values-based education for sustainability marketers: Two approaches for enhancing student social consciousness. *Journal of Marketing Education, 37*(1), 5–24. https://doi.org/10.1177/0273475314559513

Marshall, G. W., Lassk, F. G., Kennedy, K. N., & Goolsby, J. R. (1996). Integrating quality improvement tenets into the marketing curriculum. *Journal of Marketing Education, 18*(2), 28–38. https://doi.org/10.1177/027347539601800204

McAlister, A. R., Alhabash, S., & Yang, J. (2024). Artificial intelligence and ChatGPT: Exploring current and potential future roles in marketing education. *Journal of Marketing Communications, 30*(2), 166–187. https://doi.org/10.1080/13527266.2023.2289034

Means, B., Bakia, M., & Murphy, R. (2014). *Learning online-what research tells us about whether, when and how.* Routledge. https://doi.org/10.4324/9780203095959

Miller, F. L., Holmes, T. L., & Mangold, W. G. (2007). Integrating geographic information systems (GIS) into the marketing curriculum. *Marketing Education Review, 17*(3), 49–63. https://doi.org/10.1080/10528008.2007.11489013

Miller, F. L., Mangold, W. G., Roach, J., Brockway, G., Johnston, T., Linnhoff, S., McNeely, S., Smith, K., & Holmes, T. (2014). RacerGISOnline: Enhancing learning in marketing classes with web-based business GIS. *Marketing Education Review, 24*(1), 31–36. https://doi.org/10.2753/mer1052-8008240105

Muncy, J. A. (2014). Blogging for reflection: The use of online journals to engage students in reflective learning. *Marketing Education Review, 24*(2), 101–114. https://doi.org/10.2753/mer1052-8008240202

Muñoz, C. L. (2012). More than just Wikipedia: Creating a collaborative research library using a wiki. *Marketing Education Review, 22*(1), 21–26. https://doi.org/10.2753/mer1052-800822.0104

Mustafa, M. Y., Tlili, A., Lampropoulos, G., Huang, R., Jandrić, P., Zhao, J., Salha, S., Xu, L., Panda, S., Kinshuk, L.-P., & S., & Saqr, M. (2024). A systematic review of literature reviews on artificial intelligence in education (AIED): A roadmap to a future research agenda. *Smart Learning Environments, 11*(1), 1–33. https://doi.org/10.1186/S40561-024-00350-5

Mutongi, C., Rigava, B., Muchuri, T., & Chiwanza, M. R. (2025). Rethinking the Place of African Kitchen Hut as a Hub for Business Management, Marketing, Education, Health and Strategies in the Age of Artificial Intelligence. *2025 IEEE 4th International Conference on AI in Cybersecurity, ICAIC 2025*. https://doi.org/10.1109/ICAIC63015.2025.10848558

Nassif, B. W., Nofal, A., Exploring, E., Fareed, M. W., Nassif, A. B., & Nofal, E. (2024). Exploring the potentials of artificial intelligence image generators for educating the history of architecture. *Heritage, 7*(3), 1727–1753. https://doi.org/10.3390/HERITAGE7030081

Nazari, M., & Saadi, G. (2024). Developing effective prompts to improve communication with ChatGPT: A formula for higher education stakeholders. *Discover Education, 3*(1), 1–17. https://doi.org/10.1007/S44217-024-00122-W/TABLES/4

Nnanna-Ohuonu, O. (2025). The impact of artificial intelligence tools on academic performance in marketing education: Evidence from universities in south-East Nigeria. *Multidisciplinary Journal of Law, Education and Humanities, 2*(2).

Oc, Y., Gonsalves, C., & Quamina, L. T. (2024). Generative AI in higher education assessments: Examining risk and tech-savviness on student's adoption. *Journal of Marketing Education, 47*(2), 138–155. https://doi.org/10.1177/02734753241302459

OECD. (2019). *Recommendation of the Council on Artificial Intelligence (OECD AI Principles)*. OECD Legal Instruments. https://legalinstruments.oecd.org/en/instruments/oecd-legal-0449

Pan, Y., & Yang, P. (2021). The role of AI assisted socio-cultural frameworks in academic change and higher education growth. *International Journal of Technology Management, 86*(2/3/4), 196. https://doi.org/10.1504/IJTM.2021.118316

Peña, P., Riley, J., & Davis, N. (2025). Beyond the "AI" powered slide deck: Exploring emerging tools that engage, empower, and elevate student learning. *Marketing Education Review, 35*(4), 289–290. https://doi.org/10.1080/10528008.2025.2518407

Peres, R., Schreier, M., Schweidel, D., & Sorescu, A. (2023). On ChatGPT and beyond: How generative artificial intelligence may affect research, teaching, and practice. *International Journal of Research in Marketing, 40*(2), 269–275. https://doi.org/10.1016/J.IJRESMAR.2023.03.001

Pinheiro, M. M., Estima, A., & Marques, S. (Eds.). (2018). *Evaluating the gaps and intersections between marketing education and the marketing profession*. IGI Global.

Pollack, B. L., & Lilly, B. (2008). Gaining confidence and competence through experiential assignments: An exploration of student self-efficacy and spectrum of inquiry. *Marketing Education Review, 18*(2), 55–66.

Pötzsch, H., & Pereira, G. (2022). Reimagining algorithmic governance cultural expressions and the negotiation of social imaginaries. *ACM International Conference Proceeding Series, 22*. https://doi.org/10.1145/3546155.3547298

Prabhakaran, V., Qadri, R., & Hutchinson, B. (2022). *Cultural incongruencies in artificial intelligence*. https://arxiv.org/abs/2211.13069v1

Qian, Y. (2025). Pedagogical applications of generative AI in higher education: A systematic review of the field. *TechTrends*, 1–16. https://doi.org/10.1007/S11528-025-01100-1/FIGURES/6

Richter, S., Giroux, M., Piven, I., Sima, H., & Dodd, P. (2024). A constructivist approach to integrating AI in marketing education: Bridging theory and practice. *Journal of Marketing Education, 47*(2), 94–111. https://doi.org/10.1177/02734753241288876

Rogers, P. P., Allen, C., & Busby, A. (2024). Marketing educators and artificial intelligence: A perspective on productivity and innovation. *Journal of Marketing Education, 47*(2), 156–169. https://doi.org/10.1177/02734753241299095

Roll, I., & Wylie, R. (2016). Evolution and revolution in artificial intelligence in education. *International Journal of Artificial Intelligence in Education, 26*(2), 582–599. https://doi.org/10.1007/S40593-016-0110-3/TABLES/8

Romero, M. (2024). *Collaborative design of AI-enhanced learning activities*. https://arxiv.org/abs/2407.06660v1

Roy, D. (2006). Enhancing marketing curriculum through experiential education. *Marketing Management Association*, 61–62.

Roy, D. (2024). Pedagogical restructuring of business communication courses: AI-enhanced prompt engineering in an EFL teaching context. *Intelligent Systems Reference Library, 261*, 247–287. https://doi.org/10.1007/978-3-031-71232-6_12

Schiller, S. Z., Goodrich, K., & Gupta, P. B. (2013). Let them play! Active learning in a virtual world. *Information Systems Management, 30*(1), 50–62. https://doi.org/10.1080/10580530.2013.739891

Selvaratnam, D. P., Jaheer Mukhtar, K. P., Gravitiani, E., & Meiting, W. (2025). University students' Perception of Artificial Intelligence (AI) for Entrepreneurship Development in Selected Asian Countries of China, India, Indonesia, and Malaysia. In *Artificial intelligence-enabled businesses* (pp. 397–419). Wiley. https://doi.org/10.1002/9781394234028.ch22

Selwyn, N. (2019). *Should robots replace teachers?: AI and the future of education*. Wiley.

Shermis, M. D., & Burstein, J. (2013). *Handbook of automated essay evaluation*. Routledge.

Sihi, D., & Ryan, A. (2025). Crafting and evaluating generative ai prompts: Insights from students, educators, and marketers. *Marketing Education Review, 35*(2), 153–159. https://doi.org/10.1080/10528008.2024.2445816

Siu, B., & White, J. (2025). When ease becomes a barrier: What influences student intentions to use Generative AI in higher education? *British Educational Research Journal. 51*(6), 2893–2919. https://doi.org/10.1002/berj.4206

Spanjaard, D., Hall, T., & Stegemann, N. (2018). Experiential learning: Helping students to become 'career-ready. *Australasian Marketing Journal, 26*(2), 163–171. https://doi.org/10.1016/j.ausmj.2018.04.003

Sun, D., Cheng, G., Yu, P. L. H., Jia, J., Zheng, Z., & Chen, A. (2025). Personalized stem education empowered by artificial intelligence: A comprehensive review and content analysis. *Interactive Learning Environments, 33*(7), 4419–4441. https://doi.org/10.1080/10494820.2025.2462156

Tafesse, W., & Wood, B. (2024). Hey ChatGPT: An examination of ChatGPT prompts in marketing. *Journal of Marketing Analytics, 12*(4), 790–805. https://doi.org/10.1057/S41270-023-00284-W/TABLES/6

Teer, H. B., Teer, F. P., & Kruck, S. E. (2007). A study of the database marketing course in AACSB-accredited business schools. *Journal of Marketing Education, 29*(3), 245–253. https://doi.org/10.1177/0273475307306891

Thontirawong, P., & Chinchanachokchai, S. (2021). Teaching artificial intelligence and machine learning in marketing. *Marketing Education Review, 31*(2), 58–63.

Tsidylo, I. M., & Chele, E. S. (2023). Artificial intelligence as a methodological innovation in the training of future designers: Midjourney tools. *Information Technologies and Learning Tools, 97*(5), 203–214. https://doi.org/10.33407/ITLT.V97I5.5338

Von der Heidt, T., & Quazi, A. (2013). Enhancing learning-centeredness in marketing principles curriculum. *Australasian Marketing Journal, 21*(4), 250–258. https://doi.org/10.1016/j.ausmj.2013.08.005

Vos, L. (2015). Simulation games in business and marketing education: How educators assess student learning from simulations. *International Journal of Management Education, 13*(1), 57–74. https://doi.org/10.1016/j.ijme.2015.01.001

Walter, Y. (2024). Embracing the future of artificial intelligence in the classroom: The relevance of AI literacy, prompt engineering, and critical thinking in modern education. *International*

Journal of Educational Technology in Higher Education, 21(1), 1–29. https://doi.org/10.1186/S41239-024-00448-3/METRICS

Wang, S., Wang, F., Zhu, Z., Wang, J., Tran, T., & Du, Z. (2024). Artificial intelligence in education: A systematic literature review. *Expert Systems with Applications, 252*, 124167. https://doi.org/10.1016/J.ESWA.2024.124167

Weber, G., & Brusilovsky, P. (2001). ELM-ART: An adaptive versatile system for web-based instruction. *International Journal of Artificial Intelligence in Education, 12*, 351–384.

Weber, J. (2013). Advances in graduate marketing curriculum: Paying attention to ethical, social, and sustainability issues. *Journal of Marketing Education, 35*(2), 85–94. https://doi.org/10.1177/0273475313489556

Wee, L. K. N., Alexandria, M., Kek, Y. C., & Kelley, C. A. (2003). Transforming the marketing curriculum using problem-based learning: A case study. *Journal of Marketing Education, 25*(2), 150–162. https://doi.org/10.1177/0273475303254016

Weinrauch, J. D. (2005). An exploratory use of musical metaphors to enhance student learning. *Journal of Marketing Education, 27*(2), 109–121. https://doi.org/10.1177/0273475304273353

Wiboolyasarin, W., Wiboolyasarin, K., Suwanwihok, K., Jinowat, N., & Muenjanchoey, R. (2024). Synergizing collaborative writing and AI feedback: An investigation into enhancing L2 writing proficiency in wiki-based environments. *Computers and Education: Artificial Intelligence, 6*, 100228. https://doi.org/10.1016/J.CAEAI.2024.100228

Wiese, N. M., & Sherman, D. J. (2011). Integrating marketing and environmental studies through an interdisciplinary, experiential, service-learning approach. *Journal of Marketing Education, 33*(1), 41–56. https://doi.org/10.1177/0273475310389154

Yatani, K., Sramek, Z., & Yang, C.-L. (2024). *AI as Extraherics: Fostering Higher-order Thinking Skills in Human-AI Interaction*. https://arxiv.org/abs/2409.09218v2

Yin, H., Zhang, Z., & Liu, Y. (2023). The exploration of integrating the Midjourney artificial intelligence generated content tool into design systems to direct designers towards future-oriented innovation. *Systems, 11*(12), –566. https://doi.org/10.3390/SYSTEMS11120566

Yuan, B., & Hu, J. (2024). *Generative AI as a tool for enhancing reflective learning in students*. https://arxiv.org/abs/2412.02603v1

Yusuf, A., Pervin, N., & Román-González, M. (2024). Generative AI and the future of higher education: A threat to academic integrity or reformation? Evidence from multicultural perspectives. *International Journal of Educational Technology in Higher Education, 21*(1), 1–29. https://doi.org/10.1186/S41239-024-00453-6/FIGURES/11

Zawacki-Richter, O., Marín, V. I., Bond, M., & Gouverneur, F. (2019). Systematic review of research on artificial intelligence applications in higher education—Where are the educators? *International Journal of Educational Technology in Higher Education, 16*(1), 1–27. https://doi.org/10.1186/S41239-019-0171-0

Bias and Hallucinations in AI Marketing: Ethical Challenges and Emerging Responsibilities

Miguel Cachulo Pereira, Lara Mendes Bacalhau, and Joana Neves

Abstract Contemporary marketing is witnessing the growing inclusion of Artificial Intelligence (AI). AI is emerging in campaign planning, dynamic pricing, customer journeys, and content management, among others, with significant efficiency gains and enabling increasing personalization. At the same time, however, we are seeing the emergence and consolidation of two structural risks: algorithmic bias, in which data and models consolidate unfair differences between groups or individuals, and AI hallucinations, in which results appear fluent but are false. Together, these two phenomena threaten brand integrity, compliance with legal and ethical rules, and consumer confidence, creating a paradox: some consumers, despite knowing that AI results may be flawed, accept them if they appear personalized, fast, or fair. Based on recent studies in the areas of marketing, information systems, and AI ethics, this conceptual chapter synthesizes emerging evidence on (a) how bias and hallucinations arise in AI-driven marketing processes; (b) their effects on fairness, transparency, and authenticity; and (c) mitigation measures in data, algorithms, governance, and organizational capabilities. Finally, AI ethics and governance are used to emphasize that mere legal compliance is insufficient. The chapter concludes by proposing a research agenda and arguing that the adoption of AI in marketing must balance innovation with responsibility, so that AI strengthens rather than erodes long-term trust.

M. C. Pereira
GOVCOPP, ISCA, University of Aveiro, Aveiro, Portugal
e-mail: miguel.pereira@ua.pt

M. C. Pereira · L. M. Bacalhau
Polytechnic University of Coimbra, Coimbra, Portugal
e-mail: lmendes@iscac.pt

M. C. Pereira · L. M. Bacalhau · J. Neves
CEOS.PP Coimbra, Coimbra, Portugal

J. Neves (✉)
School of Economics and Management, University of Porto, Porto, Portugal

J. D. Santos et al. (eds.), *Artificial Intelligence Transforming Marketing*, Contributions to Management Science, https://doi.org/10.1007/978-3-032-22360-9_4

1 Introduction

Artificial Intelligence (AI), especially generative AI (GenAI), has been applied in many areas of marketing, such as campaign development, product information management (PIM), customer relationship management (CRM), chat support, etc. This use brings significant advances in personalization and real-time processing (Akter et al., 2022; Hardcastle et al., 2025), but also structural risks of bias and hallucinations (Yaprak, 2024), eroding expectations of transparency, fairness, and trust in marketing.

In the first case, cognitive biases such as framing or confirmation, reinforce already existing disparities (Yaprak, 2024), namely, when they are encoded in large datasets and automated via algorithms, with outcomes that are harder to detect or redress (Akter et al., 2022). In the second case, hallucinations, where outputs are fluent but false, unfounded, or disloyal to original material (Yaprak, 2024), they need not be intentional deceptions but can arise as optimization artifacts caused by systems being trained to be plausible rather than accurate. So a marketing chatbot that recommends products based on nonexistent evidence is not acting deceptively, yet can weaken brand credibility and erode consumer trust (Neves et al., 2025).

At the same time, unexpected consumer behavior has been detected: even though some individuals are aware of mistakes within some AI-produced content, they still prefer using it over trade-offs, prioritizing practicality or personalization (Christensen et al., 2024). This paradox rejects the idea that transparency or disclosure alone is all it takes to protect consumers and reframes reliability as a governance problem. This contradiction underlines the tension that GenAI imposes on ethical matters of marketing.

The guiding research question of this chapter can therefore be formulated as follows: How should marketing adapt to the challenges of biases and hallucinations in AI while safeguarding ethics and trust?

Even though the academic literature responds with approaches relating to (i) technical work (e.g., retrieval-augmented generation (RAG) and related safeguards), (ii) behavioral insights in terms of when are consumers more accepting than skeptical of AI (Hikov & Murphy, 2024; Mariani & Dwivedi, 2024), and (iii) normative response adopting a set of assurance principles for ethical GenAI design and deployment in marketing that might include, among others: autonomy, security, sustainability, representativeness/representation, accountability, non-biasedness/nondiscrimination, crediting, and empowerment (Hermann & Puntoni, 2025); these responses still operate as fragmented entities with only little integration, particularly in hyper-personalized contexts and complex technical pipelines (Hermann & Puntoni, 2025). This fragmentation constitutes the gap this chapter addresses.

Section 2 addresses the research question by exploring bias in AI-driven marketing through both cognitive and algorithmic lenses. Section 3 examines hallucinations, their structural causes, how they are perceived by consumers, and the brand risk. Finally, Sect. 4 considers ethical implications beyond compliance and, in Sect. 5, outlines future research directions, while the conclusion is that ethics needs to be seen as an ongoing commitment in AI marketing.

2 Bias in AI-Driven Marketing

This section defines bias, identifies where it arises in AI-driven marketing, and reviews diagnostic and mitigation options, preparing the ground for the subsequent discussion of hallucinations and the ethical and governance implications that cut across both topics.

2.1 Defining Bias

Marketing organizations now rely, more than ever, on AI across the pipeline from data intake and enrichment to modeling, decision-making, and customer-journey orchestration (Akter et al., 2022; Akter et al., 2023; Hardcastle et al., 2025). In this context, AI Bias can be referred to as systemic and unfair disparities in model behavior or predictions across individuals or groups that go beyond what legitimate business rules can reasonably justify (Chouldechova, 2017; Diaz et al., 2022).

Three intersecting types of bias are especially relevant in marketing: (i) Data Bias is a function of decisions about which individuals or attributes are recorded; (ii) Algorithmic Bias captures how objectives, features and learning mechanics transform data into outputs (Akter et al., 2022, 2023); and (iii) Systemic Bias reflects the role that platform structure, auction mechanisms and budget allocations play in exposure and opportunity (Ali et al., 2019; Baumann et al., 2024; Cecere et al., 2024; Lambrecht & Tucker, 2019). These three types manifest at group-level fairness level (e.g., gender or age biases in advertising exposure) (Ali et al., 2019; Cecere et al., 2024; Lambrecht & Tucker, 2019) and individual-level unfairness (where otherwise similar customers are treated differently without reasonable justification) (Jin et al., 2023; Zhao et al., 2025).

A complementary view in digital platforms concerns exposure-oriented fairness, the "attention currency" of who/what is shown, how often, and in which position across impressions and rankings (Biega et al., 2018; Diaz et al., 2022; Singh & Joachims, 2018; Wang et al., 2023).

2.2 Marketing Implications of Bias

Bias can emerge wherever objectives and cost signals determine reach, offer, and contact frequency across ad delivery, recommenders, pricing, and journey policies.

2.2.1 Target Advertising and Delivery Optimization

In auction-based settings, "delivery fairness" is measured by whether impressions align with the eligible audience implied by targeting rules (Timmaraju et al., 2023) or satisfy a given parity requirement (Baumann et al., 2024).

Field and simulation studies show that disparities frequently arise at the delivery stage: even with inclusive targeting, when platforms optimize for clicks or cost, spend shifts toward lower-CPM segments even under inclusive targeting (Ali et al., 2019; Baumann et al., 2024; Lambrecht & Tucker, 2019). Lambrecht and Tucker (2019) report roughly 20% more impressions for men in a gender-neutral STEM campaign because female viewers were costlier to reach (higher CPM). Ali et al. (2019) detect gender-and race-biased delivery for real job and housing ads with broad, non-discriminatory targeting, indicating that auction dynamics and creative cues can drive bias independently of advertiser intent. Cecere et al. (2024) show that even small ad-text changes can shift delivery toward different demographics in a field study with French high-school students. (Mehrjoo et al., 2024) document a systemic "Digital Marketing Pink Tax": a consistent CPM premium for women on Facebook, with far smaller gaps on CPC.

Representation also matters. Nowadays, ad platforms represent content (text and images) as embeddings—numeric vectors learned from large (Adomavicius & Yang, 2022). If corpora exhibit gendered stereotypes (e.g., STEM $\leftrightarrow$ male; caregiving $\leftrightarrow$ female), delivery and recommendation unfairness add combined with representational bias in training data, result in enhanced stereotyping (Ali et al., 2019; Stella, 2022). A feedback loop is formed by serving stereotype-congruent profiles, privileged click predictions, which, in turn, generate clicks, retraining the model, and CPM optimization then amplifies the original bias (Ali et al., 2019). Empirically, stereotype-congruent ads with negative valences were overdelivered to somc groups under click-optimized objectives, while impressions-based objectives reduce this skew, underlining how the choice of objective function can magnify or mitigate bias (Ali et al., 2019; Lambrecht & Tucker, 2019; Mazrekaj et al., 2024; Timmaraju et al., 2023).

2.2.2 Recommender Systems and Personalization

Beyond delivery-stage disparities, in ranked settings like recommender systems, fairness becomes less about access and more about exposure: who or what is shown, how often, and in which order. This exposure lens is two-fold: (i) consumer-side fairness is the question of whether individuals get calibrated exposure to what is relevant for them (the variety each person sees), rather than systematic disadvantage by group and (ii) provider-side fairness asks about whether small or minority sellers/creators/products consistently gain equitable exposure instead of being crowded out by popular incumbents (Jin et al., 2023; Vassøy & Langseth, 2024; Wang et al., 2023). Because improvements for one side may come at a cost to the other, recommenders need to be viewed as multi-stakeholder systems and evaluated jointly considering both fairness objectives (Diaz et al., 2022). In practice, this means specifying which notion of fairness (e.g., user-vs. provider-side) a system is optimized and what exposure-based metric will also be reported alongside accuracy.

Surveys and methodological work map these user vs. provider-side goals to exposure-based metrics (parity, coverage, calibration) and argue for their joint reporting alongside utility/accuracy in a way that allows us to reconcile trade-offs (Deldjoo et al., 2024; Diaz et al., 2022; Wang et al., 2023): ideally evaluated through online A/B tests, still relatively scarce in field settings (Vassøy & Langseth, 2024). The three emerging metrics indicate different visibility patterns: exposure parity shifts impression shares toward the ideal group target profile; coverage increases the share of users or items that receive some degree of exposure (supporting the long tail); and calibration aligns exposure closer to predicted or actual relevance for each group (Wang et al., 2023). The risk of imbalance becomes particularly clear when systems are optimized for either accuracy or short-term clicks. Jin et al. (2023) characterize popularity feedback loops in which already popular products are displayed more, receive more clicks, leading them to become even more dominant, making niche providers and some user groups increasingly less visible. Extending this approach, Zhao et al. (2025) separate individual diversity (balanced exposure across user segments) and aggregate diversity (distributed exposure across items), and demonstrate the significant impact that choice of fairness metric has on visibility patterns.

Combined, these themes highlight a central tension: short-term click optimization versus longer-term attention equity. From the marketing perspective, ranked recommenders are a primary operating site of algorithmic bias: tuned to maximize accuracy, they can distort distributions of attention, opportunities, and value, systematically under-exposing certain users and marginal providers, so that reach or sales increasingly reflect optimization artifacts rather than consumer need or product merit.

In addition to accuracy and fairness, the alignment between human expectations and system behavior is also important. Zhang and Zhang (2025) introduce the concept of misestimation: the gap between what users believe they are being targeted for and what the system actually does. In their study of Weibo women users, perceptions about algorithms, surveillance, and platform motives are crucial to explaining whether targeting is perceived as intrusive, too precise, or benign. Sometimes, even when objective performance is acceptable, misestimation can erode trust and sustain the perception of bias.

2.2.3 Pricing and Perceived Fairness

Another point of optimization is pricing for personalized or device-specific services, with often nontrivially different price choices across comparable consumers that are perceived as unfair.

In U.S. audits of e-commerce and travel-based websites identify two distinct personalization mechanisms have been identified: (i) price discrimination, where otherwise-identical items are priced differently based on an account or membership status (CheapTickets/Orbitz) or the device a user happens to be on and (ii) price steering price steering, where search results are reordered to nudge users toward higher cost options (Baumann et al., 2024; Hannak et al., 2014). Rather than a single platform quirk, these patterns appear across multiple retailers and verticals, suggesting system-level risks in web-scale pricing and ranking. For instance, Travelocity showed little differential pricing for mobile users, and Home Depot nudged iOS/mobile users more often toward higher-priced products, indicating that varying prices and rank-based nudges can be due in part to device, login state, or interaction history, even when products are otherwise comparable (Hannak et al., 2014).

On the consumer side, targeting price discrimination leads to a strong sense of unfair treatment, even among customers who benefit from discounts. These perceptions decrease purchase intention and benevolence-based trust, and increase the likelihood of complaints and search for alternatives. In turn, perceived unfairness represents a demand-side cost that might compensate for the short-run revenue increase resulting from personalization (Hufnagel et al., 2022).

Normative evaluations highlight that welfare outcomes are parameter-sensitive. Evaluating ethical trade-offs between unitary pricing and personalization using four social-welfare functions (utilitarian, prioritarian, egalitarian, and leximin), Mazrekaj et al. (2024) reveal that relatively small disutilities (such as aversion to surveillance or perceived unfairness) can flip utilitarian and prioritarian assessments in favor of unitary pricing; personalization tends to prevail only under strong egalitarian or leximin assumptions, and even then, the advantage is fragile: modest increases in surveillance aversion can reverse results.

Since little is known about end-to-end AI dynamic pricing, audited mechanisms and consumer responses suggest that optimization can conflict with equity and trust; in this context, fairness constraints such as limits on cross-group differences or price-level stabilization rules emerge as main trade-offs, though at a substantive efficiency loss.

2.2.4 Customer Journey Orchestration

Customer journey orchestration is shifting from rules-based decisioning to adaptive learning-based policies based on uplift or incremental-response modeling and constrained optimization to decide whether, when, and how to contact individuals across channels (Ascarza & Israeli, 2022; Hardcastle et al., 2025). These mechanisms estimate a marginal increment in the probability of a desired outcome caused by an action (e.g., sending a coupon, advertising, or making a call) relative to the probability of such an outcome in the absence of that action (Ascarza & Israeli, 2022). This transition introduces two orchestration-specific risks: (i) allocation bias when proxy features such as device, location, or account status correlate with sensitive attributes and focus on contact intensity or eligibility on certain groups and (ii) autonomy risk when repeated nudges or timing policies reduce perceived voluntariness or overwhelm consent mechanisms (Adomavicius & Yang, 2022; Sánchez Chamorro et al., 2023).

However, predictive precision is not the only element that defines the customer experience. During AI-controlled travels, attitudes toward privacy, data monitoring, autonomy, and algorithmic visibility have a significant impact on trust and participation. According to Hardcastle et al. (2025), these perceptions can be actively directed by the managers with the help of effective communication, practical protection, and meaningful control by the user. Examples here are to enable customers to change their access to data, have the option of personalization on or off, and track the use of their information. These steps not only facilitate compliance but also increase consumers' desire to interact with AI.

In the presence of neutral upstream segmentation, learned policies can inherit representational biases from historical interactions and optimize for short-term response signals, thereby concentrating exposure on some users while neglecting others—a mechanism that mirrors feedback patterns observed in ranked delivery (Ali et al., 2019; Singh & Joachims, 2018).

2.3 AI Bias Mitigation Mechanisms in Marketing Systems

This section moves from diagnosis to action, presenting a toolkit for AI Bias mitigation: specifying mitigation objectives, selecting fairness metrics, and acknowledging trade-offs, detailing controls for recommender ranking and pricing policies, and establishing governance and transparency across journeys.

2.3.1 Mitigation Objectives and Trade-Offs

Foundational results show that multiple fairness definitions cannot be satisfied simultaneously under realistic conditions (Chouldechova, 2017; Kleinberg et al., 2017), so mitigation must begin by selecting a concrete fairness goal (fair for whom or what?), encoding it as a constraint or KPI, and evaluating it jointly with accuracy. Each choice (e.g., exposure parity, coverage, calibration; equality of opportunity vs. statistical parity) introduces predictable trade-offs between utility/performance and equity-exposure across relevance, diversity, accuracy, coverage/reach, and business outcomes (Baumann et al., 2024; Deldjoo et al., 2024; Diaz et al., 2022; Wang et al., 2023). Simulation evidence indicates that some fairness criteria (e.g., statistical parity) can reduce utility more than alternatives like equality of opportunity or predictive parity (Baumann et al., 2024). They caution that limiting targeting options alone does not resolve discriminatory delivery and that "leveling down" effects can reduce overall exposure if one group is costlier to reach unless platforms absorb some of the fairness costs.

To make these trade-offs explicit, marketers should preregister (i) which fairness metric will be optimized, (ii) the decision thresholds and delivery-side safeguards, and (iii) the acceptable performance deltas, then run A/B tests that co-report fairness and accuracy. This prevents goal-shifting and turns "fair for whom/what" into enforceable targets that keep optimizers from drifting toward the cheapest, most stereotyped exposures (Baumann et al., 2024; Deldjoo et al., 2024; Diaz et al., 2022; Wang et al., 2023).

Because unfairness often materializes at the delivery phase (not just in segmentation/targeting), marketers should: (i) institutionalize periodic audits (impressions/CPM/conversion by proxy-protected groups); (ii) define, where appropriate, minimum-exposure floors or budget slices for under-reached groups; and (iii) add human review for stereotype-sensitive creatives. These controls complement platform optimization and reflect evidence that neutral targeting alone does not ensure neutral delivery (Baumann et al., 2024; Lambrecht & Tucker, 2019).

Data governance remains foundational. At the data stage, teams should audit and rebalance inputs before model training and delivery, ensuring that training data are not biased, when groups are under-represented or when proxies such as location or device encode sensitive attributes; broaden lookalike pools to capture missing/under-represented users; and apply inference-aware corrections when demographics are not directly observable. When popularity feedback loops or demographic stereotype reinforcement is detected, re-labeling and re-sampling can help counteract these patterns (Zhao et al., 2025).

2.3.2 Fairness in Recommender Ranking

In ranking contexts, operationalizing multi-stakeholder fairness means setting explicit objectives on both the user and provider sides (protect user exposure to relevant items and ensure equitable surfacing of items/sellers, including long-tail providers) and reporting them together with accuracy so visibility trade-offs are transparent to decision-makers (Diaz et al., 2022; Wang et al., 2023). Building on this principle, mitigation follows a standard toolbox: pre-processing to audit and rebalance inputs, in-processing with fairness-aware learning-to-rank (LTR), and post-processing via multi-objective re-ranking with joint fairness–accuracy evaluation (Deldjoo et al., 2024; Zhao et al., 2025).

During model optimization, fairness constraints can be embedded directly into recommendation systems: reinforcement-learning re-rankers can reduce demographic variance in ad/recommendation delivery while preserving privacy (Timmaraju et al., 2023), and fairness-aware learners such as Bias-Eliminating Adapted Trees (BEAT) trace efficiency-fairness frontiers, showing how efficiency gains can be balanced with group and individual fairness goals (Ascarza & Israeli, 2022).

Metric selection is a crucial design step because the metric optimized (exposure parity, coverage, calibration) determines who and what gets seen, reinforcing the need to align metric choice with the stated goal (Baumann et al., 2024; Zhao et al., 2025). In ranked environments, exposure parity redistributes impression shares toward group targets and improves coverage while preserving relevance (Timmaraju et al., 2023); coverage increases the fraction of users/items that receive any exposure (long tail); and calibration aligns exposure with predicted or true relevance for each group (Biega et al., 2018; Deldjoo et al., 2024; Singh & Joachims, 2018; Wang et al., 2023; Zhao et al., 2025). Because parity-of-outcomes objectives (e.g., statistical parity) can erode utility more than alternatives like equality of opportunity or predictive parity, teams should A/B test candidate fairness objectives and make efficiency losses explicit at decision time.

When bias surfaces at delivery time, multi-objective re-ranking and diversity-aware LTR provide post-hoc control over whom and which items are surfaced, while keeping relevance competitive; pairing the chosen objective with periodic candidate-set refresh ensures that the re-ranker has genuinely diverse options to promote, reducing popularity lock-in (Deldjoo et al., 2024; Zhao et al., 2025).

To sustain improvements in production, marketers should implement instrumentation and safeguards aligned with these objectives: dashboards that report user-side and provider-side coverage/exposure, monitoring disparities in ranked visibility over time, and, where appropriate, minimum-exposure floors for underserved user segments or long-tail suppliers so optimizers do not drift toward the cheapest, most popular items by default. Complementing these algorithmic levers with basic user controls (e.g., filters/toggles) can reduce gaps between perceived and actual system behavior and document governance choices (Deldjoo et al., 2024; Vassøy & Langseth, 2024; Wang et al., 2023).

2.3.3 Pricing Guardrails

In pricing, AI Bias mitigation is most effective when it integrates algorithm design, continuous auditing, and clear governance.

Building on the diagnosis that algorithmic personalization can produce disparate prices and rank-based price steering for otherwise comparable consumers, and that these practices erode perceived fairness and trust, mitigation focuses on policy-level constraints, continuous production auditing, and governance with human oversight (Hannak et al., 2014; Hufnagel et al., 2022).

In dynamic pricing, fairness can be encoded directly into the policy through enforceable constraints: (i) inter-group price-dispersion caps that limit like-for-like price gaps across defined groups; (ii) temporal stability limits that bound day-over-day changes for comparable offers; or (iii) demand-fairness bounds that restrict disparities in purchase probabilities/acceptance rates induced by pricing.

These constraints make the equity-utility trade-offs explicit and come with implementable learning procedures and measurable regret/efficiency costs (Cohen et al., 2025). Cohen et al. (2025) formalize these two fairness dimensions (price fairness (cross-group price caps and stability rules) and demand fairness (purchase-rate gaps)) and propose algorithms (FaPU (price fairness) and FaPD (demand fairness)) that satisfy the constraints with provable sublinear regret, showing that narrowing demand-fairness constraints typically increases regret more than dispersion caps.

Algorithmic controls should be complemented by ongoing production audits capable of detecting price discrimination and rank-based steering (e.g., unexplained differentials by device/account state and price-correlated re-ranking in specific sites/settings) supported by automated alerts and investigation workflows (Hannak et al., 2014). Maintaining feature/rationale logging improves post-hoc auditability and supports customer-facing explanations (Deldjoo et al., 2024; Wang et al., 2023). In parallel, the pricing policy should enforce standard safeguards such as cost-consistency checks (price within cost-band plus margin), proxy screens for device/account signals known to drive discrimination or steering, outlier clipping/monotonicity rules to prevent extreme personalized quotes, and exploration caps that limit the magnitude and frequency of per-user price experiments (Deldjoo et al., 2024; Wang et al., 2023), recognizing that these fairness constraints typically involve a quantifiable sacrifice in efficiency (Cohen et al., 2025).

Mitigation should also address the consumer side of fairness because perceived unfairness shapes demand, reduces purchase intention, and erodes benevolence-based trust, which means algorithmic bounds need to be paired with consumer-facing safeguards: neutral, non-personal explanations for price differences and a clear human-override path for contested or outlier quotes (Hufnagel et al., 2022). Operationally, prices that breach dispersion or stability thresholds should be routed to an exception queue for human review or approval; in sensitive categories, incident price freezes or rollbacks should be enabled when audits detect anomalies, and leadership should conduct periodic reviews of fairness dashboards and experiment results so that trade-offs are explicit and governed (Baumann et al., 2024; Wang et al., 2023).

Before deployment, it is advisable to preregister the pricing fairness objective (e.g., dispersion cap or demand fairness), decision thresholds, and acceptable revenue deltas; then run A/B tests that co-report fairness metrics alongside accuracy/utility (revenue, conversion) and transparent, reproducible evaluation protocols (Baumann et al., 2024; Deldjoo et al., 2024; Wang et al., 2023). In practice, teams should also maintain versioned artifacts and audit trails and enable human overrides where reputational risk is high, continuing postlaunch audits for steering/discrimination in ranking (Hannak et al., 2014) and documented consumer fairness effects (Hufnagel et al., 2022).

Finally, whether individualized or homogeneous pricing should be used is a strategic choice conditioned by ethical criteria and stakeholder tolerance for surveillance and inequality (Mazrekaj et al., 2024).

3 AI Hallucinations and Marketing Communication

GenAI is now embedded across marketing workflows: from creative development and social content to PIM, CRM, and service chat. These systems accelerate ideation and reduce costs, yet they also produce hallucinations: fluent but false, unfounded, or unfaithful outputs that jeopardize accuracy, compliance, and brand trust (Jiang et al., 2024; Sun et al., 2024). This section explains (i) why hallucinations arise in contemporary models (taxonomy and structural drivers), (ii) why consumers may still rely on them even when they recognize potential errors, and (iii) which marketing and brand risks emerge and how mitigation strategies, such as RAG, human-in-the-loop (HITL) review for high-stakes claims, and evaluation practices that reward calibrated uncertainty rather than confident guessing can respond (Lewis et al., 2020; Lim et al., 2025).

Conceptually, hallucinations aren't merely data-quality issues but an expected by-product of objective functions and benchmarking regimes that incentivize overly assertive outputs (Kalai et al., 2025). Managerially, perceived hallucination risk and privacy concerns shape engagement, so improving datasets alone is insufficient without operational safeguards (Lim et al., 2025).

3.1 AI Hallucinations and Consumer Behavior

Recent research treats hallucinations as a multi-faceted error class with identifiable subtypes rather than a single phenomenon (Sun et al., 2024). A taxonomy identifies several first-level error families into 31 observable subcategories, providing a practical diagnostic lens for marketing tasks that depend on factual claims, product attributes, or policy language (Sun et al., 2024). Beyond classification, structural drivers of modern language models help to explain why hallucinations persist even with clean data: common loss functions and evaluation regimes create statistical pressures that reward confident guessing, making some hallucinations structural rather than purely data-quality issues and allowing generative errors to propagate across pre-training and post-training stages (Kalai et al., 2025).

In production, lifecycle factors (e.g., data curation, RLHF reward design, and deployment without retrieval/verification guardrails) jointly shape the likelihood and severity of false outputs, highlighting the need for pipeline controls such as pre-publication checks for LLM-enriched product listings that flag unsupported attributes before release (Jiang et al., 2024).

Consumer behavior research shows that awareness does not guarantee safer choices. In a tourism decision scenario, substantial shares of respondents still selected itineraries intentionally seeded with ChatGPT errors, and self-reported concern about hallucinations did not predict better detection, suggesting overconfidence and heuristic reliance on convenience and personalization appeal (Christensen et al.,

2024). Thus, awareness alone may be insufficient to protect consumers from erroneous advice when AI content fits preference structures or task goals (Christensen et al., 2024). This pattern aligns with evidence of "algorithm appreciation", where people sometimes prefer AI algorithmic outputs over human judgment even when they know the algorithm is fallible (Logg et al., 2019), helping to explain continued use in the presence of risk. Evidence from healthcare adoption further indicates that determinants of use can operate outside a simple "exposure → intention" path: adding "hallucination exposure" to a Theory of Planned Behavior framework revealed that perceived behavioral control increased exposure to hallucinations, while subjective norms and perceived risk directly shaped intention to use chatbots; notably, hallucination exposure itself did not significantly mediate intention (Jin et al., 2025). Across these studies, a consistent behavioral vulnerability emerges: users may overweight convenience and social cues and underweight reliability signals, sustaining reliance on AI-generated content even when they know inaccuracies are present (Christensen et al., 2024; Jin et al., 2025; Logg et al., 2019).

3.2 *Marketing and Brand Risks*

When hallucinated AI-generated content is scaled through programmatic systems and owned media, brands face intertwined reputational, behavioral, and regulatory risks that can undermine campaign effectiveness and heighten legal exposure (Labrecque et al., 2024; Neves et al., 2025).

On the reputational front, authenticity risks are amplified when audiences detect or infer that content is machine-authored. Experimental and conceptual work shows that AI-authored marketing communications cues can lower perceived authenticity and trigger moral discomfort ("AI-authorship effect"), magnifying credibility losses when accuracy is uncertain (Kirk & Givi, 2025). In prosocial advertising, explicitly disclosing that content is "AI-generated" reduces perceived credibility and depresses donation intentions/amounts relative to no disclosure or human attribution; more human-like framing attenuates, but doesn't eliminate, these losses (Baek et al., 2024).

The broader "dark side" appraisal of AI in interactive marketing reinforces these concerns by highlighting harms at the individual and societal layers, such as bias, misinformation, privacy, and IP issues, and calling for safeguards and ethical governance when deploying AI at scale (Labrecque et al., 2024).

Behavioral risk transmission is non-trivial: consumers may still act on AI outputs that contain known errors, choosing flawed itineraries despite awareness of hallucination risk, suggesting that convenience and personalization appeal can outweigh reliability cues and thereby translate misinformation into real choices and downstream complaints (Christensen et al., 2024). Relatedly, interactions framed as "with AI" can depress brand trust by prompting inferences of a larger, less bounded audience, thereby increasing reputational costs when errors surface (Lefkeli et al., 2024).

Finally, from a regulatory and platform-governance perspective, risks can rise when hallucinated factual claims or unsubstantiated product attributes can trigger exposure under advertising, consumer-protection, platform-governance rules, and evolving frameworks, such as the EU Digital Services Act, which strengthens ad-transparency and oversight duties, restricts profiling using sensitive categories, and establishes special protections for minors, raising the stakes for erroneous or opaque advertising claims and disclosures (Dokumacı, 2024; Turillazzi et al., 2023; Wolters & Zuiderveen Borgesius, 2025). Where inaccurate content intersects with sensitive sectors (e.g., health, finance) or vulnerable audiences, the combination of false claims and inadequate disclosures can escalate from reputational incidents to regulatory findings (Dokumacı, 2024; Turillazzi et al., 2023).

Although not exclusively focused on hallucinations, a field-level bibliometric analysis of AI Bias in marketing documents rapid growth in fairness-related scholarship and proposes ethical and application dimensions that intersect with hallucination governance, where inaccuracies can entrench inequities or mislead vulnerable audiences (Bacalhau et al., 2025).

3.3 *Mitigation of Hallucinations in Marketing Flow*

Hallucinations arise from how contemporary models are trained (objective functions that reward confident guessing) and how they are deployed (workflows without grounding or verification), so they persist even with clean data. That makes mitigation a first-order design concern rather than a nice-to-have (Kalai et al., 2025; Sun et al., 2024).

Evidence converges on four complementary levers that should be used together: decoding-time generation controls, retrieval-anchored grounding and fact-checking, human review for high-stakes claims, and evaluation reforms that stop rewarding over-confident outputs (Kalai et al., 2025; Lewis et al., 2020; Neves et al., 2025; Wang et al., 2026).

These levers are complements, not substitutes, and should work together to reduce the frequency and impact of hallucinations in production.

3.3.1 Decoding-Time and Generation Controls

Decoding-time constraints are a first line of defense against over-assertive, ungrounded generations because they directly modulate how outputs are produced, reducing the "confident guessing" incentivized by standard training/evaluation objectives (Kalai et al., 2025). In practice, controls include conservative sampling, repetition penalties, constrained or contrastive decoding, and explicit abstention thresholds ("I don't know") that reduce pressure to guess.

In multimodal generation, Emotion-Augmented Inference reduces hallucinations and improves task performance and emotional coherence, especially under negative affect or degraded visual inputs, suggesting that affect-aware or contrastive mechanisms are useful where sentiment alignment matters for persuasion and customer experience (Wang et al., 2026).

Operationally, decoding-time controls should be chosen to match the dominant error mode: using conservative sampling or constraint-based decoding for fabrication-style errors, and reserve affect-aware or contrastive mechanisms for cases where sentiment-driven over-assertiveness is driven by emotional framing. These choices follow from taxonomy-guided diagnosis rather than one-size-fits-all settings (Sun et al., 2024; Wang et al., 2026).

3.3.2 Grounding and Human-in-the-Loop Verification

Decoding-time controls reduce over-assertiveness but do not establish factuality, so they should be combined with retrieval grounding (RAG) and HITL review to address the structural incentives to guess confidently (Kalai et al., 2025), intercepting high-impact errors before release in marketing workflows (Neves et al., 2025). RAG should be the default generation mode for any knowledge-intensive copy that makes verifiable claims (e.g., product specifications, pricing/availability, FAQs, policy text, testimonials), so that outputs are supported by documentary evidence rather than model priors (Lewis et al., 2020). In e-commerce settings, pre-publication checks for LLM-enriched product listings flag unsupported attributes before publication, block release when citations are missing, stale, or non-resolvable, and require HITL sign-off for sensitive claims (e.g., legal, safety/health, regulated pricing), illustrating how pipeline controls can reduce hallucination exposure (Jiang et al., 2024).

The most robust packages pair RAG with targeted HITL review and evaluation policies that reward calibrated uncertainty and do not penalize abstention, aligning day-to-day utility with factuality and fairness objectives. For marketers, these findings highlight the need to design safeguards that account for real decision dynamics rather than relying on warnings or passive disclosures (Christensen et al., 2024; Jin et al., 2025).

3.3.3 Operational Safeguards and Team Capability

Operational reliability rises when content teams receive targeted training, use fact-checking/verification tools before publication, and follow documented review workflows as necessary controls when deploying generative systems in content pipelines so that unsupported statements are intercepted upstream (Neves et al., 2025). Where interactions are decision-relevant, adding friction at the point of action—verification prompts or deferral to a human—helps intercept erroneous advice when risk is highest.

3.3.4 Evaluation Reform and Measurement

Finally, mitigating systemic overconfidence requires retooling metrics and acceptance criteria so models are no longer rewarded for polished guesses. Concretely, organizations should not penalize abstention, credit calibrated uncertainty, and co-report factuality with utility in both offline benchmarks and A/B tests; these shifts realign behavior away from guessing and cut hallucination incentives at the source (Kalai et al., 2025). To prevent post-hoc drift, preregister abstention/uncertainty rules, decision thresholds, and success criteria. This reframes mitigation as a socio-technical intervention in the leaderboards that guide development priorities rather than only a set of after-the-fact patches (Kalai et al., 2025).

In practice, pairing these policies with taxonomy-guided error mapping and the controls above ensures that evaluation, generation settings, and release processes reinforce one another, reducing the frequency and impact of hallucinations in production.

3.4 Synthesis and Practical Implications

Three broad consistencies stand out. First, literature consistently treats hallucination as a structural feature of contemporary models and deployments (Kalai et al., 2025; Sun et al., 2024). Second, marketing-oriented syntheses consistently highlight reputational and legal exposure and advocate layered mitigation across technical-plus-organizational mitigation controls (Labrecque et al., 2024; Neves et al., 2025). Third, consumers remain vulnerable to erroneous outputs even when aware of risk, which limits the value of disclosure-only approaches (Christensen et al., 2024; Jin et al., 2025). Perceptions of AI authorship can further reduce authenticity and increase moral disgust, which can heighten negative reactions even to minor inaccuracies (Kirk & Givi, 2025). For practice, the most reliable responses build on the four levers outlined above rather than relying on single-point fixes (Labrecque et al., 2024; Neves et al., 2025).

Two tensions also emerge: (i) normatively, creative-enablement views of hallucination clash with the imperative of factuality in public-facing communication (Labrecque et al., 2024; Patrício, 2024) and (ii) methodologically, even when decoding-time and retrieval strategies reduce errors, benchmark incentives may still favor confident guessing unless socio-technical metrics change, creating a treadmill effect for downstream mitigations (Kalai et al., 2025; Wang et al., 2026).

If teams use experiments with hallucinations as a creativity stimulus in early ideation, those activities should remain sandboxed and clearly separated from downstream market communications, with strict verification gates prior to public release to manage reputational and ethical risks (Labrecque et al., 2024; Patrício, 2024).

Finally, two findings are notable. Consumers' willingness to select itineraries seeded with known errors suggests a gap between stated concern and actual behavior in high-involvement tasks, consistent with convenience seeking, optimism bias, or perceived personalization benefits that outweigh accuracy vigilance (Christensen et al., 2024).

4 Ethics in the Age of AI Marketing

As the previous sections have shown, bias and hallucinations in AI-driven marketing shape who is reached, what is said, and how choices are presented along AI-mediated customer journeys. These dynamics raise questions that go beyond predictive performance or legal compliance: opaque personalization, quiet price divergence, and fluent but unfounded claims can put core marketing values—fairness, autonomy, transparency, and respect for persons—under pressure.

This section reframes bias and hallucinations as ethical challenges that cut across AI marketing systems. It first revisits key traditions and recent developments in marketing ethics, highlighting how emotional, organizational, and market forces jointly shape moral judgment in practice. It then examines the ethical implications of bias and hallucinations for consumer vulnerability, distributive justice, and brand authenticity, and contrasts legal baselines with broader ethical responsibilities in a rapidly evolving regulatory landscape. Throughout, ethics is treated not as a checklist layered on top of technical systems but as an ongoing negotiation that links design and governance choices to consumer welfare and long-term trust.

4.1 Foundations of Marketing Ethics in Data-Driven Contexts

Marketing ethics, at its most fundamental level, refers to the principles that guide professionals in making moral decisions when interacting with consumers, organizations, and other stakeholders in society. In practice, ethics in marketing rarely fit neatly into a checklist. It tends to play out in a gray space between personal judgment, organizational culture, and the invisible hand of market forces, which often pull in different directions. Ferrell and Gresham's contingency framework, for example, explains ethical decision-making as the joint product of individual factors, significant others in the organization, and situational opportunities in the environment (Ferrell & Gresham, 1985). From this perspective, AI does not replace these drivers but reconfigures them in data-rich, automated contexts.

Perceptions of what someone considers "ethical" are heavily shaped by emotions and by the intensity of the moral situation, especially when decisions are ambiguous. Empirical work shows that emotion, moral intensity, moral philosophy, personal norms, and intrinsic religiosity jointly influence ethical decisions, going beyond "cold" logic (Escadas et al., 2019). At the same time, institutional forces shape the moral ground marketers walk on: internal ethics training, leadership tone, and perceptions of organizational justice substantively affect how people interpret right from wrong at work, especially when market dynamics, consumer expectations, branding pressures, and competition converge (Moradi & Zihagh, 2019). Normative accounts of ethical and socially responsible marketing nonetheless propose shared aspirational principles (e.g., respect for stakeholders, justice, and stewardship) as guides for evaluating specific decisions (Laczniak & Murphy, 2006), translating diffuse concerns about fairness or autonomy in AI-mediated markets into more structured questions about what marketers ought to do. Recent updates to the Hunt-Vitell model, for example, incorporate cultural orientation, socialization, self-respect, respect from others, and information availability, offering a more granular account of ethical decision-making in marketing (Uslay, 2025).

Marketers are often in a particularly exposed and, arguably, vulnerable position as the most visible interface between companies and the public, crafting campaigns, managing pricing, collecting consumer data, and making countless perception-shaping decisions. Ethical decision-making in this role involves navigating ambiguity and competing interests, shaped not only by internal norms but also by fluctuating external pressures and personal value systems (Chowdhury, 2023).

Most ethical frameworks in marketing revolve around values such as honesty, transparency, fairness, autonomy, and privacy. While these principles remain central, their practical application is rarely straightforward. Transparency, for instance, may be formally satisfied by a legally compliant disclaimer in fine print, yet still falls short ethically if it misleads or confuses its intended audience. Similarly, respect for privacy becomes blurred when companies personalize user experiences through behavioral data, sometimes in ways perceived as more invasive than helpful (Daoud et al., 2023).

The expansion of digital platforms has further complicated the ethical landscape. Social media, targeted ads, and algorithmically generated content have expanded marketing capabilities while blurring ethical lines. Techniques such as manipulative interface designs ("dark patterns") raise concerns about manipulation and autonomy (Fassiaux, 2023; Sánchez Chamorro et al., 2023), while artificial intelligence adds another layer of complexity by scaling personalization but also intensifying risks of behavioral manipulation and data-driven persuasion (Shemshaki, 2024).

AI also creates risks that are not always easy to track. Imbalanced datasets can silently bias advice or lock out some groups, and GenAI tools can generate authoritative-looking but hallucinated content (Patrício, 2024; Sun et al., 2024) or introduce further manipulation and bias risks (Shemshaki, 2024), creating an illusion of efficiency that ultimately reinforces existing inequalities.

Subtle framing effects or confirmation bias, such as in defining success metrics or choosing campaign narratives, can seem reasonable in the moment yet reveal ethical blind spots with hindsight (Watts et al., 2020). Algorithmic systems amplify this ambiguity: assigning responsibility becomes increasingly complex when decisions are driven by opaque models with dynamic and decentralized inputs (Adomavicius & Yang, 2022). Accordingly, no single fairness criterion or mitigation technique is universally optimal; organizations face trade-offs between accuracy, transparency, and equity goals that must be managed explicitly (Jain & Menon, 2023), making ethical marketing less about rule-following and more about vigilance when efficiency gains erode fairness or displace meaningful human judgment.

The ethics of marketing can be viewed as a dynamic negotiation between technological capabilities, business-model requirements, and consumer expectations, which may never be in an optimal balance but should be taken as a necessary starting point.

4.1.1 Ethical Governance and Transparency Across Journeys

Building on these foundations, ethical marketing in AI contexts depends on governance mechanisms that make fairness and transparency operational along customer journeys.

Lasting bias mitigation depends on systematic governance that turns fairness into an operational discipline rather than a declarative principle. At the journey level, organizations should maintain version-controlled datasets and models, specify ex ante which fairness objective applies and the evaluation criteria, and conduct continuous delivery-phase audits (Deldjoo et al., 2024; Wang et al., 2023).

Regulators are likewise tightening ad transparency and data-access duties for online platforms, which raises the bar for internal auditability and external explanations (Wolters & Zuiderveen Borgesius, 2025).

In line with evaluation guidance from recommender-systems surveys, governance should link journey-level fairness objectives to measurement: co-report fairness and accuracy/utility so trade-offs are explicit at decision time (Vassøy & Langseth, 2024; Wang et al., 2023). In practice, this means running delivery-phase audits on a fixed cadence, using dashboards that track exposure and coverage by (proxy) protected groups, documenting human exceptions on sensitive decisions, and keeping feature/rationale logs to make data use visible and auditable (Deldjoo et al., 2024; Wang et al., 2023).

Sustained mitigation of AI Bias depends on organizational capacity. Akter et al. (2022, 2023) highlight three interconnected lenses: design (data, model, deployment method), context (cultural, social, personal), and application (product, price, place, promotion), that determine the extent to which firms can identify, shape, and mitigate bias in marketing ML models. Embedding these lenses into routine reviews ensures that fairness is balanced with efficiency on a scale, rather than treated as a one-off compliance task (Akter et al., 2022, 2023).

Because users frequently misestimate what the personalization systems actually do (Zhang & Zhang, 2025), organizations should align perceived and actual system behavior through clear disclosures about targeting, personalization on/off toggles with granular opt-outs, frequency limits to avoid contact pressure, and stewardship of interest tags, all wired into the internal governance stack (Wang et al., 2023; Zhang & Zhang, 2025), to narrow the gap in consumer responses to algorithmic targeting (Hardcastle et al., 2025). Operationally, these UX levers should connect to the internal governance stack (dashboards, model/data versioning, preregistered tests, audit cadence) so that fairness objectives are enforced at decision time rather than patched after the fact (Deldjoo et al., 2024; Wang et al., 2023).

Finally, governance must remain evidence-driven. Organizations should maintain versioned experiment registries, require A/B tests that co-report fairness and business outcomes for material changes, and schedule periodic leadership reviews of fairness dashboards and audit results to make equity-performance frontiers explicit and owned. This closes the loop between technical controls, UX transparency, and organizational accountability, ensuring that bias mitigation persists across journeys and over time (Akter et al., 2022; Akter et al., 2023; Deldjoo et al., 2024; Vassøy & Langseth, 2024; Wang et al., 2023; Zhang et al., 2025).

When these governance steps are routine rather than ad hoc, they not only meet regulatory expectations but also increase willingness to interact with AI systems by reducing misestimation and signaling accountability (Wang et al., 2023; Wolters & Zuiderveen Borgesius, 2025; Zhang & Zhang, 2025).

4.1.2 Content and Disclosure as Ethical Controls in Creative Operations

Fairness is not only about who sees what; it is also about what is said and how, because content itself can play a decisive role in bias. Because transparency interacts with persuasion and fairness, marketers should treat disclosure as a design variable and evaluate it alongside accuracy and equity (Deldjoo et al., 2024; Wang et al., 2023) and match it to the underlying mechanism at issue to balance moral salience, perceived fairness, and data protection rather than relying on generic transparency.

Evidence suggests that the impact of disclosure depends on the type of bias at stake: users show heightened moral awareness and reduced trust under direct discrimination, but more muted responses under indirect forms (Ebrahimi et al., 2024), so, creative operations should pair each disclosure with the assurance most relevant to the likely concern (e.g., provenance for factual claims; confidentiality and data minimization for interactions) (Baek et al., 2024; Lefkeli et al., 2024; Wang et al., 2023).

Execution details matter. In prosocial advertising, disclosing that content is "AI-generated", compared with no disclosure or human attribution, can reduce perceived credibility and lower ad evaluations and donation intentions, although anthropomorphizing the AI can attenuate these losses, underlining execution sensitivity (Baek et al., 2024).

Trust is also tested when consumers are asked to share information with an AI rather than a human. In such cases, people infer that their data may reach a larger but less defined audience. This sense of exposure increases perceptions of exploitation and, as a result, weakens brand trust, particularly among privacy-conscious individuals (Lefkeli et al., 2024). Two practical mitigation actions can be taken to reduce the loss in brand trust: (a) offering explicit confidentiality assurances that limit perceived data visibility and (b) requesting only lower-relevance information, which reduces the sense of intrusion (Lefkeli et al., 2024).

Accordingly, content-level AI Bias mitigations should focus on: (i) framing choices for "AI-generated/AI-assisted" labels; (ii) concise, non-personal confidentiality statements when copy requests user data; and (iii) data-minimizing prompts/forms during creative interactions.

4.2 Ethical Implications of Bias and Hallucinations for Fairness, Autonomy, and Authenticity

This section focuses on three values that are central to marketing ethics in AI-mediated environments: fairness, autonomy, and authenticity. Bias in data and models primarily threatens fairness by skewing who is targeted, how they are treated, and which opportunities are made visible. Hallucinations, in turn, undermine autonomy and authenticity when persuasive but unfounded outputs shape consumer decisions or misrepresent what brands stand for. The following discussion draws on recent work on AI fairness and generative models to illustrate how these risks materialize along customer journeys and what is at stake for marketers. Such distortions can alter consumer decision-making, marketing narratives, and determine the outcome of algorithm-based campaigns.

Adding to these difficulties, hallucinated outputs are not necessarily produced with ill intent but often result from AI's inability to distinguish correlation from truth. Nevertheless, such content may significantly influence consumer perception and trust when it enters marketing materials (Menard & Bott, 2024).

A central tension is that what is legal is not always ethical: a dynamic pricing algorithm may technically be compliant with the regulations yet still charge higher prices to lower-income or time-pressured users, a pattern many find ethically questionable (Kopalle et al., 2023; Seele et al., 2021).

Behavioral science also shows that well-intentioned professionals are not immune to biases. Heuristics such as anchoring, confirmation bias, or implicit stereotypes may shape how campaigns are designed, segmented, or evaluated (Stella, 2022), so ethics education needs to move beyond abstraction to help marketers recognize and mitigate such distortions in actual decision-making contexts.

AI systems add to these challenges. When trained on biased or incomplete data, they often replicate, and even amplify, existing social inequalities. A targeted ad campaign that profiles specific demographics may perform well in terms of reach, yet raise serious ethical concerns related to opacity and accountability; drawing on the New Chicago School, Lee (2022) argues that mitigating algorithmic bias requires a mix of direct and indirect regulation, through architecture (code), norms, markets, and law, rather than relying on transparency alone.

AI hallucinations introduce further complexity. Marketing content generated by AI may seem credible and persuasive yet lack factual grounding. A chatbot promoting skincare might cite fictitious studies or testimonials, not because it intends to deceive, but because of a fundamental failure to see whether something is factually accurate

(Kirk & Givi, 2025). These issues blur the line between automation and manipulation, making accountability elusive.

Ethical standards increasingly advocate transparency in AI-generated content, accountability, and responsible use of AI in marketing, supported by ethical and regulatory frameworks (Kumar & Suthar, 2024). Still, implementation remains inconsistent. Some companies use AI to write ad copy or product descriptions without disclosure; others experiment with synthetic influencers blending fiction and reality in ways imperceptible to users (Marti-Ochoa et al., 2025).

Bias and hallucinations, human and algorithmic, do not simply influence short-term credibility but also long-term brand authenticity and trust. This is especially apparent in influencer marketing as consumers are quick to perceive insincerity. Influencers who maintain a commitment to authenticity, who are transparent about sponsorship, and who resist algorithmic over-curation are more likely to develop longer-lasting, deeper relationships (Marti-Ochoa et al., 2025).

In the end, ethical marketing in the AI age will not be achieved by eliminating bias or error. Instead, it involves recognizing their presence, creating systems that minimize harm as much as possible, and promoting a culture of conversation about ethics as a continuous journey (Grewal et al., 2024).

4.3 Legal Limits and the Ethical Imperative

Although closely related, legislation and ethics occupy distinct yet complementary roles in guiding marketing practices. Laws impose enforceable boundaries, while ethics offers normative direction that extends into broader societal and moral concerns (Dokumacı, 2024). Regulatory baselines are evolving: under the EU Digital Services Act (DSA), platforms face stronger ad-transparency duties, restrictions on profiling using sensitive categories, and special protections for minors, but remaining tensions mean internal governance often needs to go beyond minimum legal duties (Wolters & Zuiderveen Borgesius, 2025).

Ethical frameworks, in contrast, are more adaptive and capable of anticipating emerging concerns, such as algorithmic opacity or hidden biases in adaptive pricing, before they become codified in law (Kulaklıoğlu, 2024). Algorithmic pricing may be entirely legal, yet still elicit public discomfort, especially when consumers in lower-income areas are silently charged more based on inferred urgency (Seele et al., 2021). The tension between what is lawful and what is fair underscores the importance of ethical reflection beyond compliance.

Ethics also becomes a lens through which the boundaries of legislation are questioned, especially where individual autonomy and social justice intersect. Marketing ethics calls for dealing with consumers fairly and with dignity, even where there are no formal requirements.

On top of that, the speed of evolution in digital marketing widens the gap between what technology can do and what the law can address, especially in privacy and data use. Complex consent mechanisms may conform to the law yet still be ethically problematic when it is unclear whether users, particularly minors, understand what they are consenting to (Turillazzi et al., 2023), which underscores the essential role of ethics in shaping corporate practice and future policy.

Ethical perspectives reveal a more active and adaptive way of responding to problems such as opaque processing, behavioral targeting, or algorithmic discrimination, issues in which regulation often follows instead of leads. The discrepancy between user comprehension and legal disclosure has been linked to broader concerns over fairness and transparency in digital ecosystems (Seele et al., 2021; Turillazzi et al., 2023).

5 Future Research Directions

5.1 Bias Research

Despite increased interest in bias in AI-driven marketing, the evidence base remains fragmented. The next generation of research needs to move beyond conceptual models and laboratory experiments and include field-level A/B tests that establish standardized exposure and calibration measures of recommender fairness (Jin et al., 2023; Zhao et al., 2025).

Further work should address metric interactions and Pareto trade-offs, recognizing that fairness, diversity, and utility objectives are interdependent rather than separate, and develop auditing methods that account for demographic inference errors and sample shifts.

In dynamic pricing, fairness-constrained mechanisms must be tested in live markets (Cohen et al., 2025), combining welfare models with behavioral evidence to identify when personalization is viable versus ethically problematic (Mazrekaj et al., 2024). Human–AI alignment deserves closer attention, especially misestimation, i.e., gaps between perceived and actual system behavior (Zhang & Zhang, 2025).

The key to balancing efficiency and equity is to embed fairness into performance measures and regular audits (Akter et al., 2022, 2023).

5.2 Hallucinations Research

Several gaps emerge from the reviewed studies that warrant targeted investigation. Field research should evaluate whether changing benchmark incentives to reward abstention measurably reduces hallucination rates in applied marketing tasks (Kalai et al., 2025) and test how affect-aware decoding and related controls generalize across formats and degraded inputs, including trade-offs between reliability and computational overhead (Wang et al., 2026). Consumer research should probe why awareness fails to translate into error detection and safer choices, isolating mechanisms such as overconfidence, personalization appeal, or effort avoidance in diverse market categories and journey stages (Christensen et al., 2024), and longitudinal and cross-population designs should access how repeated exposure to hallucinations shapes trust, continued use, and substitution patterns for human advisors (Jin et al., 2025). Marketing-specific syntheses call for rigorous detection and verification protocols, comparative evaluations of RAG, human review designs, and multimodal cross-checking in real content operations (Neves et al., 2025) and taxonomies tailored to marketing genres to improve tool support for non-expert reviewers (Sun et al., 2024). Organizational research should assess whether curated hallucination exposure improves creative outcomes without elevating downstream misinformation risk in real brand settings (Patrício, 2024). Finally, as AI-ethics scholarship expands, research should integrate hallucination management with fairness, privacy, and accountability frameworks, using models that capture multi-risk interactions in campaigns and platforms (Bacalhau et al., 2025; Labrecque et al., 2024).

5.3 Ethical Research

AI marketing presents ethical issues that are conceptually well mapped but still lack practical, company-level guidance. Future studies should consider how new rules, such as the EU AI Act, can be operationalized to inform actual governance modalities, as numerous companies remain uncertain about their obligations under these frameworks (Dokumacı, 2024; Kulaklıoğlu, 2024).

Studies should also examine how legally compliant practices are perceived by consumers, as legal practices can still be considered manipulative or unfair, such as algorithmic pricing, behavioral targeting, and data consent (Seele et al., 2021; Turillazzi et al., 2023).

Lastly, studies on adaptive ethics that follow technological change are needed, particularly in terms of regulations that drive innovation. Such work should incorporate transparency, accountability, and consumer autonomy safeguards in opaque settings that rely on automated persuasion.

Ultimately, future work should move beyond abstract principles to provide context-specific ethical playbooks, helping organizations embed fairness and dignity into marketing practice and anticipate regulatory change.

6 Conclusion

This chapter argues that algorithmic bias and AI hallucinations are central, structural risks in AI-driven marketing, shaping campaigns, pricing, and consumer interactions rather than peripheral technical bugs. Using an ethical governance lens, it integrates technical, behavioral, and normative insights to show how data, models, and deployment choices jointly affect fairness, transparency, and authenticity in the marketplace. For scholars, this calls for a shift toward field-based evidence, cross-disciplinary collaboration, and frameworks that connect mitigation techniques to behavioral and ethical outcomes, particularly in recommender fairness, dynamic pricing, and hallucination management. For practitioners, the need is equally urgent. AI should not be treated as a neutral toolkit but must be grounded in explicit decisions about fairness, transparency, accountability, and consumer autonomy. Firms that neglect these dimensions risk losing consumer trust, incurring regulatory sanctions, and eroding brand equity, whereas those that embed continuous auditing, fairness-by-design, and strong governance are better positioned to avoid harm and build long-term, trust-based relationships in increasing digital markets. Ultimately, the future of AI in marketing will be determined less by efficiency gains than by how effectively the industry balances innovation with responsibility.

References

Adomavicius, G., & Yang, M. (2022). Integrating behavioral, economic, and technical insights to understand and address algorithmic bias: A human-centric perspective. *ACM Transactions on Management Information Systems, 13*(3), 1–27. https://doi.org/10.1145/3519420

Akter, S., Dwivedi, Y. K., Sajib, S., Biswas, K., Bandara, R. J., & Michael, K. (2022). Algorithmic bias in machine learning-based marketing models: Toward a research agenda. *Journal of Business Research, 144*, 201–216. https://doi.org/10.1016/j.jbusres.2022.01.083

Akter, S., Sultana, S., Mariani, M., Wamba, S. F., Spanaki, K., & Dwivedi, Y. K. (2023). Advancing algorithmic bias management capabilities in AI-driven marketing analytics research. *Industrial Marketing Management, 114*, 243–261. https://doi.org/10.1016/j.indmarman.2023.08.013

Ali, M., Sapiezynski, P., Bogen, M., Korolova, A., Mislove, A., & Rieke, A. (2019). Discrimination through optimization: How Facebook's ad delivery can Lead to biased outcomes. *Proceedings of the ACM on Human-Computer Interaction, 3*(CSCW), 1–30. https://doi.org/10.1145/3359301

Ascarza, E., & Israeli, A. (2022). Eliminating unintended bias in personalized policies using bias-eliminating adapted trees (BEAT). *Proceedings of the National Academy of Sciences of the United States of America, 119*(11), 1–9. https://doi.org/10.1073/pnas.2115293119

Bacalhau, L. M., Pereira, M. C., & Neves, J. (2025). A bibliometric analysis of AI bias in marketing: Field evolution and future research agenda. *Journal of Marketing Analytics, 13*(2), 308–327. https://doi.org/10.1057/s41270-025-00379-6

Baek, T. H., Kim, J., & Kim, J. H. (2024). Effect of disclosing AI-generated content on prosocial advertising evaluation. *International Journal of Advertising*. https://doi.org/10.1080/02650487.2024.2401319

Baumann, J., Sapiezynski, P., Heitz, C., & Hannak, A. (2024). Fairness in online ad delivery. In *Proceedings of the 2024 ACM conference on fairness, accountability, and transparency* (pp. 1418–1432). Rio de Janeiro. https://doi.org/10.1145/3630106.3658980

Biega, A. J., Gummadi, K. P., & Weikum, G. (2018). Equity of attention: Amortizing individual fairness in rankings. In *The 41st international ACM SIGIR conference on Research & Development in information retrieval*. Ann Arbor. https://doi.org/10.1145/3209978.3210063

Cecere, G., Jean, C., Le Guel, F., & Manant, M. (2024). Artificial intelligence and algorithmic bias? Field tests on social network with teens. *Technological Forecasting and Social Change, 201*(123204), 1–16. https://doi.org/10.1016/j.techfore.2023.123204

Chouldechova, A. (2017). Fair prediction with disparate impact: A study of bias in recidivism prediction instruments. *Big Data, 5*(2), 153–163. https://doi.org/10.1089/big.2016.0047

Chowdhury, R. M. M. I. (2023). Perceived income inequality, trust, and consumers' ethical judgments. *Journal of Macromarketing, 43*(4), 476–493. https://doi.org/10.1177/02761467231187306

Christensen, J., Hansen, J. M., & Wilson, P. (2024). Understanding the role and impact of generative artificial intelligence (AI) hallucination within consumers' tourism decision-making processes. *Current Issues in Tourism, 28*(4), 545–560. https://doi.org/10.1080/13683500.2023.2300032

Cohen, M. C., Miao, S., & Wang, Y. (2025). Dynamic pricing with fairness constraints. *Operations Research, 73*(6), 3027–3043. https://doi.org/10.1287/opre.2023.0123

Daoud, M. K., Al-Qeed, M., Al-Gasawneh, J. A., & Ziani, A. (2023, November 21–24). Examining the ethical implications of data privacy and targeted advertising in digital marketing: Consumer perceptions. 2023 tenth international conference on social networks analysis, management and security (SNAMS), https://doi.org/10.1109/SNAMS60348.2023.10375481.

Deldjoo, Y., Jannach, D., Bellogin, A., Difonzo, A., & Zanzonelli, D. (2024). Fairness in recommender systems: Research landscape and future directions. *User Modeling and User-Adapted Interaction, 34*(1), 59–108. https://doi.org/10.1007/s11257-023-09364-z

Diaz, F., Burke, R., Das, A., & Ekstrand, M. D. (2022). Fairness in information access systems. *Foundations and trends®. Information Retrieval, 16*(1–2), 1–177. https://doi.org/10.1561/1500000079

Dokumacı, M. (2024). Legal frameworks for AI regulations. *Human Computer Interaction, 8*(1). https://doi.org/10.62802/ytst2927

Ebrahimi, S., Abdelhalim, E., Hassanein, K., & Head, M. (2024). Reducing the incidence of biased algorithmic decisions through feature importance transparency: An empirical study. *European Journal of Information Systems, 34*(4), 636–664. https://doi.org/10.1080/0960085x.2024.2395531

Escadas, M., Jalali, M. S., & Farhangmehr, M. (2019). Antecedents of consumer ethical decision-making: A multidimensional analysis of emotions, moral intensity, moral philosophies, personal norms, and intrinsic religiosity. In P. Rossi & N. Krey (Eds.), *Finding new ways to engage and satisfy global customers. AMSWMC 2018. Developments in marketing science. Proceedings of the academy of marketing Scienc*. Springer. https://doi.org/10.1007/978-3-030-02568-7_148

Fassiaux, S. (2023). Preserving consumer autonomy through European Union regulation of artificial intelligence: A long-term approach. *European Journal of Risk Regulation, 14*(4), 710–730. https://doi.org/10.1017/err.2023.58

Ferrell, O. C., & Gresham, L. G. (1985). A contingency framework for understanding ethical decision making in marketing. *Journal of Marketing, 49*(3), 87–96. https://doi.org/10.1177/002224298504900308

Grewal, D., Satornino, C. B., Davenport, T., & Guha, A. (2024). How generative AI is shaping the future of marketing. *Journal of the Academy of Marketing Science, 53*(3), 702–722. https://doi.org/10.1007/s11747-024-01064-3

Hannak, A., Soeller, G., Lazer, D., Mislove, A., & Wilson, C. (2014). Measuring Price discrimination and steering on E-commerce web sites. In *Proceedings of the 2014 internet measurement conference (IMC'14)* (pp. 305–318). Vancouver. https://doi.org/10.1145/2663716.2663744

Hardcastle, K., Vorster, L., & Brown, D. M. (2025). Understanding customer responses to AI-driven personalized journeys: Impacts on the customer experience. *Journal of Advertising, 54*(2), 176–195. https://doi.org/10.1080/00913367.2025.2460985

Hermann, E., & Puntoni, S. (2025). Generative AI in marketing and principles for ethical design and deployment. *Journal of Public Policy & Marketing, 44*(3), 332–349. https://doi.org/10.1177/07439156241309874

Hikov, A., & Murphy, L. (2024). Information retrieval from textual data: Harnessing large language models, retrieval augmented generation and prompt engineering. *Journal of AI, Robotics & Workplace Automation,3* (2). https://doi.org/10.69554/qafe6376

Hufnagel, G., Schwaiger, M., & Weritz, L. (2022). Seeking the perfect price: Consumer responses to personalized price discrimination in e-commerce. *Journal of Business Research, 143*, 346–365. https://doi.org/10.1016/j.jbusres.2021.10.002

Jain, L. R., & Menon, V. (2023). AI algorithmic bias: Understanding its causes, ethical and social implications. In *2023 IEEE 35th international conference on tools with artificial intelligence (ICTAI)*. https://doi.org/10.1109/ictai59109.2023.00073

Jiang, L., Jiang, K., Chu, X., Gulati, S., & Garg, P. (2024). Hallucination detection in LLM-enriched product listings. In S. Malmasi, B. Fetahu, N. Ueffing, O. Rokhlenko, E. Agichtein, & I. Guy (Eds.), *Proceedings of the seventh workshop on e-commerce and NLP @ LREC-COLING 2024*. Torino. https://aclanthology.org/2024.ecnlp-1.4/

Jin, D., Wang, L., Zhang, H., Zheng, Y., Ding, W., Xia, F., & Pan, S. (2023). A survey on fairness-aware recommender systems. *Information Fusion, 100*, 101906. https://doi.org/10.1016/j.inffus.2023.101906

Jin, L., Shen, Z., Alhur, A. A., & Naeem, S. B. (2025). Exploring the determinants and effects of artificial intelligence (AI) hallucination exposure on generative AI adoption in healthcare. *Information Development*. https://doi.org/10.1177/02666669251340954

Kalai, A. T., Nachum, O., Vempala, S. S., & Zhang, E. (2025). Why language models hallucinate. *arXiv preprint*. https://doi.org/10.48550/arXiv.2509.04664

Kirk, C. P., & Givi, J. (2025). The AI-authorship effect: Understanding authenticity, moral disgust, and consumer responses to AI-generated marketing communications. *Journal of Business Research, 186*, 114984. https://doi.org/10.1016/j.jbusres.2024.114984

Kleinberg, J., Mullainathan, S., & Raghavan, M. (2017). Inherent trade-offs in the fair determination of risk scores. 8th Innovations in Theoretical Computer Science Conference (ITCS 2017). *Leibniz International Proceedings in Informatics (LIPIcs), 67*, pp. 1–43, https://doi.org/10.4230/LIPIcs.ITCS.2017.43.

Kopalle, P. K., Pauwels, K., Akella, L. Y., & Gangwar, M. (2023). Dynamic pricing: Definition, implications for managers, and future research directions. *Journal of Retailing, 99*(4), 580–593. https://doi.org/10.1016/j.jretai.2023.11.003

Kulaklıoğlu, D. (2024). Ethical AI in autonomous systems and decision-making. *Human Computer Interaction, 8*(1). https://doi.org/10.62802/jb2ptt89

Kumar, D., & Suthar, N. (2024). Ethical and legal challenges of AI in marketing: An exploration of solutions. *Journal of Information, Communication and Ethics in Society, 22*(1), 124–144. https://doi.org/10.1108/jices-05-2023-0068

Labrecque, L. I., Peña, P. Y., Leonard, H., & Leger, R. (2024). Not all sunshine and rainbows: Exploring the dark side of AI in interactive marketing. *Journal of Research in Interactive Marketing, 18*(5), 970–999. https://doi.org/10.1108/jrim-02-2024-0073

Laczniak, G. R., & Murphy, P. E. (2006). Normative perspectives for ethical and socially responsible marketing. *Journal of Macromarketing, 26*(2), 154–177. https://doi.org/10.1177/0276146706290924

Lambrecht, A., & Tucker, C. (2019). Algorithmic bias? An empirical study of apparent gender-based discrimination in the display of STEM career ads. *Management Science, 65*(7), 2966–2981. https://doi.org/10.1287/mnsc.2018.3093

Lee, J.-A. (2022). Algorithmic bias and the new Chicago school. *Law, Innovation and Technology, 14*(1), 95–112. https://doi.org/10.1080/17579961.2022.2047520

Lefkeli, D., Karataş, M., & Gürhan-Canli, Z. (2024). Sharing information with AI (versus a human) impairs brand trust: The role of audience size inferences and sense of exploitation. *International Journal of Research in Marketing, 41*(1), 138–155. https://doi.org/10.1016/j.ijresmar.2023.08.011

Lewis, P., Perez, E., Piktus, A., Petroni, F., Karpukhin, V., Goyal, N., Küttler, H., Lewis, M., Yih, W. T., Rocktäschel, T., Riedel, S., & Kiela, D. (2020). Retrieval-augmented generation for knowledge-intensive NLP tasks. In *Proceedings of the 34th international conference on neural information processing systems*.

Lim, J. S., Shin, D., Lee, C., Kim, J., & Zhang, J. (2025). The role of user empowerment, AI hallucination, and privacy concerns in continued use and premium subscription intentions: An extended technology acceptance model for generative AI. *Journal of Broadcasting & Electronic Media, 69*(3), 183–199. https://doi.org/10.1080/08838151.2025.2487679

Logg, J. M., Minson, J. A., & Moore, D. A. (2019). Algorithm appreciation: People prefer algorithmic to human judgment. *Organizational Behavior and Human Decision Processes, 151*, 90–103. https://doi.org/10.1016/j.obhdp.2018.12.005

Mariani, M., & Dwivedi, Y. K. (2024). Generative artificial intelligence in innovation management: A preview of future research developments. *Journal of Business Research, 175*, 114542. https://doi.org/10.1016/j.jbusres.2024.114542

Marti-Ochoa, J., Martin-Fuentes, E., & Ferrer-Rosell, B. (2025). AI-driven virtual travel influencers and ethical consumerism: Analysing engagement with Sena Zaro's Instagram content. *Young Consumers*. https://doi.org/10.1108/yc-08-2024-2204

Mazrekaj, D., Verhagen, M. D., Kumar, A., & Muzio, D. (2024). Does Price personalization ethically outperform unitary pricing? A thought experiment and a simulation study. *Journal of Business Ethics, 199*(1), 207–227. https://doi.org/10.1007/s10551-024-05828-3

Mehrjoo, A., Cuevas, R., & Cuevas, Á. (2024). Online advertisement in a pink-colored market. *EPJ Data Science, 13*(1), 36. https://doi.org/10.1140/epjds/s13688-024-00473-2

Menard, P., & Bott, G. J. (2024). Artificial intelligence misuse and concern for information privacy: New construct validation and future directions. *Information Systems Journal, 35*(1), 322–367. https://doi.org/10.1111/isj.12544

Moradi, M., & Zihagh, F. (2019). Moderating effects of contextual and individual factors on the relationship between cultural precedents and marketing-related norms. *Business Ethics and Leadership, 3*(3), 39–46. https://doi.org/10.21272/bel.3(3).39-46.2019

Neves, J., Pereira, M. C., & Bacalhau, L. M. (2025). AI hallucinations on marketing: A systematic review of risks, impacts, and mitigation strategies and future directions. In *ICBTOxford'2024—The international conference on business and technology*. United Kingdom. https://icbtoxford.com/

Patrício, J. G. (2024). Is Delulu the new Trululu? Artificial intelligence hallucinations as input in the creative process. *Revista de Comunicação e Linguagens*, (60–61), 226–245. https://doi.org/10.34619/jwrp-nbht

Sánchez Chamorro, L., Bongard-Blanchy, K., & Koenig, V. (2023). Ethical tensions in UX design practice: Exploring the fine line between persuasion and manipulation in online interfaces. In *Proceedings of the 2023 ACM designing interactive systems conference* (pp. 2408–2422). https://doi.org/10.1145/3563657.3596013

Seele, P., Dierksmeier, C., Hofstetter, R., & Schultz, M. D. (2021). Mapping the ethicality of algorithmic pricing: A review of dynamic and personalized pricing. *Journal of Business Ethics, 170*(4), 697–719. https://doi.org/10.1007/s10551-019-04371-w

Shemshaki, M. (2024). Exploring the ethical implications of AI-powered personalization in digital marketing. *Data Intelligence, 3*. https://doi.org/10.3724/2096-7004.di.2024.0055

Singh, A., & Joachims, T. (2018). Fairness of exposure in rankings. In *Proceedings of the 24th ACM SIGKDD international conference on Knowledge Discovery & Data Mining*. United Kingdom. https://doi.org/10.1145/3219819.3220088

Stella, M. (2022). Cognitive network science for understanding online social cognitions: A brief review. *Topics in Cognitive Science, 14*(1), 143–162. https://doi.org/10.1111/tops.12551

Sun, Y. J., Sheng, D. F., Zhou, Z. H., & Wu, Y. F. (2024). AI hallucination: Towards a comprehensive classification of distorted information in artificial intelligence-generated content. *Humanities & Social Sciences Communications, 11*(1). https://doi.org/10.1057/s41599-024-03811-x

Timmaraju, A. S., Mashayekhi, M., Chen, M., Zeng, Q., Fettes, Q., Cheung, W., Xiao, Y., Kannadasan, M. R., Tripathi, P., Gahagan, S., Bogen, M., & Roudani, R. (2023). *T*owards fairness in personalized ads using impression variance aware reinforcement learning. In *Proceedings of the 29th ACM SIGKDD conference on knowledge discovery and data mining*. Long Beach. https://doi.org/10.1145/3580305.3599916

Turillazzi, A., Taddeo, M., Floridi, L., & Casolari, F. (2023). The digital services act: An analysis of its ethical, legal, and social implications. *Law, Innovation and Technology, 15*(1), 83–106. https://doi.org/10.1080/17579961.2023.2184136

Uslay, C. (2025). Toward a more general theory of marketing ethics. *Journal of Research in Marketing and Entrepreneurship, 27*(1), 126–161. https://doi.org/10.1108/jrme-03-2024-0083

Vassøy, B., & Langseth, H. (2024). Consumer-side fairness in recommender systems: A systematic survey of methods and evaluation. *Artificial Intelligence Review, 57*(4), 101. https://doi.org/10.1007/s10462-023-10663-5

Wang, Y., Ma, W., Zhang, M., Liu, Y., & Ma, S. (2023). A survey on the fairness of recommender systems. *ACM Transactions on Information Systems, 41*(3), 1–43. https://doi.org/10.1145/3547333

Wang, Z., Wang, J., Lu, Z., & You, F. (2026). Large language modeling of hallucinatory problem mitigation based on the wheel of emotions. *Neural Networks, 193*, 107996. https://doi.org/10.1016/j.neunet.2025.107996

Watts, L. L., Medeiros, K. E., McIntosh, T. J., & Mulhearn, T. J. (2020). Decision biases in the context of ethics: Initial scale development and validation. *Personality and Individual Differences, 153*, 109609. https://doi.org/10.1016/j.paid.2019.109609

Wolters, P., & Zuiderveen Borgesius, F. (2025). The EU digital services act: What does it mean for online advertising and adtech? *International Journal of Law and Information Technology, 33*. https://doi.org/10.1093/ijlit/eaaf004

Yaprak, B. (2024). Generative artificial intelligence in marketing: The invisible danger of AI hallucinations. *Journal of Economy Business and Management (Ekonomi İşletme ve Yönetim Dergisi), 8*(2), 133–158. https://doi.org/10.7596/jebm.1588897

Zhang, W., Li, W., Rao, X., Zou, L., Luo, X., Zhuang, C., Hong, Y., Qin, Z., Chang, H., Li, C., & Zheng, B. (2025). AIGuard: A benchmark and lightweight detection for E-commerce AIGC risks. In W. Che, J. Nabende, E. Shutova, & M. T. Pilehvar (Eds.), *Findings of the Association for Computational Linguistics: ACL 2025* (pp. 12437–12450). https://doi.org/10.18653/v1/2025.findings-acl.643

Zhang, Y., & Zhang, S. X. (2025). Human-AI alignment in ad targeting: Addressing misestimation for vulnerable groups. *Journal of Advertising, 54*(2), 196–212. https://doi.org/10.1080/00913367.2025.2465381

Zhao, Y., Wang, Y., Liu, Y., Cheng, X., Aggarwal, C. C., & Derr, T. (2025). Fairness and diversity in recommender systems: A survey. *ACM Transactions on Intelligent Systems and Technology, 16*(1), 1–28. https://doi.org/10.1145/3664928

Strategic Decision-Making Using Artificial Intelligence

José Ramón Saura, Felipe Debasa, and Senka Borovac Zekan

Abstract Artificial intelligence (AI) has become a structural force in contemporary organizations, reshaping how strategic decision-making is conceived and executed. This chapter explores the intersection of AI and strategy, emphasizing its impact on managerial activities, organizational routines, governance mechanisms, and long-term competitiveness. Drawing on previous theories like bounded rationality, behavioural strategy, dynamic capabilities, and algorithmic governance, this chapter conceptualizes how predictive, generative, and prescriptive AI systems alter problem framing, option generation, evaluation processes, and managerial commitment to action. Beyond technical efficiency, the integration of AI raises questions of transparency and ethical legitimacy, making governance and trust decisive factors for sustainable adoption. The review summarizes the fragmented literature across management, information systems, and organizational studies, offering a coherent framework that situates AI as both an enabler and a constraint in strategic contexts. The implications presented contribute to the ongoing debate on digital transformation, algorithmic decision-making, and responsible innovation, while providing a future research questions to examine hybrid human–AI systems in strategic leadership.

J. R. Saura (✉) · F. Debasa
Rey Juan Carlos University, Madrid, Spain
e-mail: joseramon.saura@urjc.es

F. Debasa
e-mail: felipe.debasa@urjc.es

S. B. Zekan
Split University, Split, Croatia
e-mail: sborovac@oss.unist.hr

J. D. Santos et al. (eds.), *Artificial Intelligence Transforming Marketing*, Contributions to Management Science, https://doi.org/10.1007/978-3-032-22360-9_5

1 Introduction

Today, senior managers and board members face a business world where data-driven technologies are central to competitiveness and added value. Artificial intelligence (AI) is no longer a tool for support; it has become part of how organizations decide on investments, innovation, creativity, supply chains, and risk management (Benbya et al., 2020). Firms that once depended mainly on human intuition and expertise, now rely on AI models that process vast amounts of structured and unstructured data (Mishra & Tripathi, 2021). Likewise, competitors use AI to detect market shifts and test multiple scenarios, changing the speed and transparency of competitive interactions (Kemp, 2024). These developments do more than improve existing tools. They change the balance of power in strategic conversations, the evidence used to justify choices, and the way in which the environment factors become a key variable (Khanfar et al., 2025). Universities, hospitals, banks, and industrial firms all face similar pressures related to the strategy that is now shaped by the combination of human judgement and algorithmic recommendations (Ghasemaghaei & Kordzadeh, 2025). Likewise, in platform-based industries, AI models not only analyse markets but also intervene in them (Saura et al., 2025a), narrowing the distance between decision and action strategies (Marvi et al., 2025).

In this way, strategic decision-making using AI is linked to task automation in the business industry, as it concerns how AI shifts attention, evaluation, and commitment when organizations must decide under uncertainty (Booyse & Scheepers, 2024). This chapter considers predictive, generative, and prescriptive forms of AI, the routines that integrate them into organizations, and the governance structures that hold decision makers responsibilities (Chung et al., 2022). These changes matter because strategic choices affect long-term survival, reputation, and the well-being of stakeholders (Al-Surmi et al., 2022). Likewise, regulators and investors expect leaders to understand model risk, data quality, and explainability (Bessa & Barbosa, 2025). This turns AI into both a technical and a strategic concern.

The literature in this field has grown but remains fragmented. Research comes from management, business economics, information systems, operations, and computer science. There are valuable studies (Jobstreibizer et al., 2025) on prediction accuracy (Vudugula et al., 2023), optimization (Hernández-Tamurejo et al., 2025), and digital transformation (Shatila et al., 2025). Yet, few works explain how AI affects the actual process of strategy or how top teams focus their attention, how options are generated, or how disagreements between managers' strategic decision and algorithms are resolved (Berman et al., 2020).

This review chapter aims to fill part of that gap. First, we organize the terminology and provide clear definitions so that readers can distinguish technologies, organizational practices, and governance mechanisms. Second, we synthesize evidence on how AI changes strategy, identifying conditions that support or limit its value, such as decision importance, time pressure, and learning capacity. Third, we offer the main outputs that connect model capabilities, human judgement, and governance, with suggestions for future research. In this way, two research questions guide this chapter: RQ1: How does AI change the stages of strategic decision-making: framing problems, generating options, evaluating alternatives, and committing to action? Under which conditions does AI improve or reduce strategic outcomes, and which governance practices ensure legitimacy over time?

To answer these questions, we apply a systematic literature review (SLR) method. We define inclusion criteria, search the Web of Sciences (WoS) database, screen studies in stages, evaluate their quality, and synthesize results with thematic coding following authors like Saura and Bužinskienė (2025). Details of the SLR approach are explained in the Methodology section.

This chapter is structured as follows. The next section develops the theoretical framework, linking AI-driven decision-making to existing theories such as bounded rationality, dynamic capabilities, and algorithmic governance. The methodology section explains the search and coding process. The findings section presents themes such as changes in attention, option portfolios, human/AI role division, and governance practices. The discussion integrates these themes into a framework with implications for theory and practice. The conclusion outlines future research and practical recommendations.

2 Literature Review

The study of strategic decision-making supported by AI requires a clear theoretical foundation. Without such a framework, research risks becoming fragmented across disciplines, with overlapping concepts and little integration. The objective of this section is to establish the main theoretical perspectives that help explain how AI interacts with organizational strategy and to clarify the key concepts that will guide the analysis. Thus, a central starting point is the theory of bounded rationality (Simon, 1990). Since Herbert Simon's work, it has been recognized that decision makers face limits in their ability to process information, foresee consequences, and evaluate alternatives. Organizations rely on simplified models and heuristics because the real world is too complex to analyse fully (Khan, 2025). AI changes this condition but does not eliminate it. On the one hand, predictive and generative models expand the amount of data and patterns that can be processed (Ooi et al., 2025). On the other hand, new forms of bounded rationality emerge, defined not by human cognitive limits but by the quality of data, the assumptions of algorithms, and the ability of managers to interpret outputs (Saura, 2025a).

The behavioural strategy perspective also offers insights. Research in this area emphasizes how executives' values, emotions, biases, and social interactions shape strategic choices (Levinthal, 2011). AI interacts with these human tendencies in complex ways. For instance, algorithmic recommendations may reduce some biases by providing systematic analysis (Varsha, 2023), but they may also introduce other distortions, such as overreliance on model outputs or the tendency to ignore contextual knowledge. Theories of behavioural strategy (Anwar et al., 2022) remind us that

AI influence depends on how managers perceive, trust, and incorporate its outputs into their judgements (Glikson & Woolley, 2020).

Also, dynamic capabilities form another relevant foundation (Teece et al., 1997). Teece and others have explained how organizations must sense opportunities, seize them, and reconfigure resources to maintain competitiveness. AI contributes to sensing by enabling faster detection of weak signals, such as changes in customer behaviour or shifts in regulatory conditions. It assists in seizing opportunities by allowing simulations and scenario analyses that guide investment or diversification (Saura et al.,2024). It also facilitates reconfiguration through optimization of processes, supply chains, and resource allocation. However, dynamic capabilities require more than technological tools (Konlechner et al., 2018), they also depend on leadership vision, organizational culture, and the ability to learn from experience. AI may accelerate processes, but without strong human capabilities, the benefits may be temporary or misdirected (Siaw & Ali, 2025).

Additionally, organizational routines understood as patterns of action through which organizations coordinate work and achieve stability becomes important in terms of AI use (Raisch & Fomina, 2025). When AI becomes part of these routines, for example through decision-support systems or automated alerts, new patterns emerge (Brauner et al., 2022). A key issue is the degree of delegation and responsibility: under what conditions do managers follow AI advice, and when do they override it? How are conflicts resolved when machine outputs contradict human intuition? The literature suggests that trust and feedback loops are key in shaping these routines, among other variables (Hurley, 2023). Over time, the integration of AI may stabilize into new forms of socio-technical routines, where human and machine actions are closely interdependent.

A more recent contribution is the debate on algorithmic governance (Gritsenko & Wood, 2022). In this case, the term governance refers to the rules, structures, and oversight mechanisms that ensure decisions are legitimate, transparent, and aligned with ethical standards. In strategic contexts, AI raises specific governance challenges. Stakeholders demand clarity on how decisions are made, especially when they affect jobs, investments, or societal outcomes. Issues of explainability, bias, and fairness have become central when governments deploy AI strategies. Boards, regulators, and policymakers increasingly require evidence that organizations can manage algorithmic risks responsibly (Saura, 2025b). This perspective situates AI not only as a tool but as an institutional actor that shapes organizational legitimacy (Martin & Waldman, 2023). Following authors like Danaher et al. (2017), algorithmic governance can be described as a set of computational methods that allow machines to perform tasks traditionally requiring human cognition, such as perception, prediction, and decision-making. Within AI, predictive systems focus on estimating future states, generative systems create new scenarios or content, and prescriptive systems recommend actions to achieve desired outcomes. When combining these two fields, strategic decision-making represents a set of processes through which organizations identify problems, generate and evaluate options, and commit to actions that affect their long-term direction (Campbell-Verduyn et al., 2017). Unlike operational decisions, strategic ones involve greater uncertainty, higher stakes, and more irreversible consequences. Therefore, the combination of these theoretical elements suggests that AI should be seen as both an enabler and a source of new constraints. It increases the range of data that can be considered and improves the quality of forecasting, but it also introduces risks related to bias and opacity (Mühlhoff, 2025). Its influence is mediated by human cognition, embedded in organizational routines, and regulated through governance structures (Saura et al., 2025b).

3 Methodology

To address this chapter's research questions, this study follows a SLR approach (Lame, 2019). A SLR offers a transparent and replicable method to identify, evaluate, and synthesize academic knowledge on a given topic (Hossain et al., 2022). Compared with traditional narrative reviews, it reduces subjectivity and ensures that the process of selecting and analysing studies is consistent (Mishra & Mishra, 2023). This is particularly relevant in the field of AI and strategic decision-making, where research is dispersed across multiple disciplines and methods.

The review process followed several steps. First, we defined inclusion and exclusion criteria to ensure that only relevant and high-quality studies were considered. We included peer-reviewed journal articles but not conference papers. The studies should directly address the use of AI in strategic or managerial decision-making. Studies focusing exclusively on technical aspects of algorithms, without a connection to organizational strategy, were excluded. Likewise, we did not include non-academic sources, book reviews, or papers in journals identified as predatory. The time window was set between 1992 and 2025, covering the period in which AI applications in management became a significant field of study as the first and the last studies were published.

Second, WoS was selected as the source database for this SLR because it offers a curated and highly reliable collection of peer-reviewed journals that meet rigorous quality and citation standards. Its long-standing use in academic research provides assurance of consistency, transparency, and reproducibility, which are essential features in SLR. Furthermore, WoS facilitates bibliometric analysis through its structured indexing and citation tracking capabilities, allowing for a precise identification of influential works and intellectual connections across disciplines. The database's emphasis on scholarly rigour and global coverage of top-tier journals ensures that the literature included in this review represents the most validated and impactful contributions to the field of AI and strategic management. This study focuses on the WoS database to ensure methodological consistency and the inclusion of high-quality, peer-reviewed publications indexed under rigorous standards (Poggi et al., 2025). However, future research may extend this review by incorporating other databases such as Scopus or specialized repositories to compare patterns, validate trends, and explore potential variations in the coverage or emphasis of AI-related studies across platforms.

Search strings combined keywords related to "artificial intelligence," "strategic decision-making," AND "management." The exact query in WoS was performed on 15 September 2025 as follows: "TS = ("artificial intelligence" AND "strategic decision-making" AND "management")." To minimize bias, we tested different keyword combinations and verified that key studies already known in the field appeared in the results. This helped ensure that the search was comprehensive. Third, we conducted a screening process in two stages. In the first stage, we reviewed titles and abstracts to remove papers clearly outside the scope. In the second stage, we examined the full texts to verify their relevance to strategic decision-making. Two reviewers independently performed the screening, and disagreements were resolved through discussion until consensus was reached. This dual process strengthened the reliability of the selection (Shaheen et al., 2023).

Fourth, we assessed the quality of the studies. Quality assessment included factors such as clarity of research design, appropriateness of methodology, transparency of data collection, and strength of conclusions (Fleming et al., 2013). Studies that lacked methodological rigour or provided only anecdotal evidence were excluded. This step ensured that the review did not rely on weak or unreliable sources. Fifth, we applied thematic synthesis. This involved grouping the findings into broader themes that reflected how AI influences strategic decision-making. Themes included, for example, the role of AI in shaping attention and sensemaking, its contribution to the generation and evaluation of options, and the governance challenges linked to its use. The synthesis emphasized conceptual integration rather than a simple listing of results.

Finally, we validated the findings by comparing them with similar insights in linked fields, such as decision-support systems, big data analytics, and digital transformation (Gandomi & Haider, 2015). This comparison helped confirm that our findings were consistent with broader trends while also highlighting what is specific to AI in strategic contexts. Each step, from search design to coding, was documented to allow other scholars to reproduce the review if needed. Likewise, the use of WoS database, clear criteria, and independent screening reduced the risk of bias.

4 Analysis of Results

4.1 Results of the Systematic Literature Review

The review identified a total of 448 studies published between 1992 and 2025 that explicitly examine AI in strategic decision-making contexts within management decisions. Out of the 448 studies found, the present chapter selected 18 final studies for analysis. Most of these studies appeared in journals from management, information systems, and operations research, with a smaller number in interdisciplinary outlets. The literature shows clear growth in the last decade, reflecting the rising importance of AI for organizations.

The review highlighted fragmentation across disciplines. Computer science studies often emphasize algorithmic performance, while management studies concentrate on strategic processes and outcomes. Few articles integrate these perspectives like Pu et al. (2025) or Schneider and Leyer (2019). Definitions of AI also varied considerably. Some authors described AI broadly as any data-driven technology, while others focused specifically on machine learning or natural language processing (NLP). This lack of definitional clarity complicates comparison and limits theory development.

In terms of bibliometric statistics, from the total number of studies identified in the review, the most common category is Management, which accounts for 125 studies, representing 27.9% of the total. This is followed by Business, with 82 studies (18.3%), and Computer Science Information Systems, with 48 studies (10.7%). A smaller but still notable proportion belongs to Engineering, with 35 studies (7.8%). Additional relevant categories include Operations Research Management Science with 29 studies (6.12%), Computer Science Artificial Intelligence with 28 studies (5.91%), and Green Sustainable Science Technology with 25 studies (5.27%). Other areas such as Information Science Library Science (21 studies, 4.43%), Computer Science Interdisciplinary Applications (20 studies, 4.22%), Business Finance (19 studies, 4.00%), and Telecommunications (19 studies, 4.00%) also contribute meaningfully to the field. Together, these distributions confirm that while the topic of AI in strategic decision-making is predominantly situated within management and business research, it also attracts increasing attention from adjacent technical and interdisciplinary domains, illustrating its cross-cutting and integrative nature. The remaining studies do not represent a proportion higher than 3% each and are distributed across diverse minor categories that do not show consistent trends or meaningful thematic groupings. These papers are linked among areas such as psychology, economics, operations research, and communication, among others, reflecting isolated contributions rather than consolidated research streams within the field of AI and strategic decision-making.

The temporal distribution of publications also illustrates a clear pattern of growth in academic interest (Tedja et al., 2024). In the early years, contributions were minimal, with only one study in 2017 (0.22%) and small numbers between 2018 and 2019 (1.79% each year). The field began to gain momentum in 2020 with 15 studies (3.35%) and stabilized at 27 publications in both 2021 and 2022 (6.03% each). A sharp increase occurred in 2023, with 49 studies (10.94%), followed by a major expansion in 2024 (134 studies, 29.91%) and 2025 (154 studies, 34.38%).

Of the 448 studies initially retrieved from the WoS database, an initial screening was carried out based on titles, abstracts, and keywords. During this first phase, 272 articles were excluded because they contained inadequate terms or their focus was not conclusive in relation to the research objectives. This process yielded 176 potentially apt articles that were subjected to a more detailed review. In the second phase, the full texts of these 176 studies were analysed to assess their direct relevance to the research topic and the quality of their methodological approaches. After this full-text evaluation, 158 articles were excluded for one or more of the following reasons: they did not fit the research objectives, lacked direct connection to the topic under study, did not present an adequate quality evaluation, or failed to specify or clearly describe the key terms used (Nazir & Das, 2025). As a result, 18 studies met all inclusion criteria and were selected for the final synthesis and analysis.

In relation to the bibliometric profile of the final sample, the 18 studies that satisfied the inclusion criteria display a distribution that reflects the interdisciplinary nature of research on AI and strategic decision-making, yet with a stronger concentration within high-level management and strategy outlets. The most prevalent category is Management and Business. This category contains 11 of the 18 studies, which represents 61.1% of the final sample. These publications emphasize strategic implications, managerial practices, competitive advantage, and leadership, which confirms that the core of the selected literature aligns closely with the disciplinary foundations of the review. A smaller, though significant, proportion belongs to categories associated with Computer Science and Information Systems. This group accounts for 4 studies (22.2%), and it reflects the contribution of technical and analytical perspectives to the understanding of decision processes augmented with artificial intelligence. Additionally, 2 studies (11.1%) fall within Operations Research and related analytical domains. These papers incorporate decision-support mechanisms, multi-criteria approaches, and quantitative modelling relevant to strategic choices. The remaining 1 study (5.5%) corresponds to Communication and Public Relations, which highlights the ethical and strategic concerns that accompany AI adoption in organizational communication.

The temporal distribution of the selected studies also reveals a pattern that differs from the general corpus. The earliest contribution dates from 1998, followed with isolated publications in 2014 and 2020, which indicates that foundational perspectives on heuristics, crisis management, and intelligence emerged long before the contemporary expansion of AI research. From 2021 onwards, publication frequency increases with 1 study in 2021, 2 studies in 2022, and another in 2023. The concentration intensifies in 2024 and 2025, which together account for 11 of the 18 studies (61.1%). This temporal pattern confirms that the most conceptually relevant and methodological work on AI and strategic decision-making has emerged in the last few years, with scholars increasingly focusing on leadership, competitive advantage, evaluation of strategic decisions, and digital transformation. Compared with the full dataset, which shows a broad surge in publication volume, the selected subset reflects a more focused and qualitatively refined consolidation of the research domain.

In this way, the papers included in the SLR that are directly linked to the study objectives and research questions are the following (see Table 1).

5 Conclusions

This chapter sets out to examine the role of AI in strategic decision-making through a SLR. Two research questions guided the analysis: (RQ1) How does AI reshape the stages of strategic decision-making problem framing, option generation, evaluation, and commitment, and through which mechanisms within organizations? (RQ2)

Table 1 Selected articles included in SLR results

Authors	Title	Journal	Main objectives
Petrescu et al. (2022)	AI-based innovation in B2B marketing: An interdisciplinary framework incorporating academic and practitioner perspectives	*Industrial Marketing Management*	• Explore AI-driven innovation in B2B marketing • Develop an interdisciplinary framework • Integrate academic and practitioner perspectives
Bevilacqua et al. (2025)	Enhancing top managers' leadership with artificial intelligence: insights from a systematic literature review	*Review of Managerial Science*	• Examine how AI enhances leadership • Provide insights from a systematic review • Assess implications for top managers
Mashiah and Avidar (2025)	The paradox of technology acceptance: ethics and strategic implications of artificial intelligence in public relations	*Journal of Communication Management*	• Investigate technology acceptance paradox in public relations • Analyse ethical concerns in AI adoption • Assess strategic implications for communication management
Hillebrand et al. (2025)	Managing with artificial intelligence: An integrative framework	*Academy of Management Annals*	• Explore how managers use AI in organizations • Develop an integrative framework • Clarify managerial implications of AI
Schneider and Leyer (2019)	Me or information technology? Adoption of artificial intelligence in the delegation of personal strategic decisions	*Managerial and Decision Economics*	• Study AI adoption in personal strategic decisions • Examine delegation between humans and AI • Analyse adoption factors influencing choices

(continued)

Table 1 (continued)

Authors	Title	Journal	Main objectives
Lam et al. (2024)	A multi-criteria intelligence aid approach to selecting strategic key opinion leaders in digital business management	*Journal of Innovation & Knowledge*	• Propose a multi-criteria AI approach • Improve selection of strategic key opinion leaders • Apply to digital business management
Saura and Bužinskienė (2025)	Behavioural economics, artificial intelligence and entrepreneurship: an updated framework for management	*International Entrepreneurship and Management Journal*	• Connect behavioural economics with AI • Update frameworks for entrepreneurship • Provide implications for management practice
Allal-Chérif et al. (2021)	Intelligent purchasing: How artificial intelligence can redefine the purchasing function	*Journal of Business Research*	• Examine AI in intelligent purchasing • Analyse redefinition of purchasing function • Explore managerial implications
Pu et al. (2025)	The analysis of strategic management decisions and corporate competitiveness based on artificial intelligence	*Scientific Reports*	• Analyse strategic management decisions using AI • Examine links to corporate competitiveness • Assess AI's strategic role in firm performance
Krakowski et al. (2023)	Artificial intelligence and the changing sources of competitive advantage	*Strategic Management Journal*	• Investigate AI's role in competitive advantage • Identify changing sources of advantage • Explore strategic implications of AI adoption
Doshi et al. (2025)	Generative artificial intelligence and evaluating strategic decisions	*Strategic Management Journal*	• Explore role of generative AI in decision evaluation • Analyse impact on strategic decision-making • Assess implications for managerial judgement

(continued)

Table 1 (continued)

Authors	Title	Journal	Main objectives
Koliousis et al. (2024)	Artificial intelligence and policy making; can small municipalities enable digital transformation?	*International Journal of Production Economics*	• Study AI in public policy-making • Evaluate digital transformation in small municipalities • Assess strategic enablers for adoption
Choi et al. (2025)	How does artificial intelligence improve human decision-making? Evidence from the AI-powered Go programme	*Strategic Management Journal*	• Examine AI's effect on human decision quality • Provide empirical evidence from AI-powered Go • Analyse implications for strategic decision-making
Krabuanrat and Phelps (1998)	Heuristics and rationality in strategic decision making: An exploratory study	*Journal of Business Research*	• Investigate heuristics in decision-making • Explore rationality in strategic choices • Provide exploratory insights into managerial practice
Barnea (2020)	How will AI change intelligence and decision-making?	*Journal of Intelligence Studies in Business*	• Assess how AI changes intelligence • Analyse impact on decision-making processes • Discuss implications for business environments
Cesta et al. (2014)	Training for crisis decision making–An approach based on plan adaptation	*Knowledge-Based Systems*	• Develop training for crisis decisions • Apply plan adaptation methods • Enhance decision-making under uncertainty

(continued)

Table 1 (continued)

Authors	Title	Journal	Main objectives
Gupta et al. (2022)	Artificial intelligence for decision support systems in the field of operations research: review and future scope of research	*Annals of Operations Research*	• Review AI in decision-support systems • Assess role in operations research • Identify future research opportunities
Nazemi et al. (2022)	Visual analytics for technology and innovation management: An interaction approach for strategic decision making	*Multimedia Tools and Applications*	• Explore visual analytics for management • Study applications in innovation strategy • Analyse AI's role in strategic decision-making

Source Authors

Under what contingencies does AI enhance or weaken strategic outcomes, and what governance arrangements sustain legitimacy over time?) The evidence synthesized in this review suggests that AI influences each stage of strategic decision-making in distinctive ways.

In relation to the first question (RQ1), the literature shows that AI redirects managerial attention by scanning large datasets and detecting weak signals that human actors may overlook. This extends the "sensing" capacity described in dynamic capabilities theory, but it also introduces new forms of bounded rationality, as attention becomes narrowly tied to what is measurable. In terms of option generation, AI expands the range of strategic alternatives through simulations and generative tools, confirming earlier insights from behavioural strategies applied in corporations (Anwar et al., 2022). Yet the review contributes by emphasizing the risks of false diversity and cognitive overload, issues that remain underexplored in the literature. For evaluation, AI improves predictive rigour and enables scenario analysis, aligning with research on evidence-based management. The contribution here lies in showing that increased technical sophistication also creates challenges of opacity and explainability, raising legitimacy concerns not sufficiently addressed in earlier studies. Finally, regarding commitment to action, the review finds that organizations rarely delegate final decisions to AI, reflecting governance as an imperative.

Next, regarding the second research question, the review finds that the benefits of AI are highly contingent. Positive outcomes occur when organizations possess strong data infrastructures, clear governance frameworks, and a culture that values both evidence and judgement. Likewise, risks emerge when governance is weak, when trust in AI outputs is low, or when overreliance on algorithms narrows strategic attention. This aligns with prior work on algorithmic governance (Latzer & Festic, 2019) but contributes by specifying how trust and accountability operate across different stages of strategy. The review also shows that the interaction between human managers and AI systems is not linear but co-constructed through organizational routines.

Finally, it should be highlighted that the present chapter makes several contributions. Conceptually, it clarifies the role of AI in strategy by mapping its influence across four stages of decision-making and by integrating perspectives from bounded rationality, behavioural strategy, dynamic capabilities, and governance. Empirically, it consolidates fragmented findings into a coherent synthesis, providing evidence of both benefits and limitations. Theoretically, it identifies process mechanisms (such as algorithmic framing of attention, option filtering, and the preservation of human legitimacy in commitments) that extend existing debates. Practically, it highlights the need for organizations to adopt governance mechanisms that ensure transparency, accountability, and trust, recognizing that AI adoption is as much a cultural and ethical challenge as a technical one. Likewise, AI has become a central actor in strategic decision-making, not as a substitute for human judgement but as a force that reshapes its boundaries. Future research should examine longitudinally how human–AI interaction evolves, under what conditions trust consolidates or erodes, and which governance structures best support responsible adoption. For practice, the challenge is to design decision systems that combine the analytical power of AI with the contextual sensitivity and accountability of human leadership.

5.1 Theoretical Implications

This review offers several contributions to theory. First, it reinterprets bounded rationality considering AI adoption. Classical theory emphasized that decision makers face cognitive limits in processing information and therefore rely on simplified models. The findings of this review suggest that AI shifts these limits rather than removing them. While algorithms extend the ability to analyse data and forecast outcomes, new constraints arise from the quality of data, the architecture of models, and the interpretability of results. This refinement updates Simon's framework for the digital era, illustrating that rationality remains bounded, though in new ways. Second, the study contributes to behavioural strategy. Prior research highlights how executives rely on heuristics and are influenced by cognitive biases when making strategic decisions. AI introduces a complex interaction with these behavioural dynamics. On the one hand, algorithms can reduce bias by offering systematic analysis and by challenging intuitive judgements. On the other hand, they may reinforce distortions if managers develop blind trust in machine outputs or if algorithmic biases remain hidden. This duality suggests that the study of biases in strategy must now consider both human and algorithmic factors, opening a new line of theoretical inquiry into hybrid rationality. Third, the findings enrich dynamic capabilities theory, especially the processes of sensing, seizing, and reconfiguring. AI strengthens sensing by scanning weak signals in markets and environments. It supports seizing by enabling simulations and comparative evaluations of strategic alternatives. However, in reconfiguration processes, tensions appear. The acceleration provided by AI may favour rapid resource adjustments, but it can also create fragility if organizations prioritize speed over resilience. This adds nuance to existing dynamic capability frameworks, highlighting trade-offs between efficiency and adaptability in AI-enabled strategy.

Finally, the review integrates perspectives on organizational routines and algorithmic governance. The evidence shows that strategic processes increasingly take the form of socio-technical routines, in which human actions and AI outputs interact continuously. This complements existing theories of routines, which have largely treated technology as a background enabler rather than an active participant. At the same time, algorithmic governance theory gains empirical support, as trust, transparency, and accountability emerge as decisive conditions for AI integration. Together, these insights encourage a rethinking of how organizational theory conceptualizes agency, responsibility, and legitimacy when decision-making involves non-human actors.

5.2 *Practical Implications*

The findings also have significant relevance for practice. For managers and executives, one key implication is the need to design governance systems that ensure trust, transparency, and accountability. AI-generated insights may offer speed and rigour, but without clear governance, their value is undermined by doubts about legitimacy and responsibility. Boards should establish oversight structures that clarify who remain accountable when strategic decisions involve AI inputs. This is not only a compliance issue but also a matter of sustaining stakeholder confidence.

Another implication concerns the management of AI-generated options. While generative and simulation tools can expand the range of alternatives, managers risk being overwhelmed by excessive or repetitive scenarios. Organizations must implement processes that filter and prioritize options so that strategic portfolios remain both diverse and manageable. This requires not only technical tools for ranking alternatives but also organizational routines that encourage debate and human judgement.

These implications are observable across diverse sectors. In manufacturing, companies such as Siemens (van Giffen & Ludwig, 2023) or Toyota (Subrahmanyam, 2025) have adopted predictive AI to anticipate supply chain disruptions and optimize production scheduling, illustrating how strategic agility can emerge from algorithmic foresight. In healthcare, hospital networks (Kamel Rahimi et al., 2024) increasingly rely on AI systems to support resource allocation and long-term investment in medical technologies. However, ethical governance mechanisms remain essential to balance efficiency with patient safety and equity. In the banking and financial services sector (Weber et al., 2024), AI-driven risk models assist strategic investment and credit decisions, yet regulators demand explainability to ensure and prevent algorithmic bias. Meanwhile, in the public sector, local governments use AI to guide policy priorities demonstrating that strategic decision-making assisted by AI requires not only technical expertise but also transparency towards citizens. These examples highlight that the practical application of AI in strategic contexts depends as much on institutional maturity and governance quality as on data analytics capability.

A third implication is the importance of capacity building within leadership teams. Managers should be trained to interpret AI outputs critically, developing the ability to question assumptions, detect possible biases, and integrate qualitative knowledge with quantitative forecasts. Overreliance on AI can lead to passivity, while outright scepticism can block innovation. The most effective organizations will be those that foster "informed trust," where leaders recognize the strengths of AI while remaining attentive to its limitations. In practice, such informed trust has been achieved, for instance, in multinational retailers that use AI to personalize marketing strategies (Cao, 2021) while maintaining human oversight of ethical boundaries, and in logistics firms (Boute & Udenio, 2022) that use prescriptive algorithms to optimize routes but still rely on managerial judgement to adapt to conditions. These cross-sector experiences reinforce that human capacity are irreplaceable complements to algorithmic intelligence.

Finally, the review suggests that organizations should approach AI adoption as a strategic and cultural transformation, not simply a technological upgrade. This means aligning AI practices with organizational values, ethical commitments, and stakeholder expectations. For regulators and policymakers, the implication is that AI in strategic contexts requires guidance and standards that go beyond technical metrics, addressing fairness, explainability, and long-term impact. In short, successful adoption depends on balancing the efficiency gains of AI with the ethical and cultural requirements of legitimacy.

5.3 Limitations

This study also has limitations that should be recognized. As a systematic review, it relies on the availability and quality of published literature, which remains uneven across regions, sectors, and methods. Areas such as longitudinal studies of human–AI collaboration, cross-industry comparisons, and board-level decision-making remain underexplored, limiting the generalizability of the findings. The focus on peer-reviewed sources may exclude valuable insights from practice-oriented reports, policy papers, unpublished work, or similar academic databases. Another limitation arises from definitional inconsistencies: while some studies use AI as an umbrella term, others focus narrowly on machine learning, analytics, or decision-support systems. This variation complicates direct comparison across studies. Finally, although this article integrates several theoretical perspectives, it does not test the proposed objectives empirically. This creates opportunities for future research to validate and refine the conceptual contributions presented here.

Statement on the Use of Artificial Intelligence Artificial intelligence tools were employed in this chapter exclusively to assist with proofreading and to enhance the clarity and flow of the English language. No AI was used for generating substantive content or for the analysis presented.

References

Al-Surmi, A., Bashiri, M., & Koliousis, I. (2022). AI based decision making: Combining strategies to improve operational performance. *International Journal of Production Research, 60*(14), 4464–4486. https://doi.org/10.1080/00207543.2021.1966540

Allal-Chérif, O., Simón-Moya, V., & Ballester, A. C. C. (2021). Intelligent purchasing: How artificial intelligence can redefine the purchasing function. *Journal of Business Research, 124*, 69–76. https://doi.org/10.1016/j.jbusres.2020.11.050

Anwar, J., Bibi, A., & Ahmad, N. (2022). Behavioral strategy: Mapping the trends, sources and intellectual evolution. *Journal of Strategy and Management, 15*(1), 140–168. https://doi.org/10.1108/JSMA-01-2021-0002

Barnea, A. (2020). How will AI change intelligence and decision-making?. *Journal of Intelligence Studies in Business, 10*(1), 75–80. https://doi.org/10.37380/jisib.v10i1.564

Benbya, H., Davenport, T. H., & Pachidi, S. (2020). Artificial intelligence in organizations: Current state and future opportunities. *MIS Quarterly Executive, 19*(4). https://doi.org/10.2139/ssrn.3741983

Berman, S., Marshall, A., & Ikeda, K. (2020). How leading CEOs drive a differentiating advantage through AI, data analytics and insight. *Strategy & Leadership, 48*(3), 39–50. https://doi.org/10.1108/SL-02-2020-0028

Bessa, G., & Barbosa, B. (2025). Integrating artificial intelligence into scenario analysis: A validated framework for strategic planning under economic uncertainty. *Global Economics Research*, 100007. https://doi.org/10.1016/j.ecores.2025.100007

Bevilacqua, S., Masárová, J., Perotti, F. A., & Ferraris, A. (2025). Enhancing top managers' leadership with artificial intelligence: insights from a systematic literature review. *Review of Managerial Science*, 1–37. https://doi.org/10.1007/s11846-025-00836-7

Booyse, D., & Scheepers, C. B. (2024). Barriers to adopting automated organisational decision-making through the use of artificial intelligence. *Management Research Review, 47*(1), 64–85. https://doi.org/10.1108/MRR-09-2021-0701

Boute, R. N., & Udenio, M. (2022). AI in logistics and supply chain management. In *Global logistics and supply chain strategies for the 2020s: Vital skills for the next generation* (pp. 49–65). Springer International Publishing. https://doi.org/10.1007/978-3-030-95764-3_3

Brauner, P., Vervier, L., Brillowski, F., Dammers, H., Steuer-Dankert, L., Schneider, S., Baier, R., Ziefle, M., Gries, T., Leicht-Scholten, C., Mertens, A., & Nagel, S. K. (2022). Organization routines in next generation manufacturing. In *Forecasting next generation manufacturing: digital shadows, human-machine collaboration, and data-driven business models* (pp. 75–94). Springer International Publishing. https://doi.org/10.1007/978-3-031-07734-0_5

Campbell-Verduyn, M., Goguen, M., & Porter, T. (2017). Big data and algorithmic governance: The case of financial practices. *New Political Economy, 22*(2), 219–236. https://doi.org/10.1080/13563467.2016.1216533

Cao, L. (2021). Artificial intelligence in retail: Applications and value creation logics. *International Journal of Retail & Distribution Management, 49*(7), 958–976. https://doi.org/10.1108/IJRDM-09-2020-0350

Cesta, A., Cortellessa, G., & De Benedictis, R. (2014). Training for crisis decision making–An approach based on plan adaptation. *Knowledge-Based Systems, 58*, 98–112. https://doi.org/10.1016/j.knosys.2013.11.011

Choi, S., Kang, H., Kim, N., & Kim, J. (2025). How does artificial intelligence improve human decision-making? Evidence from the AI-powered Go program. *Strategic Management Journal, 46*(6), 1523–1554. https://doi.org/10.1002/smj.3694

Chung, K., Thaichon, P., & Quach, S. (2022). Types of artificial intelligence (AI) in marketing management. In *Artificial intelligence for marketing management* (pp. 29–40). Routledge. https://doi.org/10.4324/9781003280392-4

Danaher, J., Hogan, M. J., Noone, C., Kennedy, R., Behan, A., De Paor, A., Felzmann, H., Haklay, M., Khoo, S. M., Morison, J., Murphy, M. H., & Shankar, K. (2017). Algorithmic governance: Developing a research agenda through the power of collective intelligence. *Big Data & Society, 4*(2), 2053951717726554. https://doi.org/10.1177/2053951717726554

Doshi, A. R., Bell, J. J., Mirzayev, E., & Vanneste, B. S. (2025). Generative artificial intelligence and evaluating strategic decisions. *Strategic Management Journal, 46*(3), 583–610. https://doi.org/10.1002/smj.3677

Fleming, P. S., Seehra, J., Polychronopoulou, A., Fedorowicz, Z., & Pandis, N. (2013). A PRISMA assessment of the reporting quality of systematic reviews in orthodontics. *The Angle Orthodontist, 83*(1), 158–163. https://doi.org/10.2319/032612-251.1

Gandomi, A., & Haider, M. (2015). Beyond the hype: Big data concepts, methods, and analytics. *International Journal of Information Management, 35*(2), 137–144. https://doi.org/10.1016/j.ijinfomgt.2014.10.007

Ghasemaghaei, M., & Kordzadeh, N. (2025). Ethics in the age of algorithms: Unravelling the impact of algorithmic unfairness on data analytics recommendation acceptance. *Information Systems Journal, 35*(4), 1166–1197. https://doi.org/10.1111/isj.12572

Glikson, E., & Woolley, A. W. (2020). Human trust in artificial intelligence: Review of empirical research. *Academy of Management Annals, 14*(2), 627–660. https://doi.org/10.5465/annals.2018.0057

Gritsenko, D., & Wood, M. (2022). Algorithmic governance: A modes of governance approach. *Regulation & Governance, 16*(1), 45–62. https://doi.org/10.1111/rego.12367

Gupta, S., Modgil, S., Bhattacharyya, S., & Bose, I. (2022). Artificial intelligence for decision support systems in the field of operations research: Review and future scope of research. *Annals of Operations Research, 308*(1), 215–274. https://doi.org/10.1007/s10479-020-03856-6

Hernández-Tamurejo, Á., González-Padilla, P., & Sepúlveda, Á. S. (2025). The economics of AI adoption in OTAs: Market dynamics and future research. *Global Economics Research*, 100001. https://doi.org/10.1016/j.ecores.2025.100001

Hillebrand, L., Raisch, S., & Schad, J. (2025). Managing with artificial intelligence: An integrative framework. *Academy of Management Annals, 19*(1), 343–375. https://doi.org/10.5465/annals.2022.0072

Hossain, M. R., Akhter, F., & Sultana, M. M. (2022). SMEs in covid-19 crisis and combating strategies: A systematic literature review (SLR) and A case from emerging economy. *Operations Research Perspectives, 9*, Article 100222. https://doi.org/10.1016/j.orp.2022.100222

Hurley, R. (2023). An organizational capacity for trustworthiness: A dynamic routines Perspective. *Journal of Business Ethics, 188*(3), 589–601. https://doi.org/10.1007/s10551-022-05318-4

Jobstreibizer, J., Beliaeva, T., Ferasso, M., Kraus, S., & Kallmuenzer, A. (2025). The impact of artificial intelligence on business models: A bibliometric-systematic literature review. *Management Decision, 63*(13), 372–396. https://doi.org/10.1108/MD-10-2024-2309

Kamel Rahimi, A., Pienaar, O., Ghadimi, M., Canfell, O. J., Pole, J. D., Shrapnel, S., van der Vegt, A. H., & Sullivan, C. (2024). Implementing AI in hospitals to achieve a learning health system: Systematic review of current enablers and barriers. *Journal of Medical Internet Research, 26*, e49655. https://doi.org/10.2196/49655

Kemp, A. (2024). Competitive advantage through artificial intelligence: Toward a theory of situated AI. *Academy of Management Review, 49*(3), 618–635. https://doi.org/10.5465/amr.2020.0205

Khan, S. (2025). From constraints to cognition: Integrating bounded rationality into AI design for realistic decision-making. *The Critical Review of Social Sciences Studies, 3*(3), 1511–1535. https://doi.org/10.59075/n96xaa33

Khanfar, A. A., Kiani Mavi, R., Iranmanesh, M., & Gengatharen, D. (2025). Factors influencing the adoption of artificial intelligence systems: A systematic literature review. *Management Decision, 63*(10), 3727–3755. https://doi.org/10.1108/MD-05-2023-0838

Koliousis, I., Al-Surmi, A., & Bashiri, M. (2024). Artificial intelligence and policy making; can small municipalities enable digital transformation? *International Journal of Production Economics, 274*, Article 109324. https://doi.org/10.1016/j.ijpe.2024.109324

Konlechner, S., Müller, B., & Güttel, W. H. (2018). A dynamic capabilities perspective on managing technological change: A review, framework and research agenda. *International Journal of Technology Management, 76*(3–4), 188–213. https://doi.org/10.1504/IJTM.2018.091285

Krabuanrat, K., & Phelps, R. (1998). Heuristics and rationality in strategic decision making: An exploratory study. *Journal of Business Research, 41*(1), 83–93. https://doi.org/10.1016/S0148-2963(97)00014-3

Krakowski, S., Luger, J., & Raisch, S. (2023). Artificial intelligence and the changing sources of competitive advantage. *Strategic Management Journal, 44*(6), 1425–1452. https://doi.org/10.1002/smj.3387

Lam, H. Y., Tang, V., Wu, C. H., & Cho, V. (2024). A multi-criteria intelligence aid approach to selecting strategic key opinion leaders in digital business management. *Journal of Innovation & Knowledge, 9*(3), Article 100502. https://doi.org/10.1016/j.jik.2024.100502

Lame, G. (2019, July). Systematic literature reviews: An introduction. In *Proceedings of the Design Society: International Conference on Engineering Design* (Vol. 1, No. 1, pp. 1633–1642). Cambridge University Press. https://doi.org/10.1017/dsi.2019.169

Latzer, M., & Festic, N. (2019). A guideline for understanding and measuring algorithmic governance in everyday life. *Internet Policy Review, 8*(2). https://doi.org/10.14763/2019.2.1415

Levinthal, D. A. (2011). A behavioral approach to strategy—what's the alternative? *Strategic Management Journal, 32*(13), 1517–1523. https://doi.org/10.1002/smj.963

Martin, K., & Waldman, A. (2023). Are algorithmic decisions legitimate? The effect of process and outcomes on perceptions of legitimacy of AI decisions. *Journal of Business Ethics, 183*(3), 653–670. https://doi.org/10.1007/s10551-021-05032-7

Marvi, R., Foroudi, P., & Cuomo, M. T. (2025). Past, present and future of AI in marketing and knowledge management. *Journal of Knowledge Management, 29*(11), 1–31. https://doi.org/10.1108/JKM-07-2023-0634

Mashiah, I., & Avidar, R. (2025). The paradox of technology acceptance: Ethics and strategic implications of artificial intelligence in public relations. *Journal of Communication Management*, 1–21. https://doi.org/10.1108/JCOM-01-2025-0024

Mishra, S., & Tripathi, A. R. (2021). AI business model: An integrative business approach. *Journal of Innovation and Entrepreneurship, 10*(1), 18. https://doi.org/10.1186/s13731-021-00157-5

Mishra, V., & Mishra, M. P. (2023). PRISMA for review of management literature–method, merits, and limitations–an academic review. *Advancing Methodologies of Conducting Literature Review in Management Domain*, 125–136. https://doi.org/10.1108/S2754-586520230000002007

Mühlhoff, R. (2025). Opacity in machine learning and predictive analytics. In *The ethics of AI* (pp. 146–155). Bristol University Press. https://doi.org/10.51952/9781529249262.ch009

Nazemi, K., Burkhardt, D., & Kock, A. (2022). Visual analytics for technology and innovation management: An interaction approach for strategic decision making. *Multimedia Tools and Applications, 81*(11), 148. https://doi.org/10.1007/s11042-021-10972-3

Nazir, J., & Das, P. K. (2025). A systematic literature review on factors of perception impacting entrepreneurial success based on PRISMA framework. *Journal of Innovation and Entrepreneurship, 14*(1), 49. https://doi.org/10.1186/s13731-025-00491-y

Ooi, K. B., Tan, G. W. H., Al-Emran, M., Al-Sharafi, M. A., Capatina, A., Chakraborty, A., Dwivedi, Y. K., Huang, T. L., Kar, A. K., Lee, V. H., Loh, X. M., & Wong, L. W. (2025). The potential of generative artificial intelligence across disciplines: Perspectives and future directions. *Journal of Computer Information Systems, 65*(1), 76–107. https://doi.org/10.1080/08874417.2023.2261010

Petrescu, M., Krishen, A. S., Kachen, S., & Gironda, J. T. (2022). AI-based innovation in B2B marketing: An interdisciplinary framework incorporating academic and practitioner perspectives. *Industrial Marketing Management, 103*, 61–72. https://doi.org/10.1016/j.indmarman.2022.03.001

Poggi, F., Pena, S., Cunha, N., Müller, A., & Romão, B. (2025). Digital land-use decision support tools in Europe: A systematic review using the PRISMA method. *European Planning Studies, 33*(10), 1840–1863. https://doi.org/10.1080/09654313.2025.2524002

Pu, Y., Li, H., Hou, W., & Pan, X. (2025). The analysis of strategic management decisions and corporate competitiveness based on artificial intelligence. *Scientific Reports, 15*(1), 17942. https://doi.org/10.1038/s41598-025-02842-x

Raisch, S., & Fomina, K. (2025). Combining human and artificial intelligence: Hybrid problem-solving in organizations. *Academy of Management Review, 50*(2), 441–464. https://doi.org/10.5465/amr.2021.0421

Saura, J. R. (2025a). AI, data economy, and behavioral intention: Towards ethical paths. In *Global perspectives on AI, ethics, and business economics: Charting the future* (pp. 3–16). Springer Nature Switzerland. https://doi.org/10.1007/978-3-031-88781-9_1

Saura, J. R. (Ed.). (2025b). *Global perspectives on AI, ethics, and business economics: Charting the future*. Springer Nature. https://doi.org/10.1007/978-3-031-88781-9

Saura, J. R., & Bužinskienė, R. (2025). Behavioral economics, artificial intelligence and entrepreneurship: An updated framework for management. *International Entrepreneurship and Management Journal, 21*(1), 1–33. https://doi.org/10.1007/s11365-025-01076-7

Saura, J. R., Barbosa, B., & Rana, S. (2025a). Decoding the privacy puzzle: A study on AI deployment in public governance. In *Handbook on governance and data science* (pp. 239–263). Edward Elgar Publishing. https://doi.org/10.4337/9781035301348.00020

Saura, J. R., Gelashvili, V., & Gabriel Martínez-Navalón, J. (2025b). *The impact of social media on Gen Z's mental health and privacy. Journal of Competitiveness, 17*(1). https://doi.org/10.7441/joc.2025.01.11

Saura, J. R., Škare, V., & Dosen, D. O. (2024). Is AI-based digital marketing ethical? Assessing a new data privacy paradox. *Journal of Innovation & Knowledge, 9*(4), Article 100597. https://doi.org/10.1016/j.jik.2024.100597

Schneider, S., & Leyer, M. (2019). Me or information technology? Adoption of artificial intelligence in the delegation of personal strategic decisions. *Managerial and Decision Economics, 40*(3), 223–231. https://doi.org/10.1002/mde.2982

Shaheen, N., Shaheen, A., Ramadan, A., Hefnawy, M. T., Ramadan, A., Ibrahim, I. A., Hassanein, M. E., Ashour, M. E., & Flouty, O. (2023). Appraising systematic reviews: A comprehensive guide to ensuring validity and reliability. *Frontiers in Research Metrics and Analytics, 8*, 1268045. https://doi.org/10.3389/frma.2023.1268045

Shatila, K., Aránega, A. Y., & Urueña, R. C. (2025). The role of digital transformation in shaping academic entrepreneurship. *Global Economics Research*, 100002. https://doi.org/10.1016/j.ecores.2025.100002

Siaw, C. A., & Ali, W. (2025). Substitution and complementarity between human and artificial intelligence: A dynamic capabilities view. *Journal of Managerial Psychology, 40*(5), 539–554. https://doi.org/10.1108/JMP-06-2024-0398

Simon, H. A. (1990). Bounded rationality. In *Utility and probability* (pp. 15–18). Palgrave Macmillan. https://doi.org/10.1007/978-1-349-20568-4_5

Subrahmanyam, S. (2025). Leveraging AI and ML for enhanced efficiency and innovation in manufacturing. In *AI's role in enhanced automotive safety* (pp. 319–344). IGI Global Scientific Publishing. https://doi.org/10.4018/979-8-3373-0442-7.ch021

Tedja, B., Al Musadieq, M., Kusumawati, A., & Yulianto, E. (2024). Systematic literature review using PRISMA: Exploring the influence of service quality and perceived value on satisfaction and intention to continue relationship. *Future Business Journal, 10*(1), 39. https://doi.org/10.1186/s43093-024-00326-4

Teece, D. J., Pisano, G., & Shuen, A. (1997). Dynamic capabilities and strategic management. *Strategic Management Journal, 18*(7), 509–533. https://doi.org/10.1002/(SICI)1097-0266(199708)18:7%3C509::AID-SMJ882%3E3.0.CO;2-Z

van Giffen, B., & Ludwig, H. (2023). How Siemens democratized artificial intelligence. *MIS Quarterly Executive, 22*(1), 1–21.

Varsha, P. S. (2023). How can we manage biases in artificial intelligence systems–A systematic literature review. *International Journal of Information Management Data Insights, 3*(1), Article 100165. https://doi.org/10.1016/j.jjimei.2023.100165

Vudugula, S., Chebrolu, S. K., Bhuiyan, M., & Rozony, F. Z. (2023). Integrating artificial intelligence in strategic business decision-making: A systematic review of predictive models. *International Journal of Scientific Interdisciplinary Research, 4*(1), 01–26. https://doi.org/10.63125/s5skge53

Weber, P., Carl, K. V., & Hinz, O. (2024). Applications of explainable artificial intelligence in finance—a systematic review of finance, information systems, and computer science literature. *Management Review Quarterly, 74*(2), 867–907. https://doi.org/10.1007/s11301-023-00320-0

The Intersection of Relationship Marketing and Artificial Intelligence

José Duarte Santos and Paulo Botelho Pires

Abstract This chapter analyses the integration of artificial intelligence (AI) into relationship marketing practices, examining strategic applications, benefits, and organizational challenges. The study identifies six key dimensions: content personalization, predictive analytics, advanced segmentation, customer lifetime value (CLV) forecasting, process automation, and customer service optimization. The literature review shows that AI enhances large-scale data analysis, supporting more informed decisions geared towards maximizing relational value. The results indicate measurable gains in operational efficiency, customer satisfaction, and return on investment. At the same time, challenges related to data privacy, algorithmic biases, and organizational resistance are identified, requiring governance frameworks that articulate transparency, ethics, and regulatory compliance. Trends point to more automated, predictive, and customer-centric CRM systems, supported by omnichannel architectures and algorithmic explainability.

1 Introduction

Artificial intelligence (AI) has been reshaping marketing by expanding organizations' ability to generate actionable insights from large volumes of data, optimize operations, and strengthen customer engagement, contributing to competitive advantage (Achour & Ayadi, 2025). In this context, AI is also conceptualized as a strategic driver of relationship marketing, working in conjunction with trust and commitment mechanisms to strengthen customer-company relationships. By facilitating and intensifying the management of multiple points of contact, AI applications tend to shape customer experience and, consequently, competitive differentiation (Cheng et al., 2023).

J. D. Santos (✉) · P. B. Pires
CEOS.PP, ISCAP, Polytechnic of Porto, Porto, Portugal
e-mail: jdsantos@iscap.ipp.pt

P. B. Pires
e-mail: paulo.pires@iscap.ipp.pt

J. D. Santos et al. (eds.), *Artificial Intelligence Transforming Marketing*, Contributions to Management Science, https://doi.org/10.1007/978-3-032-22360-9_6

The adoption of AI in customer relationship management (CRM) supports more personalized experiences through large-scale data analysis, product recommendations, and automated interactions, establishing itself as a competitive resource in relational marketing practices (Deb et al., 2018). From an analytical point of view, Customer Lifetime Value (CLV) prediction emerges as a structuring application, enabling data-driven decisions that maximize profitability and strengthen links between customers and organizations (Egorenkov, 2024). The literature points out that AI reinforces personalization and loyalty—fundamental elements in customer relationships—and supports strategic decisions in relational marketing (Ahmed et al., 2024a), while accelerating the digital transition and enabling continuous and interactive dialogue in multichannel environments, with an impact on the customer experience throughout the journey (Figueiredo et al., 2024). It should also be noted that the effects of AI are not limited to theoretical benefits: there is evidence of measurable improvements in customer experience following its adoption, with reported gains of up to 10%, suggesting an operationally relevant impact on service quality and retention capacity (Chintalapati & Pandey, 2022).

This chapter aims to highlight the contribution of artificial intelligence (AI) to specific dimensions of relationship marketing. To this end, it begins with a summary of the main principles of relationship marketing, followed by a presentation of basic AI concepts. Subsequently, the applications and strategic benefits of AI in the context of relationship marketing are discussed, as well as the challenges and ethical concerns associated with its adoption. This chapter also analyses emerging trends in the field and concludes with some final considerations.

2 Fundamentals of Relationship Marketing

Relationship marketing has its origins in service marketing and industrial marketing and emerged in response to the need to place greater emphasis on customer relations (Olson & Levy, 2017), considering the specific characteristics of services, such as their intangibility, and recurring purchases in industrial marketing. Relationship marketing emphasizes building and maintaining strong relationships with customers to create mutual value and loyalty (Gupta & Sahu, 2012).

Relationship marketing is based on lasting relationships founded on trust, information sharing, and commitment, replacing isolated transactions with ongoing interactions that aim to generate mutual value and loyalty (Figueiredo et al., 2024). Relationship marketing emphasizes customer retention and satisfaction rather than simply acquiring new customers, recognizing that building strong, lasting relationships with existing customers can be more profitable in the long term (Vasconcelo & Silva, 2022), in contrast to transactional marketing, which tends to end at the moment the transaction takes place. It goes beyond traditional marketing approaches, which focuses on individual transactions, and seeks to establish long-term connections with customers through personalized communication, customized offers, and exceptional service (Nugroho & Hati, 2020). For Averineni et al. (2024), personalization is essential for fostering loyalty and satisfaction over time.

This approach involves strategies that focus on developing long-term, mutually beneficial relationships between an organization and its customers, with the goal of creating mutual value for both parties supported by relationships based on trust and commitment (Badrinarayanan & Ramachandran, 2024). Ultimately, the aim is to cultivate brand advocates who are deeply invested in the company's success and actively promote the brand to their networks (Yulisetiarini, 2015).

With the advent of digital marketing, artificial intelligence presents novel opportunities to deepen customer relationships by enabling marketers to understand and cater to individual needs at an unprecedented level, thus enhancing the overall shopping experience (Figueiredo et al., 2024).

3 Artificial Intelligence: Concept and Technological Evolution

3.1 Definition and Evolution of AI

Artificial intelligence has been gaining prominence over the last three years, but the concept is not new. Generative artificial intelligence has come to give a new approach to the area, and, with this, also countless benefits and facilities. The term AI refers to the simulation of human intelligence in machines that are programmed to think and act like humans (Vlačić et al., 2021).

Artificial intelligence is described as the ability of computer systems to simulate intelligent behaviour, with an emphasis on artificial and deep neural networks (Ahmed et al., 2024b). In turn, Achour and Ayadi (2025) consider that AI is composed of mechanisms that simulate human intelligence in computational and digital forms, learning and adapting autonomously from data, surpassing human capabilities in mechanical and cognitive tasks, enabling intelligent decisions based on data, without additional programming. Artificial intelligence refers to the use of computational algorithms, including machine learning and deep learning, to interpret patterns and predict complex consumer behaviours (Ahmed et al., 2024a, 2024b), enabling machines to simulate human cognitive processes such as reasoning, learning, and decision-making, applying them effectively in business environments (Almahairah, 2023).

Another definition states that AI is the underpinning of a set of projects that have in common the desire to build an artificial equivalent of the human brain or, equivalently, to simulate the functioning of human intelligence outside the human brain (Figueiredo et al., 2024). AI systems are designed to perceive their environment, reason, learn, and make decisions to achieve specific goals (Yau et al., 2021), encompasses a wide range of techniques, including machine learning, natural language processing, computer vision, and robotics, all of which contribute to its ability to perform tasks that typically require human intelligence (Naz & Kashif, 2025).

The evolution of AI can be traced back to the mid-twentieth century with the advent of the Turing test, which tested a machine's ability to exhibit intelligent behaviour equivalent to, or indistinguishable from, that of a human (Vlačić et al., 2021). The field has experienced periods of both excitement and stagnation, known as "AI winters," but recent advances in computing power, data availability, and algorithmic development have led to a resurgence of AI in various industries.

The reduction in technological costs has contributed to the widespread adoption of AI (Deb et al., 2018), which has evolved with the advancement of big data, machine learning, and Natural Language Processing (NLP), becoming an indispensable tool in various areas of management, particularly in relationship marketing (Almahairah, 2023), enabling more personalized marketing approaches and real-time services (Achour & Ayadi, 2025). Thus, AI has moved from simple statistical methods to advanced models, such as deep neural networks, capable of handling unstructured and large-scale data (Ahmed et al., 2024a).

Currently, AI contributes to the existence of sophisticated human-computer interaction systems capable of simulating empathy and accurately predicting behaviour (Badrinarayanan & Ramachandran, 2024).

3.2 AI Applied to Marketing

AI applications in marketing are diverse, ranging from analysing large data volumes to identifying patterns, enabling well-informed decisions, and reshaping online customer engagement (Lakshmipriyanka et al., 2023). One of the primary areas where AI has transformed marketing is in consumer behaviour analysis (Tadimarri et al., 2024). AI algorithms can process vast amounts of data from various sources, including social media, website traffic, and customer databases, to identify patterns and trends in consumer behaviour. This information can be used to create more targeted and personalized marketing campaigns, improve customer segmentation, and optimize pricing strategies.

Artificial intelligence (AI) can be understood as a set of technologies capable of learning from data, making predictions, and automating decisions, and is increasingly being applied to customer relationship management and relationship marketing (Averineni et al., 2024). In the context of marketing, AI enables the analysis of large volumes of complex data in real time, enabling sales and behavioural predictions, more accurate segmentation, and the creation of highly personalized experiences (Almahairah, 2023; Averineni et al., 2024). These capabilities contribute to the automation of interactions and responses throughout the customer journey, reinforcing the effectiveness of communication and the consistency of customer-brand relationships (Bu et al., 2022; Deb et al., 2018). In this context, sentiment analysis is another area where AI can enhance marketing, as natural language processing techniques can be used to analyse customer feedback, social media posts, and online reviews to determine the sentiment behind them, enabling organizations to capture consumer perceptions, emotions, and attitudes systematically and in real time.

Based on these capabilities, AI has been widely recognized as a driver of business performance and organizational efficiency. Its application allows for optimized data management, personalized offers, and improved customer experience in sales interactions, both in digital and hybrid environments (Badrinarayanan & Ramachandran, 2024; Chen & Prentice, 2025). AI-based solutions enable personalized recommendations for "next-best action," predictive lead scoring, programmatic ad buying, and follow-up offers, maximizing revenue and sector efficiency (Cao & Zhu, 2022; Davenport et al., 2020). At the same time, conversational agents and virtual assistants, such as Alexa, illustrate how AI can reconfigure decision-making processes, brand preferences, and consumer choices, offering real-time recommendations and alternatives that make the purchasing process more agile, transparent, and sophisticated (Chaturvedi et al., 2024; Figueiredo et al., 2024).

4 Applications of AI in Relationship Marketing

4.1 Content Personalization

Artificial intelligence (AI) has played a central role in the evolution of personalization in marketing, enabling the adaptation of strategies, content, and offers based on individual consumer behaviour. AI-driven personalization involves tailoring marketing messages and offers to individual customers based on their preferences, behaviours, and past interactions (Alghizzawi et al., 2024). Through audience analytics, marketers gain insights into individual customer preferences, enabling AI to curate customized content that resonates with potential customer segments (Olson & Levy, 2017). AI algorithms can analyse customer data to predict their needs and preferences, allowing businesses to deliver personalized recommendations, product suggestions, and content that is more likely to resonate with them. This level of personalization can significantly enhance customer engagement, increase conversion rates, and foster stronger relationships. AI algorithms tailor content and recommendations based on individual user data, leading to higher customer satisfaction and engagement (Kumar et al., 2024). This enhances customer engagement and fosters enduring brand loyalty by ensuring communications are relevant and valued.

By analysing large volumes of explicit, implicit, and contextual behavioural data, AI-based systems can identify individual preferences and adjust products, prices, channels, and communication timing in real time (Davenport et al., 2020; Egorenkov, 2024; Figueiredo et al., 2024). Metrics such as frequency, recency, and monetary value of purchases, as well as interaction histories, are used to predict preferences and guide targeted marketing campaigns, promoting greater relevance, engagement, and conversion rates (Achour & Ayadi, 2025; Ahmed et al., 2024a).

In this context, advanced techniques such as neural networks, recommendation algorithms, and conversational agents make it possible to decipher complex behaviour patterns throughout the customer journey, enabling individualized recommendations and personalized content in a continuous and dynamic way (Chaturvedi et al., 2024). AI also enables the creation of humanized content that is psychographically tailored to the consumer profile, reinforcing the relevance of messages and the quality of customer-brand interactions (Almahairah, 2023; Bu et al., 2022). Consequently, AI-driven personalization has been associated with increased communication relevance, relational engagement, satisfaction, and customer lifetime value (CLV), establishing itself as a key element in the effectiveness of contemporary CRM strategies (Averineni et al., 2024; Badrinarayanan & Ramachandran, 2024).

Finally, the growing adoption of AI-based technology platforms, such as Adobe and Amazon, highlights the centrality of personalization in today's marketing, especially considering the exponential increase in unstructured data (Chintalapati & Pandey, 2022). These personalized systems allow multiple data sources to be integrated to offer relevant and consistent experiences, strengthening the relational bond and enhancing long-term customer loyalty (Egorenkov, 2024; Figueiredo et al., 2024).

4.2 Predictive Analytics

Predictive analytics supported by artificial intelligence (AI) has established itself as a key tool for anticipating consumer behaviour and optimizing marketing and CRM strategies, especially in conversions and retention (Averineni et al., 2024). By analysing large volumes of historical, transactional, demographic, and behavioural data, AI algorithms identify latent patterns and emerging trends, enabling the prediction of future behaviours, customer needs, and market dynamics with a high degree of accuracy (Almahairah, 2023; Islam et al., 2024). This predictive capability supports data-driven decisions regarding product development, pricing, and promotional planning, promoting proactive approaches that increase customer satisfaction and foster lasting relationships with the brand (Averineni et al., 2024). By anticipating customer needs, predictive analytics enables companies to customize marketing efforts, optimize customer experiences, and cultivate enduring relationships by resolving potential issues before they escalate (Kumar et al., 2024).

Based on these predictions, organizations can personalize interactions, anticipate problems, and dynamically adapt offerings, strengthening customer engagement and business performance. AI-based predictive analytics allows, for example, anticipating churn, estimating customer lifetime value (CLV), and identifying opportunities for retention, up-selling, and cross-selling, supporting a more efficient allocation of marketing resources (Egorenkov, 2024; Figueiredo et al., 2024; Ahmed et al., 2024b). At the same time, recommendation systems and collaborative filters use purchasing and behaviour patterns to predict future consumption decisions, enabling timely interventions throughout the customer journey and increasing conversion and retention rates (Badrinarayanan & Ramachandran, 2024; Bu et al., 2022; Deb et al., 2018).

In addition to supporting behavioural and value predictions, AI has been applied substantially to price management as a component of the marketing mix. Algorithms enable real-time price optimization and dynamic adjustment, forecasting and monitoring of market conditions and competition, as well as price and promotion personalization and segmentation, supported by automated testing and compliance verification mechanisms, reinforcing the capacity for proactive, data-driven intervention (Pires & Santos, 2023).

Finally, recent advances in predictive models, such as reinforced recurrent neural networks and post-purchase analytical solutions, expand the strategic reach of predictive analytics in marketing. These models make it possible to anticipate future rewards (Cao & Zhu, 2022), project revenues, optimize operational efficiency (Chen & Prentice, 2025), anticipate purchases, and even redefine logistics and information processes, as in "shipping-then-shopping" models (Davenport et al., 2020). Thus, AI-powered predictive analytics is establishing itself as a pillar of contemporary relationship marketing by enabling more informed, personalized decisions geared towards creating sustainable long-term value (Achour & Ayadi, 2025).

4.3 Customer Segmentation

Artificial intelligence (AI) has profoundly transformed customer segmentation by enabling the integrated analysis of large volumes of demographic, psychographic, behavioural, and transactional data, making it possible to identify patterns, correlations, and distinct segments with a high degree of accuracy (Islam et al., 2024; Luthra et al., 2024). Through machine learning algorithms, deep neural networks (DNNs), and supervised techniques, organizations can divide their consumer base into homogeneous groups with different needs, preferences, and value levels, using metrics such as recency, frequency, and monetary value (RFM) of purchases, among others (Ahmed et al., 2024a, 2024b). This approach allows for a deeper understanding of the nuances of each segment, supporting the development of more targeted, relevant, and effective campaigns (Almahairah, 2023).

Based on this analytical capability, AI-driven segmentation evolves from static models to dynamic and continuous logic, in which profiles, interactions, and consumption patterns are analysed in real time to adjust marketing and sales strategies in a contextualized manner (Averineni et al., 2024; Bu et al., 2022). AI-based tools enable automatic micro-segmentation of consumers based on behavioural patterns, social data, and anonymous information, enabling personalized communications by specific interest groups and increasing engagement and conversion rates (Achour & Ayadi, 2025; Chintalapati & Pandey, 2022; Islam et al., 2024). The integration of multiple types of data also enables the identification of niches with high profitability potential, supporting more granular and value-oriented strategies (Egorenkov, 2024).

In this context, AI-powered CRM and e-CRM systems play a central role in operationalizing advanced segmentation and strengthening customer relationship management. These systems make it possible to identify potential customers, differentiate consumers according to their relevance and value, and automate personalized recommendations, including up-selling and cross-selling strategies, dynamic pricing, and offers tailored to each segment (Bu et al., 2022; Egorenkov, 2024; Figueiredo et al., 2024). In addition to improving customer experience, intelligent automation reduces the operational burden on customer service teams, allowing human resources to focus on more complex and higher value-added interactions (Wilson et al., 2024). Thus, AI-based segmentation is consolidating itself as a strategic pillar of contemporary marketing, supporting more informed, efficient, and value-oriented decisions in the long term (Badrinarayanan & Ramachandran, 2024; Davenport et al., 2020).

4.4 Customer Lifetime Value Prediction

Relationship marketing is based on retaining valuable customers, with CLV being a key metric for decisions focused on maximizing value and long-term profitability. CLV is considered a critical indicator in customer relationships, essential for prioritizing resources and building lasting relationships based on expected future value (Badrinarayanan & Ramachandran, 2024). CLV is calculated based on transactional and behavioural data, allowing the future revenue of each customer to be estimated using accurate predictive models (Ahmed et al., 2024a). Artificial intelligence can help improve lifetime value calculation models, as it can automatically collect information that contributes to the application of the model (Egorenkov, 2024).

AI-driven predictive customer lifetime value models are crucial for maximizing long-term profitability, enabling businesses to develop intricately personalized marketing strategies that cater to individual customer behaviours and preferences (Egorenkov, 2024). These models employ advanced analytical techniques to synthesize transactional records, engagement metrics, and demographic profiles, ultimately generating a probabilistic forecast of the total economic value a customer will contribute to a business throughout the duration of their relationship (Egorenkov, 2024).

Conventional customer segmentation methodologies frequently depend on demographic information, like age, gender, and income, to categorize customers into extensive groupings, which, although beneficial, may overlook essential subtleties in customer behaviour and preferences that could enable more focused targeting (Egorenkov, 2024).

When calculating lifetime value, companies should consider the channels used to interact with customers to optimize customer value as much as possible (Libai et al., 2020). Firms can leverage AI-CRM systems to personalize dialogues with customers, adapting marketing mix elements to individual customer needs based on purchasing history and interactions. By understanding the value each customer brings over time, businesses can allocate resources more effectively, enhance customer experiences, and develop targeted marketing strategies that boost retention and revenue (Egorenkov, 2024). Notably, the cost of acquiring new customers generally exceeds the investment required to retain existing ones, thereby underscoring the strategic and economic importance of leveraging AI to enhance customer loyalty and prolong customer lifetime value (Egorenkov, 2024).

The analysis of historical and behavioural data using AI allows the value of the customer to be estimated over time, guiding retention actions (Ahmed et al., 2024b). AI-supported predictive models estimate future revenues considering purchase frequency, interactive communications across multiple channels, churn, and customer acquisition costs, offering more dynamic predictions than purely historical approaches (Egorenkov, 2024). Thus, it is possible to estimate customer value over time, guiding strategic retention decisions (Almahairah, 2023), such as decisions about relationship investment and loyalty strategies (Averineni et al., 2024), optimizing marketing investments in retention and marketing actions based on expected profitability (Bu et al, 2022). AI-driven predictive analytics not only refines the precision of sales forecasting but also significantly bolsters the efficacy of customer retention models, leading to more accurate projections and decreased churn rates (Somashekhar et al., 2024).

4.5 Marketing Automation and CRM

The integration of artificial intelligence (AI) has been automating marketing and customer relationship management processes, namely A/B testing, advertising campaign optimization, and real-time adjustments, reducing the need for human intervention and increasing operational efficiency (Achour & Ayadi, 2025) and productivity (Almahairah, 2023). This automation is often supported by predictive models that feed systems capable of dynamically reconfiguring campaigns, maximizing effectiveness and minimizing waste of resources, while contributing to the reduction of operating costs in digital contexts (Ahmed et al., 2024a, 2024b). At the same time, AI enables the automation of communications, scheduling, and follow-up activities, freeing up human resources for higher value-added tasks and boosting organizational productivity. At scale, this capability supports rapid responses and mass interactions without sacrificing relevant levels of personalization (Almahairah, 2023; Averineni et al., 2024).

This automation movement extends to the commercial cycle and service, where AI facilitates proactive customer relationship management, supporting sales process efficiency and coordination of interactions throughout the funnel. Automated systems can prioritize tasks, recommend actions, and reduce errors, redistributing human effort to creative and strategic dimensions of relationship management (Bu et al., 2022), with reported impacts on economic results such as increased revenues and reduced operating costs (Ahmed et al., 2024b). The operationalization of these capabilities is manifested, for example, in the use of platforms and applications that automate campaigns, score leads, and generate content, as well as in the automation of routine processes, increasing speed, consistency, and scale (Chintalapati & Pandey, 2022; Davenport et al., 2020). In addition, automation manifests itself through bots and automatic response tools—such as chatbots and virtual assistants—that process data in real time and interact autonomously. Furthermore, AI can automate the reading of interests and preferences from digital data (e.g., hyperlinks), accelerating two-way communication and adjusting content without continuous supervision (Deb et al., 2018; Figueiredo et al., 2024).

In this context, CRM remains focused on building lasting relationships, promoting retention, loyalty, and personalization, which are particularly critical objectives in e-commerce due to their connection to sustainability and competitiveness. However, contemporary CRM tends to go beyond the strictly informational function of data management, evolving into more intelligent systems that support sales, marketing, and service with personalized interactions, aiming for greater satisfaction, loyalty, and profitability (Almahairah, 2023; Bu et al., 2022; Ahmed et al., 2024b). In this process, AI is often presented as a response to the limitations of traditional CRM approaches in e-commerce, given its ability to process large volumes of data, automate routine tasks, predict behaviours, and improve the customer experience; as a result, it acts as a catalyst for personalization and as a mechanism for efficiency and reduction of operating costs in communication with customers (Almahairah, 2023; Averineni et al., 2024; Bu et al., 2022; Ahmed et al., 2024b).

It is worth highlighting the technical sophistication of CRM systems, which have kept pace with the evolution of AI models, moving from simpler approaches to deep architectures (DNN), which allow complex patterns to be captured and more robust decisions to be made in CRM, expanding the potential for automation, prediction, and personalization described above (Ahmed et al., 2024b).

4.6 Customer Service and Support

AI-powered chatbots and virtual assistants have reshaped customer service by providing immediate and continuous support (24/7) (Achour & Ayadi, 2025; Davenport et al., 2020), answering frequently asked questions and resolving incidents with less friction, contributing to greater satisfaction and operational efficiency. These systems, including virtual agents and voice recognition (Deb et al, 2018), enable fast and consistent responses, reduce error rates and operating costs (Achour & Ayadi, 2025; Davenport et al., 2020), and automatically scale with demand variability (Davenport et al., 2020), strengthening pre- and post-purchase support capabilities (Chintalapati & Pandey, 2022). In after-sales applications, even less complex chatbots can streamline complaint registration and basic customer service, demonstrating efficiency gains in standardized tasks (Chaturvedi et al., 2024).

In addition to availability, the value of these systems lies in personalization and proactivity, supported by interaction, intention, and sentiment analysis (Ahmed et al., 2024b). AI models applied to support can anticipate needs, recommend actions, and tailor responses based on behavioural and emotional cues, increasing the relevance of the interaction and promoting retention and satisfaction (Egorenkov, 2024; Ahmed et al., 2024a). Sentiment analysis provides actionable information about customer opinions and emotions (Bu et al., 2022), allowing engagement strategies to be adjusted and concerns to be addressed more effectively (Somashekhar et al., 2024), while techniques such as NLP and rule-based approaches contribute to more accurate and contextualized responses in real time (Averineni et al., 2024). In this context, service improvement is not limited to speed: the ability to respond in a "correct" and contextual manner tends to reinforce commitment and trust in the commercial relationship (Badrinarayanan & Ramachandran, 2024).

AI-supported CRM systems can operationalize highly personalized and consistent interaction frameworks, freeing human agents for more complex situations that require advanced analysis and empathetic engagement (Hossain et al., 2024), while e-CRM centralizes multichannel contacts to ensure consistency throughout the customer journey (Figueiredo et al., 2024). More broadly, AI-driven personalization tends to transcend marketing communication, influencing multiple dimensions of the experience—including product design, pricing architecture, and service protocols—which reinforces the centrality of intelligent support as a structural component of the value proposition and customer relationship (Kumar et al., 2019).

5 Strategic Benefits of AI in Relationship Marketing

5.1 Customer Experience Optimization

Customer experience occurs at every point of contact with the organization and is determined by consumer perception, assuming increasing centrality in marketing geared towards retention and loyalty. In this context, it becomes crucial to identify "moments of truth" throughout the journey, as these critical points guide priorities for improving service and customer relations (Bu et al., 2022). AI thus emerges as a tool for operationalizing this experiential management by integrating data and systematically optimizing touchpoints, reinforcing the consistency and overall quality of the interaction (Bu et al., 2022; Chen & Prentice, 2025).

One of the main contributions of AI today focuses on improving and optimizing the customer experience through faster, more personalized, and contextual interactions, associated with greater engagement, perceived value, loyalty, and satisfaction (Achour & Ayadi, 2025). Predictive models adjust offers and communications based on consumption patterns and preferences, while AI-based personalization makes interactions more relevant and effective—an especially critical aspect in e-commerce, where the quality of the journey directly influences conversion and retention (Figueiredo et al., 2024; Ahmed et al., 2024b). Additionally, the analysis of interactions and behaviours supports more relevant and real-time responses, reinforcing the perception of usefulness and reducing operational friction (Almahairah, 2023; Deb et al., 2018).

This experiential improvement also results from AI's ability to anticipate needs and intervene proactively across multiple channels, promoting more fluid and consistent journeys (Chintalapati & Pandey, 2022). By combining data integration, needs prediction, and touchpoint personalization, AI contributes to longer-lasting relationships and evidence-based relationship management, extending service consistency across omnichannel ecosystems (Averineni et al., 2024; Badrinarayanan & Ramachandran, 2024; Bu et al., 2022). Furthermore, by predicting value and preferences, AI can guide interventions that smooth the journey and adjust elements such as pricing in real time, reinforcing perceptions of value for the customer (Egorenkov, 2024).

Recent developments highlight the expansion of AI towards more immersive and emotionally engaging experiences, linking AI functions to touchpoints to promote consistent and potentially immersive experiences, while holistic agent/ "assistant" proposals seek to intensify emotional engagement, mitigating limitations such as the uncanny valley (Chaturvedi et al., 2024; Chen & Prentice, 2025). In service applications, service robots and sensory technologies can increase engagement and reduce friction, accelerating purchasing decisions and raising interaction standards, suggesting an expansion of the experiential domain beyond the "traditional" digital (Chintalapati & Pandey, 2022).

5.2 *Sales Funnel Management*

AI contributes to sales funnel optimization by combining personalization, forecasting, and automation, with consistent impacts on conversion rates, ROI, and loyalty (Achour & Ayadi, 2025). Personalizing content and engagement throughout the potential customer's journey reduces friction and increases the likelihood of progression between funnel stages, while simultaneously reinforcing relational value (Achour & Ayadi, 2025) and optimizing each stage of the funnel (Bu et al., 2022). This ability, based on the use of demographic and historical data to tailor offers and messages, makes interaction more relevant, increases commercial effectiveness at different touchpoints (Badrinarayanan & Ramachandran, 2024; Bu et al., 2022), and increases conversion rates and relational efficiency (Badrinarayanan & Ramachandran, 2024).

AI also enhances funnel management through predictive mechanisms that support efficient screening and resource allocation. Customer Lifetime Value (CLV) forecasting allows you to prioritize leads and calibrate conversion efforts based on future potential value, balancing short-term efficiency with long-term profitability goals (Ahmed et al., 2024a). Complementarily, models that anticipate behaviours and conversion probabilities facilitate lead qualification and opportunity prioritization, contributing to higher commercial success rates and relational efficiency (Almahairah, 2023; Badrinarayanan & Ramachandran, 2024).

In addition, AI supports continuous funnel improvement by enabling monitoring and optimization of each stage, identifying bottlenecks, opportunities, and points of loss, and proposing data-driven interventions—including automated actions and real-time adjustments. This approach promotes more proactive management of commercial performance by articulating diagnosis (detection of constraints) and action (interventions to increase conversions) with greater operational granularity (Averineni et al., 2024; Ahmed et al., 2024b). Thus, AI tends to "fill gaps" in the commercial process by connecting scattered behavioural signals to recommendations and actions that increase funnel effectiveness (Almahairah, 2023; Ahmed et al., 2024b).

Studies report that voice assistants reduce decision time and facilitate purchase completion, reducing friction in the conversion path (Chaturvedi et al., 2024). Similarly, AI-powered digital assistants monitor and interpret responses on a large scale—forwarding only the most promising leads to human salespeople—linking screening automation to concrete gains in conversion (Davenport et al., 2020).

5.3 Increased Customer Satisfaction and Loyalty

AI enhances customer satisfaction and loyalty primarily through personalization and greater responsiveness, by making campaigns, services, and interactions more relevant and agile. AI-supported personalization tends to align the experience with individual expectations, reinforcing trust, improving perceived service quality, and increasing retention rates, loyalty (Badrinarayanan & Ramachandran, 2024; Ahmed et al., 2024a), and, consequently, sales. This effect is also explained by the ability to reduce service failures and anticipate needs and behaviours, which supports a more consistent value proposition over time (Almahairah, 2023; Averineni et al., 2024; Badrinarayanan & Ramachandran, 2024).

On a relational level, the strategic integration of AI into CRM enhances not only personalization, but also predictability and proactivity (Averineni et al., 2024), enabling data-driven retention interventions (e.g., relevant offers and preventive actions) (Almahairah, 2023), which reduce churn and increase satisfaction and loyalty in the long term (Ahmed et al., 2024b). In terms of adoption mechanisms and relational consolidation, trust and perceived usefulness emerge as determinants of increased satisfaction and intention to use, which is consistent with loyalty trajectories sustained by experiential value (Cheng et al., 2023).

According to Chaturvedi et al. (2024), studies suggest that AI can contribute to "profitable loyalty" when it combines technological capabilities and human intervention in hybrid models, sustaining value and relationship continuity over time. With AI, companies offer more relevant and agile services, increasing satisfaction and strengthening emotional bonds with customers which promotes loyalty (Achour & Ayadi, 2025). In line with this perspective, other studies show that AI tools can generate loyalty by promoting satisfaction and a predisposition for continued use and recommendation, reinforcing the role of intelligent support and personalization as drivers of advocacy and retention (Deb et al., 2018).

5.4 *Improved Performance Relational Marketing*

AI has measurable effects on relationship marketing performance by supporting more informed decisions, improving communication, and optimizing resource allocation. In terms of results, a 17% increase in brand awareness associated with AI-supported marketing has been reported, indicating that gains are not limited to tactical metrics but can translate into brand value indicators (Achour & Ayadi, 2025). This performance improvement is consistent with AI's ability to support data-driven marketing decisions and coordination, reinforcing relational effectiveness and evidence-driven execution (Badrinarayanan & Ramachandran, 2024).

The use of AI increases campaign effectiveness by combining trend forecasting with real-time personalization and continuous optimization, increasing response rates and the quality of matching between supply and consumer preferences (Bu et al., 2022). The robustness of these effects is supported by evidence of gains in large-scale personalized recommendations, reinforcing the role of AI as a personalization infrastructure with a direct impact on performance (Cao & Zhu, 2022). When integrated with real-time operational capacity and operational efficiency, this logic tends to translate into substantial ROI by simultaneously improving results and processes (Chintalapati & Pandey, 2022).

It should also be noted that AI contributes to superior commercial performance by enabling more disciplined investment management, combining predictive insights with digital measurement. Budget redistribution to more profitable segments, supported by predictive analytics, can increase conversions and ROI, reinforcing the efficiency of the marketing action portfolio (Egorenkov, 2024). In online environments, continuous measurement and experimentation enable targeted testing and near-instantaneous adjustments, which amplify optimization capabilities and reduce waste in digital campaigns (Figueiredo et al., 2024).

5.5 *Building Brand Awareness*

By enabling predictive analytics and personalization, AI simultaneously strengthens consumer engagement and builds a customer-centric, value-driven brand image (Ahmed et al., 2024a). Personalized campaigns supported by predictive data tend to increase the perceived relevance of communication and the quality of the experience, favouring a more positive, memorable brand image that is consistent with consumer expectations (Averineni et al., 2024). This effect is also explained by AI's analytical ability to identify trends and behavioural patterns, allowing for greater campaign impact and contributing to the brand's competitive positioning in the market (Almahairah, 2023).

In addition to communication effectiveness, AI can support brand awareness and recognition by enabling more "humanized" and tailored messages that generate empathy and closeness, which tends to reinforce brand affinity and recall (Bu et al., 2022). In this sense, proposals such as AI-animated brand characters have been pointed out as mechanisms to foster awareness and emotional connection, complementing personalization as a differentiation strategy (Chaturvedi et al., 2024). At the same time, the consolidation of relationships based on trust and commitment favours advocacy behaviours—by customers and also by sellers—amplifying notoriety and reputation through credible recommendations and social signals (Badrinarayanan & Ramachandran, 2024).

AI can contribute to brand value and consistency by strengthening brand protection and governance in the digital environment. AI techniques support brand and trademark management activities, such as brand research and monitoring, detection of potential infringements, content moderation, automated contract analysis, and monitoring of misuse in domains and visual media, enabling faster and more informed responses in the defence of critical intangible assets (Pires & Santos, 2023).

In turn, brand awareness and reputation should be understood as results partially mediated by digital dissemination dynamics. In online ecosystems, word of mouth—fuelled by both advocates and critics—multiplies the circulation of opinions and accelerates the formation of collective perceptions, which can amplify (or deteriorate) the visibility and meaning of the brand (Figueiredo et al., 2024). Thus, the gains obtained through personalization and experience can be intensified when converted into advocacy and public discussion, given their potential for network propagation (Badrinarayanan & Ramachandran, 2024).

6 Challenges and Ethical Considerations

The literature identifies a consistent set of challenges associated with the adoption of AI in CRM and relationship marketing, with an emphasis on data privacy, algorithmic biases, and increased demands for transparency and accountability (Bu et al., 2022). These aspects are often presented as conditions for preserving consumer trust, given that the collection, processing, and prediction of customer data—often sensitive—amplify the risks of misuse, discrimination, and opaque decisions (Achour & Ayadi, 2025; Almahairah, 2023; Averineni et al., 2024). In line with this concern, there is also a need to recognize methodological limitations and ethical implications when using simulated data or automated processing of sensitive information, emphasizing the importance of rigour, auditability, and prudence in the interpretation and application of results (Ahmed et al., 2024b).

In addition to technical and data governance risks, potential adverse effects on the company-consumer relationship are mentioned, including power imbalances, manipulation, and erosion of trust, which reinforces the centrality of transparency in

AI-mediated interactions (Badrinarayanan & Ramachandran, 2024). In the context of conversational agents, specific risks such as emotional dependence, bias, and privacy are added, requiring additional safeguards in the design and implementation of these solutions (Chaturvedi et al., 2024). Thus, there is a need for regulation and responsible practices, as well as standardized protocols, to balance business innovation and consumer protection, mitigating biases and reinforcing the legitimacy of AI applications (Bu et al., 2022; Chintalapati & Pandey, 2022).

Organizational adoption also faces internal constraints, such as skills gaps and resistance to change, making technical training and ethical capacity building critical components of implementation (Achour & Ayadi, 2025). In this perspective, the creation of governance strategies—combining skills development, operational standards, accountability, transparency, privacy, and other ethical principles—is presented as a requirement for sustainable AI adoption (Almahairah, 2023; Averineni et al., 2024; Chintalapati & Pandey, 2022).

7 Trends

The integration of AI into marketing and CRM has been framed by theoretical perspectives that explain both its adoption and the generation of competitive advantage. Innovation Diffusion and Resource-Based View (RBV) support the interpretation of AI as organizational innovation and as a strategic capability that improves efficiency and performance, while approaches such as Stakeholder Theory reinforce the need to articulate technology, strategy, and ethics to preserve legitimacy and trust (Achour & Ayadi, 2025). In terms of conceptual operationalization, models and frameworks have been proposed that guide personalized decisions and the application of AI throughout the customer journey, including the CRN model for personalized decisions (Cao & Zhu, 2022) and frameworks that integrate AI experience, functions, and services at touchpoints (Chen & Prentice, 2025).

There is also a trend in technological and organizational evolution towards more automated, predictive, and customer-centric CRM, supported by omnichannel architectures and increasingly "humanized" interactions. Averineni et al. (2024) highlight the adoption of strategic frameworks with an emphasis on scalability, ethics, and continuous adaptation, adding models that integrate human capabilities and artificial intelligence in a synergistic way, promoting more agile and consumer-oriented management practices (Almahairah, 2023). Along the same lines, trends related to omnichannel sales and marketing, the central role of trust in digital environments, and interorganizational dynamics such as coopetition stand out, suggesting a more interdependent and data-driven relational ecosystem (Badrinarayanan & Ramachandran, 2024; Bu et al., 2022).

In the analytical domain, there has been an intensification in the use of heterogeneous and unstructured data, as well as the combination of external sources (e.g., social networks) to increase predictive accuracy, including in metrics such as CLV. At the same time, a methodological concern has emerged regarding the trade-off between interpretability and performance, with frameworks being proposed that contrast linear, ensemble, and deep learning models according to the objectives and constraints of the context (Ahmed et al., 2024a). This movement is reinforced by trends such as deep learning applied to unstructured data, integration with IoT and Big Data, and the development of explainable AI (XAI), aiming at transparency and strengthening trust (Egorenkov, 2024).

These trajectories coexist with the rapid spread of conversational agents and generative models in consumption, which has led to proposals for capability matrices and application frameworks throughout the customer journey, as well as research agendas focused on the quality, functions, and ethics of AI in the customer experience (Chaturvedi et al., 2024; Chen & Prentice, 2025). At the thematic level, there is a growing predominance of experiential marketing, followed by integrated digital and operations, while content remains relatively underexplored, signalling opportunities for future research (Chintalapati & Pandey, 2022). In terms of adoption dynamics and impact, the literature suggests that benefits tend to appear incremental in the short term and potentially transformative in the long term, in line with Amara's law and readings associated with the hype cycle (Davenport et al., 2020), and continued investment and reconfiguration of the competitive environment is anticipated, penalizing organizations that do not adapt (Deb et al., 2018).

It should be added that the projected trends are accompanied by governance and risk mitigation requirements, given that algorithmic biases, privacy, and model opacity can compromise trust and performance. Thus, recommendations such as audits, data diversity, and explainability emerge as structural conditions for the sustainable evolution of AI in marketing and CRM (Egorenkov, 2024).

8 Conclusions

This chapter highlights the structuring role of artificial intelligence in the reconfiguration of contemporary relationship marketing. The analysis conducted demonstrates that AI transcends the role of mere technological support, consolidating itself as a strategic capability that allows organizations to operationalize relationship models based on data, personalization at scale, and behavioural prediction, with measurable impacts on customer experience, operational efficiency, and competitive performance.

The reviewed literature maintains that the integration of AI into relational marketing materializes through multiple applications—including content personalization, predictive analytics, advanced segmentation, customer lifetime value forecasting, process automation, and customer service optimization—which, together, support more informed, agile management geared towards creating mutual value between organizations and consumers. AI's ability to process large volumes of structured and unstructured data in real time, identify latent patterns, and anticipate future behaviours stands out, enabling contextual, relevant, and proactive interactions throughout the customer journey.

From a strategic perspective, the adoption of AI has been associated with tangible benefits, namely improved customer experience, increased satisfaction and loyalty, optimized sales funnel, and enhanced brand awareness. Empirical evidence reported in the literature indicates quantifiable gains that suggest that the effects of AI are not limited to operational efficiency gains but extend to relational and value perception dimensions. These results are supported by the ability of AI systems to personalize offers, predict needs, automate responses, and dynamically adjust strategies, promoting consistency, timeliness, and relevance in company-customer interactions.

It is also evident that the adoption of AI in relational contexts is not without challenges and critical implications. The literature highlights ethical and operational concerns related to privacy and data protection, algorithmic biases, opacity of decision-making processes, and risks of manipulation or power imbalances in consumer relations. These constraints require the development of robust governance frameworks that articulate principles of transparency, accountability, auditability, and protection of rights, as well as the creation of organizational competencies that enable the ethical and sustainable implementation of AI. The absence of adequate oversight mechanisms and ethical safeguards can undermine trust—a central element in relationship marketing—and consequently limit the effectiveness of AI-based strategies.

In addition, the literature review identifies emerging trends that point to a continuous evolution of AI capabilities and reach in relationship marketing. Among these, we highlight the growing sophistication of predictive models—using deep neural networks and advanced machine learning techniques—the integration of heterogeneous and unstructured data sources (including social and sensory data), the expansion of conversational agents and virtual assistants, and the development of explainable AI models that seek to mitigate opacity issues and reinforce trust. These trends suggest that the role of AI in relationship marketing is likely to intensify, expanding its domain of application and reconfiguring the processes of interaction, decision-making, and value co-creation between companies and customers.

In summary, artificial intelligence is shaping up to be a driver of transformation in relational marketing, enabling data-driven decisions, personalization at scale, behaviour prediction, and process automation, with positive impacts on experience, satisfaction, loyalty, and organizational performance. Nevertheless, fully realizing its potential requires a balanced approach that combines technological innovation, ethical responsibility, and skills development, ensuring that AI systems are implemented in a transparent, fair, and sustainable value-oriented manner. The future evolution of relationship marketing will be largely determined by the ability of organizations to strategically, ethically, and effectively integrate the emerging capabilities of artificial intelligence, consolidating deeper, more resilient, and mutually beneficial customer-company relationships in a constantly reconfiguring digital ecosystem.

References

Achour, S., & Ayadi, S. (2025). Artificial intelligence in marketing: A strategic tool for enhancing business growth. *JEFB, 10*(1), 985–1000.

Ahmed, M. P., Das, A. C., Akter, P., Mou, S. N., Tisha, S. A., Shakil, F., Das, P., Rahman, M. K., & Ahmed, A. (2024a). Harnessing machine learning models for accurate customer lifetime value prediction: A comparative study in modern business analytics. *Academic Research Library for International Journal of Computer Science & Information System, 9*(12), 06–22.

Ahmed, S. R., Alhashmi, L. Q., Hussein, A. J., Radhi, A. D., Radhi, A. A., Ahmed, M. R., Hussain, A. S. T., & Tawfeq, J. F. (2024b). Deep learning for customer relationship management in e-commerce. In *2024 international congress on human-computer interaction, optimization and robotic applications (HORA)* (pp. 1–7). IEEE.

Alghizzawi, M., Ahmed, E., Ezmigna, I., Ezmigna, A. A. R., & Omeish, F. (2024). The relationship between artificial intelligence and digital marketing in business companies. In *Studies in systems, decision and control* (p. 885). Springer International Publishing. https://doi.org/10.1007/978-3-031-54383-8_67

Almahairah, M. S. (2023). Artificial intelligence application for effective customer relationship management. In *2023 International Conference on Computer Communication and Informatics (ICCCI)* (pp. 1–7). IEEE.

Averineni, A., Vamsi, V. S., Manikanta, A. M., Reddy, A. R., & Reddy, K. D. S. (2024, March). Strategic integration of artificial intelligence in customer relationship management: A path to personalization. In *2024 2nd International Conference on Disruptive Technologies (ICDT)* (pp. 107–111). IEEE.

Badrinarayanan, V., & Ramachandran, I. (2024). Relational exchanges in the sales domain: A review and research agenda through the lens of commitment-trust theory of relationship marketing. *Journal of Business Research, 177*, Article 114644.

Bu, Y., Quach, S., & Thaichon, P. (2022). Artificial intelligence (AI)-empowered customer relationship management. In *Artificial intelligence for marketing management* (pp. 142–159). Routledge.

Cao, L., & Zhu, C. (2022). Personalized next-best action recommendation with multi-party interaction learning for automated decision-making. *PLoS One, 17*(1), Article e0263010.

Chaturvedi, R., Verma, S., & Srivastava, V. (2024). Empowering AI companions for enhanced relationship marketing. *California Management Review, 66*(2), 65–90.

Chen, Y., & Prentice, C. (2025). Integrating artificial intelligence and customer experience. *Australasian Marketing Journal, 33*(2), 141–153.

Cheng, C. F., Huang, C. C., Lin, M. C., & Chen, T. C. (2023). Exploring effectiveness of relationship marketing on artificial intelligence adopting intention. *SAGE Open, 13*(4), 21582440231222760.

Chintalapati, S., & Pandey, S. K. (2022). Artificial intelligence in marketing: A systematic literature review. *International Journal of Market Research, 64*(1), 38–68.

Davenport, T., Guha, A., Grewal, D., & Bressgott, T. (2020). How artificial intelligence will change the future of marketing. *Journal of the Academy of Marketing Science, 48*(1), 24–42.

Deb, S. K., Jain, R., & Deb, V. (2018, January). Artificial intelligence—creating automated insights for customer relationship management. In *2018 8th International Conference on Cloud Computing, Data Science & Engineering (Confluence)* (pp. 758–764). IEEE.

Egorenkov, D. (2024). AI-powered predictive customer lifetime value: Maximizing long-term profits. *International Journal of Scientific Research and Management (IJSRM), 12*(9), 7339. https://doi.org/10.18535/ijsrm/v12i09.em02

Figueiredo, J., Oliveira, I., Silva, S., Pocinho, M., Cardoso, A., & Pereira, M. (2024). Artificial intelligence in relational marketing practice: CRM as a loyalty strategy. In *The use of artificial intelligence in digital marketing: Competitive strategies and tactics* (pp. 73–96). IGI Global.

Gupta, A., & Sahu, G. P. (2012). A literature review and classification of relationship marketing research. *International Journal of Customer Relationship Marketing and Management, 3*(1), 56. IGI Global. https://doi.org/10.4018/ijcrmm.2012010104

Hossain, Q., Hossain, A., Nizum, M. Z., & Naser, S. B. (2024). Influence of artificial intelligence on customer relationship management (crm). *International Journal of Communication Networks and Information Security, 16*(3), 653–663.

Islam, M. A., Fakir, S. I., Masud, S. B., Hossen, M. D., Islam, M., & Siddiky, M. R. (2024). Artificial intelligence in digital marketing automation: Enhancing personalization, predictive analytics, and ethical integration. *Edelweiss Applied Science and Technology, 8*(6), 6498–6516. https://doi.org/10.55214/25768484.v8i6.3404

Kumar, V., Ashraf, A. R., & Nadeem, W. (2024). AI-powered marketing: What, where, and how? *International Journal of Information Management, 77*, Article 102783. https://doi.org/10.1016/j.ijinfomgt.2024.102783

Kumar, V., Rajan, B., Venkatesan, R., & Lecinski, J. (2019). Understanding the role of artificial intelligence in personalized engagement marketing. *California Management Review, 61*(4), 135. https://doi.org/10.1177/0008125619859317

Lakshmipriyanka, A., Harihararao, M., Prasanna, M., & Deepika, Y. (2023). A study on artificial intelligence in marketing. *International Journal for Multidisciplinary Research, 5*(3), 1–12. https://doi.org/10.36948/ijfmr.2023.v05i03.3789

Libai, B., Bart, Y., Gensler, S., Hofacker, C. F., Kaplan, A., Kötterheinrich, K., & Kroll, E. B. (2020). Brave new world? On AI and the management of customer relationships. *Journal of Interactive Marketing, 51*(1), 44–56. https://doi.org/10.1016/j.intmar.2020.04.002

Luthra, L., Sharma, S., Krishna, M. H., Limbore, N. V., & Sobti, R. (2024, May). Intelligent marketing: Using AI to segment and target customers. In *2024 International Conference on Communication, Computer Sciences and Engineering (IC3SE)* (pp. 1508–1513). IEEE. https://doi.org/10.1109/ic3se62002.2024.10593574

Naz, H., & Kashif, M. (2025). Artificial intelligence and predictive marketing: An ethical framework from managers' perspective. *Spanish Journal of Marketing-ESIC, 29*(1), 22–45. https://doi.org/10.1108/sjme-06-2023-0154

Nugroho, A. P., & Hati, S. R. H. (2020). Determinants of repurchase intention and switching intention: Analysis of online travel agent, peer-to-peer accommodation, and virtual hotel operator platforms. *Market-Tržište, 32*(1), 79–96. https://doi.org/10.22598/mt/2020.32.1.79

Olson, C. A., & Levy, J. (2017). Transforming marketing with artificial intelligence. *Applied Marketing Analytics, 3(*4), 291–297. https://doi.org/10.69554/ydwt3570

Pires, P. B., & Santos, J. D. (2023). Artificial intelligence and marketing - progressive or disruptive transformation?: A review of the literature. In Paulo Botelho Pires, José Duarte Santos, Inês Veiga Pereira and Ana Isabel Torres (Eds.), *Confronting security and privacy challenges in digital marketing* (pp. 95–118). IGI Global. https://doi.org/10.4018/978-1-6684-8958-1.ch005

Somashekhar, I., Hema, P., Prasad, H., Rakesh, D., Prakruthi, P., & Mahesh, K. S. (2024). Customer relationship management and artificial intelligence: Revolutionizing business-customer interactions. *Nanotechnology*, 752–776.

Tadimarri, A., Jangoan, S., Sharma, K. K., & Gurusamy, A. (2024). AI-powered marketing: Transforming consumer engagement and brand growth. *International Journal for Multidisciplinary Research, 6*(2), 1–11. https://doi.org/10.36948/ijfmr.2024.v06i02.14595

Vasconcelo, I. R., & Silva, F. R. (2022). A importância do marketing de relacionamento para construir uma fidelização com os clientes de uma clínica na cidade de Imperatriz- MA. *Revista de Psicologia, 16*(60), 682. https://doi.org/10.14295/idonline.v16i60.3452

Vlačić, B., Corbo, L., Silva, S. C. E., & Dabić, M. (2021). The evolving role of artificial intelligence in marketing: A review and research agenda. *Journal of Business Research, 128*, 187–203. https://doi.org/10.1016/j.jbusres.2021.01.055

Wilson, G., Johnson, O., & Brown, W. L. (2024). *The impact of artificial intelligence on customer relationship management*. https://doi.org/10.20944/preprints202408.0766.v1

Yau, K. A., Saad, N. M., & Chong, Y.-W. (2021). Artificial Intelligence Marketing (AIM) for enhancing customer relationships. *Applied Sciences, 11*(18), 8562. https://doi.org/10.3390/app11188562

Yulisetiarini, D. (2015). The effect of relationship marketing towards costumer satisfaction and customer loyalty on franchised retails in East Java. *Mediterranean Journal of Social Sciences, 7*(1), 333–339. https://doi.org/10.5901/mjss.2016.v7n1p333

The Use of Artificial Intelligence to Advance Green Marketing: Balancing Ethics and Technology

João Morais and Alexandra Leandro

Abstract In an era defined by climate crises, sustainability has evolved from an optional marketing add-on to a strategic imperative. Businesses face pressure from consumers, regulators, and investors to demonstrate authentic environmental and social commitments. Within this landscape, green marketing emerges as a critical lever to align corporate messaging, operations, and consumer engagement with sustainable development goals. Recent advancements in artificial intelligence (AI) add transformative potential to this evolution, enabling organizations to optimize green marketing practices through predictive analytics, personalization, generative content, and smart nudging. This chapter examines how AI can drive real progress in green marketing while acknowledging the ethical, organizational, and social risks that accompany its adoption. By integrating empirical findings, conceptual models, and systematic review insights, this chapter explores AI's role in customer segmentation, sustainable supply chain optimization, emotional storytelling, and the mitigation of greenwashing risks. The discussion highlights how trust, algorithmic transparency, and human oversight remain essential to realizing AI's sustainability promise. Practical implications include best practices for implementing AI ethically, governance frameworks, and recommendations aligned with the UN Sustainable Development Goals (SDGs). This chapter concludes that AI can indeed be a powerful enabler of sustainability in marketing, but only when adopted with a genuine commitment to authenticity, accountability, and multi-stakeholder collaboration.

J. Morais · A. Leandro (✉)
School of Education, CEOS.PP – Coimbra Extension, Polytechnic University of Coimbra, Coimbra, Portugal
e-mail: aleandro@esec.pt

J. Morais
e-mail: jmorais@esec.pt

J. D. Santos et al. (eds.), *Artificial Intelligence Transforming Marketing*, Contributions to Management Science, https://doi.org/10.1007/978-3-032-22360-9_7

1 Introduction

In an era of mounting environmental crises, intensifying regulatory frameworks, and rising consumer demands for corporate responsibility, the concept of sustainability has become a cornerstone of modern business strategy (Delmas & Burbano, 2011). Organizations today face mounting pressure to move beyond superficial sustainability claims and embed genuine environmental and social considerations throughout their operations. This transformation extends directly to marketing practices (Peattie & Belz, 2010). Once understood as "mere" green labels or recycled packaging, green marketing has evolved into a systemic approach that integrates environmental stewardship into product design, supply chain management, consumer engagement, and brand identity (Darban & Kabbaj, 2023). Over the past three decades, sustainability has evolved from a niche concern into a mainstream business priority, driven by scientific consensus on climate change, increasingly stringent regulatory frameworks, and shifting consumer expectations (Peattie & Belz, 2010; Kumar et al., 2025). Companies that fail to address environmental and social impacts risk reputational damage, regulatory penalties, and declining consumer trust. Indeed, green marketing has emerged as a key strategy to communicate sustainability values, influence consumer behavior, and differentiate brands in competitive markets (Gündüzyeli, 2024).

At the same time, the ongoing digital transformation is radically reshaping how marketing strategies are conceived and delivered. AI now sits at the center of this digital evolution, offering unprecedented capabilities for real-time data analysis, hyper-personalization, predictive trend forecasting, and smart automation (Patil, 2025). In fact, the digital revolution has overturned traditional marketing paradigms, empowering brands to reach consumers with unprecedented precision, speed, and interactivity (Kumar et al., 2024). Companies across sectors, from retail and tourism to logistics and services, are exploring how AI tools can streamline processes, reduce waste, and better align offerings with the values of sustainability-minded consumers. The intersection of AI and sustainability has attracted increasing scholarly attention. Early contributions highlight AI's promise for optimizing energy use, waste reduction, and supply chain logistics (Alsalhy et al., 2023), emphasizing its role in shaping consumer perceptions, amplifying authentic sustainability narratives, and supporting transparent, data-backed claims. For example, blockchain-enabled AI systems can empower consumers to verify carbon footprints or fair-trade certifications through QR codes embedded in product packaging (Darban & Kabbaj, 2023).

Recent studies emphasize that AI integration into sustainable marketing is not just technological but also strategic. For example, Emon and Khan (2025) highlight how AI-driven analytics and insights enhance marketing intelligence by improving customer engagement and environmental outcomes simultaneously. This integration requires careful governance, addressing ethical concerns such as algorithmic bias and data privacy to ensure alignment with sustainability goals (Emon & Khan, 2025).

However, this "hype" is not without paradoxes.

Critics caution that the same technologies that enable granular targeting and smart nudging can also be used unethically, manipulating consumers' cognitive biases or masking the true environmental costs of production (Zaharia et al., 2024). Algorithmic bias, data privacy breaches, and a lack of explainability in complex AI models threaten to erode the very trust that green marketing seeks to build (Tatavarthy et al., 2025; Zhang et al., 2025).

Emerging research points to nuanced consumer responses: while some segments welcome AI-enabled personalization, others, especially premium or value-driven consumers, may recoil from excessive automation, perceiving it as inauthentic or intrusive (Tatavarthy et al., 2025). Indeed, there is a need for balanced, human-AI hybrid approaches that preserve the relational dimension of sustainability messaging. While AI has the potential to drive significant efficiencies and deepen engagement, it also raises questions around algorithmic transparency, fairness, and data privacy. Moreover, there is growing concern that AI, if misused, can enable sophisticated forms of greenwashing, undermining consumer trust and threatening the credibility of sustainability efforts overall (Zaharia et al., 2024).

These dynamics have given rise to an emerging body of research examining the dual role of AI as both an enabler and a possible threat to sustainable marketing practices. Academia and industry are both debating how best to leverage AI's technical power while safeguarding human oversight, relational trust, and accountability. There is growing recognition that realizing AI's sustainability promise demands robust governance frameworks, clear industry standards, and the co-creation of ethical guidelines that balance innovation with transparency (Kumar et al., 2025; Sohaib et al., 2025).

Following this context, this chapter critically examines the transformative potential and limitations of AI in advancing green marketing. It asks: How can AI tools be applied responsibly to enhance sustainable business practices? What organizational and ethical barriers stand in the way of meaningful progress? And what best practices and theoretical frameworks can guide companies as they navigate this rapidly evolving intersection of technology and sustainability? To answer these questions, this chapter drawns on a diverse body of literature, including conceptual frameworks, empirical case studies, and systematic reviews (Kumar et al., 2025; Sohaib et al., 2025). This chapter is structured in such a way that Sect. 2 provides a literature review on green marketing's evolution, AI in marketing, and integration frameworks linking the two. Then, Sect. 3 outlines the theoretical approach used. Next, Sect. 4 presents the key findings and critical discussion of applications, impacts on trust, and barriers. In a more direct way to practitioners and researchers, Sect. 5 offers practical implications and recommendations. Section 6 focuses on governance issues and identified research gaps to be followed up. Conclusion comes in the end, with a call for multi-stakeholder collaboration to realize AI's sustainability promise.

2 Literature Review

AI has rapidly emerged as a transformative force in marketing, enabling companies to process and interpret vast quantities of data in real time. Core applications include advanced customer segmentation, personalized recommendations, predictive analytics for trend forecasting, and automation of routine marketing tasks. AI-powered chatbots and virtual assistants now play an integral role in providing round-the-clock customer support and improving the overall consumer experience (Kravets et al., 2025; Patil, 2025).

Personalization has become a powerful tool for engaging consumers with tailored messages that align with their values and behaviors. However, the same algorithms that allow companies to fine-tune their marketing campaigns also raise concerns about privacy, bias, and consumer manipulation. Trust is therefore a recurring theme in literature: while personalization can strengthen relationships when done transparently, it risks alienating consumers when perceived as intrusive or when it replaces valued human interaction (Tatavarthy et al., 2025; Zaharia et al, 2024).

Emerging technologies like generative AI and emotional AI add another dimension, allowing brands to craft dynamic content and adapt messaging in real time based on sentiment analysis (Aarzoo & Lal, 2024). While these innovations hold promises for creating compelling sustainability narratives, they also highlight the importance of ethical guidelines to ensure that such tools do not mislead or exploit consumers' emotional vulnerabilities.

2.1 Green Marketing: Concepts and Evolution

"Green marketing refers to all activities designed to generate and facilitate any exchanges intended to satisfy human needs or wants, such that the satisfaction of these needs and wants occurs with minimal detrimental impact on the natural environment" (Sohaib et al., 2025, p. 2), and has emerged as an academic and managerial discipline during the environmental movements of the 1970s and early 1980s, driven by a growing recognition that industrial growth could have irreversible ecological impacts (Peattie & Belz, 2010). Early definitions framed green marketing narrowly as the promotion of products with minimal environmental harm. Peattie's seminal work later expanded this, positioning green marketing as a strategic orientation encompassing eco-design, life-cycle thinking, sustainable logistics, and transparent stakeholder communication.

In the decades since, rising consumer awareness, international climate agreements, and stricter environmental regulations have pushed companies beyond symbolic green gestures toward more systemic sustainability integration (Kumar et al., 2025). Scholars differentiate between symbolic green marketing, superficial claims that often amount to greenwashing, and substantive green marketing, where environmental goals are embedded in core business models (Zaharia et al., 2024).

Recent frameworks stress that consumer trust is fragile and easily eroded by misleading claims. The reputational costs of greenwashing can be severe, as evidenced by high-profile cases in the fashion and fast-moving consumer goods sectors (Darban & Kabbaj, 2023). Consequently, brands increasingly adopt third-party certifications, transparent supply chain reporting, and blockchain-enabled traceability to substantiate claims (Sohaib et al., 2025).

Greenwashing, however, continues to create information asymmetrically and exposes consumers to deceptive practices (Delmas & Burbano, 2011), which undermines trust not only in individual firms but also in the broader green market. This erosion of credibility translates into reputational risks such as boycotts and declining loyalty, while also weakening the legitimacy of the sustainable sector and hindering the advancement of conscious consumption. Beyond avoiding symbolic or merely rhetorical "green" narratives, the integration of sustainability into marketing requires consistency between brand positioning, value proposition, and tangible socio-environmental commitments, so that marketing effectively fosters practices aligned with structural sustainability goals. In this perspective, consumption transcends transactional exchanges and acquires a civic and political dimension, in which individual choices reflect responsibility and critical awareness of social and environmental contexts (Prothero et al., 2010).Key drivers of this evolution include regulatory pressure (e.g., the European Green Deal), investor focus on ESG metrics, and the growing purchasing power of sustainability-minded Millennials and Gen Z consumers (Gündüzyeli, 2024). However, the literature also highlights gaps: substantive green marketing demands not only credible communication but also robust measurement of environmental impact and the ability to translate abstract goals into concrete consumer-facing actions (Peattie & Belz, 2010).

2.2 *Artificial Intelligence in Marketing*

AI has become integral to marketing strategies worldwide, enabling firms to manage unprecedented volumes of consumer data and automate decision-making at scale (Kumar et al., 2024). Early applications centered on machine learning for customer segmentation and predictive analytics. Today, natural-language processing, computer vision, and generative AI expand this toolkit, powering applications from chatbots and virtual assistants to dynamic content creation (Sohaib et al., 2025). For instance, Hemalatha (2023) demonstrates that AI-powered customer engagement tools such as recommendation engines, sentiment analysis, and chatbots significantly enhance customer experience. These tools allow firms to predict consumer behavior more accurately, deliver real-time, personalized interactions, and ultimately improve loyalty—all while aligning with green marketing goals when deployed responsibly (Hemalatha, 2023).

For example, predictive analytics allows marketers to forecast shifts in green consumption trends and tailor products accordingly (Alsalhy et al., 2023). Recommendation systems now match eco-conscious consumers with sustainable product options, creating alignment between values and purchasing behavior (Kumar et al., 2025). These systems are very popular in retail and streaming, for instance. In tourism, Yu and Meng (2025) describe how image generative AI can craft aspirational visuals that promote sustainable destinations, though they warn of risks such as idealized stereotypes that may misrepresent actual in-person experiences.

Automated chatbots and virtual agents deliver 24/7 service and scalable outreach but pose risks if not humanized effectively. Studies show that premium segments in hospitality and luxury goods, for instance, often reject purely automated interactions that lack a relational element. As Tatavarthy et al. (2025) highlight, "premium customers perceive chatbots as impersonal, reducing perceived service quality and threatening relational trust" (p.6). There is definitely a conundrum: while AI improves efficiency, trust and authenticity remain decisive for marketing success.

Critics further note that AI's dependence on massive datasets raises ethical concerns. Algorithmic biases can exclude minority groups or perpetuate stereotypes (Zhang et al., 2025). Data privacy breaches erode consumer trust, especially in the EU context where GDPR imposes strict requirements on data use transparency (Zaharia et al., 2024).

Despite these risks, industry reports highlight rapid adoption. From 2017 to 2021, AI-based marketing solutions more than doubled in sectors such as retail, tourism, and B2B commerce (Gündüzyeli, 2024). Rustholllkarhu et al. (2022) demonstrate that B2B firms can leverage AI-empowered tools to manage complex digital customer journeys. By supporting activities such as analyzing buying patterns, designing touchpoints, and guiding engagement, AI enables B2B marketers to create seamless and sustainable customer experiences across digital channels (Rustholllkarhu et al., 2022). Small and medium-sized enterprises (SMEs) are increasingly using affordable AI tools to personalize communications, optimize ad spending, and automate content production (Tulbure et al., 2024). Emotional AI, as tools that analyze sentiment and adapt messages in real time, is emerging in e-commerce to foster more empathetic and sustainable shopping experiences (Aarzoo & Lal, 2024).

2.3 *Integrating Artificial Intelligence and Sustainability*

The convergence of AI and sustainability goals offers businesses a powerful lever for advancing green marketing. AI's predictive capabilities can help companies forecast demand more accurately, reducing overproduction and minimizing waste. Smart supply chain tools can optimize logistics, improve energy efficiency, and facilitate circular economy practices by tracking materials throughout their life-cycle (Patil, 2025).

At the same time, AI-enabled marketing can promote sustainable consumer behaviors through smart nudging, gamification, and real-time feedback mechanisms. For example, digital prompts encouraging customers to choose low-emission shipping options or loyalty programs rewarding eco-friendly purchases illustrate how behavioral science and AI can combine to influence decision-making (Ganesh et al., 2024; Von Zahn et al., 2024).

But the integration of AI and sustainability is not without tension. One concern is the risk of "AI-enabled greenwashing," where sophisticated algorithms are used to craft compelling but misleading sustainability claims (Delmas & Burbano, 2011; Zaharia et al., 2024).

Another is the challenge of ensuring algorithmic fairness: biased training data can perpetuate existing inequalities, undermining broader social sustainability objectives (Gündüzyeli, 2024; Kaddour et al., 2025). The literature highlights a lack of standard frameworks for auditing and verifying the environmental claims generated through AI systems (Emon & Khan, 2025; Kumar et al., 2025).

In response to these challenges, researchers and industry bodies advocate for robust governance structures, explainable AI, and participatory design approaches that involve stakeholders early in the development process. There is also a recognized need for more empirical research that assesses the long-term impacts of AI-enabled green marketing, including how repeated exposure to personalization affects consumer trust and whether digital nudges lead to sustained behavior change. As von Zahn et al. (2024) state, "the increasing use of AI for sustainable behavioral interventions raises new ethical and methodological questions that require more empirical investigation" (p.10).

Integrating AI with sustainability-oriented marketing has become a focal point for researchers seeking to understand how digital intelligence can align business growth with climate goals. Kumar et al. (2025) propose the Theory–Context–Methodology (TCM) framework to bridge fragmented studies on AI-enabled green marketing. This model highlights that AI must be implemented with a clear sustainability objective, adapted to organizational and market contexts, and critically monitored for unintended consequences.

Gündüzyeli (2024) finds that AI-driven supply chain analytics can reduce resource waste and emissions by optimizing routes, predicting demand, and coordinating circular loops. In e-commerce, von Zahn et al. (2024) show that causal machine learning[1] can personalize digital "green nudges" at checkout, significantly reducing product returns, which in turn cuts carbon emissions associated with reverse logistics.

Some scholars highlight novel dimensions: semantic ecological analysis[2] aligns brand content with sustainability values by ensuring consistent, credible messaging across platforms (Ganesh et al., 2024). Emotional storytelling powered by generative AI can foster stronger consumer-brand ties by creating immersive narratives that make sustainability feel relevant and personal (Aarzoo & Lal, 2024). Others point

---

[1] Causal Machine Learning (CausalML) is an umbrella term for machine learning methods that formalize the data-generation process as a structural causal model (Kaddour et al., 2025).

[2] Or "semantic environmental" analysis is the study of the meanings of words, expressions, and constructions that pertain to climate, weather, and associated social phenomena (Bromhead & Levisen, 2022).

to "green gamification" (the use of gamified interactions to motivate eco-friendly behaviors) as an emerging area where AI can enhance engagement.

Inevitably, barriers remain. Small firms often lack technical expertise and financial resources to implement advanced AI systems (Tulbure et al., 2024). Algorithmic opacity makes it difficult for stakeholders to verify whether claimed efficiencies or carbon reductions are real (Zhang et al., 2025). This opacity can also fuel new forms of AI-enabled greenwashing, undermining consumer trust (Zaharia et al., 2024).

3 Theoretical Framework

This study's theoretical lens synthesizes concepts from sustainable marketing, technology adoption, and governance studies. At its core, it draws on Sustainable Marketing Theory, which builds on the triple bottom line concept—emphasizing that economic success must align with positive environmental and social outcomes. This perspective frames green marketing not as an isolated tactic but as a systemic approach that permeates all stages of value creation.

To understand how AI fits into this landscape, this chapter draws from technology adoption frameworks like the Technology–Organization–Environment (TOE) model, which posits that technological innovation success depends on organizational capabilities and external pressures. It also considers the Theory–Context–Methodology (TCM) framework, which highlights the importance of aligning AI tools with clear sustainability objectives and robust monitoring mechanisms.

Another key element is the inclusion of governance and trust as mediating factors. Theoretical contributions from critical marketing and digital ethics scholarship stress that transparency, explainability, and stakeholder participation are vital for ensuring that AI-driven solutions enhance consumer trust. The growing field of explainable AI (XAI) reflects this need by calling for algorithms that can be interpreted and scrutinized by non-technical stakeholders. Figure 1 summarizes this chapter's conceptual logic linking AI-enabled green marketing tools to sustainability outcomes through governance-related mediators.

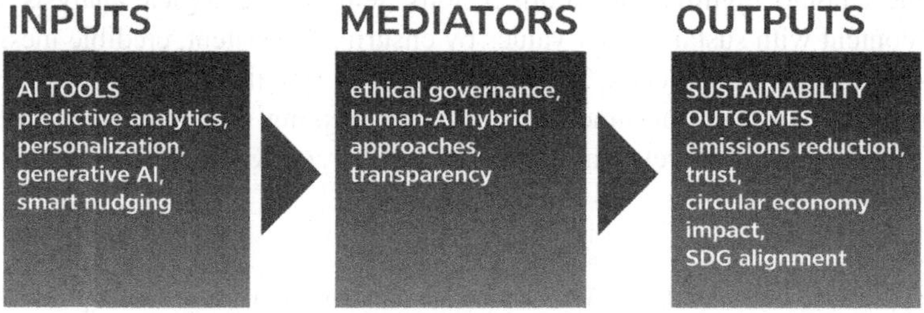

Fig. 1 Conceptual framework for responsible AI-enabled green marketing. *Source* Authors

Finally, this chapter adopts a Better Marketing for a Better World perspective, which recognizes that technological progress must serve broader societal and planetary well-being. This aligns with calls for multi-stakeholder collaboration and participatory co-design, ensuring that AI-enabled green marketing reflects diverse consumer values and cultural contexts. Together, this theoretical framework positions AI as a potentially transformative enabler of sustainability, but only when its use is grounded in rigorous governance, ethical oversight, and a clear commitment to creating real, measurable environmental value.

Research on AI's role in advancing green marketing is multi-disciplinary, drawing from sustainable marketing theory, technology adoption frameworks, and critical perspectives on digital ethics. To navigate this terrain, this chapter adopts a synthesis approach combining conceptual frameworks, empirical findings, and systematic review insights (Kumar et al., 2025).

At its core, the theoretical foundation aligns with Sustainable Marketing Theory, which builds on Peattie and Belz's (2010) work emphasizing the integration of environmental, social, and economic value: the triple bottom line (Elkington, 1994). This lens rejects symbolic gestures in favor of systemic changes that reduce ecological footprints and strengthen stakeholder trust (Zaharia et al., 2024).

The Technology–Organization–Environment (TOE) Framework and the TCM Model (Kumar et al., 2025) provide structure for understanding how AI adoption in marketing depends on internal capabilities, industry norms, and external pressures. For example, firms with high digital maturity and clear sustainability KPIs are more likely to align AI implementation with real environmental outcomes.

Emerging models highlight pressures that must be navigated for AI to genuinely advance green marketing initiatives:

- Efficiency vs. Authenticity: While AI undeniably enhances operational efficiency and scalability—from content automation to predictive analytics—it can erode perceived human authenticity, especially among premium or loyal customer segments who expect bespoke, humanized interactions (Tatavarthy et al., 2025). For instance, studies show high-tier customers may feel entitled to personalized service and react negatively to AI-driven touchpoints, demanding careful balancing between automation gains and authentic human engagement.
- Transparency vs. Complexity: AI-enabled marketing models, particularly those relying on black-box algorithms and large-scale data processing, often lack transparency. As Zhang et al. (2025) note in the context of live-streaming e-commerce, opaque AI systems complicate risk management and consumer trust by making it harder to verify the authenticity of sustainability claims. This tension necessitates robust explainability frameworks and clearer disclosure to align AI-driven messaging with genuine green commitments.
- Scalability vs. Context-Sensitivity: Universal AI solutions can fail to account for nuanced local contexts, cultural differences, and market-specific sustainability priorities. Tulbure et al. (2024) highlight that for SMEs, especially in diverse regions like Romania, the adoption of AI in content development brings clear productivity gains but also challenges related to cost, learning curves, and the

need for localized relevance. A one-size-fits-all AI model risks producing generic sustainability messaging that undermines the authenticity of green marketing.

These conflicts illustrate that the integration of AI into green marketing is not merely a technological upgrade but a socio-technical transformation that demands careful governance, ethical design, and adaptive strategies to safeguard trust, relevance, and sustainability impact.

4 Key Findings

The integration of artificial intelligence into green marketing practices is yielding advances across multiple dimensions. One of the most widely adopted applications is advanced predictive analytics, which helps companies create differentiated consumer segments based on environmental attitudes, behaviors, and purchase histories (Sohaib et al., 2025). This allows marketers to tailor sustainability messages and product recommendations to specific micro-segments, enhancing relevance and overcoming the limitations of generic campaigns. For instance, e-commerce platforms can identify frequent purchasers of organic or eco-labeled products and reward them with loyalty incentives that emphasize verified environmental benefits. While this level of personalization can improve conversion rates, it also introduces concerns about privacy and manipulation, underscoring the importance of transparent consent and clear opt-out options (Tatavarthy et al., 2025).

Beyond conventional segmentation, AI's ability to analyze vast amounts of unstructured data, including social media, search trends, and real-time feedback, enables companies to detect emerging sustainability preferences early (Alsalhy et al., 2023). In the fashion industry, for example, brands use AI to identify growing demand for biodegradable fabrics and circular design models, aligning production with eco-conscious consumer values. In tourism, Yu and Meng (2025) illustrate how AI-generated images can showcase low-impact destinations, allowing firms to test interest before significant investments. Yet as von Zahn et al. (2024) note, these tools require robust verification mechanisms to avoid superficial "green hype" that lacks measurable environmental impact: "the increasing use of AI for sustainable behavioral interventions raises new ethical and methodological questions that require more empirical investigation" (p.10).

In supply chain contexts, AI plays an important role in emissions reduction. Gündüzyeli (2024) demonstrates how machine learning algorithms improve demand forecasting and route optimization, cutting overproduction and fuel consumption. Von Zahn et al. (2024) show that causal learning combined with digital tracking can reduce product returns in e-commerce, thereby lowering carbon emissions from reverse logistics. In manufacturing, predictive maintenance powered by AI extends the lifespan of machinery, further minimizing waste. However, these gains come with caveats: efficiency improvements can produce rebound effects[3] if increased productivity drives higher consumption unless coupled with clear sustainability safeguards (Zhang et al., 2025).

AI-enabled "green nudging" is another promising practice. Smart prompts at checkout can encourage customers to choose low-emission shipping or eco-friendly packaging (von Zahn et al., 2024). Gamification techniques, such as rewarding households for meeting carbon reduction targets or offering points for sustainable purchases, illustrate how behavioral science and AI can combine to influence consumer behavior (Ganesh et al., 2024). Yet scholars warn that these strategies must be designed carefully to avoid "dark nudges" that manipulate consumers or promote superficial actions without real impact (Zaharia et al., 2024).

Emotional AI and semantic analysis emerge as powerful storytelling tools. Generative models can craft dynamic sustainability narratives, adapting messages in real time to resonate with different consumer mindsets (Aarzoo & Lal, 2024). This can help brands communicate complex climate goals more personally, increasing consumer engagement. However, overly stylized or idealized representations—such as AI-generated visuals of pristine ecotourism sites—can backfire if perceived as manipulative or inauthentic (Yu & Meng, 2025). Studies emphasize the need for clear editorial guidelines and human checkpoints to ensure emotional AI supports trust rather than undermines it (Ganesh et al., 2024).

One consistent insight across the literature is that algorithmic opacity remains a significant barrier to trust. Consumers often struggle to understand how AI-driven recommendations, nudges, or sustainability scores are produced (Zhang et al., 2025). As Sohaib et al. (2025) point out, "while AI-driven tools can increase consumers' perceived transparency, excessive personalization and algorithmic opacity may simultaneously undermine trust and weaken green purchase intentions" (p. 8). These trust dynamics vary across segments: Tatavarthy et al. (2025) found that premium customers in luxury and hospitality contexts prefer humanized interactions and may react negatively to purely automated touchpoints. Similarly, Xia and Shannon (2025) suggest that hybrid models—in which AI complements, rather than replaces, human contact—are more effective in preserving relational trust.

This pattern extends to influencer marketing and social media campaigns. Zaharia et al. (2024) show that AI-generated endorsements can boost reach and engagement but risk damaging authenticity if followers perceive interactions as artificial rather than genuine. As emotional AI becomes more sophisticated, this tension between efficiency and authenticity will demand clear boundaries for automated content.

Finally, the literature highlights organizational barriers to responsible AI adoption. Tulbure et al. (2024) emphasize that SMEs often lack technical expertise and financial resources to implement advanced AI systems, creating gaps between large firms and smaller market players. Even in digitally mature firms, limited AI literacy among

[3] Cambridge Dictionary defines "rebound effect" as "a situation in which new technologies or developments do not become as effective as they might be in allocating resources (= making sure that people use things well) because people change their behaviour to take advantage of new opportunities provided by the technology or development." Retrieved from: https://dictionary.cambridge.org/dictionary/english/rebound-effect on 19 September 2025.

marketing teams can lead to unintended bias or ineffective safeguards against greenwashing (Zhang et al., 2025). Governance frameworks remain underdeveloped, with industry bodies and policymakers calling for standardized impact audits, algorithmic bias testing, and explainability requirements (Darban & Kabbaj, 2023).

In summary, the key findings point to significant opportunities for AI to advance green marketing by improving segmentation, supply chain optimization, and personalized engagement. Yet these advances hinge on robust governance, transparent data practices, and hybrid models that maintain the relational trust essential for credible sustainability communication (Sohaib et al., 2025; Zaharia et al., 2024). Without these safeguards, AI risks reinforcing the very greenwashing and consumer skepticism that sustainability marketing seeks to overcome.

Focus: Sectoral Variations and Emerging Use Cases

The literature also highlights important sectoral differences in how AI supports sustainable marketing. In tourism, for instance, AI tools are being used not only for sentiment analysis but to co-create immersive, sustainability-focused experiences in the metaverse (Yu & Meng, 2025). This offers novel pathways for encouraging pro-environmental behavior before consumers make physical travel decisions. However, such digital storytelling must be carefully curated to avoid reinforcing exoticized or idealized images that misrepresent destinations.

In the fashion sector, predictive analytics and generative design tools help brands adapt collections in line with consumer demand for circular fashion models, such as second-hand or upcycled garments (Alsalhy et al., 2023). However, Gündüzyeli (2024) notes that without transparent life-cycle data and third-party certification, these innovations may inadvertently fuel rebound effects, with increased consumption offsetting sustainability gains.

These sectoral insights underscore that while AI provides powerful tools for aligning products and messaging with sustainability goals, its real impact depends on context-sensitive implementation, robust data governance, and credible third-party verification (Darban & Kabbaj, 2023). They also reveal opportunities for cross-sector learning: for example, blockchain-enabled traceability, already common in high-value food supply chains, could be adapted to fashion and tourism to verify carbon footprints and fair labor practices (Zhang et al., 2025). This reinforces this chapter's broader finding that AI's contribution to sustainability is shaped not only by technical innovation but by sector-specific dynamics, stakeholder trust, and clear governance frameworks.

5 Implications and Practical Guidelines

The combination of recent literature makes clear that simply adopting advanced AI tools does not guarantee meaningful sustainability outcomes (Gündüzyeli, 2024). Managers must ensure that AI systems are implemented thoughtfully, with human oversight, data governance, and measurable sustainability objectives (Kumar et al., 2025). As Kumar et al. (2025) underscore, "firms must ensure that the implementation of AI for sustainability is guided by robust governance frameworks, transparent data practices, and continuous human oversight to avoid unintended negative consequences" (p. 12). Efficiency gains alone are insufficient if they do not translate into verifiable environmental benefits (von Zahn et al., 2024).

To ensure that AI genuinely contributes to sustainability goals rather than undermining them through unintended consequences or superficial green claims, organizations should adopt a multi-layered approach rooted in the best practices identified across recent studies (Kumar et al., 2025; Zaharia et al., 2024).

5.1 Balance Automation with Human Interaction

Hybrid human–AI models remain essential for preserving trust in green marketing. Research consistently shows that while chatbots, recommendation systems, and predictive tools deliver operational efficiencies, they should complement rather than replace human interactions, especially in trust-sensitive or premium segments (Tatavarthy et al., 2025). Xia and Shannon (2025) emphasize that consumers value relational authenticity, which means organizations should map customer journeys to identify touchpoints where human empathy and ethical judgment add value. This balance helps prevent alienation and supports deeper stakeholder relationships.

5.2 Design for Transparency and Explainability

Explainable AI (XAI) is a cornerstone of responsible AI-enabled sustainability. Zhang et al. (2025) argue that marketing algorithms should produce interpretable outputs that help consumers understand how sustainability scores, recommendations, or digital nudges are derived. Blockchain-based traceability tools can further reinforce credibility by providing tamper-proof records of product life-cycles, carbon footprints, or fair-trade certifications (Darban & Kabbaj, 2023). Sohaib et al. (2025) caution that transparency should extend beyond compliance; it must be embedded into data collection, model training, and consumer-facing communications to reduce skepticism and prevent AI-enabled greenwashing.

5.3 Use Emotional and Semantic AI Responsibly

Tools like emotional AI and semantic ecological analysis allow marketers to craft compelling narratives that connect consumers with sustainability values (Ganesh et al., 2024). For example, generative AI can adapt messages in real time based on sentiment analysis, increasing engagement. However, overly stylized or idealized content, such as AI-generated visuals of pristine tourism sites can undermine credibility if perceived as manipulative (Yu & Meng, 2025). Clear editorial guidelines, human oversight, and ethical storytelling principles are essential to prevent exploitation of consumers' cognitive or emotional biases.

5.4 Leverage Gamification to Encourage Sustainable Behaviors

Gamification is a practical tool for transforming passive awareness into active engagement. Energy providers can reward households for meeting carbon reduction targets, while retailers can use points systems or digital challenges to nudge consumers toward greener choices (Ganesh et al., 2024). Von Zahn et al. (2024) highlight that well-designed nudges can significantly reduce product returns, cutting emissions from reverse logistics. However, these mechanisms must be designed to promote long-term behavioral change, not just short-term clicks or sales.

5.5 Democratize AI Access for SMEs

The resource gap that prevents many SMEs from adopting advanced AI systems risks deepening sustainability divides. Tulbure et al. (2024) argue that policymakers and industry associations should invest in shared data platforms, affordable AI-as-a-service tools, and training programs to help smaller firms integrate AI responsibly. This approach aligns with calls to make the benefits of AI-enabled green marketing more inclusive (Kumar et al., 2025).

5.6 Establish Robust Governance and Industry Standards

Governance remains the bedrock of credible AI-enabled sustainability. Zaharia et al. (2024) stress that industry bodies should develop clear cross-sector standards to define what qualifies as legitimate AI-driven sustainability claims. Such frameworks should mandate third-party audits of AI outputs, algorithmic bias testing, and environmental impact verification (Darban & Kabbaj, 2023). Certification schemes could even include AI explainability statements alongside traditional eco-labels, clarifying how carbon data or product footprints are calculated (Zhang et al., 2025). Stakeholder co-creation can make governance meaningful in practice. Involving consumers, community organizations, and regulators early in the design of AI tools ensures that these systems align with cultural contexts, digital literacy levels, and privacy expectations (Sohaib et al., 2025). Von Zahn et al. (2024) demonstrate how participatory design can prevent digital nudges from backfiring by ensuring they feel supportive rather than intrusive.

5.7 *Align AI with Measurable Sustainability KPIs*

First, AI projects must be anchored in clear, measurable sustainability objectives, such as carbon footprint reduction or waste minimization, and these should be systematically tracked using robust life-cycle assessment tools (Darban & Kabbaj, 2023; Gündüzyeli, 2024). Companies should avoid deploying AI solely for efficiency gains without verifying whether those gains translate into real environmental benefits. For example, predictive analytics that reduce product returns can cut associated emissions, but only if the metrics are transparent and verifiable (von Zahn et al., 2024).

5.8 *Expand AI Literacy and Build an Ethics-First Culture*

A recurring barrier is the lack of internal AI literacy, which can lead to blind spots around bias or unfair outcomes (Zhang et al., 2025). Companies should invest in regular training for marketing teams, data scientists, and senior managers to build awareness of ethical pitfalls, algorithmic explainability, and governance mechanisms (Sohaib et al., 2025). Clear internal guidelines can help teams recognize early signs of AI-enabled greenwashing, ensuring that sustainability claims remain credible (Darban & Kabbaj, 2023).

5.9 *Operationalize Transparency at Every Stage*

Beyond regulatory compliance, transparency should be built into data collection, model training, and communication practices. For example, AI-generated sustainability scores or product impact labels should be accompanied by explainable AI outputs that consumers can easily interpret (Zaharia et al., 2024; Zhang et al., 2025). Blockchain-enabled traceability can further reinforce confidence by allowing third parties to audit sustainability data in real time (Darban & Kabbaj, 2023).

5.10 Design Inclusive, Participatory AI Campaigns

In line with the Better Marketing for a Better World perspective (von Zahn et al., 2024), companies should co-create AI-driven green marketing strategies with stakeholders, including consumers, community groups, and advocacy organizations. This ensures that digital nudges, gamified incentives, or generative AI content align with local cultural contexts and avoid unintended manipulative effects (Yu & Meng, 2025). Participatory design can be particularly useful in emerging markets, where digital literacy varies widely (Tatavarthy et al., 2025).

5.11 Align AI Strategies with Global Sustainability Goals

Integrating AI-enabled marketing practices with the United Nations Sustainable Development Goals (SDGs) provides a shared language for accountability (Kumar et al., 2025). For example, using AI to optimize supply chains supports SDG 12 (Responsible Consumption and Production) and SDG 13 (Climate Action); democratizing AI access for SMEs aligns with SDG 8 (Decent Work and Economic Growth) and SDG 9 (Industry, Innovation and Infrastructure); and ethical AI governance and stakeholder partnerships reflect SDG 16 (Peace, Justice and Strong Institutions) and SDG 17 (Partnerships for the Goals), as summarized in Table 1.

Kravets et al. (2025) provide practical evidence that AI-enabled digital marketing ecosystems strengthen companies' adaptability to changing consumer behavior. By combining big data, predictive models, and real-time customer interaction tools, these ecosystems can optimize marketing campaigns, reduce waste, and align communication strategies with sustainability metrics. This operational agility is vital for accelerating progress toward SDG-related targets (Kravets et al., 2025).

Additionally, as Arantes and Costa (2025, p. 240) state, "integrating artificial intelligence (AI) with sustainable marketing practices marks a revolutionary stride toward addressing global challenges such as climate change, social inequality, and sustainable economic growth. This synergy (…) promise[s] to make companies more

Table 1 AI strategies in Marketing and the UN SDGs

Focus area	Best practice	Linked SDGs
Responsible Consumption	Use of AI to reduce waste and carbon emissions in supply chains	SDG 12 and 13
Inclusive Innovation	Democratize AI access for SMEs	SDG 8 and 9
Ethical Communication	Implement explainable AI for transparent sustainability claims	SDG 16
Multi-stakeholder Partnership	Involve communities in participatory AI design	SDG 17

Source Authors

agile, significantly aligned with the United Nations' Sustainable Development Goals (SDGs), and responsive to the dynamic market environment."

In summary, these practical implications emphasize that the promise of AI-enabled green marketing depends not on technology alone, but on how it is governed, explained, and embedded within authentic sustainability commitments. Indeed, responsible AI use in green marketing requires that businesses move beyond "green tech" hype to a practice anchored in clear environmental impact, stakeholder trust, and continuous learning. By aligning technological innovation with ethical design, human oversight, and participatory governance, companies can avoid the pitfalls of AI-enabled greenwashing and instead position AI as a credible catalyst for real sustainability transformation (Gündüzyeli, 2024; Sohaib et al., 2025).

Organizations must resist the lure of superficial AI applications that risk greenwashing and instead invest in approaches that balance innovation with accountability, relational trust, and measurable environmental impact.

6 Governance and Future Research Directions

The promise of AI as an enabler of green marketing does not operate in a regulatory vacuum. Recent years have seen the rapid evolution of legal frameworks that directly shape how organizations can deploy AI tools for sustainability communications and personalized engagement. At the forefront is the European Union's Artificial Intelligence Act (Regulation (EU) 2024/1689), which entered into force in 2024 and establishes the world's first comprehensive AI regulatory framework (European Union, 2024).

Under the EU AI Act, AI systems used in marketing could fall under "high-risk" categories if they influence consumer behavior in ways that significantly affect fundamental rights, such as privacy or freedom of choice. Von Zahn et al. (2024) point out that AI-driven personalization, nudging, or automated environmental claims could trigger enhanced compliance obligations, including robust transparency measures, algorithmic explainability, and human oversight. Failure to comply could expose organizations to substantial penalties.

Alongside the AI Act, the General Data Protection Regulation (GDPR) remains a cornerstone of data governance within the EU. The GDPR's emphasis on explicit consent, data minimization, and the right to explanation (Article 22) means that AI-powered profiling for green marketing must be carefully designed to respect individual privacy (Zhang et al., 2025). Sohaib et al. (2025) observe that many companies lack sufficient AI literacy to interpret how GDPR obligations intersect with machine learning systems that continuously adjust recommendations in real time. This gap increases the risk of unintentional non-compliance.

Beyond Europe, similar developments are unfolding globally. The OECD AI Principles and the G7 Hiroshima AI Process both advocate for explainability, fairness, and human-centered design in AI operation (OECD, 2022). Countries such as Canada, Japan, and Australia are developing national AI frameworks that stress the need for risk-based oversight, sector-specific codes of conduct, and industry standards for algorithmic bias detection. These evolving regimes are increasingly relevant for multinational firms whose marketing campaigns cross jurisdictions.

Specific to sustainability claims, there is also growing attention to greenwashing litigation and advertising standards. The EU's Green Claims Directive (European Commission, 2023) will require companies to substantiate environmental marketing statements with verifiable evidence and could explicitly extend this standard to AI-generated claims. Zaharia et al. (2024) warn that as AI tools enable increasingly sophisticated storytelling—for example, dynamically generated eco-labels or personalized carbon impact statements—the line between legitimate claims and deceptive marketing may blur. Clear legal definitions of acceptable AI-enabled sustainability representations will be critical to prevent consumer deception and maintain trust.

Some countries are already tightening oversight. For example, the United Kingdom's Competition and Markets Authority (CMA) has launched sector-specific investigations into misleading sustainability claims amplified by AI-powered marketing systems (Zhang et al., 2025). Similarly, the United States Federal Trade Commission (FTC) recently signaled that algorithmic transparency and disclosure requirements will extend to digital marketing contexts where AI shapes environmental messaging (Anning-Dorson et al., 2025).

For practitioners, these overlapping frameworks mean that governance must account for both technological and legal dimensions. Darban and Kabbaj (2023) recommend that firms conduct regular algorithmic audits that not only test for bias but also verify that AI-generated sustainability content aligns with evolving advertising laws. Third-party certification bodies could play a critical role by developing audit standards that address explainability, data privacy compliance, and environmental impact verification simultaneously (Zaharia et al., 2024).

Policymakers, meanwhile, face the challenge of designing adaptive regulatory approaches that balance innovation with consumer protection. Sohaib et al. (2025) argue that sandbox initiatives—where AI-enabled green marketing tools are tested in controlled environments under regulatory supervision—could provide valuable insights into best practices and potential pitfalls. Cross-sector collaboration among industry associations, regulators, civil society groups, and academic researchers will be vital for developing policy frameworks that are both robust and flexible enough to keep pace with technological evolution.

The emerging legal landscape reinforces this chapter's core argument that AI's sustainability promises hinges on transparency, accountability, and credible verification. Without rigorous regulatory guardrails and clear industry standards, the risk of AI-enabled greenwashing remains high, threatening consumer trust and undermining the transition to more sustainable markets.

Despite significant advances, the integration of AI into green marketing remains constrained by persistent governance gaps, empirical blind spots, and practical barriers. The literature highlights that robust, standardized frameworks for auditing AI sustainability claims are still underdeveloped (Darban & Kabbaj, 2023). Calls for explainable AI (XAI), algorithmic fairness testing, and independent third-party verification are becoming more vocal, yet implementation often lags industry rhetoric (Zaharia et al., 2024; Zhang et al., 2025).

Clear governance structures are essential for ensuring that AI-driven sustainability narratives do not become a new channel for sophisticated greenwashing. Scholars stress that certification labels could evolve to include explainability statements, just as eco-labels verify environmental performance (Zaharia et al., 2024). Blockchain-enabled traceability can further reinforce transparency by allowing consumers to track carbon footprints, fair-trade compliance, and life-cycle impacts in real time (Darban & Kabbaj, 2023). However, governance must go beyond technological fixes. Participatory co-design approaches that involve consumers, civil society, and regulators early in development can help align AI tools with diverse cultural norms and privacy expectations (Sohaib et al., 2025). Von Zahn et al. (2024) demonstrate that without local contextualization, AI nudges risk appearing intrusive or manipulative, undermining trust.

Alongside governance, the literature identifies clear directions for future research. First, there is a need for longitudinal studies on trust. While recent work shows that explainable, human–AI hybrid models can strengthen consumer trust (Sohaib et al., 2025; Tatavarthy et al., 2025), few studies track how trust evolves across repeated AI interactions. Future research should examine whether repeated personalization or nudging fosters deeper brand loyalty or, conversely, increases skepticism about data use. Comparative studies could assess these dynamics across product cycles, campaigns, or multi-year periods to reveal the conditions under which AI sustains, erodes, or reconfigures consumer trust in sustainability claims (Zaharia et al., 2024).

Second, more work is needed on cultural contexts and digital literacy. The global reach of AI-enabled green marketing raises questions about how personalization and smart incentives are perceived across different markets. Tatavarthy et al. (2025) show that what feels supportive in one context can seem intrusive in another, especially in regions with lower levels of trust in digital tools. Cross-cultural studies could explore how institutional trust, privacy norms, and environmental awareness modulate the effectiveness of AI-driven sustainability campaigns.

Third, future research should address the democratization of AI for SMEs, particularly in emerging economies. Tulbure et al. (2024) emphasize that smaller firms often lack the financial and technical resources needed for advanced AI adoption. Studies could investigate practical pathways to close this gap—such as shared data platforms, sectoral AI hubs, or publicly funded training programs—ensuring that the benefits of AI-enabled green marketing do not accrue solely to large, well-resourced corporations (Kumar et al., 2025). Rathore (2018) suggests that future green marketing could extend into the metaverse, where AI, immersive technologies, and virtual economies interact to promote sustainability. This emergent perspective invites scholars to examine how AI's predictive and behavioral analytics may shape green consumer practices within digital worlds, opening a new frontier for sustainable marketing research (Rathore, 2018).

6.1 Emerging Technologies and Future Research Opportunities

While current research emphasizes predictive analytics, recommender systems, and personalization, emerging technologies such as the metaverse, synthetic influencers, and digital product passports are likely to shape the next frontier of AI-enabled green marketing (Yu & Meng, 2025). These innovations raise new questions about how brands can craft sustainability narratives that resonate with consumers while maintaining transparency and trust.

For example, virtual worlds and immersive experiences in the metaverse could allow brands to demonstrate sustainability initiatives interactively—letting consumers explore supply chains or regenerative practices in real time (Kamyabi et al., 2025). Early experiments show potential for stronger emotional connections to sustainability goals, but they also risk amplifying digital greenwashing if virtual claims are not grounded in verifiable environmental impacts (Zaharia et al., 2024).

The rise of synthetic influencers (AI-generated personas that promote products or causes) adds another layer of complexity. These virtual agents can deliver hyper-personalized sustainability messages 24/7 across social media channels, but they blur the line between authentic advocacy and algorithmically driven persuasion (Tatavarthy et al., 2025). Future research could investigate how consumers perceive the credibility of synthetic influencers compared to human ambassadors, and whether they deepen or erode trust in sustainability claims.

Another area requiring empirical study is the impact of digital product passports—blockchain-enabled records that store information about a product's origin, materials, carbon footprint, and circularity potential (Darban & Kabbaj, 2023). While technology promises transparency and traceability, little is known about how consumers interpret these data points at scale or whether they influence purchasing behavior in meaningful ways (Sohaib et al., 2025). Comparative research could explore how product passports function across sectors such as fashion, FMCG, and consumer electronics.

All in all, these emerging tools highlight the need for ongoing interdisciplinary research that integrates insights from marketing, data science, behavioral psychology, and policy studies. Future work should also examine the unintended consequences of these innovations, including new forms of greenwashing or consumer fatigue, ensuring that technological advances support authentic sustainability transitions.

Finally, there is scope for deeper empirical examination of novel AI modalities like generative AI, metaverse experiences, and smart green incentives. Yu and Meng (2025) and von Zahn et al. (2024) show that these tools can immerse consumers in emotionally resonant sustainability narratives. Yet questions remain about whether such interventions translate into measurable changes in purchasing behavior or lifestyle choices. Experimental research, case studies, and sector-specific pilot projects could illuminate when and how these emerging technologies produce genuine environmental value (Gündüzyeli, 2024).

Academia thus agrees that realizing AI's sustainability promise requires moving beyond a technology-for-technology's-sake mindset. It demands rigorous governance, robust stakeholder oversight, and empirical evidence that demonstrates real, verifiable impact.

Policy Recommendations

To ensure AI genuinely supports green marketing goals, recent studies propose actionable policy measures. First, regulatory bodies should develop clear guidelines for AI explainability in sustainability claims, aligning with emerging legal frameworks like the EU AI Act (Zaharia et al., 2024). Second, public funding and tax incentives could help SMEs invest in modular, affordable AI solutions that include built-in sustainability metrics (Tulbure et al., 2024). Third, mandatory independent audits of AI-generated sustainability data, similar to financial audits, could reduce the risk of algorithmic greenwashing (Darban & Kabbaj, 2023). Finally, multi-stakeholder councils should co-create sector-specific standards for acceptable AI use in marketing—balancing innovation with transparency and privacy safeguards (Sohaib et al., 2025). Such measures align with international frameworks like the UN Sustainable Development Goals and ensure that AI-enabled marketing remains accountable to both regulators and the communities it serves.

7 Conclusions

This chapter has critically examined how artificial intelligence can advance green marketing while balancing the ethical, organizational, and trust-related challenges that arise at this intersection. The findings show that AI's transformative capabilities—predictive analytics, personalization, generative storytelling, and supply chain optimization—can meaningfully support sustainability objectives when integrated with clear governance and robust human oversight (Kumar et al., 2025; Sohaib et al., 2025).

However, the same algorithms that enable greater efficiency and engagement can also perpetuate bias, threaten privacy, and enable sophisticated greenwashing (Zaharia et al., 2024). Consumers' trust remains fragile, especially when AI-driven personalization feels intrusive or manipulative (Tatavarthy et al., 2025). These tensions underscore that technology alone cannot ensure authentic sustainability outcomes.

The practical implications outlined in this chapter emphasize the need for hybrid human–AI models, explainable algorithms, participatory co-design, and industry-wide standards that link AI adoption with measurable environmental and social value (Darban & Kabbaj, 2023; Zhang et al., 2025). Aligning these practices with the UN

Sustainable Development Goals provides organizations with a shared framework for accountability (Kumar et al., 2025).

Ultimately, AI holds the potential to become a powerful enabler of more credible, impactful green marketing—but only when guided by principles of transparency, fairness, and collaboration among multiple stakeholders. Managers, policymakers, and researchers must work together to ensure that the use of AI in marketing does not undermine trust or authenticity but contributes meaningfully to the collective transition toward a sustainable and equitable future.

Acknowledgements The authors would like to thank Pedro Alexandre Teixeira for the graphic design for Fig. 1.

References

Aarzoo, A., & Lal, R. (Prof., Dr.). (2024). Artificial Intelligence-Driven Emotional Storytelling for Brand Narrative Strategies and Consumer Perception. *SSRN Electronic Journal*. https://doi.org/10.2139/ssrn.4954803

Alsalhy, M. J., Sharif, H., Haroon, N. H., Kadhim Mohsin, S., Khalid, R., & Ali, A. (2023). Integrating AI-based Smart-Driven Marketing to Promote Sustainable and Green Systems. *International Conference on Emerging Research in Computational Science (ICERCS), 2023*, 1–6. https://doi.org/10.1109/ICERCS57948.2023.10434138

Anning-Dorson, T., Baba, F., Zulu, M., & Acheampong, G. (2025). Data-driven dynamic capabilities in emerging markets: A grounded theory approach to digital transformation in african retail banking. *International Journal of Information Management, 84*, 102914. https://doi.org/10.1016/j.ijinfomgt.2025.102914

Arantes, L., & Costa, S. (2025). Converging Theories: The Fusion of Artificial Intelligence and Sustainable Marketing for a Responsible Future. In J. Santos, P. Pires, & N. Grigoriou (Eds.), *Leveraging AI for Effective Digital Relationship Marketing* (pp. 223–256). IGI Global Scientific Publishing. https://doi.org/10.4018/979-8-3693-5340-0.ch008

Bromhead, H., & Levisen, C. (2022). Environmental Semantics. *Scandinavian Studies in Language, 13*(1), 78–87. https://doi.org/10.7146/sss.v13i1.135073

Darban, K., & Kabbaj, S. (2023). The Transformative Potential of AI in Green Marketing Strategies. *Traditional Journal of Law and Social Sciences, 2*(2). https://ojs.traditionaljournaloflaw.com/index.php/TJLSS/article/view/109

Delmas, M. A., & Burbano, V. C. (2011). The Drivers of Greenwashing. *California Management Review, 54*(1), 64–87. https://doi.org/10.1525/cmr.2011.54.1.64

Elkington, J. (1994). Towards the Sustainable Corporation: Win-Win-Win Business Strategies for Sustainable Development. *California Management Review, 36*(2), 90–100. https://doi.org/10.2307/41165746

Emon, M. M. H., & Khan, T. (2025). A Systematic Literature Review on Sustainability Integration and Marketing Intelligence in the Era of Artificial Intelligence. *Review of Business and Economics Studies, 12*(4), 6–28. https://doi.org/10.26794/2308-944X-2024-12-4-6-28

European Commission. (n.d.). *Green Claims*. https://environment.ec.europa.eu/topics/circular-economy/green-claims_en

European Union. (2024). Regulation (EU) 2024/1689 of the European parliament and of the council of 13 June 2024 laying down harmonised rules on artificial intelligence (Artificial Intelligence Act). *Official Journal of the European Union*. https://data.europa.eu/eli/reg/2024/1689/oj

Ganesh, C., Podila, N., Vamsi, G. B. K., Rao, C. M., & Bhardwaj, N. (2024). AI-Enhanced Content Marketing for Sustainability: A Theoretical Perspective on Eco-Friendly Communication Strategies. In *MATEC Web of Conferences* (Vol. 392, p. 01045). EDP Sciences. https://doi.org/10.1051/matecconf/202439201045

Gündüzyeli, B. (2024). Artificial Intelligence in Digital Marketing Within the Framework of Sustainable Management. *Sustainability, 16*(23), 10511. https://doi.org/10.3390/su162310511

Hemalatha, A. (2023). *AI-Driven Marketing: Leveraging Artificial Intelligence for Enhanced Customer Engagement* (1st ed.). Jupiter Publications Consortium. https://doi.org/10.47715/jpc.b.978-93-91303-61-7

Kaddour, J., Lynch, A., Liu, Q., Kusner, M. J., & Silva, R. (2025). Causal Machine Learning: A Survey and Open Problems. *Foundations and Trends® in Optimization, 9*(1–2), 1–247. https://arxiv.org/pdf/2206.15475

Kamyabi, M., Özgit, H., Ahmed, J. N. (2025). Sustaining digital marketing strategies to enhance customer engagement and brand promotion: Position as a moderator. *Sustainability, 17*, 3270. https://doi.org/10.3390/su17073270

Kravets, O., Korolova, U., Nosachenko, O., Vasiltsova, O., & Koberniuk, S. (2025). AI-Powered Digital Marketing: Enhancing Customer Behaviour Predictions. *European Journal of Sustainable Development, 14*(2), 84. https://doi.org/10.14207/ejsd.2025.v14n2p84

Kumar, P., Kumar, N., & Kavita. (2024). The future of AI in marketing: Trends, challenges, and opportunities for businesses. *International Journal of Research Publication and Reviews, 5*(5), 1534–1540. https://ijrpr.com/uploads/V5ISSUE5/IJRPR27259.pdf

Kumar, S., Sharma, C., Mishra, M. K., Sharma, S., & Bhardwaj, V. (2025). Smart, Sustainable, and Green: The Digital Transformation of Green-Marketing. *Discover Sustainability, 6*(1). https://doi.org/10.1007/s43621-025-01242-5

OECD. (2022). OECD AI principles. OECD AI Policy Observatory. https://oecd.ai/en/ai-principles

Organisation for Economic Co-operation and Development. (n.d.). *Artificial Intelligence*. https://www.oecd.org/en/topics/artificial-intelligence.html

Patil, D. (2025). *Artificial Intelligence in Retail and E-Commerce: Enhancing Customer Experience Through Personalization, Predictive Analytics, And Real-Time Engagement*. Elsevier BV. https://doi.org/10.2139/ssrn.5057420

Peattie, K., & Belz, F. M. (2010). Sustainability Marketing—An Innovative Conception of Marketing. *Marketing Review St. Gallen, 27*, 8–15. https://doi.org/10.1007/s11621-010-0085-7

Prothero, A., McDonagh, P., & Dobscha, S. (2010). Is Green the New Black? Reflections on a Green Commodity Discourse. *Journal of Macromarketing, 30*(2), 147–159. https://doi.org/10.1177/0276146710361922

Rathore, B. (2018). Emergent Perspectives on Green Marketing: The Intertwining of Sustainability, Artificial Intelligence, and the Metaverse. *International Journal of New Media Studies, 05*(02), 22–30. https://doi.org/10.58972/eiprmj.v5i2y18.115

Rusthollkarhu, S., Toukola, S., Aarikka-Stenroos, L., & Mahlamäki, T. (2022). Managing B2B Customer Journeys in Digital Era: Four Management Activities with Artificial Intelligence-Empowered Tools. *Industrial Marketing Management, 104*, 241–257. https://doi.org/10.1016/j.indmarman.2022.04.014

Sohaib, O., Alshemeili, A., & Bhatti, T. (2025). Exploring AI-Enabled Green Marketing and Green Intention: An Integrated PLS-SEM and NCA Approach. *Cleaner and Responsible Consumption, 17*, Article 100269. https://doi.org/10.1016/j.clrc.2025.100269

Tatavarthy, A. D., Martuza, J., & Thorbjørnsen, H. (2025). Express: Human Is Gold: Why Premium Customers Hate Chatbots and What to Do About It. *Journal of Interactive Marketing*, 10949968251322512. https://doi.org/10.1177/10949968251322513

Tulbure, A., Popescu, A., & NeacŞu, N. A. (2024). The Role of AI in Content Development among Romanian Small Businesses. *Proceedings of the International Conference on Business Excellence, 18(*1), 2353–2364. https://doi.org/10.2478/picbe-2024-0199

Von Zahn, M., Bauer, K., Mihale-Wilson, C., Jagow, J., Speicher, M., & Hinz, O. (2024). Smart Green Nudging: Reducing Product Returns Through Digital Footprints and Causal Machine Learning. *Marketing Science, 44*(4), 954–969. https://doi.org/10.1287/mksc.2022.0393

Xia, Z., & Shannon, R. (2025). Navigating the Digital Frontier: Exploring the Dynamics of Customer-Brand Relationships Through AI Chatbots. *Sustainability, 17*(5), 2173. https://doi.org/10.3390/su17052173

Yu, J., & Meng, T. (2025). Image Generative AI in Tourism: Trends, Impacts, and Future Research Directions. *Journal of Hospitality & Tourism Research,* 10963480251324676. https://doi.org/10.1177/10963480251324676

Zaharia, G.-E., Apostol, I. G., Savin, P. S., & Tanase, I. (2024). Digital Frontiers: Assessing the Influence and Ethical Challenges of AI in Online Marketing. *Proceedings of the International Conference on Business Excellence, 18*(1), 3699–3710. https://doi.org/10.2478/picbe-2024-0300

Zhang, C., Wang, Y., & Zhang, J. (2025). Risk Assessment of Live-Streaming Marketing Based on Hesitant Fuzzy Multi-Attribute Group Decision-Making Method. *Journal of Theoretical and Applied Electronic Commerce Research, 20*(2), 120. https://doi.org/10.3390/jtaer20020120

Empowering the Sales Force: How AI Is Revolutionizing Modern Sales Management

Joaquim Pratas, Ana Pinto Lima, and Pedro Mendonça Silva

Abstract This chapter explores the transformative impact of artificial intelligence on modern sales management, emphasizing its role in empowering the sales force. Tracing the evolution from intuition-driven practices to data-centric strategies, it highlights how AI, through tools like CRM automation, predictive analytics, generative AI, and emotion recognition, enhances decision-making, customer engagement, and operational efficiency across both B2B and B2C contexts. Case studies from leading firms illustrate AI's versatility, while the shift toward first-party data underscores the need for deeper behavioral insights. Ultimately, the chapter argues that successful AI adoption depends on ethical integration, strategic alignment, and human-AI collaboration to drive sustainable sales performance.

1 Introduction

The sales function has always played a strategic role in organizations, focusing on understanding customers' needs and guiding them through their buying journeys, in order to "help the customer to buy" (Churchill et al., 2016; Kowalkowski et al., 2025; Padilla et al., 2024). Traditionally, sales management used to rely on personal relationships and persuasive communication, with informal conversations guided by loose scripts focused on showing the product and answering customer questions. Over time, this evolved into a more professional approach, clearly distinguishing strategies for acquiring new customers from those aimed at retaining existing ones

J. Pratas (✉) · A. P. Lima · P. M. Silva
Polytechnic of Porto, Porto, Portugal
e-mail: jmpratas@iscap.ipp.pt

A. P. Lima
e-mail: analima@iscap.ipp.pt

P. M. Silva
e-mail: psilva@iscap.ipp.pt

J. Pratas
GOVCOPP, University of Aveiro, Aveiro, Portugal

J. D. Santos et al. (eds.), *Artificial Intelligence Transforming Marketing*, Contributions to Management Science, https://doi.org/10.1007/978-3-032-22360-9_8

(Echchakoui & Ghilal, 2019; Vieira et al., 2019). The 1990s marked another development phase, through the introduction of customer relationship management (CRM) systems and relationship marketing to build and enhance customer relationships through mutual value and promises fulfillment over time (Grönroos, 1996). These tools enabled personalized strategies that allowed cross-selling and upselling maximizing customer lifetime value (Kamakura et al., 1991). These strategies are still used today, in almost all the most evolved organizations. Paradigmatic examples of pioneering companies using these strategies include the first e-commerce retailers and early CRM software developers, many of which remain leaders in their industries today.

Further developments occurred with digital technologies (such as cloud computing, mobile technologies, and social media) and more informed buyers, revolutionizing sales into a data-driven, digital-first environment (Subramaniyan & Muthuraman, 2023). This structural trend was accelerated by the COVID-19, reinforcing the shift toward virtual commerce (Jílková & Králová, 2021).

The rise of AI especially since the launch of the first generative AI chatbot achieving global mainstream popularity, in November 2022, has also transformed sales through predictive analytics, lead scoring, and automated communication (Li et al., 2025), enabling sales teams to perform their functions more effectively. Today, AI empowers rather than replaces sales teams, boosting productivity, customer satisfaction, and commercial impact (Wengler et al., 2021).

The aim of this study is to explore how AI is reshaping modern sales management, particularly in sales teams' empowerment. It begins by tracing the evolution of sales force management, then examines how AI collaborates with human agents to enhance sales performance. The analysis develops spanning both B2B and B2C contexts, highlighting the distinct dynamics and challenges of each. The work also delves into the most impactful AI tools used in sales, their core applications, and how they're integrated into today's sales platforms. Through exploratory data and real-world case examples, it showcases the tangible benefits of AI from boosting efficiency to deepening customer engagement. Finally, it addresses emerging opportunities, ethical challenges and considerations, and the future outlook for AI in sales management.

In order to provide a coherent and systematic examination of the ways in which AI is reshaping sales management, this chapter is organized into nine sections. Following the introduction, the literature review situates AI within the historical and theoretical evolution of sales force management, with subsections addressing the trajectory from traditional practices to AI-empowered human sales forces, and exploring transformations in both B2B and B2C contexts, as well as contemporary challenges and the tools currently supporting sales processes. The subsequent section examines core AI techniques, namely machine learning, predictive analytics, natural language processing, and recommendation systems, before turning to the integration of these techniques with existing sales platforms. This is followed by descriptive data insights and case-based applications that illustrate AI's impact in practice. The discussion then considers opportunities, risks, and ethical implications, paving the way for a forward-looking analysis of AI's role in the future of sales management. The chapter concludes by synthesizing these insights, underscoring the central argument that the empowerment of the sales force through AI requires not only technological adoption but also strategic alignment, ethical safeguards, and the cultivation of human-AI collaboration.

2 Literature Review

2.1 The Evolution of Sales Force Management

Sales force management has undergone major shifts over the past century, evolving from intuition-driven and decentralized practices to data-centric and AI-enhanced strategies. Early sales relied on sellers' field experience and charisma, with sales representatives working independently and mainly incentivized by commissions (Powers, 2015). This early "experiential-intuitive era" was marked by territory-based management and field-based experience of sales representatives. As corporations grew in complexity, a "formal-training and interaction era" emerged. Organizations introduced recruitment standards, training programs, and performance metrics, transitioning from product-centric transactions to customer-oriented, consultative selling. Industry-specific specialization became the norm, supporting long-term relationship-building with clients.

By the 1990s, sales entered the "strategic integration phase". Sales became strategically integrated into corporate planning, contributing to CRM initiatives, cross-functional collaboration, account management, and value-based approaches (Piercy & Lane, 2011). This integration reflected a need to respond to commoditization pressures and evolving customer expectations.

Today, digital transformation and AI have transformed sales management and operations, enabling predictive analytics, hyper-personalization, and real-time decisions, among other functions (Blum, 2020). AI now automates up to between 30% and 40% routine tasks, positioning sales teams as agile, customer-centric drivers of performance (Deveau et al., 2023; Fischer et al., 2022).

2.2 The Future of Sales Management: Human Sales Force Empowered by AI

Advancements in information and communication technologies have fundamentally redefined the sales force role, shifting them from groups of capable individuals into strategic, data-enabled units. Contemporary sales teams leverage real-time access to customer data to anticipate individual needs and tailor offerings with precision, operating under a customer-centric framework (Amosu et al., 2024). Consequently, Silva (2025) presents the Informational Advantage Theory, according to which the positive impact of sales technologies on performance depends on the strategic use of information systems. Digital transformation has redefined the role of sales professionals, requiring integration between human and analytical skills.

AI significantly enhances data analysis by deepening organizational insight into both current and potential customers. These capabilities support the formulation of customized marketing mix strategies and facilitate real-time, data-driven decision-making, increasingly accessible via mobile devices by sales representatives. Across both B2B and B2C markets, AI enhances lead prioritization, outbound campaigns, and personalization (Rodriguez & Peterson, 2024). Integrated throughout the sales cycle, AI boosts both productivity of sales teams and customer satisfaction (Fischer et al., 2022).

2.3 *Transforming Business-to-Business (B2B) Markets Through AI*

In B2B markets, the customers are organizations with multiple decision-makers and professional buyers. Sales cycles are long, complex, and negotiation-driven, with decisions based on return on investment (ROI), efficiency, and long-term value. Relationships hinge on trust and strategic partnerships, and sales teams typically feature account managers, technical experts, and solution consultants. Commercial dynamics are shaped by the strategic interplay between account managers (on the seller's side) and procurement managers (on the buyer's side). These professionals are not merely transactional agents, as they engage in strategic planning of purchases and sales, possess technical expertise, and cultivate consultative relationships grounded in mutual value creation. Their interactions are increasingly evaluated through performance metrics such as transaction volumes (both purchases and sales), customer lifetime value, customer retention rates, and the duration and quality of sales engagements leading up to deal closure. This reality underscores the need for strategic account planning in B2B market environments. Sales initiatives must be designed around seasonal campaigns and client support programs, with customers viewed not as only "targets" but as long-term partners. Sales professionals, therefore, must evolve into technical consultants capable of delivering deep product knowledge, personalized service, and strategic insight. Training programs should be oriented toward developing these capabilities, enabling sellers to act as trusted advisors rather than mere intermediaries (Gosai, 2023; Sandesh et al., 2023). Accordingly, performance metrics in B2B markets should reflect the complexity and depth of these relationships, focusing on indicators such as deal size, pipeline velocity, and customer lifetime value (Han et al., 2022).

Sales and CRM tools include advanced CRM systems, AI-powered predictive analytics, and account management platforms (Cravens et al., 2011; Oracle, n.d.).

AI is reshaping B2B markets by significantly shortening the sales cycle (especially during the prospecting and customer engagement phases), while also streamlining transactional steps and minimizing time spent on administrative tasks (Rajeb, 2020). Beyond time savings, AI technologies are fundamentally redefining how sales organizations operate and strategize. By 2025, an estimated 35% of companies are expected to establish centralized generative AI operations teams focused on developing go-to-market strategies (Gartner, 2023), reinforcing AI's strategic importance across the sales funnel. Thus, AI can enhance sales productivity through three core functions: the automation of repetitive tasks, personalization of customer interactions, and advanced predictive analytics.

Automation of repetitive tasks includes lead prioritization, qualification, scoring, email marketing, forecasting, and pipeline management (DigitalOcean, 2023). These efficiencies allow sales teams to focus on revenue-generating activities.

The personalization of customer interactions, with generative AI, produces hyper-targeted proposals that elevate conversion rates and reframe client engagement strategies (Comite et al., 2025).

The advanced predictive analytics can also improve audience targeting and boost conversion performance (Chui et al., 2023; Salesforce Research, 2023). Ultimately, AI empowers data-driven decision-making by delivering actionable insights that improve strategic foresight and forecasting accuracy solidifying its role as a cornerstone of sales optimization.

2.4 *Transforming Business-to-Consumer (B2C) Markets through AI*

In business-to-consumer (B2C) markets the focus is on individual consumers purchasing for themselves, their families, or as gifts. Buying decisions are generally fast, emotional, and often impulsive, driven by desire, price sensitivity, and brand perceptions. Loyalty, convenience, and emotional connection shape the customer relationship. Sales teams typically include retail representatives, customer service agents, or digital platforms, supported by e-commerce systems, chatbots, and personalized recommendation engines (Cravens et al., 2011; Oracle, n.d.). Performance metrics center on conversion rates, cart abandonment, and repeat purchases, reflecting a transactional, volume-driven model (Kukar-Kinney et al., 2022).

AI is transforming B2C markets by enabling hyper-personalization, optimizing consumer journeys, powering conversational technologies, and revolutionizing product search (Katyayan & Kushwaha, 2025).

Machine learning allows companies to deliver tailored experiences at scale, generating personalized recommendations, dynamic pricing, and targeted promotions based on browsing and purchase history (Cherukuri, 2024).

AI also refines omnichannel strategies by analyzing behavior across digital touchpoints, improving timing and content delivery.

Predictive analytics anticipate purchase intent, while chatbots and automated emails boost responsiveness and cohesion (Wang et al., 2025). Conversational AI through virtual assistants and smart chat interfaces enhances product discovery, upselling, and decision-making through real-time, need-based suggestions. Voice and image recognition are also redefining search and consequently sales management. Voice commerce is rising with smart speakers, while other tools enable visual product identification, deepening brand-consumer engagement (Dagan et al., 2023). These innovations create a data-driven, intuitive, and highly personalized shopping experience. Meanwhile, agile start-ups continue to accelerate AI adoption, reshaping competition and embedding intelligent solutions across B2C ecosystems (Manner, 2020).

2.5 Contemporary Challenges in Sales Force Management

Sales teams today face crowded and competitive markets, where demanding customers and advanced data systems from all players (e.g., competitors) make it harder to reach their business goals. These strategic goals typically encompass sales targets, profitability ratios, client base expansion, and a diverse array of key performance indicators (KPIs) that assess commercial effectiveness. Navigating such complexity demands not only consistent performance but also a dynamic capacity to adapt within rapidly evolving ecosystems. A central challenge lies in balancing productivity with performance management. Globalization, digital transformation, and increasingly sophisticated buyers also require sales leaders to align organizational strategy with individual motivation of sales representatives.

This dual imperative calls for leadership that fosters coherence while cultivating accountability (Cravens et al., 2011). HubSpot's 2025 Sales Trends Report from HubSpot & The Science of Scaling (2025) confirms this tension: 64% of sales leaders prioritize pipeline growth and revenue, yet many still grapple with inefficiencies, such as poor time use, fragmented workflows, and underleveraged tech, undermining responsiveness in data-driven environments.

Hyper-personalization adds further complexity. Customers expect tailored, context-rich experiences, but delivering them demands deep customer insight, ongoing training, integrated data systems, and cross-functional coordination (Treadgold & Reynolds, 2020). While 53% of sales professionals deem personalization essential, many lack the infrastructure to execute it. AI offers promise, but only when thoughtfully embedded into workflows and interactions (HubSpot & The Science of Scaling, 2025; Medallia, 2024; Treadgold & Reynolds, 2020).

Forecasting accuracy also remains pivotal. Effective planning hinges on real-time, high-quality data and robust predictive models. Yet outdated datasets and weak data collection persist, distorting forecasts. The complexity of long sales cycles and behavioral variability compounds the issue (Treadgold & Reynolds, 2020). Nearly 70% of sales leaders struggle to align forecasts with actual customer behavior, especially in hybrid environments (Stronger Sales Teams, 2024).

Talent management is equally critical. Recruiting, developing, and retaining top performers (especially in B2B contexts) directly impacts competitive advantage.

Attrition risks eroding trust and exposing sensitive data, making retention strategies vital. These must blend financial incentives with career growth, recognition, and meaningful engagement with customer systems.

Building resilient sales teams requires a fusion of technical skill, emotional intelligence, and strategic alignment. This is not optional; it is essential in today's market. According to Stronger Sales Teams (2024), 67% of leaders cite talent management as their top concern, exacerbated by phenomena like "Quiet Quitting" and "Quiet Resignation" which reveal cracks in traditional engagement models.

These shifts underscore a broader imperative: sales leadership must evolve beyond transactional management to embrace a more holistic, human-centered approach. Investing in continuous professional development, particularly in areas related to customer data stewardship and digital fluency, is no longer optional. It is foundational to building resilient, future-ready sales organizations.

2.6 AI Tools Supporting Sales Teams' Processes

Modern customers behave like digital chameleons, fluidly navigating through online and offline touchpoints and always searching for better options, while generating vast behavioral data. Yet, despite this behavior and data surge, many sales teams still rely on outdated tools and intuition, ill-equipped to manage today's complex, real-time commercial ecosystems.

Sales managers face high-stakes decisions, such as forecasting, budgeting, territory planning, and resource allocation, often under pressure and with limited analytical support. Likewise, sales representatives must respond strategically during customer interactions, where crafting personalized, commercially viable proposals is increasingly difficult without advanced technologies.

Thus, AI has become indispensable, enhancing predictive accuracy and strategic agility. AI systems, through advanced statistical models, extract actionable insights from large datasets, as predictive analytics and recommendation engines significantly improve forecasting precision (Jamarani et al., 2024). Gartner (2025) adds that AI accelerates decision-making by automating analysis and surfacing buyer intelligence in real-time, enhancing pipeline management. Leoni et al. (2024) also demonstrate how AI-integrated knowledge systems elevate commercial decision quality. IDC (2024) confirms that AI-powered tools outperform traditional models, enabling real-time risk detection and market anticipation.

Sales performance also benefits from AI-enabled assistants that coach in real-time, automate follow-ups, and prioritize leads using engagement metrics. Baierle et al. (2019) introduced a knowledge-based AI platform that boosts decision speed and responsiveness. Case studies from SalesMind and Momentum.io report productivity gains via CRM automation, data hygiene, and workflow orchestration (Gadea, 2024; Oromy, 2025).

Most transformative, however, is AI's ability to deliver hyper-personalization at scale. Deep learning and customer analytics now enable tailored outreach aligned with individual preferences. Ali et al. (2023) highlight intelligent decision-support systems using machine learning and multi-criteria frameworks to navigate complex sales scenarios with precision. Several tools, platforms, and software exemplify this shift, leveraging enriched datasets and real-time buying signals to craft personalized engagement across diverse segments (Maram, 2025).

3 AI Techniques Applied to Sales: The Role of Machine Learning, Predictive Analytics, Natural Language Processing, and Recommendation Systems

AI replicates traditional human cognitive functions such as learning, reasoning, and self-correction, through computational systems. In sales, AI drives automation, personalization, and data-informed decision-making, enhancing customer engagement and operational efficiency (Gartner, 2025). Subfields of AI used in terms of techniques are such as machine learning (ML), predictive analytics, natural language processing (NLP), and recommendation systems. These techniques are reshaping sales strategies.

ML algorithms learn from behavioral and engagement data to optimize lead scoring, forecasting, and churn prediction (Pavlyshenko, 2019). Lead scoring ranks prospects by conversion likelihood, streamlining CRM pipelines and improving outreach (Ozay et al., 2024). For churn prediction, ML detects disengagement signals (such as reduced usage or complaints), while generative AI segments customers by risk and automates retention strategies (Pecan Team, 2024; Prompts.ai, 2025). Firms using AI for churn management report up to 20% higher retention rates (Comarch, 2025).

Predictive analytics integrates statistical modeling with ML to forecast outcomes from historical data. In sales, it refines pipeline projections and demand planning, improving resource allocation and strategic agility (Aljbour & Avci, 2024). AI-enhanced forecasting correlates internal and external variables for more accurate revenue predictions (Aguilar-Alonso & Espinoza, 2025; Venkataramanan et al., 2024).

NLP enables machines to interpret and generate human language, powering chatbots, sentiment analysis, and automated communications (Rani, 2024). Chatbots handle FAQs, qualify leads, and deliver instant feedback, freeing sales teams for high-value tasks (Labadze et al., 2023). Conversational AI, combining NLP and ML, simulates human dialogue to enrich customer journeys through context-aware interactions (Rainsberger, 2022), also automating some digital contacts of the customer with organizations and sales representatives.

Recommendation systems on the other hand personalize offers using behavioral data, driving cross-selling and upselling (Habil et al., 2023). CRM automation enhances engagement and retention by streamlining segmentation, data entry, and follow-ups. Intelligent platforms centralize customer data, uncover patterns, and trigger timely recommendations, boosting transaction value and customer satisfaction (Leelavathi et al., 2024).

4 Integration of AI Tools with Existing Sales Platforms

Sales management and CRM platforms have become essential to modern sales operations, supporting processes from pipeline tracking to segmentation. The rise of AI has significantly expanded their functional scope.

Leading systems from several providers and vendors now embed AI through native modules, application programming interfaces (APIs), or third-party extensions to enhance decision-making, automate tasks, and personalize engagement.

Salesforce (2023) reports that the top five tool types used by sales organizations include CRM systems, reporting/analytics, account and contract management, mobile sales apps, and forecasting tools. Yet, most firms aim to consolidate their tech stacks, reflecting a shift toward integrated, AI-powered ecosystems.

AI adoption within CRM spans client interaction automation, lead qualification, chatbot deployment, and predictive analytics.

CRM automation now includes AI-driven data entry, dynamic profile enrichment, and timely follow-ups. Leelavathi et al. (2024) highlight that the integration of AI enhances data fidelity and reduces manual workload. This boosts segmentation and engagement capabilities.

Several examples of chatbots developed by information technologies' (IT) companies exemplify this shift, automating tasks like email extraction and meeting scheduling. Empirical data shows AI reduces manual operations by over two hours daily per user (Leelavathi et al., 2024; Shahid, 2024).

Ultimately, AI transforms CRM platforms into predictive engines that enhance strategic agility and commercial effectiveness.

AI has also redefined lead scoring and qualification by enabling predictive models that analyze behavioral and firmographic data, such as engagement history, organizational traits, and purchase patterns, to estimate conversion likelihood. This strategic integration allows sales teams to prioritize outreach and allocate resources more effectively. Empirical evidence supports this shift. Ozay et al. (2024) show that machine learning embedded in enterprise CRM systems significantly improves lead ranking accuracy, enhancing both operational efficiency and pipeline quality. These models adapt dynamically to changing customer behaviors and market signals, creating a feedback loop that continuously refines prioritization. Several tools, platforms, and software's exemplify this evolution, leveraging thousands of data points to classify prospects by conversion probability. This empowers sales professionals to focus on high-value leads, boosting closing rates and shortening sales cycles (Ozay et al., 2024; Shahid, 2024).

Chatbots and conversational AI have become integral to digital sales infrastructure, embed across websites, CRM systems, and messaging platforms to automate inquiries, qualify leads, and coordinate logistics. Their deployment reflects a broader shift toward continuous, real-time engagement in sales processes. Labadze et al. (2023) highlight the transformative impact of AI chatbots, noting their ability to enhance responsiveness and reduce wait times, thereby improving customer experience. Their asynchronous availability extends engagement beyond traditional business hours, fostering dynamic interaction environments. These systems leverage natural language processing (NLP), machine learning, and dialog management to simulate human-like conversations that guide users through complex decisions. Several tools, platforms, and software exemplify this evolution, integrating NLP-based virtual assistants into sales workflows. According to the Floworks.ai (2025), these agents deliver real-time insights and actionable recommendations during live interactions, augmenting sales representatives' cognitive capacity and streamlining the customer journey. Such strategic integration demonstrates how conversational AI can elevate sales execution, lead nurturing, and client retention.

AI has also redefined sales forecasting and analytics, evolving from a support function to a strategic augmentation of enterprise resource planning (ERP) and CRM systems. Intelligent forecasting modules embedded in dashboards and linked to data lakes enable real-time analysis of revenue trajectories, pattern shifts, and operational risks, marking a transition from reactive management to anticipatory planning. Aguilar-Alonso and Espinoza (2025) affirm that AI-powered forecasting tools significantly improve the accuracy and relevance of financial projections. These systems employ complex algorithmic models that integrate historical data, buyer behavior, market dynamics, and pipeline trends to produce agile, granular forecasts. This fosters a more adaptive decision-support environment, where planning and resource allocation respond proactively to emerging signals. Several tools, platforms, and software exemplify this integration, synchronizing pipeline data to generate real-time revenue projections and scenario models. By illuminating future sales trajectories, such tools empower teams to refine tactics and align strategies with predictive insights (HubSpot, 2025).

Specifically in sales management, leading AI tools include enterprise-grade CRM platforms with embedded intelligence, cognitive computing systems developed by global tech firms, conversational assistants integrated into marketing workflows, and predictive lead scoring solutions (Salesforce Careers, 2024). The main topics about the utilization of AI in sales are expressed in Table 1.

5 Descriptive Data Insights: AI in Action

AI remains in a developmental phase, with organizations increasingly acknowledging its transformative potential. However, despite growing enthusiasm, a significant proportion of AI initiatives, particularly those involving generative AI, continue to fall short of expectations in terms of revenue generation and operational efficiency (Deloitte, 2024).

Table 1 AI utilization in sales (main topics)

Strategic impact	AI capabilities	Sales applications (B2B and B2C)	Tools and technologies	Main challenges
Customer-centric sales teams	Predictive analytics	Lead scoring; email campaigns; pipeline tracking; forecasting; hyper-personalized offers	CRM automation; workflow engines	Data quality; talent gaps
Tailored offerings	Hyper-personalization	Smart recommendations; dynamic pricing; targeted promotions; chatbots; automated emails	Machine learning; natural language processing (NLP); recommendation engines	Algorithmic bias
Higher customer satisfaction	Real-time decisions	Upsell and cross-sell; need-based solutions; voice & image recognition of products and customers	Predictive platforms; conversational AI	Over-dependence on automation
Faster B2B sales cycles	Task automation	Real-time insights; optimized timing and content delivery	Mobile integrations; sales platforms; communication tools	Opaque "black-box" models; privacy concerns
Better prospecting and retention	Conversational AI	Audience targeting; purchase-intent prediction	Embedded AI in platforms	Privacy risks; data quality issues

Source Authors

Importantly, the core impediment is not rooted in the technical limitations of AI models but rather in their deployment within organizational systems. While organizations often cite regulatory constraints or technological immaturity as primary barriers, recent findings from the Massachusetts Institute of Technology's NANDA project challenge this narrative. According to Challapally et al. (2025), the underperformance of generative AI projects is predominantly attributable to poor integration into core business processes. Ineffective implementations are frequently characterized by fragile workflows, insufficient contextual learning, and misalignment with daily operations. Furthermore, the study reveals a pronounced disparity in success rates between organizations that collaborate with external AI specialists and those that rely solely on internal development. Companies engaging specialized vendors report a success rate of approximately 67%, whereas in-house efforts yield positive outcomes in only one-third of cases.

Despite rapid technological advancements, broader AI adoption remains constrained by persistent structural and strategic barriers (Gartner, 2024). High implementation costs, regulatory compliance complexities, and ambiguity surrounding practical applications continue to deter investment. Pratas et al. (2024) identify the principal inhibitors as: lack of clear business use cases (33.9%), prohibitive implementation costs (33.2%), and insufficient internal knowledge of AI solutions (25.3%). Paradoxically, AI's versatility, while promising, often exacerbates uncertainty regarding its specific utility, leaving many organizations unable to assess its tangible impact. Consequently, hesitancy to invest in AI stems not only from economic considerations but also from a deficit in strategic clarity and organizational readiness.

Nevertheless, when effectively implemented, AI has demonstrated substantial gains, particularly in sales management. In 2025, AI continued its accelerated diffusion across industries, albeit with sectoral variation. According to GPT Zero (2025) and Hostinger (2025), the highest levels of AI integration were observed in information technology (67%), followed by marketing and sales (58%), customer service (56%), cybersecurity (51%), and both supply chain logistics and finance/accounting (30%). Despite this uptake, AI technologies largely remain in the introductory or early growth stages of the technology diffusion curve, suggesting that while experimentation is widespread, full-scale integration and maturity are still evolving. This reflects a landscape in which AI is increasingly viewed as a strategic asset, yet industries continue to grapple with the complexities of adoption, scalability, and long-term value realization.

Empirical evidence further substantiates AI's impact on sales operations. Gearset (2025) reports that 61% of sales teams have adopted AI tools, with 41% of employees perceiving widespread integration across their organizations. This adoption correlates with a 30% increase in productivity and a 19% reduction in labor costs (Salesforce, 2025), highlighting AI's dual role in enhancing output and reducing operational overhead.

From an analytical standpoint, AI-powered forecasting tools consistently outperform traditional models, offering superior accuracy and enhanced risk detection (Aguilar-Alonso & Espinoza, 2025). Externally, AI contributes to a 39% improvement in customer experience and a 33% increase in employee efficiency among adopters (McKinsey & Company, 2021).

Sales performance metrics have also shown marked improvement post-AI adoption. Conversion rates rose from 12–15% to 18–22%, while deal cycle duration decreased from 45 to 30 days. Customer satisfaction scores increased from 72% to 85%, and forecast accuracy improved from 60–65% to 80–90%, enabling more reliable planning and resource allocation.

Moreover, AI has significantly enhanced sales representative productivity. According to SuperAGI (2025) and Sybill (2025), time spent on direct selling activities doubled from 25% to 50%, while administrative workload dropped from 20 to 8 hours per week. Monthly deal closures increased from 8 to 11, and average revenue per representative surged by 37.5%. These outcomes illustrate AI's capacity to streamline operations, automate routine tasks, and empower sales professionals to focus on strategic engagement and customer interaction.

6 Case Examples and Applications

The integration of AI into sales and customer engagement strategies has enabled organizations to extract valuable lessons from pioneering case studies. These examples illustrate how AI is reshaping operational efficiency, customer experience, and team performance across industries.

A notable case is a multinational technology corporation headquartered in the United States, recognized for its operating systems, productivity software, cloud computing platforms, and enterprise solutions that transformed its lead qualification process. Faced with the limitations of manual lead scoring (which frequently overlooked high-value prospects) this company deployed a new AI-powered system. This tool leveraged behavioral and demographic data to prioritize sales-ready leads, resulting in a dramatic improvement: the lead-to-sales-qualified conversion rate surged from 4% to 18%, quadrupling performance and accelerating sales cycles (GoBeyond AI, 2025). This case underscores the strategic advantage of AI-driven lead scoring in enabling sales teams to concentrate efforts on the most promising opportunities, thereby enhancing both conversion rates and operational velocity.

Beyond this company, several global enterprises have embraced AI to address diverse challenges. A multinational energy company known for its operations in oil, natural gas, petrochemicals, and increasingly, renewable energy solutions, for instance, utilizes AI for predictive maintenance scheduling, significantly reducing equipment downtime. A leading Scandinavian bank, implemented an AI chatbot to manage high volumes of customer queries with efficiency and scalability. A multinational financial institution that provides services across investment banking, asset management, retail banking, and wealth advisory has integrated AI across its banking operations to optimize sales, mitigate risks, and elevate client experiences. Meanwhile, a global leader in event management market employs AI for matchmaking and virtual assistance in conference planning, enhancing networking outcomes. A leading company of athletic apparel and footwear industry, in collaboration with an award-winning creative agency specializing in digital experiences, brand strategy, and technological innovation, leveraged machine learning to simulate a virtual tennis match between one of the most well-known tennis players past and present selves, showcasing AI's creative potential in brand storytelling (GoBeyond AI, 2025).

AI's capabilities extend beyond automation and analytics, increasingly being used to coach and develop sales talent. One organization, aiming to scale personalized coaching across its global sales force, introduced a digital coaching assistant modeled after a top-performing sales leader. This AI solution delivered real-time, conversational guidance, replicating expert knowledge at scale. While current research does not claim AI coaching surpasses or equals human coaching, studies affirm its effectiveness in fulfilling core competencies required for impactful sales development.

Key benefits include reduced onboarding time for new hires, improved deal execution, and consistent coaching across geographies (Passmore et al., 2025; Tribe AI, 2023).

A pioneering enterprise software company that specializes in cloud-based platforms for customer relationship management, sales automation, and marketing intelligence offers another compelling example of AI innovation through the launch of its AI assistant embedded within its CRM platform. Traditional CRM systems often lacked personalization and demanded extensive manual input. The AI assistant addressed these limitations by harnessing unified customer data to automate over fifty tasks and personalize engagement across departments. The result was enhanced customer satisfaction, improved engagement metrics, and strengthened data governance and trust. This evolution transforms CRM from a static repository into a dynamic engine for proactive customer interaction (Leelavathi et al., 2024; SuperAGI, 2025).

Collectively, these cases illustrate AI's transformative impact across sales, customer service, coaching, and engagement. As organizations continue to experiment and refine AI applications, the potential for scalable, intelligent, and human-centered solutions grows exponentially.

7 Opportunities, Risks, and Ethical Considerations

AI is reshaping the landscape of sales management by driving efficiency, enhancing personalization, improving forecasting accuracy, and reducing customer churn. Its integration into sales processes offers transformative potential for both operational productivity and strategic agility.

One of AI's most immediate advantages lies in its ability to automate routine and repetitive tasks (such as data entry, scheduling, and follow-ups) thereby liberating sales professionals to concentrate on high-value activities like relationship-building and closing deals (Potwora et al., 2024). Beyond operational streamlining, AI enables hyper-personalized customer engagement by analyzing behavioral data to tailor content, offers, and communication strategies to individual preferences (Rane et al., 2024). This personalization not only enhances customer satisfaction but also contributes to retention, as AI systems can proactively identify at-risk clients and trigger targeted retention campaigns (Rane et al., 2024).

AI also strengthens organizational forecasting capabilities. Through predictive analytics, sales teams gain deeper visibility into pipeline dynamics and market trends, allowing for more accurate revenue projections and resource allocation (Prasad et al., 2024). These capabilities collectively position AI as a catalyst for smarter, faster, and more customer-centric sales operations.

However, the adoption of AI in sales is not without its challenges. Over-reliance on automated systems can erode human judgment, especially when decision-makers defer to algorithmic outputs without critical scrutiny. This dependency may lead to flawed conclusions, particularly in contexts where AI misinterprets data or lacks situational nuance (Stanford Institute for Human-Centered Artificial Intelligence, 2023). Moreover, algorithmic bias remains a pressing concern. Machine learning models trained on historical datasets may inadvertently perpetuate discriminatory patterns in customer segmentation or lead scoring, thereby compromising fairness and inclusivity (Trotta et al., 2023).

Compounding these risks is the opacity of many AI systems. The "black-box" nature of algorithmic decision-making impedes transparency and accountability, making it difficult for users to audit or justify AI-generated recommendations (Vasconcelos et al., 2023). This lack of explainability raises ethical questions around responsibility and trust in commercial environments. AI presents vast opportunities for sales teams, but its implementation comes with challenges that must be addressed to ensure success.

The main implementation challenges of AI and possible solutions (DigitalOcean, 2024):

- Data Accuracy & Responsible Use: AI's effectiveness depends on high-quality, unbiased data. Poor data leads to unreliable outcomes and unethical practices. To mitigate this, enforce strict data quality controls and promote responsible use of generative AI in sales content.
- Customer Experience versus Automation: Over-automation risks impersonal interactions. AI should enhance (not replace) human engagement. Sales reps must know when to step in to build relationships.
- Privacy & Security: Trust is essential. Ensure transparency about AI's role and implement strong security protocols to protect customer data.
- Job Security Concerns: AI may raise fears of job displacement. Open communication is key—clarify AI's role in handling repetitive tasks and highlight how it empowers reps to focus on strategic, human-centric activities.

Thus, several steps can leverage AI for sales success (DigitalOcean, 2024):

- Identify pain points: audit sales processes to uncover repetitive tasks like manual lead qualification. These are prime candidates for AI-driven automation.
- Align AI goals with business objectives: setting measurable, time-bound goals (e.g., reduce lead qualification time by 17%, boost productivity by 23%, or increase customer lifetime value by 13%). Ensure these align with broader business strategies.
- Evaluate Tech Infrastructure: review current tools (CRM, analytics, marketing platforms) and assess compatibility with AI. Identify gaps, gather cross-departmental feedback, and budget for necessary upgrades. External consultants may help with system audits.
- Calculate ROI & Budget: conduct a cost-benefit analysis covering software, hardware, training, and staffing. Estimate efficiency gains and revenue impact. Use ROI formulas to guide investment decisions and set realistic break-even timelines.
- Research & Shortlist AI Tools: explore market options through demos, reviews, and user feedback. Compare features like lead scoring and CRM integration. Choose tools that align with your needs and budget.

- Pilot AI Tools: test selected tools with a small group (1–10 users) over 2–3 months. Collect feedback, monitor performance metrics, and identify usability or integration issues before full deployment.
- Train & Manage Change: offer hands-on training to help staff integrate AI into daily workflows. Address concerns through town halls and one-on-one meetings. Consider external trainers if needed. Focus on buildsing confidence and skills.
- Track Performance: establish KPIs such as conversion rates and lead quality. Compare pre-and post-AI data to evaluate impact. Balance AI insights with human intuition to optimize results.

By addressing these challenges and following a structured implementation plan, organizations can unlock AI's full potential to enhance sales performance, efficiency, and customer engagement.

However, privacy concerns further complicate AI deployment. The data-intensive nature of AI applications necessitates the collection and processing of vast amounts of personal information, prompting debates around user consent, data ownership, and the potential for misuse. Ensuring compliance with data protection regulations and maintaining consumer trust are therefore critical imperatives (Gomstyn & Jonker, 2024).

In addition to ethical and operational risks, AI's environmental footprint warrants attention. The energy demands of training and running large-scale models are substantial, with projections indicating that AI could consume up to 1.3% of global electricity by 2030 (Durmus Senyapar & Bayindir, 2025). This surge is driven by data centers reliant on fossil fuels and water-intensive cooling systems, creating a paradox wherein AI both enables and threatens sustainable development (World Economic Forum, 2025; Zewe, 2025).

To navigate these complexities, organizations must embrace a model of hybrid intelligence, where human creativity, empathy, and ethical reasoning complement AI's analytical prowess. This collaborative approach is especially vital in B2B sales and complex negotiations, where contextual understanding and interpersonal nuance are irreplaceable (Lehner, 2025; Petrescu & Krishen, 2023). AI excels at processing data, recognizing patterns, and delivering real-time insights, but it is human judgment that ensures these outputs are interpreted and applied responsibly.

In conclusion, AI is not a substitute for human expertise in sales. It is a strategic partner. Its potential to enhance productivity and customer engagement is immense, but realizing this promise requires thoughtful integration, ethical safeguards, and a commitment to human-AI collaboration. The future of sales lies not in choosing between humans or machines, but in empowering both to work better together (Petrescu & Krishen, 2023).

8 Future Outlook

AI is rapidly emerging as a transformative force in sales force management, reshaping how organizations strategize, engage customers, and optimize performance. While AI currently functions as a complementary tool (supporting human sellers through automation and data-driven insights) its trajectory suggests a shift toward more autonomous and strategic roles in the near future.

As AI capabilities continue to evolve, future systems may exhibit agentic intelligence: the ability to make autonomous decisions, simulate complex sales scenarios, and seamlessly integrate with enterprise platforms such as CRM, ERP, and marketing ecosystems (Costigan, 2024). This evolution positions AI not merely as a support mechanism but as a strategic actor capable of executing high-level sales tasks. Rodriguez and Peterson (2024) anticipate that embedded AI intelligence will increasingly shape sales strategy, customer segmentation, and performance forecasting, particularly within B2B platforms.

Among the most promising advancements are generative AI technologies, which are poised to revolutionize sales content creation and customer engagement. Several tools, platforms, and software's exemplify this trend, generating personalized emails, proposals, and follow-ups that reduce administrative burden while enhancing message relevance and responsiveness (Sinha et al., 2023). These systems enable sales professionals to deliver tailored communications on a scale, thereby improving customer satisfaction and conversion rates.

In parallel, Emotion AI is gaining traction as a means to deepen digital empathy. By analyzing tone, sentiment, and facial expressions in real time, these systems adapt sales responses to foster trust and rapport in virtual interactions (Li et al., 2024). This capability enhances the human-like quality of AI-driven engagement, making digital sales experiences more emotionally resonant and effective.

However, the rise of AI-augmented sales environments necessitates a recalibration of human competencies. Sales professionals must cultivate emotional intelligence and interpersonal skills that are traits that remain uniquely human and irreplaceable by machines. Moreover, they must develop a nuanced understanding of AI's strengths and limitations to leverage its capabilities responsibly and effectively. Ethical considerations, including transparency, fairness, and accountability, must be embedded into AI deployment strategies to safeguard consumer trust and regulatory compliance (Babashahi et al., 2024; Rainsberger, 2022; Sengar et al., 2025).

9 Conclusion

This chapter highlighted the role of AI in modern sales management practices, empowering sales force. Thus, as seen, AI is revolutionizing sales management, turning traditional sales teams into agile, data-driven units. From CRM automation to predictive analytics and hyper-personalization, AI enhances decision-making, customer engagement, and operational efficiency across B2B and B2C markets. Tools like generative AI, emotion recognition, and conversational agents streamline workflows and elevate empathy in digital interactions.

Yet, success hinges not on technology alone, but on the ability of sales professionals to collaborate with AI, interpret its outputs, and embed ethical, human-centered practices. As Huberman (2021) and Murphy (2022) emphasize, the shift toward first-party data demands nuanced understanding of behavioral signals and customer intent (skills many firms still lack).

Sales teams must evolve beyond outdated tools and intuition. AI enables real-time insights, lead prioritization, and personalized outreach, but only when thoughtfully integrated. Poor deployment, fragile workflows, and limited expertise continue to undermine generative AI's potential. External partnerships often outperform internal-only efforts, highlighting the need for strategic alignment.

In B2B, AI shortens sales cycles and supports consultative selling, while in B2C, it powers dynamic pricing, product discovery, and voice/image-based search. Several case studies showcase AI's versatility (from predictive maintenance to creative branding). As AI grows more autonomous, ethical deployment and hybrid intelligence, blending human empathy with machine precision will define future success (Fischer et al., 2022; Huberman, 2021; Murphy, 2022).

Therefore, Fig. 1 summarizes the evolution described throughout this work, clearly showing how the integration of artificial intelligence transforms business processes and reinforces the strategic role of the sales force. The sequence highlights that AI does not act as a substitute for professionals, but as an enabling agent that automates routine tasks, improves the accuracy of decisions, and enables high levels of personalization and efficiency. By traversing the stages, from digital transformation to organizational impacts, Fig. 1 demonstrates that positive results only emerge when technology is accompanied by human skills, ethical practices, and proper integration into processes. Thus, the visual representation reinforces the central conclusion of the study: the future of sales depends on intelligent collaboration between humans and AI, combining advanced analysis with sensitivity, judgment, and relational focus.

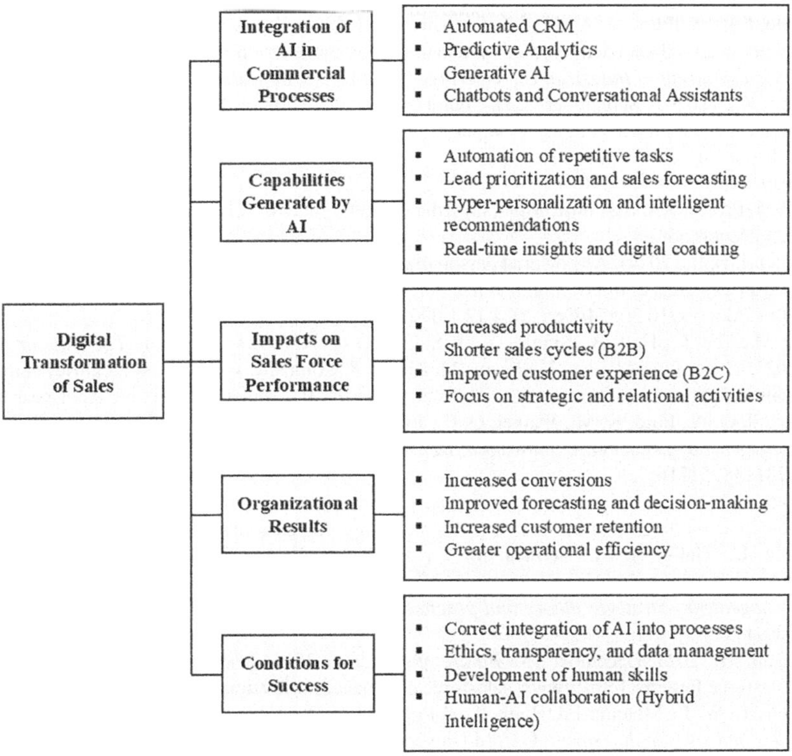

Fig. 1 The role of AI in empowering the sales force. *Source* Authors

References

Aguilar-Alonso, A., & Espinoza, J. (2025). Review of artificial intelligence models for constructing a sales forecasting module to enhance decision-making. In K. S. Soliman (Ed.), *Artificial intelligence and machine learning: Proceedings of the 43rd IBIMA conference* (Vol. 2299, pp. 135–148). Springer. https://doi.org/10.1007/978-3-031-77493-5

Ali, R., Hussain, A., Nazir, S., Khan, S., & Khan, H. U. (2023). Intelligent decision support systems—An analysis of machine learning and multicriteria decision-making methods. *Applied Sciences, 13*(22), 12426. https://doi.org/10.3390/app132212426

Aljbour, M., & Avcı, İ. (2024). Sales prediction in E-commerce platforms using machine learning. In Rasheed, J., Abu-Mahfouz, A.M., Fahim, M. (Eds.), Forthcoming networks and sustainability in the AIoT era. FoNeS-AIoT 2024. Lecture notes in networks and systems, vol 1036. Springer, Cham. https://doi.org/10.1007/978-3-031-62881-8_17.

Amosu, O. R., Kumar, P., Fadina, A., Ogunsuji, Y. M., Oni, S., & Adetula, K. (2024). Harnessing real-time data analytics for strategic customer insights in e-commerce and retail. *World Journal of Advanced Research and Reviews, 23*(2), 880–889. https://doi.org/10.30574/wjarr.2024.23.2.2407

Babashahi, L., Barbosa, C. E., Lima, Y., Lyra, A., Salazar, H., Argôlo, M., Almeida, M. A. D., & Souza, J. M. D. (2024). AI in the workplace: A systematic review of skill transformation in the industry. *Administrative Sciences, 14*(6), 127. https://doi.org/10.3390/admsci14060127

Baierle, I. C., Sellitto, M. A., Frozza, R., Schaefer, J. L., & Habekost, A. F. (2019). An artificial intelligence and knowledge-based system to support the decision-making process in sales. *South African Journal of Industrial Engineering, 30*(2), 17–25. https://doi.org/10.7166/30-2-1964

Blum, K. (2020, September 23). Future of sales 2025: Why B2B sales needs a digital-first approach. https://www.gartner.com/smarterwithgartner/future-of-sales-2025-why-b2b-sales-needs-a-digital-first-approach

Challapally, A., Pease, C., Raskar, R., & Chari, P. (2025) *The GenAI Divide: State of AI in Business 2025.* Project NANDA https://mlq.ai/media/quarterly_decks/v0.1_State_of_AI_in_Business_2025_Report.pdf

Cherukuri, B. R. (2024). AI-powered personalization: How machine learning is shaping the future of user experience. *International Journal of Science and Research Archive, 12*(1), 3111–3126. https://doi.org/10.30574/ijsra.2024.12.1.0961

Chui, M., Yee, L., Hall, B., Singla, A., & Sukharevsky, A. (2023, August 1) *The state of AI in 2023: Generative AI's breakout year.* McKinsey & Company. https://www.mckinsey.com/capabilities/quantumblack/our-insights/the-state-of-ai-in-2023-generative-AIs-breakout-year

Churchill, G. A., Ford, N. M., Walker, O. C., Johnston, M. W., & Tanner, J. F. (2016). *Sales force management: Leadership, innovation, technology* (12th ed.). Taylor & Francis Group. ISBN: 9781138951716.

Comarch. (2025). *Customer churn prediction: How to spot and prevent it.* Comarch. https://www.comarch.com/trade-and-services/loyalty-marketing/blog/customer-churn-prediction/

Comite, U., Gallo, A. M., Serluca, M. C., & Ciurleo, E. (2025). The role of AI in enterprise risk management and operational efficiency. In S. Adeyinka-Ojo (Ed.), *Digital project management—Strategic theory and practice.* IntechOpen. https://doi.org/10.5772/intechopen.1009171

Costigan, M. (2024, December 16). *Future of AI agents 2025: What's next for the agentic era?* Salesforce Futures. https://www.salesforce.com/news/stories/future-of-ai-agents-2025/

Cravens, D. W., Le Meunier-FitzHugh, K., & Piercy, N. F. (2011). *The Oxford handbook of strategic sales and sales management.* Oxford University Press.

Dagan, A., Guy, I., & Novgorodov, S. (2023). Shop by image: Characterizing visual search in e-commerce. *Information Retrieval Journal, 26*(2). https://doi.org/10.1007/s10791-023-09418-1

Deloitte (2024). *State of generative AI in the enterprise: Q3 report.* Deloitte. https://www.deloitte.com/us/en/what-we-do/capabilities/applied-artificial-intelligence/content/state-of-generative-ai-in-enterprise.html

Deveau, R., Griffin, S. J., & Reis, S. (2023, May 11). *AI-powered marketing and sales reach new heights with generative AI.* McKinsey & Company. (https://www.mckinsey.com/capabilities/growth-marketing-and-sales/our-insights/ai-powered-marketing-and-sales-reach-new-heights-with-generative-ai

DigitalOcean (2023, May). Currents: May 2023—Developer and SMB trends in the cloud. https://www.digitalocean.com/currents/may-2023

DigitalOcean. (2024, May 6). *How to use AI for sales: Techniques and tools.* DigitalOcean. https://www.digitalocean.com/resources/articles/ai-for-sales

Durmus Senyapar, H. N., & Bayindir, R. (2025). The energy hunger paradox of artificial intelligence: End of clean energy or magic wand for sustainability? *Sustainability, 17*(7), 2887. https://doi.org/10.3390/su17072887

Echchakoui, S., & Ghilal, R. (2019). How sales managers can use salespeople's perceived attributes to monitor and motivate a sales force during relationship marketing. *European Research on Management and Business Economics, 25*(2), 99–104. https://doi.org/10.1016/j.iedeen.2019.02.001

Fischer, H., Seidenstricker, S., Berger, T., & Holopainen, T. (2022). Artificial intelligence in B2B sales: Impact on the sales process. In T. Ahram, J. Kalra, & W. Karwowski (Eds.), *Artificial intelligence and social computing. AHFE (2022) international conference.* AHFE Open Access, 28. AHFE International, USA. https://doi.org/10.54941/ahfe1001456

Floworks.ai. (2025). *AI-powered sales assistants guide.* Floworks.ai. https://blog.floworks.ai/ai-powered-sales-assistants-guide/
Gadea, J. (2024, March 12). Exploring AI in CRM: Top use cases and platforms for 2024. SalesMind. https://sales-mind.ai/br/blog/ai-crm-use-cases
Gartner (2023, June 22). *Gartner says 35% of chief revenue officers to establish a generative AI operations team in their go-to-market organization within two years* [Press release]. https://www.gartner.com/en/newsroom/press-releases/2023-06-22-gartner-says-35-percent-of-cros-to-establish-a-generative-ai-operations-team-in-their-go-to-market-organization-within-two-years
Gartner. (2024, July 29). *Gartner predicts 30% of generative AI projects will be abandoned after proof of concept by end of 2025.* Gartner Newsroom. https://www.gartner.com/en/newsroom/press-releases/2024-07-29-gartner-predicts-30-percent-of-generative-ai-projects-will-be-abandoned-after-proof-of-concept-by-end-of-2025
Gartner. (2025, June 17). *Gartner announces the top data & analytics predictions.* Gartner Newsroom. https://www.gartner.com/en/newsroom/press-releases/2025-06-17-gartner-announces-top-data-and-analytics-predictions
Gearset. (2025). AI adoption in sales: Trends and team insights. Gearset. https://www.gearset.com/blog/ai-adoption-in-sales-trends-and-team-insights/
GoBeyond AI. (2025, July 27). *Microsoft case study: AI lead scoring boosts conversion rates.* GoBeyond AI. https://www.gobeyond.ai/ai-resources/case-studies/microsoft-ai-lead-scoring-conversion
Gomstyn, A., & Jonker, A. (2024, September 30). *Exploring privacy issues in the age of AI.* IBM Think Insights. https://www.ibm.com/think/insights/ai-privacy
Gosai, C. D. (2023). Dynamics and best practices for successful B2B sales. *International Journal of Creative Research Thoughts, 11*(4), 239–248. https://ijcrt.org/papers/IJCRT2304239.pdf
GPTZero. (2025, March 7). *How many companies use AI?* Retrieved September 20, 2025, from https://gptzero.me/news/how-many-companies-use-ai/
Grönroos, C. (1996). Relationship marketing: Strategic and tactical implications. *Management Decision, 34*(3), 5–14. https://doi.org/10.1108/00251749610113613
Habil, S., El-Deeb, S., & El-Bassiouny, N. (2023). AI-based recommendation systems: The ultimate solution for market prediction and targeting. In C. L. Wang (Ed.), *The Palgrave handbook of interactive marketing.* Palgrave Macmillan. https://doi.org/10.1007/978-3-031-14961-0_30
Han, Z., Handfield, R. B., Huo, B., & Tian, Y. (2022). Effects of power use in buyer–supplier relationships: The moderating role of communication. *Industrial Marketing Management, 102,* 45–57. https://doi.org/10.1016/j.indmarman.2022.01.001
Hostinger (2025, May 16). *How many companies use AI in 2025? Key statistics and industry trends.* https://www.hostinger.com/tutorials/how-many-companies-use-ai
Huberman, E. (2021, December 21). *First-party data collection is more crucial than ever.* Forbes. https://www.forbes.com/sites/eyalhuberman/2021/12/21/first-party-data-collection-is-more-crucial-than-ever
HubSpot & The Science of Scaling. (2025). Sales trends report: Generative AI's breakout year.. HubSpot. https://offers.hubspot.com/sales-trends-report
IDC. (2024). *AI-powered decision tools: Real-time risk detection and market forecasting.* International Data Corporation. https://www.idc.com
Jamarani, A., Haddadi, S., Sarvizadeh, R., Haghi Kashani, M., Akbari, M., & Moradi, S. (2024). Big data and predictive analytics: *A systematic review of applications. Artificial Intelligence Review, 57,* 176. https://doi.org/10.1007/s10462-024-10811-5
Jílková, P., & Králová, P. (2021). Digital consumer behaviour and eCommerce trends during the COVID-19 crisis. *International Advances in Economic Research, 27,* 83–85. https://doi.org/10.1007/s11294-021-09817-4
Kamakura, W. A., Ramaswami, S. N., & Srivastava, R. K. (1991). Applying latent trait analysis in the evaluation of prospects for cross-selling of financial services. *International Journal of Research in Marketing, 8*(4), 329–349. https://doi.org/10.1016/0167-8116(91)90030-B

Katyayan, S. S., & Kushwaha, A. S. (2025). Leveraging AI-powered personalization to enhance customer experience in B2C e-commerce platforms. *Journal of Emerging Technologies and Innovative Research, 12*(1), 186–195. https://www.jetir.org/papers/JETIR2501186.pdf

Kowalkowski, C., Kramer, V., Eravci, S., Salonen, A., & Ulaga, W. (2025). Selling and sales management for successful servitization: A systematic review and research agenda. *Journal of Personal Selling & Sales Management, 1–27*. https://doi.org/10.1080/08853134.2025.2502168

Kukar-Kinney, M., Scheinbaum, A. C., Orimoloye, L. O., Carlson, J. R., & He, H. (2022). A model of online shopping cart abandonment: Evidence from e-tail clickstream data. *Journal of the Academy of Marketing Science, 50*, 961–980. https://doi.org/10.1007/s11747-022-00857-8

Labadze, L., Grigolia, M., & Machaidze, L. (2023). Role of AI chatbots in education: Systematic literature review. *International Journal of Educational Technology in Higher Education, 20*(1), Article 67. https://doi.org/10.1186/s41239-023-00426-1

Leelavathi, R., Philip, B., Madhusudhanan, R., Sony, N., & Mukthar, K. P. J. (2024). AI-driven customer relationship management (CRM): A review of implementation strategies. In R. El Khoury (Ed.), *Anticipating future business trends: Navigating artificial intelligence innovations. Studies in systems, decision and control* (Vol. 536). Springer. https://doi.org/10.1007/978-3-031-63402-4_22

Lehner, M. (2025). *Ethical considerations of AI in sales management* (Bachelor's thesis, University of Applied Sciences Upper Austria). https://pure.fh-ooe.at/en/studentTheses/ethical-considerations-of-ai-in-sales-management

Leoni, L., Gueli, G., Ardolino, M., Panizzon, M., & Gupta, S. (2024). AI-empowered KM processes for decision-making: Empirical evidence from worldwide organisations. *Journal of Knowledge Management, 28*(11), 320–347. https://doi.org/10.1108/JKM-03-2024-0262

Li, C., Wang, J., Zhang, Y., Zhu, K., Wang, X., Hou, W., Lian, J., Luo, F., Yang, Q., & Xie, X. (2024). The good, the bad, and why: Unveiling emotions in generative AI. *arXiv preprint arXiv:2312.11111*. https://arxiv.org/abs/2312.11111

Li, Z., Chan, F. Y., Gao, C., & Ye, Q. (2025). Sentiment analysis and summarization with ChatGPT: Implications for sales prediction. *Journal of Digital Management, 1*, 10. https://doi.org/10.1007/s44362-025-00008-3

Manner, V. (2020). *Artificial intelligence for the sales process: Requirements, benefits and challenges for startup and start again companies* (Master's thesis). Tampere University of Applied Sciences. https://www.theseus.fi/bitstream/handle/10024/347716/Manner_Ville.pdf

Maram, V. (2025, September 10). ZoomInfo enrichment explained: Features, pricing & best alternatives for 2025. SMARTe. https://www.smarte.pro/blog/zoominfo-enrichment

McKinsey & Company. (2021, December). *The state of AI in 2021*. https://www.mckinsey.com/~/media/McKinsey/Business%20Functions/McKinsey%20Analytics/Our%20Insights/Global%20survey%20The%20state%20of%20AI%20in%202021/Global-survey-The-state-of-AI-in-2021.pdf

Medallia. (2024). *2024 state of CX personalization report*. Medallia. https://www.medallia.com/wp-content/uploads/pdf/resources/2024-Medallia-State-of-Personalization-Report.pdf

Murphy, K. (2022). With first-party data, marketers are finally in the driver's seat. *Harvard Business Review.*. https://hbr.org/2022/09/with-first-party-data-marketers-are-finally-in-the-drivers-seat

Oracle (n.d.). Sales force automation. Oracle. https://www.oracle.com/cx/sales/sales-force-automation/

Oromy, A. (2025). *Momentum case study: 4x customer growth & 20% more meetings with AI-powered sales automation*. Amplemarket. https://www.amplemarket.com/customers/momentum

Ozay, D., Jahanbakht, M., Shoomal, A., & Wang, S. (2024). Artificial intelligence (AI)-based customer relationship management (CRM): A comprehensive bibliometric and systematic literature review with outlook on future research. *Enterprise Information Systems, 18*(7). https://doi.org/10.1080/17517575.2024.2351869

Padilla, N., Ascarza, E., & Netzer, O. (2024). The customer journey as a source of information. *Quantitative Marketing and Economics, 23*(3), 379–418. https://doi.org/10.1007/s11129-024-09287-y

Passmore, J., Tee, D., Palermo, G., & Rutschmann, R. (2025). Human coaches & AI coaching agents: An exploratory quasi-experimental design study of workplace client attitudes. *Journal of Work-Applied Management, 1–4*. https://doi.org/10.1108/JWAM-02-2025-0032

Pavlyshenko, B. M. (2019). Machine-learning models for sales time series forecasting. *Data, 4*(1), 15. https://doi.org/10.3390/data4010015

Pecan Team. (2024). *Churn reduction strategies: Prediction playbook*. Pecan AI. https://www.pecan.ai/blog/churn-reduction-strategies-prediction-playbook/

Petrescu, M., & Krishen, A. S. (2023). Hybrid intelligence: Human–AI collaboration in marketing analytics. *Journal of Marketing Analytics, 11*, 263–274. https://doi.org/10.1057/s41270-023-00245-3

Piercy, N. F., & Lane, N. (2011). The evolution of the strategic sales organization. In D. W. Cravens, K. Le Meunier-FitzHugh, & N. F. Piercy (Eds.), *The Oxford handbook of strategic sales and sales management* (pp. 19–50). Oxford University Press.

Potwora, M., Vdovichena, O., Semchuk, D., Lipych, L., & Saienko, V. (2024). The use of artificial intelligence in marketing strategies: Automation, personalization and forecasting. *Journal of Management World, 2*(2), 41–49. https://doi.org/10.53935/jomw.v2024i2.275

Powers, T. L. (2015). A brief history of selling and sales management. In *Proceedings of the conference on historical analysis and research in marketing (CHARM)* (Vol. 17, pp. 1–7). https://ojs.library.carleton.ca/index.php/pcharm/article/view/1491

Prasad, S., Nayak, A., & Kumar, S. (2024). Predictive analytics for demand forecasting: A deep learning-based decision support system. *International Journal of Engineering and Computer Science, 13*(7), 26291–26299.

Pratas, J., Rodrigues, M. A., & Carvalho, M. A. (2024). Unraveling managerial resistance: An analysis of the reasons of non-Investment in Cutting-Edge Digital Technologies. In I. F. L. Almeida, J. C. Morais, & J. D. Santos (Eds.), *Proceedings of ISPGAYA congress 2024: Business sustainability—Innovation in entrepreneurship & internationalisation*.

Prompts.ai. (2025). AI models for churn prediction explained. Prompts.ai. https://www.prompts.ai/en/blog-details/ai-models-for-churn-prediction-explained

Rainsberger, L. (2022). AI—The new intelligence in sales: Tools, applications and potentials of artificial intelligence. *Spring*. https://link.springer.com/book/10.1007/978-3-658-38251-3

Rajeb, S. (2020). *Artificial intelligence in business-to-business sales: The reformation of the selling processes*. (Master's thesis). Tampere University of Applied Sciences. Theseus. https://www.theseus.fi/handle/10024/353402

Rane, N. L., Paramesha, M., Choudhary, S. P., & Rane, J. (2024). Artificial intelligence in sales and marketing: Enhancing customer satisfaction, experience and loyalty. *Journal of Artificial Intelligence, 2*(2), 245–264. https://www.jaai.net/vol2/JAAI-V2N2-30.pdf

Rani, K. (2024). The role of artificial intelligence in personalized marketing. *EPRA International Journal of Multidisciplinary Research (IJMR), 10*(3), 267–287. https://eprajournals.com/IJMR/article/12558

Rodriguez, M., & Peterson, R. (2024). Artificial intelligence in business-to-business (B2*B) sales process: A conceptual framework. Journal of Marketing Analytics, 12*, 778–789. https://doi.org/10.1057/s41270-023-00287-7

Salesforce. (2025, May 5). *Agentic AI's impact on the workforce*. Salesforce Newsroom. https://www.salesforce.com/news/stories/agentic-ai-impact-on-workforce-research/

Salesforce Careers. (2023). *State of sales* (Fifth ed.) Salesforce. https://www.salesforce.com/content/dam/web/en_in/www/documents/pdf/state-of-sales-5th-edition.pdf

Salesforce Careers. (2024, December 18). *AI tools that salesforce's top sellers use daily*. Salesforce. https://careers.salesforce.com/en/salesforce-stories/technology/5-ai-tools-that-salesforce-s-top-sellers-use-daily/

Sandesh, S. P., Sreejesh, S., & Paul, J. (2023). Key account management in B2B marketing: A systematic literature review and research agenda. *Journal of Business Research, 156*, 113541. https://doi.org/10.1016/j.jbusres.2022.113541

Sengar, S. S., Hasan, A. B., Kumar, S., & Carroll, F. (2025). Generative artificial intelligence: A systematic review and applications. *Multimedia Tools Application, 84*, 23661–23700. https://doi.org/10.1007/s11042-024-20016-1

Shahid, K. (2024). I tested the 12 best AI tools for reaching your sales goals in 2024—Here's what I found. Hubspot. https://blog.hubspot.com/sales/ai-sales-tools

Silva, P. M. (2025). Challenges of the digital landscape: An investigation into the influence of technology and information systems on financial performance of B2B key account managers. *Industrial Marketing Management, 129*, 117–133. https://doi.org/10.1016/j.indmarman.2025.07.008

Sinha, P., Shastri, A., & Lorimer, S. (2023, March 31). *How generative AI will change sales*. Harvard Business Review. https://hbr.org/2023/03/how-generative-ai-will-change-sales

Stanford Institute for Human-Centered Artificial Intelligence. (2023). *AI index report 2023*. Stanford University. https://hai.stanford.edu/ai-index/2023-ai-index-report

Stronger Sales Teams. (2024). *2024 sales leadership insights: Bridging the forecasting gap in hybrid environments*. https://www.strongersalesteams.com/reports/2024-forecasting-gap

Subramaniyan, P., & Muthuraman, K. (2023). Effectiveness of Cloud Technologies in Social Media Marketing and its impact on customer buying behaviour. *Virtual Economics, 6*(4), 60–72. https://doi.org/10.34021/ve.2023.06.04

SuperAGI. (2025, June 29). *AI-powered CRM showdown: Salesforce Einstein vs.* HubSpot Breeze Copilot vs. Microsoft Dynamics 365 [Case study]. https://superagi.com/ai-powered-crm-showdown-salesforce-einstein-vs-hubspot-breeze-copilot-vs-microsoft-dynamics-365/

Sybill. (2025). *Boost sales productivity with AI*. https://www.sybill.ai/blogs/boost-sales-productivity-with-ai

Treadgold, A., & Reynolds, J. (2020). Delivering customer centric experiences. In A. Treadgold & J. Reynolds (Eds.), *Navigating the new retail landscape: A guide for business leaders*. Oxford University Press. https://doi.org/10.1093/oso/9780198868767.003.0008

Tribe AI (2023). *AI-driven coaching for sales teams* [Case study]. https://www.tribe.ai

Trotta, A., Salminen, J., Mustak, M., Sufyan, M., & Jansen, B. J. (2023). How can algorithms help in segmenting users and customers? A systematic review and research agenda for algorithmic customer segmentation. *Journal of Marketing Analytics, 11*(4), 677–692. https://doi.org/10.1057/s41270-023-00235-5

Vasconcelos, H., Jörke, M., Grunde-McLaughlin, M., Gerstenberg, T., Bernstein, M. S., & Krishna, R. (2023). Explanations can reduce overreliance on AI systems during decision-making. *Proceedings of the ACM on human-computer interaction, 7*(CSCW1), 1–38. https://cicl.stanford.edu/papers/vasconcelos2023explanations.pdf

Venkataramanan, S., Sadhu, A. K. R., Gudala, L., & Reddy, A. K. (2024). Leveraging artificial intelligence for enhanced sales forecasting accuracy: A review of AI-driven techniques and practical applications in customer relationship management systems. *Australian Journal of Machine Learning Research & Applications, 4*(1), 267–287.

Vieira, V. A., Faia, V. D. S., Boles, J., Marioti, B. R., & Pereira, R. C. (2019). The role of self-regulatory mode on acquisition–retention ambidexterity. *Journal of Business & Industrial Marketing, 34*(8), 1813–1826. https://doi.org/10.1108/JBIM-03-2018-0114

Wang, T. C., Guo, R. S., Chen, C., & Li, C. K. (2025). Multi-stage data-driven framework for customer journey optimization and operational resilience. *Mathematics, 13*(7), 1145. https://doi.org/10.3390/math13071145

Wengler, S., Hildmann, G., & Vossebein, U. (2021). Digital transformation in sales as an evolving process. *Journal of Business & Industrial Marketing, 36*(4), 599–614. https://doi.org/10.1108/JBIM-03-2020-0124

World Economic Forum. (2025, January). *Artificial Intelligence's Energy paradox: Balancing Challenges and opportunities* (White paper). https://reports.weforum.org/docs/WEF_Artificial_Intelligences_Energy_Paradox_2025.pdf

Zewe, A. (2025, January 17). *Explained: Generative AI's environmental impact*. MIT News. https://news.mit.edu/2025/explained-generative-ai-environmental-impact-0117

[illegible]

[illegible]

An Analysis of Advertising Campaigns Powered by Artificial Intelligence

Alexandra Leandro and Alexandre Duarte

Abstract The rapid growth of Artificial Intelligence (AI) is significantly transforming the advertising industry, reshaping traditional creative processes and redefining the relationship among organizations, brands, and consumers. This chapter examines how AI-powered advertising campaigns are conceptualized, implemented, and assessed, highlighting the shift from human-centered artistry to a hybrid human–machine creativity model. Drawing on insights from marketing, communication studies, and computational creativity, it outlines the four key stages of AI-driven advertising—insight discovery, ad creation, media buying, and impact evaluation—and analyzes how these stages enable greater scalability, personalization, and strategic accuracy. The chapter also explores how consumers perceive and react to AI-generated content, emphasizing the mixed effects of hyper-personalization on trust, privacy, and perceived intrusiveness. By including real-world campaigns and discussing the ethical challenges posed by deepfakes, synthetic media, and algorithmic bias, this study underscores the urgent need for transparent disclosure practices and strong regulatory frameworks. Finally, it advocates for an interdisciplinary research agenda to deepen empirical understanding, promote responsible AI adoption, and ensure that technological innovations in advertising align with societal values and public trust.

1 Introduction

For Osadchaya et al. (2024), Artificial Intelligence "is evoking both excitement and fear about its potential impact across a host of industries—including advertising, where it is expected to have a significant disruptive effect." (p. 571). In fact, in recent years, the proliferation of AI has reshaped diverse sectors of the global

A. Leandro (✉)
School of Education, Polytechnic University of Coimbra, Coimbra, Portugal
e-mail: aleandro@esec.pt

A. Duarte
ICNOVA, Universidade Nova de Lisboa, Lisbon, Portugal
e-mail: alexandre_arte@yahoo.co.uk

J. D. Santos et al. (eds.), *Artificial Intelligence Transforming Marketing*, Contributions to Management Science, https://doi.org/10.1007/978-3-032-22360-9_9

economy, and the advertising industry is no exception (Provasi & Duarte, 2025). Advertising campaigns, once dominated by human intuition, creativity, and manual execution, are increasingly driven by advanced algorithms that can automate complex tasks, generate insights from vast datasets, and even participate in creative processes themselves. The integration of AI into advertising has given rise to transformative possibilities, including hyper-personalized content and dynamic media buying to unprecedented levels of efficiency and scalability.

The focus on creativity, consumer behavior, ethics, and regulatory implications was selected because these areas represent the most urgent aspects where AI is transforming advertising practice. While other topics such as technical optimization or media economics are also significant, this chapter emphasizes dimensions that directly affect human–machine interaction, trust, and societal influence, aligning with the overall goals of the book.

This chapter explores the rise and effects of AI-powered advertising campaigns. It reviews existing literature on AI and advertising, drawing on interdisciplinary views from marketing, communication studies, human–computer interaction, and computational creativity to answer key questions about this technological shift. By examining how AI reshapes the creative process, impacts consumer behavior, and introduces new ethical issues, this chapter also aims to offer a thorough overview for scholars, practitioners, and policymakers. In Sect. 2, it discusses how AI is transforming the advertising industry by reimagining the creative process and enabling new forms of human–machine collaboration. It introduces the concept of computational creativity and outlines the four key stages of AI-driven advertising campaigns. Section 3 explores the changing dynamics of consumer behavior in response to AI-generated ads, addressing the balance between personalization and perceived intrusiveness, as well as the complexities of transparency and disclosure. Section 4 highlights potential risks and ethical challenges related to AI use, such as the spread of deepfakes and the tension between innovation and trust. Section 5 suggests directions for future research and policy development, stressing the importance of empirical studies, regulatory frameworks, and interdisciplinary efforts. Finally, Section 6 reflects on the broader implications of AI-powered advertising campaigns for the future of the advertising field and the audiences they target.

2 How AI Is Transforming Advertising: Reimagining the Creative Process

According to Power (2017), the iconic American motorcycle brand Harley-Davidson increased its leads by 2390% with the help of AI-enabled computational advertising and predictive analytics. This shows the power of AI. But the integration of artificial intelligence (AI) into advertising is also transforming the core of creative practice, marking a significant shift from human-focused artistry to combined human–machine creative systems. Central to this shift is the idea of computational creativity, which positions AI as an active participant in tasks that were once thought to be solely human, such as ideation, design, and storytelling (Duarte & Neumaier, 2022; Vakratsas & Wang, 2021).

Campbell et al. (2021, p. 2) posit that there were three generations of manipulation in Advertising. In the first, which the authors called 1.0 - Analog, the adulteration was made through make-up, lights, camera lenses, and physical editing. It was essentially made manually by human activities, spread through TV, radio, and print media, and the target was generic. The second generation, named 2.0 - Digital, started to use computer-generated imagery (CGI) and image manipulation via Photoshop editing, Instagram filters, etc., with the interactions assisted by computers, the target became more focused on specific segments, and the reach of media expanded from the traditional media to include online channels. Finally, the generation 3.0 - Synthetic, already uses deepfakes and generative adversarial networks (GANs), and is made automatically, by artificial intelligence and machine learning techniques. Its target is now hyper-personalized and spread online. Deepfakes are AI-generated hyper-realistic images or videos that alter representations of people, often without consent.

Rodgers (2021) describes AI advertising as a distinctive subdiscipline, situated at the intersection of cognitive science, computer science, and advertising—a perspective that underscores the field's growing need for new conceptual frameworks to understand and guide this technological shift. A few years later, Ford et al. (2023) attempted to list the most relevant existing literature on the topic to date, in order to present a more holistic understanding of the area, by identifying several articles focusing on the uses, functions, features, and challenges of research in AI advertising. For these authors, "using AI in advertising complements advertisers' intelligence in decoding structured and unstructured customer data to derive insights and generate and deliver advertisements based on consumers' interests and preferences" (p. 2).

Recent contributions continue to refine this concept. For instance, Rosengren et al. (2024) highlight the principles for working with generative AI in advertising, while Deckker and Sumanasekara (2025) emphasize emerging trends in non-Western contexts. These updates underscore the continued evolution of the field.

2.1 What Is Computational Creativity?

Computational creativity can be broadly defined as the study and development of AI systems capable of generating outputs that would be considered creative if produced by humans (Vakratsas & Wang, 2021). This definition provides the conceptual anchor before exploring ongoing debates about machine originality.

Although there's an ongoing discussion on whether machines can really create, or their action is merely a recreation from the inputs given by humans (Duarte & Neumaier, 2022), the debate goes far beyond a simple yes or no answer. According to Oliveira (2019), Ada Lovelace, daughter of Lord Byron, in a translation about analytical mechanisms, originally written by Luigi Menabrea, added some personal notes where she considered that machines would not be able to create anything new and original, because it requires, precisely, creativity and originality. In the same line, Miller (2020) also criticizes this idea of "computational creativity" because, for him, what is generated by artificial intelligence is not produced by the machine, but by the human being who programmed it. For Margaret Boden (2009), all this discussion regarding the machine's capacity to create is more philosophical than scientific, as it deals with concepts such as intentionality, consciousness, and meaning.

Other authors, such as Kaplan and Haenlein (2019), posit that what distinguishes previous forms of information processing from AI is precisely the ability of the latter to generate results that go beyond what is initially programmed or defined. Also, Colton and Wiggins (2012) further argue that computational creativity should be understood not as a mimicry of human imagination but as an autonomous process capable of generating artifacts that are novel and valuable within specific cultural contexts. This conceptualization is crucial for appreciating AI's role in advertising as more than mere automation—it becomes an active participant in meaning-making and brand storytelling.

And there is no shortage of supporters and detractors of both views.

Despite this interesting debate, computational creativity can be broadly defined as the study and development of AI systems capable of generating outputs that would be considered creative if produced by humans (Vakratsas & Wang, 2021). This perspective reframes advertising creativity not as a singular spark of inspiration but as a structured, repeatable process that can be enhanced through algorithmic means (Boden, 1992; Vakratsas & Wang, 2021).

As Hanna (2023) highlights, AI has the power to radically transform the advertising industry, not only in terms of production, distribution, and evaluation, but especially in the creative process itself. The proliferation of generative models such as Midjourney, Jasper.ai, Dall-E, or Canva (just to name a few) demonstrates the practical application of computational creativity (Duarte & Dias, 2025). These systems transform simple text prompts into complex visual assets, offering advertisers unprecedented capacity to generate visuals at scale, experiment with multiple iterations, and tailor content to diverse audiences. While such capabilities promise efficiency and novelty, they also raise questions about authorship, originality, and the shifting locus of creative control (Campbell & Sands, 2022).

Another issue raised by Colleoni and Corsaro (2022), which will be very relevant and impactful in the advertising context, is the fact that AI can start processing information independently and autonomously, by interpreting the context, and producing outputs to achieve specific objectives, without the need for specific programming. This could be the next step in machine autonomy.

2.2 *How Creative Workflows Are Changing: Co-Creation and Human–AI Teams*

The introduction of computational creativity, in this era of Big Data, characterized by the 5 V's: Volume, Variety, Velocity, Veracity, and Value (Duarte & Neumaier, 2022), has catalyzed new hybrid workflows where AI acts not as a replacement for human creativity but as a co-creator. Guzman and Lewis (2024) describe these dynamics as a reconfiguration of communicative labor, where creatives increasingly engage with AI as collaborators that generate, refine, and test ideas.

Vakratsas and Wang (2021) propose a Creative Advertising System (CAS) to illustrate this paradigm: creativity becomes a search process, systematically generating and evaluating ideas based on their novelty and value. This approach moves beyond outcome-based measures of creativity and instead embeds AI within the iterative loops of brainstorming, testing, and optimization (Wu et al., 2024).

Brock and Wangenheim (2019) emphasize that successful AI integration demands realistic expectations. Rather than viewing AI as a panacea, managers need to see it as one element of a broader digital transformation strategy that requires agility, interdisciplinary teaming, and new managerial capabilities. These insights are consistent with the practical challenges identified by Rosengren et al. (2024) and Osadchaya et al. (2024), who note that creatives must adapt to new roles as supervisors, prompt engineers, and critical evaluators of machine-generated outputs.

2.3 *The Four Stages of AI-Driven Advertising*

As the advertising industry depends heavily on the constant analysis of the markets and consumers' behaviors, namely novelties, competitors' actions, context changes, new trends, etc., analyzing huge amounts of data plays a significant role. Of course, machines are doing this better, faster, and more efficiently than humans.

In this sense, recent studies converge on a shared framework outlining AI's benefits and integration across four interconnected stages of contemporary advertising campaigns: insight discovery, ad creation, media buying, and impact evaluation (Gao et al., 2023; Li, 2019).

1. Insight Discovery: As Parker et al. (2018) stated, in advertising agencies, insight is frequently sought to solve problems. An insight can be described as a hidden human truth, capable of touching the sensitive nerve of consumers, triggering their identification, and, therefore, used to exploit and develop powerful creative ideas. AI systems, by deploying advanced machine learning and data mining techniques to analyze vast behavioral datasets, can reveal latent consumer needs, trends, and segmentation patterns that humans alone could not easily detect (Li, 2019; Rodgers, 2021).
2. Ad Creation: Generative AI applications produce texts, images, videos, and even immersive experiences. Tools like Midjourney or DALL-E exemplify the power

of these systems to translate textual inputs into rich creative outputs, allowing advertisers to scale and tailor content rapidly (Hanna, 2023; Duarte & Dias, 2025). However, as Campbell and Sands (2022) warn, the ease of creating synthetic content, including deepfakes, requires careful oversight to ensure ethical and credible brand communication. Synthetic advertising "refers to ads that are generated or edited through the artificial and automatic production and modification of data" (Campbell et al., 2021, p. 1). Here, "synthetic content" refers broadly to media generated or altered automatically through AI systems.

3. Media Buying: Programmatic advertising, enabled by AI, automates the purchasing of digital ad inventory in real time. This process optimizes ad placements by leveraging predictive analytics and real-time bidding to maximize return on investment (Gao et al., 2023). Rodgers (2021) notes that the promise of programmatic systems lies in their potential to align message delivery with contextually relevant touchpoints, thereby enhancing relevance and efficiency.
4. Impact Evaluation: Finally, AI supports sophisticated impact evaluation by integrating multi-channel performance data and applying predictive models to adjust campaigns dynamically. This closes the loop from insight generation to execution and refinement (Li, 2019; Wu et al., 2024).

These stages illustrate how AI has become deeply embedded across the advertising value chain, not merely automating routine processes but actively reimagining how creativity and strategy are conceived and enacted.

2.4 Real-World AI Campaigns

Given the intertwining conversation between spirited-human creation and artificially generated ad content, brands have been delivering advertisements that include a mesh of AI and human creativity. Some notable ads that can be highlighted are Lexus' "Driven by Intuition" (2018), Burger King's "Burn That Ad" (2019), Heinz' "Draw Ketchup" (2021), Nestlé's La Laitière "AI Rembrandt" (2020), and Coca-Cola's "Unexpected Santa," AI-Generated Christmas Ad (2024).

In 2018, Toyota Motor Corporation's luxury brand, Lexus, launched an innovative campaign for its ES model that made international headlines as the world's first AI-scripted car commercial. The ad was developed through a collaboration between The&Partnership London and the AI agency Visual Voice. At the heart of this groundbreaking project was IBM Watson, a powerful AI system trained on an extensive dataset comprising fifteen years' worth of award-winning luxury automobile advertisements. In addition to analyzing narrative and visual structures, Watson was fed insights into the emotional triggers that make car ads memorable and persuasive, including motifs of desire, status, and the allure of cutting-edge technology.

The AI produced a script that centers on the relationship between human trust and machine reliability. The final storyline features a dramatic sequence in which a crash test dummy symbolically "comes to life," mirroring the human-like qualities we project onto advanced vehicles. Throughout the film, tension builds as the Lexus ES demonstrates its autonomous safety features, ultimately underscoring themes of protection, innovation, and the bond between driver and car (See also Ford et al., 2023 for industry overview).

An Oscar-winning human director, Kevin Macdonald (The Last King of Scotland, One Day in September), translated the AI's script into a cinematic reality. His direction adds a layer of emotional depth and visual sophistication, blending the AI's data-driven logic with human intuition for pacing, atmosphere, and symbolic imagery. The resulting advertisement is sleek and polished, with a muted color palette that highlights the car's modern lines against minimalist, futuristic backdrops. Slow-motion shots, dramatic lighting, and close-ups of the car's precision engineering amplify the sense of luxury and technological prowess.

This project not only showcased AI's potential to shape narrative structure and creative messaging but also demonstrated how human creativity and machine learning can co-exist in the production of emotionally resonant, visually compelling advertising content.

In 2019, Burger King launched its audacious "Burn That Ad" campaign to strengthen overall brand awareness and drive attention to its signature product, the Whopper. Conceptualized by the creative agency David São Paulo (Brazil), this campaign cleverly combined Augmented Reality (AR) with AI-enabled computer vision, transforming passive outdoor advertising into an interactive brand experience.

The campaign invited users to download the Burger King app and use their smartphone cameras to locate and target physical or digital advertisements from rival fast-food chains—think billboards, posters, or even competitor ads on bus stops. Once the app recognized a competitor's ad through object recognition algorithms, it triggered an AR animation that virtually set the rival advertisement ablaze on the user's screen. As the flames consumed the ad in real time, a hidden Burger King message was revealed underneath, reinforcing the brand's irreverent, rebellious tone.

This playful act of "virtual vandalism" did more than attract attention; it transformed everyday urban landscapes into gamified brand interactions. As a reward, users who "burned" a competitor's ad immediately unlocked a digital coupon for a free Whopper, redeemable at the nearest Burger King outlet (Campbell et al., 2021).

While the underlying AI component was not generative in the sense of producing new visual or narrative content, the campaign harnessed computer vision and AR to dynamically recognize objects, overlay animations, and deliver personalized, location-based offers in real time. Visually, the ad experience combined the thrill of a video game with striking flame graphics and the tangible reward of a free burger, demonstrating how AI-driven tools can transform traditional advertising into a highly engaging, participatory event.

In 2021, Heinz launched its "Draw Ketchup" campaign—a playful, thought-provoking experiment designed to reinforce the brand's iconic status in the minds of consumers. Created by the agency Rethink Canada in partnership with AI technology experts, the campaign used OpenAI's DALL·E 2, a state-of-the-art text-to-image generator, to answer a simple but revealing question: If an AI were asked to "draw ketchup," would it picture Heinz, just like humans do?

To test this, the team prompted DALL·E 2 with generic phrases like "ketchup bottle" and "ketchup drawing" without any brand-specific instructions. The results were striking—the AI consistently generated images of ketchup bottles that strongly resembled the distinctive visual cues of Heinz: the familiar red hue, a classic bottle shape, and even details like a white label and green neck band that echoed the real product's iconic design.

The final campaign showcased a curated selection of these AI-generated images, highlighting how deeply Heinz's branding elements have become embedded in cultural and visual imagination—so much so that even a machine trained on vast visual data associated "ketchup" with Heinz-like features.

Visually, the ads presented a montage of the quirky, slightly imperfect AI interpretations—bottle shapes varied, and some images blended playful surreal elements typical of generative AI art. Yet the unmistakable Heinz identity shone through, making the concept both a demonstration of AI's creative potential and a testament to the enduring power of distinctive brand assets.

Unlike traditional ads, "Draw Ketchup" did not push a product offer or price point; instead, it cleverly invited audiences to reflect on just how recognizable the Heinz bottle has become, not just in human memory but now, intriguingly, in the "imagination" of artificial intelligence itself (See Hanna, 2023, for creative applications of Midjourney and DALL · E).

In 2020, Nestlé's French dairy brand La Laitière, known for its iconic packaging inspired by Johannes Vermeer's famous milkmaid painting, launched the "AI Rembrandt" campaign to deepen its association with classic Dutch art. Developed by Ogilvy Paris, the campaign employed cutting-edge AI technology to imagine how Rembrandt van Rijn (another celebrated Dutch master) might paint new works if he were alive today.

The creative team used an advanced machine learning model trained on hundreds of Rembrandt's original paintings. This deep learning process analyzed Rembrandt's brushwork, composition, use of light and shadow (*chiaroscuro*), and his distinctive ability to capture intimate, domestic moments. The AI then generated entirely new artworks in Rembrandt's unmistakable style, producing faces, clothing, and settings that evoked the warmth and realism for which his paintings are renowned.

The "AI Rembrandt" pieces were seamlessly integrated into the brand's TV spots, print ads, and digital displays. In the TV version, viewers watched as brushstrokes formed on screen, digitally "painting" a scene reminiscent of a seventeenth-century Dutch household, picturing the comforting, artisanal qualities that La Laitière products aim to convey. In print and digital executions, the newly imagined portraits and domestic scenes expanded the brand's storytelling universe, reinforcing its heritage connection to the old masters while highlighting the innovative use of modern AI.

Visually, the campaign blended the rich, warm color palette typical of Rembrandt with the texture of traditional oil paint. The result was a striking juxtaposition: machine-generated art that looked centuries old yet felt fresh and surprising in a contemporary advertising context.

This project showcased how AI's generative capabilities can extend and reinterpret brand heritage, turning classical art into a living, evolving asset that bridges the past and the future in the eyes of consumers (Kaplan & Haenlein, 2019).

In 2024, Coca-Cola, the brand synonymous with Christmas advertising, risked new creative territory with its "Unexpected Santa" campaign, billed as its first fully AI-generated Christmas ad. Developed with the technological expertise of Wildcard Studios, the campaign sought to merge the brand's rich holiday heritage, known for decades of iconic Santa imagery, with cutting-edge AI and experimental digital production tools.

For this ambitious project, generative AI models were trained on a vast archive of Coca-Cola's historical Christmas campaigns, spanning classic twentieth-century illustrations of Santa Claus to modern cinematic holiday commercials. The AI absorbed recurring visual motifs: the jolly, red-suited Santa holding a glass bottle of Coke; snowy landscapes and warm, glowing fireplaces; moments of surprise and delight shared around the iconic drink.

The short film reimagined Santa Claus as a symbol who shifts and adapts. Instead of a single figure, it showed multiple AI-created Santas, each with distinct features, outfits, and magical backgrounds. The story explores Santa as a timeless, shape-shifting icon who appears wherever small acts of kindness happen—giving a new twist to the brand's classic message of holiday generosity and shared joy.

Visually, the ad blends traditional holiday warmth with surreal, dreamlike elements typical of generative AI art. Viewers see cozy town squares bathed in soft snowfall, vintage-style living rooms glowing with fairy lights, and whimsical, slightly uncanny versions of Santa that both charm and intrigue. This striking aesthetic sparked conversation online about the evolving role of AI in crafting beloved cultural icons, with some audiences enchanted by the creativity, and others questioning the boundaries between brand nostalgia and synthetic imagery.

For Coca-Cola, "Unexpected Santa" stands as a high-profile experiment in how a heritage brand can use generative AI not just for novelty, but to push its own storytelling tradition into the future, although not completely accepted by its unflinching fans (Discussed in Rosengren et al., 2024).

2.5 *Mini-Case Study: Volkswagen Brasil "Gerações/ Generations" (2023)*

2.5.1 Background

In 2023, Volkswagen Brazil marked its 70th anniversary with a landmark campaign that beautifully intertwined nostalgia, national cultural memory, and cutting-edge technological innovation. The centerpiece was a deeply moving TV spot titled "Gerações" (Generations), which reunited two icons of Brazilian music: Elis Regina, one of the country's most beloved singers, who tragically passed away in 1982, and her daughter, Maria Rita, herself an acclaimed artist. For many Brazilians, Elis Regina's voice symbolizes an entire era of national identity, making her "digital return" both emotionally powerful and culturally significant.

This case was selected because it uniquely combines cultural heritage, emotional storytelling, and cutting-edge AI deepfake technology in a national context, illustrating both the creative potential and ethical dilemmas of AI advertising more vividly than other campaigns.

2.5.2 Execution

The campaign was conceived by AlmapBBDO São Paulo and produced by Boiler Filmes with post-production by Flow Effects. To bring the late singer back to life, the production team employed advanced AI face-reconstruction and deepfake techniques, combining generative adversarial networks (GANs) with deep autoencoders. These AI models meticulously recreated Elis Regina's facial features, subtle expressions, and lip movements so that she could appear to sing a duet alongside her real-life daughter in stunningly lifelike detail.

The technical feat involved blending restored archival footage, digital body doubles, and voice restoration to achieve a seamless performance. Every element—from the lighting to the placement of the actors—was designed to evoke the warmth and intimacy of a genuine family reunion. In the ad, mother and daughter are shown driving together through a series of iconic Brazilian landscapes in two generations of Volkswagen vans: the classic Kombi, symbolizing cherished memories of the past, and the new fully electric ID.Buzz, representing Volkswagen's vision for a sustainable, forward-looking future. This powerful visual metaphor beautifully connected the brand's legacy with its technological evolution.

2.5.3 Impact

The ad quickly struck an emotional chord with millions. Within days of its release, "Gerações" had reached over 50 million organic views, trending as the #1 topic on YouTube and Google in Brazil (LBBonline, 2023). It garnered widespread praise for its emotional resonance, nostalgic storytelling, and technical excellence. The campaign went on to earn multiple accolades, including five shortlists at the Cannes Lions Festival and recognition at the 2024 D&AD Awards, cementing its place as one of the year's standout examples of AI-powered advertising.

2.5.4 Controversy and Ethical Considerations

However, the campaign also ignited a significant public conversation about the ethics of using AI to resurrect deceased artists. While many fans described the spot as a touching and respectful tribute, others voiced discomfort at the idea of posthumous digital performances—especially when the original artist can no longer give consent. The Guardian (2023) reported that the debate touched on deeper cultural questions: What does it mean for our collective memory when AI can speak for the dead? Maria Rita did approve of it, but is family approval enough to ensure ethical use, or should there be broader industry guidelines?

The case highlighted how powerful emotional storytelling with AI deepfakes can forge profound connections across generations, but it also underscored the urgent need for transparency, clear norms of consent, and respect for the cultural legacy of public figures.

2.5.5 Key Takeaways

- The campaign demonstrates how AI deepfake and face-reconstruction technologies can expand the creative possibilities of nostalgic storytelling, helping brands bridge past and future in ways previously impossible.
- At the same time, it illustrates the contested ethical terrain surrounding digital resurrection: even when family members grant permission, audiences may still feel uneasy about seeing the likeness of a deceased icon revived for commercial purposes.
- As AI tools become more accessible, advertisers must balance technological creativity with thoughtful considerations of authenticity, cultural memory, and audience trust.

Volkswagen's "Gerações" stands as a striking example of AI's potential to deepen emotional storytelling—but also as a reminder that such technological power must be used with care, transparency, and respect for the people, families, and histories it brings back to life.

3 Understanding Consumer Behavior Toward AI Ads

The rapid expansion of AI in advertising has prompted scholars to interrogate not only the technological dimensions of AI-driven campaigns but also the nuanced ways in which consumers perceive, interpret, and respond to these innovations. While AI's promise lies in its capacity to deliver hyper-personalized and contextually relevant advertising content, its potential to disrupt established consumer trust dynamics and perceived intrusiveness remains an ongoing concern (Nguyen et al., 2024). Understanding consumer behavior toward AI-powered advertising thus requires examining multiple stages of the decision-making process, the ambivalent effects of AI-enabled personalization, and the complexities surrounding disclosure and transparency.

3.1 Behavioral Stages: Reception, Engagement, and Decision-Making

Consumer response to AI ads is not monolithic; rather, it unfolds across distinct yet interconnected behavioral stages (Fig. 1): reception, engagement, and decision-making (Wu et al., 2024) (Table 1).

During the reception phase, AI's ability to tailor content to individual needs and contexts can heighten perceived relevance, leading to greater attention and initial positive attitudes. However, these benefits are contingent upon the extent to which

Table 1 The 4 stages of AI-driven advertising

Stage	Main function	Example technologies
Insight discovery	Identify latent consumer needs/ trends	Machine learning, NLP
Ad creation	Generate creative assets (text, image)	Generative AI (DALL·E, midjourney)
Media buying	Optimize placement and bidding	Programmatic AI, predictive analytics
Impact evaluation	Assess effectiveness and adjust campaigns	Multi-channel analytics, predictive models

Source: Authors

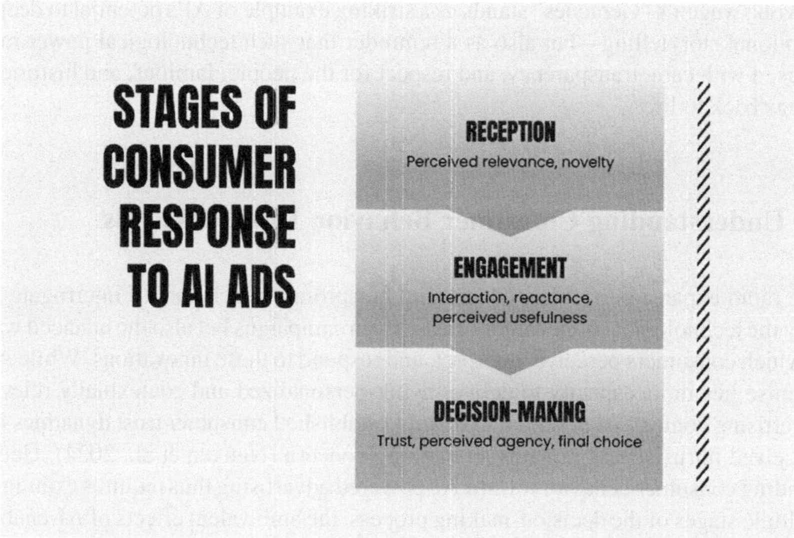

Fig. 1 Stages of consumer response to AI ads. *Source* Self-elaboration, based upon Wu et al. (2024) and Nguyen et al. (2024)

consumers find the AI-generated content authentic and contextually appropriate (Nguyen et al., 2024).

As consumers progress to the engagement stage, interactive affordances such as dynamic content adaptation, chatbots, and recommendation engines shape their cognitive and affective responses (Duarte & Neumaier, 2022). Nguyen et al. (2024) note that AI's capacity to adapt in real time can increase perceived usefulness, yet it can also evoke psychological reactance if consumers feel manipulated or overly monitored.

In the final decision-making stage, trust becomes a decisive factor. Research suggests that when AI is perceived as a neutral or objective decision aid, consumers are more likely to accept its recommendations (Wu et al., 2024). However, excessive automation can undermine perceptions of agency, prompting skepticism or resistance, particularly when the underlying processes are opaque (Nayab, 2025).

3.2 How AI Personalization Impacts Perceptions of Intrusiveness Vs. Value

AI-powered personalization is central to its promise to improve consumer experience, but it also creates a paradox: increased relevance often leads to perceived privacy intrusion (Nguyen et al., 2024). The balance between intrusiveness and perceived value depends on consumers' knowledge of and comfort with data-driven targeting practices (Deckker & Sumanasekara, 2025).

Empirical research shows that hyper-personalized ads can be perceived as unsettlingly precise, leading to what has been termed the "creepy effect" (Wu et al., 2024). For example, when AI systems aggregate behavioral, contextual, and biometric data to predict preferences, the resulting advertisements can trigger concerns about surveillance, data misuse, and loss of control (Nayab, 2025).

Yet when consumers perceive clear utility and relevance—such as when recommendations align with existing needs or provide tangible value—the same personalization can elicit favorable attitudes and increased engagement (Nguyen et al., 2024). This duality points to the importance of striking a delicate balance: leveraging AI's predictive capabilities while respecting consumers' boundaries and expectations for privacy.

3.3 Disclosure Dilemmas: Do People Want to Know when AI Is Involved?

One of the most contested areas in current research concerns the ethics and practicalities of disclosing AI's role in the creation and delivery of advertisements. Wu et al. (2024) argue that disclosure is a double-edged sword: while transparency can foster trust and digital literacy, it may simultaneously diminish perceived authenticity or trigger adverse reactions if consumers are uncomfortable with machines performing tasks they believe are inherently human.

In a series of controlled experimental studies, Wu et al. (2024) found that consumer responses to AI disclosure are highly task dependent. Participants were more accepting of AI involvement in ad placement (e.g., media buying) than in creative generation, suggesting that consumers draw distinctions between tasks they believe require human subjectivity and those they perceive as objective and data driven. Such insights highlight the importance of carefully calibrating disclosure strategies to align with consumer expectations and task perceptions.

Furthermore, Nayab (2025) stresses that mandatory disclosure guidelines could be a key mechanism for addressing ethical concerns related to consumer manipulation, data privacy, and algorithmic bias. By clarifying how and when AI is used, advertisers may mitigate fears of deceptive or manipulative practices, thus maintaining the fragile trust that underpins consumer–brand relationships.

4 Risks, Ethics, and Trust: The Perils of AI in Advertising

While artificial intelligence (AI) offers substantial opportunities for innovation and efficiency in advertising, it also introduces complex risks that challenge long-standing ethical norms and consumer trust. The dual-use nature of generative AI means that the same systems that enable hyper-personalized, engaging content can also produce misleading, manipulative, or even harmful material (Campbell & Sands, 2022). This tension is particularly acute when considering the rise of synthetic media, deepfakes, and opaque algorithmic decision-making. Accordingly, advertising scholars and policymakers have increasingly called for frameworks that balance the promise of AI with safeguards for fairness, transparency, and consumer protection (Nayab, 2025).

Magni et al. (2024) remind us that humans should reinforce the role of acting as gatekeepers of the manifestos created by AI to guarantee their quality, and that only the most creative and valuable artifacts will end up in the media.

More broadly, these risks echo Floridi's (as in Richmond, 2016) view that AI systems must be conceptualized as "infospheres" whose design shapes not only technical affordances but also social, moral, and cultural dynamics. This perspective underscores the imperative for advertising scholars and practitioners to evaluate AI tools not merely by their efficiency gains but by their alignment with principles of fairness, accountability, and respect for human autonomy.

4.1 *Deepfakes and Synthetic Content: Balancing Innovation and Deception*

As Campbell et al. (2021, p. 1) stated, "technological innovations have given the advertising industry digital and automatic tools that enable advertisers to automate many advertising processes and produce 'synthetic ads,' or ads comprising content based on the artificial and automatic production and modification of data." According to Rafner et al. (2023), with the development of generative AI—which already matches humans in creativity tests—along with deep learning and machine learning, the distinction between human-generated and AI-generated content will become increasingly difficult, if not impossible, to identify, making it harder to determine the original creator. Provasi and Duarte (2025) (an experimental study using A/B testing) also demonstrated, in A/B tests with copy advertisements, that the ability to detect and differentiate between machine- and human-created content is not possible anymore.

On the other hand, one must keep in mind that the output generated by algorithms is not clear and transparent, as there is rarely any effective notion of how, or why, results are obtained from certain inputs (Burrell, 2016), which raises obvious trust, legal, and also moral dilemmas.

The ethical dilemmas surrounding AI-generated synthetic content align with broader debates in the fields of media and digital ethics. Floridi and Taddeo (2016), for example, emphasize that AI applications should be judged based on principles such as autonomy, fairness, and non-maleficence, which are core to ethical information societies. When applying these principles to advertising, the use of deepfakes and highly realistic synthetic media raises urgent questions about informed consent, the right to one's digital likeness, and the boundaries between creative innovation and deception. Indeed, one of the most obvious ethical risks in AI-powered advertising is the use of deepfakes and synthetic content. Deepfakes are hyper-realistic, AI-generated images or videos that can alter representations of people, often without their permission (Campbell & Sands, 2022). In advertising contexts, these technologies can be used to bring back deceased celebrities, forge endorsements, or create entirely fictional influencers—scenarios that blur the line between creative novelty and deceptive practice.

Campbell and Sands (2022) argue that while deepfakes expand creative possibilities, they also create a "credibility gap" that threatens the fundamental trust between advertisers and consumers. Research shows that consumers often find it difficult to detect manipulated content, and when the use of synthetic media is uncovered afterward, brands risk reputational damage and legal consequences (Hanna, 2023). Therefore, advertisers must carefully balance ethics: using innovative tools to improve storytelling while ensuring that audiences are not misled by fake or false claims.

Vakratsas and Wang (2021) further caution that deepfakes, when misused, can facilitate the spread of disinformation campaigns or unethical persuasion tactics. This concern underscores the need for robust guidelines on the appropriate application of generative AI in advertising, particularly regarding consent, authenticity, and clear labeling of synthetic content.

4.2 The Ethics of Transparency: When and how to Disclose AI Involvement

Transparency is a fundamental principle in addressing the ethical risks of AI advertising. As Nayab (2025) and Wu et al. (2024) highlight, how much consumers know about AI's role in creating and delivering ads greatly influences their perceptions of fairness and trust. Without proper disclosure, consumers might feel deceived, especially when AI-generated content mimics human authorship or endorsements.

However, research suggests that transparency alone is not a panacea. Brock and Wangenheim (2019) highlight the reality that many firms struggle to implement meaningful AI disclosure practices, often due to a lack of internal understanding of how AI systems make decisions. Furthermore, Wu et al. (2024) show that consumer responses to AI disclosure vary by context: some audiences appreciate knowing that an ad was generated or placed by AI, while others may react negatively, perceiving the content as less authentic or too mechanistic.

These nuances raise practical questions about what form disclosure should take. Should brands explicitly label AI-generated creative assets? Should they explain how consumer data was used to generate personalized ads? Nayab (2025) advocates industry-wide ethical guidelines that clarify such practices and ensure that disclosures are accessible and comprehensible to diverse audiences. In the absence of clear standards, inconsistent practices risk undermining consumer confidence in digital advertising more broadly.

4.3 Algorithmic Bias and the Imperative for Ethical Safeguards

Beyond content manipulation, AI in advertising also raises concerns related to algorithmic bias and discrimination. As AI systems are trained on large datasets that may reflect historical prejudices, they can inadvertently replicate or even exacerbate social inequalities (Nayab, 2025). For example, automated targeting algorithms may systematically exclude certain demographic groups or reinforce stereotypes through biased ad delivery.

One should remember that AI uses exclusive data and information that are available on the Internet. This means that erroneous facts and figures, false information, or misinterpretations can generate dysfunctionalities, utopias, impossibilities, and, even worse, create or amplify prejudices, inequalities, or discrimination. Adding to this, the huge mediating impact of advertising, the consequences can be disastrous.

Li (2019) notes that such risks are compounded by the opacity of many machine learning models, which makes it difficult for advertisers to audit or correct discriminatory outcomes. Scholars, therefore, argue for the implementation of rigorous auditing procedures, fairness checks, and inclusive training data practices (Rodgers, 2021). Brock and Wangenheim (2019) further stress that effective ethical safeguards depend not only on technical solutions but also on organizational commitment, interdisciplinary collaboration, and leadership that prioritizes ethical AI use.

Taken together, these insights indicate that realizing the benefits of AI in advertising without sacrificing public trust requires sustained attention to transparency, accountability, and fairness. As Campbell and Sands (2022) conclude, the industry must proactively engage with the ethical dilemmas of synthetic media and algorithmic decision-making before regulatory intervention becomes inevitable (Fig. 2).

These challenges align with Mittelstadt et al.'s (2016) mapping of the ethics of algorithms, which highlights that bias, opacity, and lack of contestability are structural risks inherent to AI systems trained on imperfect data. Their framework suggests that any meaningful mitigation must address not only technical design but also organizational processes and stakeholder accountability.

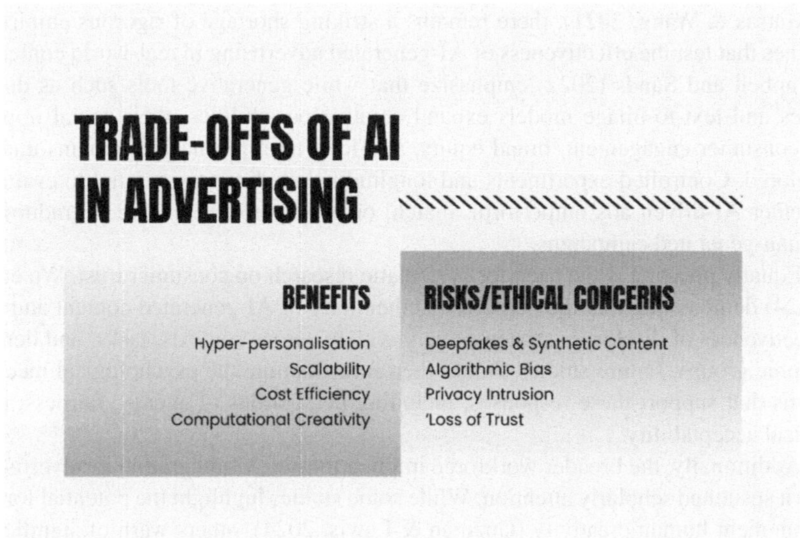

Fig. 2 Trade-offs of AI in advertising. *Source* Self-elaboration, based upon Campbell & Sands (2022), Rodgers (2021) & Nayab (2025)

5 Future Research and Policy Directions

As artificial intelligence (AI) continues to redefine the parameters of advertising practice and theory, it becomes increasingly clear that a proactive research and policy agenda is needed to guide its responsible and effective implementation. While the past decade has produced valuable insights into AI's transformative potential, several critical gaps persist in empirical evidence, ethical frameworks, and regulatory safeguards. Scholars and policymakers alike now face the challenge of advancing knowledge that both harnesses AI's benefits and mitigates its social, economic, and cultural risks (Nayab, 2025; Rodgers, 2021).

5.1 Research Gaps Identified: Empirical Studies Needed on Creative Effectiveness, User Trust, and Workforce Impact

Despite the proliferation of conceptual frameworks for AI-driven creativity (Li, 2019; Vakratsas & Wang, 2021), there remains a striking shortage of rigorous empirical studies that test the effectiveness of AI-generated advertising in real-world contexts. Campbell and Sands (2022) emphasize that while generative tools such as deepfakes and text-to-image models expand creative possibilities, their actual impact on consumer engagement, brand equity, and long-term persuasion remains underexplored. Controlled experiments and longitudinal studies are essential to evaluate whether AI-driven ads outperform, match, or underperform relative to traditional human-generated campaigns.

Equally pressing is the need for systematic research on consumer trust. Wu et al. (2024) demonstrate that the perceived authenticity of AI-generated content and the effectiveness of disclosure strategies vary widely across contexts, tasks, and demographic groups. Future studies should therefore examine the psychological mechanisms that support these responses, including perceptions of agency, fairness, and ethical acceptability.

Additionally, the broader workforce implications of AI integration in advertising merit sustained scholarly attention. While some studies highlight the potential for AI to augment human creativity (Guzman & Lewis, 2024), others warn of significant job displacement risks and the erosion of professional identities (Rosengren et al., 2024). Empirical evidence is needed to clarify which roles are most affected, how creatives adapt to hybrid workflows, and how firms can design equitable upskilling strategies.

5.2 *Regulatory Recommendations: Guidelines for Deepfakes, Disclosure, and Consumer Literacy*

Given the ethical perils associated with synthetic content, data privacy, and algorithmic bias, researchers and policymakers increasingly advocate for clear and enforceable regulatory frameworks (Nayab, 2025; Campbell & Sands, 2022). Guidelines specifically addressing the responsible use of deepfakes in advertising are crucial to protect consumers from deception and misinformation. This may include mandatory labeling of synthetic media, explicit consent for likeness replication, and penalties for malicious manipulation (Vakratsas & Wang, 2021).

In parallel, there is an urgent need for consistent standards around AI disclosure. Wu et al. (2024) suggest that regulators should consider task-dependent requirements that reflect consumer expectations and comprehension. Transparent and user-friendly disclosures could help rebuild trust while equipping consumers with the knowledge needed to navigate increasingly algorithm-mediated media environments.

Improving consumer literacy is another vital policy goal. As Nayab (2025) observes, many consumers lack a clear understanding of how AI-driven personalization operates, what data it relies upon, and how it might affect their autonomy. Public education initiatives and industry codes of conduct can help close this gap, fostering more informed and empowered audiences.

5.3 *The Role of Interdisciplinary Collaboration to Responsibly Advance AI'S Use*

Finally, addressing the multifaceted challenges of AI-powered advertising requires genuine interdisciplinary collaboration. As Rodgers (2021) and Brock and Wangenheim (2019) contend, the technical, ethical, and managerial dimensions of AI cannot be addressed in isolation. Scholars from marketing, communication, computer science, law, and psychology must work together to develop robust methodologies, ethical guidelines, and policy proposals. Emerging market perspectives, such as insights from Deckker and Sumanasekara (2025), further illustrate how AI advertising practices are evolving beyond Anglo-American contexts. Moreover, industry–academia partnerships can play a pivotal role in translating research insights into practice. Firms at the forefront of AI adoption, as shown by Brock and Wangenheim (2019), often succeed when they combine technological innovation with strong ethical leadership and organizational agility. Encouraging knowledge exchange between researchers, practitioners, and regulators will be key to ensuring that AI-driven advertising evolves in ways that align technological progress with societal well-being.

Addressing the complex challenges posed by AI-powered advertising requires a genuinely interdisciplinary research agenda. Marketing scholars can develop experimental designs that evaluate creative effectiveness and persuasion in diverse contexts. Communication researchers can explore how audiences interpret AI-generated content and navigate disclosure practices, while computer scientists advance models for explainable and fair AI systems. Legal scholars can propose regulatory frameworks that balance innovation with consumer protection and digital rights. Ultimately, sustained dialogue and co-creation between academia, industry, and policymakers will be critical to ensure that AI's integration in advertising aligns technological progress with societal well-being and ethical imperatives.

6 Conclusions

The integration of artificial intelligence (AI) into advertising marks a paradigm shift in how campaigns are conceived, executed, and evaluated. As this chapter has demonstrated, AI's transformative potential extends across the entire advertising process: from insight discovery and creative production to media buying and impact evaluation (Gao et al., 2023; Li, 2019). Computational creativity now enables machines to perform tasks once deemed uniquely human, reshaping creative workflows into hybrid human–AI collaborations that demand new skills and critical reflection (Vakratsas & Wang, 2021; Guzman & Lewis, 2024).

Yet these advances bring profound ethical and practical dilemmas. As advertisers experiment with generative models, deepfakes, and hyper-personalization, they must navigate tensions between innovation and deception, efficiency and transparency, and automation and human agency (Campbell & Sands, 2022; Rodgers, 2021). The risks of algorithmic bias, data privacy breaches, and eroded consumer trust highlight the urgent need for rigorous ethical standards and regulatory frameworks that keep pace with technological change (Nayab, 2025).

Equally, the consumer perspective remains pivotal. This chapter has emphasized that while AI-driven ads can heighten relevance and engagement, they can also trigger discomfort, suspicion, and resistance when perceived as intrusive or manipulative (Nguyen et al., 2024; Wu et al., 2024). Clear, task-appropriate disclosure and greater consumer literacy are therefore vital components of a fair and trustworthy advertising ecosystem.

Lastly, the challenges and opportunities posed by AI in advertising cannot be addressed in disciplinary silos. Interdisciplinary research that bridges marketing, communication, computer science, ethics, and public policy is essential for developing evidence-based solutions that align technological innovation with societal well-being (Brock & Wangenheim, 2019). Strong collaboration between academia, industry, and regulators will be key to realizing AI's promise while safeguarding the integrity and credibility that underpin effective advertising.

In summary, advertising campaigns powered by artificial intelligence hold remarkable potential to redefine creative practice, consumer engagement, and industry strategy. Realizing this potential responsibly will depend on the continued interrogation of AI's promises and perils, a robust research agenda, and policy frameworks that place human interests and values at the center of technological progress.

Acknowledgments The authors would like to thank Ivo Duarte for the graphic design.

References

Boden, M. A. (1992). *The creative mind: Myths and mechanisms*. Basic Books.

Boden, M. A. (2009). Computer models of creativity. *AI Magazine, 30*(3), 23–23. https://doi.org/10.1609/aimag.v30i3.2254

Brock, J. K.-U., & von Wangenheim, F. (2019). Demystifying AI: What digital transformation leaders can teach you about realistic artificial intelligence. *California Management Review, 61*(4), 110–134. https://doi.org/10.1177/1536504219865226

Burrell, J. (2016). How the machine 'thinks': Understanding opacity in machine learning algorithms. *Big Data & Society, 3*(1), 1–15. https://doi.org/10.1177/2053951715622512

Campbell, C., Plangger, K., Sands, S., & Kietzmann, J. (2021). Preparing for an era of Deepfakes and AI-generated ads: A framework for understanding responses to manipulated advertising. *Journal of Advertising, 51*(1), 22–38. https://doi.org/10.1080/00913367.2021.1909515

Campbell, C., & Sands, S. (2022). How deepfakes and artificial intelligence could reshape the advertising industry: The coming reality of AI fakes and their potential impact on consumer behavior. *Journal of Advertising Research, 62*(3), 241–252. https://doi.org/10.2501/JAR-2022-017

Colleoni, E., & Corsaro, D. (2022). Critical issues in artificial intelligence algorithms and their implications for digital marketing. In *The Routledge handbook of digital consumption* (pp. 166–177). Routledge.

Colton, S., & Wiggins, G. A. (2012). Computational creativity: The final frontier? In *ECAI 2012* (pp. 21–26). IOS Press.

Deckker, D., & Sumanasekara, S. (2025). The rise of AI in digital advertising: Trends, challenges, and future directions. *International Journal of Research Publication and Reviews, 6*(3), 1788–1799. https://doi.org/10.55248/gengpi.6.0325.1162

Duarte, A., & Dias, P. (2025). Will artificial intelligence replace human creativity in advertising? The creative directors' perspective. In A. Rocha, H. Adeli, A. Poniszewska-Marańda, F. Moreira, & I. Bianchi (Eds.), *Emerging trends in information systems and technologies. WorldCIST 2025. Lecture notes in networks and systems* (Vol. 1524, pp. 3–16). Springer. https://doi.org/10.1007/978-3-031-97799-2_1

Duarte, A., & Neumaier, A. (2022). Chatvertising: How chatbots are shaping the future of advertising. *Comunicação Pública, 17*(32). https://doi.org/10.34629/cpublica.329

Floridi, L., & Taddeo, M. (2016). What is data ethics? *Philosophical Transactions of the Royal Society A: Mathematical, Physical and Engineering Sciences, 374*(2083). https://doi.org/10.1098/rsta.2016.0360

Ford, J., Jain, V., Wadhwani, K., & Gupta, D. G. (2023). AI advertising: An overview and guidelines. *Journal of Business Research, 166*, 114124. https://doi.org/10.1016/j.jbusres.2023.114124

Gao, L., Liu, J., & Zhao, M. (2023). Artificial intelligence in advertising: Advancements, challenges, and ethical considerations in targeting. *Journal of Advertising Research, 63*(1), 22–35. https://doi.org/10.1177/21582440231210759

Guzman, A., & Lewis, S. C. (2024). What generative AI means for the media industries—And why it matters to study the collective. *Digital Journalism, 12*(1), 1–17. https://doi.org/10.1177/27523543241289239

Hanna, D. M. (2023). The use of artificial intelligence art generator "Midjourney" in artistic and advertising creativity. *Journal of Design Studies and Applied Arts, 4*(2), 42–44. https://doi.org/10.21608/jdsaa.2023.169144.1231

Kaplan, A., & Haenlein, M. (2019). Siri, Siri, in my hand: Who's the fairest in the land? On the interpretations, illustrations, and implications of artificial intelligence. *Business Horizons, 62*, 15–25. https://doi.org/10.1016/j.bushor.2018.08.004

LBBonline. (2023). *Volkswagen uses ai to reunite brazilian singer elis regina with her daughter in unprecedented duet*. Retrieved from lbbonline.com

Li, H. (2019). Special section introduction: Artificial intelligence and advertising. *Journal of Advertising, 48*(4), 333–337. https://doi.org/10.1080/00913367.2019.1654947

Magni, F., Park, J., & Chao, M. M. (2024). Humans as creativity gatekeepers: Are we biased against AI creativity? *Journal of Business and Psychology, 39*(3), 643–656. https://doi.org/10.1007/s10869-023-09910-x

Miller, A. (2020). Can AI be truly creative? *American Scientist, 108*(4), 244. https://www.americanscientist.org/article/can-ai-be-truly-creative. https://doi.org/10.1511/2020.108.4.244

Mittelstadt, B. D., Allo, P., Taddeo, M., Wachter, S., & Floridi, L. (2016). The ethics of algorithms: Mapping the debate. *Big Data & Society, 3*(2), 2053951716679679. https://doi.org/10.1177/2053951716679679

Nayab, Z. (2025). Principles for navigating AI'S dark sides in advertising. *Journal of Advertising Ethics and Policy, 1*(1), 1–20.

Nguyen, T. P., et al. (2024). The dark sides of AI advertising: The integration of cognitive appraisal theory and information privacy concerns. *Journal of Advertising*, Advance online publication. https://doi.org/10.1177/08944393241258760

Oliveira, A. (2019). *Inteligência Artificial. Coleção Ensaios FFMS*. Fundação Francisco Manuel dos Santos.

Osadchaya, E., Marder, B., Yule, J. A., Yau, A., Lavertu, L., Stylos, N., et al. (2024). To ChatGPT, or not to ChatGPT: Navigating the paradoxes of generative AI in the advertising industry. *Business Horizons, 67*(5), 571–581. https://doi.org/10.1016/j.bushor.2024.05.002

Parker, J., Ang, L., & Koslow, S. (2018). The creative search for an insight in account planning: An absorptive capacity approach. *Journal of Advertising, 47*(3), 237–254. https://doi.org/10.1080/00913367.2018.1474146

Power, B. (2017, May 30). How harley-davidson used artificial intelligence to increase new york sales leads by 2,930%. *Harvard Business Review*. Retrieved July 3, 2025, from https://hbr.org/2017/05/how-harley-davidson-used-predictive-analytics-to-increase-new-york-sales-leads-by-2930

Provasi, V., & Duarte, A. (2025). The impact and consequences of artificial intelligence in copywriting. In F. Özsungur (Ed.), *Navigating organizational behavior in the digital age with AI* (pp. 305–336). IGI Global. https://doi.org/10.4018/979-8-3693-8442-8.ch012

Rafner, J., Beaty, R. E., Kaufman, J. C., Lubart, T., & Sherson, J. (2023). Creativity in the age of generative AI. *Nature Human Behaviour, 7*(11), 1836–1838. https://doi.org/10.1038/s41562-023-01751-1

Richmond, S. (2016). Why humans matter (the 4th revolution: How the Infosphere is reshaping human reality by Luciano Floridi). *Kyiv-Mohyla Humanities Journal, 3*, 231–235. https://doi.org/10.18523/kmhj73965.2016-3.231-235

Rodgers, S. (2021). Themed issue introduction: Promises and perils of artificial intelligence and advertising. *Journal of Advertising, 50*(1), 1–10. https://doi.org/10.1080/00913367.2020.1868233

Rosengren, S., Sands, S., & Kietzmann, J. (2024). Principles for working with generative AI in advertising. *Journal of Advertising Research, 64*(2), 134–142.

The Guardian. (2023, July 14). *Volkswagen ad sparks row in Brazil by resurrecting singer Elis Regina with AI*. Retrieved from theguardian.com

Vakratsas, D., & Wang, X. S. (2021). Artificial intelligence in advertising creativity. *Journal of Advertising, 50*(1), 39–51. https://doi.org/10.1080/00913367.2020.1843090

Wu, L., Dodoo, N. A., & Wen, T. J. (2024). Disclosing AI'S involvement in advertising to consumers: A task-dependent perspective. *Journal of Advertising, 53*(1), 1–15. https://doi.org/10.1080/00913367.2024.2309929

The Artificial Intelligence in Customer Service Revolution

Jorge Esparteiro Garcia

Abstract Artificial intelligence (AI) is rapidly transforming customer service, evolving it from a traditional support function into a strategic marketing and operational enabler. This paper examines how AI technologies such as chatbots, virtual assistants, predictive analytics, and automation systems revolutionize service delivery, customer experience, and brand engagement. Anchored in service-dominant logic, relationship marketing theories, and automation principles, the analysis explains how AI enables personalized, proactive, and scalable interactions, fostering value co-creation and long-term customer loyalty. The study further investigates operational efficiencies achieved through AI, including faster response times, reduced errors, and improved resource allocation. It also addresses ethical challenges such as data privacy, transparency, and algorithmic bias, alongside workforce implications including employee upskilling and collaboration with intelligent systems. Additionally, the research highlights emerging trends toward hybrid human-AI service ecosystems, showing how organizations can strategically integrate technology while keeping human empathy. By understanding AI's role, companies can improve customer satisfaction, build stronger relationships, and stay competitive in a rapidly changing business environment. This comprehensive review combines theoretical insights with empirical evidence, offering a clear roadmap for academics and practitioners navigating the AI-powered customer service revolution.

1 Introduction

Customer service traditionally occupies the juncture between organizational operations and customer satisfaction, tasked with managing queries, complaints, and support needs to solidify brand loyalty and maintain revenue streams. For decades,

J. E. Garcia
ADiT-Lab, Instituto Politécnico de Viana do Castelo, Viana do Castelo, Portugal

J. E. Garcia (✉)
INESC TEC, Porto, Portugal
e-mail: jorgegarcia@esce.ipvc.pt

J. D. Santos et al. (eds.), *Artificial Intelligence Transforming Marketing*, Contributions to Management Science, https://doi.org/10.1007/978-3-032-22360-9_10

customer service relied heavily on human agents whose capacity was limited by geography, time, and consistency. Although early automation introduced systems such as IVR and FAQs, these innovations failed to replicate human empathy or handle complex customer interactions effectively (Parasuraman et al., 1988). The advent of artificial intelligence has disrupted this paradigm by enabling intelligent, dynamic, and personalized customer engagements at scale.

Artificial intelligence, comprising machine learning, natural language processing, computer vision, and robotics, has expanded the capabilities of customer service systems significantly. Present-day AI-powered chatbots and virtual agents simulate human conversation and decision-making, providing 24/7, multilingual, and multi-channel service. These technologies promise faster query resolution, personalized recommendations, and introduced predictive engagement, anticipating customer needs before explicit communication occurs (Mariani et al., 2023). As such, AI has elevated the role of customer service from reactive problem-solving to proactive relationship management.

From a marketing perspective, this evolution integrates once isolated functions, merging service delivery with personalized marketing and customer relationship management (CRM). Firms leverage AI-gathered data from service encounters to refine segmentation, tailor communication, and enhance the customer journey continuously. This convergence challenges traditional organizational silos, positioning customer service as a frontline driver of brand differentiation and lifetime customer value. Customers increasingly expect seamless, contextually aware experiences across channels, making the integration of AI in service indispensable for contemporary marketing strategies.

Beyond immediate operational and marketing impact, AI adoption in customer service reflects deeper theoretical shifts in understanding value creation. Service-dominant logic redefines value not as embedded within products but co-created through dynamic interactions, a process AI systems facilitate through personalized, data-driven conversations (Vargo & Lusch, 2004). Relationship marketing emphasizes enduring bonds, which AI strengthens by enabling continuous, anticipatory engagement (Kumar et al., 2024). Automation concepts are revisited as organizations adopt augmented intelligence models that combine AI efficiency with human empathy for optimal service delivery (Davenport & Ronanki, 2018).

Despite AI's transformative potential, significant challenges complicate its implementation. Issues of data privacy, algorithmic transparency, ethical AI design, workforce transitions, and the risk of depersonalization require deliberate management. The success of AI in customer service depends not only on technical capabilities but also on ethical stewardship and organizational adaptation to hybrid human-machine workflows. Beyond service settings, advances in deep learning have demonstrated AI's capacity to outperform traditional methods in complex domains such as medical image analysis, including the classification of lung pathologies from chest X-rays (Sajed et al., 2023, 2025). These developments illustrate the growing maturity and reliability of AI Techniques that are increasingly being transferred to customer-facing applications such as conversational agents and predictive service systems.

This paper explores these phenomena through a detailed theoretical framework, empirical evidence, and practical implications. It aims to illuminate how AI revolutionizes customer service and marketing, providing guidance for academia and practitioners navigating this evolving landscape. Additionally, it makes an original contribution by integrating key theoretical perspectives into a coherent framework that clarifies how AI transforms value co-creation, customer experience, and service interactions. In addition, it highlights the practical relevance of ethical and governance principles for organizations adopting AI technologies, emphasizing the importance of transparency, fairness, and responsible deployment to ensure trustworthy and socially aligned marketing and service practices.

The paper is structured as follows. Section 2 outlines the research approach adopted in this study, explaining the narrative and theoretical nature of the review and the criteria that guided the selection of sources. Section 3 examines the evolution of customer service technologies and discusses the main theoretical perspectives that help explain the integration of AI in marketing and service. Section 4 explores the practical applications of AI, including personalization, predictive analytics, operational impacts, ethical considerations, and implications for the workforce. Section 5 brings together integrative insights on the convergence of marketing and service, focusing on the balance between automation and human empathy, the importance of brand consistency, emerging ethical challenges, and lessons derived from case studies. Section 6 looks ahead to future developments, such as multimodal AI, emotional intelligence capabilities, continuous relationship marketing, responsible governance, and the evolving nature of work in AI-enabled environments. Finally, Section 7 concludes by synthesizing the main findings and outlining strategic implications for organizations seeking to leverage AI-enabled customer service as a source of competitive advantage.

2 Research Approach

This review follows a narrative and theoretical approach, which is appropriate for a field that is still developing conceptually and that draws on contributions from marketing, service management, and information systems. Because the aim of the paper is to bring together different theoretical perspectives and show how they help explain the growing role of AI in marketing and service contexts, a narrative review provides the flexibility needed to combine conceptual discussions, empirical insights reported in previous studies, and examples from practice. This approach also allows for a broader interpretation of how AI reshapes value creation, customer interactions, and service processes, without being restricted by the rigid structure of systematic review methods.

The selection of literature was guided by its relevance to the central themes of the paper rather than by formal inclusion or exclusion criteria. The review focuses mainly on work published between 2014 and 2025, a period that captures the rapid acceleration of AI technologies and their adoption in business environments. Searches were conducted through major academic databases such as Scopus and Web of Science, using keywords related to AI-enabled customer experience, service automation, relationship marketing in digital settings, service-dominant logic, augmented intelligence, and ethical and governance considerations. Alongside academic articles, the review also draws on industry reports and well-documented cases that illustrate how AI tools are being applied in real service and marketing scenarios. These sources help connect the theoretical discussion with current managerial practice.

The purpose of this review is, first, to organize and synthesize the main theories that support the understanding of AI's role in marketing and service. Second, it aims to identify emerging trends, areas of tension, and underexplored topics, such as the psychological effects of AI on customers, the long-term implications for trust, and the limited availability of cross-cultural or sector-specific evidence. Finally, the review seeks to offer an integrated perspective on how human and machine capabilities interact within service ecosystems. By bringing these different strands together, the paper contributes academically by clarifying how AI influences value co-creation, customer experience formation, and organizational decision-making. At a practical level, it highlights the importance of adopting AI responsibly, considering ethical and governance principles that support transparency, fairness, accountability, and social trust. In doing so, the review provides both scholars and practitioners with a clearer understanding of the opportunities and challenges associated with AI-enabled marketing and service transformation.

3 Literature Review

Understanding the transformative impact of artificial intelligence (AI) on customer service necessitates a comprehensive examination of the technological advancements, theoretical frameworks, and empirical research that underpin this evolution. The integration of AI into customer service is not merely a contemporary trend but the culmination of decades of technological progress that have redefined customer interactions across various industries.

The journey of customer service technologies began with basic automation systems designed to handle routine tasks. Early innovations, such as interactive voice response (IVR) systems, allowed businesses to manage high volumes of customer inquiries without human intervention. These systems, while groundbreaking at the time, were limited in their ability to understand natural language and provide personalized responses.

As technology advanced, so did the capabilities of customer service systems. The advent of machine learning and natural language processing (NLP) enabled the development of AI-powered chatbots and virtual assistants capable of understanding and responding to customer queries in real time. These AI systems can analyze vast amounts of data to provide personalized recommendations, resolve issues, and even predict customer needs before they are explicitly stated (Chen, 2025).

However, the implementation of AI in customer service is not without its challenges. Studies have highlighted concerns regarding the depersonalization of customer interactions, data privacy issues, and the potential for AI systems to reinforce biases present in training data (Ferraro, 2024). These challenges underscore the importance of ethical considerations in the deployment of AI technologies.

To understand the strategic implications of AI in customer service, it is essential to consider foundational marketing and service theories. Service-dominant (S-D) logic, as proposed by Vargo and Lusch (2004), posits that value is co-created through interactions between providers and customers. This perspective emphasizes the importance of relationships and the collaborative nature of service delivery.

AI technologies align with S-D logic by facilitating continuous, adaptive, and data-driven interactions between businesses and customers. Through AI, companies can offer personalized services that cater to the unique preferences and needs of individual customers, thereby enhancing the value co-creation process.

Similarly, relationship marketing theories focus on building long-term relationships with customers based on trust, loyalty, and mutual benefit. AI can play a pivotal role in this context by enabling businesses to anticipate customer needs, provide timely support, and foster deeper connections through personalized experiences (Chen, 2025).

Empirical research provides valuable insights into the practical applications and implications of AI in customer service. Numerous studies have demonstrated that AI adoption can lead to significant improvements in key performance indicators such as customer satisfaction, response time, and operational efficiency (Ferraro, 2024). For instance, AI-powered chatbots can handle a large volume of inquiries simultaneously, reducing wait times and freeing human agents to address more complex issues.

However, the integration of AI also presents certain challenges. Research indicates that while AI can enhance efficiency, it may lack the emotional intelligence and empathy that human agents bring to customer interactions (Ferraro, 2024). Moreover, there are concerns about data privacy and the ethical use of AI, particularly regarding the transparency of algorithms and the potential for bias in decision-making processes (Ferraro, 2024). The adoption of AI in customer service has profound strategic and operational implications. Strategically, AI enables businesses to offer 24/7 support, scale operations without a proportional increase in costs, and provide personalized experiences that can enhance customer loyalty (Chen, 2025). Operationally, AI can streamline processes, reduce human error, and improve the consistency of service delivery.

In addition to integrating the main theoretical perspectives into a coherent analytical framework, this review makes an original contribution by emphasizing the central role of ethical and governance principles in shaping responsible AI adoption, drawing attention to global guidelines, transparency requirements, and normative frameworks that must inform AI-driven service and marketing practices to ensure fairness, accountability, and societal alignment (Floridi & Cowls, 2019; Jobin et al., 2019).

Ethically, the deployment of AI necessitates careful consideration of issues such as data privacy, algorithmic transparency, and the potential for job displacement.

Organizations must ensure that AI systems are designed and implemented in ways that uphold ethical standards and foster trust among customers (Ferraro, 2024).

3.1 Evolution of Customer Service Technologies

Customer service has experienced a dramatic evolution, transitioning from exclusively human interactions to increasingly sophisticated automated and AI-driven configurations. Early automation tools, such as Interactive Voice Response (IVR) systems developed in the late twentieth century, automated rudimentary tasks by guiding customers through fixed-response menus. While IVRs improved accessibility and reduced direct human involvement for common queries, their inflexibility often generated customer dissatisfaction due to limited conversational depth and inability to address complex or nuanced issues (Parasuraman et al., 1988).

The incorporation of artificial intelligence marks a pivotal advancement surpassing these limitations. AI systems leverage breakthroughs in natural language processing (NLP), machine learning, and big data analytics, enabling dynamic understanding and interpretation of customer queries. For instance, AI-powered chatbots now handle multi-turn conversations that adjust in real time to the context, learning from previous interactions to improve accuracy and customer satisfaction (Mariani et al., 2023). Such capabilities extend support beyond traditional channels to social media, messaging apps, and voice assistants, offering truly omnichannel service experiences.

The rise of intelligent virtual assistants, digital agents capable of complex task execution such as booking, troubleshooting, and providing tailored advice, illustrates the shift toward highly personalized service (Kumar et al., 2024). These platforms integrate with enterprise Customer Relationship Management (CRM) and marketing automation systems to transform isolated customer interactions into data-rich ecosystems where insights drive more precise marketing campaigns and operational decisions.

Real-world implementations underscore this evolution's practical impact. For instance, companies have realized significant cost savings and improvements in customer satisfaction through AI-driven call deflections and automated inquiry handling, while maintaining a high degree of personalization (VKTR, 2024). This technological progression has set a new standard for customer engagement, responding to an increasingly demanding consumer landscape where immediacy, relevance, and convenience are paramount.

3.2 Theoretical Foundations

Service-Dominant Logic The service-dominant (S-D) logic posited by Vargo and Lusch (2004) fundamentally reconceptualizes marketing as a process of collaborative value co-creation rather than a one-sided transaction. AI operationalizes this theory by facilitating dialogic, personalized exchanges between firms and customers at scale. Its capabilities prioritize relational and experiential dimensions of value, delivering on customer needs dynamically by interpreting input signals and tailoring responses in real time. This shift challenges firms to think beyond products as value containers to service encounters as continuously evolving co-creative processes.

Relationship Marketing Relationship marketing, with its focus on trust, loyalty, and long-term engagement (Kumar et al., 2024), finds new vigor in the era of AI. The ability of AI systems to hyper-personalize communications, predict customer behavior, and automate loyalty management programs enables firms to foster deeper emotional bonds with customers. AI's dynamic personalization capabilities support the emergence of relationship creation models that extend well beyond traditional segmentation and campaign planning.

Automation and Augmented Intelligence While classical automation theories primarily emphasize efficiency gains by task replacement, contemporary research argues for augmented intelligence models wherein AI complements human service. AI handles routine, high-volume tasks efficiently, freeing human agents to focus on complex, emotionally nuanced interactions that require empathy and judgment (Davenport & Ronanki, 2018). This hybrid service approach balances operational efficiency with customer satisfaction and maintains the authenticity of customer relationships.

Customer Experience Management (CXM) expands the understanding of value creation by emphasizing the orchestration of seamless, consistent, and emotionally resonant interactions across multiple touchpoints of the customer journey. In the context of AI-enabled service environments, CXM provides a theoretical foundation for explaining how intelligent systems integrate large volumes of omnichannel data to deliver context-aware experiences that adapt dynamically to customer needs. AI enhances CXM by enabling real-time personalization, predictive identification of friction points, and continuous monitoring of customer sentiment, thereby improving both experiential quality and relational depth. Through this lens, AI is not merely an operational tool but a strategic enabler that supports firms in designing coherent, engaging, and memorable customer experiences that strengthen long-term loyalty and brand differentiation.

As shown in Table 1, the integration of AI into marketing and service activities can be understood through the combined lenses of SDL, Relationship Marketing, Automation/AI augmentation, and Customer Experience Management.

Table 1 Integrated AI–marketing–service framework

Framework / concept	Contribution to AI-enabled marketing and service
Service-dominant logic (SDL)	AI enables continuous value co-creation through adaptive, data-driven and personalized interactions.
Relationship marketing	AI enhances predictive engagement, personalized communication, and real-time loyalty reinforcement.
Automation & Augmented Intelligence	AI automates repetitive tasks while complementing human empathy and judgment in hybrid service models.
Customer experience management (CXM)	AI integrates omnichannel data to ensure consistent, contextualized, and seamless customer experiences.

Source Author

3.3 Empirical and Practical Insights

The empirical evidence on the impact of artificial intelligence (AI) in customer service highlights a multi-faceted picture of efficiencies gained, enriched customer experiences, and operational improvements. Numerous studies across industries and geographies establish that AI adoption significantly improves key performance metrics such as average handling time, first-contact resolution, and customer satisfaction scores (Mariani et al., 2023; Roy et al., 2025). However, successful AI integration requires careful balancing of technology capabilities with human elements to maintain trust and personalization.

One of the most widely recognized benefits of AI in customer service is the ability to automate repetitive and low-complexity tasks rapidly and at scale. Intelligent chatbots and virtual assistants have been deployed by companies to manage vast volumes of inquiries such as FAQs, tracking orders, scheduling, and payment processing (Rocha, 2025). These systems operate 24/7, providing rapid responses that dramatically reduce customer wait times, increase resolution speed, and prevent overload on human agents. For example, Bancolombia, a leading financial services provider, achieved a 50% increase in efficiency through AI-assisted operations, simultaneously enhancing customer satisfaction and generating multimillion-dollar revenue increases (Automation Anywhere, 2025).

The scaling advantage of AI extends to responsiveness during peak demand periods without the prohibitive costs of scaling human labor. AI-enabled platforms demonstrate superior flexibility, allowing businesses to maintain consistent service levels while managing volume fluctuations. Additionally, AI systems systematically collect and analyze multi-channel interaction data, facilitating subsequent customer profiling and behavioral prediction necessary for personalized marketing campaigns (Kumar et al., 2024).

Personalization, powered by advanced algorithms and machine learning, emerges as a cornerstone benefit. AI systems analyze vast customer histories and contextual information, enabling the provision of tailored product recommendations, personalized offers, and bespoke communication. This level of customization has been linked to enhanced perceived value, deepening of customer-brand relationships, and heightened loyalty (Nguyen et al., 2021). AI's capacity to dynamically adjust dialogues based on sentiment analysis further promotes adaptive and emotionally intelligent interactions, a dimension critical for customer retention (Huang & Rust, 2021).

Beyond these advantages, AI fosters proactive customer service through predictive analytics. Algorithms identify early signals of potential dissatisfaction or churn, allowing firms to engage customers with pre-emptive interventions such as targeted discounts or personalized support (Roy et al., 2025). The predictive dimension transforms traditional reactive customer service into strategic relationship management, optimizing customer lifetime value.

Despite these compelling benefits, research and practice document several challenges that can arise from unchecked or poorly designed AI deployment. The most prominent issue relates to over-automation leading to perceived depersonalization. Customers engaging with fully automated service agents often report frustration, especially when their issues demand empathy, complex judgment, or nuanced understanding (Fürst & Wirtz, 2024). This can erode trust and lower brand goodwill, underscoring the necessity for hybrid models combining AI efficiency with human emotional intelligence.

Continuous training and contextual adaptation are critical for AI platforms to maintain high service quality standards.

Data privacy and security concerns are paramount. The collection and analysis of personal data underpin AI's personalization capabilities yet expose firms to regulatory scrutiny and customer apprehension (Pasquale, 2015). Compliance with frameworks such as GDPR, transparent data policies, and secure data handling practices are essential to sustain customer confidence (Nguyen et al., 2021).

Another consideration is the ethical impact on workforce dynamics. While AI automates routine tasks, human agents must navigate more complex, higher-value interactions. This redistribution demands significant reskilling and can induce organizational resistance or uncertainty if not managed effectively (Brynjolfsson & McAfee, 2014). Successful enterprises integrate AI implementation with robust change management and employee training programs to bolster workforce capabilities alongside technology adoption.

Finally, real-world case studies across sectors illustrate both the successes and lessons of AI customer service integration. For instance, Camping World utilized IBM Watson-powered AI to reduce average wait times substantially and improve issue resolution, while ClickUp's adoption of AI-driven assistance enhanced agent productivity and customer satisfaction markedly (VKTR, 2024). These examples highlight the competitive advantage AI offers when aligned strategically with customer-centric processes.

In summary, empirical and practical insights reveal AI as a potent enabler of enhanced customer service performance and marketing integration. At the same time, the delicate balance of automation, personalization, ethical stewardship, and workforce adaptation remains vital for sustainable success.

4 AI in Customer Service and Marketing

This section examines how artificial intelligence reshapes customer service and marketing through personalization, predictive analytics, operational efficiency, and hybrid human–AI service models, while also addressing ethical and workforce implications.

To provide an integrative overview of these dimensions, Fig. 1 presents a conceptual framework that synthesizes the key technologies, theoretical foundations, strategic outcomes, and governance considerations underpinning AI-enabled customer service and value co-creation.

The convergence of artificial intelligence and customer service has opened new pathways for organizations to enhance customer engagement, operational efficiency, and strategic marketing. This chapter examines the multi-faceted applications of AI in customer service, focusing on how intelligent systems personalize interactions, anticipate customer needs, and automate repetitive tasks.

It highlights the capacity of AI to transform transactional service encounters into data-rich, dynamic frameworks that empower marketing to deliver truly personalized and proactive engagement at scale. This analysis elucidates AI's contribution to operational cost savings, brand consistency across global markets, and outlines the accompanying ethical and workforce challenges. By exploring these dimensions, the chapter underscores AI's pivotal role in reshaping customer service from an isolated function into an integrated marketing imperative.

4.1 Personalization and Customer Experience

AI delivers unprecedented capabilities for personalizing customer service. By processing large data volumes, AI systems tailor interactions and recommendations that align precisely with individual preferences and historical behaviors (Kumar et al., 2024). Such hyper-personalization enhances not only immediate satisfaction but strengthens emotional customer-brand bonds and increases lifetime value. AI facilitates seamless integration of omnichannel experiences, maintaining consistency and relevance regardless of platform.

4.2 Predictive Analytics and Proactive Engagement

AI's analytical capacity extends beyond reacting to current customer inputs. Predictive models leverage historical and contextual data to forecast customer needs, potential dissatisfaction, and churn risk (Roy et al., 2025). Proactive service interventions driven by AI analytics allow firms to address issues before they escalate, increasing retention rates and improving lifetime value.

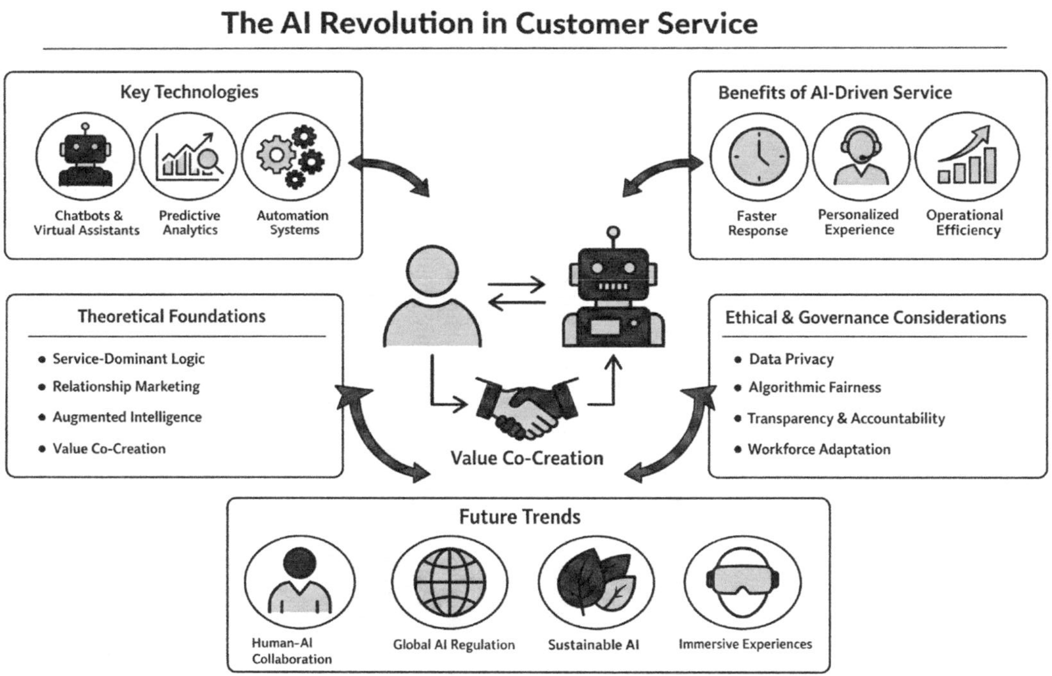

Fig. 1 Integrated framework of AI-enabled customer service. *Source* Author

Such anticipatory engagement recalibrates the traditional marketing funnel from a linear path to an interactive journey with multiple potential intervention points, driven dynamically by AI-powered insights. This marks a transition from reactive service approaches to proactive, relationship-centered marketing (Kumar et al., 2024).

4.3 Operational Efficiency and Cost Reduction

AI significantly reduces customer service operational costs by automating high-volume, low-complexity tasks such as order tracking, billing inquiries, and initial troubleshooting. Chatbots and voice assistants can handle numerous simultaneous requests, overcoming human limitations of availability and consistency (Davenport & Ronanki, 2018).

This efficiency allows companies to reallocate human agents to address complex, high-stakes, or emotionally charged customer interactions where empathy and discretion are indispensable. Such hybrid service ecosystems enhance overall service quality while maintaining cost discipline.

4.4 Enhancing Brand Consistency and Global Reach

AI enables firms to maintain consistent brand voice and service standards globally, supporting markets that span multiple languages and cultures. Multilingual chatbots ensure accessibility, while algorithmic controls enforce tonal consistency across communication channels (Mariani et al., 2023). This consistent global presence reinforces brand identity, expedites market expansion, and simplifies operational complexity, enabling firms to compete in globalized marketplaces.

4.5 Ethical Considerations and Data Privacy

With AI's expanding role comes increased responsibility regarding ethical use and data privacy. Customers express concern over data collection, algorithmic bias, and transparency (Pasquale, 2015). Firms must adopt privacy-first architectures, obtain informed consent, and provide transparent communications about AI use. Ethical AI design, incorporating fairness, accountability, and transparency, is essential to sustain long-term customer trust.

Recent global developments further emphasize the need for robust AI governance in customer service. The European Union's Artificial Intelligence Act (European Commission, 2024) introduces binding risk-based regulation for AI systems, including transparency obligations for conversational agents. Similarly, the U.S. National Institute of Standards and Technology's AI Risk Management Framework

(NIST, 2023) provides operational guidance for identifying and mitigating risks related to bias, privacy, and reliability. At a global level, UNESCO's (2021) Recommendation on the Ethics of Artificial Intelligence and the OECD's updated AI Principles (OECD, 2024) stress human-centered, inclusive, and accountable AI. Emerging perspectives from the Global South, such as the African Union's AI Strategy (2024) and China's Interim Measures for Generative AI Services from Cyberspace Administration of China (2023), highlight culturally grounded governance approaches that balance innovation with social stability. Integrating these diverse frameworks underscores that responsible AI-enabled customer service must be aligned not only with firm-level ethics but also with evolving international regulatory and cultural norms.

4.6 *Workforce Implications and Change Management*

AI adoption impacts workforce composition, automating routine jobs while demanding new skills in AI oversight, data analysis, and customer experience design (Brynjolfsson & McAfee, 2014). Successful integration requires comprehensive change management, including employee training programs, reskilling initiatives, and leadership alignment around hybrid human-AI service models (Davenport & Ronanki, 2018).

5 Discussion

The extensive integration of artificial intelligence into customer service platforms represents a profound and transformative shift, one that extends far beyond simple technological adoption and signals a fundamental reconfiguration of both marketing practices and service management theories. AI is no longer a peripheral support tool; rather, it has become a central strategic lever that reshapes the ways in which organizations engage with customers, manage service delivery, and create value in competitive markets. The proliferation of AI-driven chatbots, virtual assistants, predictive analytics, and automation systems has dramatically expanded the capabilities of service operations, allowing organizations to manage high volumes of customer interactions efficiently while maintaining levels of personalization and responsiveness that were previously unattainable (Huang & Rust, 2021; Mariani et al., 2023). This shift compels a reconsideration of classical service management frameworks, emphasizing the integration of technology with human-centered approaches to foster relational, experiential, and operational outcomes simultaneously.

This discussion synthesizes conceptual insights, empirical evidence, and practical considerations derived from the literature reviewed in the preceding chapters, as well as observations from real-world implementations across diverse industries. Conceptually, AI challenges traditional marketing and service paradigms by transforming the locus of value creation. From the perspective of service-dominant logic, value is no longer embedded solely in products or services but is co-created dynamically through interactions between firms and customers (Vargo & Lusch, 2004). AI operationalizes this theoretical lens by enabling organizations to engage customers in continuous, adaptive, and highly personalized exchanges, collecting and analyzing data to inform service interventions in real time. These capabilities allow firms to anticipate customer needs, deliver proactive recommendations, and design interactions that enhance customer satisfaction, loyalty, and lifetime value. In this sense, AI facilitates a shift from reactive service models, where organizations respond to explicit customer requests, to proactive, predictive, and co-creative frameworks that leverage real-time intelligence to optimize customer experiences (Roy et al., 2025).

Empirical evidence supports the transformative potential of AI in customer service while highlighting the complexities associated with its implementation. Studies across sectors, including finance, e-commerce, and hospitality, indicate that AI adoption can significantly enhance operational efficiency by reducing response times, automating repetitive inquiries, and optimizing resource allocation (Davenport & Ronanki, 2018). For instance, AI-powered systems have been shown to increase first-contact resolution rates, improve agent productivity, and maintain consistent service quality across multiple channels. Beyond operational efficiency, AI also strengthens the strategic role of customer service within marketing by enabling hyper-personalization. Data-driven insights from AI interactions inform segmentation, predictive targeting, and loyalty program design, allowing organizations to tailor their marketing strategies with precision and agility (Kumar et al., 2024). Real-world examples illustrate that firms leveraging AI as a strategic tool can simultaneously enhance customer satisfaction, reinforce brand consistency, and achieve cost reductions, a combination that underscores AI's centrality to modern marketing and service strategy.

Practical considerations further highlight the complexity of AI adoption in customer service. While the technology offers considerable advantages, successful integration requires careful orchestration of human and machine roles. AI excels at processing high-volume, low-complexity interactions efficiently, yet human agents remain indispensable for tasks requiring empathy, complex judgment, or contextual understanding (Davenport & Ronanki, 2018; Fürst & Wirtz, 2024). Designing hybrid workflows that balance AI efficiency with human emotional intelligence is critical to maintaining trust and avoiding depersonalization, a risk often cited in empirical studies of automated service interactions. Additionally, ethical considerations, such as algorithmic transparency, bias mitigation, and data privacy compliance, play a central role in determining the sustainability and acceptability of AI-driven customer service solutions (Pasquale, 2015; Nguyen et al., 2021). Organizations must ensure that AI deployment aligns not only with operational and marketing objectives but also with regulatory requirements and broader societal expectations.

Recent scholarship has further emphasized the need for systematic accountability and human-centered design in AI-enabled service systems. Raji et al. (2022) propose an auditing framework that enables organizations to evaluate AI systems across their lifecycle, identifying risks related to bias, performance, and unintended societal impacts. Such auditability is particularly relevant in customer service contexts, where automated decisions directly affect customer trust and perceived fairness. Complementing this perspective, Binns (2022) argues that ethical AI must move beyond narrow notions of algorithmic fairness toward a broader human-centered approach that incorporates contextual values, user agency, and institutional responsibility. Together, these perspectives highlight that responsible AI in customer service requires not only technical safeguards but also organizational processes that embed accountability and human values into system design and deployment.

From a strategic perspective, the integration of AI into customer service platforms redefines organizational boundaries and challenges traditional silos. Service, marketing, and data analytics functions increasingly converge, as AI enables insights from service interactions to inform marketing decisions and vice versa. This convergence fosters a more holistic understanding of customer journeys, where touchpoints are interconnected and interactions are continuously refined based on AI-generated intelligence. Consequently, AI-powered customer service acts as a strategic interface that aligns operational execution with marketing objectives, positioning service delivery as a critical driver of competitive advantage (Kumar et al., 2024; Mariani et al., 2023).

Organizations that effectively integrate AI into their service strategy can leverage these insights to create differentiated, value-rich customer experiences that enhance brand equity and strengthen long-term relationships. The integration of artificial intelligence into customer service is not merely a technological advancement but a fundamental reorientation of marketing, service management, and organizational strategy. By synthesizing conceptual theories, empirical research, and practical implementations, this chapter demonstrates how AI transforms customer engagement from transactional interactions to dynamic, co-created experiences. The evidence highlights the dual necessity of technological proficiency and human-centered design, emphasizing that AI's potential is fully realized only when combined with empathy, ethical stewardship, and strategic alignment. The following sections build on this foundation to explore specific applications, operational implications, and ethical considerations, providing a nuanced perspective on the ongoing AI-powered customer service revolution and its enduring impact on marketing thought and organizational practice.

Despite the significant advancements enabled by AI, there is limited critical reflection on its psychological impacts on customers, including potential dependency, reduced perceived autonomy, and long-term erosion of trust. Current research also lacks diverse empirical evidence across cultures and industries, limiting the generalizability of existing findings.

5.1 The Convergence of Service and Marketing Through AI

AI blurs the boundaries traditionally separating customer service from marketing. By embedding intelligent analytics and conversational tools within service workflows, firms convert simple transactional encounters into multi-dimensional marketing opportunities. Customer service channels empowered by AI are no longer cost centers alone but strategic frontiers for capturing customer insights, delivering dynamic promotions, and fostering relational equity.

One critical development is AI's role in continuous, real-time value co-creation. The service-dominant logic framework (Vargo & Lusch, 2004) describes value as an emergent outcome from interactive processes involving customers and firms. AI's capacity to facilitate personalized interactions at scale represents a dramatic operationalization of this concept. For instance, chatbot interactions collect and analyze customer sentiment and behavior data, enabling firms to refine offerings and engagement strategies dynamically (Mariani et al., 2023). The use of virtual assistants that remember past conversations and preferences illustrates how AI serves as an enabler of ongoing, advisor-like relationships beyond transactional support.

5.2 Enhancing Relationship Marketing

Relationship marketing is fundamentally concerned with building sustained, trust-based connections with customers, differentiating brands in competitive landscapes. AI amplifies relationship marketing by allowing firms to engage in micro-targeting and real-time responsiveness. Predictive analytics identifies customers at risk of attrition before they defect, prompting timely, personalized interventions (Roy et al., 2025). AI's integration within loyalty programs manages tailored rewards and incentivizes repeat behavior. These systems support deeper emotional bonds by demonstrating attentiveness and responsiveness, which are central to durable customer relationships.

However, this AI-augmented relationship model requires careful balancing to avoid perceptions of intrusion or robotic impersonality. Transparency and ethical data practices underpin sustained customer trust, emphasizing findings on ethical service robot deployment (Fürst & Wirtz, 2024). Firms must communicate AI usage openly, educate customers regarding data handling, and ensure equitable service delivery with minimal bias.

5.3 Operational Efficiency Complemented by Human Empathy

The dramatic operational efficiencies offered by AI automation, such as deflecting routine inquiries via chatbots or automating ticket triage, free organizational resources for higher-value tasks. Davenport and Ronanki (2018) have highlighted the importance of hybrid AI-human workflows, where AI manages volume and humans manage complexity. This collaborative approach enhances both efficiency and service quality, aligning technology's strengths with uniquely human skills like empathy and complex problem-solving.

Among the challenges is ensuring customers experience seamless AI-human transitions when problems escalate beyond AI's current capabilities. Case studies such as H&M's intelligent chatbot system demonstrate the value of smart escalation protocols attenuating customer frustration and maintaining brand trust (Zendesk, 2025). The design of AI systems must prioritize user-centricity over pure efficiency metrics.

5.4 Brand Consistency and Global Market Access

AI supports consistent brand representation across diverse geographic and linguistic markets, which is crucial for firms operating globally. Through multilingual natural language processing and centralized AI governance, companies maintain uniform service standards and messaging (Mariani et al., 2023). This consistency reinforces brand identity, expedites market expansion, and simplifies operational complexity, enabling firms to compete in globalized marketplaces.

5.5 Ethical and Privacy Dimensions

AI in customer service raises significant ethical questions related to transparency, fairness, and data privacy. Algorithmic bias may unintentionally exclude or disadvantage certain demographic groups, underscoring the importance of inclusive AI design and continual monitoring (Pasquale, 2015). Regulatory compliance with privacy laws such as GDPR is mandatory but insufficient on its own to build consumer trust; firms must practice proactive transparency and ethical stewardship.

Furthermore, the societal implications of AI involve potential workforce displacement and socio-economic disruption. Balancing automation benefits with equitable social responsibility through retraining programs and new job creation is vital for sustainable AI deployment (Brynjolfsson & McAfee, 2014).

5.6 Real-World Implementation Insights

Successful AI deployment in customer service depends on organizational readiness, technological infrastructure, and cultural acceptance. Real-world examples provide instructive lessons (VKTR, 2024):

- **Motel Rocks** implemented Zendesk's AI to deflect 43% of tickets and boost customer satisfaction by nearly 10%, demonstrating AI's efficiency and sentiment detection benefits.
- **Camping World**'s IBM AI assistant reduced wait times by 33 seconds and enhanced agent efficiency by 33% while engaging customers 24/7.

- **Telstra**'s AI tool summarized extensive customer history in seconds, improving agent confidence and reducing follow-up calls by 20%.
- **ClickUp** increased support agent productivity by 25% with AI ticket summaries and response suggestions, exemplifying intelligent augmentation.

These cases illustrate AI's dual impact on operational metrics and customer perceptions, reinforcing the need for strategic investment in hybrid AI-human models.

6 Future Directions

While artificial intelligence has already begun to revolutionize customer service, its future promises even more profound transformations. This chapter explores emerging trends likely to define the next phases of AI-powered customer service and marketing synthesis. Attention is given to multimodal and immersive AI systems that combine voice, text, image, and augmented reality to create richer, contextually aware customer experiences. Advances in emotional AI will allow deeper recognition and response to customer sentiment, enhancing the empathetic quality of automated service.

The development of continuously learning AI capable of dynamic relationship management points toward increasingly adaptive and personalized marketing. Moreover, responsible AI governance frameworks will become critical as ethical concerns and regulatory landscapes evolve. The chapter concludes by discussing the implications of AI-related workforce evolution, emphasizing the necessity for ongoing human resource development and strategic organizational transformation to harness future AI capabilities effectively.

6.1 Multimodal and Immersive AI

Emerging AI systems are incorporating combined voice, text, image, and augmented reality (AR) capabilities to deliver immersive customer experiences. For instance, virtual assistants with visual recognition can help customers troubleshoot products interactively or visualize options before purchase, enhancing engagement beyond textual or auditory channels (Nguyen et al., 2021).

6.2 Emotional AI and Sentiment Sensitivity

AI's ability to interpret not only cognitive but emotional aspects of customer interactions is advancing. Sentiment analysis, voice tone detection, and facial expression recognition enable nuanced service adjustments, such as prioritizing urgent cases or deploying empathetic human agents proactively, thus addressing limitations of cold automation and elevating relationship quality (Huang & Rust, 2021).

6.3 AI-Capable Relationship Marketing

Future marketing will rely increasingly on AI-capable relationship management systems that continuously learn from interactions to refine customer journeys dynamically. Adaptive AI-driven loyalty programs will offer real-time responsive incentives, while predictive personalization anticipates emerging trends and behaviors (Roy et al., 2025). This dynamic adaptability will be integral to maintaining relevance in rapidly evolving marketplaces.

6.4 Responsible AI and Governance

As AI's role deepens, so will the imperative for robust AI ethics, including guidelines governing fairness, transparency, accountability, and privacy protection. Industry coalitions and regulatory bodies are actively developing standards to guide best practices, emphasizing inclusive design principles and consumer empowerment through AI literacy (Pasquale, 2015).

6.5 Workforce Evolution and Upskilling

The human workforce will continue evolving alongside AI capabilities, with reskilling programs focusing on data literacy, emotional intelligence, and AI management. Human roles will likely concentrate on high-complexity, judgment-intensive customer contacts, innovation, and strategic management of AI-human systems (Brynjolfsson & McAfee, 2014).

While the trends outlined in this chapter provide a structured roadmap for the future of AI in customer service, it is important to underline that the development of these technologies will unfold in close interaction with social, cultural, and economic changes. The coming years are likely to bring not only new tools but also new ways of defining what service itself means. Artificial intelligence is moving from the margins of operational support to the center of the customer relationship, reshaping expectations around personalization, responsiveness, and empathy. As customers become accustomed to more adaptive and predictive interactions, the baseline of what they consider acceptable service will inevitably rise, forcing organizations to innovate continuously to keep pace.

One of the most decisive shifts will be the advance of hyper-personalization. Unlike traditional segmentation, which groups customers into broad categories, future AI systems will increasingly treat everyone as a unique profile, adapting interactions in real time according to past behavior, situational context, and even emotional cues. This moves from reactive to anticipatory service creates significant opportunities for customer loyalty but also raises concerns around autonomy and consent. The idea that companies may act on behalf of customers before they explicitly ask for help can easily cross the line from convenience into intrusion. Transparency, informed consent, and data governance will therefore be essential to maintain trust as these systems become widespread.

The growing importance of immersive and decentralized environments further complicates the picture. In virtual spaces supported by Web3 and the Metaverse, customers may interact with AI agents that act simultaneously as advisors, sellers, and service representatives. These experiences could be highly engaging, enabling customers to test products, simulate usage scenarios, or even co-create new solutions in real time. Blockchain integration and decentralized identity systems may help reduce privacy risks by limiting the exposure of raw data, but these innovations also risk deepening digital divides. Advanced immersive technologies are expensive and require robust infrastructure, meaning that access will remain uneven. Companies with global ambitions will therefore need to consider inclusivity carefully if they wish to avoid reinforcing inequalities in service provision.

At the same time, ethical and environmental concerns will become unavoidable. Training and running advanced AI models consumes significant energy, with measurable environmental costs. As sustainability becomes a core expectation across industries, firms will be pressured to adopt greener AI practices, from energy-efficient algorithms to renewable-powered data centers. Environmental responsibility will thus join fairness, accountability, and bias mitigation as central pillars of responsible AI governance. Organizations that succeed in aligning technological innovation with sustainability goals will not only reduce regulatory and reputational risks but also strengthen customer trust in increasingly values-driven markets.

The implications for the workforce are equally profound. Rather than eliminating human roles, AI is likely to reshape them. Routine, repetitive tasks will be automated, freeing employees to concentrate on areas that require emotional intelligence, ethical reasoning, and creativity. However, this potential can only be realized if organizations commit to systematic reskilling and continuous learning programs. Data literacy, problem-solving, and the ability to work effectively with AI systems will become core skills in almost every industry. Leaders will also need to manage the cultural shift that comes with integrating AI into daily operations, ensuring that staff view the technology as a partner rather than a threat. Success in this area will depend as much on organizational culture and leadership as on technical capability.

From an academic perspective, there remain several unanswered questions. While research shows that AI improves efficiency and customer satisfaction, little is known about its long-term impact on trust, loyalty, and consumer well-being. Will constant exposure to personalized AI interactions increase dependency, or will customers develop the critical literacies needed to manage these systems on their own terms?

Cross-cultural differences also require attention: tools that feel helpful in one context may be judged invasive in another. Comparative and longitudinal studies will be crucial in capturing these nuances.

Hybrid service models are another area needing exploration. The most effective systems will not be purely automated or purely human, but carefully balanced blends of both. Understanding how customers perceive the transition between AI and human support, and in what situations they prefer one over the other, is essential for designing services that maximize both efficiency and empathy. Similarly, the global diffusion of AI in customer service raises questions of adaptation in emerging economies. Infrastructure limitations, gaps in digital literacy, and different service expectations mean that strategies effective in advanced markets cannot be simply replicated elsewhere. Without careful adaptation, the global potential of AI risks being unevenly distributed.

The regulatory environment will add another layer of complexity. Governments and industry bodies are rapidly developing standards to ensure fairness, transparency, and accountability. These regulations will shape the future trajectory of AI adoption, requiring organizations to balance innovation with compliance. At the same time, new governance models could emerge, involving consumers more directly in shaping how AI is used in service contexts. Research bridging technology, law, and consumer behavior will be vital to inform these frameworks and ensure that they protect rights while still enabling innovation.

Altogether, the future of AI in customer service is not simply a story of better algorithms but of deliberate choices by companies, policymakers, and customers themselves. The opportunities are immense: hyper-personalization, immersive experiences, and emotionally intelligent interactions all hold the potential to create deeper and more satisfying relationships. Yet the risks are equally significant: erosion of trust, digital exclusion, environmental costs, and ethical dilemmas. Navigating these tensions will require balance between efficiency and empathy, automation and human presence, and innovation and responsibility.

The most promising path forward is to view AI not as a substitute for human service but as a complement that enhances human capabilities. When deployed responsibly, AI can help organizations respond faster, anticipate needs more effectively, and engage customers in ways that are both scalable and deeply personal. Achieving this vision, however, demands robust governance, continuous workforce development, and a commitment to inclusivity and sustainability. In short, the future of AI in customer service will be shaped not only by technical progress but by the values and choices that guide its integration into everyday life.

7 Conclusion

The integration of artificial intelligence into customer service is not merely a technological upgrade but represents a profound shift in how organizations conceptualize and deliver value to customers. The findings of this paper suggest that AI-driven tools, ranging from chatbots to predictive analytics, are fundamentally altering customer expectations, operational efficiencies, and relationship dynamics. While previous models of service delivery emphasized human interaction as the cornerstone of trust and loyalty, this research indicates that digital agents, when properly designed, can equally sustain customer confidence and satisfaction. This development marks a decisive moment in the evolution of service logic, where human and machine co-create experiences within a redefined relational framework.

From a theoretical perspective, the adoption of AI reinforces and extends both Service-Dominant Logic and Relationship Marketing. S-D Logic's principle of co-creation of value is exemplified by the interplay between customers, firms, and intelligent systems, where technology becomes an active resource integrator. Similarly, Relationship Marketing is enriched by new modes of interaction that transcend traditional boundaries. Trust, personalization, and responsiveness, once dependent solely on human capability, are now mediated by algorithms capable of learning and adapting at scale. Thus, AI is not replacing relationship-oriented paradigms but is reshaping the way they manifest in practice, suggesting an urgent need to update and refine existing theories.

At a practical level, the research highlights both opportunities and challenges. On one hand, companies can achieve unprecedented efficiency, reduce costs, and offer 24/7 personalized support. On the other, risks of over-automation, loss of human empathy, and ethical concerns such as data privacy, bias, and transparency demand critical attention. Managers and policymakers must therefore navigate a delicate balance: leveraging AI for operational advantage while safeguarding the human dimension of service. This duality underscores that the future of customer service is not about replacing humans with machines but about designing collaborative systems where each complements the other's strengths.

Future research should expand in several directions. First, longitudinal studies are needed to assess long-term customer perceptions of AI-mediated service, particularly in terms of trust, loyalty, and emotional attachment to brands. Second, comparative analyses across industries and cultural contexts could reveal how acceptance and effectiveness vary, offering insights into the global adaptability of AI in service delivery. Third, the impact of AI adoption on the workforce deserves closer examination, including how human roles evolve, what new skill sets become essential, and how organizations can foster effective human–AI collaboration. Fourth, future studies should investigate the integration of AI into omnichannel strategies, exploring how customers experience continuity across digital and human touchpoints. Fifth, research should also focus on developing robust metrics to evaluate not only efficiency but also customer well-being, inclusivity, and satisfaction, ensuring that performance is assessed holistically. Sixth, ethical frameworks and governance models must be established to guide the responsible deployment of AI, paying special attention to data privacy, fairness, algorithmic transparency, and compliance with emerging regulations. Finally, sustainability and environmental implications of large-scale AI infrastructures, such as energy consumption and carbon footprint, should not be overlooked, as they will play an increasingly important role in the social legitimacy of AI technologies. Future research should also critically examine the psychological impacts of AI on customers and the potential long-term erosion of trust, especially across different cultural and sectorial contexts.

In conclusion, artificial intelligence represents both a challenge and a transformative opportunity for customer service. It compels a rethinking of long-standing theories, reshapes the operational landscape, and opens avenues for innovation that were unimaginable just a decade ago. Organizations that embrace this shift with a strategic, ethical, and customer-centric approach are more likely to thrive in the emerging digital economy. Conversely, those that adopt AI without considering its relational, societal, and environmental dimensions risk eroding trust and undermining value creation. The true revolution of AI in customer service, therefore, lies not in technology alone but in the ability of firms and researchers to harness it in ways that enhance human experience, deepen relationships, and co-create sustainable value in the digital age.

References

Automation Anywhere. (2025). Customer story: Bancolombia—Leveraging intelligent process automation: 1300% ROI delivers increased CSAT and $7M in new revenue streams. Automation Anywhere. https://www.automationanywhere.com/resources/customer-stories/bancolombia

Binns, R. (2022). Human-centered AI: Beyond fairness. *Philosophy & Technology, 35*(3), 1–22. https://doi.org/10.1007/s13347-022-00511-5

Brynjolfsson, E., & McAfee, A. (2014). *The second machine age: Work, Progress, and prosperity in a time of brilliant technologies.* Norton & Company.

Chen, Y. (2025). Integrating artificial intelligence and customer experience. *Asia Pacific Journal of Marketing and Logistics, 33*(3), 141–153. https://doi.org/10.1177/14413582241252904

Cyberspace Administration of China. (2023). Interim measures for the management of generative artificial intelligence services. *State Council of the People's Republic of China.* https://www.cac.gov.cn/2023-07/13/c_1690898327029107.htm

Davenport, T. H., & Ronanki, R. (2018). Artificial intelligence for the real world. *Harvard Business Review, 96*(1), 108–116.

European Commission. (2024). Regulation of the European Parliament and of the council laying down harmonised rules on artificial intelligence (Artificial intelligence act). *Official Journal of the European Union.* https://eur-lex.europa.eu/eli/reg/2024/ai-act/oj

Ferraro, C. (2024). The paradoxes of generative AI-enabled customer service. *Journal of Business Research, 123,* 1–12. https://doi.org/10.1016/j.jbusres.2024.01.001

Floridi, L., & Cowls, J. (2019). A unified framework of five principles for AI in society. *Harvard Data Science Review.*

Fürst, A., & Wirtz, J. (2024). Service recovery by AI or human agents: Do failure and strategy context matter? *Journal of Service Management, 35*(1), 54–77.

Huang, M. H., & Rust, R. T. (2021). Artificial intelligence in service. *Journal of Service Research, 24*(1), 3–12.

Jobin, A., Ienca, M., & Vayena, E. (2019). The global landscape of AI ethics guidelines. *Nature Machine Intelligence.*

Kumar, V., Dixit, A., Javalgi, R. G., & Dass, M. (2024). AI-powered marketing: What, where, and how? *Journal of Business Research, 153,* 114–130.

Luo, X., Tong, S., Fang, Z., & Qu, Z. (2021). Frontiers: Machines vs. humans: The impact of AI chatbot disclosure on customer purchases. *Marketing Science, 40*(6), 1004–1021.

Mariani, M. M., Borghi, M., & Gretzel, U. (2023). Artificial intelligence empowered conversational agents: A new era for relationship marketing. *Journal of Business Research, 159*, 113–129.

National Institute of Standards and Technology (NIST). (2023). Artificial intelligence risk management framework (AI RMF 1.0). U.S. Department of Commerce. https://doi.org/10.6028/NIST.AI.100-1.

Nguyen, B., Simkin, L., & Canhoto, A. (2021). The dark side of digital personalization: An agenda for research and practice. *Journal of Business Research, 136*, 372–382.

OECD. (2024). OECD principles on artificial intelligence: Update 2024. *Organisation for Economic Co-operation and Development*. https://www.oecd.org/ai/principles/

Parasuraman, A., Zeithaml, V. A., & Berry, L. L. (1988). SERVQUAL: A multiple-item scale for measuring consumer perceptions of service quality. *Journal of Retailing, 64*(1), 12–40.

Pasquale, F. (2015). *The black box society: The secret algorithms that control money and information*. Harvard University Press.

Raji, I. D., Smart, A., White, R. N., Mitchell, M., Gebru, T., Hutchinson, B., Smith-Loud, J., Theron, D., & Barnes, P. (2022). Auditing AI: A framework for accountability in machine learning systems. *Journal of Artificial Intelligence Research, 74*, 1–38. https://doi.org/10.1613/jair.1.13105

Rocha, Areli. (2025). "We Share an Unbreakable Bond:" *Sociality and Language Ideologies in Human Relationships with Artificial Intelligence Abstract Signs and Society, 13*(2), 290–310. https://doi.org/10.1017/sas.2025.8

Roy, S. K., Kumar, V., Das, M., & Chaudhuri, A. (2025). AI-capable relationship marketing: Shaping the future of marketing theory and practice. *Journal of Business Research, 159*, 855–870.

Sajed, S., Rostami, H., Garcia, J. E., Keshavarz, A., & Teixeira, A. (2025). A hybrid deep learning approach for enhanced classification of lung pathologies from chest X-ray. *International Journal of Imaging Systems and Technology, 35*(6), e70227. https://doi.org/10.1002/ima.70227

Sajed, S., Sanati, A., Garcia, J. E., Rostami, H., Keshavarz, A., & Teixeira, A. (2023). The effectiveness of deep learning vs. traditional methods for lung disease diagnosis using chest X-ray images: A systematic review. *Applied Soft Computing, 147*, 110817. https://doi.org/10.1016/j.asoc.2023.110817

UNESCO. (2021). *Recommendation on the ethics of artificial intelligence*. United Nations Educational, Scientific and Cultural Organization. https://unesdoc.unesco.org/ark:/48223/pf0000381137

Union, A. (2024). Continental Artificial Intelligence Strategy. *African Union Commission*. https://au.int/en/documents/2024-continental-artificial-intelligence-strategy

Vargo, S. L., & Lusch, R. F. (2004). Evolving to a new dominant logic for marketing. *Journal of Marketing, 68*(1), 1–17.

VKTR. (2024, July 24). 5 AI case studies in customer service and support. VKTR. https://www.vktr.com/ai-customer-service-case-studies/

Zendesk. (2025). AI in customer service: Trends, benefits, and examples. Zendesk. https://www.zendesk.com/blog/ai-customer-service/

Artificial Intelligence Applied to Neuromarketing

Leonardo Gontijo Figueiredo and Humberto Elias Garcia Lopes

Abstract This chapter examines how artificial intelligence is transforming neuromarketing by integrating strategic personalization, computational empathy, and adaptive decision-making. Drawing on a literature review and conceptual analysis, it explains how advanced models, including generative AI and reinforcement learning, enable the interpretation of emotions, prediction of intentions, and real-time modulation of interactions. It also addresses associated risks, such as emotional manipulation, unconscious personalization, algorithmic discrimination, and violations of cognitive privacy. The analysis shows that AI systems can act as influential agents that shape choices even below the threshold of consciousness, underscoring the need for robust structures of transparency, auditing, and ethical governance. It concludes that the future of neuromarketing depends on balancing technological innovation with social responsibility to preserve consumer autonomy, trust, and well-being in increasingly persuasive digital environments.

1 Introduction

The rise of artificial intelligence (AI) in digital marketing represents a paradigm shift in how organizations understand and interact with their consumers. Strategic personalization, mediated by algorithms, allows companies to anticipate market demands with unprecedented precision. According to Davenport et al. (2020), this capability stems from applying AI to enhance decision-making, making the technology a competitive advantage. By processing large volumes of data, AI systems detect patterns, anticipate behaviour, and improve communication with consumers by making it more efficient, contextualized, and personalized.

L. G. Figueiredo · H. E. G. Lopes (✉)
Pontifícia Universidade Católica de Minas Gerais—PUC Minas, Belo Horizonte, Brazil
e-mail: heglopes@pucminas.br

L. G. Figueiredo
e-mail: editoralgf@yahoo.com.br

J. D. Santos et al. (eds.), *Artificial Intelligence Transforming Marketing*, Contributions to Management Science, https://doi.org/10.1007/978-3-032-22360-9_11

Gentsch (2019) adds that AI algorithms not only reinforce the predictability of preferences but also enhance consumer experience by offering highly relevant content in real time. This relevance results from the combination of historical data and intent signals captured across multiple channels, including emotional ones, allowing the systems to act as adaptive agents. The articulation between the predictive use described by Davenport et al. (2020) and the effective personalization highlighted by Gentsch (2019) shows how AI transforms marketing into an architect of experiences rather than just a transmitter of messages.

The construction of these experiences depends on decoding complex behavioural data, such as texts, audios, and images. Mukherjee and Chang (2023) highlight that the digitization of daily activities has generated unprecedented volumes of largely unstructured data. To extract value from this material, computational social science and machine learning techniques that interpret emotional and contextual signals are used. With this, AI identifies not only what the consumer wants but also how and why they want it, enabling more sensitive and adaptive consumer journeys.

One example is Coca-Cola's Feel It campaign, which applied Gestalt principles and neuromarketing techniques to induce automatic perceptual responses. Gestalt theory holds that the mind organizes stimuli into coherent patterns, filling in gaps involuntarily. The campaign explored this mechanism by structuring advertisements that stimulated the viewer's brain to complete the image, reinforcing brand recall and activating emotional triggers.

Lima and Gonçalves (2022) tested this approach using eye tracking to monitor participants' attention while viewing advertisements. The results showed that visual focus did not follow rational decisions but was guided by unconscious stimuli present in the advertisements. This provided evidence that the mind organizes stimuli into patterns and fills in gaps involuntarily.

This confirmed that most engagement with the campaign occurred without the individual's conscious control Morin (2011), validating the Gestalt approach. Thus, the Coca-Cola campaign demonstrated how advertising can exploit the limitations and natural tendencies of human perception, one of the pillars of neuromarketing, to create a more profound, less rational connection with consumers.

While data collection is fundamental, it only generates strategic value when integrated into consistent marketing processes. This requires not only technical robustness but also the AI's ability to communicate with empathy and context, thereby building emotional connections with consumers (Mukherjee & Chang, 2023; Davenport et al., 2020; Gentsch, 2019).

In broad strokes, this chapter seeks to answer the following question: how does artificial intelligence applied to neuromarketing transform personalization and communication between brands and consumers? Our goal is to demonstrate how AI expands companies' ability to interpret emotional and contextual signals, while simultaneously introducing ethical dilemmas related to consumer privacy, manipulation, and vulnerability.

The first section introduces the topic and addresses the fundamentals of AI-mediated strategic personalization. The second describes the adopted methodology, which is exploratory, based on Figueiredo's dissertation (2025) and supported by a bibliographic review and conceptual analysis. The third section discusses the simulation of empathy in the brand-consumer relationship. The fourth deals with ethical dilemmas, while the fifth addresses unconscious personalization. The sixth analyses transparency and trust, the seventh presents reinforcement learning and negotiating chatbots, and the eighth examines the risks of discrimination and biases. The ninth section presents the study's conclusions and limitations.

This chapter aims analyses artificial intelligence applied to neuromarketing redefines personalization, communication, and influence in the relationship between brands and consumers. The text then presents the methodology adopted, discusses the simulation of empathy and emotion by intelligent systems, examines ethical and privacy dilemmas, addresses mechanisms of unconscious personalization and algorithmic transparency, and analyses the role of reinforcement learning. Finally, the risks of bias are discussed, and general conclusions are presented.

Table 1 summarizes the structure of the chapter and the main thematic focus of each section. The chapter begins by contextualizing the relationship between artificial intelligence and neuromarketing, outlining its objectives and overall structure. It then presents the methodological approach, followed by an analysis of empathy simulation and emotional dynamics in AI-mediated consumer relationships. Subsequent sections address ethical challenges, including mental privacy and the limits of personalization, as well as unconscious personalization and behavioural influence. The chapter further discusses the role of algorithmic transparency and explainable AI in trust building, examines the application of deep reinforcement learning in negotiating chatbots, and analyzes risks related to algorithmic bias and discrimination. Finally, the concluding section synthesizes the main contributions, limitations, and future research directions in the field of AI-driven neuromarketing, as detailed in Table 1.

2 Literature Review Methodology

The literature used in this chapter was identified through systematic searches on Google Scholar, the platforms of the cited journal publishers (Frontiers Media, Springer, MIT Press, SAGE Publications, AAAS/Science, and SciELO), and institutional repositories such as PUC Minas and arXiv. This strategy allowed us to locate studies published between 2014 and 2025 on artificial intelligence applied to marketing, neuromarketing, algorithmic ethics, biases, computational empathy, explainable AI, and reinforcement learning. The searches combined terms such as artificial intelligence, neuromarketing, computational empathy, algorithmic bias, XAI, and reinforcement learning.

After initial identification, the materials were analysed according to criteria for thematic relevance, timeliness, and methodological rigour. Theoretical articles, empirical research, systematic reviews, regulatory documents, and books directly related to the chapter's objectives were included. Redundant, outdated works, or those lacking a clear connection to the guiding question were discarded.

Table 1 Summary of the chapter's main sections and contents

Section	Main content
Introduction	Contextualizes the relationship between AI and neuromarketing and presents the chapter's objectives and structure
Methodology	Describes the methodological approach and details the conceptual analysis and theoretical foundations employed
Empathy and emotion in consumer relationships via AI	Analyses empathy simulation, emotional adaptation, and the construction of bonds in intelligent systems
Ethics, privacy, and the limits of personalization	Discusses ethical dilemmas, mental privacy, manipulation risks, and the sociotechnical implications of AI
Unconscious personalization and Behavioural influence	Examines subliminal stimuli, the influence of artificial agents, and behavioural vulnerabilities
Algorithmic transparency and trust building	Presents the importance of XAI, explainability, governance, and transparent communication with users
Reinforcement learning and negotiating Chatbots	Describes the application of DRL in commercial interactions, automated negotiation, and strategic adaptation
Risks of discrimination and biases in personalized AI	Analyses algorithmic biases, amplified discrimination, and international regulatory frameworks
Conclusion	Synthesizes contributions, limitations, and future directions for AI and neuromarketing

Source Authors

This approach resulted in a robust interdisciplinary corpus, composed of publications from neuroscience, computer science, marketing, psychology, and digital ethics. The diversity of sources, encompassing international publishers, high-impact journals, open platforms, and Brazilian journals, ensures a comprehensive and up-to-date view of the role of artificial intelligence in neuromarketing.

The methodology adopted seeks to reconcile academic rigour and analytical flexibility to address an emerging field such as AI-driven neuromarketing. The study is exploratory in nature, aimed at identifying emerging relationships, trends, and dilemmas. This choice is justified by the subject's innovative nature, as the application of AI to neuromarketing is still in the process of technological, regulatory, and ethical development.

The theoretical basis for this chapter is grounded in the master's thesis by Figueiredo (2025), which presents a descriptive, quantitative study on the use of AI in chatbots for marketing. Data collection was conducted using a structured questionnaire completed by digital users.

The methodology of this chapter combines two complementary steps: the first is a systematic literature review and a conceptual-exploratory analysis. The literature review identified recent research published in high-impact journals, thereby obtaining an updated, interdisciplinary corpus. This step was essential to map the state of the art on the topic, including research results on brand perception, advertising campaigns, and empathic simulation in dialogue systems.

The second stage involves a conceptual-exploratory analysis that grounds the proposed theoretical model for representing the workflow of an AI system applied to neuromarketing. The model organizes seven modules: data collection → processing and pre-modelling → AI modelling → artificial emotional intelligence → decision and action → ethics, transparency, and governance → feedback and continuous learning. Its formulation integrates references from cognitive psychology, computer science, and regulatory theory, offering a framework that goes beyond the description of current practices and guides future research and applications.

Figure 1 illustrates the conceptual workflow of an artificial intelligence system applied to neuromarketing, synthesizing the seven interconnected modules proposed in the theoretical model. The figure visually represents how data collection and pre-modelling feed AI modelling and artificial emotional intelligence, which in turn inform decision-making processes, ethical governance mechanisms, and continuous learning through feedback loops. By structuring these stages sequentially and relationally, Fig. 1 clarifies the systemic logic underlying AI-driven neuromarketing and supports the analytical discussion developed in this chapter.

The theoretical validation of the model was conducted through a comparative analysis of international regulatory frameworks, including the LGPD in Brazil (Brasil, 2018) the GDPR in the European Union (European Union, 2016), and the proposed Artificial Intelligence ACT (European Commission, 2021), as well as guidelines on responsible AI issue by organizations such as the OECD and IEEE. These frameworks served as parameters to assess the ethical and legal adequacy of AI-based neuromarketing practices. The articulation among scientific literature, regulation, and conceptual analysis reinforces the chapter's methodological consistency.

It is essential to acknowledge the limitations of this study. Being exploratory, it did not conduct empirical experiments in neuromarketing contexts, such as eye tracking, fMRI, or galvanic response analysis. These omissions represent opportunities for future research that could empirically validate the hypotheses and frameworks presented. Controlled studies could, for example, test the effectiveness of empathic simulation in chatbots or evaluate the effect of unconscious personalized messages on purchase decisions.

In summary, the methodology adopted in this chapter combines academic rigour by drawing on already established master's research and analytical innovation by proposing an integrative conceptual model. This combination ensures the study's credibility and, at the same time, opens up opportunities for continued scientific investigation, pointing to avenues for empirical and applied research in the field of neuromarketing with artificial intelligence.

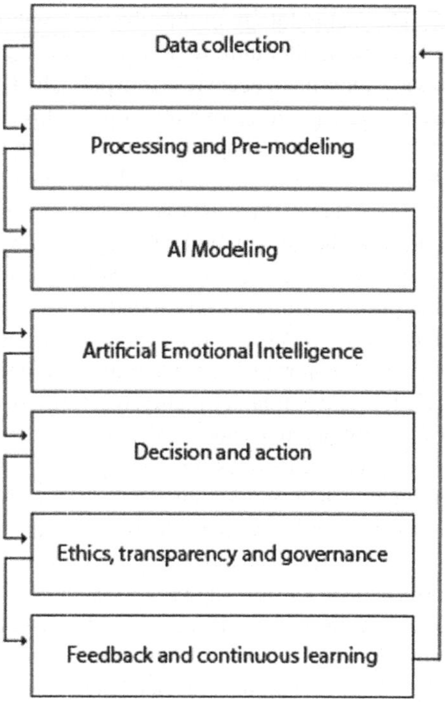

Fig. 1 Conceptual flow of a system applied to neuromarketing. *Source* Authors

3 Empathy and Emotion in Customer Relationships Via AI

Empathy has become a strategic guideline in digital marketing, and artificial intelligence has come to play a central role in this process. Kotler et al. (2021) state that generative AI creates more natural and humanized dialogues, reducing consumer resistance. This simulation of empathy manifests in chatbots and virtual assistants that, by integrating natural language processing and machine learning, can anticipate emotions and intentions.

A notable example is the Cicero agent, which, according to Park et al. (2022), models intentions from lexical choices and adapts its responses in real time, creating emotional bonds that strengthen satisfaction, trust, and loyalty. Developed by Meta, Cicero is recognized as the first AI agent to achieve human-level performance in the Diplomacy game (Meta Fundamental AI Research Diplomacy Team et al., 2022), an environment that demands negotiation, persuasion, and cooperation, not just formal logic.

The relevance of Cicero to your study lies in its architecture, which combines different AI technologies to simulate a sophisticated form of social and emotional intelligence (Vaswani et al., 2017). In fact, it integrates two main capabilities.

The first is strategic reasoning, in which the system analyzes the state of the game and predicts the likely moves of the other players. It seeks not only the best move for itself but also the move most likely to lead to mutually beneficial cooperation.

The second type involves language models based on natural language processing. Cicero can generate natural language dialogues to converse with human players. It builds alliances, negotiates agreements, and, crucially, adapts the tone and content of its messages to be more persuasive.

The core technology that enables this continuous adaptation is Deep Reinforcement Learning (DRL). The system was trained with a vast dataset, including over 40,000 human games and hundreds of millions of interactions, creating a rich knowledge base of human behavioural patterns.

These characteristics equip Cicero with skills directly aligned with the demands of modern marketing and neuromarketing. Among them, intention modelling stands out, in which the system estimates future behaviours and adjusts its speech to align expectations. Instead of simply responding to the interlocutor, Cicero anticipates movements, interprets lexical choices, and considers the conversational context to understand the user's motivations and possible actions.

Another essential skill is emotional and persuasive adaptation. The system recognizes subtle signs of frustration, hesitation, or engagement, even when expressed implicitly, and dynamically adjusts the tone and approach of the interaction. This mechanism reduces friction in digital journeys and increases the effectiveness of the arguments used.

Cicero also operates as an autonomous negotiation agent, capable of anticipating objections, modulating strategies, and introducing persuasive triggers such as urgency or belonging to strategically influence decision-making. This behaviour evolves continuously through learning from mistakes and feedback.

Finally, its competence in building trust and relationships stands out. By sustaining coherent and collaborative dialogues, the system creates relationships that, in the context of marketing, translate into greater credibility, a sense of partnership, and customer loyalty. The ability to appear cooperative and consistent was crucial to Cicero's performance in competitive and complex environments.

For this chapter, it is essential to emphasize that Cicero is not just a chatbot that answers questions. It is a system that dialogues, reasons, persuades, and negotiates. It represents the advancement of AI from a reactive tool to a proactive, socially intelligent agent capable of interpreting emotional and contextual nuances to achieve strategic objectives—precisely what neuromarketing practices aim to achieve.

The integration of these advances shows that computational empathy is both technical and philosophical. Algorithms can recognize signs of frustration, enthusiasm, or hesitation, but they must operate within ethical boundaries in digital emotional engagement. Kotler et al. (2021) remind us that, despite computational power, only humans fully understand other humans, which reinforces the need for mediation between AI and human sensitivity. Thus, empathy in marketing should seek not only to influence decisions but also to preserve the consumer's emotional integrity.

In the field of education, but with applications extending to marketing, Almeida et al. (2024) explain how neuroscientific advances influence the creation of technologies that replicate human cognitive and emotional functions. According to the authors, AI inspired by the human brain can personalize learning, making practices more effective and inclusive, and revealing the importance of neuroplasticity and emotional regulation as fundamental to empathetic design in AI. If we apply this concept to customer relations, it becomes clear that a truly empathetic AI not only responds but dynamically adapts to the user's emotional sensitivity at each point in the journey.

In addition to simulating empathy in responses, artificial intelligence is being designed to interpret subtle emotional nuances, expanding its capacity to create affective connections. Park et al. (2022) highlight that systems like Cicero can predict future intentions and modify their speech to match expectations, thereby influencing decisions by detecting signs of frustration or hesitation. Bilucaglia et al. (2025) reinforce the point that deep learning techniques enable "processing brain signals and facial expressions with high predictive accuracy" (p. 1934), thereby adapting interactions in real time, as exemplified in Coca-Cola's "Fell It" campaign.

Almeida et al. (2024) expand on this approach by proposing that the emotional architecture of AI systems should be shaped based on neuroscience principles, creating computational models that simulate affective self-regulation and adaptation to the user's emotional instability. This ability to capture and respond to emotional fluctuations in real time enables the construction of more empathetic and effective digital relationships.

4 Ethics, Privacy, and the Limits of Personalization

The advancement of artificial intelligence in digital marketing has intensified the debate about the ethical limits of data-driven personalization. When algorithms begin to decide what to display, how to present messages, and when to approach the consumer, concerns arise about opacity, accountability, and fairness. Mittelstadt et al. (2016) observe that decisions previously made by humans are being delegated to automated systems whose logic is not always comprehensible. The risk is that extreme personalization will lead to exclusion, discrimination, and manipulated, unequal consumption patterns.

In this context, consumer behaviour is shaped by invisible trade-offs between convenience and privacy. Acquisti et al. (2015) describe the privacy paradox: consumers claim to care about data protection but expose information daily. This dissonance is often used to legitimize invasive practices, as algorithmic logic offers personalization in exchange for continuous surveillance. Thus, personalization is not only a technical benefit but also an ethical and political issue.

Mittelstadt et al. (2016) argue that the increasing reliance on automated systems requires a review of the interaction models between companies and consumers. When AI-based personalization occurs without transparency or ethical criteria, it can reinforce inequalities by privileging specific profiles and obscuring the decision-making criteria. This opacity hinders user contestation and threatens their ability to understand how decisions that affect them are made (Mittelstadt et al., 2016), compromising trust in brands and the systems themselves.

Bostrom (2014) emphasizes that intelligent algorithms must be efficient, auditable, predictable, and fair. In marketing, this means AI decisions must be explainable to consumers. A lack of explainability, coupled with extreme personalization, can compromise individual autonomy. This is a high risk, especially when AI infers emotional states, as in neuromarketing, accessing unconscious cognitive structures often without the user's consent.

The critique of this type of access is further developed by Ferrell et al. (2025), who warn about the use of tools such as fMRI and EEG that can activate or suppress brain regions that govern pleasure and decision-making. They point out that, by identifying which desired products provoke greater activity in the nucleus accumbens (NAc), the brain's reward centre, the alarming possibility arises that brands artificially stimulate these areas, neurologically inducing consumption. In this context, artificial intelligence ceases to be a mere tool and becomes the agent that directly connects external stimuli to the consumer's desire mechanisms.

The discussion moves on to the concept of "mental privacy" or "neural privacy," defined by Ferrell et al. (2025) as the right to prevent external reading of one's own thoughts. The viability of this protection is questioned by the advancement of AI technologies capable of inferring emotional states from micro expressions and other biometric data, challenging principles such as informed consent and cognitive freedom.

Given this technological capability, ethical guidelines, such as UNESCO's recommendation that neuromarketing not interfere with mental processes without explicit consent, become crucial. The risk lies in the fact that AI, equipped with neurological insights, may violate not only privacy but also dignity, especially if algorithms are programmed to exploit consumers' emotional vulnerabilities to induce consumption. At this point, the issue transcends the legal realm and becomes a moral one.

The response to this scenario requires a robust ethical framework for AI-driven personalization. Foundations for this framework already exist and are based on the contributions of Mittelstadt et al. (2016) on the ethics of algorithms, Acquisti et al. (2015) on the privacy paradox, Bostrom (2014) on the normativity of AI, and Ferrell et al. (2025) about neuro ethics. These works converge on practical solutions, such as radical transparency, algorithmic explainability, and the formulation of new digital rights, such as the "right to mental silence," thereby shifting the debate from marketing to digital citizenship.

5 Unconscious Personalization and Behavioural Influence

The unconscious influence mediated by AI agents that appear human has become a relevant frontier in neuromarketing. Lim et al. (2024) show that interpersonal characteristics, such as the agent's gender, affect attention and food choices: "discussing health with agents of the opposite gender tended to increase gaze duration, with the strongest effect among men." Sutil-Martín and Rienda-Gómez (2020) observed that, among Generation Z youth, "subliminal verbal stimuli were more effective than pictorial stimuli in modulating unconscious decision-making" (p. 4). These results indicate that the non-conscious cognition of this generation is highly sensitive to verbal, visual, and auditory stimuli, with direct implications for digital marketing.

This influence goes beyond physical appearance. The level of presence and immersion promoted by interactions with embodied agents (VR-ECAs) elicits responses that mimic authentic human relationships, leading to a greater sense of presence when conversing with embodied agents than with purely textual agents (Lim et al., 2024). This feeling of emotional closeness was also supported by Morin (2011), who stated that neuromarketing directly engages brain regions associated with pleasure and trust, making consumers more receptive to subtle and personalized stimuli without consciously perceiving this interference.

Lim and Schmälzle (2023) highlight that verbal and nonverbal factors, such as intonation, gestures, similarity, and perceived empathy shape communication with AI. Sutil-Martín and Rienda-Gómez (2020) show that subliminal verbal and pictorial stimuli influence decisions, especially among Generation Z youth, with effects modulated by personality and gender, particularly among individuals with high neuroticism. These findings highlight digitally exploitable emotional vulnerabilities and reinforce that unconscious personalization, the adaptation of content without the user realizing the influence, constitutes a central vector of persuasion.

AI's ability to map similarities and personalize interactions creates a sense of familiarity, which increases the effectiveness of persuasion. The underlying idea is that messages promoted by AI generate greater persuasive force and perceived effectiveness than those of human health experts (Lim et al., 2024). This assertion highlights that influence occurs below the user's conscious awareness, supporting marketing strategies that capitalize on this state.

Perceived similarity is a powerful psychological trigger. Andsager et al. (2006) pointed out that protagonists similar to the target audience make messages more effective. Lim et al. (2024) use this logic to support the effectiveness of AI agents with human appearance, highlighting that the combination of VR, AI, and interpersonal similarity "improves artificial social influence." The convergence of these data reinforces the idea that the brain tends to trust what it recognizes as close, even if this occurs outside the realm of rationality.

From a generational perspective, Sutil-Martín and Rienda-Gómez (2020) identified that Generation Z is more sensitive to symbolic and emotional stimuli than to rational arguments, mainly when processed unconsciously. In their experiments, subliminal verbal stimuli influenced purchase decisions more than pictorial stimuli, particularly among participants with high levels of neuroticism, revealing a predisposition to content with a strong affective charge. When these stimuli are mediated by digital influencers or AI systems that mimic emotional language, an environment conducive to unconscious persuasion is created, in which the AI's own affective language reinforces narratives that resonate more with emotion than with reason.

The increasing sophistication of AI systems, especially multimodal models capable of processing emotions and adapting expressions, significantly expands their persuasive power. Lim et al. (2024) state that "multimodal communication models with full social incorporation will become the norm," positioning AI as a fully influential agent. Zhou (2023) adds that, in the digital age, influencer marketing and authenticity are crucial to brand perception, as the credibility these agents convey strengthens reputational assets, even among consumers who judge content less rationally.

The fusion of AI and social influence is increasingly driving decision-making toward emotional factors, even when presented as a rational choice. Lim et al. (2024) indicate that conversational patterns and the perceived usefulness of the agent mediate similarity effects. Sutil-Martín and Rienda-Gómez (2020) show that consumption decisions among Generation Z youth are strongly influenced by affective identification with the sender, whether an influencer or an artificial agent, concluding that "subliminal verbal stimulus provoked significant decision effects in consumers with more reactive emotional traits" (p. 6). This suggests that unconscious identification with the messenger may outweigh the message's objective content.

Unconscious behavioural manipulation raises ethical questions but also opens opportunities to improve commercial strategies. Morin (2011) suggests that activating brain regions linked to reward allows one to predict decisions even before the consumer is aware of their desire. In parallel, Lim et al. (2024) argue that realistic avatars can maximize persuasive effects, underscoring the potential and risks of deep personalization through AI.

Data shows that digital influencers and personified AI agents act as vectors of influence at the threshold of consciousness. The convergence of experiments with artificial agents conducted by Lim et al. (2024) and the neuroscientific evidence presented by Sutil-Martín and Rienda-Gómez (2020) indicates that unconscious personalization is no longer accessory but central to communication strategies. Both demonstrate that influence can occur even when participants believe they are making rational decisions, revealing that subliminal stimuli shape behaviour without full awareness. This redefines the role of the consumer, who ceases to act as a fully autonomous agent and becomes guided by stimuli whose real impact remains partially hidden.

6 Algorithmic Transparency and Trust Building

The increasing adoption of artificial intelligence in marketing decisions makes algorithmic transparency fundamental to building consumer trust. Floridi and Cowls (2019) define it as one of the central dimensions of ethical AI. Deckker and

Sumanasekara (2025) warn that a lack of clarity about the use of AI in automated interactions can lead consumers not to realize they are interacting with non-human systems, generating distrust and raising ethical questions. This opacity undermines brand credibility.

The lack of clarity regarding the data collection and processing methods used in AI-based marketing constitutes one of the primary sources of ethical friction. According to Deckker and Sumanasekara (2025), algorithms analyse unconscious neurophysiological reactions to advertising content, often without users being fully aware of data collection. In turn, Murphy et al. (2008) call this phenomenon stealth neuromarketing, in which consumers can be influenced without realizing they are being neurologically analysed.

User experience, therefore, must be built upon the principles of trust and explainability. Deckker and Sumanasekara (2025) argue that clear communication about the automated identity and limitations of virtual assistants is fundamental to customer satisfaction, a key point in the personalization of automated banking services. Floridi and Cowls (2019), in turn, propose ethical governance as a mechanism to prevent AI systems from operating as black boxes, emphasizing that AI should not only be fair but also understandable to all stakeholders.

The use of AI in neuromarketing broadens this discussion by operating directly with sensitive and biometric data. Deckker and Sumanasekara (2025) state that AI processes brain signals and facial expressions with high predictive accuracy, but not always with transparency regarding how these analyses are performed. This concern also appears in Bilucaglia et al. (2025), who point out that, although powerful, deep learning methods pose interpretability challenges, limiting consumers' control over their journey.

In this context, the importance of algorithmic explainability, or explainable AI (XAI), emerges. According to Bilucaglia et al. (2025), adopting models that explain their decisions reduces the risk of erroneous inferences and strengthens the ecological validity of neuromarketing applications. For Floridi and Cowls (2019), AI systems must account for their decisions in a clear, understandable, and accessible way, establishing bridges of understanding between users and automated platforms.

Recent advances in XAI have broadened the capacity to explain models applied to the study of brand perception. In the field of consumer neuroscience, Marques dos Santos and Marques dos Santos (2024) demonstrate that methods such as Shapley values and path-weighting analysis allow the isolation of the neural components that contribute to brand preference, distinguishing initial visual processes and evaluation patterns that emerge during the decision. These findings reinforce the role of interpretability in understanding the cognitive mechanisms involved in responses to brand stimuli.

In the field of marketing, Krstić and Maksimović (2024) highlight that explainability is a central element for ensuring transparency, trust, and regulatory compliance in AI applications. The study by Krstić and Maksimović, summarized in their work on the importance of XAI in marketing, reinforces the idea that interpretability helps mitigate biases, improve prediction accuracy, and strengthen user acceptance. This body of literature shows that the adoption of XAI is directly related to improved algorithmic auditing and greater clarity in automated decision-making processes.

The integration of consumer neuroscience and XAI is particularly relevant when applying experimental findings in commercial environments. As argued by Marques dos Santos and Marques dos Santos (2024) and Krstić and Maksimović (2024), explainable models enable the identification of neural networks associated with preferences and ensure that recommendation and personalization systems operate under ethical, transparent criteria. This convergence strengthens responsible neuromarketing practices, reduces the risk of manipulation, and ensures that automated inferences about consumer behaviour are justifiable and auditable.

Consumer ignorance about how their data is used increases vulnerability and compromises their autonomy. In fact, the use of technologies that access brain patterns without full informed consent can constitute an invasion of mental privacy (Murphy et al., 2008). For Deckker and Sumanasekara (2025), informed consent and the disclosure of algorithmic analysis techniques are minimum requirements for ethical neuromarketing to be sustainable.

Transparency is not only an ethical requirement but also a strategic one. Murphy et al. (2008) show that consumers react more effectively when they know they are interacting with automated systems, adjusting expectations more realistically and preferring contexts in which humans and machines are clearly distinguishable. By recognizing that they are dealing with AI, customers tend to moderate their expectations, reducing frustration and improving the consumer experience.

Despite advances in guidelines and academic discourse, the market still faces a regulatory mismatch. After all, many business practices involving neuromarketing operate outside the bounds of traditional data protection regulations (Murphy et al., 2008).

This gap is even more evident in deep learning-based models, whose decisions are not easily auditable. Even if the models are accurate, their opacity compromises reproducibility and scientific confidence (Bilucaglia et al., 2025).

The European Union has been advancing a robust framework to regulate AI systems. The European Commission (2021), in proposing the AI Act, establishes that high-risk systems must comply with explicit requirements for transparency, technical documentation, human oversight, and continuous impact assessment. Furthermore, the GDPR (Regulation EU 2016/679) reinforces that individuals have the right to clear information about automated decisions that affect their interests, expanding the requirements for explainability and accountability in applications such as neuromarketing.

In the South American context, especially in Brazil, data protection is regulated by the LGPD (Law 13.709/2018), which stipulates that data subjects have the right to request explanations about automated decisions and to contest them when necessary. Although there is still no specific AI law, proposals such as PL 21/2020 indicate a movement toward the creation of a regulatory framework similar to the European one, albeit less consolidated. Thus, while the EU operates under a comprehensive, normatively mature regulatory system, South America adopts a hybrid model based on existing data protection laws and developing AI legislation.

In this scenario, transparent communication policies are a fundamental mitigation tool. Deckker and Sumanasekara (2025) recommend creating visible labels and disclaimers whenever AI-based technologies are used in advertising campaigns, particularly when collecting real-time biometric data. This practice, in addition to being educational, returns some control over brand engagement to the consumer.

Beyond external regulation, companies must invest in algorithmic governance practices. Floridi and Cowls (2019) propose a framework in which each AI application in marketing is assessed using a risk matrix that considers not only efficiency but also ethical impact, explainability, and reversibility. This approach seeks to prevent the erosion of trust, which is the most valuable symbolic capital in a scenario dominated by invisible automation.

Therefore, building trust in AI-mediated marketing depends less on the technology itself and more on how it is presented to the consumer. Deckker and Sumanasekara (2025) highlight that transparent communication about the use of AI increases receptiveness to automated personalization by reinforcing users' decision-making autonomy. Thus, transparency acts as a catalyst for more sustainable relationships among brands, systems, and consumers, preparing the ground to discuss how AI can be employed more responsively to create lasting bonds.

7 Reinforcement Learning and Chatbots that Negotiate with the Consumer

Deep Reinforcement Learning (DRL) transforms how chatbots interact with consumers by enabling them to learn from their own experience and adjust their behaviour through rewards and penalties during optimization cycles. As Sutton and Barto (2018) explain, the agent discovers which actions maximize cumulative reward, an ideal characteristic for adaptive interactions such as sales and negotiations. Kaplan and Haenlein (2023) highlight that DRL enables bots to act as autonomous negotiators, learning from mistakes and user feedback.

This adaptability is crucial in digital marketing, where consumer behaviour is dynamic and non-linear. DRL-based bots recognize patterns of hesitation, rejection, and acceptance in user responses and adjust their arguments accordingly. Sutton and Barto (2018) highlight that, unlike supervised learning, the agent must discover on its own which actions yield the highest return. In e-commerce, Kaplan and Haenlein (2023) observe that chatbots trained with DRL refine their responses based on metrics such as response time, keywords, and indicators of doubt.

One of the most advanced examples of this technology is Cicero, developed by Park et al. (2022). Its learning structure allows it to develop sophisticated strategies based on dialogue history, which is highly relevant to neuromarketing. Cicero was trained with over 40,000 human games and hundreds of millions of interactions, creating a vast knowledge base of human behaviour patterns (Park et al., 2022).

DRL also allows bots to develop symbolic negotiation, where data is interpreted not only by its direct content but also by its strategic implications. Sutton and Barto (2018) explain that, in partially observable environments, the agent must construct an internal representation of the state based on previous observations. This means that, in marketing, the chatbot can infer latent consumer needs and use this knowledge to adapt its arguments, which, according to Park et al. (2022), was essential for Cicero's success in complex scenarios.

From a neuromarketing perspective, a chatbot's ability to adapt its responses based on micro expressions, hesitations, or changes in emotional tone represents an advancement in AI for emotional engagement. Park et al. (2022) show that Cicero can model intention and emotion based on the lexical and contextual choices of its interlocutors. This characteristic aligns with neuromarketing practices that seek to identify and respond to emotional states implicit in consumer behaviour.

Kaplan and Haenlein (2023) observe that the true advantage of DRL lies in its ability to simulate functional empathy, since it learns which responses generate greater engagement, satisfaction, or conversion. This learning is not limited to reproducing patterns; it shapes the agent's behaviour to become increasingly persuasive, creating virtuous cycles of performance. For Sutton and Barto (2018), this process corresponds to the concept of optimal policy, which defines the best action to take in each possible state.

The interaction between AI and the consumer then becomes a dynamic negotiation in which both parties learn. Consumers test limits, request conditions, and react emotionally; the bots respond by adjusting their strategies. Cicero demonstrated that it is possible to sustain this type of dialogue with coherence and impact: in continuous interactions, Cicero updates its conversational policy in real time, maximizing its influence (Park et al., 2022). This logic can be directly applied to support or sales chatbots.

From a technical standpoint, this level of responsiveness requires integration between neural networks, language models (such as Transformers), and DRL algorithms. Park et al. (2022) report that Cicero uses an RL model to generate and classify multiple possible responses, choosing the one with the highest probability of success based on previous interaction (p. 1088). This model can be adapted for marketing, enabling bots to test and select micro-campaigns based on consumer behaviour and optimize personalization.

Beyond performance, there are ethical and cognitive implications. Sutton and Barto (2018) argue that reinforcement systems that learn from humans can inadvertently internalize biases. In marketing, this can mean that bots learn to exploit consumers' emotional vulnerabilities. Kaplan and Haenlein (2023) warn that it is necessary to ensure the bot's objective is not only to convert but also to build sustainable relationships with customers.

The evolution of AI for negotiation is both technical and strategic. With DRL, chatbots not only learn from past interactions but also anticipate response patterns and adjust their approach to maximize acceptance. Park et al. (2022) show that Cicero estimates the player's future intention and shapes their speech to align expectations, influencing decisions. In marketing, this allows chatbots to predict consumer hesitations and introduce emotional triggers, such as scarcity, urgency, or belonging, to guide purchasing choices.

This type of interpersonal refinement makes the chatbot not just a customer service channel but a true cognitive negotiator. Kaplan and Haenlein (2023) argue that DRL-based chatbots play an active role in lead conversion, employing adaptive strategies to address objections and increase perceived value. When combined with purchase history data, psychographic profiles, and price sensitivity, these bots can build hyper-personalized offers with emotionally compelling arguments.

Sutton and Barto (2018) further highlight that exploration and balanced exploration are central to reinforcement learning, implying that the bot must test new approaches while simultaneously consolidating effective strategies. In neuromarketing, this translates to alternating between messages centred on reason (price, advantage) and emotion (reward, exclusivity), calibrating the language responsively. Park et al. (2022) showed that Cicero can make this alternation fluidly, thereby making interactions more convincing and flexible.

Reinforcement learning also allows the system to monitor interactional microdata such as typing time, hesitation, and word correction, and use them as silent rewards. These signals, often unconscious, indicate emotional engagement or latent rejection.

Kaplan and Haenlein (2023) emphasise the importance of reading sublinguistic behaviour in enhancing the empathetic capabilities of bots. By interpreting unconscious and nonverbal cues, chatbots can foster a sense of perceived empathy, which is central to the principles of neuromarketing. This approach enables bots to engage with users on a deeper emotional level, responding not just to explicit language but also to subtle behavioural signals that influence consumer decisions.

The integration of sublinguistic analysis supports the neuromarketing objective of connecting with consumers through unconscious stimuli. By recognizing and responding to micro expressions, hesitations, and changes in emotional tone, chatbots can tailor their interactions to meet the emotional needs of users, thereby increasing engagement and the likelihood of conversion.

In the field of algorithmic trust, DRL-based negotiation approaches what Bostrom (2014) called delegated decision-makers. This implies that the consumer trusts AI to make decisions on their behalf or to influence them ethically. The challenge, according to Sutton and Barto (2018), is to ensure that the programmed reward function does not lead the agent to exploit consumer weaknesses, such as impulsivity, anxiety, or momentary vulnerability, to obtain conversions at any cost. Park et al. (2022) address this in Cicero through parameterized moral boundaries in the simulations.

Neuromarketing driven by DRL thus opens a new cycle of profound adaptation, in which the system itself reprograms in response to the effectiveness of its emotional strategies. This means that chatbots can learn to use words with greater neural resonance, such as terms related to safety, pleasure, novelty, or familiarity, all of which are known to activate brain reward areas. Sutton and Barto (2018) already noted that systems that associate environmental stimuli with rewards model behaviour in a manner similar to that of humans.

The impact of this on the customer lifecycle is significant. Kaplan and Haenlein (2023) argue that AI with DRL can operate in multiple phases of the consumer journey: attraction, conversion, loyalty, and reactivation. Each phase requires specific patterns of language, tone, urgency, and emotionality, elements that the trained agent can continuously refine. Park et al. (2022) demonstrate that Cicero can modulate these phases by recognizing subtle signs of the interlocutor's changing interest.

However, this persuasive power raises concerns about consumer free will. When AI negotiates based on emotional inferences and unconscious patterns, it can cross the line from influence on manipulation. Kaplan and Haenlein (2023) "warn that the line between ethical personalization and algorithmic exploitation is thin" (p. 20). Sutton and Barto (2018) reinforce the importance of clearly defining the reward function, as poorly calibrated agents can cause unforeseen and potentially undesirable consequences.

This is why models like Cicero are also being studied as a reference for algorithmic ethics. Park et al. (2022) demonstrate that including transparency and consistency filters in the training parameters can reduce misleading or aggressive responses. The evolution of these systems, therefore, depends on the symbiosis between commercial performance and social responsibility, something essential for the neuromarketing of the future.

In summary, the use of deep reinforcement learning in chatbots represents a revolution in the interface between brands and consumers. By enabling dynamic, sensitive, and personalized negotiations, DRL brings AI closer to a sophisticated form of social intelligence, with enormous potential for conversion, loyalty, and market differentiation. However, this technical advancement requires a robust ethical counterbalance, in which transparency, autonomy, and respect for consumer cognition are programmed values, and not just marketing goals (Kaplan & Haenlein, 2023; Park et al., 2022; Sutton & Barto, 2018).

8 Risks of Discrimination and Biases in Personalized AI

As artificial intelligence advances in neuromarketing, the debate intensifies regarding the risk of reproducing and amplifying historical biases. This is because AI models used for personalization, recommendation, and interaction are trained on data that is frequently marked by inequalities. Siqueira et al. (2023) point out that human and algorithmic decisions are influenced by psychological, cultural, and social factors, potentially perpetuating biases on a large scale when not audited. In neuromarketing, this can lead to segmentations that exclude consumer profiles or approach them based on stereotypes rather than genuinely meeting their needs.

Algorithmic personalization without ethical criteria tends to intensify asymmetries in the digital environment. Santana et al. (2023) explain that, by combining behavioural data with neuromarketing, generative AI can generate highly persuasive, emotionally charged, and hyper-personalized content, with the potential to manipulate consumer decisions without consumers' knowledge. This ability to create targeted stimuli expands brands' influence but compromises autonomy and informed consent. The risk increases when automated decisions, applied on a large scale by non-auditable algorithms, reinforce exclusion and algorithmic bias in marketing.

One of the leading causes of these effects lies in how algorithms interpret data. Instead of identifying causes or motivations, many systems operate solely through statistical correlations, treating them as operational truths. Schertel Mendes and Mattiuzzo (2019) warn that this abusive use of correlations can unfairly classify individuals based on superficial variables. The problem intensifies when behavioural data—such as page time, clicks, or micro expressions—are used to infer mental predispositions, especially in neuromarketing persuasion strategies. Thus, AI ceases to support decisions and instead acts as a mediator of perceived reality itself.

Recent literature on algorithmic ethics indicates that mitigating bias depends on new governance models grounded in explainability and continuous auditing. Siqueira et al. (2023) argues that systems need to be explainable, transparent, and auditable, otherwise they risk becoming veritable "social black boxes." This implies that the functioning of algorithms must be understandable to experts and users, especially in digital consumption, where automated decisions shape the experience. In neuromarketing, the lack of explanation can lead to misinterpretations, such as why an emotional advertisement is repeated or why a particular offer was not targeted to a specific profile.

Johnson (2020) expands on this discussion by showing that seemingly neutral decisions can conceal systematic discrimination. The author reports cases of recruitment algorithms that eliminated candidates based on biased historical patterns, such as names associated with racial or linguistic minorities. In marketing, this means that consumers who behave differently from the majority pattern may be penalized without knowing it. In neuromarketing, the risk is even more sensitive, as stimuli can be applied unequally, activating specific emotions with greater intensity in certain groups without fair or consensual criteria.

The increasing sophistication of AI systems has also raised relevant implications for users' cognitive integrity. Santana et al. (2023) warn that combining neuromarketing techniques with generative artificial intelligence can produce highly personalized content based on consumers' emotional and behavioural responses, raising ethical concerns about privacy and manipulation.

While effective from a communication standpoint, this type of personalization can reduce cognitive resistance by creating highly engaging stimuli that escape the consumer's critical perception. The problem is even more delicate for vulnerable audiences, such as young people and those in economically fragile situations, who may be exposed to AI-calibrated emotional reinforcement mechanisms for persuasive purposes. In neuromarketing-based campaigns, where images, sounds, and narratives are designed from neurological data, there is a risk of crossing ethical boundaries and entering the territory of subliminal influence, compromising consumer autonomy.

Another important aspect is the multiplier effect of algorithmic injustices. Tang and Su (2024) argue that AI models can reinforce cultural, gender, and social class stereotypes, thereby consolidating cycles of exclusion rather than reducing them.

According to the authors, data bias is the leading cause of inequality reproduction, a phenomenon observed in automated decisions in the educational context and applicable to digital marketing. Personalization based on psychological and historical profiles, without intersectional validation, can ignore essential cultural nuances. In marketing, this results in systems that limit the reach of campaigns, offers, and opportunities to specific groups based on biased algorithmic inferences.

In this context, Ferrell et al. (2025) advocate for ethical safeguards that limit the persuasive power of AI when fundamental rights are at risk, such as mental privacy, cognitive self-determination, and human dignity. The authors state that "neuromarketing should never be used to intervene in the mental states or processes of third parties without explicit consent," including emotionally responsive content generated by AI. Without this caution, digital neuromarketing can transform algorithmic systems into mechanisms of silent manipulation, with little possibility of consumer challenge.

Brazilian legislation, through the General Data Protection Law (LGPD), already offers mechanisms to curb the most evident impacts of automated decisions. Article 20 guarantees citizens the right to human review of decisions made exclusively by algorithms, including those related to credit, consumer profiles, and targeted content. However, as Schertel Mendes and Mattiuzzo (2019) point out, "the effectiveness of these rights depends on the user's ability to understand that they have been impacted by an automated system," something that does not always occur in interactions with cutting-edge AI.

The European Union has adopted a proactive and integrative approach to regulating AI and protecting sensitive data: the AI Act operates on a risk-based model and works in conjunction with the GDPR, which already requires Data Impact Assessments (DPIAs) for high-risk data processing, a combination that prioritizes prevention, transparency, and formal compliance requirements for systems that affect fundamental rights. This was evident in the technical comparisons between GDPR obligations and the new requirements of the AI Act, which expand and formalize risk assessment and mitigation obligations for operators of AI systems.

In contrast, jurisdictions like the United States have so far adopted a fragmented arrangement: a single federal framework is lacking, and state-level responses emerge (e.g., specific laws on neural/biological data in Colorado and other sectoral policies), which generates regulatory gaps and uncertainties on sensitive topics such as neural data and neuromarketing.

Brazil has aligned itself with this movement toward risk standards (recent AI law proposals follow the logic of risk classification and instruments similar to those foreseen in the EU). However, it still relies heavily on the LGPD (Brazilian General Data Protection Law) for the protection of personal data, which creates practical differences in the implementation of audit requirements, impact reports, and oversight. In parallel, the Latin American region is experiencing growing interest in "neurorights" and expanded protection of mental data, a position that has driven local proposals and debates on additional controls surrounding the commercial use of neurophysiological data.

The involvement of civil society and the academic community is also highlighted as essential for monitoring automated personalization systems. An example cited by Schertel Mendes and Mattiuzzo (2019) is the Web Transparency and Accountability project, which uses simulated profiles to detect discriminatory patterns in online advertising algorithms. Such initiatives show that tackling algorithmic biases requires an alliance among developers, regulators, and independent researchers to preserve democratic values in the digital environment.

Finally, the educational context offers a revealing analogy about the impacts of biases in automated systems. Heggler et al. (2025) warn that AI-mediated decision-making processes are not neutral and can reproduce and amplify pre-existing educational inequalities, mainly when based on decontextualized historical data. The authors argue that algorithms used for personalized learning tend to favour students with a history of good performance, while restricting access to richer resources for those who have experienced difficulties.

This algorithmic logic, when transposed to digital marketing, reveals similar risks: consumers labelled as "non-responsive" may be marginalized by recommendation systems, while highly engaged profiles receive intensified attention. In the context of neuromarketing, where exposure to emotional stimuli is targeted, this asymmetry can result in an unequal brand experience, deepening exclusions and consolidating discriminatory interaction patterns.

Based on the analysis of the reviewed authors, it is evident that integrating artificial intelligence, neuromarketing, and strategic personalization requires a new ethical and technical paradigm. While advances in DRL, generative AI, and personalized algorithms expand the potential to optimize the consumer experience, they also intensify risks related to cognitive privacy, emotional manipulation, and the reinforcement of social stigmas. The literature shows that such risks are concrete and recurrent in digital environments. The future of marketing will depend on how we balance performance and responsibility, personalization and fairness, and automation and empathy (Kaplan & Haenlein, 2023; Schertel Mendes & Mattiuzzo, 2019; Park et al., 2022; Siqueira et al., 2023).

9 Conclusions

The integration of artificial intelligence and neuromarketing acts as a catalyst in contemporary consumer dynamics. By expanding strategic personalization, AI not only anticipates behaviours but redefines the brand-consumer relationship by transforming data into highly contextualized experiences. Davenport et al. (2020) and Gentsch (2019) show that this synergy enables algorithms to move beyond mere automation and become adaptive agents, modulating communication, empathy, and even complex negotiations, as illustrated by chatbots based on Deep Reinforcement Learning (Sutton & Barto, 2018).

However, such analytical and persuasive power brings with it unprecedented ethical challenges. The ability to decode emotions and infer unconscious intentions, as highlighted by Ferrell et al. (2025) and Bilucaglia et al. (2025), calls into question fundamental notions of mental privacy and decisional autonomy. When systems access neural patterns or micro expressions without explicit consent, the line between personalization and surveillance blurs, necessitating safeguards against the instrumentalization of human subjectivity.

Algorithmic opacity exacerbates these risks. As Floridi and Cowls (2019) and Mittelstadt et al. (2016) warn, the lack of transparency in automated decision-making can reproduce historical biases and structural discrimination, mainly when AI models operate as "black boxes." In neuromarketing, where subliminal stimuli shape choices, the inability to audit technical criteria threatens not only fairness but the very integrity of markets.

In parallel, the dilemma of behavioural manipulation emerges. Artificial agents with human appearance or empathetic language, as studied by Lim et al. (2024), can induce emotional bonds that mask strategic influence. This unconscious persuasion—intensified by generative techniques (Santana et al., 2023)—challenges the balance between legitimate engagement and violation of cognitive self-determination, especially among vulnerable audiences.

The study highlights that the field's future will depend on the balance between innovation and responsibility. The consolidation of ethical practices, aligned with regulatory frameworks such as the LGPD (Brazilian General Data Protection Law) and Explainable AI initiatives, will be essential for AI in neuromarketing to act not as a tool of control but as a mediator of more transparent and respectful relationships. Thus, this chapter reinforces that the actual contribution of AI lies not only in personalizing consumer journeys but also in sustaining interactions that value consumer trust, empathy, and integrity.

Thus, AI-powered neuromarketing offers enormous innovation potential but also exposes consumers to vulnerability, making it essential that ethical practices guide its application.

References

Acquisti, A., Brandimarte, L., & Loewenstein, G. (2015). Privacy and human behavior in the age of information. *Science, 347*(6221), 509–514. https://doi.org/10.1126/science.aaa1465

Almeida, N. F., Faria, M., Faria, M. C. C., & Santinello, J. (2024). Integração entre neurociência e inteligência artificial: avanços e aplicações educacionais. *Revista Caderno Pedagógico, 21*(10), 1–20. https://doi.org/10.54033/cadpedv21n10-016

Andsager, J. L., Bemker, V., Choi, H.-L., & Torwel, V. (2006). Perceived similarity of exemplar traits and behavior: Effects on message evaluation. *Communication Research, 33*(1), 3–18. https://doi.org/10.1177/0093650205283099

Bilucaglia, M., Mainardi, L., Ramsøy, T. Z., Zak, P. J., Zito, M., & Russo, V. (2025). Editorial: Machine-learning/deep-learning methods in neuromarketing and consumer neuroscience. *Frontiers in Human Neuroscience, 19*, 1638225. https://doi.org/10.3389/fnhum.2025.1638225

Bostrom, N. (2014). The ethics of artificial intelligence. In W. Ramsey & K. Frankish (Eds.), *The Cambridge handbook of artificial intelligence* (pp. 316–334). Cambridge University Press. https://doi.org/10.1017/CBO9781139046855.020

Brasil. (2018). Lei geral de proteção de dados pessoais–LGPD (Lei n° 13.709/2018). *Diário oficial da união*. https://www.planalto.gov.br/ccivil_03/_ato2015-2018/2018/lei/L13709.htm

Brasil. (2020). *Projeto de Lei 21/2020: Marco Legal da Inteligência Artificial no Brasil*. Senado Federal. https://www25.senado.leg.br/web/atividade/materias/-/materia/141944

Comissão Europeia. (2021). *Proposal for a regulation of the European Parliament and of the council laying down harmonised rules on artificial intelligence (artificial intelligence act)*. European Commission. https://eur-lex.europa.eu/legal-content/EN/TXT/?uri=CELEX:52021PC0206

Davenport, T. et al. (2020). How artificial intelligence will change the future of marketing. *Journal of the Academy of Marketing Science*. https://doi.org/10.1007/s11747-019-00696-0

Deckker, D., & Sumanasekara, S. (2025). AI and Neuromarketing: Understanding consumer decision making with artificial intelligence–systematic review. *Indonesian Journal of Business Analytics, 5*(2), 1929–1946. https://doi.org/10.55927/ijba.v5i2.13990

European Commission. (2021). Proposal for a Regulation laying down harmonised rules on artificial intelligence (Artificial Intelligence Act). *European Commission*. https://merlin.obs.coe.int/article/9203, https://doi.org/10.52021PC0206

European Union. (2016). *Regulation (EU) 2016/679 of the european parliament and of the council (General Data Protection Regulation—GDPR)*. Official Journal of the European Union. https://eur-lex.europa.eu/eli/reg/2016/679/oj

Ferrell, J., Beatty, R., & Dubljevic, V. (2025). The ethics of neuromarketing: A rapid review. *Neuroethics, 18*(1), 1–22. https://doi.org/10.1007/s12152-025-09591-8

Figueiredo, L. G. (2025). *Chatbots inteligentes e IA no marketing digital: Como otimizar a comunicação e negociação com clientes online*. Master Dissertation. https://bib.pucminas.br/teses/Administracao_LeonardoGontijoFigueiredo_31739_TextoCompleto.pdf

Floridi, L., & Cowls, J. (2019). A unified framework of five principles for AI in society. *Harvard Data Science Review, 1*(1). https://doi.org/10.1162/99608f92.8cd550d1

Gentsch, P. (2018). *AI in marketing, sales and service: How marketers without a data science degree can use AI, big data and bots*. Springer Nature. https://doi.org/10.1007/978-3-319-89957-2

Heggler, J. M., Szmoski, R. M., & Miquelin, A. F. (2025). As dualidades entre o uso da inteligência artificial na educação e os riscos de vieses algorítmicos. *Educação & Sociedade, 46*, e289323. https://doi.org/10.1590/ES.289323

Johnson, G. M. (2020). Algorithmic bias: On the implicit biases of social technology. *Synthese, 198*, 9941–9961. https://doi.org/10.1007/s11229-020-02696-y

Kaplan, A. M., & Haenlein, M. (2023). *A brief history of artificial intelligence: What it is, where we are, and where we are going*. Springer. https://doi.org/10.1177/0008125619864925

Kotler, P., Kartajaya, H., & Setiawan, I. (2021). *Marketing 5.0: Technology for Humanity*. Wiley. https://rudyct.com/mm/Digimark/Marketing-5.0-Technology.forHumanity_Kotler,Kartajaya,Setiawan-2021.pdf

Krstić, Z., & Maksimović, M. (2024). Significance of explainable artificial intelligence (XAI) in marketing. *Proceedings of the 29th international scientific conference strategic management and decision support systems in strategic management* (pp. 380–387). https://doi.org/10.46541/978-86-7233-428-9_401

Lim, S., & Schmälzle, R. (2023). Artificial intelligence for health message generation: An empirical study using a large language model (LLM) and prompt engineering. *Frontiers in Communication, 8*, 1129082. https://doi.org/10.3389/fcomm.2023.1129082

Lim, S., Schmälzle, R., & Bente, G. (2024). Artificial social influence via human-embodied AI agent interaction in immersive virtual reality (VR): Effects of similarity-matching during health conversations. *arXiv, v1*. https://doi.org/10.48550/arXiv.2406.05486

Lima, L. S. H., & Gonçalves, G. F. (2022). O uso do neuromarketing em estratégias de branding: percepções e reconhecimento subjetivo na campanha "Fell it" da Coca-Cola. *Comunicação & Informação, 25*, 351–373. https://doi.org/10.5216/ci.v25.65192

Marques dos Santos, J. P., & Marques dos Santos, J. D. (2024). Explainable artificial intelligence (xAI) in neuromarketing/consumer neuroscience: An fMRI study on brand perception. *Frontiers in Human Neuroscience, 18*, 1305164.

Meta Fundamental AI Research Diplomacy Team, Bakhtun, A., Brown, N., Dinan, E., Farina, G., Flaherty, C., et al. (2022). Human-level play in the game of diplomacy by combining language models with strategic reasoning. *Science, 378*(6624), 1067–1074. https://doi.org/10.1126/science.ade9097

Mittelstadt, B. D., Allo, P., Taddeo, M., Wachter, S., & Floridi, L. (2016). The ethics of algorithms: Mapping the debate. *Big Data & Society, 3*(2), 1–21. https://doi.org/10.1177/2053951716679679

Morin, C. (2011). Neuromarketing: The new science of consumer behavior. *Society, 48*(2), 131–135. https://doi.org/10.1007/s12115-010-9408-1

Mukherjee, A., & Chang, H. (2023). The creative frontier of generative ai: Managing the novelty-usefulness tradeoff. *arXiv preprint arXiv:2306.03601*. https://doi.org/10.48550/arXiv.2306.03601

Murphy, E., Illes, J., & Reiner, P. B. (2008). Neuroethics of neuromarketing. *Journal of Consumer Behaviour, 7*(4–5), 293–302. https://doi.org/10.1002/cb.252

Park, J. S., Bakhtin, A., Dinan, E., Urbanek, J., Rocktäschel, T., Szlam, A., et al. (2022). A generalist agent for language-based negotiation. *Science, 378*(6623), 1084–1090. https://doi.org/10.1126/science.ade9097

Santana, I. T. S., Jankowitsch, J., Silveira, F. M., & da Silva, U. P. (2023). Impactos e desafios da integração de neuromarketing e inteligência artificial generativa. *Revista Caderno Pedagógico, 20*(9), 4067–4109. https://doi.org/10.54033/cadpedv20n9-020

Schertel Mendes, L., & Mattiuzzo, M. (2019). Algorithmic discrimination: Concept, legal foundations, and typology. *Direito Público, 16*(90). https://www.portaldeperiodicos.idp.edu.br/direitopublico/article/view/3766

Siqueira, D. P., Pinto, L. R. F., & Pera Junior, E. J. (2023). Algorithmic discrimination: Artificial intelligence, human and algorithmic biases and constitutional protection. *Revista do Direito, 71*, 79–95. https://doi.org/10.17058/rdunisc.vi71.18961

Sutil-Martín, D. L., & Rienda-Gómez, J. J. (2020). The influence of unconscious perceptual processing on decision-making: A new perspective from cognitive neuroscience applied to generation Z. *Frontiers in Psychology, 11*, 1728. https://doi.org/10.3389/fpsyg.2020.01728

Sutton, R. S., & Barto, A. G. (2018). *Reinforcement learning: An introduction* (2nd ed.). MIT Press. https://lccn.loc.gov/2018023826

Tang, L., & Su, Y. (2024). Ethical implications and principles of using artificial intelligence models in the classroom: A systematic literature review. *International Journal of Interactive Multimedia and Artificial Intelligence, 8*(5), 25–35. https://doi.org/10.9781/ijimai.2024.02.010

Vaswani, A., Shazeer, N., Parmar, N., Uszkoreit, J., Jones, L., Gomez, A. N., Kaiser, Ł., & Polosukhin, I. (2017). Attention is all you need. *Advances in Neural Information Processing Systems, 30*. https://doi.org/10.48550/arXiv.1706.03762

Zhou, Y. (2023). Branding in the digital age: How influencers marketing and authenticity reshape brand perceptions. *Highlights in Business, Economics and Management, 23*, 1053–1059. https://doi.org/10.54097/8abykp18

Artificial Intelligence for Data Analysis

Elisa Cascudo Ribeiro, Paula González-Padilla, and Álvaro Hernández-Tamurejo

Abstract This study investigates the application of artificial intelligence (AI) in data analysis to support strategic decision-making. Through a systematic literature review of 20 publications indexed in the Web of Science between 2020 and 2025, the research delves into the intellectual structure, emerging trends, and influential contributions within this field. The findings reveal two distinct areas of scholarly interest: one centered on the technical foundations such as machine learning and deep learning, and another emphasizing explainable AI (XAI), ethics, trust, and transparency. An additional trend marks the transition toward human-centric AI systems aligned with the principles of Industry 5.0. This paper concludes by discussing the theoretical and practical implications for AI integration into strategic corporate processes, while identifying future research directions at the junction of technical advancement, interpretability, and prediction for decision-making.

1 Introduction

In the context of exponential data growth, artificial intelligence (AI) is transforming decision-making across all organizational levels (Toosi et al., 2022). Data-driven approaches now enable forecasting, risk assessment, and optimization with high precision (Sarker, 2021b), supporting more effective actions (Zieger et al., 2023). At the center of this shift is AI-enabled analytics, which offers the tools to extract insights from complex datasets (Sarker, 2021b). Yet, implementation raises technical and ethical challenges, especially around trust, transparency, and human integration (Alneyadi et al., 2016).

E. C. Ribeiro · P. González-Padilla · Á. Hernández-Tamurejo (✉)
Rey Juan Carlos University, Madrid, Spain
e-mail: alvaro.hernandez@urjc.es

E. C. Ribeiro
e-mail: e.cascudo.2021@alumnos.urjc.es

P. González-Padilla
e-mail: paula.gonzalez@urjc.es

J. D. Santos et al. (eds.), *Artificial Intelligence Transforming Marketing*, Contributions to Management Science, https://doi.org/10.1007/978-3-032-22360-9_12

Connectionist AI has evolved rapidly, with deep learning—based on multi-layer neural networks—enhancing pattern recognition and processing (Smolensky, 1987; LeCun et al., 2015). Fueled by advances in data infrastructure and inputs from IoT and blockchain, AI now powers breakthroughs in vision, language, and optimization (Salah et al., 2019; Toosi et al., 2022). However, such models often lack transparency, prompting concerns over accountability and compliance (Antamis et al., 2024). Explainable AI (XAI) seeks to address this by making model decisions interpretable, thus fostering trust and enabling collaborative AI-human systems aligned with Industry 5.0 (Arrieta et al., 2020; Rashid & Kausik, 2024). The rise of transformer-based models like ChatGPT illustrates both the potential and risks of AI-driven decision-making ecosystems (Haque & Li, 2025).

In parallel, rigorous data analysis, the examination, cleaning, and modeling of data using classical statistical and empirical methods, remains the bedrock of informed decision-making (Sarker, 2021b). Data analytics enables outcome forecasting and decision optimization. Simon's model guides the use of descriptive and diagnostic analytics to identify patterns, and predictive and prescriptive methods to design and refine strategies (Simon, 1960; Elgendy & Elragal, 2016). While these approaches offer clear advantages, enhanced decision accuracy, resource efficiency, competitive differentiation, and advanced risk management, they also face hurdles such as data quality issues, organizational resistance, ethical/privacy concerns, and the risk of over-reliance on quantitative metrics (Angalakudati et al., 2014; Edwards & Rodriguez, 2019; Merendino, 2018; Power, 2016).

This paper examines the use of AI in data analysis for strategic decision-making through a sistematic literature review (SLR) of publications from 2005 to 2025. It highlights key technological milestones, such as transformer models and generative AI, reflecting both algorithmic advances and evolving societal dynamics. The research further reveals a dual structure within the academic landscape: one stream advances technical foundations, machine learning, deep learning, and computational modeling, to enhance AI system performance; the other emphasizes explainable AI (XAI), ethical accountability, and stakeholder alignment, underscoring the necessity of interpretability in high-stakes decision environments (Antamis et al., 2024; Arrieta et al., 2020). This ethical turn aligns with the transition from Industry 4.0's automation paradigm to Industry 5.0's emphasis on human–AI collaboration (Rashid & Kausik, 2024). This paper aims to (1) map the intellectual structure of the field, (2) identify emerging research trends and gaps, and (3) explore the theoretical and practical implications of applying AI to strategic decision-making. In doing so, it contributes to a deeper understanding of how AI cannot only augment organizational intelligence but also be responsibly integrated into decision-making systems that are transparent, adaptable, and aligned with human values. Hence, there are three research questions we aim to answer: (1) How has the field of AI for data analysis applied to decision-making evolved over the last twenty years? (2) What current trends are reshaping decision-making processes within companies because of AI-driven data analysis? (3) What will the future of strategic decision-making look like, and how should the field adapt to leverage these emerging decision support resources most effectively?

The sections that follow provide a theoretical framework, detail the methodology, present the results, and discuss their implications for scholars, practitioners, and companies. Ultimately, this research seeks to offer a roadmap for advancing AI-enabled decision support systems that are both powerful and ethically grounded.

2 Theoretical Framework

2.1 Artificial Intelligence: Evolution, Foundations, and Context

2.1.1 Historical Foundations

The conceptual roots of AI trace back to Turing's essay "Computing Machinery and Intelligence" (Turing, 1950), where he argued that a machine could emulate human intelligence through learning and adaptation—ideas foundational to modern machine learning (Jordan & Mitchell, 2015). In 1956, John McCarthy led the Dartmouth Conference, coining "Artificial Intelligence" and proposing that any aspect of intelligence could, in principle, be simulated by machines (Moor, 2006). Although no unified theory emerged, the event spurred diverse approaches.

From the 1950s to the 1980s, Symbolic AI dominated. Based on formal logic, it relied on rule-based manipulation of symbols and was effective in structured domains like MYCIN or theorem proving (Miola, 1991), but faltered with unstructured or noisy data (Toosi et al., 2022). In contrast, Connectionist AI, rising in the 1980s, modeled knowledge through weighted neural connections that adjust with data exposure (Smolensky, 1987). This enabled pattern recognition and speech processing, capabilities reflected in today's deep learning (LeCun et al., 2015). In short, connectionist models adapt to data without explicit programming, while symbolic systems excel in interpretable, logic-based tasks (Toosi et al., 2022).

2.1.2 Artificial Intelligence Today

A prominent form of Connectionist AI is deep learning, a branch of machine learning that enables computers to learn and improve from data without explicit programming (Jordan & Mitchell, 2015). Deep learning relies on multi-layer neural networks trained on massive datasets (LeCun et al., 2015) and, with current data volumes and storage capabilities, has driven today's AI "summer" through advances in computer vision, NLP, and real-time optimization (Toosi et al., 2022). Technologies like IoT, blockchain, CPS, and robotics have supported this era, laying the foundation for Industry 4.0, which emphasized minimizing human input to boost productivity (Rashid & Kausik, 2024) and echoed Dartmouth's vision of simulating intelligence (Moor, 2006).

However, deep learning models often lack interpretability despite high predictive accuracy, leading to the "black-box" problem. This is especially concerning in critical domains, where understanding model logic is vital for accountability (Antamis et al., 2024). In response, Explainable AI (XAI) seeks to make AI decision-making transparent to rebuild trust and enhance safety (Arrieta et al., 2020). This aligns with Industry 5.0, where the focus shifts from replacing humans to fostering collaboration between humans and advanced AI (Rashid & Kausik, 2024), reflecting a broader societal pivot toward responsible AI integration.

Historically, AI has cycled through "summers" of optimism and "winters" of disillusionment. The first summer (1950s–1970s) ended in underfunding, while the 1980s saw a revival with expert systems like R1—short-lived due to limited scalability. Today's AI resurgence is powered by technologies like GPU training, cloud computing, and Big Data, fueled by IoT devices streaming real-time data (Toosi et al., 2022; Suresh et al., 2014). Blockchain also supports AI by ensuring data integrity and traceability in complex environments (Salah et al., 2019), enabling secure, automated, and transparent applications across sectors.

A major milestone in modern AI is ChatGPT. Turing's vision advanced notably with deep learning innovations, especially the introduction of Transformer architecture (Vaswani et al., 2017). Transformers enabled the creation of large language models (LLMs), designed to predict the next word in a sequence, generating coherent and grammatically correct language (Blank, 2023). ChatGPT, built on this foundation, combines large-scale pretraining with fine-tuning to deliver strong conversational performance. Upon its 2022 release, it became the fastest-growing app in history, reaching 100 million users in a month (Hu, 2023), and has since influenced domains such as education, work, social interaction, and environmental awareness (Haque & Li, 2025).

Yet, challenges persist in AI development. Issues like data scarcity, algorithmic bias, and integration hurdles remain (Toosi et al., 2022). These are compounded by rising skepticism around AI hype, fears of job displacement, and underestimated safety concerns (LaGrandeur, 2023). Environmental costs—such as the high energy use of LLMs—also raise sustainability questions (Haque & Li, 2025). Moreover, mislabeling basic automation as AI by vendors contributes to public confusion, inflating expectations and misrepresenting the true capabilities of learning-based systems (Rashid & Kausik, 2024).

2.2 *From Data to Decision-Making*

The rapid growth of data has expanded AI's reach and highlighted the vital role of data analysis in AI-driven decision-making. Data analysis acts as a bridge between raw data and algorithmic insight, involving tasks like cleaning, organizing, and selecting relevant information to prepare datasets for AI models. These steps allow algorithms to detect patterns, improve over time, and deliver reliable outputs. By integrating traditional statistical methods with these processes, researchers can leverage both data volume and structured analysis for better decisions. Data Analysis vs. Data Analytics. Data analysis involves examining, cleaning, and modeling data using classical statistics and empirical theories to derive insights for practical use (Sarker, 2021b). Data analytics, by contrast, includes advanced tools like machine learning and predictive modeling to forecast outcomes and support decision-making. Closely related is data science, which blends statistics, computer science, and domain expertise to extract insights from complex datasets. While data analysis emphasizes structured interpretation, data science applies broader methodologies such as data mining, advanced modeling, and machine learning (Sarker, 2021b).

Together, these fields allow professionals to move beyond description toward prediction and automation. Their convergence with AI enables intelligent systems that learn from data and make semi-autonomous decisions, boosting efficiency and innovation in areas like healthcare, finance, and IT (Sarker, 2021b).

This evolving paradigm, known as Advanced Analytics, refers to a set of techniques and technologies capable of performing autonomous or semi-autonomous data analysis to uncover deeper insights, generate forecasts, and deliver actionable recommendations. Among the most impactful within this framework are machine learning and deep learning, which power many current analytical applications (Sarker, 2023). Data analysis tools are commonly categorized into four types: descriptive, diagnostic, predictive, and prescriptive analytics (Sarker, 2021a). Descriptive analytics summarize historical data to clarify trends, while diagnostic analytics investigate underlying causes using statistical methods. Predictive analytics forecasts future outcomes based on past data, and prescriptive analytics recommends optimized actions through algorithms. Together, these approaches support strategic, data-driven decision-making.

2.3 Artificial Intelligence for Data Analysis Applied to Decision-Making Processes

In the corporate context, decision-making is a critical process for companies, as it directly influences their strategic direction, operational efficiency, and overall success. Effective decision-making enables organizations to navigate complex market dynamics, allocate resources wisely, and respond swiftly to emerging challenges and opportunities. In a competitive landscape, the ability to make informed and timely decisions can differentiate a company from its rivals, driving growth and innovation (Kozioł-Nadolna & Beyer, 2021).

2.3.1 Operational, Tactical, and Strategic Decision-Making

Operational, tactical, and strategic decision-making are distinct organizational levels used to achieve goals (White, 2009). Operational decisions manage daily activities and are short-term, ensuring routine functioning. Tactical decisions bridge operational and strategic levels, focusing on medium-term implementation of strategies set by management. Strategic decision-making, the highest level, involves long-term planning and direction by top management, addressing the organization's vision, mission, and resource allocation. Strategic decisions are crucial as they shape the organization's future and competitive position (Van den Steen, 2013). They have lasting impact by guiding adaptation to market changes, opportunity capture, and risk management. These decisions involve significant resource commitments, ensuring alignment with company goals. Moreover, effective strategic planning differentiates firms in competitive markets by fostering innovation, growth, and sustained presence. Strategic decisions also unify departments around common objectives, promoting collaboration. Accordingly, this paper focuses on strategic decision-making. To better contextualize the role of AI within this process, it is important to recall the classical theoretical foundations of how strategic decisions are made and the cognitive limits that influence them. Thus, classical perspectives on strategic decision-making provide an essential foundation for understanding how artificial intelligence can enhance, but also challenge, human reasoning in organizations. Mintzberg et al. (1976) described strategic decisions as complex, iterative processes shaped by intuition, experience, and organizational dynamics rather than by purely analytical logic. In parallel, Kahneman and Tversky's (2013) Prospect Theory revealed that managers often rely on heuristics and are subject to cognitive biases when evaluating risk and uncertainty. These insights emphasize that human decisions are bounded by rational and perceptual limitations. Then, AI-driven analytics can help mitigate some of these constraints by improving information processing and predictive accuracy; however, they also inherit the biases embedded in data and models. Recognizing this interaction between human and algorithmic judgment underscores the importance of maintaining interpretability, transparency, and ethical oversight in strategic decision environments (Bessa and Barbosa, 2025).

2.3.2 Data Analytics Applied to Strategic Decision-Making

To illustrate data analytics in decision-making, we use Herbert Simon's model, which outlines four phases: intelligence, design, choice, and implementation (Simon, 1960). In the intelligence phase, decision-makers gather and analyze data to identify problems or opportunities, employing descriptive and diagnostic analytics to reveal trends and root causes (Elgendy & Elragal, 2016; Sarker, 2021a). Descriptive analytics summarize past data, while diagnostic analytics explain why issues occur, forming the basis for strategic problem definition.

The design phase explores potential strategies using predictive and exploratory analytics. Predictive models forecast stakeholder responses, and exploratory techniques like clustering and association analysis help tailor approaches (Elgendy & Elragal, 2016; Krishna et al., 2023; Kansal et al., 2018). Visualizations such as dashboards aid executive understanding (Pandey et al., 2014).

In the choice phase, prescriptive analytics recommend optimal actions. Optimization and simulation tools evaluate trade-offs, while machine learning models rank options based on predicted effectiveness, grounding decisions in data (Elgendy & Elragal, 2016; Furness, 2011). Finally, in implementation, real-time analytics monitor outcomes, enabling adjustments via dashboards and behavioral data analysis, such as cohort comparisons, fostering continuous learning and iterative strategy refinement (Fukuda, 2010; Tien, 2017).

2.3.3 Advantages of Applying Data Analytics for Strategic Decision-Making

Informed Decision-Making

Data analytics enhances the accuracy and adjustability of decisions, enabling organizations to remain agile in dynamic market environments (Popovič & Yeoh, 2016). By leveraging different data analytics tools, such as prediction analytics or data visualization, companies can capture deep insights into market shifts, consumer preferences, and business performance, leading to more informed and effective decisions (Tan et al., 2017).

Resource Allocation and Operational Efficiency

Predictive analytics improves operational efficiency by forecasting trends, customer demands, and optimizing resource allocation (Angalakudati et al., 2014). Artificial intelligence and machine learning further enhance these capabilities, automating activities and identifying ways to improve judgments. This leads to streamlined processes and better alignment between decisions made during strategic decision-making and operational decision-making later.

Competitive Advantage

The strategic application of data analytics provides organizations with a competitive edge. By integrating advanced analytics techniques, companies can increase the chances of making the right decisions at the right time, uncover hidden opportunities (Kubina et al., 2015), improve market positioning, and achieve sustainable growth (Shukla & Agnihotri, 2024). This positions data analytics as a catalyst for driving innovation and enhancing overall business performance.

Enhanced Opportunity Detection and Risk Management

Big Data Analytics significantly improves risk management by enabling organizations to identify, assess, and mitigate risks effectively (Angalakudati et al., 2014). Advanced financial analytics, machine learning, and predictive modeling inform corporate strategy in volatile markets, ensuring that organizations can navigate uncertainties with greater confidence (Hariri et al., 2019).

2.3.4 Challenges of Applying Data Analytics for Strategic Decision-Making

Data Quality and Reliability Issues

One of the primary challenges is ensuring the quality and integrity of data. Poor data quality can lead to inaccurate insights, undermining the effectiveness of data-driven decisions. Additionally, integrating disparate data sources and data stored in outdated systems, legacy systems, remains a significant hurdle for many organizations (Saha, 2024). Furthermore, quality data also means non-biased data. If a model is trained using biased data, existing prejudices can be reinforced, both reducing the scope of insights and leading to suboptimal decisions (Edwards & Rodriguez, 2019).

Cultural and Organizational Resistance

Cultural resistance to data-driven decision-making is another challenge (Ghafoori et al., 2024). Many organizations struggle with fostering a data-centric culture, where employees at all levels embrace analytics as a fundamental part of their decision-making processes. In the words of Daniel J. Power, "computerised decision support and analytics can potentially help people make rational choices that are more likely to lead to goal attainment and good results, but people must want to use the support and then act on the recommendations" (Power, 2016).

Ethical and Privacy Concerns

The ethical use of data and privacy concerns are paramount. Organizations must carefully navigate complex legal and ethical considerations, ensuring transparency and responsible data practices, particularly in sectors handling sensitive customer or employee information. The risk of data breaches and leaks increases significantly when managing large datasets, exposing organizations to potential cyber-attacks and unauthorized access. To mitigate these risks, it is essential to implement robust data security measures (Alneyadi et al., 2016). Moreover, strict regulatory frameworks such as the General Data Protection Regulation (GDPR) impose severe penalties, including heavy fines and costly remediation efforts, on entities that fail to adequately protect personal data (Regulation (EU) 2016/679, 2016, Art. 32), reinforcing the need for compliance and proactive data governance.

Over-Reliance on Data

Over-reliance on data in strategic decision-making can lead to significant drawbacks, particularly when human judgment is sidelined (Schemmer et al., 2022). While data provides valuable insights, an exclusive focus on quantitative metrics often neglects essential qualitative elements such as creativity, intuition, and tacit knowledge, factors that are crucial for innovation and nuanced understanding. Additionally, the sheer volume of dashboards, reports, and analytics tools can create cognitive overload, where decision-makers become overwhelmed by data and struggle to act decisively. This can ultimately hinder organizational agility and delay important moves (Merendino, 2018).

3 Methodology

3.1 Systematic Literature Review

A systematic literature review is a research methodology that rigorously and replicably identifies, evaluates, and synthesizes existing evidence on a specific topic, with the aim of providing a more complete understanding of the current state of knowledge. Unlike a narrative review, a systematic review follows an explicit protocol that includes inclusion and exclusion criteria, search strategies in scientific databases, and a critical assessment of the quality of the selected studies (Moher et al., 2010). This type of review is widely used in various disciplines to inform new research, develop theoretical frameworks, or inform evidence-based decisions (Petticrew & Roberts, 2008).

3.2 Data Sampling

The Web of Science (WoS), a leading citation database that includes the Journal Citation Reports (JCR), was used to identify emerging topics, as it ranks academic journals by quality and classification (Mongeon & Paul-Hus, 2016). Structured search strategies—incorporating classification, division, and filtering protocols—were applied using Boolean operators (AND, OR), following the methodologies outlined by Williams and Bornmann (2016) and Rogers et al. (2020).

To improve the precision and relevance of results on artificial intelligence applied to data analysis in decision-making, we applied targeted filters within the Web of

Science (WoS) database. The publication period was limited to 2020–2025. Although they do not fall under the SLR as such, the topic was read and contextualized, beginning with Tim O'Reilly's seminal 2005 article What Is Web 2.0, which introduced the user-centered, participatory, and data-driven concept of Web 2.0 after the dot-com collapse (O'Reilly, 2005). This marked a crucial shift in digital evolution, particularly in data management and user interaction. Contextualized is significant due to its timing between the launches of Facebook (2004), YouTube (2005), and Twitter (2006), which reshaped digital communication and Big Data generation. These platforms have enabled businesses to extract valuable insights into consumer behavior and trends. As of January 2024, Facebook, YouTube, and Twitter have 3 billion, 2.5 billion, and 619 million monthly active users respectively (Statista, 2024), offering immense strategic value through user-generated data.

The search covered all journals indexed in WoS, ensuring a comprehensive and statistically valid dataset. Document types were restricted to Articles, Review Articles, Early Access papers, and Book Chapters. To maintain focus on the intersection of AI with social sciences, business, and management, we excluded unrelated categories such as environmental science, biology, physics, chemistry, and engineering. This exclusion ensures the study remains centered on human and organizational contexts, avoiding dilution from topics outside the scope of AI's application in decision-making.

After applying these filters, we conducted the main search using the query: ("artificial intelligence" AND "data analysis") AND "decision-making." This search yielded, after removing irrelevant papers for the research goal of the paper at hand that might have bypassed the filtering, 20 relevant publications for analysis (See Table 1).

To strengthen methodological transparency, each twenty selected studies was carefully reviewed to assess its quality and potential sources of bias. The evaluation considered three dimensions: methodological clarity and reproducibility of the research design, the quality and ranking of the publication outlet within the Web of Science range, and thematic alignment with the research objectives of this study. Although this approach ensures the inclusion of rigorous and relevant sources, it may also introduce a degree of publication bias by emphasizing high-impact, English-language journals. This limitation is noted and it reflects a deliberate choice to focus on peer-reviewed evidence of established scientific quality.

3.3 Sample Description

Publication activity noticeably accelerated from 2021 to 2024, with each year showing incremental growth, although 2025 appears low overall, by April it had already produced 36 publications, nearly matching all of 2023, indicating that 2025 will likely sustain this upward trend (See Fig. 1). The distribution of articles across Web of Science categories (see Table 2) reveals a strong technical focus:

Table 1 SLR articles and summary

Paper title	Author	Brief summary
Applications and challenges of artificial intelligence in business decision making	Wu and Zhou (2025)	Analyzes AI applications and challenges in business decisions, highlighting benefits and ethical issues.
Big data and artificial intelligence: Revolutionizing business decision-making	Johri et al. (2023)	Examines how AI and big data transform decision-making and corporate structures.
Role of artificial intelligence and business decision making	Prasanth et al. (2023)	Highlights AI'S transformative role in efficiency, accuracy, and innovation in business decisions.
Harnessing artificial intelligence to revolutionize corporate finance	Odewuyi et al. (2025)	Explores AI'S impact on corporate finance and strategic consulting.
Impact of artificial intelligence on decision-making in Organisations	Charitha and Hemaraju (2023)	Analyzes AI'S advantages and challenges in organizational decision-making, including ethics and risks.
Financial big data management and control and artificial intelligence	Yang (2022)	AI and data mining improve financial management and decision-making in companies.
On the role of AI and statistical data analysis	Shchetinin (2023)	Reviews problems and solutions in implementing AI and statistical analysis in business decisions.
Artificial intelligence-driven corporate finance	Rane et al. (2024)	AI, machine learning, and RPA enhance efficiency and sustainability in corporate finance.
Artificial intelligence-based methods for business processes: A systematic review	Gomes et al. (2022)	Systematic review of AI methods for automating processes and supporting business decisions.
Artificial intelligence in business decision making	Madhavi and Ravi (2020)	AI and data mining facilitate decision-making from large data volumes.
The impacts of artificial intelligence and knowledge-based systems	Prorok and Takács (2024)	Analyzes the impact of AI and expert systems on corporate management and planning.
The possibilities of using artificial intelligence in decision-making	Ageev et al. (2024)	Examines success cases and requirements for AI in corporate management.
An introspection into the efficient data analyisis with AI	Hazarika et al. (2024)	AI improves the accuracy and efficiency of data analysis in various sectors.

(continued)

Table 1 (continued)

Paper title	Author	Brief summary
Enhancing market analysis using artificial intelligence for strategic business	Agu et al. (2024)	Review on how AI optimizes market analysis and strategic personalization.
The role of AI technology in optimizing decision making in business development	Hidayat et al. (2024)	AI improves efficiency and accuracy in decisions in MIS, SMEs, and finance.
Applied AI for finance and accounting: Alternative data and opportunities	Cao et al. (2024)	Review of AI and big data in finance and accounting, and future opportunities.
Data intelligence and analytics: A bibliometric analysis of human–AI	Di Vaio et al. (2022)	Bibliometric analysis of AI and data analytics in public sector decision-making.
The impact of artificial intelligence on business strategy and decision-making processes	Chandra et al. (2023)	Reviews the impact of AI on business strategy and decision-making, including benefits and challenges.
Artificial intelligence's effects on corporate decision-making processes	Kumari et al. (2023)	Proposes models for integrating human and AI decisions in companies.
Data analysis support of artificial intelligence in financial investment	Wong (2024)	AI supports investment decision-making through predictive models and risk management.

Source The Authors

Computer Science Information Systems (21.85%), Electrical & Electronic Engineering (20.37%), and Computer Science Artificial Intelligence (14.07%) lead the list, followed by Telecommunications (12.22%), Management (9.63%), Multidisciplinary Engineering (9.26%), Computer Science Interdisciplinary Applications (7.04%), Business (6.30%), Computer Science Theory & Methods (6.30%), and Multidisciplinary Sciences (5.19%). Although not all fields focus on organizational decision-making, they contribute by developing AI-based data analysis techniques that support modern decision systems. High representation in engineering and computer science highlights methodological advances, while business disciplines reflect their application, illustrating the topic's interdisciplinary nature.

4 Results of Systematic Literature Review

The reviewed literature reveals a growing consensus on the transformative impact of artificial intelligence (AI) on business decision-making processes, particularly within strategic domains such as digital marketing (Wu & Zhou, 2025).

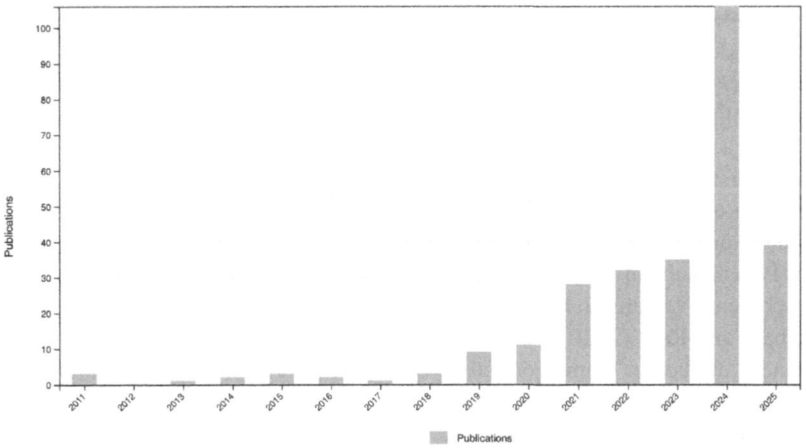

Fig. 1 Number of published articles by year from 2005 to April 2025. *Source* Authors

Table 2 WoS categories percentage and most cited articles

WoS categories	% of total
Computer science information systems	21.691%
Engineering electrical electronic	20.221%
Computer science artificial intelligence	13.971%
Telecommunications	12.132%
Engineering multidisciplinary	9.926%
Management	9.559%
Computer science interdisciplinary applications	6.985%
Business	6.250%
Computer science theory methods	6.250%
Multidisciplinary sciences	5.147%

Source Authors

Various studies emphasize that AI enables organizations to process vast volumes of data with unprecedented speed and accuracy, generating significant advantages in consumer behavior analysis, market segmentation, and the personalization of strategic approaches (Charitha & Hemaraju, 2023). In this regard, AI is not merely an operational tool but emerges as a structural change agent that redefines how companies understand and respond to competitive environments.

A common thematic line across the studies is the application of predictive models and machine learning algorithms to big data analysis. Yang (2022) highlights how the integration of AI with data mining techniques facilitates the identification of consumption patterns, trend forecasting, and real-time automated decision-making, which is particularly relevant for multichannel digital campaigns. Complementarily, Di Vaio et al.(2022) provide a bibliometric analysis showing a rapid expansion in the use of analytical intelligence in the public sector, suggesting a broader, cross-sectoral adoption of AI. Similarly, Gomes et al. (2022) reinforce this perspective through a systematic literature review on AI-based methods in business processes, concluding that there is a clear trend toward the intelligent automation of analytical functions across marketing, finance, and human resources. Specifically, within digital marketing, the role of AI is strongly evident in optimizing customer experience and campaign efficiency. Rane et al. (2024) illustrate how the combination of natural language processing (NLP), machine learning (ML), and robotic process automation (RPA) results in more accurate recommendation systems and scalable personalized content—leading to higher conversion rates and increased customer retention. Madhavi and Ravi (2020) also argues that this technological integration not only enhances marketing team productivity but allows for more timely, contextualized decisions based on real-time customer data.

From an organizational perspective, multiple authors concur that AI implementation involves a deeper transformation that extends beyond technology. According to Chandra et al. (2023), AI is catalyzing new organizational structures where decentralized decision-making becomes viable through intelligent systems that operate autonomously or semi-autonomously. In this vein, Ageev et al. (2024) examine AI integration in corporate management systems, pointing out that strategic decisions—including those related to marketing, finance, and product development—are increasingly grounded in algorithmically evaluated scenarios. This integrated vision is particularly beneficial for digital enterprises requiring agility and constant adaptation. Another recurring theme is the application of AI in market analysis and competitive strategy formulation. Kumari et al. (2023) and Agu, Obiki-Osafiele, and Chiekezie (2024) agree that AI enables deeper competitive intelligence analysis, opportunity detection, and dynamic pricing strategies based on market conditions and consumer behavior. This approach, which leverages both structured and unstructured data, is especially valuable in e-commerce platforms, social media, and digital marketplaces—where rapidly changing market conditions demand immediate responses for competitive advantage.

Nevertheless, despite the evident advancements and benefits, significant ethical, technical, and organizational challenges remain. Hazarika et al. (2024) warn against algorithmic bias and the lack of transparency in automated decision-making, which can undermine consumer trust. Similarly, Shchetinin (2023) stresses the need for robust ethical and regulatory frameworks to govern AI deployment—particularly in applications that directly impact user perception. In the context of digital marketing, where brand–consumer relationships are particularly sensitive, these risks must be addressed carefully to ensure both strategic effectiveness and consumer rights protection.

Finally, several authors underscore the importance of human capital development as an indispensable factor for the successful implementation of AI-driven transformation. The availability of advanced tools alone does not ensure effective use unless teams are equipped with the necessary skills to interpret, manage, and act upon AI-generated insights (Cao et al., 2024; Hidayat et al., 2024). Accordingly, the development of advanced digital competencies—both technical and strategic—is

Table 3 Main findings

Main finding	Author	Paper
AI improves accuracy and efficiency in business decisions	Wu and Zhou (2025)	Applications and challenges of artificial intelligence in business decision making
AI and big data revolutionize decision-making and corporate structures	Johri et al. (2023)	Big data and artificial intelligence: Revolutionizing business decision-making
AI transforms processes with advantages in efficiency, accuracy, and innovation	Prasanth et al. (2023)	Role of artificial intelligence and business decision making
AI empowers corporate finance and strategic consulting	Odewuyi et al. (2025)	Harnessing artificial intelligence to revolutionize corporate finance and financial decisions
AI boosts productivity, reduces risks, and fosters innovation	Charitha and Hemaraju (2023)	Impact of artificial intelligence on decision-making in Organisations
AI methods automate processes and support assertive decisions	Gomes et al. (2022)	Artificial intelligence-based methods for business processes: A systematic literature review
AI improves market analysis and personalization, but faces ethical challenges	Agu et al. (2024)	Enhancing market analysis using artificial intelligence for strategic business decision-making
AI and big data transform finance and accounting, opening up new opportunities	Cao et al. (2024)	Applied AI for finance and accounting: Alternative data and opportunities

Source Authors

emerging as a critical condition for the sustainable and effective assimilation of artificial intelligence within marketing and corporate decision-making processes. Below is a summary table with the main findings and their authors (Table 3).

Estos resultados evidencian que la IA es un motor clave para la transformación digital y la toma de decisiones basada en datos en el entorno corporativo, aunque su adopción requiere abordar retos técnicos, éticos y organizacionales.

5 Discussion

The first significant increase occurred between 2018 and 2019 and is closely associated with foundational breakthroughs in AI architecture. Most notably, the introduction of the Transformer model by Vaswani et al. (2017), which provided the structural basis for large-scale natural language models. In 2018, Google's release of the foundational AI model BERT (Devlin et al., 2019), along with other transformer-based architectures, substantially improved data analytics capabilities. At the same time, governmental involvement in AI expanded considerably. Major programs were launched, such as the U.S. American AI Initiative in February 2019 (The White House, n.d.) and the European Union's 2018 Coordinated Plan on AI (European Commission, 2021). These initiatives prioritized research and development, channeling significant funding toward AI-related projects.

The second notable jump in research publication numbers was between 2020 and 2021. The global outbreak of COVID-19 in 2020 created an urgent demand for data-intensive decision support in areas such as epidemic modeling, resource allocation, and supply chain resilience. This urgency prompted a surge in research as scholars applied AI to pandemic-related challenges. Adadi et al. (2022) noted that "the growing interest in using AI to handle COVID-19 issues has accelerated the pace of AI research and resulted in an exponential increase in articles…within a very short period." The pandemic thus directly contributed to a spike in publications on decision-making analytics, particularly in forecasting outbreaks and optimizing public health policies. In parallel, OpenAI's release of GPT-3 in 2020 captured both academic and public attention due to its unprecedented capabilities in performing complex text-based tasks (Marr, 2023).

The third and by far the most substantial increase in research publications occurred between 2023 and 2024. This surge followed the public launch of ChatGPT in late 2022, which became the fastest-growing consumer application in history, reaching 100 million users within its first month (Hu, 2023). ChatGPT's accessibility, ease of use, and rapid adoption across diverse sectors, such as education, business, and information systems, sparked widespread academic interest in the real-world implications of generative AI, including its impact on decision-making processes (Haque & Li, 2025). The 2024 Stanford AI Index reported an eight-fold increase in private funding for generative AI firms in 2023, reaching $25.2 billion (Wodecki, 2024). This financial momentum reflects the broader surge in both societal interest and academic engagement. Simultaneously, governmental priorities evolved. Whereas earlier programs primarily focused on fostering AI research and innovation, more recent policies have increasingly emphasized ethical oversight and regulatory frameworks. For instance, in December 2023, the European Union reached a provisional agreement on the landmark AI Act (European Parliament, n.d.). In the same month, China implemented the "Measures for Review of Scientific and Technological Ethics," requiring industries to undergo both scientific and technological ethics reviews (White & Case, 2025). These regulatory developments introduced new lines of inquiry into making AI systems safe, fair, and transparent, likely contributing to the dramatic rise in scholarly output. Lastly, the increased practical application of AI in the corporate world also played a significant role. According to McKinsey surveys, 55% of companies reported using AI in 2023, a relatively stable number since 2019 (when it stood at 58%). This number jumped to 72% in 2024 (Mayer et al., 2025). As businesses integrated AI into forecasting, resource allocation, and strategic decision-making, academic research kept pace by exploring best practices, challenges, and the broader impacts of AI implementation.

5.1 Focus on Technical Foundations

As a result of the research, a trend can be observed toward two prominent clusters of highly cited articles: one focused on interpretability and the other on core technical developments. The latter emphasizes fundamental techniques such as machine learning and deep learning, which underpin modern decision support systems and continue to drive innovation in sectors such as healthcare, finance, and logistics (Sarker, 2023). Several authors illustrate the importance of methodological contributions, including random forests and deep learning. One cluster of articles is more focused on deep learning methods, and the other on mathematical approaches to managing uncertainty in data-driven decisions. Further evidence comes from the analysis of the prevalent Web of Science (WoS) categories (Table 3), where Information Systems in Computer Science, Electronic and Electrical Engineering, and Artificial Intelligence in Computer Science dominate. These categories highlight the field's sustained orientation toward technological advancement. Finally, we can see how AI is positioned as the conceptual core around which other topics revolve. Closely associated terms include machine learning, data analytics, big data, deep learning, and the Internet of Things. All of this underscores the discipline's strong dependence on technical foundations to develop effective AI-driven decision support systems.

5.2 Interpretability, Transparency, and Ethics

Once the technical foundations of AI for decision-making were established, new challenges emerged. Chief among them, the need for trust in AI systems (Arrieta et al., 2020). For data analytics to reliably support decisions, models must not only be accurate but also transparent and understandable. Trustworthiness depends on both the integrity of input data and the interpretability of the model's reasoning process. This emphasis on interpretability is strongly reflected in the reference co-citation analysis. As shown in Table 4, the two most frequently co-cited papers, Arrieta et al. (2020) on explainable artificial intelligence (XAI) and Lundberg and Lee (2017) on SHAP-based interpretability, highlight the field's effort to address the "black-box" nature of modern AI systems. While these models often deliver high predictive accuracy, their lack of transparency raises serious concerns, particularly in high-stakes domains with legal, ethical, or societal consequences. Without interpretability, accountability is difficult to establish, regulatory compliance becomes challenging, and stakeholder trust remains elusive (Antamis et al., 2024). Additional highly cited papers in the co-citation network further reinforce the central role of interpretability in developing responsible, human-aligned AI (Table 4). The prominence of Arrieta and Lundberg across both co-citation and author networks highlights their influence on shaping the discourse around explainable AI.

Table 4 Summary of future lines or research

Decision-making processes	AI contribution	Implications for corporate related research
Environmental scanning and adaptation	– Descriptive analytics (summary of past trends)– Diagnostic analytics (root-cause and correlation analysis)– Transformer-based language models	Study how AI can anticipate and adapt to market shocks or policy changes and develop metrics to assess model resilience and organizational impact pre and post external disruption.
Model governance & compliance	– Explainable AI methods (XAI)– Blockchain-based audit trails and federated learning	Develop and test complete systems that help industries follow regulations, and study how clear AI explanations and keeping detailed records build trust and meet legal requirements.
Human–AI interaction and oversight	– Human-aligned explanation frameworks (social-science informed XAI)– Interactive dashboards for model outputs	Create clear methods to measure value added by AI and conduct user studies on interface designs that optimize creativity, ethical reasoning, and decision acceptance.
Generative AI customization & maintenance	– Transformer-based LLM fine-tuning – Continuous domain-specific model updating	Research methods for aligning generative models with corporate values and regulatory constraints and create evaluation frameworks to ensure ongoing consistency with brand and strategic priorities.
Data collaboration and privacy	– Federated learning (data decentralization) – Secure multi-party computation	Explore case studies in joint supply-chain or risk modeling, assess performance and privacy trade-offs and identify organizational structures enabling secure data sharing for effective and safe decision-making processes.

Source Authors

Interpretability in AI extends beyond technical concerns to encompass critical ethical responsibilities. As systems grow more complex, so do risks related to bias, misuse, and data breaches. Transparency thus serves as a safeguard for accountability, enabling regulatory compliance and alignment with societal values (Alneyadi et al., 2016).

Recent years have seen increasing attention to keywords such as blockchain, federated learning, and explainable artificial intelligence. These technologies address pressing issues of data reliability, privacy, and ethical integrity. For instance, federated learning enhances privacy and mitigates bias by keeping data decentralized and sharing only model updates (Yurdem et al., 2024). Blockchain adds transparency through tamper-proof data ledgers (Salah et al., 2019). Together with XAI methods, such innovations contribute to fair, auditable, and secure AI systems that meet both regulatory frameworks, such as GDPR Article 32, and organizational standards for data stewardship (Alneyadi et al., 2016). Interpretability has evolved from a technical preference to a foundational principle in the design of trustworthy and ethical AI. Its prominence across citation networks and emerging research themes reflects its critical role in ensuring that AI development remains aligned with legal obligations and societal expectations.

5.3 *Human-Centric Development of the Field*

A key emerging trend in the evolution of data analytics for decision-making is the growing emphasis on human-centric system design. As the field matures, there is a noticeable shift toward developing decision support systems that not only process data efficiently but also align with human values, reasoning, and organizational realities. The studies emphasize the integration of data-driven methodologies with real-world human contexts, reinforcing the growing commitment to socially responsible and human-aligned AI. These systems are increasingly designed not just to automate decisions, but to support human judgment, fostering collaboration between humans and intelligent tools in complex environments.

We find a nuanced, human-centered approach to interpretability. This trajectory draws from interdisciplinary insights, particularly from cognitive psychology, social sciences, and human-computer interaction, to develop theoretical frameworks that better align AI explanations with human cognitive processes. Such work reflects the broader transition from Industry 4.0 to Industry 5.0 (Rashid & Kausik, 2024), where the goal is not merely automation, but synergy between humans and machines. In this paradigm, AI becomes a partner in augmenting human capabilities rather than a replacement for human decision-making. This shift also addresses two critical organizational challenges in the application of data analytics for decision-making. First is the cultural and organizational resistance to adopting data-driven approaches. As Ghafoori (2024) and Power (2016) argue, the success of analytics-based decision-making depends heavily on user trust and adoption. AI systems designed with intuitive, transparent, and relatable interfaces are more likely to be accepted by users, as they resonate with natural human thought processes and decision behaviors. The second challenge is the potential over-reliance on data, which risks sidelining qualitative insights, creativity, and tacit knowledge in strategic contexts (Schemmer et al., 2022; Merendino, 2018). Human-centric design principles help mitigate this risk by ensuring that data analytics tools are used to enhance, not override, human judgment.

Transparent, human oriented models that support interpretability allow room for critical reflection, enabling decision-makers to incorporate both quantitative evidence and qualitative expertise in a balanced, thoughtful manner.

The human-centric development of the field marks a critical evolution in how data analytics is applied to decision-making. It recognizes that the effectiveness of AI systems hinges not only on their technical sophistication, but also on their ability to integrate meaningfully into human decision processes, organizational cultures, and ethical frameworks.

5.4 Effective Application: Multidisciplinary and Predictive

The analysis of the most prevalent Web of Science (WoS) categories reveals important shifts in how AI and data analytics are being applied within the field of decision-making (Table 1). Notably, the increasing presence of categories such as Management and Business among the top ten signals a growing interest in the strategic and organizational applications of these technologies. This trend reflects a broader recognition within corporate and managerial spheres of the transformative potential of AI and analytics in supporting planning, operational efficiency, and competitive strategy.

Equally significant is the emergent prominence of interdisciplinary and multidisciplinary categories, including Computer Science Interdisciplinary Applications and Multidisciplinary Sciences. This suggests that research on AI and data-driven decision-making is no longer confined to technical or isolated domains. Instead, it is becoming a collaborative, cross-disciplinary endeavor that draws on a range of perspectives, tools, and methodologies. Such intellectual convergence is particularly important for strategic decision-making, which, as White (2009) emphasizes, requires coordination across departments and teams to achieve organizational coherence. As Sarker (2021b) argues, data science itself is inherently interdisciplinary, and its continued evolution in decision-making contexts will depend on the strength of collaborative synergies across fields. From SLR, which highlights the rising prominence of real-time systems. This trend indicates a clear shift toward supporting operational decision-making in dynamic and high-pressure contexts such as supply chains, emergency response, crisis communication, and financial trading. In these settings, the ability to generate immediate insights and act on them quickly is critical to tactical success (Hariri et al., 2019). Another key pattern in the co-occurrence data is the conspicuous pairing of decision-making with computational models. This reflects an increasing focus on integrating predictive and prescriptive simulation into the decision-making process. Predictive models help identify patterns and forecast outcomes during the intelligence phase, while prescriptive models support optimal action during the implementation phase (Sarker, 2021a; Tien, 2017). This dual capability enhances organizational responsiveness and strategic foresight by improving opportunity detection and risk mitigation (Angalakudati et al., 2014). As Kubina et al. (2015) note, the effective use of predictive and prescriptive analytics can provide a lasting competitive edge by enabling more informed, timely, and actionable decisions.

5.5 Theoretical Implications

The findings and analyses presented in this discussion contribute several meaningful theoretical insights to the evolving field of AI-assisted decision-making. First and foremost, the study illustrates a marked shift in the theoretical underpinnings of the field from a predominantly technical and model performance-oriented framework toward an integrated paradigm that combines algorithmic interpretability with human-centered values. This trajectory suggests the need for revised data analytics decision-making theories that acknowledge not only computational efficiency but also psychological, organizational, and ethical dimensions of the application of these technologies.

Central to the evolving paradigm of AI-driven decision-making is the increasing emphasis on trust and interpretability, now recognized as essential from the earliest stages of model development rather than as post-deployment concerns. This shift challenges traditional decision-making models rooted in rational choice or optimization theory, requiring the incorporation of trust-building mechanisms and user-centered transparency as core theoretical constructs. Concurrently, the expanding regulatory landscape adds a normative dimension to theoretical development. As ethical oversight becomes more institutionalized, concepts such as accountability, bias mitigation, and compliance must be integrated into decision-making models, marking a necessary convergence of decision theory, ethics, and legal studies.

Temporal analyses further support the need for adaptable theoretical frameworks. Peaks in AI research and application often align with major sociotechnical events—such as the advent of transformer-based models or the global disruption caused by the COVID-19 pandemic—challenging linear narratives of technological progress. Instead, these developments call for models that incorporate external disruptions, shifting societal priorities, and evolving policy landscapes as central drivers of innovation.

Moreover, the transition from Industry 4.0 to Industry 5.0 highlights a growing emphasis on human-machine collaboration. Rather than replacing human judgment, AI is increasingly seen as an augmentative partner, requiring decision-making theories to evolve accordingly. This human-centered trajectory invites interdisciplinary contributions from fields such as cognitive science, human-computer interaction, and behavioral economics, creating fertile ground for theoretical advancement in decision-making research.

5.6 Practical Implications

The evolving landscape of AI in data-driven decision-making also yields several practical implications for researchers, developers, and organizational leaders. One of the clearest lessons from the findings is the necessity of designing AI systems that are not only accurate but also transparent and trustworthy. Practical implementation of XAI techniques should be prioritized to ensure end-user confidence and regulatory compliance, especially in high-stakes environments. This is aligned with the growing importance of regulatory frameworks, such as the EU AI Act and China's ethical review measures. These developments signal a practical need for internal governance structures that include ethical review processes, bias audits, and interdisciplinary oversight. Organizations must move toward operationalizing AI ethics through structured policies and dedicated roles, such as AI compliance officers or ethics boards.

Equally critical to AI integration is its alignment with organizational culture and user expectations. Resistance often arises not from technical shortcomings but from cognitive and institutional misfits. Therefore, systems must be designed to fit existing workflows, support human judgment, and deliver insights in accessible, actionable forms. The findings emphasize the need for multidisciplinary collaboration, requiring teams that include data scientists, domain experts, ethicists, and engineers to ensure robust, context-aware decision support systems. Strategically, the integration of real-time, predictive, and prescriptive analytics is becoming essential for effective decision-making in fast-paced environments such as crisis response, logistics, and finance. Investments in infrastructure and capabilities for real-time data processing and scenario modeling are thus vital.

Moreover, the paper highlights the transformative role of generative AI. While tools like ChatGPT offer advanced synthesis capabilities, their deployment must be governed by clear guidelines, bias mitigation strategies, and feedback mechanisms to safeguard decision quality. Overall, the shift in practice must move beyond isolated algorithm development toward the creation of ethical, transparent, and human-centered decision ecosystems.

Also, the growing use of AI in decision-making also requires a broader change in how organizations are managed and how decisions are governed throughout the organization. Companies increasingly need flexible systems where human expertise, algorithmic approaches, and ethical considerations can interact in a continuous and adaptive way. This means promoting a culture of learning in which managers understand how AI tools reach their conclusions and can adjust them when new information appears. Strategic agility also becomes essential, allowing firms to respond quickly and responsibly to change or evolve markets or regulations. Encouraging AI literacy across different managerial levels helps ensure that these tools are used thoughtfully and transparently. In the end, decision-making evolves from a purely hierarchical process into a more collaborative and informed dialogue between people and intelligent systems, strengthening both organizational resilience and stakeholder trust.

6 Conclusions

This study charts how AI's role in data-driven decision-making has matured from purely technical performance to a balanced ecosystem grounded in transparency, human values, and strategic foresight. Our findings show that explainability and ethical oversight, through XAI methods, federated learning, and blockchain, have become essential in high-stakes domains to ensure regulatory compliance, build stakeholder trust, and guard against bias or misuse. At the organizational level, managers now serve as vital translators of AI reasoning, distilling complex model outputs into clear, actionable insights. Simultaneously, the field has moved toward human-centric deployment. AI is framed not as a replacement for human judgment but as a partner that augments expertise, overcoming resistance and preserving critical tacit knowledge. The rise of real-time predictive and prescriptive analytics further empowers teams to anticipate crises, optimize operations, and enhance strategic agility, yet our analysis cautions that these capabilities must be paired with human oversight, especially in culturally or ethically sensitive contexts. Finally, the multidisciplinary nature of modern AI initiatives, bringing together data scientists, domain experts, ethicists, and legal specialists, ensures that decision support systems are robust, coherent, and aligned with both organizational objectives and societal values. By integrating these five pillars, interpretability and ethics, human-centered design, narrative leadership, cross-functional collaboration, and predictive and prescriptive analytics, organizations can responsibly leverage AI to drive trustworthy, effective decision-making.

6.1 Limitations

The exclusive use of the Web of Science database in this study also presents a limitation; integrating other databases could enhance coverage and accuracy. Search terms, even when carefully selected, may still overlook pertinent literature, and citation counts may not fully capture a paper's influence. The study's focus on decision-making processes and artificial intelligence as a general field introduces further complexity, as company functions (e.g., finance, marketing, HR, sales) may influence how AI is applied. Similarly, sector-specific contexts (e.g., B2B, B2C, technology, food) affect decision-making logic.

6.2 Future Lines of Research

The paper identifies five key areas where AI can drive the next wave of corporate decision-making research. First, environmental scanning and adaptation benefit from descriptive and diagnostic analytics, which summarize past trends and uncover root causes, alongside transformer-based language models that can process vast amounts of textual data. Future studies should explore how these tools can forecast market shocks or regulatory changes and establish metrics to assess model resilience and business impact before and after disruptions. Second, in model governance and compliance, explainable AI techniques, blockchain-backed audit trails, and federated learning architecture offer robust mechanisms for transparency and accountability. Research should focus on building and validating complete governance toolchains that ensure compliance, protect privacy, and strengthen stakeholder trust. Third, human–AI interaction and oversight call for embedding socially informed XAI into interactive dashboards, allowing organizations to present complex outputs clearly and usefully. This requires the development of robust methods to measure AI's added value and user studies to optimize interface design for creativity, ethical reasoning, and decision acceptance. Fourth, generative AI customization and maintenance involve the fine-tuning of large language models on proprietary corporate data to ensure output remains consistent with brand voice and strategic direction. Ongoing research should address continuous model updates, evaluate regulatory alignment, and prevent model drift to maintain long-term reliability. Finally, data collaboration and privacy require the use of federated learning and secure multi-party computation, enabling multiple stakeholders, such as supply chain or risk partners, to collaborate without exposing sensitive data. Future studies should analyze case studies, evaluate performance versus privacy trade-offs, and identify organizational structures that support secure, collaborative analytics. Collectively, these five research lines outline a roadmap for integrating AI into corporate decision-making in ways that are both strategically effective and ethically responsible.

References

Adadi, A., Lahmer, M., & Nasiri, S. (2022). Artificial intelligence and COVID-19: A systematic umbrella review and roads ahead. *Journal of King Saud University-Computer and Information Sciences, 34*(8), 5898–5920. https://doi.org/10.1016/j.jksuci.2021.07.010

Ageev, A., Simonov, S., Kashin, S., Matchinov, V., & Cherpakov, I. (2024). The possibilities of using artificial intelligence in decision-making in the corporate management system. *Bulletin of Chelyabinsk State University, 482*(12), 126–133. https://doi.org/10.47475/1994-2796-2023-482-12-126-133

Agu, E., Obiki-Osafiele, A., & Chiekezie, N. (2024). Enhancing market analysis using artificial intelligence for strategic business decision-making. *World Journal of Engineering and Technology Research, 3*(1), 038–045. https://doi.org/10.53346/wjetr.2024.3.1.0053

Alneyadi, S., Sithirasenan, E., & Muthukkumarasamy, V. (2016). A survey on data leakage prevention systems. *Journal of Network and Computer Applications, 62*, 137–152. https://doi.org/10.1016/j.jnca.2016.01.008

Angalakudati, M., Balwani, S., Calzada, J., Chatterjee, B., Perakis, G., Raad, N., & Uichanco, J. (2014). Business analytics for flexible resource allocation under random emergencies. *Management Science, 60*(6), 1552–1573. https://doi.org/10.1287/mnsc.2014.1919

Antamis, T., Drosou, A., Vafeiadis, T., Nizamis, A., Ioannidis, D., & Tzovaras, D. (2024). Interpretability of deep neural networks: A review of methods, classification and hardware. *Neurocomputing, 601*, 128204. https://doi.org/10.1016/j.neucom.2024.128204

Arrieta, A. B., Díaz-Rodríguez, N., Del Ser, J., Bennetot, A., Tabik, S., Barbado, A., Garcia, S., Gil-Lopez, S., Molina, D., Benjamins, R., Chatila, R., & Herrera, F. (2020). Explainable artificial intelligence (XAI): Concepts, taxonomies, opportunities and challenges toward responsible AI. *Information Fusion, 58*, 82–115. https://doi.org/10.1016/j.inffus.2019.12.012

Bessa, G., & Barbosa, B. (2025). Integrating artificial intelligence into scenario analysis: A validated framework for strategic planning under economic uncertainty. *Global Economics Research*, 100007. https://doi.org/10.1016/j.ecores.2025.100007

Blank, I. A. (2023). What are large language models supposed to model? *Trends in Cognitive Sciences, 27*(11), 987–989. https://doi.org/10.1016/j.tics.2023.08.006

Cao, S., Jiang, W., Lei, L., & Zhou, Q. (2024). Applied AI for finance and accounting: Alternative data and opportunities. *Pacific-Basin Finance Journal, 84*, 102307. https://doi.org/10.1016/j.pacfin.2024.102307

Chandra, D., & Menon, R., Paulin, S., Yerasuri, S., Saha, H., & Dongol, P. (2023). The impact of artificial intelligence on business strategy and decision-making processes. *European Economic Letters, 13*(3). https://doi.org/10.52783/eel.v13i3.386

Charitha, C., & Hemaraju, B. (2023). Impact of artificial intelligence on decision-making in organisations. *International Journal For Multidisciplinary Research, 5*(4). https://doi.org/10.36948/ijfmr.2023.v05i04.5172

Devlin, J., Chang, M.-W., Lee, K., & Toutanova, K. (2019). BERT: Pre-training of deep bidirectional transformers for language understanding. *arXiv*. https://doi.org/10.48550/arXiv.1810.04805

Di Vaio, A., Hassan, R., & Alavoine, C. (2022). Data intelligence and analytics: A bibliometric analysis of human–artificial intelligence in public sector decision-making effectiveness. *Technological Forecasting and Social Change, 174*, 121201. https://doi.org/10.1016/j.techfore.2021.121201

Edwards, J. S., & Rodriguez, E. (2019). Remedies against bias in analytics systems. *Journal of Business Analytics, 2*(1), 74–87. https://doi.org/10.1080/2573234X.2019.1633890

Elgendy, N., & Elragal, A. (2016). Big data analytics in support of the decision making process. *Procedia Computer Science, 100*, 1071–1084. https://doi.org/10.1016/j.procs.2016.09.251

European Commission. (2021). *Coordinated plan on artificial intelligence 2021 review*. https://digital-strategy.ec.europa.eu/en/policies/plan-ai

European Parliament. (n.d.). Regulation on artificial intelligence. *Legislative Train Schedule*. https://www.europarl.europa.eu/legislative-train/theme-a-europe-fit-for-the-digital-age/file-regulation-on-artificial-intelligence

Fukuda, K. (2010). A cohort analysis of household vehicle expenditure in the U.S. and Japan: A possibility of generational marketing. *Marketing Letters, 21*(1), 53–64. https://doi.org/10.1007/s11002-009-9077-2

Furness, P. (2011). Applications of Monte Carlo simulation in marketing analytics. *Journal of Direct, Data and Digital Marketing Practice, 13*(2), 132–147. https://doi.org/10.1057/dddmp.2011.25

Ghafoori, A., Gupta, M., Merhi, M. I., Gupta, S., & Shore, A. P. (2024). Toward the role of organizational culture in data-driven digital transformation. *International Journal of Production Economics, 271*, 109205. https://doi.org/10.1016/j.ijpe.2024.109205

Gomes, P., Verçosa, L., Melo, F., Silva, V., Filho, C., & Bezerra, B. (2022). Artificial intelligence-based methods for business processes: A systematic literature review. *Applied Sciences, 12*(5), 2314. https://doi.org/10.3390/app12052314

Haque, M. A., & Li, S. (2025). Exploring ChatGPT and its impact on society. *AI and Ethics, 5*, 791–803. https://doi.org/10.1007/s43681-024-00435-4

Hariri, R. H., Fredericks, E. M., & Bowers, K. M. (2019). Uncertainty in big data analytics: Survey, opportunities, and challenges. *Journal of Big Data, 6*(1), 44. https://doi.org/10.1186/s40537-019-0206-3

Hazarika, A., Madhukullya, S., & Hazarika, A. (2024). An introspection into the efficient data analysis with artificial intelligence. *Journal of Trends and Challenges in Artificial Intelligence, 1*(3), 81–84. https://doi.org/10.61552/jai.2024.03.001

Hidayat, R., Kusumasari, I., Sophia, Z., & Puspita, D. (2024). Peran Teknologi AI dalam Mengoptimalkan Pengambilan Keputusan dalam Pengembangan Bisnis. *Sosial Simbiosis: Jurnal Integrasi Ilmu Sosial dan Politik, 1*(4), 167. https://doi.org/10.62383/sosial.v1i4.905

History Timelines. (n.d.). *Social media—History timelines.* https://historytimelines.co/timeline/social-media

Hu, K. (2023, February 1). *ChatGPT sets record for fastest-growing user base—Analyst note.* Reuters. https://www.reuters.com/technology/chatgpt-sets-record-fastest-growing-user-base-analyst-note-2023-02-01/

Johri, S., Rawal, K. V., Aishwarya, B. K., Singh, N., & Shaaker, A. M. (2023). Big data and artificial intelligence: Revolutionizing business decision-making. In *2023 10th IEEE Uttar Pradesh section international conference on electrical, electronics and computer engineering (UPCON)* (Vol. 10, pp. 1689–1693). IEEE. https://doi.org/10.1109/UPCON59197.2023.10434500

Jordan, M. I., & Mitchell, T. M. (2015). Machine learning: Trends, perspectives, and prospects. *Science, 349*(6245), 255–260. https://doi.org/10.1126/science.aaa8415

Kahneman, D., & Tversky, A. (2013). Prospect theory: An analysis of decision under risk. In *Handbook of the fundamentals of financial decision making: Part I* (pp. 99–127). https://doi.org/10.1142/9789814417358_0006

Kansal, T., Bahuguna, S., Singh, V., & Choudhury, T. (2018). Customer segmentation using K-means clustering. In *2018 international conference on computational techniques, electronics and mechanical systems (CTEMS)* (pp. 135–139). https://doi.org/10.1109/CTEMS.2018.8769171

Kozioł-Nadolna, K., & Beyer, K. (2021). Determinants of the decision-making process in organizations. *Procedia Computer Science, 192*, 2375–2384. https://doi.org/10.1016/j.procs.2021.09.006

Krishna, S. H., Oyebode, O. J., Joshi, A., Reddy, G. S., Karthikeyan, P., & Ganesh, K. (2023). The technical role of regression analysis in prediction and decision making. In *2023 3rd international conference on advance computing and innovative Technologies in Engineering (ICACITE)* (pp. 183–187). https://doi.org/10.1109/ICACITE57410.2023.10182872

Kubina, M., Varmus, M., & Kubinova, I. (2015). Use of big data for competitive advantage of company. *Procedia Economics and Finance, 26*, 561–565. https://doi.org/10.1016/S2212-5671(15)00955-7

Kumari, N., Singh, K., Gangwar, K., Arul, S., Vijay, A., Gaur, V., & Tamkhade, J. (2023). Artificial intelligence's effects on corporate decision-making processes. In *2023 6th international conference on contemporary computing and informatics (IC3I)* (Vol. 6, pp. 2102–2106). https://doi.org/10.1109/IC3I59117.2023.10397768

LeCun, Y., Bengio, Y., & Hinton, G. (2015). Deep learning. *Nature, 521*(7553), 436–444. https://doi.org/10.1038/nature14539

Madhavi, M., & Vijay, D. R. (2020). Artificial intelligence in business decision making. *Institute of Scholars (InSc).*

Marr, B. (2023, May 19). A short history of ChatGPT: How we got to where we are today. *Forbes.* https://www.forbes.com/sites/bernardmarr/2023/05/19/a-short-history-of-chatgpt-how-we-got-to-where-we-are-today/

Mayer, H., Yee, L., Chui, M., & Roberts, R. (2025, January 28). *Superagency in the workplace: Empowering people to unlock AI's full potential.* McKinsey & Company. https://www.mckinsey.com/capabilities/mckinsey-digital/our-insights/superagency-in-the-workplace-empowering-people-to-unlock-ais-full-potential-at-work

Merendino, A., Dibb, S., Meadows, M., Quinn, L., Wilson, D., Simkin, L., & Canhoto, A. I. (2018). Big data, big decisions: The impact of big data on board level decision-making. *Journal of Business Research, 93*, 67–78. https://doi.org/10.1016/j.jbusres.2018.08.029

Mintzberg, H., Raisinghani, D., & Theoret, A. (1976). The structure of "unstructured" decision processes. *Administrative Science Quarterly*, 246–275. https://doi.org/10.2307/2392045

Miola, A. (1991). Symbolic computation and artificial intelligence. In P. Jorrand & J. Kelemen (Eds.), *Fundamentals of Artificial Intelligence Research* (Vol. 535, pp. 243–255). Springer. https://doi.org/10.1007/3-540-54507-7_20

Moor, J. (2006). *The Dartmouth College artificial intelligence conference: The next fifty years.*

Moher, D., Liberati, A., Tetzlaff, J., Altman, D. G., & Prisma Group. (2010). Preferred reporting items for systematic reviews and meta-analyses: The PRISMA statement. *International Journal of Surgery, 8*(5), 336–341. https://doi.org/10.1016/j.ijsu.2010.02.007

Mongeon, P., & Paul-Hus, A. (2016). The journal coverage of Web of Science and Scopus: A comparative analysis. *Scientometrics, 106*(1), 213–228. https://doi.org/10.1007/s11192-015-1765-5

Odewuyi, O., Shodimu, O., Kazeem, O., Phillips, A., Okpo, S., & Ogundipe, A. (2025). Harnessing artificial intelligence to revolutionize corporate finance and financial decisions in strategic consulting for businesses. *International Journal of Science and Research Archive, 14*(02), 205–128. https://doi.org/10.30574/ijsra.2025.14.2.0353

O'Reilly, T. (2005). What is Web 2.0: Design patterns and business models for the next generation of software. *O'Reilly Media.* https://www.oreilly.com/pub/a/web2/archive/what-is-web-20.html

Pandey, A. V., Manivannan, A., Nov, O., Satterthwaite, M., & Bertini, E. (2014). The persuasive power of data visualization. *IEEE Transactions on Visualization and Computer Graphics, 20*(12), 2211–2220. https://doi.org/10.1109/TVCG.2014.2346419

Petticrew, M., & Roberts, H. (2008). *Systematic reviews in the social sciences: A practical guide.* Wiley.

Popovič, A. & Yeoh, W. (2016). Extending the understanding of critical success factors for implementing business intelligence systems. *Journal of the Association for Information Science and Technology, 67*(1), 134–147. https://doi.org/10.1002/asi.23366

Power, D. J. (2016). Data science: Supporting decision-making. *Journal of Decision Systems, 25*(4), 345–356. https://doi.org/10.1080/12460125.2016.1171610

Prasanth, A., Vadakkan, D., Surendran, P., & Thomas, B. (2023). Role of artificial intelligence and business decision making. *International Journal of Advanced Computer Science and Applications, 14*(4). https://doi.org/10.14569/ijacsa.2023.01406103

Prorok, M., & Takács, I. (2024). The impacts of artificial intelligence and knowledge-based systems on corporate decision support. In *2024 IEEE 18th international symposium on applied computational intelligence and informatics (SACI)* (pp. 000065–000070). https://doi.org/10.1109/SACI60582.2024.10619820

Rane, N., Choudhary, S., & Rane, J. (2024). Artificial intelligence-driven corporate finance: Enhancing efficiency and decision-making through machine learning, natural language processing, and robotic process automation in corporate governance and sustainability. *SSRN Electronic Journal.* https://doi.org/10.2139/ssrn.4720591

Rashid, A. B., & Kausik, M. A. K. (2024). AI revolutionizing industries worldwide: A comprehensive overview of its diverse applications. *Hybrid Advances, 7*, 100277. https://doi.org/10.1016/j.hybadv.2024.100277

Rogers, M., Briscoe, S., & Bethel, A. (2020). Conduct and reporting of citation searching in Cochrane systematic reviews: A cross-sectional study. *Research Synthesis Methods, 11*(2), 169–180. https://doi.org/10.1002/jrsm.1355

Salah, K., Rehman, M. H. U., Nizamuddin, N., & Al-Fuqaha, A. (2019). Blockchain for AI: Review and open research challenges. *IEEE Access, 7*, 10127–10149. https://doi.org/10.1109/ACCESS.2019.2893041

Sarker, I. H. (2021a). Data science and analytics: An overview from data-driven smart computing, decision-making and applications perspective. *SN Computer Science, 2*(5), 377. https://doi.org/10.1007/s42979-021-00765-8

Sarker, I. H. (2021b). Machine learning: Algorithms, real-world applications and research directions. *SN Computer Science, 2*(3), 160. https://doi.org/10.1007/s42979-021-00592-x

Sarker, I. H. (2023). Machine learning for intelligent data analysis and automation in cybersecurity: Current and future prospects. *Annals of Data Science, 10*(6), 1473–1498. https://doi.org/10.1007/s40745-022-00444-2

Schemmer, M., Hemmer, P., Kühl, N., Benz, C., & Satzger, G. (2022). Should I follow AI-based advice? Measuring appropriate reliance in human-AI decision-making. *arXiv preprint*. https://arxiv.org/abs/2204.06916

Sharma, A., Rana, N. P., & Slade, E. L. (2021). Artificial intelligence and big data analytics in digital economy: A systematic literature review. *Information Systems Frontiers, 23*, 1407–1431. https://doi.org/10.1007/s10796-020-10067-2

Shchetinin, E. (2023). On the role of artificial intelligence and statistical data analysis in business decision making. *Soft Measurements and Computing*. https://doi.org/10.36871/2618-9976.2023.11-2.007

Shukla, A., & Agnihotri, A. (2024). AI-driven smart management processes: Transforming decision-making and shaping the future. *Library Progress International, 44*(3), 5471–5493.

Simon, H. A. (1960). *The new science of management decision*. Harper & Brothers.

Smolensky, P. (1987). On the proper treatment of connectionism. *Behavioral and Brain Sciences, 11*(1), 1–23. https://doi.org/10.1017/S0140525X00052432

Statista. (2024). *Number of internet and social media users worldwide*. https://www.statista.com/statistics/617136/digital-population-worldwide/

Suresh, P., Daniel, J. V., Parthasarathy, V., & Aswathy, R. H. (2014). A state of the art review on the Internet of Things (IoT) history, technology and fields of deployment. *2014 International Conference on Science Engineering and Management Research (ICSEMR)*, 1–8. https://doi.org/10.1109/ICSEMR.2014.7043637

Tien, J. M. (2017). Internet of things, real-time decision making, and artificial intelligence. *Annals of Data Science, 4*(2), 149–178. https://doi.org/10.1007/s40745-017-0112-5

Toosi, A., Bottino, A., Saboury, B., Siegel, E., & Rahmim, A. (2021). A brief history of AI: How to prevent another winter (a critical review). *PET Clinics, 16*(4), 449–469. https://doi.org/10.1016/j.cpet.2021.07.001

Turing, A. M. (1950). I—Computing machinery and intelligence. *Mind, 59*(236), 433–460. https://doi.org/10.1093/mind/LIX.236.433

Van den Steen, E. (2013). A formal theory of strategy (Harvard Business School Strategy Unit Working Paper No. 14-058). https://doi.org/10.2139/ssrn.2383981

Vaswani, A., Shazeer, N., Parmar, N., Uszkoreit, J., Jones, L., Gomez, A. N., Kaiser, L., & Polosukhin, I. (2017). Attention is all you need. *Advances in Neural Information Processing Systems, 30*, 5998–6008. https://arxiv.org/abs/1706.03762

Wong, E. (2024). Data analysis support of artificial intelligence in financial investment decision-making. In *Modern economics & management forum* (Vol. 5, N°. 5, p. 784). https://doi.org/10.32629/memf.v5i5.2840

White, C. (2009). *Strategic management*. Palgrave Macmillan.

White & Case LLP. (2025). *AI Watch: Global regulatory tracker—China*. White & Case LLP. https://www.whitecase.com/insight-our-thinking/ai-watch-global-regulatory-tracker-china

Williams, R., & Bornmann, L. (2016). Sampling issues in bibliometric analysis. *Journal of Informetrics, 10*(4), 1225–1232. https://doi.org/10.1016/j.joi.2015.11.004

Wodecki, B. (2024, April 23). Generative AI funding hits $25.2 billion in 2023, report reveals. *AI Business*. https://aibusiness.com/verticals/generative-ai-funding-hits-25-2-billion-in-2023-report-reveals

Wu, T., & Zhou, Y. (2025). Applications and challenges of artificial intelligence in business decision making. In *Proceedings of the 4th international conference on business and policy studies* (pp. 156–162). https://doi.org/10.54254/2754-1169/2025.21777

Yang, N. (2022). Financial big data management and control and artificial intelligence analysis method based on data mining technology. *Wireless Communications and Mobile Computing, 2022*, 7596094. https://doi.org/10.1155/2022/7596094

Yurdem, B., Kuzlu, M., Gullu, M. K., Catak, F. O., & Tabassum, M. (2024). Federated learning: Overview, strategies, applications, tools and future directions. *Heliyon, 10*(19), e38137. https://doi.org/10.1016/j.heliyon.2024.e38137

Zieger, K., Schneider, U., & Darcos, L. (2023). Designing campaigns and optimizing campaign performance: The ingredients of campaign excellence. In U. Schneider & J. Hoika (Eds.), *Digital marketing in the automotive electronics industry: Redefining customer experience through digital customer engagement* (pp. 127–151) Springer.

Designing and Optimizing Brick-and-Mortar Retail Spaces with Artificial Intelligence

Maria Antónia Rodrigues, Joaquim Pratas, and Paulo Gonçalves

Abstract This chapter explores how artificial intelligence is revolutionizing the design and management of brick-and-mortar retail spaces. It focuses on the integration of traditional, generative, and agentic AI across stores' strategic planning and daily operations. AI enhances static variables like site selection, construction processes, and layout design through data-driven insights and creative simulations. Simultaneously, dynamic variables powered by AI applications enable stores to respond in real time to customer behavior, environmental changes, and operational needs, turning retail spaces into adaptive and intelligent environments. The chapter also highlights how these technologies are reshaping professional roles such as retail designers, marketers, and technologists. Through a review of literature and practical examples, the chapter presents a clear framework for understanding how AI supports more efficient, engaging, and ethically aware retail experiences. Success factors, implementation challenges and ethical concerns are also highlighted. Finally, conclusions are developed and future research directions are suggested.

1 Introduction

The aim of this chapter is to identify the main applications of Artificial Intelligence (AI) in the designing and ongoing optimization processes of brick-and-mortar retail spaces. These processes are undergoing a transformative shift, driven by the integration of AI across strategic and operational layers.

M. A. Rodrigues · J. Pratas (✉) · P. Gonçalves
CEOS.PP, ISCAP, Polytechnic of Porto, Porto, Portugal
e-mail: jmpratas@iscap.ipp.pt

M. A. Rodrigues
e-mail: mar@iscap.ipp.pt

P. Gonçalves
e-mail: pjg@iscap.ipp.pt

J. Pratas
GOVCOPP, University of Aveiro, Aveiro, Portugal

J. D. Santos et al. (eds.), *Artificial Intelligence Transforming Marketing*, Contributions to Management Science, https://doi.org/10.1007/978-3-032-22360-9_13

Brick-and-mortar retail spaces, once shaped primarily by intuition and static planning, are now evolving into dynamic, data-responsive environments. This chapter explores how AI technologies are redefining the way retailers conceive, execute, and continuously refine their spaces, offering new possibilities for both long-term planning and real-time adaptation.

The chapter begins with a literature review that situates brick-and-mortar retail at a critical juncture in the twenty-first century, where digital disruption and changing consumer expectations demand new approaches to spatial design and operational efficiency. It introduces the distinction between static and dynamic analysis in retail, framing the former as encompassing, among other variables, store openings, construction processes and layout planning, and the latter as involving ongoing store communication, customer engagement, and operational responsiveness. The review then examines how AI supports store openings and renovation processes, including site selection, market intelligence, and digital twin simulations. It continues by analyzing the role of AI in layout design and infrastructure construction, highlighting the use of generative simulations and behavioral analytics to inform spatial decisions. The discussion extends to sensory design, customer service, merchandising, and planogram execution, showing how AI enhances emotional engagement, automates service interactions, and ensures shelf compliance. Operational improvements and ongoing store operations are also explored through the lens of AI-driven inventory management, staffing optimization, and autonomous systems. Finally, the review considers the broader evolution of smart retailing and the transformation of brick-and-mortar retail spaces in the AI era.

The chapter also focuses on the practical applications of AI in brick-and-mortar retail. It begins by defining the three main types of AI (traditional, generative, and agentic) and explains their relevance to retail environments.

It then explores how traditional and generative AI are applied in static analysis, supporting store openings, renovations, and layout optimization through predictive modeling and creative design tools.

The chapter also examines dynamic analysis powered by agentic AI, which enables real-time responsiveness in sensory design, customer service, merchandising, planogram execution, and ongoing store operations. Together, these sections provide a comprehensive framework for understanding how AI is reshaping the physical retail landscape, and are complemented with practical examples. This role of AI also introduces profound shifts in professional roles and workflows. As AI capabilities continue to evolve, the brick-and-mortar retail space is being redefined as a responsive interface between data, design, and human experience.

Finally conclusions are developed, as well as academic and managerial implications, and suggestions for future research.

2 Literature Review

2.1 *Brick-and-Mortar Retail Stores at the Crossroads of the Twenty-First Century*

Amid the rise of e-commerce, shifting consumer expectations, and omnichannel retailing, brick-and-mortar retail spaces face a mounting pressure to maintain sales and profitability (Grewal et al., 2017; Hagberg et al., 2016; Piotrowicz & Cuthbertson, 2014; Verhoef et al., 2015).

Challenges such as showrooming that can benefit other retailers (Pratas & Amorim, 2022), declining foot traffic, and escalating operational costs compel retailers to reimagine the strategic role of their brick-and-mortar spaces. In response, many are adopting smart retailing, an integration of digital technologies, data analytics, and customer-centric innovations, to enhance both operational efficiency and in-store experiences (Pantano et al., 2020). This evolution positions the brick-and-mortar retail spaces not merely as points of sale, but as experiential, data-driven environments that foster engagement, differentiation, and immersive brand storytelling.

2.2 *Static and Dynamic Analysis in Brick-and-Mortar Retail*

Retail success depends on balancing two strategic dimensions: static and dynamic variables. Static analysis encompasses enduring structural elements, such as location, layout, infrastructure, and structural design, among other variables, that shape long-term economic viability of brick-and-mortar retail spaces and customer experiences. These elements are generally fixed attributes, often tied to Capital Expenditures (CAPEX), representing high-cost investments in assets like property, equipment, and digital infrastructure (Pratas & Brito, 2019).

In contrast, dynamic analysis reflects a store's agility in responding to market shifts through adaptable elements like assortment, pricing, sales promotions, communications, and engagement strategies. These operational variables, linked to Operational Expenditures (OPEX), can be modified with relative ease to sustain competitiveness and responsiveness (Pratas & Brito, 2019; Rousseau, 2020).

2.3 *Store Openings and Renovation Processes*

Store openings and renovations are pivotal strategic levers for retail growth, enabling firms to expand market reach, elevate customer experience, and align with evolving consumer expectations (Alexander & Doherty, 2008). These complex initiatives require coordinated execution across internal teams and external partners.

Key activities include (Sandberg, 2014):

- Site selection—identifying and evaluating potential store locations based on strategic and operational criteria;
- Lease negotiation—finalizing rental or buying agreements and legal terms with property owners;
- Store design—planning the layout, aesthetics, and functional aspects of the store;
- Construction and renovation works—building or/and refurbishing the physical space to meet brand and operational standards;
- Procurement of fixtures and equipment—ordering and installing shelves, furniture, lighting, and other store infrastructure;
- IT and systems setup—implementing brick-and-mortar retail systems, inventory software, and connectivity infrastructure;
- Merchandise planning and delivery—coordinating product selection, inventory levels, and delivery schedules;
- Staff recruitment and training—hiring and onboarding employees, including training in company procedures and customer service;
- Marketing and promotion—planning and executing campaigns to generate awareness and foot traffic;
- Store setup and merchandising—arranging products, signage, and displays to align with brand standards;
- Opening day execution—with final checks, soft launch activities, and official opening to the public.

The activities are typically managed by a central establishment function, which coordinates across departments and external suppliers using a mix of six coordination mechanisms. These mechanisms are mutual adjustment, direct supervision, work processes standardization, standardization of outputs, standardization of skills, and standardization of norms. These mechanisms help balance flexibility and control, especially in dynamic retail environments (Sandberg, 2014).

2.4 Designing Layout and Infrastructure Construction Processes

Store layout definition and construction are among the most intricate and integrative phases of store openings and renovations. Layout planning establishes spatial and technical requirements that shape infrastructure development, ensuring alignment with customer flow, visibility, and operational zones. These interdependent processes demand close coordination among architects, engineers, designers, and retail managers (Andrea, 2023). A well-designed layout directly influences shopper behavior, sales outcomes, profitability, and operational efficiency.

Generally the layout definition process implies:

- Feasibility study—in order to assess the location, dimensions, accessibility, and technical conditions of the premises. It is also necessary to evaluate lighting, ventilation, fire safety, and licensing requirements;
- Functional program development—defining the store's purpose, target audience, and operational needs. It is also necessary to identify the required zones for the stores as the entrance, product displays, checkout, storage, and staff areas;
- Zoning and flow planning—in order to map customer pathways to encourage exploration and maximize exposure to products, and plan for intuitive navigation, clear signage, and strategic product placement;
- Layout proposal definition—create one or more schematic layout options using softwares and digital twins. The document should include public and private areas, evacuation routes, and service access areas;
- Client approval and refinement—e.g., presenting layout options to stakeholders, and refine the proposals based on their feedback, brand guidelines, and operational constraints.

An effective store layout strategically presents merchandise to capture attention and guide customer movement, increasing exposure to products and positively influencing sales performance (Nguyen et al., 2022). Beyond layout, Bonfanti and Yfantidou (2021) highlight five experiential dimensions essential for crafting memorable in-store environments: immersive design, sensorial ambiance, social interaction, trialability, and real experience sharing. All these features (from themed designs, mood-setting details, hands-on product experiences and community events) help customers feel more engaged, emotionally connected, and loyal to the brand in brick-and-mortar retail spaces.

Once the layout is approved, the construction phase begins. This includes the following phases (Andrea, 2023):

- Preconstruction and permits—finalize architectural plans and secure building permits, and coordinate with landlords or mall managers for approvals;
- Site preparation—conduct site surveys and utility checks, and prepare the space for construction (with demolitions, and structural adjustments);
- Build phase—execute construction namely walls, flooring, lighting, heating, ventilation, air conditioning systems (HVAC) and plumbing. It also involves fixtures, displays, shelves, furniture, and technological systems installation;
- Shop fitting and branding—add shelving, signage, POS systems, and brand elements, ensuring consistency with visual merchandising strategy;
- Final checks and handover—inspect for compliance with safety and design standards, and conduct walkthroughs, finalizing punch list items before opening.

2.5 Store Sensory Elements, Customer Service, Merchandising, and Planograms

To stay competitive in the digital era, physical retailers must redesign stores as immersive, emotionally engaging environments that go beyond simple transactions. This shift relies on multisensory design, using visuals, scents, sounds, and tactile cues, alongside personalized atmospheres and human-centered interactions such as staff engagement and in-store events (Szocs et al., 2023). High-touch experiences and customer service further reinforces loyalty and perceived value, offering a differentiated experience that counters online convenience (Sen et al., 2023).

Merchandising plays a strategic role in shaping consumer behavior through curated product presentation, assortment, and promotion (Karabiyik & Elgün, 2021). Grounded in cognitive psychology, effective merchandising employs techniques such as block merchandising, shelf framing, and adjacency planning to guide attention, stimulate impulse purchases, and enhance navigation (Liljenwall, 2013).

Central to these efforts are planograms. These visual tools dictate precise product placement to optimize visibility, sales and profitability. Each layout integrates multiple planograms tailored to product categories. Each planogram must include information about shelf location, module and shelf designation, number of facings, heights, depths, and capping (if exists), as well as the total stock of the item on display, along with details regarding the vertical or horizontal presentation of the products. These tools ensure consistency across physical stores of the retail chain, streamline restocking, and reduce stockouts (Pratas & Brito, 2019).

Planogram technology has evolved through five phases (InContext, 2024). In the pre-digital era (1950s–1970s), the planograms were manually crafted tools used to organize retail space and enhance product visibility. The digital transition phase (1980s–1990s) introduced computer-based planogramming, improving inventory tracking and layout consistency. Retailers benefited from improved consistency across locations and reduced planning errors, laying the groundwork for scalable merchandising strategies. The third phase, technological advancements in the 2000s integrated systems like Enterprise resource planning (ERP) and point-of-sale (POS) systems, enabling 3D modeling and algorithmic optimization. The fourth phase, in 2010s saw cloud and mobile solutions enhance accessibility, collaboration, and predictive analytics. Today, in the fifth phase, modern planogram tools leverage big data, AI, and immersive technologies (e.g., virtual reality (VR) and augmented reality (AR)) to simulate environments and support omnichannel merchandising, driving operational efficiency and customer engagement.

2.6 *Operational Improvements and Ongoing Store Operations*

Retail store operations encompass a network of interdependent functions executed by both management and frontline staff to ensure efficiency, adaptability, and customer satisfaction. Core activities include demand forecasting, in-store logistics, inventory management, product assortment and presentation, promotional strategies implementation, checkout processes and staff coordination (Pratas & Brito, 2019).

Demand forecasting is related with inventory levels and staffing needs that can be determined, through predictive models that align supply with expected consumer behavior.

- In-store logistics involves the use of backroom storage, timely replenishment of shelves and displays, and coordination of omnichannel flows that integrate online and offline fulfillment.
- Inventory management aims to prevent stockouts, minimize system errors, and optimize product availability through price sensitivity analysis and demand-driven ordering.
- The definition and presentation of product assortments (including category breadth, depth, and spatial allocation) are guided by planograms and visual merchandising standards to maximize shopper engagement.
- Promotional strategies and communication, whether price-related or not, further influence purchasing decisions and brand perception.
- At the checkout, operational efficiency and customer service converge through payment processing and personalized assistance.
- Finally, staff coordination, including scheduling and task management, ensures that human resources are aligned with store rhythms and service expectations (Shandong et al., 2018).

2.7 *Smart Retailing and the Evolution of Brick-and-Mortar Retail Spaces in the AI Era*

Smart retailing technologies are reshaping brick-and-mortar retail spaces into data-driven, customer-centric environments that enhance operational efficiency and elevate the shopping experience. Tools such as AI, Internet of Things (IoT), augmented reality (AR), and advanced analytics personalize customer journeys, optimize inventory, and streamline operations.

For example, AI-powered recommendation engines and AR shopping assistants help tailor product suggestions and improve decision-making (Zimmermann et al., 2023). IoT sensors and heatmap analytics refine product placement by tracking movement and dwell time (Dragonfly AI, 2025), while AR and AI tools support tailored recommendations at brick-and-mortar retail spaces.

These innovations reduce friction, foster immersive engagement, and enable seamless omnichannel integration between online and offline touchpoints (Chen & Chang, 2023), positioning smart retailing as a strategic imperative in a tech-driven marketplace.

Therefore, Table 1 summarizes the main topics regarding the differences between static and dynamic analysis in brick-and-mortar retail spaces, namely the nature of decisions, cost structure, store location and real estate, store layout and infrastructure, design and experiential environment, technology and systems setup, planograms and space management, human resources and training, operational processes, customer experience architecture, marketing and customer engagement, and merchandising foundations.

3 AI Applications in Brick-and-Mortar Retail Spaces

3.1 AI Main Types: Traditional, Generative and Agentic AI

Retail AI technologies can be broadly categorized into three evolutionary tiers, each offering distinct capabilities and strategic value. These AI technologies can be defined as (Song, 2025):

- Traditional AI encompasses rule-based, deterministic systems designed for narrowly scoped tasks using supervised learning and statistical models. These systems rely on structured data and explicit programming to drive functions such as recommendation engines, fraud detection, and inventory forecasting. For instance, collaborative filtering suggests products based on purchase history, while predictive models align stock levels with demand patterns.
- Generative AI leverages deep learning, particularly transformer architectures, to produce novel content including text, images, audio, and code. By learning from vast datasets, it enables retailers to automate content creation, deploy intelligent chatbots for customer and employee support, and offer virtual try-ons. Applications such as dynamic product descriptions and promotional visuals enhance engagement while reducing operational costs.
- Agentic AI, as described by Bandi et al. (2025), represents a new frontier: autonomous, goal-oriented systems capable of planning, tool selection, and executing multi-step tasks with minimal supervision. These entities integrate perception, reasoning, and adaptability to optimize pricing, manage inventory dynamically, and deliver personalized virtual assistance. For example, agentic systems can autonomously reconfigure shelf layouts based on real-time sales data or orchestrate supply chain actions across multiple locations.

Swagler (2025) introduces the concept of the agentic store, where AI agents autonomously orchestrate retail operations in real time. Unlike siloed systems, agentic stores integrate inventory, checkout, signage, and other functions through

Table 1 Static and dynamic analysis in brick-and-mortar retail (main topics)

Main topics	Static analysis	Dynamic analysis
Nature of decisions	Focuses on long-term, structural, and sunk-cost decisions that define the store's economic viability and customer experience. Once implemented, changes are costly or infeasible	Focuses on short-term, operational decisions that can be adjusted frequently to respond to market shifts, customer behavior, and competitive dynamics
Cost structure	Linked to CAPEX: property, construction, infrastructure, equipment, and digital systems. High-cost, long-lived assets	Linked to OPEX: assortment, pricing, promotions, staffing, communications, and day-to-day operations. Flexible adjustments
Store location and real estate	Site selection, lease negotiation, and physical constraints of the property. These choices lock the retailer into a long-term geographic and structural position	Localized marketing, neighborhood-specific promotions, and community engagement strategies that can be adapted continuously
Store layout and infrastructure	Layout definition, zoning, flow planning, feasibility studies, HVAC, lighting, plumbing, fixtures, and construction. These elements shape customer movement and operational zones and cannot be easily modified	Adjustments to product placement, signage, experiential elements, and micro-layout tweaks based on traffic patterns, seasonality, or campaign needs
Design and experiential environment	Architectural design, structural branding, permanent aesthetic elements, and multisensory infrastructure (e.g., lighting systems, sound systems)	Dynamic sensory cues such as music, scent, lighting intensity, digital signage content, and AR/VR experiences that adapt to customer profiles or time of day
Technology and systems setup	Installation of POS systems, ERP, connectivity infrastructure, security systems, and digital architecture. These are foundational and costly to replace	Software updates, content changes, digital promotions, mobile notifications, and real-time system configurations
Planograms and space management	Initial planogram design, shelf dimensions and physical module configuration. These are fixed once installed	Ongoing compliance checks, stock adjustments, dynamic facings, digital shelf labels, and real-time optimization based on sales and traffic
Human resources and training	Recruitment, onboarding, and structural staffing models. These require long-term planning and investment	Daily scheduling, task allocation, performance adjustments, and real-time labor optimization
Operational processes	Checkout infrastructure, storage layout, backroom design, and logistics pathways	Replenishment timing, omnichannel flow coordination, fraud detection responses, and service adjustments based on demand

(continued)

Table 1 (continued)

Main topics	Static analysis	Dynamic analysis
Customer experience architecture	Permanent experiential zones, trial areas, and social spaces built into the store	Dynamic events, staff interactions, live demos, and personalized service flows
Marketing and customer engagement	Brand identity, store positioning, and long-term experiential strategy	Promotions, pricing, communication content, loyalty triggers, and omnichannel engagement that can shift daily or hourly
Merchandising foundations	Planogram frameworks, category zoning, shelf hardware, and physical merchandising infrastructure. These define the store's structural merchandising logic	Assortment rotation, pricing changes, promotional campaigns, visual merchandising refreshes, and real-time planogram adjustments

Source Authors

intelligent agents capable of perceiving their environment, setting goals, and executing tasks independently to optimize performance and customer satisfaction. These systems exhibit real-time responsiveness, for instance, automatically managing refrigeration failures by triggering maintenance, rerouting inventory, and updating signage without human intervention. Key enabling technologies include IoT devices, smart shelves, computer vision, frictionless checkout, and advanced AI orchestration platforms.

3.2 AI in Brick-and-Mortar Retail Static Analysis: Store Openings and Renovations, and Store Layout Optimization

AI is increasingly transforming static analysis in retail, offering scalable solutions across store site selection, layout optimization, and renovation planning. Its integration promises operational efficiency, enhanced customer experience, and strategic decision-making (Resnick, 2022; Srinivasan, 2025).

3.2.1 Store Site Selection and Opening

AI streamlines the traditionally fragmented store opening process, marked by disjointed systems and ad hoc assessments, by consolidating market demographics, competitor footprints, and economic indicators into unified platforms that score and rank potential sites (Avula, 2024; Haque et al., 2024).

Machine learning models forecast foot traffic and sales potential, enabling retailers to prioritize high-ROI locations (Hassan & Hassan, 2025; Panai et al., 2021). Automated project management tools further optimize contractor scheduling and equipment installation, reducing delays and truck rolls (Gai, 2025; Hassan & Hassan, 2025). Key capabilities include geospatial clustering for catchment analysis, calendar-based optimization for scheduling, and risk scoring for permitting and build-out costs based on historical performance (Ahaggach et al., 2024).

3.2.2 Layout Design and Zoning

Retail layout defined as the strategic arrangement of aisles, displays, and checkout areas, directly influences shopper behavior, dwell time, and sales (Levy et al., 2022). AI supports layout design across multiple phases:

- Feasibility Studies: Geospatial analytics and computer vision assess foot traffic and accessibility (Lu et al., 2024; Zhang et al., 2025). Environmental modeling via Building Information Modeling (BIM), and IoT sensors simulates lighting, ventilation, and fire safety (Mannino et al., 2021). Natural Language Processing (NLP) tools scan regulatory documents for compliance (Zhang & El-Gohary, 2022).
- Functional Programming: Clustering algorithms segment customers by preferences, enabling tailored zone allocation (Grewal et al., 2025). Reinforcement learning simulates operational needs to optimize space usage (Choi et al., 2024).
- Flow Planning: AI enhances path optimization and behavioral prediction through heatmap analytics and computer vision (Dragonfly AI, 2025). Generative design algorithms simulate layout variations to reduce congestion (Kang, 2025), while eye-tracking data guides intuitive navigation (Šola et al., 2024).
- Client Approval: NLP analyzes stakeholder feedback to refine proposals, and AI-driven visualization platforms enable interactive layout simulations (El Nekiti et al., 2026).

3.2.3 Store Renovation and Dynamic Adaptation

During store renovations, AI helps maintain sales continuity, aligns upgrades with consumer preferences, and manages capital expenditure. Digital twins simulate renovation scenarios, while computer vision analyzes CAD plans and video footage to identify bottlenecks and optimize layout flow (Mesquita et al., 2024).

Predictive models estimate sales uplift from design changes, guiding budget allocation. Heatmap analysis, spend-to-return forecasting, and phased scheduling further enhance renovation outcomes (Tang, 2025).

3.2.4 Planogram Generation and Shelf Optimization

Planograms are static visualizations dictating product's shelf space allocation, which have been also enhanced by AI through the integration of POS data, loyalty profiles, and trend indicators (Bianchi-Aguiar et al., 2021).

Clustering algorithms position complementary products to boost cross-selling, while constraint-based optimization ensures compliance with supplier agreements and store dimensions. AI enables store-specific planograms based on customer behavior, improving sell-through rates, reducing stockouts, and balancing consistency with localized adaptation (Silverio et al., 2025). Sales and profitability are also increased in these optimization processes.

3.2.5 AI Paradigms in Retail Layout Design: Traditional, Generative, and Agentic Contributions

Retail store layout design is increasingly shaped by three distinct AI paradigms (traditional, generative, and agentic), each offering unique capabilities across planning, personalization, and operational responsiveness (Haque et al., 2024; Hassan & Hassan, 2025).

Traditional AI leverages machine learning and optimization algorithms to analyze historical data on customer flow, dwell time, and sales. These models inform strategic decisions on product placement, aisle configuration, and traffic patterns, enhancing products' exposure and reducing congestion. Beyond layout, traditional AI supports inventory and supply chain management through demand forecasting, anomaly detection, supplier risk assessment, and routing optimization.

Generative AI, on the other hand, introduces novel layout concepts by learning from existing designs and behavioral data. It generates tailored layout variations for specific customer segments or seasonal trends, including 3D simulations of store interiors with personalized displays. Applications extend to planogram design, automated marketing content, product recommendations, and customer service automation through chatbots and virtual assistants. Visual search capabilities allow customers to locate products using images, while virtual try-on tools enhance pre-purchase engagement.

Finally, agentic AI has functions as autonomous agents capable of perceiving, deciding, and acting in real time. It dynamically reconfigures store layouts and communication tools such as adjusting digital signage, shifting product zones, or rerouting foot traffic based on live environmental feedback. For instance, overcrowded areas can be alleviated through instant layout adjustments or staff alerts (Ghosh, 2025; Retail Prowess, 2025).

According to Dutta (2024), AI technologies collectively enable:

- Personalized marketing via recommendation engines and dynamic content creation
- Virtual shopping assistants for cross-channel support

- Fulfillment optimization, including "buy online, pick up in store" (BOPIS) strategies and predictive pickup scheduling
- Automated retail messaging across platforms
- Enhanced customer insights through real-time feedback and sentiment analysis
- Immersive AR/VR experiences integrating digital and physical shopping environments

Together, these AI approaches redefine retail layout design, balancing operational efficiency with customer-centric innovation.

Table 2 summarizes the main topics of brick-and-mortar retail static analysis covered through traditional AI, generative AI, and agentic AI, as well as their opportunities.

3.3 AI in Brick-and-Mortar Retail Dynamic Analysis: Sensory Elements, Customer Service, Merchandising, Planograms and Ongoing Store Operations

3.3.1 Sensory Design and Experiential Retail

AI orchestrates sensory elements to influence customer perception and emotional engagement:

- Personalized Sensory Stimuli: AI tailors lighting, scent, and ambiance based on customer data such as demographics and dwell time. Smart systems adjust environmental conditions dynamically (Solanki, 2025).
- Environmental Optimization: IoT sensors and AI algorithms monitor temperature, noise, and crowd density, adapting music, displays, and signage to maximize engagement (Solanki, 2025).
- Immersive Design: AR/VR technologies simulate tactile and visual experiences, creating "phygital" environments that resonate with Gen Z and experience-driven consumers (Rudkovska, 2025).
- Digital Integration: AI synchronizes mobile notifications and digital signage to guide shoppers through high-impact zones, aligning sensory design with personalized journeys (Solanki, 2025).
- Adaptive Feedback Loops: AI continuously learns from customer interactions, adjusting sensory layouts in real time to boost engagement (O'Brien, n.d.).

3.3.2 Intelligent Customer Service

AI enhances retail service delivery through automation, personalization, and omnichannel integration:

Table 2 AI in brick-and-mortar retail static analysis (main topics)

Main topics	Traditional AI	Generative AI	Agentic AI
Store site selection and opening	Uses demographic, competitive, and economic data to score sites; forecasts foot traffic and sales; optimizes contractor scheduling and permitting through historical-pattern analysis; applies geospatial clustering and risk scoring to reduce delays and CAPEX uncertainty	Produces alternative site-selection scenarios, synthesized market briefs, and visual comparisons; generates simulated demand forecasts and optimized construction schedules; creates automated feasibility reports to support decision-making	Monitors permitting, contractor availability, and site readiness in real time; autonomously adjusts schedules, reallocates resources, and triggers operational actions to maintain project timelines and reduce overruns
Layout design and zoning	Applies geospatial analytics and environmental modeling for feasibility; uses clustering for zoning and reinforcement learning for space optimization; predicts flow through heatmaps to reduce congestion	Generates multiple layout variations, zoning concepts, and 3D simulations; explores thousands of design permutations to improve flow and exposure; produces interactive visualizations for stakeholder approval	Dynamically adapts layouts based on live or predictions about foot-traffic and congestion data; autonomously adjusts signage, routing cues, and temporary zones to maintain optimal flow and customer experience
Store renovation and dynamic adaptation	Uses digital twins to simulate renovation scenarios; predicts sales uplift and CAPEX impact; analyzes CAD and video to detect bottlenecks; optimizes phased scheduling and spend-to-return allocation	Generates renovation concepts, visual mock-ups, and alternative design schemes; synthesizes customer behavior and stakeholder feedback into refined proposals; produces immersive visualizations for faster approvals	Monitors renovation progress and disruptions in real time; autonomously adjusts phases, reallocates space or staff, and maintains sales continuity during remodels
Planogram generation and Shelf optimization	Integrates POS, loyalty, and trend data to create store-specific planograms; uses clustering for complementary placement and constraint optimization for compliance; reduces stockouts and improves sell-through	Produces multiple planogram variations tailored to local behavior, trends, or promotions; generates visual shelf simulations and adaptive layouts aligned with emerging patterns	Adjusts shelf layouts based on live sales, stockouts, and movement data; triggers micro-optimizations such as shifting facings or activating digital shelf labels to maintain performance

Source Authors

- Task Automation: Chatbots and virtual assistants manage routine inquiries and streamline scheduling, queues, and checkout (Pratas et al., 2024; Wavetec, 2025).
- Predictive Support: Machine learning segments customers by behavior, enabling proactive assistance and targeted promotions (Pathak, 2024; Pavion, n.d.).
- Omnichannel Consistency: AI unifies customer profiles across platforms, ensuring seamless support from online to in-store (Buehler, 2024).
- Operational Insights: AI monitors sentiment and service metrics, optimizing staffing and inventory availability (Spencer, 2024).
- Conversational Interfaces: NLP enables empathetic, context-aware interactions, fostering trust in digital service channels (Pavion, n.d.).

3.3.3 Merchandising and Planogram Innovation

AI empowers retailers to make smarter, faster merchandising decisions through:

- Demand Forecasting: Predictive analytics improve assortment planning and product availability tailored to local preferences (Nicasio, 2025).
- Process Automation: Computer vision and machine learning automate shelf layout and inventory management, reducing waste and stockouts (Ross, 2024; Spencer, 2024).
- Hyper-Personalization: AI drives dynamic pricing and real-time promotional content via digital signage (Ross, 2024; Spencer, 2024).
- Visual Merchandising: Customer movement analytics refine product placement and display strategies (Ross, 2024).
- Agentic Adaptability: Autonomous systems adjust inventory and promotions based on live data (Salesforce, n.d.).

3.3.4 Planogram Creation and Compliance

AI also revolutionizes planogram creation and compliance, through:

- Automated Layouts and templates: AI generates shelf designs using real-time sales and behavioral data, ensuring optimal product placement (Beam, 2024).
- Compliance Verification: Image recognition tools detect planogram discrepancies across store locations (Max, 2024).
- Localized Adaptation: Layouts are customized to store-specific dimensions and traffic patterns (Beam, 2024).
- Dynamic Updates: POS and inventory integration enables real-time planogram adjustments (Matellio, 2025).
- Efficiency Gains: AI-driven planogram tools can increase sales by 10–30%, reduce stockouts by 80%, and cut labor costs by 40% (Matellio, 2025).

3.3.5 Operational Excellence and Real-Time Responsiveness

AI enhances store operations by automating tasks and enabling data-driven decisions:

- Inventory Management: AI predicts demand using historical and contextual data, optimizing stock levels and automating replenishment (Rudkovska, 2025; Spencer, 2024).
- Customer Engagement: Chatbots and AR mirrors support shoppers across channels, improving satisfaction and reducing returns (Pratas et al., 2024; Rudkovska, 2025).
- Analytics and Layout Optimization: AI analyzes foot traffic and sales trends to adjust staffing and store configurations (Aviso, 2025; Downie & Hayes, n.d.).
- Robotic Automation: Autonomous systems handle cleaning, scanning, and checkout, while AI detects fraud and shrinkage patterns (Cummings, 2025; Downie & Hayes, n.d.).
- Targeted Promotions: AI personalizes offers and signage content based on real-time shopper profiles (Spencer, 2024).

3.3.6 Bridging Static Design and Dynamic Behavior

AI integrates static layout strategies with dynamic shopper behavior:

- Personalized Navigation: Digital signage and mobile prompts guide customers to high-impact zones using dwell time and QR code analytics (Pratas, 2023; Pratas et al., 2025).
- Seasonal Adaptation: Wi-Fi sensors and beacons inform layout changes aligned with customer flow and campaign timing (Dai et al., 2023).
- Shelf Compliance and Inventory Health: Edge-AI cameras and robotics detect misplaced items, monitor stock, and trigger automated replenishment. Technologies include object recognition, RFID/barcode validation, and real-time alert dashboards (Grewal et al., 2017; Pratas et al., 2022).

Table 3 summarizes the main topics of brick-and-mortar retail dynamic analysis covered through traditional AI, generative AI and agentic AI, as well as their opportunities.

4 Case Studies in AI-Driven Brick-and-Mortar Retail Spaces

A growing number of companies are using AI to reshape how physical retail environments are designed and optimized. These applications now span site selection, layout planning, renovation, merchandising, and customer engagement, reflecting the rising sophistication of AI in brick-and-mortar retail.

Table 3 AI in brick-and-mortar retail dynamic analysis (main topics)

Main topics	Traditional AI	Generative AI	Agentic AI
Sensory design and experiential retail	Uses customer data to tailor lighting, scent, and ambiance; monitors temperature, noise, and crowd density via IoT; adjusts music, displays, and signage to optimize engagement; analyzes interactions to refine sensory layouts	Generates immersive AR/VR experiences and "phygital" environments; produces personalized sensory journeys and digital-physical integrations; creates adaptive content for signage and mobile touchpoints	Continuously adapts sensory conditions in real time based on live customer behavior; autonomously tunes lighting, ambiance, and digital cues to maximize emotional engagement
Intelligent customer service	Automates routine inquiries, queueing, and checkout; segments customers for predictive support; unifies profiles across channels; monitors sentiment and service metrics; enables empathetic NLP-based interactions	Generates personalized responses, service scripts, and promotional content; creates dynamic knowledge bases and conversational flows; simulates customer scenarios for improved service design	Provides proactive, real-time assistance across channels; autonomously adjusts staffing cues, service routing, and support actions based on live customer needs and sentiment
Merchandising and planogram innovation	Forecasts demand for assortment planning; automates shelf layout and inventory checks; drives dynamic pricing and real-time promotions; analyzes movement data to refine displays	Generates merchandising concepts, promotional content, and visual layouts; produces adaptive pricing and display variations tailored to local behavior	Adjusts inventory, pricing, and promotions autonomously based on live sales and traffic data; continuously optimizes merchandising decisions
Planogram creation and compliance	Creates shelf layouts using sales and behavioral data; verifies compliance via image recognition; adapts layouts to store dimensions and traffic patterns; updates planograms using POS and inventory data	Generates automated planogram templates, visual simulations, and localized variations; produces optimized shelf configurations for different scenarios	Monitors shelves in real time, detecting discrepancies and triggering adjustments; autonomously updates planograms to maintain compliance and performance

(continued)

Table 3 (continued)

Main topics	Traditional AI	Generative AI	Agentic AI
Operational excellence and real-time responsiveness	Predicts demand and automates replenishment; analyzes foot traffic and sales to adjust staffing; detects fraud and shrinkage; supports targeted promotions and AR-based engagement	Generates operational insights, promotional content, and scenario simulations; creates adaptive layouts and customer-engagement scripts	Automates cleaning, scanning, checkout, and replenishment; dynamically adjusts store operations, staffing, and promotions based on real-time conditions
Bridging Static Design and Dynamic Behavior	Uses analytics to guide navigation, seasonal layout changes, and inventory health; detects misplaced items and stock issues via computer vision and RFID	Generates adaptive navigation prompts, seasonal layout concepts, and visual merchandising variations; produces predictive scenarios for shopper behavior	Continuously aligns static layouts with live behavior; autonomously guides customers, updates layouts, and triggers replenishment through edge-AI and robotics

Source Authors

In-store site selection, AI-powered location analytics have become essential. These platforms combine demographic data, competitive context, and economic indicators to score and rank potential locations with high precision. Computer-vision systems focused on autonomous store operations complement this by analyzing shopper behavior and store performance, helping retailers make informed, data-driven expansion decisions (Anderson, 2025).

For layout design and zoning, real-time visual intelligence tools use heatmaps and computer vision to optimize product placement and signage based on customer movement and attention. In-store spatial intelligence platforms deepen this analysis by tracking shopper journeys, dwell times, and interactions to guide planogram development and zone allocation. Generative AI adds dynamic layout simulations, traffic-flow optimization, and smart shelving strategies. These improvements have driven sales increases of 10–15% for some retailers.

Renovation and ongoing adaptation are increasingly supported by AI-driven digital twin platforms. These tools let retailers test renovation scenarios virtually, reducing disruption and improving design outcomes. When paired with computer vision, they also enable real-time monitoring of construction progress and workflow efficiency, ensuring renovation efforts align with operational goals and customer expectations.

In planogram generation and shelf optimization, AI is streamlining execution across store networks. Computer-vision systems automate compliance checks, shelf scanning, and inventory tracking, while other platforms generate planograms based on real-time sales and customer behavior. These solutions deliver store-specific layouts that remain consistent with supplier agreements and merchandising standards.

Cross-functional improvements are emerging from platforms that merge personalization with spatial intelligence. AI engines power recommendation systems, virtual assistants, and omnichannel support, while spatial analytics optimize fulfillment, engagement, and layout performance using real-time location data. This fusion of personalization and operational intelligence is reshaping how retailers serve and interact with customers.

Sensory design and experiential retail are also evolving. AI platforms now tailor in-store music, scent, and lighting to shopper profiles and contextual cues. IoT sensors integrated with AI monitor environmental conditions and adjust sensory elements dynamically to enhance emotional engagement. AR and VR technologies further extend this by creating hybrid digital-physical shopping experiences that appeal to experience-driven consumers.

Customer service is being transformed by AI systems that automate up to 70% of inquiries through chatbots, reducing response times and improving satisfaction. These platforms deliver predictive support, unify customer profiles across channels, and use NLP to enable empathetic, context-aware interactions. Virtual assistants add another layer of personalization and streamline routine service tasks.

Merchandising and planogram innovation benefit from platforms specializing in retail analytics, inventory management, and demand forecasting. Machine-learning models support accurate sales predictions, assortment planning, and dynamic pricing. Computer-vision tools automate shelf audits and compliance, while AI-driven planogram systems adjust layouts based on behavioral data and real-time sales, ensuring consistent execution and localized optimization.

Operational excellence and real-time responsiveness are increasingly driven by AI applications that analyze shopper behavior, optimize inventory, and detect loss-prevention risks. Edge-AI cameras and IoT systems support shelf scanning, inventory-health monitoring, and robotic automation. Retailers are also adopting AI for predictive inventory management, dynamic staffing, and autonomous checkout, improving efficiency and customer flow.

To connect static and dynamic analysis, retail automation platforms now integrate spatial intelligence with layout and planogram optimization. These systems evaluate dwell time, customer flow, and zone engagement to enable dynamic layout adjustments and targeted promotions. AI tools also support personalized navigation and campaign-linked updates, while POS-integrated planogram software delivers real-time responsiveness and measurable efficiency gains (often boosting sales by up to 30%).

As AI adoption accelerates, evidence increasingly shows that these technologies deliver substantial financial returns for brick-and-mortar retailers. Recent studies report that AI-enabled retail operations can improve profitability. For example, Boileau (2023) finds that AI-driven analytics significantly increase retail profitability by improving decision-making and operational efficiency. Similarly, Gajjar (2024) demonstrates that AI and AR integration boosts operational efficiency and customer experience, contributing to measurable revenue growth. AI-driven pricing and inventory systems have also been shown to reduce costs and improve margin performance, with machine-learning-based pricing models yielding notable gains in inventory turnover and cost management (Köksal et al., 2024). Industry-wide projections reinforce these findings: AI-enabled retail transformations are expected to generate double-digit revenue uplifts, with layout and planogram optimization alone contributing 10–30% sales increases in some contexts. Although implementation costs vary, ranging from modest investments in analytics platforms to more substantial expenditures for computer-vision infrastructure, the studies consistently conclude that the long-term ROI outweighs initial costs, particularly as AI systems scale across store networks. Collectively, these projections underscore that AI is not only reshaping operational practices but also establishing a clear economic case for sustained investment in intelligent retail environments.

5 Success Factors, Implementation Challenges and Future Directions

AI-driven site selection succeeds when retailers unify diverse data (such as demographics, competition, and economic indicators) into a single platform. Foot-traffic and ROI models guide location choices, while automated scheduling streamlines contractor and installation workflows. Key challenges include fragmented legacy systems, uneven data quality, and stakeholder resistance. Early alignment and historical performance data remain essential for forecasting risks. Emerging directions include federated learning for cross-brand insights, sustainability-based scoring, and AR walkthroughs for pre-approval.

AI-powered layout design uses geospatial analytics, behavioral clustering, and reinforcement learning to create intuitive zoning and optimized space use. Barriers persist, such as the cost of generative simulations, difficulty operationalizing AI outputs, and varying regulatory requirements. Eye-tracking, heatmaps, NLP feedback tools, and BIM integration have improved design accuracy, but are in its infancy in terms of utilization. Future advances will enable real-time layout adaptation, persona-based zoning, and dynamic pricing integration.

Renovation planning also benefits from digital twins, predictive modeling, and heatmap analysis to maintain sales and align upgrades with customer preferences. Challenges include managing traffic during construction, budget limits, and shifting design expectations. Phased scheduling, CAD, video analysis, and real-time sensors improve continuity and responsiveness. Next-generation tools will feature evolving digital twins, AI-driven sentiment analysis, and sustainability-focused simulations.

Planogram optimization has improved through POS and loyalty data, clustering, and compliance algorithms, boosting sell-through and reducing stockouts. Obstacles include format variability, supplier constraints, and pushback against automation. Store-specific planograms and real-time updates enhance relevance. The next wave will bring AR previews, dynamic inventory-linked planograms, and federated learning for cross-brand innovation.

Traditional AI strengthens layout and inventory decisions through historical analysis; generative AI adds creative concepts and simulations; agentic AI enables real-time adaptation. Challenges include balancing creativity with feasibility, maintaining brand consistency, and training staff to interpret outputs. Hybrid models outperform single approaches, and generative simulations improve stakeholder engagement. Future work will focus on multi-agent systems, immersive AR/VR design, and live shopper data.

In sensory design, AI personalizes lighting, scent, and ambiance using customer data. IoT sensors enable dynamic adjustments, and AR/VR creates immersive experiences. High infrastructure costs, privacy issues, and format consistency remain hurdles. Adaptive feedback loops and synchronized mobile-signage systems improve engagement and navigation, while emotion analytics refine stimuli. Future innovations include sentiment-linked sensory design, profile-based zones, and sustainability metrics.

Customer service has been transformed by chatbots and virtual assistants that automate tasks and deliver predictive support. AI unifies customer profiles and provides real-time sentiment insights. Challenges include NLP accuracy, expectation management, and privacy. Retailers report reduced wait times, higher satisfaction, and better staffing decisions. The next stage will bring emotion-aware conversational AI, context-driven personalization, and in-store voice interfaces.

Merchandising and operations benefit from predictive analytics, computer vision, and autonomous systems that optimize inventory, improve layout responsiveness, and reduce shrinkage. Legacy integration, training, and data latency remain issues. Dynamic staffing and personalized promotions boost efficiency and conversion. Future developments include full-store robotics, behavior-linked merchandising, and sustainability-driven inventory planning.

AI now connects static design with real-time shopper behavior. Digital signage and mobile prompts guide navigation, while Wi-Fi sensors and beacons support seasonal adjustments. Edge-AI cameras and robotics improve shelf compliance and inventory health. Challenges include layout consistency and accurate object recognition. Dynamic prompts and layout recalibration enhance engagement and prevent stockouts. Future directions include real-time layout evolution, predictive navigation, and automated replenishment tied to behavioral analytics. Therefore multiple opportunities exist, but the implementation challenges are also significant.

6 Conclusion

AI is reshaping brick-and-mortar retail by transforming how brick-and-mortar retail spaces are designed, executed, and continuously optimized. It replaces intuition-driven decisions with data-driven precision across both static and dynamic aspects of store management.

Traditional AI has strengthened static analysis through historical data, geospatial intelligence, and optimization models, ensuring that locations, layouts, and planograms align with demand and efficiency goals. Generative AI expands this by producing creative, personalized layout simulations and adaptive merchandising strategies tailored to customer segments and seasonal shifts.

Dynamic analysis reflects the real-time adaptability of modern retail. Agentic AI systems autonomously respond to shopper behavior, environmental changes, and operational fluctuations. These tools enhance sensory design, customer service, inventory management, and layout adjustments, creating immersive experiences while preserving agility.

As AI advances, future innovation will emphasize deeper personalization, sustainability, and cross-brand collaboration, positioning the brick-and-mortar stores as dynamic interfaces between data, design, and human experience.

The convergence of traditional, generative, and agentic AI is also reshaping roles and workflows across retail functions. Designers must shift from static planners to dynamic experience architects, working closely with data and technology teams. Marketers gain new precision through AI-driven personalization, sentiment analysis, and dynamic content delivery, moving from broad segmentation to micro-targeting while navigating privacy and emotional-data ethics.

Technologists lead the deployment of AI infrastructure (from edge computing and IoT to federated learning and autonomous systems), while ensuring interoperability, scalability, and real-time responsiveness. Their role now includes coordinating across teams so AI outputs translate into actionable decisions, all while maintaining transparency and trust.

7 Future Research Directions

AI is transforming brick-and-mortar retail spaces by enabling smarter design, planning, and real-time responsiveness. This shift highlights the need for research on integrating traditional, generative, and agentic AI into unified retail systems. Key opportunities include hybrid models that blend data-driven optimization with creative spatial design, as well as deeper human–AI collaboration through generative simulations and digital twins. Ethical concerns such as emotional analytics, biometric data, and privacy require strong governance. Sustainability is also becoming a priority, with AI supporting energy-efficient layouts and waste reduction. As agentic AI gains autonomy in store operations and customer interactions, retailers will need robust frameworks to ensure transparency, accountability, and brand alignment. Together, these developments point toward a future where intelligent retail spaces are efficient, adaptive, and ethically grounded.

References

Ahaggach, H., Abrouk, L., & Lebon, E. (2024). Systematic mapping study of sales forecasting: Methods, trends, and future directions. *Forecasting, 6*(3), 502–532. https://doi.org/10.3390/forecast6030028

Alexander, N., & Doherty, A. M. (2008). *International retailing*. Oxford University Press.

Anderson, C. C. (2025, December 13). *Retail site selection software: Compare top AI platforms (2025)*. Growth Factor. Retrieved December 17, 2025, from https://www.growthfactor.ai/blog-posts/retail-site-selection-software?

Andrea. (2023, February 24). *The stages in a retail architecture and construction project*. Retrieved June 25, 2025, from https://grupidea.com/en/stages-retail-architecture-construction-project/

Aviso, A. (2025, September 4). *How AI in retail is driving growth and efficiency*. TechRepublic. Retrieved December 16, 2025, from https://www.techrepublic.com/article/ai-in-retail/

Avula, A. K. R. (2024). AI-powered location intelligence: Revolutionizing site selection and investment decisions. *International Journal of Scientific Research in Computer Science, Engineering and Information Technology, 10*(6), 1735–1742. https://doi.org/10.32628/CSEIT241061217

Bandi, A., Kongari, B., Naguru, R., Pasnoor, S., & Vilipala, S. V. (2025). The rise of agentic AI: A review of definitions, frameworks, architectures, applications, evaluation metrics, and challenges. *Future Internet, 17*(9), 404. https://doi.org/10.3390/fi17090404

Beam. (2024, May 3). *The transformative impact of AI on planogram creation and approval*. Retrieved July 10, 2025, from https://beam.ai/articles/the-transformative-impact-of-ai-on-planogram-creation-and-approval

Bianchi-Aguiar, T., Hübner, A., Carravilla, M. A., & Oliveira, J. F. (2021). Retail shelf space planning problems: A comprehensive review and classification framework. *European Journal of Operational Research, 289*(1), 1–16. https://doi.org/10.1016/j.ejor.2020.06.018

Boileau, W. (2023). AI in retail industry: Valuable insights that improve profitability and drive growth. In K. Arai (Ed.), *Proceedings of the Future Technologies Conference (FTC) 2023* (Vol. 1). Lecture Notes in Networks and Systems, Vol. 813. Springer. https://doi.org/10.1007/978-3-031-47454-5_25

Bonfanti, A., & Yfantidou, G. (2021). Designing a memorable in-store customer shopping experience: Practical evidence from sports equipment retailers. *International Journal of Retail and Distribution Management, 49*(9), 1295–1311. https://doi.org/10.1108/IJRDM-09-2020-0361

Buehler, T. L. (2024, February 5). *AI in customer service: Revolutionizing digital retail*. American Public University—Digital Learning for Real Life. Retrieved June 28, 2025, from https://www.apu.apus.edu/area-of-study/business-and-management/resources/ai-in-customer-service/

Chen, J., & Chang, Y.-W. (2023). How smart technology empowers consumers in smart retail stores? The perspective of technology readiness and situational factors. *Electronic Markets, 33*(1). https://doi.org/10.1007/s12525-023-00635-6

Choi, H., Yu, S., Lee, D., Noh, S. D., Ji, S., Kim, H., Yoon, H., Kwon, M., & Han, J. (2024). Optimization of the factory layout and production flow using production-simulation-based reinforcement learning. *Machines, 12*(6), 390. https://doi.org/10.3390/machines12060390

Cummings, A. R. (2025, March 11). *AI in retail: Use cases, examples & adoption (2025)*. Shopify. Retrieved July 10, 2025, from https://www.shopify.com/retail/ai-in-retail

Dai, J., Wang, M., Wu, B., Shen, J., & Wang, X. (2023). A survey of latest Wi-Fi assisted indoor positioning on different principles. *Sensors, 23*(18), 7961. https://doi.org/10.3390/s23187961

Downie, A., & Hayes, M. (n.d.). *AI in retail*. IBM. Retrieved July 10, 2025, from https://www.ibm.com/think/topics/ai-in-retail

Dragonfly AI. (2025). *Computer vision and heatmap analytics that track customer movement to refine product placement and signage*. Retrieved June 28, 2025, from https://dragonflyai.co/amazon-heat-map

Dutta, S. S. (2024). Revolutionizing retail: An empirical study on the impact of generative AI in omnichannel retail. *International Journal for Multidisciplinary Research, 6*(5), 1–12. https://www.ijfmr.com/papers/2024/5/28799.pdf

El Nekiti, A., Mukala, P., Ullah, O., & Yatsyshyn, D. (2026). Advanced learning analytics with AI: Analyzing stakeholder perceptions of feedback, assessment, engagement, and faculty development in MENA higher education using NLP. In V. Bhateja, M. El Barachi, A. T. Azar, & D. K. Sharma (Eds.), *Information system design: Big data analytics and data science*. ISDIA 2025. Lecture Notes in Networks and Systems, Vol. 1539. Springer. https://doi.org/10.1007/978-981-96-9248-4_9

Gai, T. (2025). Machine learning approaches for accurate sales forecasting in supermarket chains. In G. A. Tsihrintzis, M. N. Favorskaya, R. Kountcheva, & S. Patnaik (Eds.), *Advances in computational vision and robotics. ICCVR 2024*. Learning and Analytics in Intelligent Systems, 47. Springer. https://doi.org/10.1007/978-3-031-85952-6_26

Gajjar, T. (2024). Revolutionizing retail: The synergy of AI and AR. *International Journal of Science and Research Archive, 13*(2), 3944–3966. https://doi.org/10.30574/ijsra.2024.13.2.2656

Ghosh, D. (2025). *How agentic AI is redesigning the retail architecture*. Tata Consultancy Services. Retrieved June 28, 2025, from https://www.tcs.com/what-we-do/industries/retail/white-paper/agentic-ai-redesigning-retail-architecture

Grewal, D., Roggeveen, A. L., & Nordfält, J. (2017). The future of retailing. *Journal of Retailing, 93*(1), 1–6. https://doi.org/10.1016/j.jretai.2016.12.008

Grewal, D., Satornino, C. B., Davenport, T., & Guha, A. (2025). How generative AI is shaping the future of marketing. *Journal of the Academy of Marketing Science, 53*, 702–722. https://doi.org/10.1007/s11747-024-01064-3

Hagberg, J., Sundstrom, M., & Egels-Zandén, N. (2016). The digitalization of retailing: An exploratory framework. *International Journal of Retail and Distribution Management, 44*(7), 694–712. https://doi.org/10.1108/IJRDM-09-2015-0140

Haque, A., Akther, N., Khan, I., Agarwal, K., & Uddin, N. (2024). Artificial intelligence in retail marketing: Research agenda based on bibliometric reflection and content analysis (2000–2023). *Informatics, 11*(4), 74. https://doi.org/10.3390/informatics11040074

Hassan, D., & Hassan, B. (2025). A comprehensive systematic review of machine learning in the retail industry: Classifications, limitations, opportunities, and challenges. *Neural Computing & Applications, 37*, 2035–2070. https://doi.org/10.1007/s00521-024-10869-w

InContext. (2024, August 1). *The evolution of planogram software: 1950 to 2024*. Incontext. Retrieved June 20, 2025, from https://incontextsolutions.com/blog/evolution-planogram-software-1950-2024/

Kang, N. (2025). Generative AI-driven design optimization: Eight key application scenarios. *JMST Advances, 7*, 105–111. https://doi.org/10.1007/s42791-025-00097-1

Karabiyik, H. Ç., &Elgün, M. N. (2021). An examination about merchandising: How merchandising should be defined as a theory and practice. *Business and Management Studies: An International Journal, 9*(1), 155–163. https://doi.org/10.15295/bmij.v9i1.1743

Köksal, A. G., Çelik, M. E., & Yeldan, G. (2024). AI-driven pricing algorithms for efficient inventory and cost management in retail. *The European Journal of Research and Development, 4*(4), 298–308. https://doi.org/10.56038/ejrnd.v4i4.607

Levy, M., Weitz, B., & Grewal, D. (2022). *Retailing management* (11th ed.). McGraw-Hill.

Liljenwall, R. (2013). *O Poder do marketing no ponto de venda: manual essencial para vender mais & melhor*. Top Books.

Lu, J., Zheng, X., Nervino, E., Li., Y., Xu, Z., & Xu, Y. (2024). Retail store location screening: A machine learning-based approach. *Journal of Retailing and Consumer Services, 77*, 103620, https://doi.org/10.1016/j.jretconser.2023.103620

Mannino, A., Dejaco, M. C., & Re Cecconi, F. (2021). Building information modelling and internet of things integration for facility management—Literature review and future needs. *Applied Sciences, 11*(7), 3062. https://doi.org/10.3390/app11073062

Matellio. (2025, March 24). *Retail planogram software development: AI-Driven merchandising for optimized Shelf placement and Sales growth*. Matellio. Retrieved June 28, 2025, from www.matellio.com/blog/retail-planogram-software-development/

Max, A. (2024, August 6). *Planogram compliance perfection with the latest technologies and AI*. Leafio—Optimizing retail. Retrieved June 28, 2025, from https://www.leafio.ai/blog/planogram-compliance-perfection-with-the-latest-technologies-and-ai/

Mesquita, R. P., Leal, F., & De Queiroz, J. A. (2024). Digital twins in the retail industry: A systematic literature review. *International Journal of Simulation Modelling, 23*(3), 424–434. https://doi.org/10.2507/IJSIMM23-3-690

Nguyen, K., Le, M., Martin, B., Cil, I., & Fookes, C. (2022). When AI meets store layout design: A review. *Artificial Intelligence Review, 55*, 5707–5729. https://doi.org/10.1007/s10462-022-10142-3

Nicasio, F. (2025, February 4). *AI merchandising in retail: How-Tos, best practices and examples*. iWD. Retrieved June 27, 2025, from https://magazine.iwd.io/ai-merchandising-in-retail-how-tos-best-practices-and-examples

O'Brien, K. (n.d.). *Keys to introducing AI in retail environments*. IBM Consulting. Retrieved June 28, 2025, from https://www.ibm.com/think/insights/keys-to-implement-ai-in-retail-environments

Panai, B., Baloian, N., Pino, J., Penafiel, S., Frez, J., Fuenzalida, C., Sanson, H., & Zurita, G. (2021). Forecasting key retail performance indicators using interpretable regression. *Sensors, 21*(5), 1874. https://doi.org/10.3390/s21051874

Pantano, E., Pizzi, G., Scarpi, D., & Dennis, C. (2020). Competing during a pandemic? Retailers' ups and downs during the COVID-19 outbreak. *Journal of Business Research, 116*, 209–213. https://doi.org/10.1016/j.jbusres.2020.05.036

Pathak, A. (2024, May 16). *How is AI transforming customer service for retail companies*. Synergize.ai. Retrieved June 28, 2025, from https://vsynergize.com/blog/how-is-ai-transforming-customer-service-for-retail-companies/

Pavion. (n.d.). *The future of AI in retail customer service*. Pavion. Retrieved June 28, 2025, from https://pavion.com/resource/the-future-of-ai-in-retail-customer-service/

Piotrowicz, W., & Cuthbertson, R. (2014). Introduction to the special issue: Information technology in retail: Toward omnichannel retailing. *International Journal of Electronic Commerce, 18*(4), 5–16. https://doi.org/10.2753/JEC1086-4415180400

Pratas, J. (2023). Metaverse and digital twins: An opportunity to increase retailers' profitability? An exploratory research using Nike case study and retail managers' in-depth interviews. In J. D. Santos, P. B. Pires, & I. V. Pereira (Eds.), *Management and marketing for improved retail competitiveness and performance* (pp. 217–235). IGI Global Publishing. https://doi.org/10.4018/978-1-6684-8574-3.ch011

Pratas, J., & Amorim, C. (2022). Consumer research shopping and buying behaviors in sports footwear omni-channel. Retailing: A conceptual model. In J. L. Reis, M. K. Peter, R. Cayolla, & Z. Bogdanović (Eds.), *Marketing and smart technologies*. Smart Innovation, Systems and Technologies, Vol. 280, (pp. 297–309). Springer. https://doi.org/10.1007/978-981-16-9272-7_25

Pratas, J., Amorim, C., Oliveira, Z., Carlos, V., & Reis, J. L. (2024). Retail Chatbots' main themes and research over time: A bibliometric and content analysis. In J. L. Reis, J. Zelený, B. Gavurová, & J. P. M. d. Santos (Eds.), *Marketing and smart technologies*. ICMarkTech 2023. Smart Innovation, Systems and Technologies, Vol. 386 (pp. 87–103). Springer. https://doi.org/10.1007/978-981-97-1552-7_7

Pratas, J., Amorim, C., & Reis, J. L. (2022). Smart retailing technologies impact in brand leadership and market performance: A conceptual model. In J. L. Reis, M. K. Peter, R. Cayolla, & Z. Bogdanović (Eds.), *Marketing and smart technologies*. Smart Innovation, Systems and Technologies, Vol. 280, (pp. 311–324). Springer. https://doi.org/10.1007/978-981-16-9272-7_26

Pratas, J., & Brito, P. Q. (2019). *Distribuição: gestão de pontos de venda e de retalho – gestão eficiente do negócio*. Actual Editora.

Pratas, J. M., Gonçalves, P. J., & Kaswengi, J. (2025). Retail evolution using Artificial Intelligence of Things (AIoT): An exploratory analysis and innovative ideas using literature review and creativity techniques. In J. M. Pratas, M. A. Rodrigues, & M. A. Carvalho (Eds.), *Artificial Intelligence of Things (AIoT) for retail and services management* (pp. 41–76). IGI Global Publishing. https://doi.org/10.4018/979-8-3693-8512-8.ch002

Resnick, N. (2022, November 29). 5 ways AI technology can modernize brick-and-mortar retail. *Forbes*. Retrieved June 28, 2025, from https://www.forbes.com/sites/allbusiness/2022/11/29/5-ways-ai-technology-can-modernize-brick-and-mortar-retail/

Retail Prowess. (2025). *Agentic AI in retail: Transforming operations and customer experience*. Retrieved June 27, 2025, from https://retailprowess.com/agentic-ai-in-retail/

Ross, M. (2024, July 9). *AI retail merchandising: Benefits, examples and future trends*. Leafio—Optimizing retail. Retrieved June 20, 2025, from https://www.leafio.ai/blog/ai-retail-merchandising-benefits-examples-and-future-trends/

Rousseau, J. A. (2020). *Manual de Distribuição* (3rd ed.). Principia Editora.

Rudkovska, O. (2025, May 19). *AI in retail: Use Cases, benefits, and implementation*. Euristiq. Retrieved June 10, 2025, from https://euristiq.com/ai-in-retail/

Salesforce. (n.d.). *How agentic AI is reshaping retail*. Salesforce. Retrieved June 11, 2025, from https://www.salesforce.com/retail/artificial-intelligence/agentic-ai-in-retail/

Sandberg, E. (2014). Coordination mechnisms in the store opening process. *International Journal of Retail and Distribution Management, 42*(6), 482–499. https://doi.org/10.1108/ijrdm-01-2013-0024

Sen, S. S., Alexandrov, A., Jha, S., McDowell, W. C., & Babakus, E. (2023). Convenient = competitive? How brick-and-mortar retailers can cope with online competition. *Review of Managerial Science, 17*, 1615–1643. https://doi.org/10.1007/s11846-022-00566-0

Shandong, M., Robb, D. J., & DeHoratius, N. (2018). Retail store operations: Literature review and research directions. *European Journal of Operational Research, 265*(2), 399–422. https://doi.org/10.1016/j.ejor.2017.07.003

Silverio, F., Cantalupo, M., Custode, L. C., & Iacca, G. (2025). A customer behavior-driven clustering method in the planogram design domain. *Applied Soft Computing, 172*. https://doi.org/10.1016/j.asoc.2025.112836

Šola, H. M., Qureshi, F. H., & Khawaja, S. (2024). Predicting behaviour patterns in online and PDF magazines with AI eye-tracking. *Behavioral Sciences, 14*(8), 677. https://doi.org/10.3390/bs14080677

Solanki, A. (2025, June 12). *The future of retail: How AI, experience, and sensory design are reshaping brick-and-mortar*. Colliers Knowledge Leader. Retrieved June 28, 2025, from https://knowledge-leader.colliers.com/anjee-solanki/the-future-of-retail-how-ai-experience-and-sensory-design-are-reshaping-brick-and-mortar/

Song, P. (2025) *Traditional AI vs generative AI vs agentic AI*. ML Journey. Retrieved June 29, 2025, from http://mljourney.com/traditional-ai-vs-generative-ai-vs-agentic-ai/

Spencer, A. (2024, October 24). Artificial intelligence in retail: 6 use cases and examples. *Forbes*. Retrieved June 20, 2025, from https://www.forbes.com/sites/sap/2024/04/19/artificial-intelligence-in-retail-6-use-cases-and-examples/

Srinivasan, V. (2025, March 18). *Brick-and-mortar is back—With AI as a key sidekick*. Cognizant. Retrieved June 20, 2025, from https://www.cognizant.com/us/en/insights/insights-blog/brick-and-mortar-retail-is-back-with-ai

Swagler, J. (2025, April 16). *AWS for industries: The agentic store: How AI orchestration will revolutionize physical retail*. Amazon Web Services. Retrieved June 28, 2025, from https://aws.amazon.com/blogs/industries/the-agentic-store-how-ai-orchestration-will-revolutionize-physical-retail

Szocs, C., Kim, Y., Lim, M., Mera, C. A., & Biswas, D. (2023). The store of the future: Engaging customers through sensory elements, personalized atmospherics, and interpersonal interaction. *Journal of Retailing, 99*. https://doi.org/10.1016/j.jretai.2023.11.005

Tang, J. (2025). Unlocking retail insights: Predictive modeling and customer segmentation through data analytics. *Journal of Theoretical and Applied Electronic Commerce Research, 20*(2), 59. https://doi.org/10.3390/jtaer20020059

Verhoef, P. C., Kannan, P. K., & Inman, J. J. (2015). From multi-channel retailing to omni-channel retailing: Introduction to the special issue on multi-channel retailing. *Journal of Retailing, 91*(2), 174–181. https://doi.org/10.1016/j.jretai.2015.02.005

Wavetec. (2025, February 25). *The impact of artificial intelligence on retail customer service.* Retrieved June 15, 2025, from https://www.wavetec.com/blog/impact-of-artificial-intelligence-on-retail-customer-service/

Zhang, R., & El-Gohary, N. (2022). Building information modeling, natural language processing, and artificial intelligence for automated compliance checking. In C. Eastman, R. Sacks, & P. Teicholz (Eds.), *Research companion to building information modeling* (pp. 248–267). Edward Elgar. https://doi.org/10.4337/9781839105524.00022

Zhang, J., Song, J., & Zeng, J. (2025). Toward resilience: Assessing retail location's complex impact mechanism using PLS-SEM aided by machine learning. *Sustainability, 17*(16), 7461. https://doi.org/10.3390/su17167461

Zimmermann, R., Mora, D., Cirqueira, D., Helfert, M., Bezbradica, M., Werth, D. W. J., Riedl, R., & Auinger, A. (2023). Enhancing brick-and-mortar store shopping experience with an augmented reality shopping assistant application using personalized recommendations and explainable artificial intelligence. *Journal of Research in Interactive Marketing, 17*(2), 273–298. https://doi.org/10.1108/JRIM-09-2021-0237

Crisis Communication with AI: Organisational Impacts and Strategic Challenges

Susana Pinto

Abstract Artificial intelligence (AI) has become an essential element in defining and developing crisis communication strategies. Its implementation brings a set of advantages and challenges for the organisation that can impact its image and reputation. Considering the different stages of crisis communication, crisis management teams must know which tools to use, how to act, and how to respond according to their level of responsibility. This research presents an analysis of four organisational case studies, including Vodafone, Coca-Cola, McDonald's, and Sports Illustrated, which aims to understand the influence of AI tools and their implementation in organisational communication strategies, as well as their impact on the public's perception of and trust in these organisations. The results reveal that the effectiveness of a crisis communication strategy depends not only on the tactics chosen but also on factors such as human analysis and supervision during planning and implementation, transparency, and ethical conduct in the use of technology. The study proposes practical recommendations for communication professionals and reinforces the importance of having a crisis management plan in place when implementing AI platforms within organisations.

1 Introduction

Organisations are currently facing increasingly complex challenges in managing their institutional image and reputation amid digital transformation and constant media exposure. Crisis communication is one of the areas of strategic public relations, fundamental to preserving a positive organisational image and reputation, as well as the normal functioning of the organisation. Nowadays, organisations face a range of challenges related to the new information society and the consequent development of new technologies, such as Artificial Intelligence (AI). With the development of various AI tools, there is a greater risk of incidents and negative messages emerging and proliferating, which can affect the credibility and reputation of the organisation.

S. Pinto (✉)
CEOS.PP, ISCAP, Polytechnic of Porto, Porto, Portugal
e-mail: spinto@iscap.ipp.pt

J. D. Santos et al. (eds.), *Artificial Intelligence Transforming Marketing*, Contributions to Management Science, https://doi.org/10.1007/978-3-032-22360-9_14

The development of AI tools has led to a reconfiguration of communication processes within organisations. This transformation brings new opportunities and challenges in crisis management. Its ability to analyse large volumes of information in real-time, monitor sentiment on social media, predict certain behaviours, and automate responses positions it as a tool with enormous potential. Nowadays, its adoption or implementation still raises some important ethical, technical, and organisational issues, particularly regarding privacy, data reliability, transparency, and building beneficial relationships with different institutional audiences.

This study aims to understand how AI is being used by organisations in crisis management and what effects this use has on the organisational image. The central aim of this analysis is to examine how AI is being applied in organisational communication during crises, to understand its impact on organisational reputation, the ethical challenges it presents, and its operational limitations. In this study, we propose a critical analysis of four specific cases of organisations that have faced media crises due to the use/implementation of AI technologies in the day-to-day running of the company.

Despite the proliferation of studies on crisis communication and the growing literature on AI, there is a lack of research examining how AI relates to the attribution of responsibility, ethical decision-making, and the establishment of trust between parties during a crisis. This study contributes to filling this gap by integrating classic crisis communication frameworks, such as Situational Crisis Communication Theory (SCCT), with emerging empirical evidence on AI-driven communication practices.

This chapter seeks to address a gap in research on the strategic and ethical implications of AI in crisis communication, an area in which empirical and theoretical integration remains limited. After introducing concepts of crisis communication, the chapter discusses key theoretical models, particularly SCCT. It then explores the relationship between digital communication and AI, followed by an analytical discussion of four organisational case studies. Finally, the chapter concludes by identifying implications and challenges for management, theoretical contributions, and suggestions for future research.

2 Crisis Communication

As a part of their daily activities, organisations face various challenges and threats that can expose their reputation. According to Lampreia (2007), negative events that interfere with an organisation's day-to-day activities do not necessarily constitute a crisis.

Before analysing the concept of crisis, it is essential to distinguish between an incident and a crisis. In an organisation, an incident can occur at any time that has an impact on the normal functioning and routine of the business, without, however, requiring great difficulty to resolve. This incident can develop into a crisis if it is not properly resolved (Lampreia, 2007). According to Lampreia (2007), a crisis refers to an exceptional situation, characterised by uncertainty regarding its outcomes, which represents a significant threat to the overall organisational structure or to specific areas of production. From one moment to the next, organisations can be confronted with unexpected situations that pose challenges to their normal functioning. A crisis refers to a situation of great complexity, while an incident, as described above, is less severe in terms of resolution.

2.1 Crisis Concept

In recent decades, numerous studies have been conducted on crisis management, with various authors and perspectives emerging. According to Fearn-Banks and Hooper (2006), a crisis is an event with a potentially harmful outcome that affects an organisation, company, or area of activity, as well as the public, including its products, services, and reputation. This event interrupts everyday business transactions and, considering its scale, could threaten the organisation's existence.

Wilcox et al. (2015) define a crisis as an extraordinary event, or series of events, that affects the integrity of the product, the reputation or financial stability of the organisation, or the health and well-being of different stakeholders.

Fearn-Banks (2011) offers a systematisation arguing that there are five stages in a crisis: detection, prevention, containment, recovery, and learning. These five stages of crisis correspond to different moments and activities, which are listed below:

1. **Detection** of a critical situation (incident/emergency) that could lead to a crisis is crucial, which is why it is essential to have systems and processes in place to quickly identify emerging threats/risks, and alert those responsible for crisis management.
2. **Prevention/Preparation**: a set of preventive measures are taken to reduce the risk of the problematic situation becoming a crisis. This may include identifying and mitigating risks, developing contingency plans, training human resources and implementing effective communication systems.
3. **Containment**: measures are taken to contain the crisis and minimise its effects. This may include coordinating response efforts, managing communication with stakeholders, and damage control.
4. **Recovery**: the primary objective is to restore normalcy and rebuild trust following the crisis. This may include assessing damage, repairing damage, compensating affected parties, and implementing changes to prevent future crises.
5. **Learning**: organisations and individuals involved in a crisis should learn from the experience and implement changes to improve crisis management in the future. This may include reviewing and updating contingency plans, training, implementing new practices and continuously improving crisis management.

An organisation in a crisis must prove to its institutional audiences in general that the prevalence of negative opinion is not factual. As a result of new environmental developments, terrorism, and the proliferation of media are leading to increased exposure, and companies are now playing a key role in crisis management (Coombs, 2015).

In this sense, it is understood that a crisis refers to an unexpected situation with high visibility and a strong repercussion on the performance and reputation of an organisation, calling into question its existence if it is not handled correctly. According to Bittar (2012), if a crisis is well-managed, it can be an opportunity to strengthen a brand, as it is a period of heightened visibility in the eyes of public opinion. This opportunity can be used to present positive behaviour and discourse on how to solve a problem. Any organisation can face a crisis; the difference lies in how the institution manages times of difficulty.

Forni (2019) draws attention to the fact that a crisis consists of a disruption in the normal functioning of an organisation, presenting itself as an adverse event that often challenges the company's management, with implications for the business, reputation, and future of the organisation.

Crisis communication is the approach adopted when an adverse event has already occurred, and the company must manage the situation. Crisis communication aims to manage the public's perception of the organisation during a crisis and minimise its effects. Within the scope of crisis communication, it is up to the organisation to disseminate a set of information to its audiences about what has happened, the measures being taken to deal with the situation, and what lessons have been learned to prevent this event from happening again (Forni, 2019).

2.2 Origins of the Crisis

Seeger (2006) considers that organisations are expected to proactively identify the risks they face, to anticipate potential crises, mapping vulnerable areas, and establishing response strategies that enable swift and effective problem resolution.

Coombs (2015), in turn, proposes nine categories of events that can give rise to crisis: natural disasters, sabotage/terrorism, violence at work, accident due to technological error, accident due to human error, accident due to defective product, transgression, mixed, and general type of crisis.

Natural disasters refer to crisis caused by environmental events. Sabotage and terrorism refer to a type of crisis that occurs when an external agent attacks the organisation. Another type of negative event suggested by the author is workplace violence perpetrated by an employee or former employee against current employees of the organisation. An accident due to a technological error is related to a failure in equipment or technology that could lead to an industrial accident. A crisis may also arise when a defective product is placed on the market, which may be caused by a failure in equipment or technology. An accident due to human error occurs when a human agent triggers an industrial accident. Finally, transgression refers to a crisis that results from the organisation having violated regulations or laws (Coombs, 2015).

All organisations must understand what can lead to a crisis to plan efficiently, reducing the degree of uncertainty and surprise in the event of a negative event.

To start the crisis management process, it is necessary to identify/typify the origin of the crisis to implement appropriate actions to minimise its effects.

In this sense, if the organisation can identify the type of crisis and know its stages, this knowledge will enable strategic action (Ulmer et al., 2017), which will make it possible to:

- Manage uncertainty through consistent communication.
- Identify the cause of the problem, contact the victims, and determine present and future risks.
- Respond to the crisis, to reduce the feeling of uncertainty associated with it by disseminating valid information.
- Dispelling the crisis: renewing the organisation's reputation.
- Learning from the crisis: improving security and prevention, reviewing the communication standards applied, optimising and perfecting the communication process with the different institutional audiences.

2.3 Situational Crisis Communication Theory (SCCT)

The SCCT model was developed by Timothy Coombs in the 1990s to identify a set of response strategies that organisations can use in a crisis. This model makes it possible to define who and what is responsible for causing the crisis and the scale of the threat to the organisation's reputation.

The SCCT model provides a theoretical basis and empirically tested strategic suggestions for selecting crisis response strategies. The SCCT model manages to link two aspects in the field of crisis communication: the crisis and the response strategy.

The most obvious feature of the SCCT model is that it allows us to theorise about the importance of understanding, before defining a communication strategy, that each type of crisis affects the public differently and, consequently, their perceptions will influence the level of responsibility they will attribute to the organisation in the context of a crisis. The definition of the three phases of the crisis—Pre-crisis, Crisis and Post-crisis—structured by Coombs (2015) allows us to know the aspects to consider for each of these phases when planning.

Coombs (1995) developed the SCCT model based on two theories, the Crisis Type Matrix and the Attribution Theory. The Crisis Type Matrix assesses the intentionality behind an organisational crisis, i.e. whether it is intentional or unintentional, as well as its origin, whether it is internal or external. This matrix distributes organisational crisis into four quadrants, as can be seen in Table 1. This matrix aims to help organisations understand the nature of the crisis they face and adapt their crisis management strategies according to the category of crisis.

Attribution theory, on the other hand, describes how people make judgements about the cause of a crisis and the attribution of responsibility. According to this theory, the population/public opinion tends to "create" simple explanations for a crisis and generally attribute blame to people or organisations that are easily identifiable

Table 1 Type of crisis matrix

	Unintentional	Intentional
External origin	Faux pas	Terrorism
Internal origin	Accident	Transgression

Source Author

and that control, or exercise some form of control over, the events that led to the crisis. Furthermore, they tend to be more critical of organisations that have a history of inappropriate behaviour or a lack of transparency. The Attribution Theory served as the basis for the development of the Situational Theory of Crisis Communication, to identify the various crisis type that affect an organisation's reputation and the degree of responsibility attributed to them.

The Crisis Type Matrix and Attribution Theory help explain how people perceive and respond to a crisis, while Coombs' SCCT model provides a framework for effective communication during that same crisis.

Coombs (2007) grouped the degree of responsibility into three categories:

- Minimum Responsibility Crisis with victims: natural disasters (acts of nature, such as tornadoes or earthquakes); rumours (false and damaging information circulating about your organisation); workplace violence: attacks by former or current employees or between current employees in the organisation; product tampering/sabotage (external agent causes damage to the organisation).
- Medium Liability Accidental: challenges (the claim by stakeholders that the organisation is working improperly); accidents due to technical faults (equipment or technology failure that causes an industrial accident); technical product failure (equipment or technology failure that causes the product to be defective or harmful for consumption).
- Maximum Liability avoidable Intentional crisis: accidents due to human error (industrial accident caused by human error); product damage due to human error (the product is defective or potentially harmful due to human error); organisational misconduct or lack of ethics (management actions that put stakeholders at risk and/or violate the law).

Considering the need to recover the organisational image after a crisis, it is necessary to define concrete response strategies that can intervene in terms of reputation and the management of negative reactions from *stakeholders* (Coombs, 2007). The response strategies established by the SCCT model are implemented based on the organisation's level of responsibility and reflect the different levels of attribution of responsibility.

Crisis response strategies, as conceptualised by Coombs (2007) in the framework of SCCT, are generally divided into primary and secondary strategies. These categories reflect the different approaches organisations may adopt when attempting to mitigate the reputational impact of a crisis and restore stakeholder trust.

The primary strategies encompass denial, diminishing, and rebuilding approaches. Denial strategies are characterised by the organisation's attempt to reject any form of responsibility. This may take the form of attacking the accuser, by confronting those who claim wrongdoing; denial, which involves asserting that no crisis exists; or scapegoating, which transfers the blame to external actors. While denial strategies may protect the organisation in certain cases, they also entail the risk of further reputational damage if evidence emerges to contradict the claims. Diminishing strategies, on the other hand, seek to reduce perceived responsibility or severity. They may include excuses, which deny intentionality, and highlight the organisation's lack of control over the events, or justification, which downplays the perceived harm caused by the crisis. Such strategies may be effective when organisational culpability is low, yet they can be perceived as evasive if stakeholders expect accountability. Rebuilding strategies represent a more constructive response, aimed at repairing damaged relationships and restoring legitimacy. They include compensation, whereby the organisation offers material or financial redress to victims, and apology, which involves a direct assumption of responsibility accompanied by an expression of remorse. These approaches are generally considered the most effective in terms of long-term reputation recovery, although they may also entail significant financial or symbolic costs.

Alongside these primary strategies, SCCT model also recognises secondary reinforcement strategies, which function as complementary measures to strengthen stakeholder support. These include reminding, which highlights the organisation's good practices; ingratiation, which involves praising stakeholders and recalling past achievements; and victimisation, where the organisation presents itself as also being affected by the crisis. While not sufficient in isolation, these strategies can reinforce the organisation's narrative and foster empathy among stakeholders.

The choice of strategy depends not only on the nature and severity of the crisis but also on the expectations of stakeholders and the broader socio-cultural context in which the organisation operates.

In this model, Coombs (2007) defined a set of response strategies that organisations can use to deal with different types of crises:

- Information and fact-checking can be sufficient when crisis have minimal attributions of responsibility for the crisis (victim crisis), no history of similar crisis and a neutral or positive previous reputation.
- The victim's image can be used as part of the response in the case of workplace violence, product tampering, natural disasters, and rumours.
- Diminishing crisis response strategies should be used for crisis with minimal attributions of responsibility for the crisis, along with a history of similar crisis and/or a negative previous relationship reputation.
- Decline strategies should be used for crisis with a low attribution of responsibility for the crisis (accident crisis), no history of similar crisis and a neutral or positive previous relationship reputation.
- Rebuilding crisis response strategies should be used for crisis with a low attribution of responsibility for the crisis (accident crisis), along with a history of similar crisis and/or a negative previous relationship reputation.

- Rebuilding crisis response strategies should be used for crisis with strong attributions of crisis responsibility (avoidable crisis), regardless of crisis history or previous relationship reputation.
- Posture denial crisis response strategies should be used for rumour and challenge crisis when possible.
- Maintain consistency in crisis response strategies. Mixing denial crisis response strategies with diminishing or rebuilding strategies will erode the effectiveness of the overall response.

Once the existing response strategies have been presented, it is possible to identify a causal relationship between them and the types of crises. Response strategies must be selected considering the type of crisis and the specific situation of the organisation. Coombs (2007) stresses the importance of the organisation's need to respond to a crisis quickly and accurately, to avoid problems in terms of the demands of institutional audiences and the media's attempts to fill communication gaps. Choosing the right response strategy can have a decisive impact on the public perception of the organisation and its ability to recover from the crisis.

2.4 The Stages of Crisis Management

Institutional crisis management is a critical organisational function whose mission is to protect the organisation from threats and/or reduce their impact. Coombs (2007) defined crisis management as a set of factors with the aim of combating crisis and preventing or reducing damage to the organisation's image and reputation, thereby protecting it. Crisis management should be analysed as a process made up of different parts, namely: a set of preventative measures, planning for the different stages of the crisis and a post-crisis assessment. The set of factors that make up crisis management can be divided into three stages: pre-crisis, crisis, and post-crisis.

The pre-crisis stage involves efforts to prevent a crisis by defining its origins, the risks, and defining the actions that will allow the organisation to act effectively and quickly, avoiding damage. The prevention phase aims to reduce or contain previously defined risks that may lead to a crisis and involves creating the crisis management plan, selecting, and training the crisis management team, as well as carrying out exercises to test the crisis management plan and its management team (Fearn-Banks, 2007).

For Caetano et al. (2006), efforts to prevent and plan for a crisis can become as difficult as dealing with it. Thus, how to interact with the different publics, as well as defining the list of crisis origins, cases and scenarios whose emergence could trigger a crisis are two key issues that must be dealt with by crisis communication.

A crisis is the response to a real event. Crisis response is the stage that includes everything management does and says after being hit by a crisis, to react to its consequences. Crisis management aims to protect an organisation and its stakeholders from threats and/or reduce their impact to restore public safety, repair reputation and behavioural intentions, and recover the organisation's financial results.

The post-crisis stage defines the activities/efforts aimed at learning from the crisis event. In terms of the outcome of the crisis, there are three possible scenarios: the damage caused by the crisis may not affect the organisation and it therefore comes out of the crisis unscathed; the crisis may cause serious damage to the interested parties (stakeholders) and losses to the organisation (human, financial, and reputational) which are remedied through effective crisis management and the organisation manages to survive; the response to the crisis is not effective enough to deal with the threats or to remedy the damage caused by the crisis and the organisation does not survive.

The post-crisis phase is the stage in which management looks for ways to better prepare for the next crisis and fulfils the commitments made during the crisis response. Preparing for future crisis allows them to be managed more quickly and in a more planned manner. Preparing to act in a crisis should focus on a specific plan to assess the risk and provide guidelines to be followed.

2.5 The Relationship Between Crisis Communication and Digital Communication

Strauss et al. (2024) consider that digital institutional communication is not just the transition of content disseminated through traditional channels to online platforms, but includes a reconfiguration of communication channels, the creation of relationships and constant dialogue between the organisation and the different audiences and greater attention to the organisational image. In this context, AI has emerged as a relevant tool in the field of organisational communication, but it presents several challenges for crisis communication.

This technology can help strategic communication establish dialogue with stakeholders, as it allows for the creation of real-time response mechanisms, message personalisation, advanced monitoring of public sentiment, and evaluation of mentions of the company.

On the other hand, when AI replaces human intervention in more sensitive activities or moments, such as crisis management, the organisation's audiences may feel the lack of fundamental attributes of reputation, such as empathy, trust, authenticity, and accountability. The absence of supervision or the opacity of algorithms has contributed to the creation of a negative perception on the part of the organisation's audience, as they tend to hold the organisation directly responsible for the negative effects of automation and the replacement of human labour. Social media are digital platforms for social interaction that allow users to create and share various types of content by creating profiles. Social media are communication platforms between organisations and people, always ensuring a close relationship and interaction with the brand (Batista & Costa, 2021).

Social media has a set of unique characteristics that make it an important element of crisis communication, as it allows messages to be disseminated more quickly and have an impact on different institutional audiences. Social networks present opportunities, but also some challenges for public relations professionals. When an organisation is faced with a crisis, social media can pose a potential threat, as consumers can share information about the company very quickly to a considerable number of people, making it a difficult process to control (Effing & Spil, 2016).

Social media has changed the communication dynamics of society, as well as the dynamics of crisis situations and the way crisis managers deal with and create communication flows with affected communities (Veil et al., 2011). The relationship between organisations and their institutional publics becomes accessible and visible to a wider audience, which causes a lack of control over the messages shared, creating a feeling of institutional vulnerability (Coombs & Holladay, 2010).

Considering the role of social networks and the way content is developed, they play an important role in shaping opinion, awareness, and perception of crisis. In this sense, there are some aspects that the organisation should pay attention to effectively manage a negative event, namely:

- Monitoring social media: it is important to monitor social media daily to detect negative feedback or events that mention the company. The company should use social media monitoring tools to keep track of brand mentions, related *hashtags*, and relevant keywords.
- Respond quickly: once a crisis is detected, the company must respond quickly. The pace of social media is very fast, and users expect immediate responses. A delay or lack of response from the organisation can lead to greater public discontent.
- Humanising the discourse: it's important to show social media users that you care about resolving the negative event. A human and personal approach should be used to respond to questions and comments.
- Share updates: keep users up to date on the event and the measures being implemented to resolve the problem.
- Proactivity: in addition to responding to questions and comments from users on social media, the company may take a proactive approach to communication. For example, it may publish an official statement, create a crisis website or send an email to different audiences.

Crisis management is crucial for companies with a digital presence, as these platforms are one of the main sources of information and communication for the public. A crisis on social media can have a significant impact on a company's reputation, and the way it acts, through sharing information or responding to comments, is essential to gaining the trust of its audiences.

According to Coombs and Holladay (2014), defining a crisis management plan for companies with a social media presence is of great importance, with the following aspects standing out:

- Protecting the company's reputation: crisis management helps the company protect its image and reputation. An effective response can minimise the impact of a negative event and help restore consumer confidence.
- Demonstrate responsibility: the way a company handles a crisis can demonstrate its responsibility, transparency, and commitment to its stakeholders.
- Mitigate damage: Crisis management allows a company to minimise the damage caused by a crisis. A quick and effective response can prevent the situation from worsening.
- Maintaining transparency: a transparent response can help the company maintain public trust. Transparency can be achieved by publicising accurate and clear information about the crisis and the measures being taken to resolve it quickly and easily.
- Improving communication processes: crisis management can help the company improve communication, as well as communication processes. An effective response can establish an open and transparent communication channel that can improve the perception of the company and its relationship with its *stakeholders*.

Interactions between the company and the public(s) increasingly involve social networks. This form of communication has led to systematic changes in the relationship between organisations and *stakeholders*. Adaptation to this new reality is therefore required, especially in terms of information control, which is becoming more relevant in our daily lives, given the phenomena *of fake news* and disinformation.

Following the presentation of the SCCT conceptual framework, the next section examines how AI reshapes the traditional understanding of organisational responsibility and stakeholder perception in crisis contexts.

3 Artificial Intelligence in Crisis Communication

AI is an area of computing that allows technology to perform a set of tasks that normally require human intelligence, such as reasoning, knowledge, planning, learning, and language. The main aim of AI is to enable machines to behave in a similar way to humans (McCarthy, 2007). According to McCarthy (2007), Alan Turing's idea was to build a computer capable of imitating the human brain, stating that any calculation could be implemented digitally. Over the past 10 years, applications based on AI algorithms have played a crucial role in different areas of activity, serving as a basis for improving their structure and the platform where deep learning was developed.

AI is taking on a prominent role in organisations as it drives efficiency, productivity, innovation, and decision-making, as well as transforming the way they communicate and manage crisis. However, its success depends on the development of a strategic, ethical, and collaborative approach that combines the potential of technology with the intelligence and emotional side of human beings.

3.1 Advantages of AI in Crisis Communication

The use of AI tools in crisis management and communication offers numerous advantages for organisations, as they can locate and respond to incidents or emergencies more quickly and effectively. The processing and evaluation of large volumes of data, raw and with extreme precision, are the most important differentiating factors. According to Goldberg (2025), the integration of AI-driven tools into strategic communication processes allows organisations to move beyond reactive responses and adopt preventive, data-informed approaches that improve situational awareness and decision-making.

Cheng et al. (2024) and Hossain et al. (2025) deem that the primary benefits of employing AI in crisis communication are as follows:

- Speed and effectiveness in processing information: it allows for swift and effective response in the event of a crisis, processing information faster than a human being. Conversely, it drastically lowers the response time and effect of cyber-attacks or other serious events for the organisation.
- Automating functions and optimising formal proceedings, saving invaluable time and resources for the professionals of an organisation to apply them towards more strategy and creative functions.
- Processing and distributing data in real time: the capability for ongoing digital platform surveillance, and predictive research enables AI to discover threats in real time, test risks, and deliver instant knowledge to support the decision-making process. Conversely, the processing of sentiment on social nets enables us to make public perception, thus allowing for the formulation of certain messages and the handling of institutional image.
- Handling the origin of crises and the risks: with predictive models, AI foresees vulnerabilities before they become actualities. Such proactive actions enable preparing effective responses in a better time, given categorisation of the origin of the crises and its threats, taking into consideration the volume of intensity and the volume of responsibility, the simulation of the most complex scenarios, and the improved preparation of the crisis management team.
- Specialised communication and engagement with the different institutional audiences: there are also various tools, such as chatbots and virtual assistants, that facilitate continuous support in the communication process, provide updated content and help respond to questions in real time. AI also makes possible the personalisation of messages sent out to all the institutional audiences in different languages. It also makes possible the combating of disinformation through the verification and check of the truth of content sent out.
- Optimisation of logistical resources: in the event of an incident or emergency within the organisation, AI strengthens resource optimisation and provides useful information for decision-making at the logistical level based on real data. The use of IoT sensors and drones with AI also enables the monitoring of critical infrastructure and the collection of important data from inaccessible locations.

- Decision-making support: AI provides accurate and verified information that supports the organisation's strategic decisions, limiting subjective behaviour. In high-tension environments, this analytical power enables more reliable decision-making.
- Improved security systems and fraud prevention: AI tools monitor information systems in real time, enabling the detection of suspicious activity and sending advance alerts about security threats, such as network intrusions or fraudulent activity. This activity protects the organisation's digital assets and confidential commercial data.
- Strengthening organisational reputation: in the post-crisis phase, AI enables the sharing of personalised organisational messages through the establishment of more efficient communication channels. This action aims to improve public image. In the post-crisis phase, the organisation must gather information to ensure that the situation does not recur in the future, which is a continuous learning process.

AI provides clear advantages for crisis communication: early detection of reputational risks, information management, personalised stakeholder engagement, and improved decision-making. According to Goldberg (2025), the future of crisis communication lies in a hybrid model where AI enhances human capacity while preserving the ethical and relational dimensions essential to strategic communication practice.

3.2 Risks of AI in Crisis Communication

The use of AI in organisations continues to be a risk factor, as there are situations that give rise to critical incidents. The use of AI in crisis communication is a cause for great concern, particularly in view of the right to privacy and personal data protection. The processing of private data, often without the express consent of the user, risks violating individuals' fundamental rights to privacy. One of the most high-profile cases involved the misuse of personal data by Scatter Lab Co. Ltd, which, when developing and implementing the chatbot Lee-Luda, used private communications to train language models. This situation demonstrated the danger of using large volumes of data, security issues and ethical issues in the use of personal data (Jang & Lee, 2023).

On the other hand, there is a possibility that AI systems may exhibit algorithmic bias through machine learning processes that use historical data. These are likely to reproduce or increase levels of social discrimination and produce biased decisions in processes such as recruitment, healthcare or prioritising responses in emergency situations. The attribution of responsibility for the decisions of automated systems is among the fundamental dilemmas currently under consideration. The obscurity of the algorithm, also in most instances obscure even for experts, destroys the potential for the auditable, and makes institutional responsibility doubtful, in the case of catastrophes of serious impact (Ore & Sposato, 2022).

Transparency is now an absolute necessity, not merely for the functions of the systems, but also for the building of public confidence. The lack of explanations in the decision-making process, together with the potential for the dissemination of manipulated or false content, such as deepfakes, clickbait's or fake news, jeopardises the legitimacy of the institution and can trigger a reputation crisis (Treleaven et al., 2023).

The performance of the systems of AI directly correlates with the quality of the input. Incomplete, outdated, biased or misclassified input puts the integrity of the output in jeopardy and may result in insufficient response in high-stakes situations. The inherent complexity of the systems of AI, particularly in the case of rapid implementation, may lead to maintenance problems, continuous validation, and use in ordinary operations. Nowadays, we are still witnessing the spreading of factually inaccurate responses, particularly in the case of generative models, that may constitute a high risk for the crisis management, in the case when the accuracy and contextualisation of the information are high stakes (Cheng et al., 2024).

The use of AI in organisations triggers resistance to the change, particularly in the case of employees less close to the world of technology. Moreover, most of the companies are lacking the special technical competencies in dealing with digitalisation and innovation, because of the absence of qualified staff and the absence of in-company training plans.

Other related risk is the dehumanisation of the communication. The substitution of the classical communication channels with automated communications, such as chatbots or virtual assistants, may put in jeopardy the empathy, the active listening and the response in a customised approach, considered being mandatory in the critical environments. On the other hand, the rising in the number of the frauds because of the spreading of the software being able to very efficiently simulate the voice of the people or to fake false messages, necessitates the legal answer, on a global level (Cruz, 2023).

3.3 AI Tools in Crisis Communication

In an organisational environment with high levels of complexity and intense media coverage, crisis communication is key in terms of institutional image and reputation preservation. AI offers a toolkit that incorporates a variety of technological solutions able to optimise the organisations potential for predicting, directing, and responding to critical events.

The use of AI in crisis communication makes it possible, among other functionalities, for social networks, digital media, and digital environments to be monitored in real time, for the analysis of predictive risks, for the automation of interactions with publics, the production of custom content, and the derivation of insights for use in terms of strategic choice. Nevertheless, the use of the tool is not free of problems, including ethical and technical problems related to the preservation of privacy, the security of the datum, algorithmic biases, and limitations in the interpretation of the human language.

The constantly updated digital environment surveillance offered using AI enables the early identification of events that could evolve into crisis with damage to image and reputation. Today there are multiple types of AI tools, for example Google Alerts, which allows for the automated identification of references to an organisation and/or brand in multiple languages using sentiment analysis. The use of sentiment analysis enables content produced by multiple organisational publics to be identified and labelled as positive, negative or neutral, allowing public opinion to be assessed and the potential for crisis detected. The PRISMA Crisis Intelligence is an example of an application of the use of AI, able to monitor social media discussions and bring to the attention of professional's negative references, able to process complex documentation in multiple languages to interpret obscured sentiments (Scott, 2020).

In addition to identifying crises, AI enables the processing of large amounts of information, identifying language patterns, and/or themes that help predict changes in public opinion or anticipate disruptive events. For example, Lynguo is an AI platform that tracks conversations on social media and analyses sentiment, what is being communicated by competitors and influencers. The platform allows you to find new business opportunities, discover your brand's reputation and predict potential crises, identify viral content, and monitor the performance of marketing campaigns, among other things. It also includes filters that allow customised searches, such as searching by word, impact, category or sentiment.

One of the strengths of AI is the construction of predictive risk analyses, using complex algorithms that process old data to identify repetitive patterns of behaviour and make highly accurate predictions of future events. Predictive analysis has been introduced in different areas of business, enabling a proactive approach to risk prevention. In the field of crisis communication, predictive analysis allows us to identify potential sources and risks of crises, develop fact-based preparedness scenarios and improve the institution's response time to undesirable events (Cruz, 2023). The automation of communication systems, i.e. responses and interactions with different institutional audiences, is one of the most effective and efficient uses of AI in the field of crises. Chatbots, virtual assistants, and voice response systems (IVR) make it possible to maintain communication channels and establish dialogue with audiences daily. These are most effective in situations of information overload, such as health crises or natural disasters, where an immediate and appropriate response is imperative. AI enables the personalisation of customer service, the prediction of requests through categorisation, and the optimisation of responses in real time, whether through social media, email, or telephone.

Generative AI, such as ChatGPT and DALL-E, has revolutionised content and image creation. These tools enable the rapid and effective creation of social media posts, institutional emails, and/or graphic support, with personalised messages for different audiences and different markets. Other auxiliary software, such as QuillBot and Grammarly, enable language restructuring and tone control, making messages more effective and appropriate. On the other hand, the Synthesia platform, which involves image, video and synthesised voice, brings new opportunities for effective multimodal communication.

Analytical capacity is increasingly important in times of uncertainty, as it allows for the immediate implementation of actions with high levels of reliability. In addition, the implementation of AI tools has considerably increased the automation of procedural and operational functions, such as bank reconciliation, payment processing, or logistics management in humanitarian crisis situations. The automation of these everyday activities frees up labour for more strategic and creative tasks, optimising the organisation's productivity at critical stages.

3.4 AI's Role in Crisis Communication

According to the research by Cheng et al. (2024), AI plays a contributing role in the three stages of crisis communication through its ability to analyse, predict, and communicate with audiences in real-time. The integration of AI into crisis communication processes can be conceptualised across three distinct phases: pre-crisis, crisis, and post-crisis. In each of these stages, AI-driven learning operates in real time, thereby strengthening organisational capacity to anticipate, manage, and evaluate crises.

During the pre-crisis phase, organisations benefit from automated information scanning and predictive analysis. Automated information scanning allows for the swift processing of large volumes of data, the identification of emerging issues, and the detection of trends that can inform proactive decision-making. Predictive analysis, in turn, leverages historical data to forecast potential crisis scenarios, enabling organisations to design tailored strategies and minimise the potential impact on stakeholders. This anticipatory use of AI transforms crisis prevention into a data-informed and strategically proactive endeavour.

In the crisis phase, the focus shifts to real-time engagement through two critical mechanisms: social media monitoring and personalised communication. Social media monitoring encompasses sentiment analysis, the detection of misinformation, and the identification of disinformation and false narratives, thereby helping organisations respond quickly to evolving narratives. Personalised communication, supported by AI tools such as chatbots, facilitates the delivery of tailored crisis messages, fosters direct dialogue with stakeholders, and ensures constant supervision of digital communication processes. These AI-enhanced practices allow for rapid, adaptive, and stakeholder-focused crisis management.

The post-crisis phase emphasises evaluation, learning, and improvement. Organisations are expected to conduct rigorous assessments of the effectiveness of their crisis responses, supported by continuous monitoring and risk assessment. Benchmarking and comparative analysis play a central role in identifying areas for improvement, while educational initiatives ensure that affected populations are adequately informed and supported. In this way, the post-crisis stage not only closes the loop of crisis management but also prepares the organisation for future contingencies.

Table 2 Integration between SCCT phases and AI applications

	Pre-crisis (detection and prevention)	Crisis (response and containment)	Post-crisis (recovery and learning)
Main objectives	Identify potential risks; training	Ensure transparency and trust	Rebuild reputation
Key AI tools	– Predictive analytics for risk detection – Sentiment analysis of stakeholder discourse – Early-warning dashboards	– Real-time monitoring of social media – Fact-checking and misinformation filtering – Chatbots	– Data analytics – Feedback and reputation tracking – Scenario modelling for prevention
AI-enabled outcomes	– Earlier identification of threats – Reduced uncertainty	– Faster information dissemination – Improved message consistency	– Enhanced learning – Reputation restoration – Strengthened resilience

Source Author

According to SCCT, which categorises crisis response into pre-crisis, crisis, and post-crisis phases, this model expands the framework by incorporating AI-driven capabilities (Table 2). The integration of an AI within SCCT not only enhances message tailoring and stakeholder responsiveness but also introduces predictive and adaptive learning loops that extend the original scope of the theory.

At the core of all these phases lies AI learning in real time, which ensures that data from each stage continuously informs the next. This cyclical and reflexive process reinforces organisational resilience, transforming crises into strategic learning experiences that align with contemporary models of adaptive governance and digital-era crisis management (Coombs & Tachkova, 2023).

4 Methodology

AI is playing an increasingly important role in crisis management and the protection of institutional image and reputation, allowing organisations to respond more quickly and in an informed manner to unexpected challenges.

This research analyses four examples of organisational practices, with both positive and negative impacts on the organisational structure, following the implementation of AI tools daily. Four multinational organisations were selected—Vodafone, Coca-Cola, McDonald's and Sports Illustrated—based on two main criteria: (i) the effective application of AI tools in their communication and crisis management processes, and (ii) the public availability of relevant information for analysis (press releases, news, institutional reports, social media content and media coverage).

This analysis aims to establish a relationship between the case studies and the theoretical models of crisis communication, particularly the Situational Theory of Crisis Communication by Coombs (2007). This framework makes it possible to classify the types of crises, assess the degree of responsibility attributed to organisations and relate the strategies adopted to the effects on the company's reputation.

The analysis focused on identifying patterns of action, the advantages and risks of using AI, and the strategic implications for each organisation's image. The limitation of this study lies in the fact that the analysis is based on secondary sources, such as news articles, press releases, websites and social media posts, which may limit the depth of interpretation. Furthermore, due to a lack of information, we did not present how the organisation reacted at a strategic, tactical and operational level.

This analysis aims to offer relevant contributions to understanding the role of AI in crisis communication, paving the way for future more in-depth empirical research, namely through interviews, discourse analysis or longitudinal studies.

5 Practical Cases of the Use of AI Tools in Organisations

To deepen understanding of how AI influences crisis communication strategies, this paper presents a critical analysis of four organisations. The main goal is to develop a systematic assessment of the cases of Vodafone, Coca-Cola, McDonald's and Sports Illustrated, highlighting best practices and mistakes made. By identifying patterns, strategic divergences and contextual variables that shape the effectiveness of AI in each situation, it is possible to gain a deeper understanding of the topic.

Vodafone, with the aim of improving customer experience, has invested £120 million in generative AI technology, with significant results in Portugal. TOBi, the customer service chatbot, was implemented in Portugal using Microsoft's generative AI technology, Azure OpenAI. This tool follows a ten-year strategic partnership between Vodafone and Microsoft, established in January 2024, covering IoT, AI and cloud services. Vodafone wants TOBi to be able to better understand customer requests for information and respond more quickly and accurately. Additionally, this update will enable the chatbot to interpret complete sentences and expressions, providing more natural and detailed responses. A preliminary analysis by Vodafone on the use of TOBi based on generative AI is already showing positive results. Response times have been reduced, and customer satisfaction has improved substantially. Vodafone aims to respond to market challenges by enhancing the customer experience and processing customer inquiries more efficiently and cost-effectively. With the help of generative AI, the company hopes not only to improve the customer experience, but also to redefine customer service standards (Mesquita, 2024).

In the context of crisis communication, Vodafone will have to be attentive to the responses given by TOBi to customers, through careful planning of responses, waiting time scenarios, considering the different markets in which Vodafone operates. This action requires identifying all the problems that may arise when using it, but also carefully analysing the responses to be provided to its customers.

From a crisis communication point of view, this implementation is part of the prevention phase or pre-crisis stage, as described in the crisis management cycle, acting in advance to avoid service failures and minimise dissatisfaction. By guaranteeing faster, more natural and appropriate responses, Vodafone reduces the risk of customer frustration and the exposure of negative comments or opinions on social networks.

According to the SCCT model, when the organisation acts in contexts of minimal attribution of responsibility (for example, unintentional technical failures or occasional negative experiences), the recommended strategies focus on minimising the impact and reinforcing the perception of competence. Generative AI fulfils this role by enabling a more humanised and effective automated response, consolidating the company's image as technically innovative and customer centric. However, adopting AI in customer service also carries risks. The company must be prepared to respond to potential system failures, misinterpretations or inadequate TOBi responses, which could jeopardise user confidence. The absence of human oversight, especially in culturally distinct markets, can give rise to perception crisis, requiring Vodafone to carefully plan automated responses. In this sense, the integration of generative AI into Vodafone's communications ecosystem must be accompanied by a robust monitoring and incident response strategy. AI, when implemented well, requires ethical planning, definition and testing of different scenarios and continuous evaluation, especially in an organisation with a multinational presence and different audiences.

Coca-Cola is one of the brands that has invested the most in implementing AI technology in its different business practices. One of the success stories was the implementation of IBM's Watson platform to analyse social media data in real time. Coca-Cola's main objective is to understand consumer preferences, purchasing habits and interactions with the brand on social networks. This analysis allows the brand to improve the customer experience, but also to evaluate user interactions and mentions, creating response mechanisms to protect the institutional reputation. This tool allows comments to be analysed, creating an analysis of positive, negative and neutral comments. In terms of crisis communication strategy, the Coca-Cola brand can easily identify topics or posts that are generating negative buzz and act more quickly. On the other hand, it can check which publications have the greatest reach and the highest number of interactions, allowing it to successfully (re)define its communication tactics. Now, Coca-Cola is already working with AI tools to create adverts, buy advertising space and segment adverts according to market niches. In view of this change in the company's paradigm, the marketing and communications team will have to set up a monitoring system to control audience feedback, as well as develop a contingency plan that allows them to act quickly and communicate with different audiences on a global scale.

To modernise its service, the multinational McDonald's has started using an AI tool to record orders at its drive-thru in the United States. The partnership with IBM promised a faster and more accurate service, but the reality was quite different. During the implementation phase of the tool, customers began posting videos on social media sharing serious errors in the service. These included an order for 400 McNuggets; strange combinations such as ice cream with bacon or even the difficulty of understanding the various accents and/or noises in the surroundings. Both brands were mentioned on social media for the worst reasons, with negative or humorous comments, which had a strong negative impact on their institutional image. McDonald's suspended its tests of the new technology, recognising that it was not yet ready to be implemented. IBM, for its part, was labelled in a negative light as it presented the market with an AI tool with serious flaws. This example demonstrates that, in terms of crisis management, McDonald's should have planned before implementing the technology, as well as defining potential risks, carrying out more rigorous tests and initial monitoring by a team. This case demonstrates that implementing automated systems with the aim of direct interaction with consumers without adequate human supervision can have damaging consequences for the brand. Although this is a crisis in which the responsibility is medium because it is due to a technological failure, public perception can quickly change depending on the narrative used in the media and on social networks. According to the SCCT, in these situations compensation and correction strategies are recommended, with apologies and immediate corrective action. McDonald's response was in line with these recommendations, but the incident highlights the risks of automation without human supervision, making clear the need to combine AI with human responsibility at points of contact with the consumer.

In 2023, the prestigious magazine Sports Illustrated was involved in an editorial scandal that had a major international media impact. The magazine was accused of publishing articles developed with AI tools, such as ChatGPT, as well as creating fake author profiles. Futurism, which focuses on science and technology, published an investigation revealing that Sports Illustrated had published articles written by fake authors, whose profile photos were for sale on AI-generated image platforms. The strategy was to publish a greater diversity of content, but it ended up being a critical move with a major impact on the magazine's reputation. Initially, the Futurism team contacted Sports Illustrated's management to find out their position on the information they had, sending several questions that went unanswered. At that point, all articles were removed from the website without explanation (Dupré, 2023). When the investigation was published, the Arena Group, which owns the magazine, quickly denied the allegations, claiming that the articles in question had been purchased from AdVon Commerce, an advertising company that develops AI-powered e-commerce solutions (Sobral, 2023). Two weeks after the investigation became public, the board of directors of the Arena Group, owner of Sports Illustrated, announced the resignation of the CEO (Merdan, 2023).

This situation revealed some inconsistencies in terms of crisis management, demonstrating a lack of transparency, authenticity and an attempt to eliminate information to hide the organisation's responsibility. On the other hand, in releasing the company's official statement, they place the blame on AdVon, which was also not well received by the public, as it is an attempt to shift responsibility to a third party. This is a preventable crisis in which the organisation is held accountable by public opinion for making deliberate decisions that violate ethical standards and public expectations.

The analysis of these four examples demonstrates that AI has positive or negative impacts, depending on how it is planned, implemented, communicated and supervised. The four case studies show that the use of AI in crisis communication can take on different roles, risks and impacts, depending on variables such as the sector, the type of crisis, the strategy adopted, and the degree of responsibility assigned to the organisation (Table 3).

Following the presentation of the four case studies, a critical and comparative reflection is proposed on the main observed patterns:

- The implementation of AI in different stages of a crisis: AI tools have proven to be most effective when integrated into the detection and prevention phases of the crisis cycle (i.e. the pre-crisis stage), as evidenced in the case studies of Vodafone and Coca-Cola. In these cases, the technology was used to monitor, prevent or mitigate risks, thereby reinforcing the institution's proactive behaviour. On the other hand, when AI is implemented without adequate supervision during critical phases, as observed at McDonald's, or with a lack of transparency, as evidenced by Sports Illustrated, it can increase the impact of ongoing crises.

Table 3. Comparative analysis of AI applications in organisational crisis contexts

Criteria	Vodafone	Coca-Cola	McDonald's	Sports Illustrated
Area of activity	Communication	Retail	Food	Media
Type of crisis	–	–	Incident due to technological error	Incident due to human error
Intentionality	–	–	Unintentional	Intentional
Degree of responsibility	Minimal	Lowest	Medium	High
AI tools	TOBi chatbot	Watson (IBM)	Automated ordering system	ChatGPT/DALL-E
Purpose of AI	Customer service	Sentiment analysis	Order automation	Content production
Risks identified	Technical faults	Image/security and data analysis	Image/errors	Image/lack of trust
Response strategy	Minimisation + reinforcement	Minimisation + containment	Compensation + correction	Denial + externalisation
Impact on image	Positive	Positive	Negative	Very negative
Recommendations	Human supervision data security	Contingency plan	Tests/human supervision	Ethics and transparency

Source Author

- Relationship between level of responsibility and reputation: the perception of responsibility is a fundamental component of SCCT, exerting a significant influence on the impact of organisational image and reputation in the cases analysed. Cases such as those involving Vodafone, Coca-Cola and McDonald's demonstrate that unintentional crises with minimal or medium responsibility can be managed through the implementation of minimisation strategies and communication efforts, thereby facilitating the restoration of a positive reputation. On the other hand, in cases of intentional or avoidable crises, such as the Sports Illustrated controversy, the public reaction was predominantly negative, requiring the implementation of recovery strategies or public relations efforts. In the post-crisis stage, Sports Illustrated must develop a public relations strategy aimed at establishing trust and credibility with stakeholders.
- The role of supervision as a critical factor: an analysis of successful and unsuccessful cases reveals a common denominator: the need for human supervision and the adoption of ethical and transparent behaviour. The lack of intervention or supervision by the organisation's employees, as evidenced by the McDonald's case, and the concealment of information, as exemplified by the Sports Illustrated case, were determining factors in exacerbating the negative reputation and magnitude of the crisis. The use of automated systems in critical situations is no substitute for human judgement.
- Transparency and trust: organisational transparency has been shown to be important in mitigating the effects of an AI crisis. Coca-Cola leveraged AI as a real-time analysis and response mechanism, thereby ensuring visibility and control of its image. On the other hand, Sports Illustrated's efforts to remove content and deflect responsibility exacerbated the perception of misconduct, shaking public confidence.
- The use of AI as a means of enhancing strategic decision-making processes: the cases analysed demonstrate that AI should be conceptualised as support for communication strategy, rather than as a replacement for communication management. Technology is most effective when employed in conjunction with an organisational culture that is oriented towards ethical principles, transparency, and the establishment of a mutually beneficial relationship with various constituencies within the organisation.

6 Conclusions

The integration of AI in crisis communication represents a significant transformation in the way organisations monitor, interpret, and respond to activities or events. Throughout this research, we sought to understand how AI can be applied in crisis contexts, the risks and opportunities it presents, as well as the ethical and strategic challenges that emerge from its application.

Through the analysis of four case studies—Vodafone, Coca-Cola, McDonald's and Sports Illustrated—it was possible to identify different forms of technological appropriation, ranging from predictive monitoring to process automation and content generation. This diversity allowed us to observe that the effectiveness of AI in crisis management depends on the organisational context, the degree of human supervision, the adoption of ethical behaviour and the public perception of responsibility.

The results suggest that, although AI can increase the agility, efficiency, and personalisation of communication responses, its use without ethical criteria, transparency or human supervision can exacerbate the effects of the crisis and compromise the organisation's image and reputation. The lack of accountability, as demonstrated in the case of Sports Illustrated, exemplifies the risks of unregulated technological adoption.

In this sense, it is argued that AI should be seen as a support tool and not as a substitute for humans. Its application requires an integrated approach, centred on the principles of responsible communication, digital ethics, and building trust with *stakeholders*.

From an academic point of view, this study reinforces the need to expand the SCCT model to incorporate new variables associated with the use of AI, proposing a theoretical update that reflects the contemporary challenges of digital communication.

As a future perspective, we recommend the development of empirical studies with communication professionals and analyses of real-time crisis situations involving AI to assess its effectiveness and impact on public perception. This ongoing analysis will enable the implementation of research projects and the definition of responsible practices that will transform AI into an effective ally in crisis communication.

This study contributes to advancing crisis communication theory by updating the SCCT model to account for algorithmic mediation, ethical governance, and real-time learning. Such integration reframes SCCT as a dynamic, data-informed model suitable for digital environments where AI both augments and challenges traditional notions of responsibility.

References

Batista, D., & Costa, P. (2021). *Marketing digital—Conteúdos Vencedores*. Lidel.

Bittar, D. (2012). *O poder da assessoria de comunicação nos momentos de crise*. https://arquivo.bocc.ubi.pt/pag/bittar-danielle-o-poder-da-assessoria-de-comunicacao.pdf. Accessed April 14, 2026.

Caetano, J., Vasconcelos, M., & Vasconcelos, P. (2006). *Gestão de Crise*. Editorial Presença.

Cheng, Y., Lee, J., & Qiao, J. (2024). *Crisis communication in the age of AI: Navigating opportunities, challenges, and future horizons. Media and crisis communication*. Routledge.

Coombs, T. (2007). Protecting organisation reputations during a crisis: The development and application of situational crisis communication theory. *Corporate Reputation Review, 10*(3), 163–176.

Coombs, T. W., & Holladay, J. S. (2014). How publics react to crisis communication efforts: Comparing crisis response reactions across sub-areas. *Journal of Communication Management, 18*(1), 40–57.

Coombs, W. T. (1995). Choosing the right words: The development of guidelines for the selection of the "appropriate" crisis-response strategies. *Management Communication Quarterly, 8*(4), 447–476.
Coombs, W. T. (2015). *Ongoing crisis communication: Planning, managing and responding* (4th ed.). Sage.
Coombs, W. T., & Holladay, S. J. (2010). *The handbook of crisis communication*. Wiley-Blackwell.
Coombs, W. T., & Tachkova, E. R. (2023). How emotions can enhance crisis communication: Theorizing around moral outrage. *Journal of Public Relations Research, 36*(1), 6–22. https://doi.org/10.1080/1062726X.2023.2244615
Cruz, A. (2023). Inteligência Artificial e a comunicação nas organizações. *Revista Temática, 19*(10), 34–47. https://doi.org/10.22478/ufpb.1807-8931.2023v19n10.68280
Dupré, M. (2023). *Sports Illustrated published articles by fake, AI-generated writers*. https://futurism.com/sports-illustrated-ai-generated-writers
Effing, R., & Spil, T. (2016). The social strategy cone: Towards a framework for evaluating social media strategies. *International Journal of Information Management, 36*(1), 1–8.
Fearn-Banks, K. (2007). *Crisis communications: A casebook approach* (3rd ed.). Lawrence Erlbaum Associates, Inc.
Fearn-Banks, K. (2011). *Student workbook to accompany crisis communications*. Routledge.
Fearn-Banks, K., & Hooper, P. (2006). Introduction: Crisis communications and crisis management. *Journal of Promotion Management, 12*(3–4), 3–5.
Forni, J. (2019). *Gestão de Crises e Comunicação* (3rd ed.). Editora Atlas.
Goldberg, J. (2025). *AI and new era of crisis comms*. PRSA. https://www.prsa.org/article/ai-and-the-new-era-of-crisis-comms-ST-May25?utm_source=chatgpt.com
Hossain, M. Z., Akter, N., Hasan, L., Bepari, M., & Sultana, S. (2025). Artificial intelligence and machine learning in crisis communication: A management information system perspective. *European Journal of Innovative Studies and Sustainability, 1*(3), 149–163. https://doi.org/10.59324/ejiss.2025.1(3).12
Jang, H., & Lee, S. M. (2023). Introducing the Co-oriented Scansis (CoS) model: A case of chatbot, Lee-Luda. *Public Relations Review, 49*(4). https://doi.org/10.1016/j.pubrev.2023.102360
Lampreia, J. M. (2007). *Da Gestão de Crise ao Marketing de Crise*. Texto Editores.
McCarthy, J. (2007). *What is artificial intelligence?* Stanford University. http://jmc.stanford.edu/articles/whatisai/whatisai.pdf
Merdan, J. (2023). *Sports Illustrated magazine published articles written by authors generated by artificial intelligence*. https://expresso.pt/sociedade/tecnologia/2023-11-29-Revista-Sports-Illustrated-publicou-artigos-escritos-por-autores-gerados-pela-inteligencia-artificial-648f23ca
Mesquita, J. (2024). *Vodafone invests in generative AI with significant results in Portugal*. https://digitalinside.sapo.pt/vodafone-investe-em-ia-generativa-com-resultados-significativos-em-portugal/
Ore, O., & Sposato, M. (2022). Opportunities and risks of artificial intelligence in recruitment and selection. *International Journal of Organisational Analysis, 30*(6), 1771–1782. https://doi.org/10.1108/ijoa-07-2020-2291
Scott, D. M. (2020). *The new rules of marketing & PR: How to use content marketing, podcasting, social media, AI, live video, and newsjacking to reach buyers directly*. Wiley.
Seeger, M. W. (2006). Best practices in crisis communication: An expert panel process. *Journal of Applied Communication Research, 34*(3), 232–244.
Sobral, C. (2023). *Sports Illustrated CEO fired after scandal with articles written by artificial intelligence*. https://observador.pt/2023/12/12/ceo-da-sports-illustrated-e-despedido-depois-de-escandalo-com-artigos-gerados-por-inteligencia-artificial/
Strauss, C., Harr, M. D., & Pieper, T. M. (2024). Analysing digital communication: A comprehensive literature review. *Management Review Quarterly, 75*, 3319–3157. https://doi.org/10.1007/s11301-024-00455-8

Treleaven, P., Barnett, J., Brown, D., Bud, A., Fenoglio, E., Kerrigan, C., … Schoernig, M. (2023). The future of cybercrime: AI and emerging technologies are creating a cybercrime tsunami. *SSSRN*, 450722. https://doi.org/10.2139/ssrn.4507244

Ulmer, R. R., Sellnow, T. L., & Seeger, M. W. (2017). *Effective crisis communication: Moving from crisis to opportunity* (4th ed.). Sage.

Veil, S. R., Buehner, T., & Palenchar, M. J. (2011). A work-in-process literature review: Incorporating social media in risk and crisis communication. *Journal of Contingencies and Crisis Management, 19*(2), 110–121.

Wilcox, D., Cameron, G., & Reber, B. (2015). *Public relations: Strategies and tatics* (11th ed.). Pearson Education Ltd.

AI Applied to Business-to-Business Marketing

Paulo Botelho Pires and José Duarte Santos

Abstract This chapter synthesises the growing evidence of the transformative impact of Artificial Intelligence on Business-to-Business marketing. Using a comprehensive array of theoretical frameworks, including Activity Theory, Knowledge-Based Marketing, Diffusion of Innovation, the Resource-Based View and Dynamic Capabilities, a review of the core peer-reviewed sources from 2019 to 2025 was conducted. This review shows that AI acts as a helpful tool that speeds up knowledge sharing, reduces uncertainty in decision-making, and helps organise resources better in industrial networks. It also shows that using AI tools for data analysis, creating content, and supporting decisions together improves how well companies connect with customers, create value, and adapt to changes, leading to better financial results and relationships. Nevertheless, the adoption of these technologies remains uneven, with technical complexity, governance deficits, and cross-functional misalignment still constraining diffusion beyond early adopters.

1 Introduction

Artificial Intelligence (AI) is revolutionising the Business-to-Business (B2B) marketing landscape by offering innovative solutions that address the complexities of business activities and decisions. Recently, there has been a growing acknowledgement that this uprising requires greater attention. This has become an issue of great importance recently due to the introduction of Large Language Models (LLMs) and Agents AI. However, to fully grasp AI's impact on B2B, it's vital to analyse how AI can be integrated into the B2B market sector, even though this presents an even greater challenge due to the rapid pace of change and innovation in the field of AI.

P. B. Pires · J. D. Santos (✉)
CEOS.PP, ISCAP, Polytechnic of Porto, Porto, Portugal
e-mail: jdsantos@iscap.ipp.pt

P. B. Pires
e-mail: paulo.pires@iscap.ipp.pt

J. D. Santos et al. (eds.), *Artificial Intelligence Transforming Marketing*, Contributions to Management Science, https://doi.org/10.1007/978-3-032-22360-9_15

Since the release of ChatGPT on November 30, 2022, there has been a rapid turnover following a few years of dormancy, frustration, uncertainty, and lack of funding, collectively referred to as the AI winter. Thus, with the emergence of this technology, there has been a wide variety of applications achieved in recent years, particularly in B2B.

In the B2B sector, AI is recognised for its ability to automate and optimise various marketing processes, such as structuring, standardising, and customising data, which is crucial in a complex business environment (Chatterjee et al., 2021). AI's integration into B2B marketing allows companies to analyse large volumes of data, providing valuable insights that enhance marketing strategies and personalise product offerings (Solaz et al., 2025). This data-driven approach enables businesses to make informed decisions, improve customer service, and gain a competitive edge (Solaz et al., 2025). Furthermore, AI technologies, like conversational intelligence solutions, can analyse sales calls in real-time, helping sales teams respond effectively to customer pain points and competitive mentions (Grewal et al., 2021). The adoption of AI in B2B marketing is not just about efficiency; it also drives innovation. AI-powered tools help businesses automate routine operations, improve data analysis, and forecast market trends with greater precision (Alawamleh et al., 2024).

It is also evident that AI has the potential to offer both opportunities and challenges for B2B marketers. Overall, the use of AI mechanisms empowers marketers to develop more effective marketing activities, thereby effecting a transformation in the manner in which businesses interact with the clients (Lada et al., 2023; Petrescu et al., 2022a). This paradigm shift is particularly evident in B2B markets, where the integration of AI into operational processes has been found to enhance the efficiency of complex organisational routines, including decision support systems, relationships management, and sales administration. Prior and Marcos-Cuevas (2025) observe that such systems frequently augment managerial judgement or execute tasks plainly unattainable without algorithmic assistance. Since B2B exchanges tend to involve lengthy sales cycles and high transaction costs, firms deploy AI to coordinate complex supply chains and highly specialised offerings (Sahoo et al., 2024). On the other hand, in consumer markets, AI tends to target individual engagement and personalisation; however, B2B contexts privilege durable strategic relationships mediated by multilateral decision structures. Consequently, algorithms must coordinate dispersed stakeholders and optimise resources across hierarchical tiers, a requirement that recent studies emphasise (Garg et al., 2025; Khan & Khan, 2025). Implementation, nevertheless, remains fraught with higher integration expenses, extended timelines, and an imperative for collective executive endorsement. Indeed, Cooper (2024) reports that only a modest share of B2B marketers have operationalised AI, largely due to their limited technical comprehension. However, the ability to improve efficiency and handle complex situations is still driving companies to adopt AI, giving forward-thinking businesses a strong edge over their competitors.

The prevailing paradigm of B2B marketing, which has been shaped by the advent of personal computers and the internet, has laid the foundation for the integration of AI (Bamberger et al., 2025). And AI is increasingly recognised for its capacity to disrupt prevailing marketing theories because it combines sophisticated technological capabilities with notable cost efficiencies (Keegan et al., 2022). However, Keegan et al. (2022) and Petrescu et al. (2022a) observe that many organisations still struggle to integrate AI coherently within established frameworks.

A closer look at some reviews also reveals that AI technologies have been shown to transform routine B2B tasks, thereby enhancing human-machine collaboration (Spreitzenbarth et al., 2024). Additionally, they optimise operations and supply chain management, according to the same authors. Since innovations in e-commerce and digital technology continue to reshape conventional processes, an alignment with an expanded array of stakeholders is increasingly demanded (Skare et al., 2023). Indeed, AI-powered solutions generate richer insights, accelerate reaction times, and open new revenue channels, thereby delivering demonstrable performance gains (Mikalef et al., 2021).

Another important key point is the relationship between AI and strategy. Although the strategic use of AI remains in its infancy, Li et al. (2021) argue that early adopters secure durable competitive advantages. The same stream of research indicates that AI already enhances customer care, fortifies quality assurance, and supports data-driven business models (Mikalef et al., 2021). Consequently, Petrescu et al. (2022a) insist on a comprehensive framework that bridges theory and practice while exploiting AI's strengths for collaborative innovation.

Therefore, it can be concluded that the transition from traditional to AI-driven B2B marketing is contingent upon the capitalisation of technological advances, the overcoming of managerial impediments, and the satisfaction of evolving customer expectations, with the ultimate objective being the enhancement of marketing effectiveness and firm performance (Bamberger et al., 2025; Keegan et al., 2022). Furthermore, Petrescu et al. (2022a) and Mikalef et al. (2021) contend that such progress demands continuous innovation and systematic co-creation.

This chapter delineates the scope and defines key terms; (ii) synthesises recent peer-reviewed literature to identify the mechanisms through which AI reshapes activities, knowledge flows, adoption, and performance; (iii) advances and justifies an integrative theoretical framework combining Activity Theory, Knowledge-Based Marketing, Diffusion of Innovation, the Resource-Based View and Dynamic Capabilities, alongside Service-Dominant Logic; (iv) formulates propositions and associated questions derived from this framework; (v) outlines the methodological approach and delimitations that structure the empirical and conceptual analyses; and (vi) distils theoretical, managerial, and policy implications while setting an agenda for future research.

The main sections below explain the key effects of AI in B2B practice, highlighting its strategic importance, and include seven themes that cover different theoretical views, basic theories, and ideas. First, there is an overview of activity theory, which provides a systemic lens through which AI implementation in legacy B2B marketing routines can be understood. The second part looks at knowledge-based marketing theory and describes how AI-enabled information systems gather, combine, and change market knowledge to help with strategic decision-making in B2B situations. Thirdly, we explore innovation diffusion theory to shed light on the adoption trajectories and implementation hurdles of AI technologies in industrial marketing contexts.

Finally, a comparative mapping demonstrates how the resource-based view, dynamic capabilities, service-dominant logic, the technology acceptance model, customer lifetime value analytics, and diffusion of innovation constructs have been mobilised across the extant literature.

We conducted a targeted review of peer-reviewed sources published between 2019 and 2025 to identify frameworks that, in combination, explain how AI reshapes activities, knowledge flows, adoption, and performance in B2B markets. Articles were eligible if they focused explicitly on AI in B2B contexts, offered an identifiable theoretical contribution, and presented conceptual or empirical evidence permitting cautious generalisation. Screening proceeded in two stages: (i) title-abstract appraisal for topical relevance and (ii) full-text assessment for conceptual contribution and methodological quality. From the refined corpus, we mapped each study to core theoretical mechanisms and retained seven complementary lenses that together span the value-creation cycle under AI: Activity Theory (socio-technical mediation of actors-resources-activities), Knowledge-Based Marketing (codification, integration, and exploitation of market knowledge), Diffusion of Innovation (innovation attributes and inter-organisational adoption channels), Resource-Based View and Dynamic Capabilities (resource valuation and sensing-seizing-reconfiguring), plus customer-facing Service-Dominant Logic and adjacent constructs to capture perceived usefulness, technology acceptance, and lifecycle value.

2 The Activity Theory Perspective

Activity Theory positions AI as a transformative mediating artefact that reconfigures interactions among market actors. This perspective emphasises the dynamic interplay between actors, activities, and resources, which is central to the evolution of B2B models. According to Pardo et al. (2022), AI permeates the traditional Actor-Resource-Activity framework by endowing resources with agency, thereby enabling non-human agents to mobilise human or organisational counterparts. Consequently, Pardo et al. (2022) have deemed conventional network models inadequate because they rarely capture the salience of AI-driven activities and resources. AI also organises and analyses voluminous market data, converting dispersed facts into actionable judgements that support firms operating in volatile conditions (Alawamleh et al., 2024). Such computational capacity has been found to optimise production processes, curtail energy consumption, and strengthen competitive advantage (Lin et al., 2024). Moreover, Sahoo et al. (2024) argue that AI enables B2B firms to collaborate, co-create products, and test novel business models despite resource constraints.

Building on these insights, Mikalef et al. (2023) maintain that AI-enhanced marketing yields behavioural insights, reveals critical market signals, and mitigates inefficiencies, thereby raising organisational performance. Accordingly, the relationship among AI technologies, business actors, and market objectives is interpreted as an activity system whose components co-evolve over time, consonant with Activity

Theory. However, Zhan et al. (2024) highlight persistent knowledge gaps and call for comprehensive research that can guide strategic AI adoption while balancing benefits and risks. Without such guidance, firms may confront misalignment between technological capabilities and business goals, a tension frequently documented in earlier studies (Han et al., 2025).

Patnaik and Bakkar (2024) conceptualise B2B marketing as a collaborative activity system, suggesting that AI implementation surfaces both conflicts and synergies that must be managed for effective coordination. Indeed, subsequent analyses indicated that AI adoption remains low and its benefits uncertain, as initially documented by Gupta et al. (2020), underscoring the need for conflict-resolution mechanisms. Complementarily, Baabdullah et al. (2021) show that AI practices enhance relational governance by improving joint planning and problem-solving capabilities across partner firms. Furthermore, interdisciplinary collaboration has been reported to flourish when AI connects business, operational, and marketing personnel, thereby dismantling organisational silos (Mikalef et al., 2023). Zhan et al. (2024) accordingly frame AI implementation as a socio-technical action that both impacts and is affected by surrounding activities, reinforcing the need for holistic governance.

In conclusion, it is evident that the transformative influence of AI on B2B activities, process optimisation, and innovation has been elucidated through an Activity Theory lens. Nevertheless, there are still unresolved tensions that require further exploration.

3 Knowledge-Based Marketing Theory in B2B Markets

AI now occupies a central position within Knowledge-Based Marketing theory in B2B contexts because it gathers, organises, and interprets the fragmented knowledge resources that circulate between suppliers and customers. According to Bag et al. (2021) and Moradi and Dass (2022), AI captures fine-grained customer insights, maps how user knowledge flows across organisational boundaries, and absorbs external market signals; these combined capabilities strengthen a firm's capacity to create actionable knowledge. Chatterjee et al. (2021) likewise maintain that, once customer-related information has been codified in this way, the intricate processes of structuring, standardising, aligning, and customising data can be automated, thereby alleviating the cognitive burden that typically accompanies complex B2B transactions.

Because such automation produces timely, reliable intelligence, managers can make decisions that enhance marketing performance, raise perceived customer value, and bolster loyalty, consequently consolidating long-term competitive advantage. Gaczek et al. (2023) demonstrate that AI-driven analytics enable firms not only to detect emerging opportunities but also to seize and reconfigure them more rapidly than competitors; the transformation of raw data into strategic knowledge thus becomes a sustained source of advantage.

It is important to note that operational efficiencies go beyond discrete marketing tasks. Abou-Foul et al. (2023) contend that AI supports new value propositions by synchronising production schedules with fluctuating demand, enriching customers' experiences through real-time personalisation, and stimulating social innovation across supply networks. Their view is corroborated by Sahoo et al. (2024), who find that integrating AI into broader organisational routines encourages exploratory learning, which, in turn, nurtures strategic agility in volatile industrial environments.

Consequently, the integration of AI into knowledge-based marketing theory has the potential to enhance our understanding of knowledge creation, mobilisation, and exploitation within B2B ecosystems. Furthermore, it can refine decision-making processes, cultivate customer relationships, optimise operational performance, and catalyse innovation, thereby reinforcing firms' competitive positioning (Bag et al., 2021; Chatterjee et al., 2021; Gaczek et al., 2023).

4 Diffusion of Innovation Theory Supported by AI

Diffusion of Innovation Theory provides a robust conceptual lens through which the uptake of AI in B2B contexts may be interpreted. Because this framework elucidates how innovations traverse social systems by foregrounding inter-organisational interactions and emerging technologies, it aligns neatly with current patterns of corporate digitisation. Empirical evidence has been marshalled, as Abdalla et al. (2024) demonstrate, to confirm that organisational characteristics and perceived innovation attributes decisively shape managers' willingness to integrate AI, thereby explaining its rapid corporate penetration. When AI is implemented, B2B operations are markedly streamlined, transactional costs are lowered, and customer experience is enhanced; these outcomes are attributed by Sahoo et al. (2024) to automation, large-scale data analytics and data-driven decision-making. Nevertheless, the same authors contend that AI also catalyses open innovation since it allows resource-constrained firms to collaborate with diverse stakeholders and co-create novel offerings despite fierce rivalry. Indeed, advances in big data analytics and computational power have propelled AI's adoption in B2B marketing, where practitioners exploit predictive insights to personalise value propositions. Researchers have documented illustrative cases that reconfigure promotional strategies and upgrade service delivery (Zhan et al., 2024). Therefore, the diffusion of AI within B2B markets sustains competitive advantage and stimulates continual innovation, a point underlined by Abou-Foul et al. (2023).

A recent and relevant contribution to this field is also provided and well documented in Abdalla et al. (2024). The authors contend that Diffusion of Innovation Theory provides a rigorous lens for analysing AI adoption in B2B markets. Within this perspective, innovations are diffused progressively: early adopters experiment first, and mainstream firms imitate successful pioneers (Baffour Gyau et al., 2024). Adoption is nevertheless conditioned by technological complexity, organisational readiness, and ambient market demand, factors corroborated by Baffour Gyau et al.

(2024). The interaction of those contingencies has been demonstrated by Mubarik et al. (2025), leading to heterogeneous diffusion velocities across sectors. It is important to note that empirical evidence demonstrates a synergy between digital and innovation capabilities, whereas environmental support remains ineffectual without robust institutional scaffolding (Arroyabe et al., 2024). According to Delios et al. (2024), once implanted, AI revolutionises entrenched business models, heightens operational efficiency, and opens previously inaccessible growth avenues.

The Bass Diffusion Model, therefore, complements the Diffusion of Innovation. It distinguishes innovation from imitation and facilitates credible pre-launch sales forecasts (Keshavarz-Ghorbani & Reza Pasandideh, 2022). However, a holistic alignment of technology-organisation-environment is argued to be indispensable because technical capabilities must be embedded within supportive structures and external ecosystems (Robertson et al., 2025). When such alignment materialises, digital and innovation assets reinforce each other, thereby accelerating both experimentation and imitation. As a result, the way businesses adopt AI becomes more consistent and faster, showing how it spreads and providing significant advantages to B2B companies (Mubarik et al., 2025). The key takeaway is that AI changes how B2B companies adopt new technologies by using additional skills, following established patterns of innovation spread, and succeeding only when there is a strong effort to integrate everything together (Abdalla et al., 2024; Arroyabe et al., 2024).

Alongside this, there is another relevant and important point that requires attention. AI increasingly shapes the communication channels envisaged by Innovation Diffusion Theory, particularly in B2B settings. Because these channels govern how information circulates within social systems, optimising them remains vital. Therefore, this discussion explores the principal routes through which AI achieves optimisation. Ghasri and Vij (2021) demonstrate that AI interrogates vast datasets, discerns emerging patterns, and tailors mass-media campaigns, thereby heightening early awareness of novel offerings.

As for content creation and distribution, they are routinely automated through AI-driven tools, a practice first highlighted by Agarwal and Prasad (1998), which ensures rapid and far-reaching outreach. According to the authors, AI systems scrutinise individual preferences and behavioural traces and then deliver customised messages that answer specific organisational concerns. This customisation is enhanced by AI-powered chatbots and virtual assistants; Bobrova et al. (2021) say that these tools mimic real conversations and make persuasive communication more effective.

Moving to a different issue, Magsamen-Conrad and Dillon (2020) note that machine-learning algorithms locate pivotal influencers within digital networks, thereby accelerating diffusion through precisely targeted engagement. In addition, sentiment across social platforms is continually monitored, and corresponding strategies are adjusted, as Mahajan (1993) originally proposed, to cultivate favourable attitudes towards innovation. Cathala and Moorley (2023) argue that AI-enabled segmentation exploits homophily and heterophily by clustering audiences according to similarity or diversity and then aligning messages with those patterns. Communication efficiency is thus increased within homogeneous partner groups, while cross-group exchanges are simultaneously facilitated, insights also articulated by Cathala and Moorley (2023). Additionally, Mikhail et al. (2025) reveal that AI dashboards can track adopters' progress through the knowledge, persuasion, decision, implementation, and confirmation stages, thereby supplying real-time managerial intelligence. Marketing strategies are consequently refined since data from multiple channels are analysed and iteratively fed back, a process that the authors consider critical for successful uptake. Taken together, these capabilities demonstrate how AI automates tasks, personalises interactions, and orchestrates channel strategies, thus hastening the diffusion of innovations throughout B2B social systems. Ghasri and Vij (2021) and Agarwal and Prasad (1998) reach similar conclusions, while Mahajan (1993) foresaw the strategic potential of social networks; more recent analyses by Bobrova et al. (2021), Magsamen-Conrad and Dillon (2020), Cathala and Moorley (2023) and Mikhail et al. (2025) further substantiate this argument.

A prevalent area of study is the influence of AI in the different phases of diffusion and the different types of consumers. AI is reshaping early adopters in B2B markets because it alters every stage of innovation diffusion. Predictive analytics emboldens firms to pursue first-mover advantage by converting uncertain prospects into measurable forecasts (Shih, 2012). Consequently, perceived risk is lowered as automated engines continuously update expected outcomes. Additionally, AI-driven training tools also deepen the technical competence that typifies innovators (Gao et al., 2012). Furthermore, algorithmic content curation manufactures synthetic buzz and refines product attributes through rapid feedback loops (Yücel & van Daalen, 2011), and decision-making is streamlined by real-time dashboards, which permit more objective economic evaluations (Havas et al., 2023). It is also important to note that early trials become safer and more visible when simulation environments display tangible benefits before large investments (Bossink, 2025).

Early adopters can thus maintain a strategic vision, while the mainstream maintains its pragmatic stance (Egmond et al., 2006). Machine-learning classifiers identify influential professionals and amplify their reach, intensifying social contagion (Yousefi-Nooraie et al., 2012), and adaptive targeting also directs messages at younger, highly educated, high-status groups, reinforcing the socio-demographic tilt of adoption (Figenbaum et al., 2015). Lastly, continuous monitoring lets AI recalibrate diffusion curves and foresee saturation points with greater accuracy (Sheldon & Dua, 2024).

Because of the aforementioned, it may be concluded that AI can reduce uncertainty, augment competence, and accelerate knowledge flows among early adopters. These groups also consolidate their strategic orientation and demographic specificity, thereby accelerating the overall diffusion of the phenomenon.

5 AI Enhancing Resource-Based View

The Resource-Based View (RBV) asserts that firms gain a sustainable advantage by leveraging idiosyncratic resources; AI intensifies this leverage by augmenting both the efficiency and the strategic elasticity of such resources (Chen et al., 2025).

Scholars integrating AI into RBV in B2B markets argue that firms strengthen competitive advantage by valorising internal resources. Within this perspective, AI technologies, most notably generative systems, are strategically deployed so that collaboration, efficiency, and innovation are amplified. Such deployment enhances managerial decision-making, streamlines operations, and, by cultivating human capital alongside organisational capabilities, intensifies firms' competitiveness (Singh et al., 2024).

Indeed, the RBV posits that firms harness distinctive resources (relational knowledge and emergent AI competences) to secure differential performance. Consequently, when firms nurture these resources, they manage inter-firm relationships more adroitly and elevate customer relationship quality. The enrichment of customer insights has been reported when AI-driven analytics are employed (Wang et al., 2023). Enhanced loyalty is likewise observed when generative and predictive tools are embedded within relationship processes, as evidenced by Gaczek et al. (2023).

Beyond relational functions, AI-centred automation of data collection and analytics empowers managers to act rationally, raise performance, and curate organisational knowledge. Through these dynamic capabilities, firms are enabled to sense, seize, and reconfigure market opportunities, thereby preserving long-term advantage (Hossain et al., 2022).

Integrating AI can also lead to improved collaboration, efficiency, and innovation, which are crucial for enhanced decision-making and streamlined operations (Singh et al., 2024). The RBV framework suggests that the complementary use of resources, including AI, can significantly improve marketing integration, sales channels, and brand alignment, thereby enhancing overall firm performance (Kanungo, 2021). This integration requires not only the acquisition of AI technologies but also the development of human capital and organisational capabilities to fully realise the potential benefits (Singh et al., 2024). Moreover, the RBV highlights the importance of managing and sharing resources effectively within B2B relationships. Nurturing an open exchange of ideas, knowledge, and experience among employees from different organisations, companies can strengthen their B2B ties and optimise the use of AI technologies (Samadhiya et al., 2023). This collaborative approach can lead to better resource usage and improved corporate performance. Therefore, the RBV framework highlights the need for a systematic approach to analysing, implementing, and regulating AI resources and capabilities in B2B marketing. This approach clearly ensures that AI integration enhances operational efficiency and contributes to sustained competitive advantage (Kassa & Worku, 2025; Petrescu et al., 2022a).

Building on these theoretical insights, it is necessary to translate the RBV-guided vision for AI-enabled collaboration into a concrete set of organisational requirements. In other words, once companies recognise that the strategic value of AI resides not merely in owning advanced algorithms but in orchestrating them with complementary human, structural and relational assets, the next logical step is to identify which specific capabilities must be cultivated and how they interlock. This articulation combines the high-level argument that AI can enhance performance through resource complementarity with the operational reality of mobilising technology, data, and people. The ensuing discussion, therefore, defines the core technological, analytical, and organisational capabilities that have practical effects on RBV's prescriptions, clarifying the pathways through which AI investments are transformed into sustainable competitive advantage.

To effectively integrate AI into B2B marketing, several key resources and capabilities are essential. Firstly, technology readiness and ICT capabilities are foundational. These lower-order capabilities facilitate the development of higher-order AI-CRM capabilities, which are crucial for sensing market opportunities, seizing new prospects, and reconfiguring business strategies to adapt to technological changes (Rahman et al., 2023). Additionally, data collection, analysis, predictive modelling, and resource optimisation are critical components. These elements form the backbone of a climate-competent AI framework, which not only promotes environmental sustainability but also enhances cost savings and customer loyalty (Shankar & Gupta, 2024). Moreover, the integration of AI and big data is vital for discovering and using critical information, leading to a competitive advantage. AI aids in gathering important customer information, retaining existing customers, and increasing customer satisfaction through personalised marketing efforts (Papagiannidis et al., 2023). Furthermore, supporting resources, labour skills, and organisational coordination are necessary to develop AI capabilities, such as forecasting, planning, and learning. These capabilities help automate, augment, and transform business processes, making them more efficient and effective (Chen et al., 2022). Lastly, the adoption of AI in B2B marketing is driven by the availability of data from various sources, advances in big data analytics, increased computing power, and lower costs (Zhan et al., 2024). Consequently, the integration of AI in B2B marketing is contingent upon a combination of technological readiness, data analytics, big data integration, and organisational coordination to enhance marketing capabilities and achieve a competitive advantage.

To understand the ideas mentioned above, it's important to explain the specific resources and skills needed to effectively integrate AI into B2B marketing. The subsequent sentences will address this subject. In B2B marketing, firms within the RBV can leverage AI in several impactful ways to enhance their competitive advantage. AI serves as a transformative resource that integrates prediction, optimisation, and execution, all of which are critical for resource acquisition and integration. This capability allows firms to dynamically allocate innovation resources, reduce costs, and enhance innovation efficiency, thereby sustaining long-term competitive advantages in dynamic environments (Lang Zhao et al., 2025a, 2025b).

In addition, the following aspects must be mentioned. AI's ability to process and interpret large volumes of data makes it a valuable intangible resource. It enhances governance and decision-making, driving business efficiency and innovation (Xia et al., 2025). Just through the automation of repetitive tasks and optimising resource allocation, AI helps firms streamline operations, reduce costs, and increase productivity, which directly contributes to enhanced competitiveness (Abdelfattah et al., 2024). Furthermore, the authors state that AI enhances decision-making capabilities, which in turn further strengthens a firm's competitive position.

Overall, in the context of RBV, AI is considered a valuable, rare, inimitable, and non-substitutable resource. It facilitates operational efficiency, product innovation, customer experience customisation, and supply chain optimisation, all of which are essential for maintaining a competitive edge (Wei & Shen, 2025). AI also supports firms in transforming big data into actionable insights, enabling the development of effective marketing strategies and enhancing business operations (Petrescu et al., 2022a). AI's integration into business processes aligns with RBV principles by providing firms with unique and strategic resources that drive competitive advantage in B2B marketing.

6 Enhancing Dynamic Capabilities with AI

The dynamic capabilities view emphasises a firm's capacity to adapt and innovate in turbulent markets, because such agility sustains competitive advantage (Garg et al., 2025). AI and machine learning, increasingly employed to close empirical gaps in existing research, have transformed these adaptive activities. AI-powered customer relationship management systems combine data from various sources and provide personalised services, which enhances discussions about the basic principles of dynamic capability theory (Alnofeli et al., 2025).

Within enterprise development, opportunities are sensed more effectively when dynamic capabilities are amplified by advanced AI applications that streamline processes and reduce costs (Sun, 2025). However, strategic leaders, nurture organisational ambidexterity by deliberately balancing exploration and exploitation to seize and transform emerging opportunities (Akter et al., 2023). Under AI-enabled information systems, real-time analytics are used to reconfigure resources swiftly so that firms respond with agility (Liu et al., 2025).

Accordingly, the core capacities of sensing, seizing, and reconfiguring remain central since competitive advantage depends upon their ongoing orchestration (Pereira-Moliner et al., 2024). In Industry 4.0 environments, corporate capabilities are improved through pervasive AI technologies that embed intelligence within production and logistics networks (Shen et al., 2025). In fact, sophisticated data utilisation practices allow organisations to align rapid market responses with internal coordination, maximising the utility of dynamic routines (Lin et al., 2024). Distinctive advantages have been observed in retail healthcare, where technological infrastructures are integrated and reconfigured to differentiate offerings (Yadav et al., 2025). Future scholarship, nevertheless, must probe the boundary conditions of these effects to enrich strategic-management frameworks (Liu & Son, 2024). It is important to note that artificial intelligence ultimately amplifies dynamic capabilities by enabling firms across sectors to adapt, innovate, and respond effectively.

7 Enhancing Service-Dominant Logic (SDL) in B2B with AI

Artificial intelligence significantly fortifies Service-Dominant Logic (SDL) in business-to-business marketing because it catalyses value co-creation, augments customer experiences, refines operational processes, and supports informed strategic choices. Li et al. (2021) demonstrate that industrial AI empowers suppliers, customers, and technology partners to craft mutual value by combining essential value types with critical digital capabilities. In addition, real-time conversational intelligence has been shown to flag salient client utterances and to prompt timely responses, thereby deepening co-creation (Grewal et al., 2021).

Because AI algorithmic promotion tailors brand and product propositions with remarkable precision, AI revolutionises the customer journey and enhances the quality of the experience (Rashid & Kausik, 2024). In B2B contexts, firms deploy chatbots and predictive maintenance to streamline workflows, reduce downtime, and elevate client satisfaction (Zhan et al., 2024). It is important to note that operational data have been routinely structured, standardised, and customised by intelligent systems, a practice considered indispensable for efficiency in complex B2B environments (Chatterjee et al., 2021).

Recent implementations at organisations illustrate that AI-enabled services can overcome entrenched operational barriers and unlock novel growth avenues (Zhan et al., 2024). Strategic decision-making has likewise been influenced by neural networks and machine learning, which segment markets, prioritise sales opportunities, and optimise promotional portfolios (Petrescu et al., 2022a). Consequently, AI addresses the principal challenges identified in contemporary B2B marketing theory, namely technological advancement and the perpetual pursuit of superior value propositions (Abou-Foul et al., 2023). Therefore, AI has been shown to invigorate Service-Dominant Logic by enabling value co-creation, enhancing experiential richness, increasing operational agility, and informing strategic judgement.

8 Other Foundations and Theories Enhanced in B2B with AI

AI increasingly reshapes B2B marketing by strengthening the Technology Acceptance Model (TAM), extending customer lifetime value (CLV), and refining satisfaction and loyalty metrics.

Within TAM, AI-enabled customer-relationship-management systems automate decisions, raising relational satisfaction and firm performance; however, technology turbulence diminishes these gains (Chatterjee et al., 2022). Leadership support actively moderates this dynamic because proactive managers champion systematic adoption that maximises the aforementioned gains. Big data repositories have been transformed into actionable intelligence, allowing firms to craft incisive strategies and elevate operational efficiency, thereby intensifying long-term value extraction from individual buyers (Petrescu et al., 2022a). Jia and Wang (2024) extend this insight by modelling how predictive learning systems steadily compound customer lifetime value.

Customer experience has also been reconfigured as human-like conversational agents deliver real-time responses, and satisfaction is consequently heightened (Kushwaha et al., 2021). Grewal et al. (2021) corroborate this observation by demonstrating that seamless engagement across digital touchpoints elevates affective evaluations. Personalisation has been driven by algorithmic profiling, and suppliers are thereby enabled to establish rich yet cost-efficient relationships, an approach first articulated by Prior and Keränen (2020) and now closely linked with stronger loyalty. Building on that foundation, Hautamäki and Heikinheimo (2025) argue that sales-process analytics, predictive forecasting, and dynamic pricing algorithms integrate seamlessly to sustain engagement and reinforce the loyalty effects. Operational efficiency has also been improved, and market offerings have been aligned with wider B2B marketing goals, a trajectory examined by Abou-Foul et al. (2023), since technological advancement is causally tied to value creation.

Therefore, and as a conclusion, Shankar and Gupta (2024) contend that AI-infused strategies exploit granular data and personalised interactions, and their synthesis ultimately increases satisfaction, loyalty, and financial performance. It is important to note that, across these studies, AI has consistently been conceptualised not as a discrete tool but as an integrated capability that reshapes every customer-centric metric.

9 AI Applications in B2B Marketing

Recent scholarship contends that AI in B2B marketing has coalesced around fourteen interconnected application domains, which collectively reflect the digitally mediated, customer-facing value chain. Within customer-relationship management, personalization increasingly depends on predictive lead-classification systems that fuse firmographic data with rich behavioural streams; Benhaddou and Leray (2017) showed, through Bayesian-network elicitation on "small data", how such scoring engines emerge, whereas Gonzalez-Flores et al. (2025) subsequently illustrated, in live software-as-a-service (SaaS) environments, the incremental performance gains secured by gradient-boosting ensembles. Because these predictive layers shape every contact, AI-enabled service interfaces simultaneously recalibrate brand experience, a point emphasised both by Khoshtaria et al. (2025) and by Hitti and Ramadan (2025).

Although the same data foundations sustain AI-driven segmentation and insight generation, literature-based reviews identify this topic as merely one of five dominant clusters (Han et al., 2021); nevertheless, broader analytics syntheses still place segmentation at the very centre of "Marketing 4.0" capability building (Mahdiraji et al., 2023). Personalised content delivery, often showcased through conversational or generative agents, remains conceptually celebrated; however, Stone and Woodcock (2021) observed that robust empirical evidence in B2B settings continues to lag.

Many of the remaining themes rely on predictive analytics for their quantitative foundation. Eitle and Buxmann (2019) documented full-stack, machine-learning pipelines for sales-opportunity forecasting, and Rezazadeh (2020) complemented this work with Azure-based workflow blueprints that confirm scalability. Because causal-uplift and heterogeneous-treatment-effect estimation can now be embedded in production-grade optimisation engines, practitioners report commercially material improvements (Zhao et al., 2025a, 2025b). These predictive capacities, in turn, underpin sales-process optimisation, where frameworks that integrate forecasting, mixed-integer resource allocation, and contextual bandits deliver measurable revenue gains (Zhao et al., 2025a, 2025b). Lead-scoring automation displays a similar evolutionary arc: the field progressed from expert-oriented Bayesian networks (Benhaddou & Leray, 2017), through a systematic taxonomy of forty-four empirical studies (Wu et al., 2023), and finally to explainable-AI deployments embedded in enterprise CRMs (Jena et al., 2023).

Work on pipeline- or conversion-rate optimisation follows closely. Early probabilistic approaches, such as Hawkes-process models and regression-based classifiers, were developed by Yan et al. (2011), Yan et al. (2015), as well as by Duncan and Elkan (2015). These prototypes have since evolved into multi-class risk stratification applied to complex tendering contexts (Zahid et al., 2021) and into agent-based, autonomic revenue-operations architectures (Ramsaran, 2025b). Customer-journey optimisation now attracts dedicated theoretical attention: Khvatova et al. (2024) validated, across sixty-one industrial firms, an input–process–output framework that aligns specific AI solutions with discrete journey stages while exposing the organisational levers required for successful change management.

Content-automation studies, though still embryonic, indicate rising managerial salience. Pothukuchi (2025) supplied a practitioner-centred technical overview of generative components inside Salesforce ecosystems, whereas Ramsaran (2025a) designed orchestration layers for federating specialist bots across the lead-to-cash continuum. Campaign-optimisation scholarship remains largely speculative; Pandiya (2020) proposed deep-learning architectures for funnel management, yet these remain untested beyond simulated data.

A distinctive research stream interrogates co-creation and collaboration. Fehrenbach et al. (2024) catalogued how buyers, suppliers, and technology providers engage with AI artefacts, mapping actor constellations, process enablers, and industrial-market value mechanisms. Activity-theory examinations expose the socio-technical "contradictions" that shape adoption trajectories (Keegan et al., 2022), while multi-agent revenue-operations designs articulate orchestration layers capable of integrating autonomous specialist bots (Ramsaran, 2025b). Stakeholder-engagement models complete the loop: Bashir et al. (2024) reframed AI capabilities as dynamic resources mediating the path from data readiness to customer-lifetime-value expansion, and Onifade et al. (2022) proposed conceptual metrics for monitoring transparency, maturity, and ethical alignment.

Cross-cutting integrative reviews underline the systemic nature of these fourteen domains. Paschen et al. (2019) argued that AI building blocks reinforce market-knowledge generation, whereas Chen et al. (2021) employed organisational-learning and information-processing lenses to explain adoption heterogeneity. Although technical sophistication is advancing rapidly, as witnessed by both explainability modules (Bohanec et al., 2017) and small-enterprise conversion models (Gouveia & Costa, 2022), an asymmetry persists. Mature, model-rich investigations of scoring, pipeline management, and co-creation contrast with nascent work on campaign orchestration, content generation, and real-time stakeholder-network optimisation. To connect these gaps, we will need long-term studies involving multiple participants that combine advanced methods for understanding cause and effect with ideas about management and skill-building, ensuring that the deep knowledge gained in the established areas spreads throughout the whole B2B AI-marketing field.

Complementary studies reinforce these conclusions. Khoshtaria et al. (2025) confirmed that AI-enabled personalisation improves brand awareness and account engagement, provided information-processing demands are met and organisational learning is encouraged, a point further elaborated by Chen et al. (2021). Generative models can now translate predictive insights into next-best messages: Liyang Zhao et al. (2025a, 2025b) demonstrated that coupling causal prediction with constrained optimisation and text generation enhances revenue, while Hitti and Ramadan (2025) highlighted concomitant ethical concerns surrounding transparency and bias. Research into forecasting lead behaviour has moved from Hawkes-process and regression formulations (Yan et al., 2015) to explainable pipelines tailored for industrial software vendors (Eitle & Buxmann, 2019) and to globally oriented frameworks for industrial solutions providers (Shittu, 2025).

Sales-process optimisation now integrates heterogeneous-treatment-effect estimation, mixed-integer resource assignment, and contextual bandits; Liyang Zhao et al. (2025a, 2025b) recorded parallel gains in conversion and retention, whereas Jena et al. (2023) argued that narrative explanations are essential for securing seller adoption. Multi-classifier comparisons on contemporary SaaS datasets confirm the incremental value of feature-importance isolation (Gonzalez-Flores et al., 2025). Sequential classifiers and temporal point processes still outperform heuristic forecasts once CRM-native features and explainability overlays are incorporated (Eitle & Buxmann, 2019; Yan et al., 2015).

Khvatova et al. (2024) emphasised that multi-actor, multi-stage journeys necessitate fit-for-purpose AI tools at every touchpoint and demand explicit change management strategies. Although content automation remains nascent, generative agents embedded in revenue-operations frameworks can autonomously draft proposals and sales collateral, provided orchestration layers coordinate those agents and enforce governance (Paschen et al., 2019; Ramsaran, 2025a).

Collaboration-oriented applications underscore AI's capacity to reconfigure inter-firm relationships. Fehrenbach et al. (2024) charted how actor motives, capability requirements, and process enablers combine within co-creation initiatives, while Keegan et al. (2022) traced the socio-technical contradictions that surface when AI confronts conventional marketing praxis. Autonomous, interoperable agents foster dynamic knowledge brokering across functional silos (Ramsaran, 2025b), and interdisciplinary frameworks already integrate practitioner perspectives on innovation diffusion within such ecosystems (Petrescu et al., 2022b). Critically, stakeholder engagement models align AI competence development with ethical governance, transparency, and downstream customer lifetime value growth (Bashir et al., 2024; Hitti & Ramadan, 2025).

A thorough look at the relevant studies shows a shift from individual algorithm examples to broader ideas of AI-enabled B2B marketing that include social and technical aspects, processes, and entire ecosystems. However, bringing together content automation, campaign optimisation, and stakeholder management within cohesive, theory-based frameworks is still a key focus for future research. Nonetheless, the harmonisation of content automation, campaign optimisation, and stakeholder governance within unified, theoretically grounded frameworks remains an essential agenda for future research.

10 Conclusions

This chapter has set out to synthesise the emerging evidence on how AI is reshaping B2B marketing across more than seven complementary theoretical lenses. The findings, when considered a comprehensive body of evidence, suggest that AI is now operating as a mediating artefact. This assertion suggests that AI is capable of accelerating knowledge flows, reducing decision uncertainty, and orchestrating resources in a more adroit manner than legacy systems. Recent advancements in AI have led to significant progress in the realm of business strategy, particularly in the domains of data science and machine learning. Combining AI with data insights has been proven to improve relationships and create more value, which helps build the important skills needed to gain and keep a competitive edge in the Resource-Based View and Service-Dominant Logic frameworks.

One of the results of this analysis implies that managers who align investments in AI with change management levers throughout the customer journey are better positioned to convert the potential of analytics into quantifiable gains in performance. In addition, the body of research on the diffusion of innovation demonstrates that AI-enabled analytics reduce the adoption barriers for early adopters while amplifying social contagion effects. This, in turn, results in accelerated market penetration. Therefore, it is incumbent upon policymakers and senior executives to embed ethical governance, transparency safeguards, and cross-functional orchestration mechanisms from the outset to ensure that strategic dividends are realised sustainably.

The present review is subject to several limitations. Firstly, the extant corpus remains largely cross-sectional and concept-driven. Secondly, empirical longitudinal studies and inter-industry comparisons are still scarce. Thirdly, reported adoption levels remain modest despite strong normative advocacy. It is therefore recommended that future research efforts concentrate on multi-year, multi-actor case studies while simultaneously integrating content automation, campaign optimisation, and stakeholder governance themes within unified, theoretically grounded frameworks. The execution of such work will serve two primary objectives. First, it will serve to test the generalisability of the propositions advanced in this text. Secondly, it will shed light on the socio-technical contradictions that arise when implementing AI in established marketing praxis.

It is therefore the conclusion of this comprehensive review that the present analysis provides a comprehensive conceptual framework that elucidates how, and the reasons for, AI engenders value in the field of B2B marketing. In addition, it offers a compelling programme for scholars and practitioners seeking to navigate an AI-intensive competitive landscape.

References

Abdalla, A. A., Bhat, M. A., Tiwari, C. K., Khan, S. T., & Wedajo, A. D. (2024). Exploring ChatGPT adoption among business and management students through the lens of diffusion of Innovation Theory. *Computers and Education: Artificial Intelligence, 7*. https://doi.org/10.1016/j.caeai.2024.100257

Abdelfattah, F., Salah, M., Dahleez, K., Darwazeh, R., & Al Halbusi, H. (2024). The future of competitive advantage in Oman: Integrating green product innovation, AI, and intellectual capital in business strategies. *International Journal of Innovation Studies, 8*. https://doi.org/10.1016/j.ijis.2024.02.001

Abou-Foul, M., Ruiz-Alba, J. L., & López-Tenorio, P. J. (2023). The impact of artificial intelligence capabilities on servitization: The moderating role of absorptive capacity-A dynamic capabilities perspective. *Journal of Business Research, 157*. https://doi.org/10.1016/j.jbusres.2022.113609

Agarwal, R., & Prasad, J. (1998). The antecedents and consequents of user perceptions in information technology adoption. *Decision Support Systems, 22*. https://doi.org/10.1016/S0167-9236(97)00006-7

Akter, S., Hossain, M. A., Sajib, S., Sultana, S., Rahman, M., Vrontis, D., & McCarthy, G. (2023). A framework for AI-powered service innovation capability: Review and agenda for future research. *Technovation, 125*. https://doi.org/10.1016/j.technovation.2023.102768

Alawamleh, M., Shammas, N., Alawamleh, K., & Bani Ismail, L. (2024). Examining the limitations of AI in business and the need for human insights using Interpretive Structural Modelling. *Journal of Open Innovation: Technology, Market, and Complexity, 10*. https://doi.org/10.1016/j.joitmc.2024.100338

Alnofeli, K. K., Akter, S., & Yanamandram, V. (2025). Unlocking the power of AI in CRM: A comprehensive multidimensional exploration. *Journal of Innovation & Knowledge, 10*. https://doi.org/10.1016/j.jik.2025.100731

Arroyabe, M. F., Arranz, C. F. A., Fernandez De Arroyabe, I., & Fernandez de Arroyabe, J. C. (2024). Analyzing AI adoption in European SMEs: A study of digital capabilities, innovation, and external environment. *Technology in Society, 79*. https://doi.org/10.1016/j.techsoc.2024.102733

Baabdullah, A. M., Alalwan, A. A., Slade, E. L., Raman, R., & Khatatneh, K. F. (2021). SMEs and artificial intelligence (AI): Antecedents and consequences of AI-based B2B practices. *Industrial Marketing Management, 98*. https://doi.org/10.1016/j.indmarman.2021.09.003

Baffour Gyau, E., Appiah, M., Gyamfi, B. A., Achie, T., & Naeem, M. A. (2024). Transforming banking: Examining the role of AI technology innovation in boosting banks financial performance. *International Review of Financial Analysis, 96*. https://doi.org/10.1016/j.irfa.2024.103700

Bag, S., Gupta, S., Kumar, A., & Sivarajah, U. (2021). An integrated artificial intelligence framework for knowledge creation and B2B marketing rational decision making for improving firm performance. *Industrial Marketing Management, 92*. https://doi.org/10.1016/j.indmarman.2020.12.001

Bamberger, B., Reinartz, W., & Ulaga, W. (2025). Navigating the future of B2B marketing: The transformative impact of the industrial metaverse. *Journal of Business Research, 188*. https://doi.org/10.1016/j.jbusres.2024.115057

Bashir, T., Zhongfu, T., Sadiq, B., & Naseem, A. (2024). How AI competencies can make B2B marketing smarter: Strategies to boost customer lifetime value. *Frontiers in Artificial Intelligence, 7*, 1451228. https://doi.org/10.3389/frai.2024.1451228

Benhaddou, Y., & Leray, P. (2017). Customer relationship management and small data — application of Bayesian network elicitation techniques for building a lead scoring model. In *2017 IEEE/ACS 14th International Conference on Computer Systems and Applications (AICCSA)*, 251–255–251–255. https://doi.org/10.1109/AICCSA.2017.51

Bobrova, Y., Papachristos, G., & Chiu, L. F. (2021). Homeowner low carbon retrofits: Implications for future UK policy. *Energy Policy, 155*. https://doi.org/10.1016/j.enpol.2021.112344

Bohanec, M., Robnik-Šikonja, M., & Borštnar, M. K. (2017). Organizational learning supported by machine learning models coupled with general explanation methods: A Case of B2B sales forecasting. *Organizacija, 50*(3), 217–233. https://doi.org/10.1515/orga-2017-0020

Bossink, B. (2025). Experiments and demonstrations for environmentally sustainable technological innovation: Reviewing insights and proposing a model. *Journal of Cleaner Production, 519*. https://doi.org/10.1016/j.jclepro.2025.145971

Cathala, X., & Moorley, C. (2023). Diffusion of social media in nursing education: A scoping review. *Nurse Education Today, 127*. https://doi.org/10.1016/j.nedt.2023.105846

Chatterjee, S., Chaudhuri, R., Vrontis, D., & Basile, G. (2022). Digital transformation and entrepreneurship process in SMEs of India: A moderating role of adoption of AI-CRM capability and strategic planning. *Journal of Strategy and Management, 15*(3), 416–433.

Chatterjee, S., Rana, N. P., Tamilmani, K., & Sharma, A. (2021). The effect of AI-based CRM on organization performance and competitive advantage: An empirical analysis in the B2B context. *Industrial Marketing Management, 97*. https://doi.org/10.1016/j.indmarman.2021.07.013

Chen, D., Esperança, J. P., & Wang, S. (2022). The impact of artificial intelligence on firm performance: An application of the resource-based view to e-commerce firms. *Frontiers in Psychology, 13*. https://doi.org/10.3389/fpsyg.2022.884830

Chen, L., Jiang, M., Jia, F., & Liu, G. (2021). Artificial intelligence adoption in business-to-business marketing: Toward a conceptual framework. *Journal of Business & Industrial Marketing, 37*(5), 1025–1044. https://doi.org/10.1108/jbim-09-2020-0448

Chen, Y., Du, L., Zhang, B., Wang, L., Wang, K., Huang, X., & Shi, Y. (2025). The impact of artificial intelligence on the sustainability of international trade enterprises. *International Review of Economics & Finance, 101*. https://doi.org/10.1016/j.iref.2025.104136

Cooper, R. G. (2024). The AI transformation of product innovation. *Industrial Marketing Management, 119*. https://doi.org/10.1016/j.indmarman.2024.03.008

Delios, A., Li, J., Schotter, A. P. J., & Vrontis, D. (2024). Challenging the orthodoxy in international business research: Directions for "new" research areas. *Journal of World Business, 59*. https://doi.org/10.1016/j.jwb.2024.101552

Duncan, B., & Elkan, C. (2015). Probabilistic modeling of a sales funnel to prioritize leads. In *Proceedings of the 21th ACM SIGKDD International Conference on Knowledge Discovery and Data Mining*. https://doi.org/10.1145/2783258.2788578

Egmond, C., Jonkers, R., & Kok, G. (2006). One size fits all? Policy instruments should fit the segments of target groups. *Energy Policy, 34*. https://doi.org/10.1016/j.enpol.2005.07.017

Eitle, V., & Buxmann, P. (2019). Business analytics for sales pipeline management in the software industry: A machine learning perspective. *Unknown Journal*, 1–10–11–10. https://doi.org/10.24251/HICSS.2019.125

Fehrenbach, D., Herrando, C., & Martín-De Hoyos, M. J. (2024). Co-creation with AI in B2B markets: A systematic literature review. *Sustainability, 16*(18). https://doi.org/10.3390/su16188009

Figenbaum, E., Assum, T., & Kolbenstvedt, M. (2015). Electromobility in Norway: Experiences and opportunities. *Research in Transportation Economics, 50*. https://doi.org/10.1016/j.retrec.2015.06.004

Gaczek, P., Leszczyński, G., & Mouakher, A. (2023). Collaboration with machines in B2B marketing: Overcoming managers' aversion to AI-CRM with explainability. *Industrial Marketing Management, 115*. https://doi.org/10.1016/j.indmarman.2023.09.007

Gao, T., Leichter, G., & Wei, Y. (2012). Countervailing effects of value and risk perceptions in manufacturers' adoption of expensive, discontinuous innovations. *Industrial Marketing Management, 41*. https://doi.org/10.1016/j.indmarman.2011.09.014

Garg, V., Gabaldon, J., Niranjan, S., & Hawkins, T. G. (2025). Impact of strategic performance measures on performance: The role of artificial intelligence and machine learning. *Transportation Research Part e: Logistics and Transportation Review, 198*. https://doi.org/10.1016/j.tre.2025.104073

Ghasri, M., & Vij, A. (2021). The potential impact of media commentary and social influence on consumer preferences for driverless cars. *Transportation Research Part c: Emerging Technologies, 127*. https://doi.org/10.1016/j.trc.2021.103132

Gonzalez-Flores, L., Rubiano-Moreno, J., & Sosa-Gomez, G. (2025). The relevance of lead prioritization: A B2B lead scoring model based on machine learning. *Frontiers in Artificial Intelligence, 8*, 1554325. https://doi.org/10.3389/frai.2025.1554325

Gouveia, B., & Costa, O. (2022). Industry 4.0: Predicting lead conversion opportunities with machine learning in small and medium sized enterprises. *Procedia Computer Science, 204*, 54–64. https://doi.org/10.1016/j.procs.2022.08.007

Grewal, D., Guha, A., Satornino, C. B., & Schweiger, E. B. (2021). Artificial intelligence: The light and the darkness. *Journal of Business Research, 136*. https://doi.org/10.1016/j.jbusres.2021.07.043

Gupta, S., Leszkiewicz, A., Kumar, V., Bijmolt, T., & Potapov, D. (2020). Digital analytics: Modeling for insights and new methods. *Journal of Interactive Marketing, 51*. https://doi.org/10.1016/j.intmar.2020.04.003

Han, R., Lam, H. K. S., Zhan, Y., Wang, Y., Dwivedi, Y. K., & Tan, K. H. (2021). Artificial intelligence in business-to-business marketing: A bibliometric analysis of current research status, development and future directions. *Industrial Management & Data Systems, 121*(12), 2467–2497. https://doi.org/10.1108/imds-05-2021-0300

Han, W., Zhu, W., Song, Z., & Lu, R. (2025). Innovative resources driven artificial intelligence orientation: The moderating role of environmental and executives' characteristics. *Technology in Society, 81*. https://doi.org/10.1016/j.techsoc.2025.102837

Hautamäki, P., & Heikinheimo, M. (2025). Fully leveraging AI in B2B sales: Exploring sales managers' capabilities and organizational knowledge processes. *Journal of Business Research, 194*. https://doi.org/10.1016/j.jbusres.2025.115396

Havas, A., Schartinger, D., & Weber, K. M. (2023). Innovation studies, social innovation, and sustainability transitions research: From mutual ignorance towards an integrative perspective? *Environmental Innovation and Societal Transitions, 48*. https://doi.org/10.1016/j.eist.2023.100754

Hitti, S., & Ramadan, A. (2025). Balancing innovation and ethics: the role of artificial intelligence in transforming B2B customer experience. *Competitiveness Review: An International Business Journal*, 35(4), 772–793. https://doi.org/10.1108/cr-03-2025-0104

Hossain, M. A., Agnihotri, R., Rushan, M. R. I., Rahman, M. S., & Sumi, S. F. (2022). Marketing analytics capability, artificial intelligence adoption, and firms' competitive advantage: Evidence from the manufacturing industry. *Industrial Marketing Management, 106*. https://doi.org/10.1016/j.indmarman.2022.08.017

Jena, S., Jilei, Y., & Fangfang, T. (2023). Unlocking sales growth: Account prioritization engine with explainable AI. *ArXiv, abs/2306.07464*. https://doi.org/10.48550/arXiv.2306.07464

Jia, Y., & Wang, Z. (2024). Application of artificial intelligence based on the fuzzy control algorithm in enterprise innovation. *Heliyon, 10*. https://doi.org/10.1016/j.heliyon.2024.e28116

Kanungo, R. P. (2021). Payment choice of M&As: Financial crisis and social innovation. *Industrial Marketing Management, 97*. https://doi.org/10.1016/j.indmarman.2021.06.012

Kassa, B. Y., & Worku, E. K. (2025). The impact of artificial intelligence on organizational performance: The mediating role of employee productivity. *Journal of Open Innovation: Technology, Market, and Complexity, 11*. https://doi.org/10.1016/j.joitmc.2025.100474

Keegan, B. J., Canhoto, A. I., & Yen, D.A.-W. (2022). Power negotiation on the tango dancefloor: The adoption of AI in B2B marketing. *Industrial Marketing Management, 100*. https://doi.org/10.1016/j.indmarman.2021.11.001

Keshavarz-Ghorbani, F., & Reza Pasandideh, S. H. (2022). Incorporating a choice-based diffusion model into a bi-objective multi-generation product optimization problem under consignment stock policy. *Journal of Cleaner Production, 381*. https://doi.org/10.1016/j.jclepro.2022.135175

Khan, A. N., & Khan, N. A. (2025). Belief triggers to action in artificial intelligence arenas: Exploring the role of AI intention and top management support in multi-level investigation. *European Research on Management and Business Economics, 31*. https://doi.org/10.1016/j.iedeen.2025.100285

Khoshtaria, T., Matin, A., Abrakhamia, G., & Khuskivadze, M. (2025). Investigating the impact of AI-powered personalization on brand awareness in B2B E-commerce. *FIIB Business Review*. https://doi.org/10.1177/23197145241306831

Khvatova, T., Appio, F. P., Ray, S., & Schiavone, F. (2024). Exploring the role of AI in B2B customer journey management: Towards an IPO model. *IEEE Transactions on Engineering Management, 71*, 13852–13866. https://doi.org/10.1109/tem.2023.3284532

Kushwaha, A. K., Kumar, P., & Kar, A. K. (2021). What impacts customer experience for B2B enterprises on using AI-enabled chatbots? Insights from Big data analytics. *Industrial Marketing Management, 98*. https://doi.org/10.1016/j.indmarman.2021.08.011

Lada, S., Chekima, B., Karim, M. R. A., Fabeil, N. F., Ayub, M. S., Amirul, S. M., Ansar, R., Bouteraa, M., Fook, L. M., & Zaki, H. O. (2023). Determining factors related to artificial intelligence (AI) adoption among Malaysia's small and medium-sized businesses. *Journal of Open Innovation: Technology, Market, and Complexity, 9*. https://doi.org/10.1016/j.joitmc.2023.100144

Li, S., Peng, G., Xing, F., Zhang, J., & Zhang, B. (2021). Value co-creation in industrial AI: The interactive role of B2B supplier, customer and technology provider. *Industrial Marketing Management, 98*. https://doi.org/10.1016/j.indmarman.2021.07.015

Lin, J., Zeng, Y., Wu, S., & Luo, X. (2024). How does artificial intelligence affect the environmental performance of organizations? The role of green innovation and green culture. *Information & Management, 61*. https://doi.org/10.1016/j.im.2024.103924

Liu, D., & Son, S. (2024). Exploring the impact mechanism of collaborative robot on manufacturing firm performance: A dynamic capability perspective. *Sustainable Futures, 8*. https://doi.org/10.1016/j.sftr.2024.100262

Liu, Y. D., Zhang, J. Z., Zheng, J., & Kamal, M. M. (2025). Artificial intelligence-enabled systems and innovation in B2B firms: The role of strategic agility and decision-making performance. *Industrial Marketing Management, 127*. https://doi.org/10.1016/j.indmarman.2025.04.003

Magsamen-Conrad, K., & Dillon, J. M. (2020). Mobile technology adoption across the lifespan: A mixed methods investigation to clarify adoption stages, and the influence of diffusion attributes. *Computers in Human Behavior, 112*. https://doi.org/10.1016/j.chb.2020.106456

Mahajan, V. (1993). Chapter 8 New-product diffusion models. *Handbooks in Operations Research and Management Science, 5*. https://doi.org/10.1016/S0927-0507(05)80031-3

Mahdiraji, H. A., Sharifpour Arabi, H., & Vrontis, D. (2023). Marketing 4.0 analytics in the B2B sector: A state-of-the-art review and integrated framework. *Journal of Strategic Marketing, 32*(8), 965–986. https://doi.org/10.1080/0965254x.2023.2273501

Mikalef, P., Conboy, K., & Krogstie, J. (2021). Artificial intelligence as an enabler of B2B marketing: A dynamic capabilities micro-foundations approach. *Industrial Marketing Management, 98*. https://doi.org/10.1016/j.indmarman.2021.08.003

Mikalef, P., Islam, N., Parida, V., Singh, H., & Altwaijry, N. (2023). Artificial intelligence (AI) competencies for organizational performance: A B2B marketing capabilities perspective. *Journal of Business Research, 164*. https://doi.org/10.1016/j.jbusres.2023.113998

Mikhail, M., Pandya, A., Webster, Q., & Evins, R. (2025). Transparent communication for residential heating decarbonization: A content analysis of heat pump marketing in Canada. *Energy Research & Social Science, 124*. https://doi.org/10.1016/j.erss.2025.104066

Moradi, M., & Dass, M. (2022). Applications of artificial intelligence in B2B marketing: Challenges and future directions. *Industrial Marketing Management, 107*. https://doi.org/10.1016/j.indmarman.2022.10.016

Mubarik, M., Maciukaite-Zviniene, S., Mubarak, M. F., Ghobakhloo, M., & Pilkova, A. (2025). Strategic and organisational factors for advancing knowledge in intelligent automation. *Journal of Innovation & Knowledge, 10*. https://doi.org/10.1016/j.jik.2025.100675

Onifade, A. Y., Ogeawuchi, J. C., Abayomi, A. A., Agboola, O. A., Dosumu, R. E., & George, O. O. (2022). A conceptual framework for integrating AI adoption metrics into B2B marketing decision systems. *International Journal of Management and Organizational Research, 1*(1), 237–248. https://doi.org/10.54660/ijmor.2022.1.1.237-248

Pandiya, D. K. (2020). Optimizing sales funnels and enhancing B2B conversion rates with advanced predictive models and sales technology. *Turkish Journal of Computer and Mathematics Education (TURCOMAT), 11*(3). https://doi.org/10.61841/turcomat.v11i3.14792

Papagiannidis, E., Mikalef, P., Conboy, K., & Van de Wetering, R. (2023). Uncovering the dark side of AI-based decision-making: A case study in a B2B context. *Industrial Marketing Management, 115*. https://doi.org/10.1016/j.indmarman.2023.10.003

Pardo, C., Wei, R., & Ivens, B. S. (2022). Integrating the business networks and internet of things perspectives: A system of systems (SoS) approach for industrial markets. *Industrial Marketing Management, 104*, 258–275.

Paschen, J., Kietzmann, J., & Kietzmann, T. C. (2019). Artificial intelligence (AI) and its implications for market knowledge in B2B marketing. *Journal of Business & Industrial Marketing, 34*(7), 1410–1419. https://doi.org/10.1108/jbim-10-2018-0295

Patnaik, P., & Bakkar, M. (2024). Exploring determinants influencing artificial intelligence adoption, reference to diffusion of innovation theory. *Technology in Society, 79*. https://doi.org/10.1016/j.techsoc.2024.102750

Pereira-Moliner, J., Villar-García, M., Molina-Azorín, J. F., Tarí, J. J., López-Gamero, M. D., & Pertusa-Ortega, E. M. (2024). Using tourism intelligence and big data to explain flight searches for tourist destinations: The case of the Costa Blanca (Spain). *Tourism Management Perspectives, 51*. https://doi.org/10.1016/j.tmp.2024.101243

Petrescu, M., Krishen, A. S., Kachen, S., & Gironda, J. T. (2022a). AI-based innovation in B2B marketing: An interdisciplinary framework incorporating academic and practitioner perspectives. *Industrial Marketing Management, 103*. https://doi.org/10.1016/j.indmarman.2022.03.001

Petrescu, M., Krishen, A. S., Kachen, S., & Gironda, J. T. (2022b). AI-based innovation in B2B marketing: An interdisciplinary framework incorporating academic and practitioner perspectives. *Industrial Marketing Management, 103*, 61–72. https://doi.org/10.1016/j.indmarman.2022.03.001

Pothukuchi, A. (2025). Leveraging AI to transform the salesforce sales process: A technical overview. *International Journal of Scientific Research in Computer Science, Engineering and Information Technology, 11*(1), 2134–2141. https://doi.org/10.32628/cseit251112213

Prior, D. D., & Keränen, J. (2020). Revisiting contemporary issues in B2B marketing: It's not just about artificial intelligence. *Australasian Marketing Journal (AMJ), 28*. https://doi.org/10.1016/j.ausmj.2019.09.001

Prior, D. D., & Marcos-Cuevas, J. (2025). Transitioning to artificial intelligence-based key account management: A critical assessment. *Industrial Marketing Management, 126*. https://doi.org/10.1016/j.indmarman.2025.02.009

Rahman, M. S., Bag, S., Gupta, S., & Sivarajah, U. (2023). Technology readiness of B2B firms and AI-based customer relationship management capability for enhancing social sustainability performance. *Journal of Business Research, 156*. https://doi.org/10.1016/j.jbusres.2022.113525

Ramsaran, J. (2025a). Architecting lead-to-cash automation: The role of artificial intelligence in redefining B2B revenue systems. *European Journal of Computer Science and Information Technology, 13*(39), 163–186. https://doi.org/10.37745/ejcsit.2013/vol13n39163185

Ramsaran, J. (2025b). Multi-agent systems for autonomous revenue operations: Architectural advancements and future directions. *World Journal of Advanced Engineering Technology and Sciences, 15*(3), 557–571. https://doi.org/10.30574/wjaets.2025.15.3.0927

Rashid, A. B., & Kausik, M. D. A. K. (2024). AI revolutionizing industries worldwide: A comprehensive overview of its diverse applications. *Hybrid Advances, 7*. https://doi.org/10.1016/j.hybadv.2024.100277

Rezazadeh, A. (2020). A generalized flow for B2B sales predictive modeling: An Azure machine-learning approach. *Forecasting, 2*(3), 267–283. https://doi.org/10.3390/forecast2030015

Robertson, J., Botha, E., Oosthuizen, K., & Montecchi, M. (2025). Managing change when integrating artificial intelligence (AI) into the retail value chain: The AI implementation compass. *Journal of Business Research, 189*. https://doi.org/10.1016/j.jbusres.2025.115198

Sahoo, S., Kumar, S., Donthu, N., & Singh, A. K. (2024). Artificial intelligence capabilities, open innovation, and business performance – Empirical insights from multinational B2B companies. *Industrial Marketing Management, 117*. https://doi.org/10.1016/j.indmarman.2023.12.008

Samadhiya, A., Kumar, A., Yadav, S., Luthra, S., Jabbour, C. J. C., & Agrawal, R. (2023). Artificial intelligence - partner relationships management for climate management in B2B firms to achieve sustainable competitiveness. *Industrial Marketing Management, 115*. https://doi.org/10.1016/j.indmarman.2023.11.002

Shankar, R., & Gupta, L. (2024). An integrated AI framework for managing organizational risk and climate change concerns in B2B market. *Industrial Marketing Management, 117*. https://doi.org/10.1016/j.indmarman.2023.12.019

Sheldon, T. L., & Dua, R. (2024). The dynamic role of subsidies in promoting global electric vehicle sales. *Transportation Research Part a: Policy and Practice, 187*. https://doi.org/10.1016/j.tra.2024.104173

Shen, Y., Bai, Y., & Zhang, F. (2025). Industrial Robots application and corporate competitiveness: Evidence from China's A-share market. *Economic Analysis and Policy, 87*. https://doi.org/10.1016/j.eap.2025.05.061

Shih, H.-Y. (2012). The dynamics of local and interactive effects on innovation adoption: The case of electronic commerce. *Journal of Engineering and Technology Management, 29*. https://doi.org/10.1016/j.jengtecman.2012.06.001

Shittu, A. K. (2025). Optimizing sales operations in industrial solutions: A data-driven approach for global markets. *International Journal of Management and Organizational Research, 4*(1), 101–117. https://doi.org/10.54660/ijmor.2025.4.1.101-117

Singh, K., Chatterjee, S., & Mariani, M. (2024). Applications of generative AI and future organizational performance: The mediating role of explorative and exploitative innovation and the moderating role of ethical dilemmas and environmental dynamism. *Technovation, 133*. https://doi.org/10.1016/j.technovation.2024.103021

Skare, M., Gavurova, B., & Rigelsky, M. (2023). Innovation activity and the outcomes of B2C, B2B, and B2G E-Commerce in EU countries. *Journal of Business Research, 163*. https://doi.org/10.1016/j.jbusres.2023.113874

Solaz, F. C., Moya, V. S., & Navarrete, S. R. (2025). The digital divide in social entrepreneurship: A bibliometric analysis. *Sustainable Technology and Entrepreneurship, 4*. https://doi.org/10.1016/j.stae.2024.100095

Spreitzenbarth, J. M., Bode, C., & Stuckenschmidt, H. (2024). Designing an AI purchasing requisition bundling generator. *Computers in Industry, 155*. https://doi.org/10.1016/j.compind.2023.104043

Stone, M., & Woodcock, N. (2021). Developments in B to B and B to C marketing and sales automation systems. *Journal of Business-to-Business Marketing, 28*(2), 203–222. https://doi.org/10.1080/1051712x.2021.1920702

Sun, L. (2025). The impact of business model innovation and dynamic capabilities on enterprise development: An international business communication perspective. *Finance Research Letters, 80*. https://doi.org/10.1016/j.frl.2025.107346

Wang, X., Wei, R., Liu, Y., Xia, H., & Zhao, Y. (2023). The effects of relational knowledge emphasis on new product development strategy. *Industrial Marketing Management, 109*. https://doi.org/10.1016/j.indmarman.2023.02.005

Wei, J., & Shen, Y. (2025). Impact and mechanism of digital transformation on performance in manufacturing firms. *Innovation and Green Development, 4*. https://doi.org/10.1016/j.igd.2025.100205

Wu, M., Andreev, P., & Benyoucef, M. (2023). The state of lead scoring models and their impact on sales performance. *Information Technology and Management*, 1–30. https://doi.org/10.1007/s10799-023-00388-w

Xia, Y., Xie, L., Chen, X., & Lin, Z. (2025). Artificial intelligence and corporate fraud: Evidence from China. *Economic Analysis and Policy, 86*. https://doi.org/10.1016/j.eap.2025.04.030

Yadav, S. K., Singh, S., Vijay, T. S., & Singh, S. (2025). Strategic roadmapping for the future of retail healthcare. *Journal of Retailing and Consumer Services, 87*. https://doi.org/10.1016/j.jretconser.2025.104351

Yan, J., Zhang, C., Zha, H., Gong, M., Sun, C., Huang, J., Chu, S., & Yang, X. (2015). On machine learning towards predictive sales pipeline analytics. *Proceedings of the AAAI Conference on Artificial Intelligence, 29*(1), 1945–1951–1945–1951. https://doi.org/10.1609/aaai.v29i1.9455

Yan, T., Zijiang, Y., & Benslimane, Y. (2011). Towards an optimal classification model against imbalanced data for Customer Relationship Management. *2011 Seventh International Conference on Natural Computation, 4*, 2401–2405–2401–2405. https://doi.org/10.1109/ICNC.2011.6022593

Yousefi-Nooraie, R., Dobbins, M., Brouwers, M., & Wakefield, P. (2012). Information seeking for making evidence-informed decisions: A social network analysis on the staff of a public health department in Canada. *BMC Health Services Research, 12*. https://doi.org/10.1186/1472-6963-12-118

Yücel, G., & van Daalen, C. E. (2011). Exploratory analysis of the impact of information dynamics on innovation diffusion. *Technological Forecasting and Social Change, 78*. https://doi.org/10.1016/j.techfore.2010.11.004

Zahid, E., Ong, Y. J., Megahed, A., & Nakamura, T. (2021). Predicting loss risks for B2B tendering processes. *2021 IEEE International Conference on Big Data (Big Data)*, 2076–2083–2076–2083. https://doi.org/10.1109/BigData52589.2021.9671710

Zhan, Y., Xiong, Y., Han, R., Lam, H. K. S., & Blome, C. (2024). The impact of artificial intelligence adoption for business-to-business marketing on shareholder reaction: A social actor perspective. *International Journal of Information Management, 76*. https://doi.org/10.1016/j.ijinfomgt.2024.102768

Zhao, L., Seton, O., Reddivari, H. R., Jena, S., Zhao, S., Kumar, R., & Wei, C. (2025). Causal predictive optimization and generation for business AI. *ArXiv, abs/2505.09847*. https://doi.org/10.48550/arXiv.2505.09847

Zhao, L., Xu, J., Zhang, B., & Lu, J. (2025b). Leveraging AI to enhance firms' resource efficiency: Ecological modernization theory and resource-based view perspectives. *International Journal of Production Economics*. https://doi.org/10.1016/j.ijpe.2025.109723

[illegible]

Emotional and Social Listening with Artificial Intelligence

Luciana Oliveira, Xabier Martínez-Rolán, Joana Milhazes-Cunha, and William Ferreira

Abstract Artificial Intelligence (AI) has become the engine of digital marketing, transforming social and emotional listening by moving beyond static sentiment dictionaries to adaptive, multimodal analysis. We review the theoretical roots of affective computing, enabling technologies, and the practical applications of social listening frameworks that monitor brand mentions, segment audiences, predict trends, and optimise campaigns in real time. The chapter then explores emotional listening, integrating text, image, audio, and physiological signals to detect nuanced affective states. Ethical, privacy, and governance dimensions are critically assessed with reference to the EU AI Act and recent scholarly debates, outlining strategies to mitigate bias, ensure consent, and uphold user autonomy. To navigate these challenges, we present governance frameworks and a five-pillar risk framework, which includes fairness, privacy, manipulation, transparency, and governance. Finally, we highlight future directions, such as intercultural validation, privacy-preserving methods, and causal impact analysis, arguing that emotion-aware AI, supported by robust ethics, will drive sustainable competitive advantage in an increasingly emotion-driven marketplace.

L. Oliveira (✉) · J. Milhazes-Cunha
CEOS.PP, ISCAP, Polytechnic of Porto, Porto, Portugal
e-mail: lgo@iscap.ipp.pt

J. Milhazes-Cunha
e-mail: jmc@iscap.ipp.pt

X. Martínez-Rolán
SEPCOM, University of Vigo, Pontevedra, Spain
e-mail: xabier.rolan@uvigo.gal

W. Ferreira
FEUP, University of Porto, Porto, Portugal
e-mail: william.ferreira@elife.com.br

J. D. Santos et al. (eds.), *Artificial Intelligence Transforming Marketing*, Contributions to Management Science, https://doi.org/10.1007/978-3-032-22360-9_16

1 Introduction

Artificial Intelligence (AI) now underpins digital marketing, particularly in social and emotional listening. AI is transforming how brands collect and act on consumer feedback in real time (van Esch & Stewart Black, 2021). In an attention-scarce environment, not adopting AI risks slow crisis response, missed engagement, and weaker emotional connections. Traditional social listening, based on tracking mentions, measuring conversation volume, and using static sentiment dictionaries, provides useful data but falls short in capturing the nuance of online speech. For instance, lexicon-based methods, such as those built on the National Research Council Canada Emotion Lexicon (NRC EmoLex), cannot keep pace with rapidly changing slang, memes, or sarcasm (Mohammad & Turney, 2013). By contrast, AI models learn from fresh data, distinguishing irony from praise and subtle mood shifts.

Emotional listening merges text, image, voice, and physiological signals to reveal which emotions are felt, their intensity, and duration. Affective computing, first defined by Picard (1997), laid the foundations for machines that can respond to human feelings, and more recent work in multimodal fusion shows that combining text, facial cues, and tone yields much richer insights than a single channel alone (Gladys & Vetriselvi, 2023). For emotion categories, most systems still rely on Ekman's six basic emotions (Ekman, 1992) and Plutchik's wheel (Plutchik, 1979), but advances in models like EmoBERTa and datasets such as GoEmotions have expanded detection to dozens of refined emotional states.

Yet with great power comes great responsibility. The rapid rise of AI-driven listening raises serious concerns about privacy, bias, and manipulation. The EU AI Act underscores transparency, consent, and fairness in emotional data (European Parliament & Council, 2024), and recent studies also call for clear governance and sustained multidisciplinary debate to keep systems aligned with human values (Coeckelbergh, 2025a; Danilevskyi et al., 2025).

Organisations that invest in both technological sophistication and ethical oversight will not only understand their customers more deeply but also build stronger and more lasting relationships in an increasingly emotion-driven marketplace. Thus, in this chapter, we explore what AI tools can achieve, and the safeguards required to use them responsibly. We argue that AI-enabled social listening matures into emotional listening when multimodal models are paired with responsible governance, delivering better decisions today and a roadmap for ethical adoption tomorrow.

2 AI-Powered Social Listening

Social Media Analytics (SMA) is an interdisciplinary field devoted to the development, adaptation, and extension of digital tools, frameworks, and methods to track, collect, and analyse large volumes of social media data (structured, semi-structured, and unstructured) to extract patterns and useful information (Zachlod et al., 2022).

It is employed to monitor communities, understand group behaviour and opinion dynamics, as well as to analyse collective sentiments and/or emotions and to make predictions (Belcastro et al., 2017; Crisci et al., 2018; Liere-Netheler et al., 2019). Although the terms sometimes appear interchangeably in the literature, we distinguish them as follows: in this chapter, SMA refers to the set of methods, metrics, and models for analysing social data, while Social Listening (SL) refers to the operational procedure that consumes these outputs.

Social Listening (SL), sometimes referred to as Social Media Listening, can be defined as a strategic process that involves the continuous monitoring of websites and social media platforms to understand buzz about brands, companies, products or other relevant topics (Chumwatana & Chuaychoo, 2017), thereby enabling the extraction of valuable insights from online social interactions (Ducange et al., 2019). A central aspect in SL is identifying where conversations occur, who is participating, and what they are discussing (Micera & Crispino, 2017).

Procedures associated with SL also involve analysing conversation volume and measuring sentiment and/or emotions expressed (positive, negative, or neutral) (Widmar et al., 2020). It entails active attention, interpretation, and response to stimuli from different channels: digital, electronic, and social (Pomputius, 2019). SL improves consumer understanding and is widely used to track reviews and emerging trends. Organisations now use SL as a strategic tool to collect data on public perception and to guide marketing, communications, and product-development decisions based on the authentic voice of consumers (Reid & Duffy, 2018).

Over the last decade, greater integration of AI into digital marketing tools has transformed how organisations operate, streamlining processes, enabling data-driven decision-making, and improving customer experience. Kaplan and Haenlein (2019, p. 1) define AI as the "ability to correctly interpret external data, to learn from such data, and to use those learnings to achieve specific goals and tasks through flexible adaptation", a definition with clear potential for digital marketing as SMA platforms incorporate AI capabilities. In marketing, Xu et al. (2020) similarly defined AI as "a technology-enabled system for evaluating real-time service scenarios using data collected from digital and/or physical sources to provide personalised recommendations, alternatives, and solutions to customers' enquiries or problems, even very complex ones" (p. 1). AI-augmented SMA enables quantitative, qualitative, and contextual analysis of large-scale conversations, converting them into marketing intelligence.

Recent literature indicates that AI-powered social listening enhances consumer understanding and insight extraction, strengthens brand monitoring and risk management, and supports campaign optimisation and strategic decision-making. In Fig. 1, we summarise the most common functions and their key benefits, which we further explore in subsequent sections.

The three primary categories of Social Media Analytics functions that support SL, summarised in Fig. 1, are detailed in Sects. 2.2–2.4, after an overview of the enabling AI technologies in Sect. 2.1.

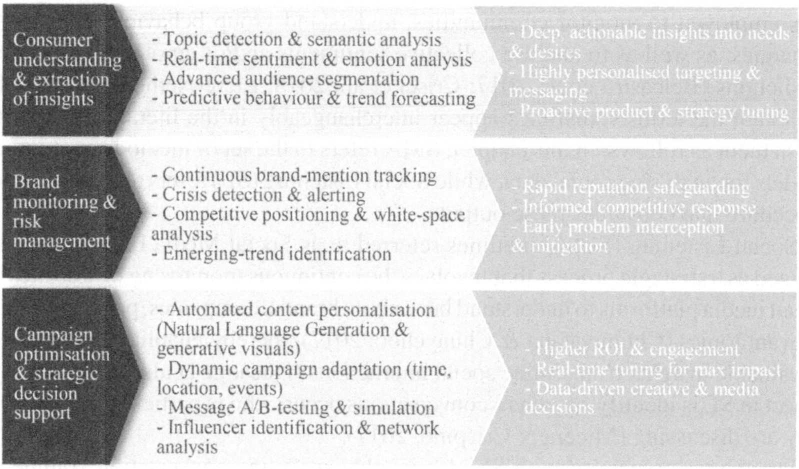

Fig. 1 AI-driven Social Media Analytics functions that support Social Listening and their key benefits. *Source* Authors

2.1 AI Technologies Supporting Social Listening Functions

As shown in Fig. 1, a broad and expanding spectrum of marketing activities is covered, each providing distinct value to how companies interact, understand, and respond to consumers.

These functions are supported by a wide range of technologies that vary in complexity and output. Foundationally, traditional machine learning models are widely applied, such as logistic regression (ideal for binary classification tasks, like identifying posts as positive or negative), Random Forests (effective for high-dimensional or heterogeneous data), and Support Vector Machines (SVMs), commonly used to distinguish between sentiments, topics, and emotions. Building on this, more advanced deep learning has been widely adopted in the past decade, including Long Short-Term Memory (LSTM) networks, used for time-series forecasting and capturing sentiment variation over time, and Deep Neural Networks (DNNs), which are capable of modelling complex patterns in large-scale unstructured data. More recently, structural deep learning models, such as Graph Neural Networks (GNNs), have been applied to social media analysis, enabling the exploration of network structures, community formation, and influential user dynamics (Navarro, 2024).

Kumar et al. (2025, p. 316) present a very comprehensive mapping of business enabled by Generative AI based on different types of models: Large Language Models (LLMs), for Natural Language Processing (NLP) (text generation, translation, and question answering); Large Vision Models (LVMs) for image recognition and object detection; Generative Adversarial Networks (GANs) for image generation, video creation, and synthesis; and Convolutional Neural Networks (CNNs) for image and video recognition, and object detection.

For instance, in the domain of natural language, AI technologies are increasingly employed to identify what people are talking about and how they feel. Transformer-based models, such as BERT, RoBERTa, and DeBERTa, originally developed for general language tasks, show excellent performance in emotion detection in texts, surpassing previous solutions like SentiMoji (Demszky et al., 2020; Gladys & Vetriselvi, 2023; Kim & Vossen, 2021). Simultaneously, tools like TopicGPT leverage the generative power of models such as GPT-4 to extract interpretable topics from large volumes of text using simple prompts, without the need for retraining. These approaches significantly expand AI-powered SL capabilities, enabling more accurate and scalable automatic analyses (Pham et al., 2023).

For sentiment classification on social media, transformer-based models consistently outperform traditional machine learning models, achieving up to 17% higher F1-score on sentiment classification tasks on social media datasets, owing to superior handling of context, emotional nuance, and linguistic ambiguity (Pham et al., 2023). In addition, Assiri et al. (2024) proposed a hybrid DeBERTa + GRU model for sentiment analysis on Twitter and achieved 96.9% accuracy, significantly outperforming models based on SVM, Naive Bayes, and XGBoost baselines.

Given the richness of social media data, emotion detection has progressively evolved from unimodal to multimodal approaches, encompassing text, image, audio, video, and even physiological signals. Initial efforts in this field were based on traditional tools such as OpenSMILE for acoustic analysis (Eyben et al., 2013) and OpenFace for facial expression recognition using convolutional neural networks (Baltrušaitis et al., 2016), which have been widely applied in audiovisual content analysis and continuously updated. More recently, OpenFace 3.0 was released in 2025 (Hu et al., 2025), integrating facial landmark detection, action units, gaze estimation, and explicit emotion recognition into a single lightweight model, improving precision and enabling real-time processing even on edge devices with low video resolution. In parallel, the development of Transformer-based models has advanced emotion recognition in text and multimodal contexts. Notable examples include EmoBERTa, a RoBERTa-based model designed for emotion detection in dialogues with speaker-awareness (Kim & Vossen, 2021), and MEmoBERT, which processes textual, visual, and auditory data to detect emotions in video content (Zhao et al., 2022). These models reflect the increasing integration of deep learning architectures for rich and context-aware emotional analysis across multiple media formats (see Sect. 3 for multimodal emotion recognition and fusion mechanisms).

For topic detection, a technique in NLP that identifies the main subject in large sets of documents, researchers previously employed methodologies such as Latent Dirichlet Allocation (LDA) to identify related words that frequently appear together statistically. Since late 2023, TopicGPT has leveraged LLMs and prompt-based strategies, which have been more efficient in interpreting semantic topic labels, marking a significant advance in the field. In research by Pham et al. (2023), aiming to identify the technology most consistent with human-labelled topics, TopicGPT misaligned 30.3% versus 62.4% for LDA.

However, AI technologies not only enable understanding and insight generation from existing content but also support the creation of new, contextually relevant content. The most recent Natural Language Generation (NLG) technologies, including GPT-4, FLAN-T5, and Claude, allow users to generate fluent text content that is coherent and context-sensitive and that can be created with instructions (prompts) or structured data (Chung et al., 2024; Fu et al., 2024; Yekta, 2024), supporting the creation of automated responses, marketing texts, summarised reports, and real-time personalised interactions. Simultaneously, generative visual models, such as DALL-E 3, Midjourney v6, and Stable Diffusion XL, enable the creation of high-quality images and creative visual assets from textual instructions (prompts). Although the first advances in this domain have been fostered by GAN-based models, such as StyleGAN and CycleGAN, more recent systems increasingly rely on diffusion-based architectures, which provide better visual fidelity, stronger semantic alignment, and greater creative control over the generated outputs (Ho et al., 2020; Nichol & Dhariwal, 2021; Ramesh et al., 2022; Saharia et al., 2022). This capability is highly relevant to digital marketing strategies that incorporate emotional storytelling or personalised content delivery, enabling dynamic ads and the creation of emotion-driven visual narratives (Fong & See, 2024; Ramesh et al., 2022; Saharia et al., 2022).

Beyond content analysis and creation, AI technologies also assist in understanding how information and content flow in networks. This covers community detection (PageRank, centrality measures, and theme clustering), and analysis of social graphs, essential tools to discover connections and influence patterns on social media, identifying opinion leaders, segmenting users by interests, and tracking how information spreads in digital spaces. In this domain, classic methods and Graph Neural Networks (GNNs), which learn representations of networks of content and/or people, have been augmented by specialised GNN variants, such as Graph Convolutional Networks (GCNs), Graph Attention Networks (GAT), and GraphSAGE, all of which have proven to be highly effective in community detection, sentiment analysis and recommendations in sparse and dynamic networks (Wu et al., 2021; Ye et al., 2022; Zhou et al., 2020).

The three primary categories of functions summarised in Table 1 are detailed in the following sections.

2.2 *Consumer Understanding and Extraction of Insights*

This is where AI-powered social listening excels: gathering the raw voice of consumers across platforms and transforming it into practical insights with strategic value.

Social listening is, therefore, extremely valuable because it captures the authenticity and spontaneity of consumer voices. Brands can capture, process, and interpret these voices from a variety of sources—social media posts and comments, opinions

Table 1 Risks, examples, and mitigation strategies

Risk category	Specific risk	Practical example	Mitigation strategy
Fairness & Cultural Validity	Algorithmic bias in emotional recognition[a]	System interpreting culturally specific expressions as negative: *A retailer's social listening flags "I'm dead" as negative in Gen-Z posts, when slang actually means "that's hilarious"*	Training with multicultural datasets and cross-cultural validation
	Exclusion of linguistic minorities[b]	AI only processing emotions in dominant languages: *The model misses sarcasm and mood shifts in Arabic-dialect tweets, so brand risk in MENA goes unseen*	Multilingual development from initial design
	Imposition of dominant cultural norms[c]	Systems assuming universal emotional expressions: *A closed-mouth smile is tagged "unfriendly" ignoring cultures where that expression signals respect*	Continuous consultation with diverse communities
Privacy & Biometric Data	Unconsented emotional profiling[d]	Apps analysing mood without clear disclosure: *A call-centre "mood detector" records and stores raw customer audio and emotions without consent*	Granular consent and opt-out options
	Secondary use of biometric data[e]	Emotional analysis data sold to third parties: *Facial-affect clips collected for "quality assurance" are later sold to a data broker*	Strict no-sharing policies for sensitive data
	Vulnerability of intimate data[f]	Leaked personal emotional profiles: *A leak exposes users' voice tone scores and stress indices from wearable-linked companies*	End-to-end encryption and data minimisation
Manipulative Persuasion	Exploitation of emotional vulnerability[g]	Targeted advertising during detected depressive states: *Ads auto-boost when sadness spikes, pushing limited-time offers during low mood*	Policies prohibiting targeting during vulnerable states
	Creation of emotional dependency[h]	Chatbots fostering excessive emotional bonds: *A brand chatbot shifts to "always-on empathy", nudging nightly check-ins that users rely on emotionally*	Clear limits on interactions and artificiality reminders
	Emotional dark patterns[i]	Interfaces exploiting emotional states for decisions: *Checkout copy escalates urgency after detecting frustration in voice, steering users to pricier bundles*	Regular ethical design audits

(continued)

Table 1 (continued)

Risk category	Specific risk	Practical example	Mitigation strategy
Transparency & Explainability	Inexplicable algorithmic decisions[j]	System rejecting candidates for unexplained "emotional indicators": *A creator is flagged "toxic/angry" with no rationale, freezing a launch campaign*	Development of intuitive explanations for complex decisions
	Inability to contest decisions[k]	Users without mechanisms to dispute emotional analyses: *Influencers can't see or challenge their "risk score", so takedowns go unreviewed*	Appeal systems with human review
	Technical complexity as barrier[l]	Explanations filled with inaccessible jargon: *The tool explains results with tech jargon ("embeddings", "AU12") so teams can't see which exact words, tone, or facial cues triggered the emotion label*	User-level adapted explanation interfaces
Governance & Standards	Regulatory fragmentation[m]	Different standards across countries for emotional data: *An EU campaign pauses because local rules bar affective targeting allowed in the U.S*	Development of coordinated international frameworks
	Normative gaps[n]	Absence of specific regulation for emotional AI: *Multimodal listening is used to tailor ads by anxiety level; no company policy defines permissible inferences*	Industry self-regulation codes while legislation develops
	Lack of interdisciplinary expertise[o]	Technical regulations without psychological/cultural understanding: *A compliance review approves biosignal capture without clinical input on stress measurement limits*	Multidisciplinary advisory committees

Source Authors
Note [a]Huang et al. (2023); Ramaswamy and Palaniswamy (2024).[b]César et al. (2024); Huang et al. (2023).[c]Ashok et al. (2022); Huang et al. (2023).[d]Brendel et al. (2021); European Parliament & Council (2024); Mehra (2025).[e]Brendel et al. (2021); Oladosu et al. (2023).[f]Brendel et al. (2021).[g]Ashok et al. (2022); European Parliament & Council (2024); Swamy et al. (2025).[h]Gunkel (2018).[i]Coeckelbergh (2025b); Wen et al. (2024)[j]Danilevskyi et al. (2025); Huang et al. (2023).[k]Coeckelbergh (2025b); European Parliament & Council (2024).[l]Danilevskyi et al. (2025); Huang et al. (2023).[m]Coeckelbergh (2025a).[n]Coeckelbergh (2025a); Oladosu et al. (2023).[o]Gao and Yu (2024)

in forums, product reviews, and more—and identify needs, expectations, frustrations, and desires. NLP and semantic analysis play a major role in these procedures, supporting the detection of topics, patterns, and emotions, which AI can turn into actionable insights to improve products, services, and customer experience (Islam et al., 2024; Panda et al., 2023; Ziakis & Vlachopoulou, 2023).

Beyond these traditional sources of social data, brands are increasingly incorporating AI-enabled chatbots as active listening channels. These interactions generate a rich corpus of text with frequent questions, complaints, queries, and purchase intentions, providing high-value inputs to Voice of Customer (VoC) analyses, because they capture real-time feedback about critical moments in the consumer journey. In this context, intention detection models, sentiment analysis, and topic classification can sharpen personalisation and improve customer touchpoints.

Real-time sentiment and emotion analysis has become central to social listening practice. AI has significantly improved brands' understanding of customers, enabling instant readings of their feelings and emotions regarding products, services, and brand attributes (Gungunawat et al., 2024; Ziakis & Vlachopoulou, 2023). Underpinning this capability are advanced technologies, such as NLP and deep learning algorithms that process and analyse large volumes of unstructured data from social media, forums, and other digital channels (Islam et al., 2024; Okeleke et al., 2024).

AI-powered social listening can also significantly improve audience segmentation by analysing extensive volumes of data from consumers, including demographics, navigation behaviours, purchase history, and interactions on social media (Gungunawat et al., 2024; Islam et al., 2024; Nitu & Gautam, 2024). Unlike traditional methods based on generic and static categories, AI integrates behavioural, psychographic, and contextual data to develop more adaptive and detailed real-time segmentation strategies (Davtyan, 2024; Hermann, 2022; Nitu & Gautam, 2024). This enables automatic segmentation across multiple criteria, boosting directed and personalised campaigns (Islam et al., 2024; Nitu & Gautam, 2024). AI-powered social listening also identifies microsegments with similar behaviours, leading to highly relevant campaigns with higher conversion rates, and it can dynamically map the entire consumer journey (Davtyan, 2024; Islam et al., 2024). A deeper understanding of psychographic profiles is also favoured, going beyond any segmentation based on demographic data alone (Anayat & Rasool, 2024; Nitu & Gautam, 2024).

When planning for the future, AI-based predictive analysis has revolutionised how organisations anticipate consumer behaviour and market trends, offering a significant competitive advantage. Machine learning algorithms analyse vast amounts of data in real time to identify patterns and predict consumers' future actions (Gungunawat et al., 2024), which is essential for guiding product development and adjusting long-term marketing strategies. In fact, AI can recommend proactive decisions by identifying high-value customers and churn risks (Islam et al., 2024; Okeleke et al., 2024), and can also forecast campaign performance and support efficient resource allocation (Okeleke et al., 2024). Additionally, predictive AI in neuromarketing combines facial recognition, EEG, and fMRI (Functional Magnetic Resonance Imaging) to anticipate reactions with high precision, continually learning to preserve predictive accuracy and adapt to shifting market dynamics (Tavishi, 2024).

2.3 Brand Monitoring and Risk Management

Along with early crisis detection, AI-powered SL provides continuous, intelligent surveillance of the brand's perception in the digital ecosystem (Haleem et al., 2022; Huang & Rust, 2021; Mustak et al., 2021), and supports the design of preventive measures to safeguard brand reputation (Nitu & Gautam, 2024; Yadav et al., 2013; Ziakis & Vlachopoulou, 2023). AI-powered sentiment further improves crisis management by rapidly identifying negative sentiment and, when combined with social media monitoring tools, delivers invaluable information for effective reputation management.

These procedures enable monitoring of brand mentions and the evaluation of tone, intensity, and sentiment dynamics, allowing organisations to react rapidly to incidents while maintaining a holistic view of their reputation. In addition, modern AI-powered social listening can also incorporate disinformation analytics, adding a second layer that detects coordinated false narratives and inauthentic actors. For example, Cyabra's analysis of the "No-Shampoo" trend identified 731 million potential views and 31 million engagements in one month, mapped the creators driving the narrative against named brands (Head & Shoulders, Pantene, and Tresemmé), and recommended detect-debunk-monitor playbooks (Baruchin, 2024). In the entertainment sector, Cyabra scanned approximately 280,000 profiles around *Wonder Woman 1984*, identified nearly 25,000 fake accounts behind a surge in negative sentiment, and helped Warner Media focus on authentic communities, thereby mitigating reputational risk (Himmelreich, n.d.). Together, these cases illustrate how anomaly alerts (volume and sentiment) combined with narrative/bot forensics enable earlier detection and targeted response before issues cascade.

AI-powered SL also advances brand-image building by mapping competitive positioning and shaping differentiation attributes (e.g., quality, trust, and innovation). This competitive surveillance keeps brands agile, enabling timely adjustments to strategy, based on up-to-date market and social data. It can also reveal white spaces—under-explored market areas—that may represent opportunities for growth and innovation. Additionally, analysing hashtags and communities is effective for consumer insight, allowing AI to anticipate emerging trends and demand, thereby creating strategic benefits.

2.4 Campaign Optimisation and Strategic Decision Support

The integration of AI in SL transforms data into intelligent insights that support strategic, personalised marketing decisions. Persistent, automated, and deep monitoring of audiences enables better-informed decisions with greater strategic value and long-term strategic success (Davtyan, 2024; Nitu & Gautam, 2024; Panda et al., 2023), improving ROI, customer retention, and overall marketing performance.

AI-powered SL also substantially increases the ability to personalise content precisely and relevantly, aligning it to the emotional and behavioural contexts of target audiences, thereby strengthening familiarity. This is accomplished by continuously analysing emerging trends, prevailing feelings, and vocabulary preferences within these groups (Davtyan, 2024; Haleem et al., 2022), and adjusting style, tone, and lexical complexity for different segments, while maximising emotional resonance with the public. Natural Language Generation (NLG) tools can generate email subject lines, product descriptions, or full articles, based on data collected from social media. Additionally, deep learning algorithms can adapt marketing campaigns to specific variations in real time (time of day, geographic location, or specific events) to improve click-through rate, conversion, and engagement with the brand (Haleem et al., 2022; Ramya et al., 2025).

In market and competitive analysis, intelligence grounded in the authentic consumer voice enables brands to adjust themes, values, and concerns, and to tailor narratives, claims, and slogans to consistently match real-world expectations. The possibilities are vast, as brands can rapidly detect regional, demographic, contextual, and cultural variations, enriching communication across digital channels and strengthening customer relationships (Haleem et al., 2022; Mustak et al., 2021). As mentioned, behavioural simulations and predictive models also allow teams to anticipate reactions to different messages before their launch, enabling virtual tests of multiple approaches and the selection of the most effective options. For example, AI systems based on social media data may trigger the need for brand repositioning—after a sudden change in the market or a reputational crisis—and indicate which values need to be reinforced or softened to re-establish the connection with audiences (van Esch & Stewart Black, 2021).

In SL, AI also plays a growing role in influencer marketing by assisting in the identification of relevant voices with a genuine impact on organisational audiences. This is accomplished by using algorithms for social network analysis and graph-based network modelling that go beyond the superficial and traditional metric of the number of followers to include indicators based on effective authority and interaction (Panda et al., 2023). The focus is on selecting influencers whose genuine interests align with their audiences', thereby enabling more efficient and relevant campaigns.

3 Emotional Listening: The Crown Jewel of Social Listening

Emotional listening has emerged as one of the most sophisticated and strategically valuable components of social listening, since it expands all the dimensions of social listening covered in the previous sections, as summarised in Fig. 2.

While social listening maps topics, polarity, and interest groups, emotional listening elevates this to the affective level, revealing not only what is said but

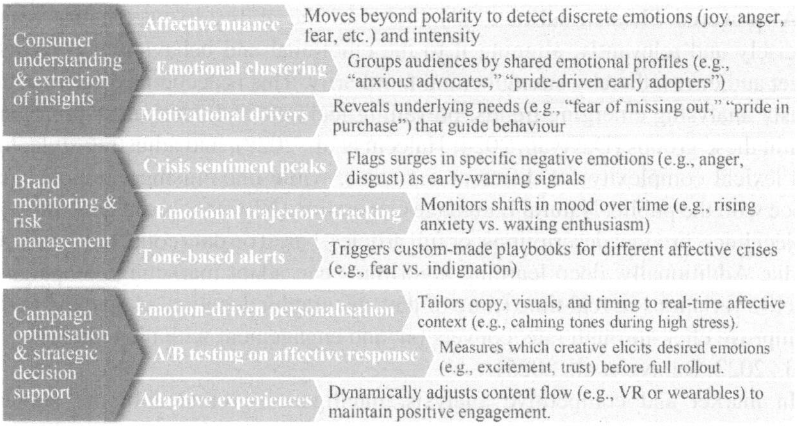

Fig. 2 Emotional Listening enhancements layered onto Social Listening function categories. *Source* Authors

how strongly audiences feel. For instance, brands gain deeper consumer understanding with nuances of motivation and apprehension, real-time analysis moves beyond simple spikes in negative mentions to capture surges of anger or enthusiasm, audience segmentation evolves into emotional clusters, and forecasting accuracy improves when affective variables are included.

The theoretical foundations that support these techniques are not merely historical; they also explain why emotional listening has become viable and reliable. Affective computing, a term coined by Rosalind Picard in 1997, argued that machines can and should respond to human affect (Picard, 1997). Subsequent advances, from deep learning to transformer architectures, have not only increased accuracy but also reduced the cost of real-time detection, opening the way for applications in digital marketing, mental health, and adaptive interfaces (Calvo & D'Mello, 2010). For emotion categorisation, most research still relies on Ekman (1992) six basic emotions and Plutchik (1979) wheel of eight emotions, but recent literature shows that these models gain explanatory detail when integrated into multimodal emotion detection. Surveys such as Ramaswamy and Palaniswamy (2024) confirm that attention-based fusion methods and multisensory models generate richer joint representations of text, voice, and image, offering a holistic, and potentially actionable, reading of the consumer's affective state.

The catalogue of emotions used in research and practice has also been expanded. For instance, contemporary datasets, such as GoEmotions, contain 27 fine-grained emotions (including pride, relief, and curiosity), allowing to train models (e.g., EmoBERTa) capable of detecting subtler affective states. If needed, these expanded sets can be remapped to basic emotion categories (Demszky et al., 2020).

On a large scale and in real time, as required to perform emotional listening on social media, this progress has been enabled by the steady introduction of AI technologies that turn emotional listening into a strategic tool for brands seeking genuine digital empathy. It is, however, worth noting that the focus here is emotions rather than sentiment. While grounded in sentiment analysis, emotion modelling goes beyond polarity by detecting fine-grained categories and, in many set-ups, their intensity across text, visual, audio, and physiological modalities (Demszky et al., 2020). By the mid-2010s, the launch of commercial emotion-AI platforms such as Affectiva (facial cues) and Cogito (voice analytics), together with more affordable webcams, microphones, and wearable biosensors, made large-scale emotional listening commercially viable, allowing the detection of discrete emotions and their intensity (Ha, 2014; Simonite, 2013).

Currently, the four main types of emotional listening are supported by their own set of methods and tools, and their combination—the multimodal fusion, traditionally designated by Multimodal Emotion Recognition (MER) (Gladys & Vetriselvi, 2023)—enables a single unique and robust emotional score.

Detecting emotions in text typically follows two approaches. First, crowdsourced affective lexicons are used, such as NRC EmoLex, where terms are annotated with basic emotions (joy, anger, fear, surprise, disgust, and sadness) to provide a quick reading of emotional charge, (e.g., if the text contains "furious" is marked as "anger") (Mohammad & Turney, 2013). Second, state-of-the-art emotion classifiers (e.g., EmoBERTa) provide fine-grained labels and more reliable intensity estimates (e.g., full sentences or social media posts, such as "I just got a call and I got my dream job" is marked as "joy", "excitement", and "pride") (Kim & Vossen, 2021). The performance is usually assessed on the GoEmotions corpus (Demszky et al., 2020), which comprises 58,000 Reddit comments annotated with 27 emotions and serves as the current benchmark.

For visual affect, the analysis of emotions, based on toolkits such as OpenFace (Baltrušaitis et al., 2016) and OpenFace 3.0 (Hu et al., 2025), enables the detection of discrete emotions (joy, anger, sadness, surprise, disgust, and fear) from facial muscle patterns. Simultaneously, as stated by Gladys and Vetriselvi (2023), recent models based on Vision Transformers (ViT) have also been applied both to still images and video streams to recognise gestures and body movements associated with affective states. Such unimodal approaches have been complemented by audio-visual fusion techniques, and the MER survey by Gladys and Vetriselvi (2023) shows that fusion typically adds 5 to 10 percentage points of accuracy in emotion detection, compared to face-only or voice-only emotion detection models.

Regarding the audio domain, emotion recognition relies on the extraction of acoustic features, such as prosody, vocal intensity, and rhythm, through libraries such as OpenSMILE (Eyben et al., 2013). Current audio encoders now leverage attention-based architectures, improving robustness in noisy conditions and enabling trajectory-level emotion estimates. Integrating acoustic cues with facial video, through cross-attention or fusion networks such as MAFN, consistently improves accuracy, for example, from 71 to 78% (Lian et al., 2023).

Finally, physiological data, such as heart rate (HR), electrodermal activity (EDA) or galvanic skin response (GSR), Electroencephalogram (EEG), and Electrocardiogram (ECG), enable continuous, objective detection of affective states, which can be integrated into multimodal fusion techniques that combine these biological signals for a more complete perception of the emotional state (Wang & Wang, 2025). To unite text, image, and audio into a single emotional score, models such as the Tensor Fusion Network (TFN) have been used, by exploring unimodal, bimodal, and trimodal interactions (Zadeh et al., 2017). More recently, approaches based on attention-based fusion (Aslam et al., 2023) and graph neural networks (Li et al., 2023) dynamically weigh each modality depending on the context, increasing the system's adaptability to real scenarios where the quality of each signal can vary.

The consolidation of the four modalities and multimodal fusion has achieved industry scale with the latest AI developments, through tools such as multilingual NLP transformers (e.g., GPT-4o-Mini) and multimodal networks that combine text, image, voice, and physiological signals (e.g., Emotion-LLaMA, Omni-Emotion, R1-Omni). For instance, Singh et al. (2025) tested a small, multilingual model called GPT-4o-Mini and scored higher than the latest SemEval benchmark for detailed story detection. Cheng et al. (2024) introduced Emotion-LLaMA, a model that reads emotions in sound, video, and text together, with over 90% accuracy on two leading video-emotion tests (DFEW and MER2023-SEMI). Yang et al. (2025) followed with Omni-Emotion, which adds detailed face and audio analysis to a video analysis system and set a record on two recent multimodal benchmarks. Subsequently, Zhao et al. (2025) introduced R1-Omni, which not only improves performance but also provides a short explanation of the facial, vocal, or textual signals that justify each emotion label, allowing users to see why the system decided someone sounded angry, happy, or sad.

In a systematic review on responsible multimodal sentiment analysis in marketing applications, César et al. (2024) reported that the most common combinations of modalities are textual + visual, in 47% of the studies analysed, followed by textual + visual + audio in 43% of the papers. Thus, 90% of research in marketing applications is focuses on textual, visual, and audio modalities, whereas only 10% include modalities supported by physiological data, such as eye-tracking and EEG. The authors argue that most marketing studies still rely on "easy" channels (text, images, and, to a lesser extent, audio) because physiological signals pose additional challenges. First, hardware such as EEG caps or eye-tracking glasses is expensive and intrusive, making large-scale or field tests difficult to run. Second, the raw biosignals are noisy and nonlinear, so researchers must spend extra time on complex pre-processing and alignment before they can fuse them with text or video. Third, there are very few public datasets that combine labelled heart rate or brain-wave data with marketing content, which limits reproducibility. Fourth, most current experiments still take place in controlled labs, and brands worry that findings will not transfer to real-world campaigns.

3.1 Applications of Emotional Listening in Marketing

Several recent studies reveal how AI-based emotion detection is transforming core marketing functions, converting affective data into tactical and strategic decisions.

In predicting purchasing behaviour, Tzafilkou et al. (2023) explored facial micro-expressions in promotional videos for yogurt and nut butters, using FaceReader™ and neural networks, and achieved 90–91% accuracy in anticipating purchase intent, allowing marketers to adjust the tone, pace, and content of creative pieces in the early A/B testing phase, thereby minimising risks before large-scale launch. This ability to predict emotional preferences suggests a paradigm shift: instead of reacting to sales data, teams can anticipate and shape behaviours before they occur, strengthening proximity to the consumer.

Next, using spectral power density and prefrontal asymmetry indices extracted via EEG, Xu and Liu (2024) focused on the e-commerce environment and predicted "purchase vs. non-purchase" with 87.1% accuracy, providing insights pinpoint the moments in a browsing session when consumers are most receptive to offer pop-ups or cross-selling recommendations, guiding real-time on-site personalisation. Dynamic prediction integrates neurophysiology with behavioural data. With explicit consent, it can reduce intrusiveness (fewer, better-timed prompts) but raises data sensitivity; privacy-by-design safeguards are therefore required. Therefore, privacy-by-design safeguards (granular opt-in, data minimisation, and on-device processing where feasible) and strict limits on persuasive use are required (see Sect. 3.2).

Also, Nandini et al. (2025) set a new standard for "always on" campaigns by integrating signals from wearables—Galaxy Watch, Empatica E4, and MUSE 2—and achieved up to 99.41% accuracy in classifying nine basic emotions and 97.8% in valence. In terms of marketing operations, this enables remarketing and the delivery of highly targeted contextual offers based on the user's current daily mood. However, these demands require rethinking the data collection infrastructure and privacy policies to ensure that the use of the sensory signals is transparent and consented to, thereby strengthening consumer confidence. In fact, implementing personalised emotional targeting and measuring its long-term effects on loyalty and advocacy can guarantee that these emotion-driven tactics both spark immediate actions and cultivate enduring brand relationships.

The study of emotion is also extending into the sustainability domain. Mukherjee et al. (2024), noting the increased worldwide prioritisation of environmental targets, study how emotional data can drive greener consumption. Their unique framework combines real-time facial emotion recognition with machine learning to tailor product suggestions and promote sustainable choices that reduce carbon footprint, boost customer retention, and support ethical marketing practices.

In optimising engagement and memorability, Strle et al. (2023) demonstrated that the fusion of skin temperature, valence indicators, and emotional fatigue, obtained by wearables and EDA (GSR), was able to correctly distinguish engaged from non-engaged viewers in about 70% of the time. Thus, by identifying peaks of fatigue, media teams can adjust the cadence of ads or space out push notifications and emails to avoid emotional overload, preserving audience attention and receptivity. This method prioritises the consumer's emotional space, suggesting more empathetic and less intrusive marketing (Wen et al., 2024).

For campaign personalisation and brand design consistency, Xu et al. (2023) found that brain activity (EEG) and skin conductance peaks (GSR) reflect people's emotional response to different visual brand styles. In practice, this means marketers can use these emotional response insights to choose colours, fonts, and images that truly appeal to their audience, making branding and packaging more attractive and effective. The authors encourage a closer collaboration between design and data science teams, promoting an organisational culture guided by emotional evidence.

Finally, in the creation of adaptive immersive experiences, Pei et al. (2023) showed that a CNN-LSTM classifier applied to a lightweight EEG headset with 32 sensors can distinguish, with 85.2% accuracy, states of happiness, fear, calm, and boredom in 360° VR scenarios. This might pave the way for future campaigns—for example, virtual showrooms that shift colour schemes as you browse or gamified demos that adjust their pace based on your emotional response—to become a two-way conversation, where the brand environment responds in real time, generating greater engagement and a deeper emotional connection.

Together, recent cases illustrate how AI-based emotion detection (from facial micro-expressions and neural signals to wearables and immersive environments) offers significant advantages: greater accuracy in purchase prediction, engagement optimisation, visual and timing personalisation, and interactive experiences that respond in real time to audience emotions, which allows us to anticipate that the future of marketing will be increasingly collaborative, ethical, and focused on the emotional well-being of the consumer, transforming affective data into insights that humanise the brand-customer relationship.

3.2 Challenges and Ethical Considerations

As outlined in the preceding sections, the opportunities presented are not without associated ethical implications. The amalgamation of computer vision, speech analytics, text mining, and bio signals in the context of emotional listening has been shown to create a broader risk surface than traditional sentiment analysis. Compared with text-only sentiment analysis, multimodal emotional listening extends the risk surface by using biometric/voice signals (higher identifiability) and fine-grained emotion inferences (greater misuse/manipulation impact), requiring explicit consent, data minimisation, and, where feasible, on-device processing. In this section, we propose a series of concrete measures with the aim of mitigating the risks identified in five specific areas.

3.2.1 Fairness and Cross-Cultural Validity

The concept of fairness in AI systems extends beyond mere technical considerations, constituting a matter of social justice. When algorithms reflect systemic biases, they do not merely perpetuate existing inequalities; they amplify the effects of these inequalities on already marginalised communities (Ashok et al., 2022). This has been identified as a particularly problematic issue in critical sectors such as finance and healthcare, where decisions made by algorithms can influence access to essential services.

The increasing ubiquity of AI requires the development of a comprehensive understanding of fairness that transcends cultural differences (Huang et al., 2023). Technical sophistication alone is insufficient; systems must recognise and respect human diversity.

Diverse perspectives must be embedded from the outset. Communities from varied backgrounds should participate meaningfully in the design and evaluation of systems. This involvement should not be regarded as mere late consultation; rather, it should be considered genuine, ongoing participation in the creative process (Huang et al., 2023). The ethical frameworks proposed by Gunkel (2018) are inclusive by nature, thus providing a solid foundation for the proposed approach. Ignoring cultural differences is not only ethically problematic but also counterproductive for technology adoption.

3.2.2 Privacy, Biometric Data, and Consent

The collection of biometric data for emotional analysis raises a number of complex ethical dilemmas that extend beyond the scope of traditional privacy concerns. The concept of emotional listening entails the capture of data that extends beyond mere verbal content, encompassing the emotional dimension. This approach facilitates the creation of comprehensive profiles that offer insights into the subtleties of personality and the nuances of mental state.

Brendel et al. (2021) emphasise that the uncontrolled aggregation of personal data poses a threat not only to individual privacy but also to individual autonomy itself. In the context of biometric data, this issue assumes particular significance. Our facial expressions, voice patterns, and physiological responses are fundamental elements of our identity; they are not merely data points.

The issue of consent becomes particularly challenging because many users do not realise how extensively their emotional signals are captured and processed. Empirical work on AI-driven personalisation in e-commerce shows that recommendation engines can steer purchasing behaviour below the threshold of conscious awareness (Swamy et al., 2025). When those same engines ingest voice inflexions, facial micro-expressions, or biosignals—a practice often called emotional listening—the scope for such covert influence widens even further.

A recent illustration is the rollout of ChatGPT's Advanced Voice Mode. The feature was withheld throughout most of 2024 in the European Union and, even after its release, still ships with a reduced set of expressive accents. OpenAI explained that some regions "require additional external reviews before launching new products" (Barlow, 2024). Analysts note that the restraint aligns with Article 5 of the EU Artificial Intelligence Act, which bans AI systems that use subliminal or purposefully manipulative techniques likely to distort user behaviour (European Parliament & Council, 2024). Because advanced voice synthesis can modulate tone, cadence, and emotional resonance, releasing it without appropriate safeguards could breach that provision. The European regulatory context, therefore, exemplifies how limits on emotional data processing are already shaping product design and deployment.

Mehra (2025) proposes the adoption of user-centred designs that promote explicit consent mechanisms; however, this would require the development of mechanisms that go beyond the typical acceptance pop-ups. It is imperative that interfaces effectively educate users on the potential consequences of sharing their emotional data.

3.2.3 Manipulative Persuasion and User Autonomy

When designed responsibly, sentiment analysis and personalisation can help customers. They surface timely support when frustration is detected (e.g., routing to service, simplifying next steps), tailor information to stated preferences to reduce noise and choice overload, improve product discovery through real-time relevance, and pace communications to avoid fatigue—benefits repeatedly noted in AI-for-marketing research (Davtyan, 2024; Huang & Rust, 2021; Mustak et al., 2021; Wen et al., 2024). At the same time, these same capabilities create new failure modes if optimisation overrides user interests.

Emotional listening systems possess a unique potential for subtle manipulation. By comprehending not only the verbal statements of users but also their underlying emotions, these systems possess the capacity to formulate remarkably persuasive interventions that have the potential to erode individual autonomy in ways that are only beginning to be comprehended.

As posited by Ashok et al. (2022), there is a potential risk of AI systems subverting user intent. This is attributable to the potential of personalised algorithms to promote content that, while superficially aligned with user interests, may ultimately yield outcomes that are not conducive to the user's best interests. From an emotional standpoint, this issue assumes a more profound significance: the existence of a system capable of detecting emotional vulnerability presents a potential vulnerability for exploitation in commercial contexts. For example, a food-delivery app that infers sustained sadness from late-night chat messages could automatically boost "limited-time comfort food" discounts and push larger-basket offers precisely when the user is emotionally vulnerable, unless policies explicitly prohibit targeting on inferred vulnerability.

Gunkel (2018) philosophical research reveals a further problematic dimension, namely the emotional complicity that users can develop towards AI entities that appear to be autonomous. The establishment of emotional connections with AI interfaces by individuals gives rise to the potential for these systems to leverage such bonds for commercial gain, thereby giving rise to significant ethical concerns.

The development of ethical frameworks is imperative, encompassing transparency measures and the articulation of algorithms' intentions and their potential influence on decision-making processes (Coeckelbergh, 2025b). Nevertheless, it is crucial that this transparency is authentic and does not manifest as a technical smokescreen that serves to obfuscate rather than elucidate.

3.2.4 Transparency, Explainability, and Contestability

This is an issue also addressed by the same philosopher (Coeckelbergh, 2025b): The inherent complexity of emotional listening systems poses unique challenges for transparency. He advances the concept of governance frameworks that prioritise transparency as a mean of ensuring accountability, empowering users to contest and challenge decisions made by AI. However, a key question remains: how can decisions be explained when they are based on the analysis of micro-expressions, subtle vocal cues, and complex biometric signals?

As emphasised by Danilevskyi et al. (2025), user comprehension is imperative for establishing trust. However, within the paradigm of emotional listening, this requires the translation of intricate technical processes into comprehensible explanations, without compromising their intricacy. The opacity of these systems is not merely a technical issue; it constitutes an inherent impediment to the exercise of fundamental rights.

Huang et al. (2023) have observed that the complexity of AI decision mechanisms frequently leads to obfuscation, thereby rendering it difficult for users to comprehend the influence of their data on outcomes. In systems that process emotions, this lack of understanding has the potential to erode trust more profoundly than in other AI applications.

Padala et al. (2021) propose a novel integration of user feedback mechanisms into the design process, with the objective of enhancing transparency. This is of particular pertinence in the domain of emotional systems, wherein the subjective experience of the user serves as the most reliable indicator of the system's accuracy.

3.2.5 Governance, Compliance, and Industry Standards

Governing emotional listening requires frameworks that transcend national and disciplinary boundaries. While Coeckelbergh (2025a) argues for a global approach to AI governance, recognizing that ethical dilemmas frequently transcend national borders and require collaborative frameworks to address them effectively, other authors such as Oladosu et al. (2023) highlight that ethical data governance must ensure technologies prioritize user privacy and fairness, establishing industry standards that benefit both organisations and consumers. In the emotional context, this means developing specific protocols for handling data that reveals intimate aspects of human experience.

Gao and Yu (2024) point out that the emergence of digital civilisation requires innovative governance structures that encompass diverse ethical considerations and methods of engagement with AI technologies. For emotional listening, this implies creating spaces where technical expertise genuinely dialogues with humanistic, psychological, and cultural perspectives.

Establishing ongoing dialogue among researchers, practitioners, and policymakers is essential for developing a coherent strategy that addresses the multidimensional challenges presented by emotional AI (Brendel et al., 2021). This dialogue must be genuine, not a cosmetic consultation.

3.2.6 Risk Assessment and Mitigation Framework

Addressing the ethical challenges of emotional listening isn't about overcoming obstacles, but about constantly navigating tensions. From concerns about fairness and privacy to imperatives of transparency and governance, the implications of these technologies demand careful navigation that promotes ethical usage while harnessing their transformative potential.

Building ethically responsible, transparent, and collaborative frameworks will be essential for steering emotional AI development towards a direction that safeguards human dignity and fosters truly inclusive progress. This requires not just good intentions, but sustained commitment to ethical reflection, community engagement, and continuous vigilance of the unintended consequences of our technological innovations.

Table 1 synthesises the key risks identified across all areas, providing concrete examples and actionable mitigation strategies.

4 Conclusions

A few years ago, it would have been impossible for companies to "read the room" across digital touchpoints with the level of detail and speed that they now can. AI-powered social and emotional listening is now central to marketing, but it delivers value only when converted into governed business actions.

Rather than monitor everything, managers should start with narrow, high-value goals (e.g., real-time service recovery; mood-matched ads) to accelerate ROI and credibility. Since most of the easily actionable insights are still produced by text analytics, organisations should incorporate more complex data (voice, image, or biometric) gradually, and only after a solid base of understanding has been built, as this lays the technical and ethical groundwork needed to extract value from those richer, but more demanding and expensive, data types. It is also more important to incorporate these into real-time alerts available to frontline teams, who can take rapid action, than just including them in dashboards.

An institutionalised ethical attitude is also fundamental because emotion data can damage a company's reputation just as quickly as it can foster it. Missteps include using inferred emotions without consent (perceived surveillance), misclassifying emotion in sensitive moments (e.g., flagging sarcasm as anger) that triggers improper responses, targeting offers at moments of detected vulnerability (seen as exploitation), and breaches exposing highly intimate affect data, any of which can spark public backlash, regulatory scrutiny, and trust erosion. Since customer sentiment and emotion analysis are high-risk data, responsible marketers should aim at treating affective signals as sensitive data, with the same controls applied to health or biometrics. To do so, the core challenges might rely on (1) consent & context (make sure inferences about feelings are opt-in and clearly explained), (2) fairness & cultural fit (avoid misreads across dialects, age, and cultures), (3) manipulation risk (prohibit targeting on inferred vulnerability and audit optimisers for "emotional dark patterns"), (4) privacy & security (minimise data, prefer on-device/ephemeral processing, and encrypt anything retained), and (5) accountability (log decisions, enable user appeals, and run red-team tests before deployment).

A holistic approach, pairing data scientists with behavioural researchers and service-design experts, is also highly beneficial, if not essential. Lastly, performance measurement needs to connect short-term results (e.g., engagement and mood variations) to long-term outcomes such as lifetime value, churn, and brand trust, and every model should be persistently revised, because language, culture, and platform features change.

Looking forward, the academic and industry research agenda can take several directions. First, emotion classifiers trained on Western datasets must be tested in intercultural settings, since models that work well in one region may fail in another. Second, researchers should extend to longitudinal studies to evaluate how a brand's sustained emotional tone affects customer loyalty and brand equity over time instead of relying on one-time snapshots. Third, rigorous causal inference methods are needed to determine if emotion-based interventions improve outcomes or simply occur alongside them. Fourth, privacy-preserving techniques, such as federated learning and on-device inference, require careful research so that marketers can deliver personalised experiences while complying with regulations like the EU AI Act.

Simplifying tools, by creating models and visualisations that are friendly to non-technical users, is also necessary to overcome current limitations in the adoption of complex emotion detection procedures, namely the multimodal ones. Additionally, the growing use of AI-generated avatars and voice clones brings new challenges. Thus, research is needed to understand how machine empathy influences customer trust and perceived authenticity, and which are the ethical risks of manipulation when interactions feel less human or more artificial.

AI-powered emotional and social listening, when governed carefully and measured with clear performance metrics, enables companies to understand customers more deeply and build a competitive advantage, but much research and practice are still needed to ensure that emotion-aware AI enhances human judgement, supports customer dignity, and delivers lasting value over the next decade.

References

Anayat, S., & Rasool, G. (2024). Artificial intelligence marketing (AIM): Connecting-the-dots using bibliometrics. *Journal of Marketing Theory and Practice, 32*(1), 114–135. https://doi.org/10.1080/10696679.2022.2103435

Ashok, M., Madan, R., Joha, A., & Sivarajah, U. (2022). Ethical framework for Artificial Intelligence and Digital technologies. *International Journal of Information Management, 62*, 102433. https://doi.org/10.1016/j.ijinfomgt.2021.102433

Aslam, A., Sargano, A. B., & Habib, Z. (2023). Attention-based multimodal sentiment analysis and emotion recognition using deep neural networks. *Applied Soft Computing, 144*, 110494. https://doi.org/10.1016/j.asoc.2023.110494

Assiri, A., Gumaei, A., Mehmood, F., Abbas, T., & Ullah, S. (2024). DeBERTa-GRU: Sentiment analysis for large language model. *Computers, Materials and Continua, 79*(3), 4219–4236. https://doi.org/10.32604/cmc.2024.050781

Baltrušaitis, T., Robinson, P., & Morency, L. P. (2016, March 7–10). OpenFace: An open source facial behavior analysis toolkit. In *2016 IEEE Winter Conference on Applications of Computer Vision (WACV)*.

Barlow, G. (2024). OpenAI's Advanced Voice mode is unavailable in the EU, and now we might know why. *TechRadar*. https://www.techradar.com/computing/artificial-intelligence/openai-s-advanced-voice-is-unavailable-in-the-eu-and-now-we-might-know-why

Baruchin, R. (2024). Hair care brands tangled up in fake news. *Cybra Blog*. https://cyabra.com/blog/hair-care-brands-tangled-up-in-fake-news/

Belcastro, L., Marozzo, F., Talia, D., & Trunfio, P. (2017, July 17–21). A parallel library for social media analytics. In *2017 International Conference on High Performance Computing & Simulation (HPCS)*.

Brendel, A. B., Mirbabaie, M., Lembcke, T.-B., & Hofeditz, L. (2021). Ethical management of artificial intelligence. *Sustainability, 13*(4), 1974. https://www.mdpi.com/2071-1050/13/4/1974

Calvo, R. A., & D'Mello, S. (2010). Affect detection: An interdisciplinary review of models, methods, and their applications. *IEEE Transactions on Affective Computing, 1*(1), 18–37. https://doi.org/10.1109/T-AFFC.2010.1

César, I., Pereira, I., Rodrigues, F., Miguéis, V. L., Nicola, S., Madureira, A., Reis, J. L., Dos Santos, J. P. M., & De Oliveira, D. A. (2024). A systematic review on responsible multimodal sentiment analysis in marketing applications. *IEEE Access, 12*, 111943–111961. https://doi.org/10.1109/ACCESS.2024.3441514

Cheng, Z., Cheng, Z.-Q., He, J.-Y., Wang, K., Lin, Y., Lian, Z., Peng, X., & Hauptmann, A. (2024). Emotion-llama: Multimodal emotion recognition and reasoning with instruction tuning. *Advances in Neural Information Processing Systems, 37*, 110805–110853.

Chumwatana, T., & Chuaychoo, I. (2017, October 21–23). Using social media listening technique for monitoring people's mentions from social media: A case study of Thai airline industry. In *2017 2nd International Conference on Knowledge Engineering and Applications (ICKEA)*.

Chung, H. W., Hou, L., Longpre, S., Zoph, B., Tay, Y., Fedus, W., Li, Y., Wang, X., Dehghani, M., & Brahma, S. (2024). Scaling instruction-finetuned language models. *Journal of Machine Learning Research, 25*(70), 1–53.

Coeckelbergh, M. (2025a). The case for global governance of AI: Arguments, counter-arguments, and challenges ahead. *Ai & Society, 40*(3), 1803–1806. https://doi.org/10.1007/s00146-024-01949-5

Coeckelbergh, M. (2025b). LLMs, truth, and democracy: An overview of risks. *Science and Engineering Ethics, 31*(1), 4. https://doi.org/10.1007/s11948-025-00529-0

Crisci, A., Grasso, V., Nesi, P., Pantaleo, G., Paoli, I., & Zaza, I. (2018). Predicting TV programme audience by using twitter based metrics. *Multimedia Tools and Applications, 77*(10), 12203–12232. https://doi.org/10.1007/s11042-017-4880-x

Danilevskyi, M., Perez-Tellez, F., & Buscaldi, D. (2025). Implementing ethical principles in AI: An initial discussion. *AI and Ethics, 5*(4), 3549–3555. https://doi.org/10.1007/s43681-025-00710-y

Davtyan, N. (2024). *AI in consumer behavior analysis and digital marketing: A strategic approach.* https://ideas.repec.org/p/bfv/sbsrec/005.html

Demszky, D., Movshovitz-Attias, D., Ko, J., Cowen, A., Nemade, G., & Ravi, S. (2020, July). GoEmotions: A dataset of fine-grained emotions. In D. Jurafsky, J. Chai, N. Schluter, & J. Tetreault (Eds.), *Proceedings of the 58th annual meeting of the association for computational linguistics* [Online].

Ducange, P., Fazzolari, M., Petrocchi, M., & Vecchio, M. (2019). An effective Decision Support System for social media listening based on cross-source sentiment analysis models. *Engineering Applications of Artificial Intelligence, 78*, 71–85. https://doi.org/10.1016/j.engappai.2018.10.014

Ekman, P. (1992). An argument for basic emotions. *Cognition & Emotion, 6*(3–4), 169–200.

European Parliament & Council. (2024). Regulation (EU) 2024/1689 of 13 June 2024 laying down harmonised rules on artificial intelligence (Artificial Intelligence Act). *Official Journal of the European Union, L, 1689*, 1–144. https://eur-lex.europa.eu/legal-content/EN/TXT/PDF/?uri=OJ:L_202401689

Eyben, F., Weninger, F., Gross, F., & Schuller, B. (2013). Recent developments in openSMILE, the Munich open-source multimedia feature extractor. In *Proceedings of the 21st ACM International Conference on Multimedia*, Barcelona, Spain. https://doi.org/10.1145/2502081.2502224

Fong, B. Q., & See, J. (2024). BrandDiffusion: Multimodal personalized marketing visual content generation. In *Proceedings of the 2nd international workshop on multimedia content generation and evaluation: New methods and practice*, Melbourne VIC, Australia. https://doi.org/10.1145/3688867.3690175

Fu, X.-Y., Laskar, M. T. R., Khasanova, E., Chen, C., & TN, S. B. (2024). Tiny titans: Can smaller large language models punch above their weight in the real world for meeting summarization? *arXiv preprint* arXiv:2402.00841

Gao, D., & Yu, D. (2024). Challenges and cracks: Ethical issues in the development of artificial intelligence. *Science, Technology and Society, 29*(3), 415–434. https://doi.org/10.1177/09717218241246372

Gladys, A., & Vetriselvi, V. (2023). Survey on multimodal approaches to emotion recognition. *Neurocomputing, 556*, 126693. https://doi.org/10.1016/j.neucom.2023.126693

Gungunawat, A., Khandelwal, N., & Gupta, N. (2024). AI-powered personalization in digital marketing: Transforming consumer engagement and strategy. *Research Review International Journal of Multidisciplinary, 9*(11), 183–191. https://doi.org/10.31305/rrijm.2024.v09.n11.026

Gunkel, D. J. (2018). The other question: Can and should robots have rights? *Ethics and Information Technology, 20*(2), 87–99. https://doi.org/10.1007/s10676-017-9442-4

Ha, A. (2014, February 13). Affectiva launches an SDK to bring emotion tracking to mobile apps. *TechCrunch*. https://techcrunch.com/2014/02/13/affectiva-mobile-sdk/

Haleem, A., Javaid, M., Asim Qadri, M., Pratap Singh, R., & Suman, R. (2022). Artificial intelligence (AI) applications for marketing: A literature-based study. *International Journal of Intelligent Networks, 3*, 119–132. https://doi.org/10.1016/j.ijin.2022.08.005

Hermann, E. (2022). Leveraging artificial intelligence in marketing for social good—An ethical perspective. *Journal of Business Ethics, 179*(1), 43–61. https://doi.org/10.1007/s10551-021-04843-y

Himmelreich, D. (n.d.). Warner Media. *Cyabra Case Studies*. https://cyabra.com/cyabra-case-studies/warner-media/

Ho, J., Jain, A., & Abbeel, P. (2020). Denoising diffusion probabilistic models. *Advances in Neural Information Processing Systems, 33*, 6840–6851.

Hu, J., Mathur, L., Liang, P. P., & Morency, L.-P. (2025). OpenFace 3.0: A lightweight multitask system for comprehensive facial behavior analysis. *arXiv preprint* arXiv:2506.02891

Huang, C., Zhang, Z., Mao, B., & Yao, X. (2023). An overview of artificial intelligence ethics. *IEEE Transactions on Artificial Intelligence, 4*(4), 799–819. https://doi.org/10.1109/TAI.2022.3194503

Huang, M.-H., & Rust, R. T. (2021). A strategic framework for artificial intelligence in marketing. *Journal of the Academy of Marketing Science, 49*(1), 30–50. https://doi.org/10.1007/s11747-020-00749-9

Islam, M. A., Fakir, S. I., Masud, S. B., Hossen, M. D., Islam, M. T., & Siddiky, M. R. (2024). Artificial intelligence in digital marketing automation: Enhancing personalization, predictive analytics, and ethical integration. *Edelweiss Applied Science and Technology, 8*(6), 6498–6516. https://doi.org/10.55214/25768484.v8i6.3404

Kaplan, A., & Haenlein, M. (2019). Siri, Siri, in my hand: Who's the fairest in the land? On the interpretations, illustrations, and implications of artificial intelligence. *Business Horizons, 62*(1), 15–25. https://doi.org/10.1016/j.bushor.2018.08.004

Kim, T., & Vossen, P. (2021). Emoberta: Speaker-aware emotion recognition in conversation with roberta. *arXiv preprint* arXiv:2108.12009

Kumar, V., Kotler, P., Gupta, S., & Rajan, B. (2025). Generative AI in marketing: Promises, Perils, and public policy implications. *Journal of Public Policy & Marketing, 44*(3), 309–331. https://doi.org/10.1177/07439156241286499

Li, J., Wang, X., Lv, G., & Zeng, Z. (2023). GraphMFT: A graph network based multimodal fusion technique for emotion recognition in conversation. *Neurocomputing, 550*, 126427. https://doi.org/10.1016/j.neucom.2023.126427

Lian, H., Lu, C., Li, S., Zhao, Y., Tang, C., & Zong, Y. (2023). A survey of deep learning-based multimodal emotion recognition: Speech, text, and face. *Entropy, 25*(10).

Liere-Netheler, K., Gilhaus, L., Vogelsang, K., & Hoppe, U. (2019). *A literature review on application areas of social media analytics*. Business Information Systems.

Mehra, C. (2025). Ethical challenges and solutions in artificial intelligence development. *International Journal for Multidisciplinary Research, 7*(2), 1–9. https://doi.org/10.36948/ijfmr.2025.v07i02.42527

Micera, R., & Crispino, R. (2017). Destination web reputation as "smart tool" for image building: The case analysis of Naples city-destination. *International Journal of Tourism Cities, 3*(4), 406–423. https://doi.org/10.1108/IJTC-11-2016-0048

Mohammad, S. M., & Turney, P. D. (2013). Crowdsourcing a word–emotion association Lexicon. *Computational Intelligence, 29*(3), 436–465. https://doi.org/10.1111/j.1467-8640.2012.00460.x

Mukherjee, S., Thapliyal, K., Manchanda, M., Jha, S., & Zeeshan. (2024, November 21–23). Sustainable E-commerce through customer emotion recognition with machine learning. In *2024 3rd Edition of IEEE Delhi Section Flagship Conference (DELCON).*

Mustak, M., Salminen, J., Plé, L., & Wirtz, J. (2021). Artificial intelligence in marketing: Topic modeling, scientometric analysis, and research agenda. *Journal of Business Research, 124*, 389–404. https://doi.org/10.1016/j.jbusres.2020.10.044

Nandini, D., Yadav, J., Singh, V., Mohan, V., & Agarwal, S. (2025). An ensemble deep learning framework for emotion recognition through wearable devices multi-modal physiological signals. *Scientific Reports, 15*(1), 17263. https://doi.org/10.1038/s41598-025-99858-0

Navarro, L. F. M. (2024). The integration of deep learning and machine learning for enhanced social media analytics. *Nuvern Machine Learning Reviews, 1*(1), 11–21.

Nichol, A. Q., & Dhariwal, P. (2021). Improved denoising diffusion probabilistic models. In *International Conference on Machine Learning.*

Nitu, N., & Gautam, T. (2024). Examining the use of Ai-powered social media analytics for target customer segmentation: A systematic review in retail industry. *Educational Administration: Theory and Practice, 30*(4), 1798–1805. https://doi.org/10.53555/kuey.v30i4.1753

Okeleke, P. A., Ajiga, D., Folorunsho, S. O., & Ezeigweneme, C. (2024). Predictive analytics for market trends using AI: A study in consumer behavior. *International Journal of Engineering Research Updates, 7*(1), 36–49.

Oladosu, S., Ike, C., Adepoju, P., Afolabi, A., Ige, A., & Amoo, O. (2023). Frameworks for ethical data governance in machine learning: Privacy, fairness, and business optimization. *Magna Scientia Advanced Research and Reviews, 7*(2), 96–106. https://doi.org/10.30574/msarr.2023.7.2.0043

Padala, M., Damle, S., & Gujar, S. (2021). Federated learning meets fairness and differential privacy. In *Neural Information Processing: 28th International Conference*, ICONIP 2021, Sanur, Bali, Indonesia, December 8–12, 2021, Proceedings, Part VI 28.

Panda, V., Mishra, A., & Sharma, M. (2023, September 14–15). Turning data into insights: Leveraging artificial intelligence for better understanding of social media consumer behaviour. In *2023 International Conference on Sustainable Emerging Innovations in Engineering and Technology (ICSEIET).*

Pei, G., Fan, C., Li, T., Jin, J., & Wang, R. (2023). *EEG-based emotion recognition in immersive virtual reality: Meeting the requirement of accuracy and computational efficiency.* In *Proceedings of the 2023 7th International Conference on Digital Signal Processing*, Chengdu, China. https://doi.org/10.1145/3585542.3585544

Pham, C. M., Hoyle, A., Sun, S., Resnik, P., & Iyyer, M. (2023). Topicgpt: A prompt-based topic modeling framework. *arXiv preprint* arXiv:2311.01449

Picard, R. W. (1997). *Affective computing MIT press* (p. 2). Massachsusetts.

Plutchik, R. (1979). *Emotion.* Harper & Row.

Pomputius, A. (2019). Can you hear me now? Social listening as a strategy for understanding user needs. *Medical Reference Services Quarterly, 38*(2), 181–186. https://doi.org/10.1080/02763869.2019.1588042

Ramaswamy, M. P. A., & Palaniswamy, S. (2024). Multimodal emotion recognition: A comprehensive review, trends, and challenges. *WIREs Data Mining and Knowledge Discovery, 14*(6), e1563. https://doi.org/10.1002/widm.1563

Ramesh, A., Dhariwal, P., Nichol, A., Chu, C., & Chen, M. (2022). Hierarchical text-conditional image generation with clip latents. *arXiv preprint* arXiv:2204.06125, *1*(2), 3.

Ramya, D. J., Swapna, D. S., Varalakshmi, D. C., Mukherjee, D. R., & Kumar, D. B. R. (2025). AI-powered marketing: Predictive consumer behavior and personalized campaigns. *Journal of Marketing & Social Research, 2*(2), 28–38. https://doi.org/10.61336/jmsr/25-02-13

Reid, E., & Duffy, K. (2018). A netnographic sensibility: Developing the netnographic/social listening boundaries. *Journal of Marketing Management, 34*(3–4), 263–286. https://doi.org/10.1080/0267257X.2018.1450282

Saharia, C., Chan, W., Saxena, S., Li, L., Whang, J., Denton, E. L., Ghasemipour, K., Gontijo Lopes, R., Karagol Ayan, B., & Salimans, T. (2022). Photorealistic text-to-image diffusion models with deep language understanding. *Advances in Neural Information Processing Systems, 35*, 36479–36494.

Simonite, T. (2013, October 23). Call centers tap voice-analysis software to monitor moods. *WIRED.* https://www.wired.com/2013/10/call-centers-voice-analysis/

Singh, I., Scarton, C., & Bontcheva, K. (2025). GateNLP at SemEval-2025 Task 10: Hierarchical three-step prompting for multilingual narrative classification. *arXiv preprint* arXiv:2505.22867

Strle, G., Košir, A., & Burnik, U. (2023). Physiological signals and affect as predictors of advertising engagement. *Sensors, 23*(15), 6916. https://www.mdpi.com/1424-8220/23/15/6916

Swamy, A., Jagadeesh, T., & Sangeet, V. (2025). Ethical considerations in e-commerce personalization: Balancing customer benefits with privacy and fairness. *Universal Research Reports, 12*(1), 167–186. https://doi.org/10.36676/urr.v12.i1.1470

Tavishi, Y. (2024). AI in neuromarketing: Understanding consumer emotions and behavior through machine learning. *International Journal for Multidisciplinary Research, 6*(5).

Tzafilkou, K., Economides, A. A., & Panavou, F.-R. (2023). You look like you'll buy it! Purchase intent prediction based on facially detected emotions in social media campaigns for food products. *Computers, 12*(4), 88. https://www.mdpi.com/2073-431X/12/4/88

van Esch, P., & Stewart Black, J. (2021). Artificial Intelligence (AI): Revolutionizing digital marketing. *Australasian Marketing Journal, 29*(3), 199–203. https://doi.org/10.1177/18393349211037684

Wang, Z., & Wang, Y. (2025). Emotion recognition based on multimodal physiological electrical signals. *Frontiers in Neuroscience, 19*, 1512799.

Wen, T. J., Chuan, C.-H., Anghelcev, G., Sar, S., Yun, J. T., & Xu, Y. (2024). Infusing affective computing models into advertising research on emotions. *Journal of Advertising, 53*(5), 710–731. https://doi.org/10.1080/00913367.2024.2409254

Widmar, N., Bir, C., Lai, J., & Wolf, C. (2020). Public perceptions of veterinarians from social and online media listening. *Veterinary Sciences, 7*(2).

Wu, Z., Pan, S., Chen, F., Long, G., Zhang, C., & Yu, P. S. (2021). A comprehensive survey on graph neural networks. *IEEE Transactions on Neural Networks and Learning Systems, 32*(1), 4–24. https://doi.org/10.1109/TNNLS.2020.2978386

Xu, Y., Shieh, C.-H., van Esch, P., & Ling, I. L. (2020). AI customer service: Task complexity, problem-solving ability, and usage intention. *Australasian Marketing Journal (AMJ), 28*(4), 189–199. https://doi.org/10.1016/j.ausmj.2020.03.005

Xu, Z., & Liu, S. (2024). Decoding consumer purchase decisions: Exploring the predictive power of EEG features in online shopping environments using machine learning. *Humanities and Social Sciences Communications, 11*(1), 1202. https://doi.org/10.1057/s41599-024-03691-1

Xu, Z., Zhang, M., Zhang, P., Luo, J., Tu, M., & Lai, Y. (2023). The neurophysiological mechanisms underlying brand personality consumer attraction: EEG and GSR evidence. *Journal of Retailing and Consumer Services, 73*, 103296. https://doi.org/10.1016/j.jretconser.2023.103296

Yadav, M. S., de Valck, K., Hennig-Thurau, T., Hoffman, D. L., & Spann, M. (2013). Social commerce: A contingency framework for assessing marketing potential. *Journal of Interactive Marketing, 27*(4), 311–323. https://doi.org/10.1016/j.intmar.2013.09.001

Yang, Q., Bai, D., Peng, Y.-X., & Wei, X. (2025). Omni-Emotion: Extending Video MLLM with detailed face and audio modeling for multimodal emotion analysis. *arXiv preprint* arXiv:2501.09502

Ye, Z., Kumar, Y. J., Sing, G. O., Song, F., & Wang, J. (2022). A comprehensive survey of graph neural networks for knowledge graphs. *IEEE Access, 10*, 75729–75741. https://doi.org/10.1109/ACCESS.2022.3191784

Yekta, M. (2024). The general intelligence of GPT–4, its knowledge diffusive and societal influences, and its governance. *Meta-Radiology, 2*(2), 100078. https://doi.org/10.1016/j.metrad.2024.100078

Zachlod, C., Samuel, O., Ochsner, A., & Werthmüller, S. (2022). Analytics of social media data – State of characteristics and application. *Journal of Business Research, 144*, 1064–1076. https://doi.org/10.1016/j.jbusres.2022.02.016

Zadeh, A., Chen, M., Poria, S., Cambria, E., & Morency, L.-P. (2017, September). Tensor fusion network for multimodal sentiment analysis. In M. Palmer, R. Hwa, & S. Riedel (Eds.), *Proceedings of the 2017 Conference on Empirical Methods in Natural Language Processing.*

Zhao, J., Li, R., Jin, Q., Wang, X., & Li, H. (2022). Memobert: Pre-training model with prompt-based learning for multimodal emotion recognition. *ICASSP 2022–2022 IEEE International Conference on Acoustics, Speech and Signal Processing (ICASSP)*, pp. 4703–4707. https://doi.org/10.1109/ICASSP43922.2022.9746910

Zhao, J., Wei, X., & Bo, L. (2025). R1-omni: Explainable omni-multimodal emotion recognition with reinforcement learning. *arXiv preprint* arXiv:2503.05379

Zhou, J., Cui, G., Hu, S., Zhang, Z., Yang, C., Liu, Z., Wang, L., Li, C., & Sun, M. (2020). Graph neural networks: A review of methods and applications. *AI Open, 1*, 57–81. https://doi.org/10.1016/j.aiopen.2021.01.001

Ziakis, C., & Vlachopoulou, M. (2023). Artificial intelligence in digital marketing: Insights from a comprehensive review. *Information, 14*(12).

Integrating Artificial Intelligence into Content Marketing: A Systematic Literature Review and a Conceptual Framework

Sara Santos and Pedro Espírito Santo

Abstract Combining generative artificial intelligence (AI) into content marketing transforms how brands generate, disseminate, and assess digital content. The rapid growth of AI tools necessitates an evaluation of academic research on their impact on digital marketing, particularly in the context of content marketing. This research systematically examines the literature on AI applications in content marketing. The main goal is to analyse the process of integrating AI into content marketing strategy, considering challenges and obstacles. The review followed PRISMA guidelines by selecting publications from 2019 to 2025 that were written in English and accessible through open access. Discussion divided findings into three main sections: (1) creation and personalisation; (2) analytics and performance; and (3) governance and trust. The CAG framework (Creation, Analytics, and Governance) connects these domains through content marketing strategy. Results show that AI enhances human-machine teamwork and enables extensive personalisation while utilising predictive models to optimise performance metrics. It also requires robust governance systems to mitigate risks such as disinformation and reputational harm. Furthermore, organisations need strategic approaches which combine creative innovation with standardised assessment methods and ethical compliance. This chapter presents a strategic framework for content marketing AI implementation, which serves as a guide for both practitioners and academicians.

S. Santos (✉)
CEOS.PP, Porto, Portugal
e-mail: sara.santos@uab.pt

NECE - Research Centre for Business Sciences, Covilhã, Portugal

Departamento de Ciências Sociais e Gestão, Universidade Aberta, Lisboa, Portugal

P. E. Santo
Centre of Applied Research in Management and Economics (CARME), Polytechnic University of Leiria, Leiria, Portugal
e-mail: pedro.m.santo@ipleiria.pt

J. D. Santos et al. (eds.), *Artificial Intelligence Transforming Marketing*, Contributions to Management Science, https://doi.org/10.1007/978-3-032-22360-9_17

1 Introduction

Artificial Intelligence (AI) tools are widely used, changing digital marketing practices, particularly content marketing. Large-scale language models and machine learning instruments enable the creation of highly customised texts, images, audio and video content (Haenlein & Kaplan, 2019; Sun et al., 2024). Therefore, marketing content generation, distribution, and monitoring have undergone significant transformations through these technologies, which enhance personalisation tactics (Alzoubi et al., 2025) and performance analysis (Chen, 2023).

The implementation of generative AI in content marketing presents both strategic and ethical challenges, which include brand authenticity (Ali et al., 2025) and algorithmic biases (Reed et al., 2025), as well as data transparency and security (Alzoubi et al., 2025) and information reliability (Sun et al., 2024). AI technologies enhance operational efficiency and audience participation, but also present risks to brand identity consistency and trust (Ali et al., 2025). Hari et al. (2025) discuss the ethical aspects of AI marketing applications, while Hue and Hung (2025) examine the influence of AI on branding. However, there is a literature gap about recommended AI integration processes in content marketing. Some studies (Ali et al., 2025; Hari et al., 2025) highlight the lack of evaluation methods to assess the marketing practices and the impact of these technologies on results, as well as methods that account for different sectors, cultural environments, and regulatory systems.

This chapter analyses scientific evidence about generative AI in content marketing to suggest improvements in integrating AI into content marketing strategy.

Building on this objective, the chapter is organised into six main sections. It begins with the introduction, which contextualises the relevance of integrating artificial intelligence into content marketing. The methodology section then details the systematic approach adopted for selecting and analysing the literature. This is followed by the results section, which synthesises the key findings and identifies dominant themes and trends. The discussion section critically examines these findings, incorporating international case studies and expanding on technical performance metrics. The chapter concludes with a section on future research and implications, highlighting avenues for further empirical exploration and a conclusion that summarises the main contributions of the study.

2 Methodology

This systematic review examines empirical evidence from the literature to identify challenges and obstacles in content marketing and AI processes. The main objective is to analyse the process of integrating AI into content marketing strategy. This study's research question is "How does artificial intelligence impact content marketing processes and results?"

The Preferred Reporting Items for Systematic Reviews and Meta-Analyses (PRISMA) guidelines (Page et al., 2021) provided the structured methodological framework for this investigation. The methodology follows a systematic approach using the PRISMA guidelines to identify, select, and evaluate studies before synthesising relevant findings.

The research uses Scopus as its exclusive bibliographic database for this review. Scopus is regarded as the largest citation and abstract database, offering broader subject coverage compared to the Web of Science database (Wang et al., 2015). This database provides comprehensive access to high-quality, peer-reviewed publications across relevant domains, along with powerful search features that enable precise and reproducible literature retrieval.

The search was conducted on August 20, 2025, using the following Boolean operators: ("artificial intelligence" OR "AI" OR "machine learning") AND ("content marketing" OR "marketing content" OR "branded content" OR "digital content") OR ("Artificial intelligence generated content" OR "AIGC").

The choice of keywords reflected the core conceptual dimensions of the study. Terms such as "artificial intelligence", "AI", and "machine learning" were included to capture the full range of technologies underpinning generative systems. These terms were combined with marketing-related terms, such as "content marketing", "marketing content", "branded content", and "digital content", to ensure comprehensive coverage of studies focusing on marketing applications. Additionally, the "artificial intelligence-generated content" (AIGC) was incorporated to target the rapidly emerging body of literature specifically addressing AI-generated outputs. The use of the Boolean operator "OR" within each conceptual cluster broadened the search to include synonymous expressions, while "AND" was applied to intersect the technological and marketing domains, thereby retrieving only those studies that intersected both fields. This approach was deliberately chosen to strike a balance between breadth and precision, ensuring methodological transparency and reproducibility in the selection of relevant literature.

The following inclusion criteria were used to choose articles: (a) have been published between 2019 and 2025; (b) be written in English; (c) be articles or conference proceedings; (d) be published in areas of Social Sciences, Business, Management and Accounting; and (e) be open access.

3 Results

In accordance with the PRISMA guidelines, the Scopus search yielded 86 records (Fig. 1). After verifying duplication, titles and abstracts were screened, and 52 items that did not address the research question were excluded. The remaining 34 records underwent a full-text review and were found to meet the established eligibility criteria, resulting in a final analytic sample of 34 studies.

The final selection encompasses diverse perspectives on utilising artificial intelligence in content marketing across various contexts. Authors emphasise creative

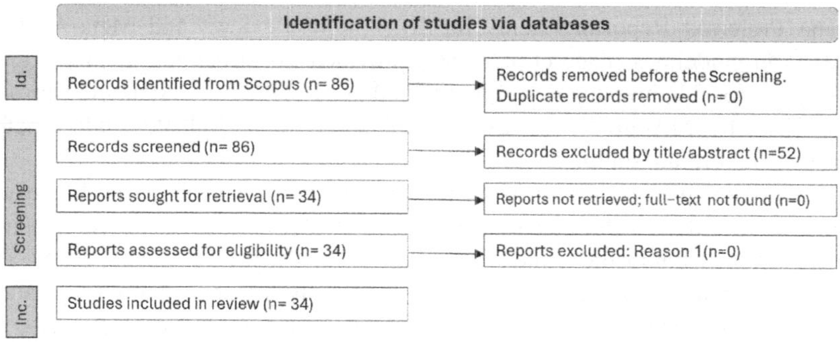

Fig. 1 PRISMA flow diagram for the systematic review process. *Source* Authors

creation and quality, brand authenticity, large-scale personalisation, predictive analytics for performance optimisation, and governance frameworks.

Table 1 summarises the research studies and their objectives.

The selected studies in Table 1, most of which were published in 2024, demonstrate various research methods and objectives that apply artificial intelligence to content marketing. The research shows evolution through its diverse collection of empirical analyses, literature reviews, benchmarking methodologies, and conceptual framework studies. It focuses on creative quality assessment, brand authenticity evaluation, the effects of AI content labelling, and human-AI collaborative content creation. Articles also investigate large-scale personalisation techniques and predictive analytics to show how AI enhances operational efficiency and digital platform audience engagement.

The ongoing difficulties in AI content marketing stem from ethical governance, transparency issues, and risk mitigation concerns, including disinformation and deepfakes. Researchers address these issues through blockchain-based innovative solutions, benchmarking standards, and hybrid validation models.

The multiple studies identified limitations show a need for more extended research periods, different cultural and regulatory assessment approaches, and standardised metrics to measure consistent real-world impacts.

Table 2 presents a comprehensive summary of the main findings from the analysed studies. The results are presented by combining key highlights to provide a better understanding of the research context.

Table 2 summarises the main contributions and findings of the 34 studies in the review, highlighting the diversity of approaches and contexts in which generative AI is applied to content marketing.

The use of AI in content marketing strategies has consequences for consumer behaviour. Alzoubi et al. (2025) and Gu et al. (2024) demonstrate that large-scale AI-powered personalisation leads to better consumer engagement and commitment when it is consistent with brand identity. In addition, Brüns and Meißner (2024) and Zhang and Prebensen (2024) demonstrate that "AI-generated" content appears less

Table 1 Description of the study's objective included in the review

Nº	Authors	Title	Journal/ Proceedings	Year	Study objective
1	Alzoubi, H. M.; Shameem, B., Mushtaq, S., Al Kurdi, B.; Joghee, S., & Hamadneh, S	Unveiling the Role of Artificial Intelligence: Navigating Personalised Content Marketing, Customer Engagement, and Commitment with Data Transparency and Security	International Review of Management and Marketing	2025	To investigate, in the UAE healthcare sector, the mediation of AI between personalised content marketing and engagement and the moderation of data transparency/ security
2	Arora, A., Bansal, S., Kandpal, C., Aswani, R., & Dwivedi, Y. K	Measuring social media influencer index: Insights from Facebook, Twitter and Instagram	Journal of Retailing and Consumer Services	2019	Develop and validate a social media influencer index by analysing key metrics from Facebook, Twitter, and Instagram to quantify influencer effectiveness and predict their impact on audience engagement
3	Brüns, J. D., & Meißner, M	Do you create your content yourself? Using generative artificial intelligence for social media content creation diminishes perceived brand authenticity	Journal of Retailing and Consumer Services	2024	Evaluate the effects of using and disseminating generative AI on brand authenticity and follower responses (three experimental studies)

(continued)

Table 1 (continued)

Nº	Authors	Title	Journal/ Proceedings	Year	Study objective
4	Buhalis, D., & Sinarta, Y. (2019)	Real-time co-creation and nowness service: Lessons from tourism and hospitality	Journal of Travel & Tourism Marketing	2019	Conceptualise how artificial intelligence, big data, and social media enable real-time co-creation and "nowness service" to deliver personalised, context-aware experiences in tourism and hospitality
5	Campbell, C., Sands, S., Montecchi, M., & Schau, H. J	That's So Instagrammable! Understanding How Environments Generate Indirect Advertising by Cueing Consumer-Generated Content	Journal of Advertising	2022	Quantify how features of "Instagrammable" physical environments stimulate UGC that functions as indirect advertising
6	Chen, Y	Comparing content marketing strategies of digital brands using machine learning	Humanities and Social Sciences Communications	2023	Integrate text mining and ensemble learning to compare content strategies of six major brands from Facebook pages
7	Dwivedi, Y. K., Ismagilova, E., Hughes, D. L.; et al	Setting the future of digital and social media marketing research: Perspectives and research propositions	International Journal of Information Management	2021	Define a digital/ social marketing research agenda with theoretical propositions, including AI, digital content, and performance metrics

(continued)

Table 1 (continued)

Nº	Authors	Title	Journal/ Proceedings	Year	Study objective
8	Fan, F., Luo, C., Gao, W., & Zhan, J	AIGCBench: Comprehensive evaluation of image-to-video content generated by AI	BenchCouncil Transactions on Benchmarks, Standards and Evaluations	2023	Propose a standardised benchmark for image-to-video generation with 11 metrics in four dimensions and evaluate correlation with human judgements
9	Gioia, G., & Lener, S. M	The protection of individuals against privacy-invasive and discriminatory inferences under European law: From the GDPR and the Digital Content and Services Directive to the Artificial Intelligence Act	Zbornik Pravnog fakulteta u Zagrebu	2024	Assess European legal protection against invasive and discriminatory inferences and identify gaps in the GDPR, DCSD, and AI Act
10	Gu, C., Jia, S., Lai, J., Chen, R., & Chang, X	Exploring Consumer Acceptance of AI-Generated Advertisements: From the Perspectives of Perceived Eeriness and Perceived Intelligence	Journal of Theoretical and Applied Electronic Commerce Research	2024	Identify determinants of acceptance of AI-generated ads based on the dimensions of perceived strangeness and perceived intelligence
11	Hartmann, J., Exner, Y., & Domdey, S	The power of generative marketing: Can generative AI create superhuman visual marketing content?	International Journal of Research in Marketing	2025	Compare AI-generated visual creativity to human-generated alternatives, measuring perceived quality and performance in field tests

(continued)

Table 1 (continued)

Nº	Authors	Title	Journal/ Proceedings	Year	Study objective
12	Jang, H. E., Kim, S. H., Jeon, J. S., & Oh, J. H	Visual Attributes of Thumbnails in Predicting YouTube Brand Channel Views in the Marketing Digitalisation Era	IEEE Transactions on Computational Social Systems	2024	Build a predictive view model with 16,278 thumbnails from 137 brand channels and isolate traffic drivers
13	Jaroucheh, Z., Alissa, M., Buchanan, W. J., & Liu, X	TRUSTD: Combat fake content using blockchain and collective signature technologies	Proceedings of the 2020 International Conference on Cyber Security and Protection of Digital Services (Cyber Security), IEEE	2020	Design a content provenance and validation architecture with blockchain and collective signatures to combat fake content
14	Joshi, S., Das, A., & Matta, M	Artificial intelligence tools for enhancing customer experience	International Journal of Recent Technology and Engineering	2019	Explores how artificial intelligence tools such as chatbots, facial recognition, and sentiment analysis enhance customer experience by enabling more personalised, efficient, and engaging interactions
15	Kshetri, N	Generative artificial intelligence in marketing: Applications, opportunities, challenges, and research agenda	International Journal of Information Management	2024	Review the applications and barriers of generative AI in marketing and propose an agenda focused on personalisation and insight generation

(continued)

Table 1 (continued)

Nº	Authors	Title	Journal/ Proceedings	Year	Study objective
16	Kupalova, H., Honcharenko, N., Andrusiv, U., Jakupova, D., Oleshko, E., & Demchenko, K	Organisational and financial aspects of the distribution management of digital content	Financial and Credit Activity: Problems of Theory and Practice	2024	Propose organisational measures and revenue models for digital content distribution (focus on e-books) and advocate for introducing AI into the platform
17	Kuzyk, O., Kabanova, O., Chyrva, H., Vlasenko, D., & Komarnytska, H	Trends and perspectives on the impact of digital technologies on the efficacy of marketing communication	Financial and Credit Activity: Problems of Theory and Practice	2023	Prioritise 32 digital solutions via cross-ranking to guide investment and reduce financial risk in marketing communications
18	Lewis, J., & Moorkens, J. (2020)	A Rights-Based Approach to Trustworthy AI in Social Media	Social Media + Society	2020	Propose a rights-based governance approach for AI in social networks, including collective data rights
19	Lou, Y	Human Creativity in the AIGC Era	She Ji: The Journal of Design, Economics, and Innovation	2024	Explore the distinctive role of human creativity in the AIGC era and outline core competencies for creators
20	Lu, Y	A Chinese perspective on artificial intelligence-generated content and copyright	Információs Társadalom	2024	Analyse the Chinese copyright framework applicable to AIGC, mapping current trends on originality and ownership

(continued)

Table 1 (continued)

Nº	Authors	Title	Journal/ Proceedings	Year	Study objective
21	Maiano, L., Benova, A., Papa, L., Stockner, M., Marchetti, M., Convertino, G., Mazzoni, G., & Amerini, I	Human Versus Machine: A Comparative Analysis in Detecting Artificial Intelligence-Generated Images	IEEE Security and Privacy Magazine	2024	Compare human and automated performance in detecting AI-generated images and evaluate the robustness of different generation methods
22	Moreira, D., Marcel, S., & Rocha, A	Synthetic Realities and Artificial Intelligence-Generated Contents: Guest Editors' Introduction	IEEE Security and Privacy Magazine	2024	Contextualise risks, forensic challenges, and methodological needs in the light of the dissemination of synthetic content
23	Oppenlaender, J., Linder, R., & Silvennoinen, J	Prompting AI art: An investigation into the creative skill of prompt engineering	International Journal of Human–Computer Interaction	2024	Assessing prompting as a creative skill in three studies analysing prompt evaluation, writing, and refinement
24	Pahari, S., Bandyopadhyay, A., Vijay Kumar, V. M., & Pingle, S	A bibliometric analysis of digital advertising in social media: the state of the art and future research agenda	Cogent Business & Management	2024	Map the production (2000–2023) on digital advertising in social media and identify trends and gaps via bibliometric analysis
25	Pellas, N	The influence of sociodemographic factors on students' attitudes toward AI-generated video content creation	Smart Learning Environments	2023	Analyse how sociodemographic factors and AI training influence attitudes towards AI-powered video creation

(continued)

Table 1 (continued)

Nº	Authors	Title	Journal/ Proceedings	Year	Study objective
26	Salminen, J., Yoganathan, V., Corporan, J., Jansen, B. J., & Jung, S.-G	Machine learning approach to auto-tagging online content for content marketing efficiency: A comparative analysis between methods and content type	Journal of Business Research	2019	Investigate how different machine learning methods can be applied to auto-tag online content across content types to improve the efficiency and accuracy of content marketing
27	Sang, N. M	Bibliometric insights into the evolution of digital marketing trends	Innovative Marketing	2024	Outline the evolution of digital marketing (2003–2024) in Scopus and propose research/ practice paths based on bibliometric indicators
28	Shoaib, M. R., Wang, Z., Taleby Ahvanooey, M., & Zhao, J	Deepfakes, Misinformation and Disinformation in the Era of Frontier AI, Generative AI and Large AI Models	International Conference on Computer and Applications (ICCA)	2023	Present an integrated defence framework against deepfakes and disinformation, combining detection techniques, watermarking, and policy tools
29	Sun, Y., Sheng, D., Zhou, Z., & Wu, Y	AI Hallucination: Towards a Comprehensive Classification of Distorted Information in Artificial Intelligence-Generated Content	Humanities and Social Sciences Communications	2024	Systematically classify hallucinations in AIGC and propose an operational taxonomy for auditing and mitigation
30	Tanase, I., Voicu, B. C., Popa Chivu, R.-G., & Grejdan, E. F	The Use of the OpenAI GPT-3 AI Technology for Marketing Content Purposes	Journal of Eastern Europe Research in Business and Economics	2024	Evaluate the usefulness of GPT-3 in generating marketing content and discuss quality and ethics requirements

(continued)

Table 1 (continued)

Nº	Authors	Title	Journal/ Proceedings	Year	Study objective
31	Wahid, R., Mero, J., & Ritala, P	Editorial: Written by ChatGPT, illustrated by Midjourney—generative AI for content marketing	Asia Pacific Journal of Marketing and Logistics	2023	Synthesise opportunities, challenges, and research priorities for using generative AI in content marketing
32	Wei, S., Ge, Z., & Tan, C	The Public Interest in the Digital Age: Exploring the Emerging Roles and Governance Models of AI as a Common Good	Journal of Ecohumanism	2024	Examine AI as a common good and analyse how public understanding and trust affect the acceptance of governance models
33	Whittaker, G., Letheren, K., & Mulcahy, R	The Rise of Deepfakes: A Conceptual Framework and Research Agenda for Marketing	Australasian Marketing Journal	2021	To provide a conceptual framework and research agenda for deepfakes in marketing, balancing opportunities and risks
34	Zhang, Y., & Prebensen, N. K	Co-creating with ChatGPT for tourism marketing materials	Annals of Tourism Research Empirical Insights	2024	Compare texts generated by ChatGPT with professional texts in terms of fluency, attractiveness, and distinctiveness in tourism marketing (two experiments)

authentic when it lacks human elements. From this perspective, the role of AI is to enhance human creativity and support authenticity, rather than replace it.

Research on content quality demonstrates two conflicting outcomes. According to Oppenlaender et al. (2024), technical measurements of realism and CTR (click-to-rate) indicate that advanced AIGC (Artificial Intelligence Generated Content) models can produce outputs at human levels. However, Lou (2024) demonstrates that the technical achievement of AIGC models producing human-level outputs fails to create brand value because it lacks narrative and culturally relevant context. These perspectives reveal a significant gap between actual and perceived quality, as content

Table 2 Key highlights from the studies

Nº	Authors	Key highlights
1	Alzoubi, H. M., Shameem, B., Mushtaq, S., Al Kurdi, B., Joghee, S., & Hamadneh, S	It confirms the positive mediation of AI between personalisation and engagement, as well as the moderating effect of transparency/security. Specifically, "Time and Delivery" has a greater impact and significant effects (partial mediation)
2	Arora, A., Bansal, S., Kandpal, C., Aswani, R., & Dwivedi, Y. K	By applying machine learning techniques to data from major social media platforms, the study identifies engagement, reach, sentiment, and growth as key variables for measuring the effectiveness of influencers. It demonstrates how these metrics can be used to predict campaign outcomes and inform strategic marketing decisions
3	Brüns, J. D., & Meißner, M	The "AI-generated" label diminishes perceived authenticity and attitudes, mitigating the effects when AI is presented as supporting human creators
4	Buhalis, D., & Sinarta, Y	Leveraging AI, big data, and social media enables dynamic co-creation, real-time personalisation, and context-aware service delivery, transforming customer engagement and value creation in the tourism and hospitality sectors
5	Campbell, C., Sands, S.,d Montecchi, M., & Schau, H. J	Colour, brightness, and interactive elements increase UGC; many design topics have zero or negative effects. It needs empirical testing
6	Chen, Y	Identifies three interaction/notification/deflection modules; continuous social listening generates actionable clues to optimise engagement and traffic
7	Dwivedi, Y. K., Ismagilova, E., Hughes, D. L., et al	Emphasises AI integration and explainable metrics; highlights ethical and transparency challenges to guide performance-based decisions
8	Fan, F., Luo, C., & Gao, W.; Zhan, J	It establishes a comparable framework (alignment, movement, temporal consistency, and quality) for selecting models with the best expected performance
9	Gioia, G., & Lener, S. M	Identifies gaps in GDPR/DCSD/AI law in protecting against invasive and discriminatory inferences, recommending additional safeguards
10	Gu, C., Jia, S., Lai, J.; Chen, R., & Chang, X	Strangeness reduces acceptance while perceived intelligence increases it, with visual verisimilitude and vitality being positive factors
11	Hartmann, J., & Exner, Y., & Domdey, S	AI-generated images achieve superior quality/realism ratings, as well as higher CTR in A/B testing, with cost and scale advantages
12	Jang, H. E., Kim, S. H., Jeon, J. S., & Oh, J. H	Thumbnail attributes, offline brand strength, and channel size explain views, providing a basis for predictive editorial planning
13	Jaroucheh, Z., Alissa, M., Buchanan, W. J., & Liu, X. (2020)	It demonstrates, through a proof-of-concept, that blockchain and collective signatures can guarantee immutable provenance and facilitate collaborative content validation

(continued)

Table 2 (continued)

Nº	Authors	Key highlights
14	Joshi, S., Das, A., & Matta, M	Demonstrates that integrating AI tools into customer interactions enables real-time personalisation, improved engagement, and more seamless service experiences
15	Kshetri, N	It argues that GenAI enables high-level personalisation and productivity gains, requiring data governance and appropriate metrics
16	Kupalova, H., Honcharenko, N., Andrusiv, U., Jakupova, D., Oleshko, E., & Demchenko, K	Links channel and investment decisions to performance dashboards; AI to optimise operations, reporting, and financial efficiency
17	Kuzyk, O., Kabanova, O., Chyrva, H., Vlasenko, D., & Komarnytska, H	It points to a clear trend towards AI in communications; a link between technological choices, risk reduction, and increased ROI
18	Lewis, J., & Moorkens, J	Advocates for rights-based governance, including collective data rights and human oversight, to increase transparency and accountability on platforms
19	Lou, Y	It argues that meaning, cultural awareness, and narrative reasoning are essential human advantages in AI-assisted creative direction
20	Lu, Y	Maps 12 currents on originality and three on ownership in AIGC, highlighting the need for legal clarification to enable creative uses
21	Maiano, L., Benova, A., Papa, L., Stockner, M., Marchetti, M., Convertino, G., Mazzoni, G., & Amerini, I	It shows that classifiers (ResFormer) outperform humans in in-domain scenarios, but with poor generalisation between generation methods and human biases in decision-making
22	Moreira, D., Marcel, S., & Rocha, A	It summarises the forensic risks and challenges associated with synthetic content and highlights the urgency of terminological standardisation and interoperable metrics
23	Oppenlaender, J., Linder, R., & Silvennoinen, J	It demonstrates that crafting effective prompts is not a trivial task and requires a nuanced understanding of stylistic vocabulary, as well as iterative practice, to unlock aesthetic quality
24	Pahari, S., Bandyopadhyay, A., Kumar, V. M., & Pingle, S	It focuses on consumer behaviour, brand engagement, and the growing adoption of analytics/AI/AR to enhance advertising effectiveness
25	Pellas, N	Training and technological experience are associated with more favourable attitudes, suggesting that upskilling facilitates the adoption and quality of new technologies

(continued)

Table 2 (continued)

Nº	Authors	Key highlights
26	Salminen, J., Yoganathan, V., Corporan, J., Jansen, B. J., & Jung, S.-G	Shows that applying machine learning algorithms, such as random forest, KNN, and neural networks, enables accurate auto-tagging of online content. Performance is evaluated through metrics like precision, recall, and F1-score, thereby improving content organisation and marketing effectiveness
27	Sang, N. M	It confirms the shift towards data-driven approaches and highlights AI/ML, content marketing, and digital transformation as structuring themes
28	Shoaib, M. R., Wang, Z., Taleby Ahvanooey, M., & Zhao, J	It presents an integrated defence framework against deepfakes and disinformation, combining multimodal detection, watermarking, and policy measures
29	Sun, Y., Sheng, D., Zhou, Z., & Wu, Y	It proposes a taxonomy of 8 types and 31 subtypes of hallucinations in AIGC, offering an operational basis for auditing and mitigation
30	Tanase, I., Voicu, B. C., Popa Chivu, R.-G., & Grejdan, E. F	It signals gains in productivity and usefulness, requiring factual verification, mitigation of biases and adherence to the brand voice
31	Wahid, R., Mero, J., & Ritala, P	It presents a framework in which GenAI complements or replaces creation steps, outlining an agenda for measuring its impacts on platforms and engagement
32	Wei, S., Ge, Z., & Tan, C	Evidence that public understanding and trust predict participation and acceptance of governance models for AI as a common good
33	Whittaker, G., Letheren, K., & Mulcahy, R	Introduces a typology and research agenda for deepfakes in marketing, highlighting the need for consent and disclosure policies
34	Zhang, Y., & Prebensen, N. K	AI-generated texts showed comparable fluency/attractiveness and were, in many cases, indistinguishable from those produced by professionals, supporting human–AI co-creation

Source Authors

depends on cultural and contextual elements, as well as narrative factors, influencing consumer perception and engagement.

The conversion of technical metrics, such as alignment scores and movement smoothness, into business Key Performance Indicators (KPIs) (Fan et al., 2023; Jang et al., 2024) follows a pattern in analytics and performance research; however, standardisation remains inadequate. Sang (2024) provides evidence that standardised benchmarks are missing, which makes it impossible for researchers to perform longitudinal and cross-platform comparisons. Methodological weakness makes it difficult to establish reliable connections between technical enhancements and their impact on sales funnel performance.

On the other hand, predictive model-derived engagement metrics help boost conversion rates when tested through A/B testing (Hartmann et al., 2025). Studies have drawn opposing conclusions because they did not consider essential elements, including audience characteristics and distribution channel preferences. Lewis and Moorkens (2020) and Jaroucheh et al. (2020) recognise the necessity of strong traceability systems, while Whittaker et al. (2021) evidence the importance of transparent disclosure requirements. However, experts disagree on the importance of these measures. Gioia and Lener (2024) emphasise ongoing deficiencies in the European legal system, but Lu (2024) notes that China and other nations have progressed despite ongoing intellectual property uncertainties. The cultural and regulatory environment determines the suitability and impact of governance practices, making a universal solution impossible.

4 Discussion

Research findings indicate that generative artificial intelligence in content marketing operates through three interconnected domains that transform content. The first domain demonstrates how these technologies produce content at human levels or surpass human capabilities, thereby delivering maximum relevance to target audiences.

The second axis focuses on developing standardised analytical metrics that translate technical generative production indicators into business KPIs, enabling cross-platform and format validation of effectiveness.

The third axis focuses on governance, transparency, and trust, including traceability, authenticity verification, and compliance with legal and ethical standards.

A content marketing framework requires these essential components to implement generative AI properly. Based on the synthesis of the results, the CAG (Creation, Analytics, and Governance) framework was developed, articulating the integration of generative AI into content marketing across three interdependent dimensions (Fig. 2). This model provides a conceptual foundation for practical applications and future research.

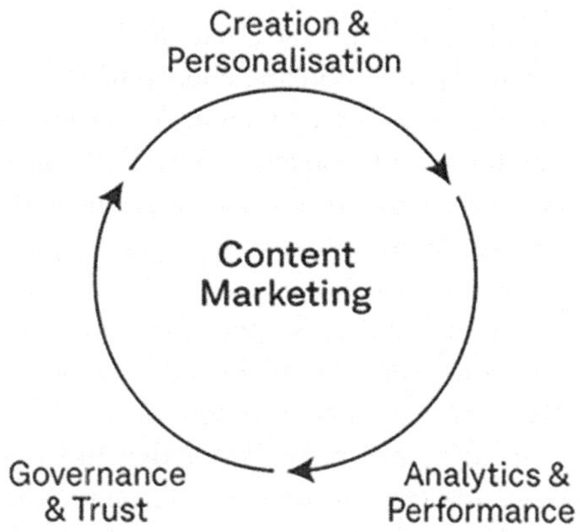

Fig. 2 CAG (Creation, Analytics, and Governance) framework for integrating generative AI into content marketing. *Source* Authors

The proposed CAG (Creation, Analytics, and Governance) framework provides a conceptual model to explain strategic and responsible integration of generative AI into content marketing. The framework consists of three interconnected dimensions which include (1) Creation and Personalisation that uses AI to develop and customise multimodal content according to brand identity and objectives; (2) Analytics and Performance that transforms technical data into business performance indicators to support continuous improvement; and (3) Governance and Trust which establishes ethical and legal and technical standards to ensure transparency and minimise risks of bias or misinformation.

These three components operate as part of a dynamic, cyclical process, where content creation metrics drive performance-based modifications that support audits and governance procedures. In contrast, governance rules govern content production to ensure compliance with ethical and regulatory standards. The CAG framework delivers an extensive plan to enhance content marketing, creative, and performance effectiveness through generative AI while preserving brand trust and integrity.

4.1 Creation and Personalisation

Research on generative creation and personalisation reveals a change in how businesses generate and distribute content to specific groups and individuals. Experiments and field tests demonstrate that properly integrated generative artificial intelligence produces content that matches or surpasses standards.

The evolving role of artificial intelligence in content personalisation is also closely linked to the concept of "nowness service" and real-time co-creation. Buhalis and Sinarta (2019) argue that AI, combined with big data analytics and social media, enables brands to dynamically co-create value with consumers. This real-time engagement enables organisations to personalise content based on historical preferences, as well as situational factors such as location, mood, and current trends.

In the tourism and hospitality sectors, for example, brands have successfully leveraged AI to deliver highly contextualised offers, recommendations, and narratives that adapt moment by moment to user interactions (Buhalis & Sinarta, 2019). Such applications illustrate how AI-driven personalisation transcends static segmentation models, transforming content marketing into an interactive and co-creative process.

Additionally, Zhang and Prebensen (2024) conducted two controlled trials in tourism marketing, demonstrating that language model-generated writings were indistinguishable from those written by humans in terms of fluency and appeal. The study advocates for a human-AI collaborative approach to copywriting tasks.

Conversely, Tanase et al. (2024) evaluated the implementation of GPT-3 in marketing environments, demonstrating its benefits in terms of productivity and usefulness. However, human oversight remains essential for maintaining factual accuracy, brand voice consistency, and bias management (Tanase et al., 2024).

Gu et al. (2024) employed experimental methods to demonstrate that AI advertisement acceptance increases when stimuli display high levels of perceived intelligence, thereby defining the conditions under which generative outputs can match or surpass human-generated references.

The way AI information reaches the public population determines how consumers will respond. Three experimental studies to demonstrate that direct labelling of AI-generated content results in decreased brand authenticity and adverse attitudinal and behavioural outcomes. However, presenting AI as a human-assistance tool instead of a standalone solution reduces these adverse effects (Brüns & Meißner, 2024). Accepting AI-generated ads depends on striking a proper balance between perceived eeriness and perceived intelligence, as eeriness signals tend to decrease acceptance. However, verisimilitude, vitality, and imagination enhance the overall creative evaluation (Gu et al., 2024). Two operational implications emerge from these findings: AI should be presented as part of a responsible authoring system with clear human supervision, and formal content attributes need to be managed to achieve maximum relevance while minimising artificial signals that cause rejection.

The importance of artificial intelligence in content personalisation is further highlighted by research on enhancing customer experience. Joshi et al. (2019) demonstrate how AI tools, such as chatbots, facial recognition, and sentiment analysis, enable brands to deliver hyper-personalised content and services in real time. These technologies analyse behavioural patterns, emotional responses, and contextual signals to tailor marketing messages and digital interactions to individual preferences. As a result, organisations can create more relevant, engaging, and seamless customer journeys that strengthen loyalty and increase satisfaction. This perspective underscores that personalisation extends beyond algorithmic targeting. It involves dynamically adapting content to evolving user expectations and emotional states.

However, it is necessary to understand the transition from traditional creation to generative creation and personalisation. Wahid et al. (2023) present a framework that explains how generative tools enhance content creation stages, demonstrating their ability to replace certain stages in specific situations and their potential to improve creative processes and user engagement. Kshetri (2024) demonstrates how AI enables genuine personalisation through dynamic messages which use near-real-time behavioural data.

Successful implementation requires particular competencies and universal quality standards. The research by Oppenlaender et al. (2024) suggests that prompt engineering requires non-intuitive creative abilities because users can assess prompts and create descriptions. They also demonstrate weaknesses in stylistic vocabulary and modifier skills, which supports the need for structured training programmes and step-by-step guidance (Oppenlaender et al., 2024). Lou (2024), based on meaning-making, cultural awareness, and narrative reasoning, should inform the direction of AI-mediated production (Lou, 2024). Pellas (2023) presents video evidence showing that students who received AI training and technological experience develop more positive attitudes towards AI creation, indicating that structured upskilling programmes enhance adoption readiness and reliability assessment.

The literature also demonstrates the importance of quantitative data about personalisation systems and their factors influencing relational success. In the UAE healthcare sector, Alzoubi et al. (2025) demonstrate how AI connects personalised content marketing to engagement, leading to higher commitment. They demonstrate how AI facilitates personalised content marketing, leading to increased engagement, responsibility, and transparency. Alzoubi et al. (2025) demonstrated how AI connects personalised content marketing to engagement, leading to higher commitment and openness. Additionally, data security strengthens the relationship between personalisation and engagement (Alzoubi et al., 2025). The study demonstrates how performance compatibility functions in conjunction with trust, as robust data governance practices enable personalisation to sustain engagement and commitment.

Quality standards need explicit editorial chains and consistent metrics for their consolidation process. The assessment of textual content requires researchers to conduct blind and A/B tests for fluency and attractiveness while maintaining strict alignment with the brand voice (Tanase et al., 2024; Zhang & Prebensen, 2024). The evaluation process for visual content requires assessment of quality and realism alongside aesthetics and brief adherence, which should be linked to behavioural metrics, including click-through rate (Hartmann et al., 2025). According to Tanase et al. (2024), human monitoring verifies facts and minimises biases.

Extending this analysis, several international case studies further illustrate how generative AI is applied in diverse cultural and sectoral contexts for content marketing. According to Whittaker et al. (2021), one notable example is the use of deepfake technology in India to adapt political messaging to regional dialects, reaching more than 15 million voters and demonstrating how AI-generated content can localise narratives to heterogeneous audiences.

In the United Kingdom, the "Malaria Must Die" campaign utilised AI-generated multilingual video content featuring David Beckham to overcome linguistic barriers and expand the global reach of a public health message.

In the United States, the Dalí Museum integrated deepfake-based storytelling to recreate the artist's presence and deepen audience engagement. These examples demonstrate that AI-generated content extends beyond commercial marketing, influencing political communication, cultural storytelling, and public-interest campaigns, while expanding the strategic possibilities of content marketing on a global scale.

Although this topic exhibits increasing dynamism, knowledge generalisation and accumulation remain restricted by several limitations.

Research studies have specific empirical contexts, such as tourism student populations, healthcare in the UAE, which require careful extrapolation to other categories, geographic regions, and regulatory frameworks (Alzoubi et al., 2025; Pellas, 2023; Zhang & Prebensen, 2024). However, longitudinal and multichannel studies are also necessary to establish correlations between tactical advantages (such as click-through rates and blind quality evaluations) and medium-term results, including brand equity and loyalty (Hartmann et al., 2025). The current research lacks a standardised taxonomy for AI disclosure (label, formulation, timing, and level of detail) and an insufficient characterisation of contingent effects by brand type, audience, and platform, despite evidence showing that penalty mitigation occurs when AI is presented as support (Brüns & Meißner, 2024). The research demands expertise in prompting and multimodal benchmarks that connect individual competencies to business indicators, as mentioned in applied research (Oppenlaender et al., 2024; Kshetri, 2024).

The evidence suggests that generative AI serves as a structuring assistant for creative and personalisation tasks under human team supervision, ensuring the maintenance of meaning, ethical standards, and editorial quality. AI-assisted production achieves its highest effectiveness through responsible co-authorship communication and content attribute measurement, reducing artificiality signs, and training programmes for prompting and editing to professionalise tool usage. The combination of personalised content with transparent data governance demonstrates the potential to transform short-term engagement into enduring customer commitment (Alzoubi et al., 2025; Brüns & Meißner, 2024; Gu et al., 2024; Hartmann et al., 2025; Kshetri, 2024; Lou, 2024; Oppenlaender et al., 2024; Tanase et al., 2024; Zhang & Prebensen, 2024).

4.2 Analytics and Performance

In analytics and performance, studies show that AI/ML-based models and metrics enable diagnosis, prediction, and optimisation of content performance across the creation-distribution cycle. The research findings stem from extensive bibliometric studies analysing content attributes, platform dynamics, and results-oriented organisational choices.

Pahari et al. (2024) analyse digital advertising literature on social media platforms, while artificial intelligence enhances advertising effectiveness. The scientific agenda focuses on measuring results (e.g., clicks, shares, and conversions) and identifying their determinants. However, Sang (2024) demonstrates how data-driven methods, AI/ML, content marketing, and digital transformation have become fundamental topics which guide analytical research for strategic decision-making and professional training. Also, Dwivedi et al. (2021) establish a digital marketing and social media agenda that combines AI with digital content management and performance metrics while emphasising transparency and ethical requirements.

Research findings about intrinsic content attributes, platform signals, and engagement metrics provide proven operational guidelines for content design and distribution practices. Chen (2023) develops a social listening system that combines text mining techniques with ensemble learning methods for brand page analysis, aiming to detect notification, interaction, and traffic diversion indicators through analysis of posting patterns and information composition. His research demonstrates that continuous competitive monitoring enables designers to create more effective content while adjusting their editorial schedule to enhance audience engagement.

On the other hand, Campbell et al. (2022) demonstrate that physical environments designed for photography and sharing ("Instagrammable") become more likely to produce consumer content and indirect brand diffusion due to their tangible features, including colour and brightness, as well as interactive elements.

Recent research has introduced standardised metrics and analytical models to assess the impact of AI-generated content across platforms. Jang et al. (2024) demonstrate how predictive models can estimate expected video performance before publication by integrating variables such as thumbnail brightness, colourfulness, and object complexity with channel-level indicators like subscriber base and offline brand awareness. These predictive analytics enable marketers to quantify potential reach and optimise visual content proactively. Similarly, Chen (2023) proposes a machine learning framework that measures interaction effectiveness through three core modules (notification, interaction, and diversion), each associated with specific behavioural KPIs, such as click-through rate (CTR), dwell time, and repeat engagement. Incorporating these standardised metrics into AI-driven strategies supports more rigorous benchmarking, facilitates cross-platform comparisons, and strengthens the feedback loops necessary for continuous optimisation. Such approaches reflect a growing emphasis on technical transparency and accountability in evaluating the performance of AI-enhanced content.

Fanet al. (2023) develop AIGCBench as an 11-indicator framework with four dimensions, focusing on control-video alignment, motion effects, temporal consistency, and video quality for image-to-video tasks in open-ended scenarios. The authors demonstrate that these metrics align with human assessments, facilitating effective model comparisons and enabling the transfer of computational indicators (such as temporal consistency) into business metrics (such as watchability and completion rate), despite the limited connection in current applied research.

A more technical perspective on performance optimisation is presented by Salminen et al. (2019), who investigate how machine learning techniques can automate the tagging and classification of online content to improve marketing efficiency. By applying algorithms such as random forest, k-nearest neighbour (KNN), and multilabel neural networks, the study demonstrates how unstructured text can be transformed into structured metadata that supports more accurate targeting and evaluation. The authors report that metrics such as precision, recall, and F1-score provide robust indicators of model performance, enabling marketers to benchmark tagging systems across platforms. This evidence reinforces the idea that standardised metrics and algorithmic classification methods are essential components of a data-driven content marketing strategy, enhancing both the scalability and the analytical rigour of AI-supported campaigns.

In addition to algorithmic tagging and content classification, the evaluation of performance in AI-driven content marketing increasingly relies on metrics that capture the dynamics of influence across social platforms. Arora et al. (2019) propose a "social media influencer index" that quantifies an influencer's effectiveness based on engagement, reach, sentiment, and growth. These metrics give more profound insights into audience behaviour and content resonance, complementing traditional indicators such as click-through rates and dwell time. Integrating influencer-level analytics into performance evaluation thus enhances the strategic use of AI-generated content, allowing marketers to better understand and leverage social influence as a driver of engagement and brand visibility.

The optimisation of content requires distribution and economic efficiency as essential contrasts. Kupalova et al. (2024) present organisational and financial aspects of digital content distribution management through AI platform implementation to enhance operational efficiency, reporting capabilities, and revenue models. Performance dashboards must guide channel and investment choices to prevent operational inefficiencies (Kupalova et al, 2024). Sovīk et al. (2023) employ the cross-ranking technology prioritisation method to analyse 32 digital communication solutions, establishing a direct relationship between AI adoption and decreased financial risk and improved return on investment. This helps organisations link analytical investments to performance gains.

The research findings yield integrative implications. The combination of intrinsic content attributes (e.g., thumbnail colour and brightness) with platform signals (channel history, publishing rhythm) and brand characteristics (offline strength) leads to better prediction performance by avoiding the use of single metrics. Jang et al. (2024) and Chen (2023) show that textual cues and editorial rhythms are interaction determinants. Social listening through AI must operate continuously with a competitive focus to utilise ensemble methods and multimodal analysis for pattern detection and publishing rhythm control and interaction quality assessment, which serves as a value proxy (Chen, 2023; Dwivedi et al., 2021).

In this perspective, Chen (2023) presents a comparative machine learning analysis of six leading global digital brands (Disney, Netflix, Microsoft, Google, YouTube, and LinkedIn) to understand how AI reshapes content structure and audience interaction dynamics. The study identifies three key "interaction modules" that underpin successful AI-enhanced strategies: notification (capturing user attention through personalised triggers), interaction (fostering two-way engagement via adaptive messaging), and diversion (sustaining long-term user interest with dynamic content evolution). By integrating social listening, predictive analytics, and automated message optimisation, these brands demonstrate how AI can be operationalised at scale across markets to tailor narratives and stimulate continuous engagement.

The findings underscore that the effectiveness of AI-driven content creation lies not only in the automation of text, images, or videos, but also in its capacity to architect complex communication ecosystems responsive to real-time audience behaviours.

However, the standardisation of metrics and benchmarks (e.g., AIGCBench) needs to be connected to decision panels (CPA, LTV) and technological prioritisation to enable cross-sectional comparison between models and content, and to accelerate organisational learning cycles. It is also essential to identify limitations that compromise external validity. Jang et al. (2024) focus on brand channels at specific scales, which challenges extrapolation to other categories and geographies; cross-sector and multi-platform replications are necessary.

Many articles establish robust associations but lack naturalistic tests (e.g., geo-A/B) that link changes in content attributes and distribution strategies to causal variations in KPIs, a gap already highlighted by Chen (2023) and consistent with the agenda of Dwivedi et al. (2021).

Although Fan et al. (2023) present coherent measures for AI-generated content, applying these metrics to commercial objectives (retention, completion rate) is still insufficient and necessitates convergent validation. Additionally, the conclusions by Pahari et al. (2024) and Sang (2024) underscore the potential of AI/ML and emphasise the importance of algorithmic transparency and accountability in data utilisation. These components are still poorly operationalised in performance-oriented predictive studies.

The literature indicates that analytics and performance maturity consists of three fundamental pillars which include (i) explainable models that combine intrinsic content attributes with platform signals and brand variables; (ii) experimentation systems which evaluate incremental effects in real-world scenarios; and (iii) standardised metrics that match technical benchmarks to business targets and serve as inputs for decision-making and technology selection (Fan et al., 2023) and technology prioritisation processes. The triple link depends on measurement culture, as recommended by several authors (Dwivedi et al., 2021; Pahari et al., 2024; Sang, 2024), and an organisation's capacity to convert analytical findings into a content-channel-monetisation model alignment (Kupalova et al., 2024).

The reviewed studies show that analysis and performance are central to technology-driven content marketing. They highlight predictive social listening (Chen, 2023) and standardised metrics for testing (Fan et al., 2023). Other contributions highlight environments that encourage user-generated content (Campbell et al., 2022), the optimisation of video thumbnails (Jang et al., 2024), and distribution and investment (Kupalova et al., 2024). Finally, several authors discuss how to shape future research agendas in this field (Dwivedi et al., 2021; Pahari et al., 2024; Sang, 2024).

4.3 Governance and Trust

The governance of artificial intelligence applied to content creation (AIGC) requires legal frameworks and technical mechanisms for abuse prevention and detection that build public trust and organisational legitimacy. The literature suggests that operational definitions of risk, traceability, and rights-based governance principles are crucial for safeguarding users and brands in digital media ecosystems.

The first axis addresses identifying the informational risks that stem from AIGC. Sun et al. (2024) present a detailed taxonomy of AI hallucinations, which includes 243 incidents and identifies eight error types (e.g., unfounded fabrication, factual error, reasoning error) and 31 subtypes. The methodology combines editorial audits with verification checklists and pre-publication control design to minimise terminological ambiguity, thereby preventing discrepancies in study and platform comparison. The taxonomy provides essential value for content marketing because it establishes clear prevention methods, measurement standards, and reporting protocols for reputational and legal risk management.

The conceptual framework of risks expands through the examination of deepfakes. Whittaker et al. (2021) introduce deepfakes into marketing research through their typology of benign versus malicious applications. Their research plan evaluates creative possibilities against threats, including consent violations, manipulation, and deviance. The authors state that disclosure methods, consent protocols, and repair systems must advance at the same rate as the development of generative technology to protect trust and prevent short-term effectiveness losses. Similarly, Shoaib et al. (2023) develop an integrated defence system that fights deepfakes, disinformation and manipulation through multimodal detection, digital watermarking, machine learning authentication, cross-platform coordination, and public policy instruments. The "defence in depth" recommendation is crucial for brands facing coordinated disinformation campaigns or falsified sponsored content.

The second axis covers detection and authenticity. Maiano et al. (2024) examine how automated models and human evaluators perform in detecting AI-generated architectural pictures. The authors demonstrate that classifiers trained and tested with the same generation techniques perform better than human evaluators. They also show that generalisation between different synthesis methods remains weak while documenting how human biases, such as aesthetic preferences, influence judgement processes. The evidence supports hybrid (human-in-the-loop) strategies and highlights the need for more representative datasets and benchmarks to improve out-of-sample robustness. Ex-post detection procedures lead to the development of provenance and traceability methods.

The third axis deals with governance, which is based on rights and responsibilities. Lewis and Moorkens (2020) advocate for a rights-based framework of AI in social media because individual rights, such as consent and privacy, do not adequately address information asymmetries and collective consequences, including inferred profiling and opaque microtargeting. They recommend collective data rights and co-regulatory mechanisms which bring together platforms, regulators, and civil society organisations to enhance transparency and human oversight. The fundamental principle of "no datafication without representation" provides a normative standard for data collection and use practices which support AIGC.

Gioia and Lener (2024) examine European protection mechanisms for machine learning-generated invasive and discriminatory outcomes by analysing the GDPR, Digital Services Directive, and AI Act coverage and identifying gaps. The authors advocate for creating operational methods that prevent discrimination in content and advertising personalisation profile processing while fighting algorithmic opacity.

The legal framework for intellectual property rights and authorship emerges within the AIGC system. Lu (2024) discusses Chinese perspectives on authorship rights by organising twelve originality concepts alongside three ownership theories within the AIGC from 2017 to 2023. A national strategy for law development, ethical standards, and AI safety assessment abilities must be established by 2025 to enable responsible creative ecosystem investment and adoption. The framework allows brands to develop contracts with creators, license AI-generated assets, and streamline rights clearance processes.

Public backing enables technical and legal governance systems to function effectively. According to Wei et al. (2024), AI functions as a common good, as demonstrated through their research, which surveyed 400 Chinese participants to show that public understanding and trust are determinants of AIGC governance framework acceptance. The study indicates that transparent procedures and public involvement methods lower resistance while generating trust. The results support the establishment of disclosure regulations and the development of collaborative relationships between regulators and platform operators.

On the other hand, Moreira et al. (2024) conduct scientific research to explain how AIGC speed and sophistication necessitate digital forensic methodological changes, alongside standardised terminology and data sharing standards, to enable replicable research. The paper creates strong academic-to-regulatory connections through its analysis of methodological limitations and its proposal for standardised measurement systems.

The identified gaps in existing research indicate multiple directions for future investigations. The field continues to experience terminological confusion about "hallucination" and lacks standardised measurement tools that connect error categories to reputation effects and regulatory expenses. There is an urgent need to verify intersubjective scales and risk metrics that enable sector-to-sector comparisons, according to Sun et al. (2024) and Moreira et al. (2024).

The detection field faces out-of-domain robustness challenges (Maiano et al., 2024), which suggest implementing shared benchmarks, open panels and cross-platform testing with diverse samples of techniques and generation model families. The regulatory framework remains unclear regarding AIGC authorship rights, ownership protection, and the prevention of opaque inferences, according to Lu (2024) and Gioia and Lener (2024). The practical effectiveness of the AI Act and national legislation requires empirical studies to evaluate their real-world impact.

The academic discourse on "Governance and Trust" in artificial intelligence emphasises that cultivating trust within AI ecosystems requires a holistic strategy, integrating regulatory structures with advanced technical safeguards. This includes the precise definition of risk factors and the establishment of measurable evaluation criteria (Sun et al., 2024), the deployment of reliable technological protections (Jaroucheh et al., 2020; Maiano et al., 2024), and the implementation of rights-oriented governance frameworks with a broad collective scope (Lewis & Moorkens, 2020), supported by legally enforceable safeguards (Gioia & Lener, 2024). Translating these principles into practice requires interoperable standards, thorough empirical testing, and sustained cooperation among institutions, ensuring that conceptual models are transformed into concrete applications.

5 Future Research and Implications

The research agenda for generative artificial intelligence in content marketing contains multiple dimensions as proposed by various authors (Table 3).

The proposed research focuses on personalisation and dissemination methods, which must be evaluated through short-term and long-term metrics to assess

Table 3 Future Research aligns with the primary authors

Theme	Research gaps	Main authors
Quality and effectiveness of generative creation	In real and controlled contexts, testing how the type of advertising, alignment with brand voice, and level of personalisation affect effectiveness metrics and medium-term effects	Alzoubi et al. (2025), Brüns and Meißner (2024), Gu et al. (2024); Hartmann et al. (2025), and Zhang and Prebensen (2024)
Standardisation and translation of analytical metrics	Develop multimodal benchmarks and metrics that translate technical indicators into business KPIs, with cross-platform validation, ensuring consistency and accuracy across all platforms	Chen (2023), Fan et al. (2023), Jang et al. (2024), Pahari et al. (2024), and Sang (2024)
AIGC Governance and Transparency	Analyse verifiable traceability and authentication protocols, reconciling legal requirements, data protection, and consumer trust	Gioia and Lener (2024), Lewis and Moorkens (2020), Lu (2024), and Wei et al. (2024)
Mitigation of risks of disinformation and deepfakes	Improve robust cross-model detection (human-in-the-loop and classifiers), interoperate with watermarks/digital signatures, and define disclosure/consent policies for the use of synthetic content	Jaroucheh et al. (2020), Maiano et al. (2024), Moreira et al. (2024), Shoaib et al. (2023), Sun et al. (2024), and Whittaker et al. (2021)
Human-AI skills and integration	Map and assess competencies (prompt engineering, curation, and editing), editorial standards, and hybrid team models; quantify the effects of upskilling on quality and effectiveness	Kshetri (2024), Lou (2024), Oppenlaender et al. (2024), Pellas (2023), Tanase et al. (2024), and Wahid et al. (2023)
Sociocultural and regulatory impact	Compare how cultural, legal, and regulatory contexts influence the perception, acceptance, and application of GenAI in content marketing, and evaluate their impact on disclosure and trust	Alzoubi et al. (2025), Gioia and Lener (2024), Kshetri (2024), Lu (2024), and Sang (2024)
Sustainability	Investigate the energy costs and environmental impacts of mass-market AI-powered content production, as well as the trade-offs between scalability, performance, and organisational sustainability	Dwivedi et al. (2021) and Sang (2024)

consumer engagement and trust levels. A crucial priority is creating fast benchmarks and measures that convert technical indicators into business KPIs for real-life comparison and application.

It is also a priority for governance and transparency, with recommendations for developing comprehensive traceability and authentication systems that adhere to legal, ethical, and operational standards. Detecting disinformation and synthetic content requires advancements in authentication and consent integration mechanisms to mitigate associated risks. The successful integration between humans and AI systems depends on professional training, which includes mapping and assessing skills such as prompt engineering and editorial curation.

The research areas of sociocultural and regulatory dimensions, as well as the environmental impacts of AI-generated content mass production, have emerged as strategic priorities for establishing sustainable practices that respect culture and meet social responsibility standards.

On the other side, given its innovative contribution to the field, the CAG model warrants further exploration and empirical validation in future research, particularly to assess its applicability across diverse industries, cultural contexts, and content marketing scenarios.

6 Conclusions

The systematic review reveals that artificial intelligence has a profound impact on content marketing, affecting creative quality, personalisation, and production capabilities. Empirical research indicates that AI-created content meets or surpasses the technical standards of human-generated content and demonstrates equal or higher levels of relevance (Hartmann et al., 2025; Zhang & Prebensen, 2024). However, at the same time, some authors (Brüns & Meißner, 2024; Gu et al., 2024) emphasise that the "AI-generated" term leads to lower perceptions of authenticity and brand attitudes, and this effect becomes less pronounced when AI functions as a human collaboration tool. Implementing GenAI leads to operational benefits for creating and delivering content faster (Alzoubi et al., 2025; Kshetri, 2024); however, it also generates problems regarding authenticity perception and consumer trust.

In addition, integrating AI-driven tools such as chatbots, sentiment analysis, and facial recognition has been shown to enhance customer experience by enabling real-time personalisation and more seamless service interactions, which can indirectly reinforce trust and brand loyalty (Joshi et al., 2019).

Brands should utilise hybrid creative models that combine AI technological skills with human supervision (Lou, 2024; Wahid et al., 2023) to align with their identity and voice while adhering to legal and ethical standards. Standardising multimodal measurements and benchmarks (Chen, 2023; Fan et al., 2023; Jang et al., 2024) transforms technical indicators into business-oriented KPIs.

Recent research further highlights the role of machine learning techniques in optimising tagging and classification processes, providing measurable indicators such as precision, recall, and F1-score that improve content discoverability and support more accurate performance evaluation (Salminen et al., 2019). Moreover, the development of influencer indices based on engagement, reach, sentiment, and growth adds an additional layer of performance-based transparency, enabling brands to evaluate their impact and refine content strategies more effectively (Arora et al., 2019).

On the other side, rights-based governance approaches (Lewis & Moorkens, 2020) and traceability/authentication protocols (Jaroucheh et al., 2020; Lu, 2024) play a crucial role in maintaining transparency and preventing disinformation, deepfakes, and copyright violations (Shoaib et al., 2023; Whittaker et al., 2021).

Also important is the capacity of AI to enable real-time co-creation and "nowness service", where content and experiences are continuously adapted to the user's context and behaviour. Such dynamic personalisation reinforces user trust and enhances the perceived relevance of brand interactions, demonstrating that ethical and responsible AI use can also become a source of value co-creation (Buhalis & Sinarta, 2019).

The digital world requires a strategic approach to balance creative content development with performance metrics and ethical responsibility to maintain sustainable content marketing and build audience trust. The field shows growing interest, but essential research gaps continue to exist.

The solution requires sustained research to study content-sharing methods (Brüns & Meißner, 2024), human-AI collaboration dynamics (Oppenlaender et al., 2024; Tanase et al., 2024), and the effects of cultural and regulatory environments (Gioia & Lener, 2024; Wei et al., 2024).

The rapid spread of AI also makes it essential to consider its ethical implications and broader social and environmental effects (Kshetri, 2024; Sang, 2024), particularly the ecological costs associated with creating digital information.

This chapter presents a strategic framework (CAG) for utilising AI in content marketing, emphasising ethical guidelines and sustainable practices. The CAG framework can serve as a strategic decision-making tool, guiding organisations in aligning AI-driven content creation, performance optimisation, and governance mechanisms. By integrating these three dimensions into a cohesive system, the model supports evidence-based decisions that balance creativity, accountability, and competitive advantage.

However, this study has some limitations. One significant limitation is its dependence on a single database and its exclusive focus on English-language sources. These factors naturally restrict the diversity of perspectives included and reduce the broader relevance of the findings. Broadening the scope to incorporate research published in multiple languages and drawing on additional well-regarded databases such as Web of Science or IEEE Xplore could have meaningfully improved both the breadth of representation and the overall methodological strength of the results.

Furthermore, the analytical emphasis has been predominantly placed on the marketing dimensions of generative artificial intelligence, with comparatively limited attention given to its technological infrastructure and data science underpinnings. Addressing these gaps should constitute a priority for future inquiries, accompanied by the formulation of standardised methodological criteria and harmonised evaluative metrics. Such measures would enable more rigorous comparative analysis across studies and facilitate the development of models with broader theoretical and practical applicability.

Acknowledgements NECE, Research Centre for Business Sciences, Research Centre and this work are funded by FCT—Fundação para a Ciência e a Tecnologia, IP, project UID/04630/2025 and DOI identifier https://doi.org/10.54499/UID/04630/2025

References

Ali, L., Abdalla, M. J., & Alotaibi, S. (2025). Beyond the hype: Evaluating the impact of generative AI on brand authenticity, image, and consumer behaviour in the restaurant industry. *International Journal of Hospitality Management, 131*, Article 104318. https://doi.org/10.1016/j.ijhm.2025.104318

Alzoubi, H. M., Shameem, B., Mushtaq, S., Al Kurdi, B., Joghee, S., & Hamadneh, S. (2025). Unveiling the role of artificial intelligence: Navigating personalised content marketing, customer engagement, and commitment with data transparency and security. *International Review of Management and Marketing, 15*(2), 343–355. https://doi.org/10.32479/irmm.18499

Arora, A., Bansal, S., Kandpal, C., Aswani, R., & Dwivedi, Y. K. (2019). Measuring social media influencer index: Insights from Facebook, Twitter and Instagram. *Journal of Retailing and Consumer Services, 49*, 86–101. https://doi.org/10.1016/j.jretconser.2019.03.012

Brüns, J. D., & Meißner, M. (2024). Do you create your content yourself? Using generative artificial intelligence for social media content creation diminishes perceived brand authenticity. *Journal of Retailing and Consumer Services, 79*, Article 103790. https://doi.org/10.1016/j.jretconser.2024.103790

Buhalis, D., & Sinarta, Y. (2019). Real-time co-creation and nowness service: Lessons from tourism and hospitality. *Journal of Travel & Tourism Marketing, 36*(5), 563–582. https://doi.org/10.1080/10548408.2019.1592059

Campbell, C., Sands, S., Montecchi, M., & Jensen Schau, H. (2022). That is so Instagrammable! Understanding how environments generate indirect advertising by cueing consumer-generated content. *Journal of Advertising, 51*(4), 411–429. https://doi.org/10.1080/00913367.2022.2053901

Chen, Y. (2023). Comparing content marketing strategies of digital brands using machine learning. *Humanities and Social Sciences Communications, 10*, 57. https://doi.org/10.1057/s41599-023-01544-x

Dwivedi, Y. K., Hughes, D. L., Coombs, C., Constantiou, I., Duan, Y., Edwards, J. S., & Upadhyay, N. (2021). Setting the future of digital and social media marketing research agenda. *International Journal of Information Management, 59*, 102168. https://doi.org/10.1016/j.ijinfomgt.2020.102168

Fan, F., Luo, C., Gao, W., & Zhan, J. (2023). AIGCBench: Comprehensive evaluation of image-to-video content generated by AI. *BenchCouncil Transactions on Benchmarks, Standards and Evaluations, 3*(4), Article 100152. https://doi.org/10.1016/j.tbench.2024.100152

Gioia, G., & Lener, S. M. (2024). The protection of individuals against privacy-invasive and discriminatory inferences under European law: From the general data protection regulation and the digital content and services directive to the artificial intelligence act. *Zbornik Pravnog fakulteta u Zagrebu, 74*(5–6). https://doi.org/10.3935/zpfz.74.56.6

Gu, C., Jia, S., Lai, J., Chen, R., & Chang, X. (2024). Exploring consumer acceptance of AI-generated advertisements: From the perspectives of perceived eeriness and perceived intelligence. *Journal of Theoretical and Applied Electronic Commerce Research, 19*, 2218–2238. https://doi.org/10.3390/jtaer19030108

Haenlein, M., & Kaplan, A. (2019). A brief history of artificial intelligence: On the past, present, and future of artificial intelligence. *California Management Review, 61*(4), 5–14. https://doi.org/10.1177/0008125619864925

Hari, H., Sharma, A., Verma, S., & Chaturvedi, R. (2025). Exploring ethical frontiers of artificial intelligence in marketing. *Journal of Responsible Technology, 21*, Article 100103. https://doi.org/10.1016/j.jrt.2024.100103

Hartmann, J., Exner, Y., & Domdey, S. (2025). The power of generative marketing: Can generative AI create superhuman visual marketing content? *International Journal of Research in Marketing, 42*, 13–31. https://doi.org/10.1016/j.ijresmar.2024.09.002

Hue, T. T., & Hung, T. H. (2025). Impact of artificial intelligence on branding: A bibliometric review and future research directions. *Humanities and Social Sciences Communications, 12*, 209. https://doi.org/10.1057/s41599-025-04488-6

Jang, D.-U., Jeong, X.-Y., Kim, T. J., & Jang, S. (2024). Visual attributes of thumbnails in predicting YouTube brand channel views in the digital marketing era. *IEEE Transactions on Computational Social Systems, 11*(6), 8169–8177. https://doi.org/10.1109/TCSS.2023.3289410

Jaroucheh, Z., Alissa, M., Buchanan, W. J., & Liu, X. (2020). TRUSTD: Combat fake content using blockchain and collective signature technologies. In *2020, IEEE 44th Annual Computers, Software and Applications Conference (COMPSAC)* (pp. 1235–1240). IEEE. https://doi.org/10.1109/COMPSAC48688.2020.00-87

Joshi, S., Das, A., & Matta, M. (2019). Artificial intelligence tools for enhancing customer experience. *International Journal of Recent Technology and Engineering, 8*(2S3), 700–706. https://doi.org/10.35940/ijrte.B1130.0782S319

Kshetri, N. (2024). Generative artificial intelligence in marketing: Applications, opportunities, challenges, and research agenda. *International Journal of Information Management, 75*, Article 102716. https://doi.org/10.1016/j.ijinfomgt.2023.102716

Kupalova, H., Honcharenko, N., Andrusiv, U., Jakupova, D., Oleshko, E., & Demchenko, K. (2024). Organisational and financial aspects of the distribution management of digital content. *Financial and Credit Activity: Problems of Theory and Practice, 5*(58). https://doi.org/10.55643/fcaptp.5.58.2024.4502

Lewis, J., & Moorkens, J. (2020). A rights-based approach to trustworthy AI in social media. *Social Media + Society, 6*(3), 1–13. https://doi.org/10.1177/2056305120954672

Lou, Y. (2024). Human creativity in the AIGC era. *She Ji: The Journal of Design, Economics, and Innovation, 9*(4). https://doi.org/10.1016/j.sheji.2024.02.002

Lu, Y. (2024). A Chinese perspective on artificial intelligence generated content and copyright. *Információs Társadalom, 24*(2), 129–142. https://doi.org/10.22503/inftars.XXIV.2024.2.8

Maiano, L., Benova, A., Papa, L., Stockner, M., Marchetti, M., Convertino, G., Mazzoni, G., & Amerini, I. (2024). Human versus machine: A comparative analysis in detecting artificial intelligence-generated images. *IEEE Security & Privacy, 22*(3), 77–86. https://doi.org/10.1109/MSEC.2024.3390555

Moreira, D., Marcel, S., & Rocha, A. (2024). Synthetic realities and artificial intelligence-generated contents: Guest editors' introduction. *IEEE Security & Privacy, 22*(3), 7–10. https://doi.org/10.1109/MSEC.2024.3388244

Oppenlaender, J., Linder, R., & Silvennoinen, J. (2024). Prompting AI art: An investigation into the creative skill of prompt engineering. *International Journal of Human-Computer Interaction.* Advance online publication. https://doi.org/10.1080/10447318.2024.2431761

Page, M. J., McKenzie, J. E., Bossuyt, P. M., Boutron, I., Hoffmann, T. C., Mulrow, C. D., Shamseer, L., Tetzlaff, J. M., Akl, E. A., Brennan, S. E., Chou, R., & Moher, D. (2021). The PRISMA 2020 statement: An updated guideline for reporting systematic reviews. *BMJ, 372,* 71. https://doi.org/10.1136/bmj.n71

Pahari, S., Bandyopadhyay, A., Vijay Kumar, V. M., & Pingle, S. (2024). A bibliometric analysis of digital advertising in social media: The state of the art and future research agenda. *Cogent Business & Management, 11*(1), 2383794. https://doi.org/10.1080/23311975.2024.2383794

Pellas, N. (2023). The influence of sociodemographic factors on students' attitudes toward AI-generated video content creation. *Smart Learning Environments, 10*, 57. https://doi.org/10.1186/s40561-023-00276-4

Reed, C., Wynn, M., & Bown, R. (2025). Artificial intelligence in digital marketing: Towards an analytical framework for revealing and mitigating bias. *Big Data and Cognitive Computing, 9*(2), 40. https://doi.org/10.3390/bdcc9020040

Salminen, J., Yoganathan, V., Corporan, J., Jansen, B. J., & Jung, S.-G. (2019). Machine learning approach to auto-tagging online content for content marketing efficiency: A comparative analysis between methods and content type. *Journal of Business Research, 101*, 203–217. https://doi.org/10.1016/j.jbusres.2019.04.018

Sang, N. M. (2024). Bibliometric insights into the evolution of digital marketing trends. *Innovative Marketing, 20*(2), 1–14. https://doi.org/10.21511/im.20(2).2024.01

Shoaib, M. R., Wang, Z., Ahvanooey, M. T., & Zhao, J. (2023). Deepfakes, misinformation, and disinformation in the era of frontier AI, generative AI, and large AI models. In the *2023 International Conference on Computing Applications (ICCA)* (pp. 1–7). IEEE. https://doi.org/10.1109/ICCA59364.2023.10401723

Sun, Y., Sheng, D., Zhou, Z., & Wu, Y. (2024). AI hallucination: Towards a comprehensive classification of distorted information in artificial intelligence-generated content. *Humanities and Social Sciences Communications, 11*, 1278. https://doi.org/10.1057/s41599-024-03811-x

Tanase, I., Voicu, B. C., Popa, R.-G., & Grejdan, E. F. (2024). The use of the OpenAI GPT-3 AI technology for marketing content purposes. *Journal of Eastern European Research in Business and Economics, 2024*, Article 350288. https://doi.org/10.5171/2024.350288

Wahid, R., Mero, J., & Ritala, P. (2023). Editorial: Written by ChatGPT, illustrated by Midjourney: Generative AI for content marketing. *Asia Pacific Journal of Marketing and Logistics, 35*(8), 1813–1822. https://doi.org/10.1108/APJML-10-2023-994

Wang, J., Zheng, T., Wang, Q., Xu, B., & Wang, L. (2015). A bibliometric review of research trends on bioelectrochemical systems. *Current Science, 109*(12), 2204–2211. https://doi.org/10.18520/v109/i12/2204-2211

Wei, S., Ge, Z., & Tan, C. (2024). The public interest in the digital age: Exploring the emerging roles and governance models of the AI as a common good. *Journal of Ecohumanism, 3*(7), 2529–2544. https://doi.org/10.62754/joe.v3i7.4397

Whittaker, G., Letheren, K., & Mulcahy, R. (2021). The rise of deepfakes: A conceptual framework and research agenda for marketing. *Australasian Marketing Journal, 29*(3), 204–214. https://doi.org/10.1177/1839334921999479

Zhang, H., & Prebensen, N. K. (2024). Co-creating with ChatGPT for tourism marketing materials: Comparing AI-generated and human-generated texts. *Annals of Tourism Research Empirical Insights, 5*, Article 100124. https://doi.org/10.1016/j.annale.2024.100124

How Artificial Intelligence Shapes Consumer Behaviour in Social Commerce

Ricardo Afonso Soares, Iviane Ramos de Luna, and Gisela Ammetller

Abstract Artificial intelligence (AI) is a cutting-edge technology transforming business-consumer engagement on social commerce platforms, where commercial activities are driven by social interactions. Together, AI and social commerce have the potential to redefine how people experience and participate in digital commerce. In this chapter, we perform a systematic literature review of the empirical research on AI within social commerce (s-commerce) environments. The review identifies how AI assists social commerce managers in optimising operations and adapting strategic content in real time. While its benefits primarily remain functionally driven, initial findings acknowledge that new AI features that unlock emotional appeals throughout consumer journeys are promising. However, the current body of research exhibits contextual and methodological heterogeneity, limiting theoretical generalisation. This chapter offers a research agenda that provides significant insights for practitioners on refining AI deployment for enhanced consumer experiences and contributes to the developing of academic discourse on the intricate intersection of social, technological, and emotional factors shaping online consumer behaviour.

1 Introduction

Artificial Intelligence has significantly transformed marketing strategies. AI-driven systems use machine learning algorithms to personalise recommendations, connect users with content that matches their interests, and automate decisions based on consumer behaviours in real time (Khrais, 2020). Rather than suggesting products

R. A. Soares (✉)
CEOS.PP, ISCAP, Polytechnic of Porto, Porto, Portugal
e-mail: rasoares@iscap.ipp.pt

R. A. Soares · I. R. de Luna · G. Ammetller
Faculty of Economics and Business, Open University of Catalonia, Barcelona, Spain
e-mail: iramosde@uoc.edu

G. Ammetller
e-mail: gammetller@uoc.edu

J. D. Santos et al. (eds.), *Artificial Intelligence Transforming Marketing*, Contributions to Management Science, https://doi.org/10.1007/978-3-032-22360-9_18

based on categories or past purchases, AI detects deeper patterns based on browser history and better predicts future needs, enhancing consumers' satisfaction (Balakrishnan & Dwivedi, 2024). The analysis of behavioural patterns of user data is what differentiates AI from any prior technological advancement. Indeed, by processing large volumes of information, marketing managers gain more accurate behavioural insights and thus develop more effective targeting strategies (Sadiq et al., 2025). Hence, AI has often been referred to as a strategic business partner for understanding consumer behaviours, optimising the delivery of content, and personalising experiences in real time (Davenport et al., 2020; Shanmugasundaram & Tamilarasu, 2023).

More recently, and building on the broader role of AI in marketing, specific research of AI in social commerce settings emerges. The rationale of the interest is similar to the intersection of AI and marketing. Social platforms rely on AI to analyse vast amounts of consumer data (Leong et al., 2023; Rahman et al., 2023), with the main goal of making the social shopping experience more personalised, engaging, and efficient (Cittadini et al., 2023). By means of conversational agents and sentiment analysis tools, AI interprets consumers' emotions, preferences, and behaviours (Brüns & Meißner, 2024) that connect emotionally with consumers. Therefore, social managers can adapt their strategies in real time (Hashmi & Bal, 2024; Kaplan & Haenlein, 2019), even stopping marketing campaigns when not performing well (Youn & Jin, 2021). In doing so, AI does not simply support social commerce, but it redefines its strategic possibilities.

However, research on the specific role of AI for enhancing consumer experiences and shaping behaviours in social commerce deserves further research attention (Laradi et al., 2024). Therefore, this chapter sets out to explore through a systematic literature review, how artificial intelligence influences consumer behaviour in social commerce, considering both consumer experiences and business strategies. This analysis will clarify the mechanisms through which AI impacts user experience and influences purchasing behaviours, ending in a proposed future research agenda. By doing so, the chapter aims to contribute to the theoretical advancement of consumer behaviour research in digital contexts and offers practical insights for the effective management and deployment of AI within social commerce (e.g. Paul, 2024).

The chapter is structured as follows: it begins by defining and tracing the evolution of social commerce, followed by the methodology employed to identify and analyse relevant literature. Subsequently, it presents the main findings from AI in social commerce and discusses their implications. Finally, we outline an agenda with specific research avenues, followed by practical implications and concluding remarks.

2 What Is Social Commerce?

Social media have become the greatest space for commercial transactions over the last years (Busalim & Asadi, 2025), as YouTube, Instagram, Snapchat, or Pinterest have launched "shoppable content" that facilitates consumers to purchase goods or services with just one click (Hund & McGuigan, 2019). Similarly, Facebook Shops simplified e-commerce for small businesses and individuals (Wongkitrungrueng & Assarut, 2020), creating a marketplace for their products.

The roots of social commerce can be traced back to the early innovations of eBay and Amazon (Curty & Zhang, 2011; Hajli, 2013) in the late 90 s. These two pioneers introduced new features like product reviews and ratings (Busalim & Hussin, 2016; Friedrich, 2015) (see Fig. 1), fostering an environment in which social interactions began to play a significant role in the shopping process, in turn generating new commercial opportunities (Salvatori & Marcantoni, 2015). Building on these early integrated functionalities, the combination of e-commerce and social networking was first coined as "social commerce" by Yahoo! in 2005 (Cui et al., 2018). Described as the way user interactions enabled commercial transactions (Kim & Srivastava, 2007), it marked the beginning of a new stage in digital commerce.

Between 2005 and 2014, social commerce evolved from traditional e-commerce, where users interact with websites, into a specific branch focused on user interactions (Zhang & Benyoucef, 2016). With the development of Web 2.0 technologies, social commerce empowered final consumers to buy and sell goods and services within online communities and marketplaces (Stephen & Toubia, 2009). Differently, IBM defined social commerce as a merger of electronic word-of-mouth (eWOM) and e-commerce (Dennison et al., 2009). However, social commerce for others was considered to be social media being the foundational platform for executing e-commerce activities and transactions (Curty & Zhang, 2013; Liang & Turban, 2011). Furthermore, scholars set social commerce apart from conventional e-commerce models (Huang & Benyoucef, 2013), by pointing out the social platform interactions among users in (the so-called Big Five) Facebook, Twitter, LinkedIn, Pinterest, and YouTube (Marsden & Chaney, 2012). While these early definitions varied, they collectively contribute to understand how, over that decade, the definition and role of social commerce evolved (Lin et al., 2017).

Still, there is not a unique and consistent definition of social commerce (Laradi et al., 2024). Rather, researchers from marketing, psychology, e-commerce, and information systems (Nakayama & Wan, 2019) have adjusted the concept within

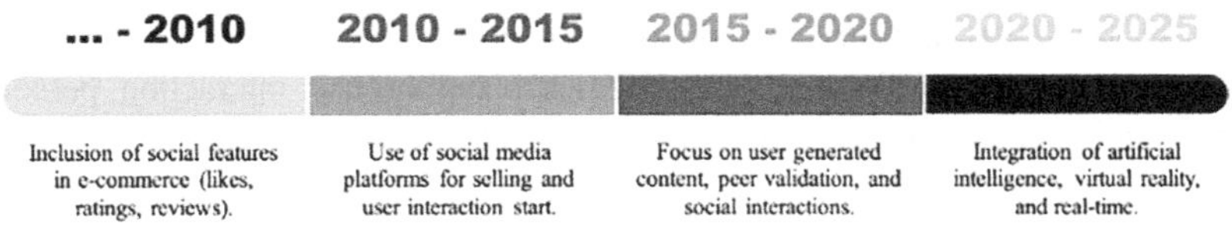

Fig. 1 Social commerce evolution timeline *Source* Authors

their research boundaries. Unsurprisingly, since 2015, the increasing interest in social commerce among practitioners and academics (Herzallah et al., 2025) has yielded much research that positions social commerce at the intersection of social and technological factors. Social commerce is broadly conceived as the execution of e-commerce activities and transactions through social media platforms, as well as e-commerce activities driven by social interactions (Hajli, 2015). These social elements, particularly social interactions, user-generated content, and peer validation, significantly influence consumers' purchase behaviours (Bazi et al., 2019; Dhaigude & Mohan, 2023; Dincer & Dincer, 2023; Wang et al., 2020). Online communities, by integrating these social interactions with purchase decisions, have emerged as a relevant space for social commerce (Sheikh et al., 2019). This development was intricately linked with the ongoing technological advancements.

A significant turning point arrived during the COVID-19 pandemic in 2020, which disrupted the retail sector (Elshaer et al., 2024). As physical stores closed, social commerce provided a flexible, low-cost, and direct way for brands to reach consumers, promote goods and services, and sustain sales (Abed, 2022). The pandemic expanded universal attention to social commerce among vendors, marketers, and researchers (Baethge et al., 2016; Ooi et al., 2018), seeking innovative differentiation. This evolution also gave rise to new forms of commerce such as live shopping commerce, also known as live-streaming commerce, that involves real-time video broadcasts where influencers or brand representatives showcase goods (Pons Julián & de Luna, 2024), mobile Facebook commerce (m-Facebook), a subtype of mobile social commerce allowing social commerce via mobile platforms, where user experiences are improved by immersive experiences (Rodríguez-Ardura & Meseguer-Artola, 2019), conversational commerce that facilitates AI-driven, real-time interactions through chatbots and digital assistants, allowing users to make purchases via platforms like Messenger or Alexa (Balakrishnan & Dwivedi, 2024; Sidlauskiene et al., 2023), or metaverse commerce, which integrates virtual reality, artificial intelligence, and user behaviour tracking to offer immersive, personalised shopping experiences (Chen & Yang, 2022; Zvarikova et al., 2022). What truly defines these emerging forms of commerce is their profound reliance on cutting-edge technologies. Artificial intelligence, industry 4.0, blockchain, machine learning, big data analytics (BDA), internet of things (IoT), and wearable devices (Leong et al., 2024) are the fundamental architects of a forever-evolving social commerce environment.

Among these defining technologies, AI stands out as a game-changing force within social commerce, reshaping consumer behaviours. While research directly linking AI's comprehensive impact with social commerce remains an evolving area (Jiang et al., 2019), its practical applications are already widespread. Brands are integrating AI into digital marketing strategies to support user interaction, personalisation, and decision-making (Mariani et al., 2018). As businesses adopt AI-driven tools and strategies, consumers are also becoming exposed to these technologies in everyday shopping. AI chatbots, virtual assistants, and dynamic recommendation engines offer real-time, personalised experiences, and continuous engagement. Sidlauskiene et al. (2023) argue that AI chatbots, in particular, contribute to customer service by answering questions, facilitating purchases, and simulating human support twenty-four hours a day.

3 Research Data and Method

Following Bandara et al. (2011) and Brocke et al. (2009), we divided the first step of the systematic review into two preliminary phases: source selection, concerning the identification of the pertinent database, and search strategy, aimed at determining the appropriate terms facilitating keyword scanning.

We conducted a search using specific combinations of the defined keywords ("artificial intelligence" and "s-commerce"; "artificial intelligence" and "social commerce"; "AI" and "social commerce"; and "AI" and "s-commerce") across titles, abstracts, or author-supplied keywords of academic publications indexed in Web of Science, renowned for its extensive repository of scholarly journals. This initial search yielded 48 journal articles. As is common with searches incorporating full terms and acronyms, this set included duplicate entries across the different keyword combinations. Figure 2 illustrates the complete process of our literature search strategy.

The second step consisted of establishing the inclusion and exclusion criteria to ensure the relevance of the identified papers (Kitchenham & Charters, 2007; Webster & Watson, 2002). The inclusion criteria focused on both AI and social commerce papers, to provide insights and dominant trends in marketing and consumer behaviour. The exclusion criteria omit recurrent papers and studies that deviated from the search main topic (Paul & Criado, 2020).

The examination of the literature began with abstracts and conclusions of the 48 papers; the main inclusion criteria were that these studies needed to be about AI and s-commerce. This screening identified 29 relevant papers. The second step ensured

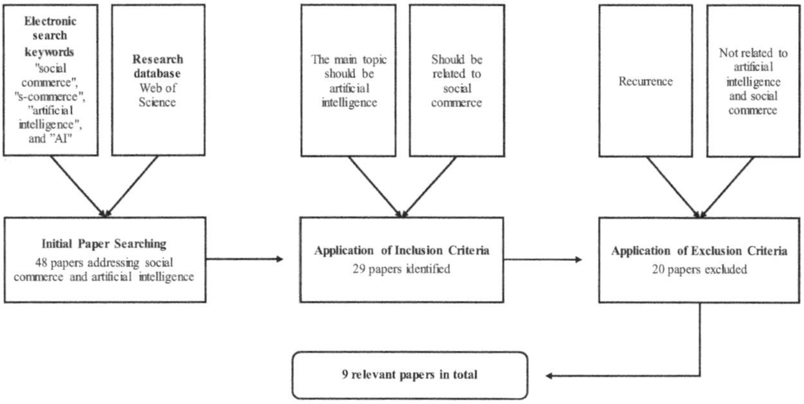

Fig. 2 The process of the literature search strategy *Source* Authors

Table 1 Inclusion and exclusion criteria

Inclusion criteria	Exclusion criteria
·Main topic is artificial intelligence ·Should be related to social commerce	·Duplicated studies ·Outside the selected themes

Source Authors

full-text scanning aligned with pre-established exclusion criteria (see Table 1) by discarding 19 recurrent papers and one study that was conducted on s-commerce, but not about s-commerce. The subset of 9 papers that provided empirical results into AI and social commerce was selected for further scrutiny. The final consideration set of manuscripts was organised by publication years, facilitating a chronological understanding of the evolving landscape of the research.

4 Artificial Intelligence in Social Commerce

AI in marketing has been approached by its predictive and generative natures, which respectively focus on using algorithms to make decisions, and the use of modelling to create new content (Hermann & Puntoni, 2024). Together, they provide the capacity for AI systems to fully leverage AI's potential in social commerce to anticipate consumer needs; create tailored content; optimise segmentation, targeting and positioning; and refine the whole strategic planning processes (Grewal et al., 2025; Kumar et al., 2024; Leong et al., 2024).

The first study of the review of AI in social commerce dates from 2020. Yuan et al. (2020) developed a method to interpret and predict user intentions in social commerce. This method employs advanced AI techniques, specifically knowledge graphs and inductive logic programming (ILP). The authors constructed a knowledge base representing the social commerce environment, integrating information on users' social relationships, social commerce model factors, and domain background knowledge. Knowledge graphs are used to visualise entities and relationships, while ILP discovers implicit information to interpret user information behaviours and intentions. The study confirmed the effectiveness and feasibility of this approach for analysing and predicting user intentions in social commerce.

Three years later, Leong et al. (2023) conducted a meta-analytic study to extend the theory of planned behaviour (TPB) for social commerce. They first proposed TPB1 by adding internal paths (subjective norms to attitude, perceived behavioural control to attitude, and subjective norms to use behaviour) and later extended this to TPB2 by integrating social support into the model. TPB2 significantly improved the predictive power for attitude, behavioural intention, and use behaviour in social commerce. The study presents an exemplary model for AI-enabled conversational commerce, discussing how AI attributes (perceived anthropomorphism, intelligence, and animacy) can be integrated to influence customer attitudes. Further, the authors show that AI-powered conversational commerce, including chatbots and voice assistants, can personalise interactions and optimise sales processes.

Next year, Boonta and Hinthaw (2024) investigated a set of technological and social factors that influence restaurant business performance on social commerce platforms in Bangkok. They demonstrated how AI positively affects business model innovation through data-driven agility and operational responsiveness. They took advantage of natural language processing AI to analyse online customer reviews from Wongnai and Facebook. This AI-powered sentiment analysis gathered data from consumers' comments to find out how satisfaction varied across different restaurant price ranges. Machine learning techniques, including artificial neural networks, decision trees, and logistic regression, were employed to build predictive models for restaurant performance on social commerce platforms. Their findings indicate that online review sentiment impacts customer decision-making on all restaurant types, deeply affecting business results.

Additionally, Chu (2024) explores live stream commerce (LSC) through the lens of sellers who enhance their sales via human-computer interaction (HCI) AI. The qualitative study, based on the assemblage theory, examines how streamers leverage technologies to reshape personal selling. In particular, how HCI AI and algorithms empower streamers to target viewers and understand their needs, enabling mass customisation beyond traditional retail. It further describes how Facebook uses AI for improving advertising strategies. By analysing existing user data to identify similar audiences for impacting potential consumers, this AI and data-driven approach in LSC allows for dynamic, tailored interactions and offers, based on real-time consumer feedback.

Until the end of June 2025, we identified five studies that met our inclusion criteria. Muhammad et al. (2025) examine factors that influence social commerce adoption among Gen-Z entrepreneurs in Nigeria. The study directly investigates AI integration into social commerce, identifying it as a crucial technological factor. The research reveals that AI integration significantly and positively influences the adoption of social commerce by micro, small, and medium enterprises (MSMEs). This adoption, in turn, positively impacts MSMEs' performance. While MSME performance was tested as a single construct in their model, the authors' findings suggest this impact encompasses improved sales, customer engagement, and business growth. AI achieves this positive impact through its capabilities, like automating customer interactions, optimising marketing efforts, and facilitating data-driven recommendations, which are identified as essential for refining business operations, and improving the overall customer experience in social commerce environments. Wu et al. (2025) introduce an AI model that uses emotions to improve how negotiation agents persuade. The study recognises social commerce as a new type of e-commerce where transactions rely on social relationships and frequent online negotiations. The model presents an intelligent negotiation agent with cognitive and emotional abilities. It shows how perceived trust affects how long a negotiation can last. Advanced AI technologies, including intelligent recommendations and robot agents, are now part of social commerce platforms. This integration creates new challenges for human-computer automated negotiation. Experiments showed that the trust-driven emotional persuasion model significantly improved negotiation performance, reducing negotiation rounds and utility differences compared to non-emotional and other existing models. Furthermore, a human-computer negotiation case study validated the agent's human-like negotiating capabilities. The paper evidences how AI agent intelligence and humanisation can be applied to complex e-commerce and social commerce environments. Grewal et al. (2025) conducted a topic modelling study to delineate current and future retailing research. Social commerce is one out of the five emerging themes in retail research. The paper discusses AI's role across various retail technologies, including the use of AI and generative AI to power chatbots that act as personal shopping assistants, enhancing customer service from pre-purchase to post-purchase stages. The authors convey a great potential to AI in increasing operational efficiencies and facilitating creative efforts, such as new product development or designing targeted ads. Within social commerce, the authors specifically point to the need for future research to define the role of AI influencers. Overall, the paper emphasises how AI contributes to technology-infused retailing by enabling faster, cheaper, and more comprehensive service, and explicitly links AI advancements to the evolving dynamics of digital selling within social commerce. Shoukat et al. (2025) drew upon the theory of planned behaviour to investigate how privacy and intrusiveness concerns influence Saudi Arabian consumers' intentions to use AI in social commerce. The study indicates that privacy concerns affect, negatively and directly, perceived usefulness. This perceived lack of usefulness then negatively affects their intention to use the platform. However, perceived intrusiveness concerns do not exert any significant effect into perceived usefulness nor behavioural intention. The authors added two control variables to their model: gender and social commerce experience. Their results evidence that consumers worry about how much access businesses have to their personal data and online activities within social commerce, as privacy concerns significantly reduce the perceived usefulness of AI-assistance tools. Consequently, this perceived lack of usefulness, driven by privacy worries, negatively impacts their intention to use these platforms. Curiously, although consumers express worries about intrusiveness, these specific concerns do not appear to significantly deter their perception of AI tools' usefulness or their overall behavioural intentions.

Lastly, Sadiq et al. (2025) examine factors influencing social commerce platform adoption from both technological and human perspectives, with a significant focus on the role of AI. This quantitative study employs the unified theory of acceptance and use of technology 2 (UTAUT2) and social cognitive theory (SCT) as its theoretical foundations and explores the moderating role of trust on purchase intention in social commerce. The authors demonstrate how AI-enabled personalisation and user experience, together with trust and social influence, shape consumers' behavioural intentions and purchase decisions in social commerce platforms. In particular, their findings reveal that AI tools (chatbots and recommendation engines) optimise the process of filtering vast quantities of data and can effectively target consumer segments by leveraging behavioural insights. Figure 3 resumes the TCCM framework, organising the literature review across four dimensions, and the *Appendix* provides a detailed overview of the implication drawn from the reviewed studies of AI in social commerce.

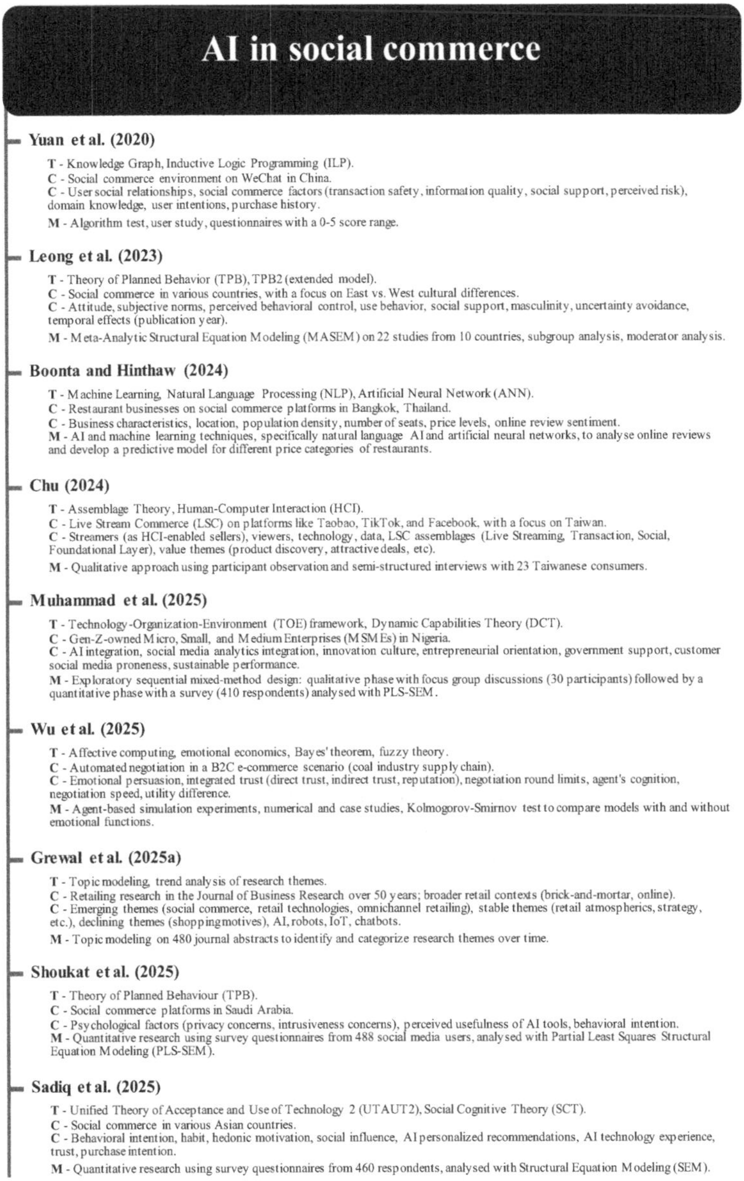

Fig. 3 TCCM framework on the existing literature of AI in social commerce *Source* Authors

5 Discussion: Insights from the Literature Review

This reviewed literature reveals that research examining the influence of AI on social commerce dynamics remains limited, with only nine studies identified that explicitly address this intersection (Boonta & Hinthaw, 2024; Chu, 2024; Grewal et al., 2025; Leong et al., 2023; Muhammad et al., 2025; Sadiq et al., 2025; Shoukat et al., 2025; Wu et al., 2025; Yuan et al., 2020). While the contributions of these studies are significant and advance our understanding of the role of AI in social commerce, they remain insufficient in volume to fully capture the complexity of this evolving field. In addition, the diversity of perspectives challenges theoretical-building and empirical inter-study comparisons.

Across the nine studies reviewed, the considerable contextual diversity reflects the global relevance of AI in social commerce, while also stressing geographic and sectoral concentrations. Several studies are conducted within Asian markets, including Pakistan, China, India, Sri Lanka, Japan, and Nepal (Sadiq et al., 2025), as well as Saudi Arabia (Shoukat et al., 2025), providing insights into consumer behaviours and technological adoption in high-growth social commerce environments. Research contexts also include Gen-Z-owned MSMEs in Nigeria (Muhammad et al., 2025) and restaurants in Bangkok (Boonta & Hinthaw, 2024), putting attention to emerging economies and sectoral variations such as food services. Studies like Chu (2024) focus on live stream commerce platforms in China, while Yuan et al. (2020) analyse social commerce data in the book and shoe retail sectors, and Wu et al. (2025) employ experimental settings with participants in China. In contrast, Leong et al. (2023) and Grewal et al. (2025) adopt broader scopes through meta-analyses and topic modelling, examining multiple countries and contexts within the retail and social commerce domains.

While the variety of contexts advances understanding of AI integration into social commerce, they also reveal limitations, with a predominance of studies in Asian and emerging markets and a lack of research in Western and cross-cultural comparative contexts. Moreover, the focus on specific industries, such as retail and food services (Boonta & Hinthaw, 2024; Yuan et al., 2020), suggests future research opportunities to investigate AI integration in social commerce in services, healthcare, education, and other sectors. Extending research to underrepresented contexts will enhance the generalisability of findings and provide insights into how cultural, economic, and infrastructural differences influence consumer interactions with AI in social commerce environments.

From a theoretical standpoint, the review demonstrates notable heterogeneity. While some authors adopt well-established behavioural models such as TPB (Leong et al., 2023; Shoukat et al., 2025), its extensions (TPB2), UTAUT2, and Social Cognitive Theory (Sadiq et al., 2025), others broaden the theoretical landscape by incorporating Assemblage Theory to explore human-machine co-creation (Chu, 2024) and TOE and Dynamic Capabilities Theory to address organisational readiness for AI integration (Muhammad et al., 2025). Contributions exploring agent-based automated negotiation and emotion modelling within social commerce (Wu et al., 2025) further enrich the theoretical diversity, while Yuan et al. (2020) demonstrate the potential of ontological frameworks using Google's Knowledge Graph and inductive logic programming for analysing social commerce interactions. Grewal et al. (2025) do not test behavioural theories directly, but their systematic topic modelling study provides an empirical mapping of emerging themes such as social commerce and AI, informing theoretical development and research agenda.

Despite this diversity of perspectives, the review reveals gaps in addressing significant aspects of AI integration. For example, drawing on the four dimensions of User and Gratification Theory (UGT) (utilitarian, technology, hedonic, and social) (Xie et al., 2024), future studies could advance towards the understanding of how AI shapes not only behavioural intentions but also emotional engagement, trust-building, and consumer experiences within the evolving landscape of social commerce (Ammetller et al., 2025; Busalim & Asadi, 2025). Additionally, trust and privacy concerns appear as variables in some studies (e.g. Shoukat et al., 2025; Wu et al., 2025). Nevertheless, frameworks explicitly addressing trust, ethical AI deployment, and consumer privacy concerns remain underexplored across the reviewed studies despite their critical importance for sustainable AI integration in social commerce environments. Upcoming research could benefit from interdisciplinary theoretical integration, combining perspectives from marketing, information systems, and human-computer interaction to comprehensively capture the complex dynamics of AI-mediated consumer interactions in social commerce (Dwivedi et al., 2021).

Methodologically, the studies reviewed span quantitative, qualitative, and advanced computational techniques. Quantitative methods using Structural Equation Modelling (Sadiq et al., 2025; Shoukat et al., 2025) dominate adoption studies, while qualitative approaches (Chu, 2024; Muhammad et al., 2025) provide in-depth explorations of user experiences. Meta-analytic SEM (Leong et al., 2023) offers aggregated evidence, and topic modelling (Grewal et al., 2025) maps the intellectual structure of retail and social commerce research. Advanced machine learning techniques (Boonta & Hinthaw, 2024) and knowledge-graph methods (Yuan et al., 2020) illustrate the potential of AI both as an analytical tool and as a phenomenon under investigation, while emotion persuasion models and experiments (Wu et al., 2025) reveal emerging intersections between affective computing and consumer responses in social commerce environments.

6 Future Research Agenda

While existing literature has established the functional benefits of AI in social commerce, there is a prevailing need to move from descriptive studies to generative theory building. To advance the field, five key theoretical directions are proposed. These directions focus on how specific AI mechanisms (e.g. generative content, affective computing) activate behavioural pathways (e.g. trust, privacy, social presence) to influence consumer outcomes. Table 2 clarifies the future research agenda and proposes direct research questions.

The first direction is about the theoretical shift from just predictive to consider generative AI mechanisms. Current research has largely focused on AI's predictive capabilities to anticipate consumer needs. Research in this domain remains essential, as predictive and generative natures work together to fully leverage AI's potential in social commerce. However, as generative AI becomes persistent, future research could investigate its impact on the consumer experience. Grewal et al. (2025) highlight the strategic choice retailers face between using AI to maximise efficiency (e.g. supply chain optimisation) beyond enhancing the customer experience (e.g. personalised advice). A critical area for future inquiry is determining the trade-offs of using generative AI trained on general data versus proprietary databases, and how these different models influence the depth and accuracy of consumer interactions. A further opportunity for research lies in understanding how hybrid systems could integrate generative and predictive artificial intelligence to optimise decision-making in marketing, addressing both the need to understand the complementarity between the two technologies highlighted by Peres et al. (2023), and the empirical evidence showing that human-AI approaches outperform isolated models (Arora et al., 2025) and that generative models add value without completely replacing traditional methods (Estévez et al., 2025).

Second, regarding the affective pathway, research has demonstrated the efficacy of emotional AI agents. Wu et al. (2025) found that agents capable of simulating emotional responses can significantly improve negotiation outcomes and efficiency compared to non-emotional agents. However, the boundary conditions of this effectiveness remain underexplored. Future research could investigate how these agents can be deployed to not just negotiate, but to build long-term trustful relationships, and whether the positive impact of emotional simulation holds true across different types of high-stakes versus low-stakes social commerce transactions.

Third, the privacy-personalisation paradox remains a critical tension. Shoukat et al. (2025) confirm that privacy concerns negatively impact the perceived usefulness of AI-enabled tools, which in turn mediates the relationship with behavioural intention. While current studies identify privacy as a barrier, they have not examined the mechanisms to mitigate this friction. Specifically, research could test how an increase in both AI algorithms' transparency and users' control over their data moderate the negative impact of privacy concerns on the adoption of AI-powered social commerce platforms.

Fourth, AI mechanisms evolve from tools into active participants, such as AI influencers, clarifying their distinct roles. Grewal et al. (2025) explicitly call for research to "define the role of social influencers, including human versus AI influencers". Thus, influencer marketing effectiveness would benefit from the best type of influencers (i.e. human or AI influencers) for evaluating products requiring consumers' subjective validation or objective data processing (Belanche et al., 2024). Understanding this distinction would shed light into the optimal deployment of human versus AI agents in retail strategies.

Table 2 Future research agenda of AI in social commerce

Dimension	Current state (descriptive)	Proposed agenda (generative)	Future research questions
1. Generative AI & content	Current research focuses on predictive AI for efficiency. Grewal et al. (2025) identify a strategic choice for retailers between using AI for just increasing operational efficiency versus enhancing customer experience.	Explore the full potential of generative AI when trained in real consumers' interactions—Beyond general public data.	- how do proprietary GenAI models influence the depth and accuracy of consumer interactions compared to general models? - how AI-driven efficiency compromises the perceived social presence that drives trust?
		Examine how hybrid AI systems outperform isolated models in decision-making.	- how do hybrid predictive-generative AI enhance consumer decision-making in social commerce?
2. Affective AI	Emotional AI agents capable of simulating responses significantly improve negotiation efficiency and utility compared to non-emotional agents.	Explore boundary conditions of affectiveness. Investigate if emotional agents can be deployed to build long-term trust, rather than just facilitating immediate negotiation outcomes.	- which is the real importance of emotional simulation during social commerce transactions? - how can emotional AI agents effectively build trust for long-term relationships?
3. Privacy paradox	Privacy concerns significantly reduce consumers' AI perceived usefulness.	Examine mechanisms (e.g. increasing algorithm transparency, providing user control) to mitigate privacy frictions.	- does algorithm transparency enhance AI perceived usefulness? - do users' control over data collection mitigate the negative impact of privacy concerns?

(continued)

Table 2 (continued)

Dimension	Current state (descriptive)	Proposed agenda (generative)	Future research questions
4. AI influencers	Clearly define distinctive roles of social influencers (human versus AI).	Develop a comparative model testing if human influencers persuade via affective processes (subjective validation) while AI influencers excel via cognitive processes (objective data processing).	- are human influencers more effective for products requiring subjective validation while AI influencers excel in objective categories? - which type of influencer is more effective for hedonic versus utilitarian product categories?
5. Cross-cultural contexts	Cultural dimensions moderate consumers' AI related behaviours in social commerce.	Move beyond broad regional labels (east vs. west) and consider additional social commerce aspects (e.g. trust in AI) that may vary across specific cultural dimensions.	- do social commerce related elements, like "trust in AI agents", vary across cultural dimensions? - how do specific cultural values moderate AI algorithmic recommendations?

Source Authors

Last but not least, the global nature of social commerce has a critical need to consider boundary conditions across cultures (e.g. Pranata et al., 2024). While Leong et al. (2023) found cultural invariance in the core TPB model between Eastern and Western cultures, they did identify specific nuances. For instance, the influence of subjective norms on behavioural intention was found to be weaker in cultures with high masculinity and high uncertainty avoidance. Future research could build on these specific findings to determine if social commerce aspects (e.g. trust in AI agents or susceptibility to algorithmic recommendations) vary significantly across different cultural dimensions beyond the standard East-West dichotomy.

7 Practical Implications

More than a trend, social commerce is the dynamic intersection between e-commerce and social media wherein users interact, recommend, and purchase. What sets social commerce settings apart from other environments is the central role of social interaction, through which user-generated content, peer feedback, and real-time engagement shape consumers' buying decisions (Dincer & Dincer, 2023; Hajli, 2015).

The two main marketing-focused findings of this review at the interplay between AI and social commerce point to the use of advanced AI features for optimising operations and acquiring new knowledge on consumer behaviour. The automation of functionalities implies more efficiency and effectiveness of tasks. By using AI, firms improve performance by better designing and managing decision processes (Sadiq et al., 2025), especially when dealing with complex and data-driven decision-making (Muhammad et al., 2025). As a result, social managers gain in smarter planning of more precise strategies. To date, social commerce managers have mostly relied on AI tools to provide quick responses and product suggestions to consumers (Shoukat et al., 2025). However, audiences are not fully satisfied with such AI automatic features. Actually, consumers often feel frustrated when AI falls short on offering the kind of empathetic communication expected in social environments (Juquelier et al., 2025). Users often describe their interaction with chatbots or AI recommendation systems as irritating, too scripted, and predictable (Mpinganjira et al., 2024). Finding their automated responses impersonal and unauthentic creates reluctance to engage for real purposes (Fathi et al., 2024), largely because users miss an actual human connection (Fang et al., 2025).

Indeed, social consumers rely on human recommendations (e.g. peers, community members), and adverse feelings elicited by automatic tools can even make them opt out of social commerce settings. Therefore, firms and individual sellers must ensure that AI-driven tools (at least) do not ruin their brands. Otherwise, consumers will seek other alternatives to satisfy their consumption needs. Hopefully, suggestions of future research (Hyman & Lukosius, 2024; Leong et al., 2023) addressing this issue yield new insights for making AI-driven content guidance more human.

At a halfway point between functional optimisation and deeper understandings of consumer experiences would set the insights yielded by Boonta and Hinthaw (2024). Their research introduces emotions and consumer satisfaction, thereby giving voice to a more hedonic appeal of AI. Nevertheless, this affective state has limited presence within the reviewed papers. Just Sadiq et al. (2025) test and confirm the influence of an AI hedonic driver on behavioural intention. Confidently, new AI personalisation features will enhance consumers' evoked hedonic appeals (Hyman & Lukosius, 2024).

Yet, some existing AI tools already identify affective tones in consumers' narratives and predict more individually relevant and emotionally engaging content that resonates better with the audience (Chu, 2024). Also, AI tools assist social commerce managers' refinement of personalisation strategies by targeting recommendations and customising content in social media platforms (Sadiq et al., 2025; Yuan et al., 2020). But involving humans is still a must for targeting effective communications (Grewal et al., 2025) that deliver more than utilitarian values (Xie et al., 2024).

Influencer marketing deserves special attention here, as a new stakeholder intertwining with AI and social commerce. Influencers are good at prompting effective communication strategies (Leung et al., 2022). Further, recent research on influencer marketing advocates for enhancing AI-related studies that optimise managerial decisions, from influencer identification to communication effectiveness (Aw & Agnihotri, 2024). So far, in social commerce settings, AI helps find influencers that align well with the promoted brands. By ensuring source-brand alignment strategies, AI becomes an effective tool for enhancing consumers' confidence towards social commerce purchases (Shoukat et al., 2025). However, both AI and influencer marketing have much to offer to social commerce environments. For example, AI can provide immediate data feedback on the consumers' responses to influencers' activity. By gaining a better knowledge of consumers' social interaction patterns with influencers, social commerce brands would benefit from new insights on cultural and contextual factors (Muhammad et al., 2025) that should serve as promising segmentation strategies for better tailoring consumers (Chu, 2024). Also, as Leong et al. (2023) assert, AI conversational tools foster consumers' experiences and simplify their decision-making processes in social commerce, and using influencers to get familiar with them (e.g. sharing informative content, posting videos of its use in their daily lives) could enhance consumers' engagement with social commerce platforms.

Luckily, in the meantime, some reviewed studies on AI and social commerce fit within the consumer-centric perspective (Grewal et al., 2017), that lies on the basis of enhancing consumers' experiences that social managers seek. It stands out here: Grewal et al.'s (2025) research on retailing scenarios reinforces the pervasive role of AI across all the stages of consumption processes, from the stimuli that trigger consumers' decision-making to the evaluation of the experience. Therefore, AI will become a resourceful tool for social managers as long as it intensifies the whole experiential journey of consumers.

8 Concluding Remarks

The aim of this chapter was to explore how artificial intelligence impacts consumer behaviour in social commerce. By systematically reviewing how AI influences consumer behaviour in social commerce, we highlight that AI exerts a dual impact in social commerce by optimising business processes and shaping consumer behaviours (see appendix).

Progressively, AI-powered technologies are being integrated into social media platforms to streamline purchasing processes while providing businesses with actionable insights into consumer behaviour, enabling more informed and strategic decision-making in social commerce environments. Additionally, more advanced psychosocial AI dimensions refine consumer perceptions and behaviours, and foster deeper cognitive and emotional connections that define marketing interactions in AI-driven environments (Labib, 2024). Therefore, AI becomes a valuable business resource for designing and delivering more interactive and personalised experiences for each user, enhancing social commerce journeys (Leong et al., 2023). Thus, when managers consider AI as a strategic enabler—and not only an operational asset—AI will effectively create more human-centric and emotionally meaningful customer experiences. Similarly, from a theoretical perspective, the affective dimensions of AI-human interaction are yet underexplored.

However, rather than viewing these gaps as shortcomings, this work leverages the limitations of the current research to propose a future research agenda that proposes to enhance AI generative capabilities for increasing value propositions that strengthen consumers' long-standing relations in each culture.

Finally, the single reliance on the Web of Science database could have restricted the scope of the reviewing sample. Although it is one of the most comprehensive and rigorous scientific databases, the inclusion of other databases could expand the insights on how AI shapes social commerce.

Appendix—Implications of Reviewed Studies about AI in Social Commerce

Authors	Practical implications	Theoretical implications
Yuan et al. (2020)	1) AI, using knowledge graphs and ILP, effectively interprets, understands, and predicts user intentions in social commerce; 2) knowledge graphs are effective AI tools for representing a knowledge base, making information understandable (both machine and human); 3) AI algorithms (especially ILP) are used for mining the knowledge base for more implicit and valuable information.	1) knowledge graphs and ILP are validated for social commerce intention analysis; 2) advances the theoretical understanding of data semantics in social commerce by focusing on intention discovery, interpretation, and prediction. 3) highlights the benefit of AI models exploiting background knowledge for robust insights in social commerce; 4) establishes a framework for explainable AI, producing both machine and human-readable outputs; 5) enables multi-perspective interpretation of user intentions by integrating diverse knowledge sources.

(continued)

(continued)

Authors	Practical implications	Theoretical implications
Leong et al. (2023)	1) AI-powered conversational tools enhance customer experience and simplify sales processes; 2) AI systems provide instant answers and information, speeding up service and improving efficiency; 3) voice assistants, powered by AI, learn customer preferences to offer personalised solutions and strengthen relationships; 4) AI attributes (perceived anthropomorphism, intelligence, and animacy) can be integrated to influence customer attitudes, used to create a resembling human-to-human interaction; 5) businesses need support for effectively integrating AI technologies; 6) using AI in social commerce can significantly boost firms' overall performance.	1) TPB2 should be extended to incorporate AI-specific characteristics (perceived anthropomorphism, perceived intelligence, and animacy) as new external variables to influence consumers' attitudes in social commerce; 2) new contextual mechanisms (managerial support and technical capacity from AI-enabled conversational commerce firm) should be integrated into theoretical frameworks to enhance explanatory power. 3) AI-enabled conversational commerce firm is theoretically introduced as an outcome variable within the extended TPB2 model. 4) AI-driven conversational commerce can serve as a new moderator within TPB2.
Boonta and Hinthaw (2024)	1) AI-powered sentiment analysis of online reviews provides valuable insights for strategically managing restaurant businesses; 2) AI-driven insights can be used to evaluate the success or failure of a business (before making decisions or during operations); 3) AI helps identify factors influencing customer satisfaction levels.	1) eWOM has a profound impact on consumer decision-making and business performance, influenced by online review sentiment analysis; 2) machine learning algorithms (including artificial neural networks, decision trees, and logistic regression) have efficient and predictive power when applied to social commerce data, predicting businesses' performance; 3) consumer satisfaction can be understood by AI-powered sentiment analysis; 4) AI facilitates business model innovation by fostering data-driven agility and operational responsiveness in social commerce environments.

(continued)

(continued)

Authors	Practical implications	Theoretical implications
Chu (2024)	1) AI enables platforms to offer tailored content and products based on immediate consumer data and feedback; 2) AI and algorithms empower precise targeting of viewers, ensuring content relevance and influencing purchasing behaviour; 3) AI assists in adapting sales tactics and informing strategies in real time (faster with a lower cost).	1) AI'S application through assemblage theory offers a novel framework for studying HCI-enabled sellers in LSC; 2) integration technology and seller agency creates innovative retail models, enriching personal selling research; 3) AI highlights mass customisation as a critical concept within the foundational layer assemblage, showing LSC platforms' potential to adapt and personalise at scale; 4) mass customisation can also serve as a valuable metric for assessing LSC seller performance in an HCI-influenced service model.
Muhammad et al. (2025)	1) AI enhances customer engagement, simplifies operations, and enables data-driven decision-making; 2) AI-integrated functions can automate complex tasks to manage social commerce environments effectively.	1) integration of AI into TOE and DCT, offering a nuanced understanding of how technological factors (specifically AI) intersect with organisational and environmental factors in social commerce adoption; 2) from a TOE perspective, AI integration improves organisational capabilities, enabling gen-Z-owned MSMEs to make data-driven decisions, automate processes, and personalise customer interactions in social commerce; 3) from a DCT perspective, AI helps MSMEs build dynamic capabilities, enabling them to quickly reconfigure operations, respond to customer behaviour, and innovate in real time, promoting sustainable growth in the digital economy; 4) AI'S influence helps to understand social commerce adoption in emerging markets.

(continued)

(continued)

Authors	Practical implications	Theoretical implications
Sadiq et al. (2025)	1) AI enables businesses to give more personalised and engaging user experiences through AI-driven content customisation and targeted product recommendations; 2) AI tools (chatbots and recommendation engines) can target specific consumer segments in social commerce; 3) AI can automate processes (order processes, inventory management, and customer support); 4) AI integration helps managers maximise productivity and cut expenses; 5) AI technologies (recommendation systems, forecasting, and conversational agents) allow relevant and appealing experiences tailored to consumer needs and wants; 6) AI features (interactive tools or real-time assistance systems) can appeal to rational self-interest and hedonic self, improving consumer trust and satisfaction.	1) Behavioural theories, specifically UTAUT2 and SCT, are integrated with AI-enabled technologies. This integration enhances the understanding of consumer behaviour on social commerce adoption; 2) AI plays a dual role as a cognitive and behavioural facilitator, linking advanced technological applications with theoretical concepts (habit, trust, and hedonic motivation) within social commerce; 3) AI technologies and their influence extend existing technology acceptance models, contributing to understand how new constructs derived from AI (e.g. personalised recommendations, AI technology experience) fit within frameworks like UTAUT2 and SCT.
Shoukat et al. (2025)	1) AI-powered tools enhance consumers' buying experiences; 2) integrating chatbots and AI-powered customer service improves customer interactions by enabling rapid responses to inquiries and product recommendations; 3) AI assists influencer marketing by identifying influencers whose values and brand alignment are relevant to the target audience; 4) AI in influencer marketing leads to less concerned and more confident consumers, boosting purchases on social commerce; 5) businesses can increase trust by improving platform attributes (data integrity, simplicity, safety, and secrecy).	1) strengthens the theory of planned behaviour by applying it to AI-powered social commerce platforms; 2) improves understanding of how privacy concerns and fear of intrusion influence buying decisions within AI-powered social commerce environments; 3) consumers' perceived advantage, identified as a primary purchasing motivation, impacts their privacy and intrusion worries.

(continued)

(continued)

Authors	Practical implications	Theoretical implications
Wu et al. (2025)	1) AI helps automate and improve online negotiations (smarter and more human-like); 2) AI improves risk management, allowing businesses to adjust negotiation lengths; 3) businesses can set AI agents to be more eager or less eager to negotiate.	1) introduce trust-driven adjustment of negotiation rounds in agent-based negotiations, enhancing theoretical models of trust in AI-mediated negotiations; 2) theoretical models on negotiation agents should include both internal (cognitive and emotional) and external (opponent offers) factors; 3) the cognitive and emotional computing theory helps explain agent-based negotiations in social commerce.
Grewal et al. (2025)	1) AI contributes to operational efficiencies, which, in social commerce contexts, might involve automating aspects of businesses to optimise processes; 2) AI-powered aids consumers chatbots serve as personal shopping assistants across the whole stages of consumers' decision-making processes (pre-purchase, purchase, and post-purchase); 3) generative AI supports creativity in targeting strategies, specifically by assisting with the design of targeted advertisements; 4) AI can strengthen trust, deliver clear value, and encourage social support on social commerce platforms to drive consumer engagement; 5) customised large language models enable retailers to provide store-specific and merchandise-specific information to customers through various AI interfaces, allowing for highly personalised content delivery on social commerce platforms.	1) user interactions and user-generated content are what distinguish social commerce from e-commerce; 2) the identification of gaps in the literature: The interaction of user-generated content with product information in social commerce environments; The identification of social commerce drivers; The role of AI influencers vs. human influencers in social commerce contexts; 3) social commerce, omnichannel retailing, retail technologies, experiential retailing, and online shopping behaviour deserve future theoretical advances; 4) research in social commerce needs theoretical advances in consumer motivation, trust, and engagement.

References

Abed, S. S. (2022). A literature review exploring the role of technology in business survival during the Covid-19 lockdowns. *International Journal of Organizational Analysis, 30*(5), 1045–1062. https://doi.org/10.1108/IJOA-11-2020-2501

Ammetller, G., de Luna, I. R., & Soares, R. A. (2025). Flowing through social commerce: A systematic review and research agenda. *International Journal of Consumer Studies, 49*(6). https://doi.org/10.1111/ijcs.70148

Arora, N., Chakraborty, I., & Nishimura, Y. (2025). AI–human hybrids for marketing research: Leveraging large language models (LLMs) as collaborators. *Journal of Marketing, 89*(2), 43–70. https://doi.org/10.1177/00222429241276529

Aw, E. C. X., & Agnihotri, R. (2024). Influencer marketing research: Review and future research agenda. *Journal of Marketing Theory and Practice, 32*(4), 435–448. https://doi.org/10.1080/10696679.2023.2235883

Baethge, C., Klier, J., & Klier, M. (2016). Social commerce—State-of-the-art and future research directions. *Electronic Markets, 26*(3), 269–290. https://doi.org/10.1007/s12525-016-0225-2

Balakrishnan, J., & Dwivedi, Y. K. (2024). Conversational commerce: Entering the next stage of AI-powered digital assistants. *Annals of Operations Research, 333*(2), 653–687. https://doi.org/10.1007/s10479-021-04049-5

Bandara, W., Miskon, S., & Fielt, E. (2011). A systematic, tool-supported method for conducting literature reviews in information systems. In V. K. Tuunainen, M. Rossi, & J. Nandhakumar (Eds.), *19th European conference on information systems, ECIS 2011*, Helsinki, Finland, June 9–11, 2011 (p. 221). http://aisel.aisnet.org/ecis2011/221

Bazi, S., Hajli, A., Hajli, N., Shanmugam, M., & Lin, X. (2019). Winning engaged consumers: The rules of brand engagement and intention of co-creation in social commerce. *Information Technology & People, 33*(2), 456–476. https://doi.org/10.1108/ITP-09-2018-0415

Belanche, D., Casaló, L. V., & Flavián, M. (2024). Human versus virtual influences, a comparative study. *Journal of Business Research, 173*, 114493. https://doi.org/10.1016/j.jbusres.2023.114493

Boonta, S., & Hinthaw, K. (2024). Forecasting the business performance of restaurants on social commerce. *Journal of Distribution Science, 22*(4), 11–22. https://doi.org/10.15722/jds.22.04.202404.11

Brocke, J. V., Simons, A., Niehaves, B., Niehaves, B., Riemer, K., Plattfaut, R., & Cleven, A. (2009). Reconstructing the giant: On the importance of rigour in documenting the literature search process. *ECIS 2009 Proceedings*, 161. https://aisel.aisnet.org/ecis2009/161

Brüns, J. D., & Meißner, M. (2024). Do you create your content yourself? Using generative artificial intelligence for social media content creation diminishes perceived brand authenticity. *Journal of Retailing and Consumer Services, 79*, 103790. https://doi.org/10.1016/j.jretconser.2024.103790

Busalim, A., & Asadi, S. (2025). What drives customers to engage with social commerce: A systematic review and factor derivation approach. *Information Systems and e-Business Management, 23*, 717–743. https://doi.org/10.1007/s10257-025-00700-x

Busalim, A. H., & Hussin, A. R. C. (2016). Understanding social commerce: A systematic literature review and directions for further research. *International Journal of Information Management, 36*(6, Part A), 1075–1088. https://doi.org/10.1016/j.ijinfomgt.2016.06.005

Chen, B. J., & Yang, D. N. (2022). User recommendation in social metaverse with VR. In *Proceedings of the 31st ACM international conference on Information & Knowledge Management* (pp. 148–158). https://doi.org/10.1145/3511808.3557487

Chu, H. (2024). HCI-enabled sellers in live stream commerce: Forging new value from an assemblage theory perspective. *International Journal of Human-Computer Interaction, 41*(13), 8464–8480. https://doi.org/10.1080/10447318.2024.2410054

Cittadini, A., Chierichetti, C., Lembo, L., & Morsanuto, S. (2023). Multisensory-learning-environments: Artificial intelligence for the domotisation and replication of lights and sounds that foster the state of flow. *Journal of Inclusive Methodology and Technology in Learning and Teaching, 3*(4). https://doi.org/10.32043/jimtlt.v3i4.115

Cui, Y., Mou, J., & Liu, Y. (2018). Knowledge mapping of social commerce research: A visual analysis using CiteSpace. *Electronic Commerce Research, 18*(4), 837–868. https://doi.org/10.1007/s10660-018-9288-9

Curty, R. G., & Zhang, P. (2011). Social commerce: Looking back and forward. *Proceedings of the American Society for Information Science and Technology, 48*(1), 1–10. https://doi.org/10.1002/meet.2011.14504801096

Curty, R. G., & Zhang, P. (2013). Website features that gave rise to social commerce: A historical analysis. *Electronic Commerce Research and Applications, 12*(4), 260–279. https://doi.org/10.1016/J.ELERAP.2013.04.001

Davenport, T., Guha, A., Grewal, D., & Bressgott, T. (2020). How artificial intelligence will change the future of marketing. *Journal of the Academy of Marketing Science, 48*(1), 24–42. https://doi.org/10.1007/s11747-019-00696-0

Dennison, G., Bourdage-Braun, S., & Chetuparambil, M. (2009). *Social Commerce Defined*. White Paper No. 23747, IBM, Research Triangle Park.

Dhaigude, S. A., & Mohan, B. C. (2023). Customer experience in social commerce: A systematic literature review and research agenda. *International Journal of Consumer Studies, 47*(5), 1629–1668. https://doi.org/10.1111/ijcs.12954

Dincer, C., & Dincer, B. (2023). Social commerce and purchase intention: A brief look at the last decade by bibliometrics. *Sustainability, 15*, 846. https://doi.org/10.3390/su15010846

Dwivedi, Y. K., Hughes, L., Ismagilova, E., Aarts, G., Coombs, C., Crick, T., Duan, Y., Dwivedi, R., Edwards, J., Eirug, A., Galanos, V., Ilavarasan, P. V., Janssen, M., Jones, P., Kar, A. K., Kizgin, H., Kronemann, B., Lal, B., Lucini, B., et al. (2021). Artificial intelligence (AI): Multidisciplinary perspectives on emerging challenges, opportunities, and agenda for research, practice and policy. *International Journal of Information Management, 57*, 101994. https://doi.org/10.1016/j.ijinfomgt.2019.08.002

Elshaer, I. A., Alrawad, M., Lutfi, A., & Azazz, A. M. S. (2024). Social commerce and buying intention post COVID-19: Evidence from a hybrid approach based on SEM—fsQCA. *Journal of Retailing and Consumer Services, 76*, 103548. https://doi.org/10.1016/j.jretconser.2023.103548

Estevez, M., Ballestar, M. T., & Sainz, J. (2025). Market research and knowledge using generative AI: The power of large language models. *Journal of Innovation & Knowledge, 10*(5), 100796. https://doi.org/10.1016/j.jik.2025.100796

Fang, C. M., Liu, A. R., Danry, V., Lee, E., Chan, S. W. T., Pataranutaporn, P., Maes, P., Phang, J., Lampe, M., Ahmad, L., & Agarwal, S. (2025). *How AI and human behaviors shape psychosocial effects of chatbot use: A longitudinal randomized controlled study*. https://doi.org/10.48550/arXiv.2503.17473

Fathi, J., Rahimi, M., & Derakhshan, A. (2024). Improving EFL learners' speaking skills and willingness to communicate via artificial intelligence-mediated interactions. *System, 121*, 103254. https://doi.org/10.1016/j.system.2024.103254

Friedrich, T. (2015). Analyzing the factors that influence consumers' adoption of social commerce: A literature review. *Proceeding of twenty-first americas conference on information systems*, 1–16. https://www.researchgate.net/publication/279975923

Grewal, D., Roggeveen, A. L., Benoit, S., Andrade, L. O., & M., Wetzels, R., & Wetzels, M. (2025). A new era of technology-infused retailing. *Journal of Business Research, 188*, 115095. https://doi.org/10.1016/j.jbusres.2024.115095

Grewal, D., Roggeveen, A. L., Sisodia, R., & Nordfält, J. (2017). Enhancing customer engagement through consciousness. *Journal of Retailing, 93*(1), 55–64. https://doi.org/10.1016/j.jretai.2016.12.001

Grewal, D., Satornino, C. B., Davenport, T., & Guha, A. (2025). How generative AI is shaping the future of marketing. *Journal of the Academy of Marketing Science, 53*(3), 702–722. https://doi.org/10.1007/s11747-024-01064-3

Hajli, M. (2013). A research framework for social commerce adoption. *Information Management & Computer Security, 21*(3), 144–154. https://doi.org/10.1108/IMCS-04-2012-0024

Hajli, N. (2015). Social commerce constructs and consumer's intention to buy. *International Journal of Information Management, 35*(2), 183–191. https://doi.org/10.1016/J.IJINFOMGT.2014.12.005

Hashmi, N., & Bal, A. S. (2024). Generative AI in higher education and beyond. *Business Horizons, 67*(5), 607–614. https://doi.org/10.1016/j.bushor.2024.05.005

Hermann, E., & Puntoni, S. (2024). Artificial intelligence and consumer behavior: From predictive to generative AI. *Journal of Business Research, 180*, 114720. https://doi.org/10.1016/j.jbusres.2024.114720

Herzallah, D., Liébana-Cabanillas, F., Muñoz-Leiva, F., & Zarco, C. (2025). Past, present, and future of social commerce: A bibliometric analysis. *Quality and Quantity, 59*(4), 3079–3111. https://doi.org/10.1007/s11135-025-02103-z

Huang, Z., & Benyoucef, M. (2013). From e-commerce to social commerce: A close look at design features. *Electronic Commerce Research and Applications, 12*(4), 246–259. https://doi.org/10.1016/j.elerap.2012.12.003

Hund, E., & McGuigan, L. (2019). A shoppable life: Performance, selfhood, and influence in the social media storefront. *Communication, Culture and Critique, 12*(1), 18–35. https://doi.org/10.1093/ccc/tcz004

Hyman, M. R., & Lukosius, V. (2024). Refocusing and futuring perspectives on AI in marketing. *Journal of Macromarketing, 44*(4), 906–919. https://doi.org/10.1177/02761467241280364

Jiang, C., Rashid, R. M., & Wang, J. (2019). Investigating the role of social presence dimensions and information support on consumers' trust and shopping intentions. *Journal of Retailing and Consumer Services, 51*, 263–270. https://doi.org/10.1016/j.jretconser.2019.06.007

Juquelier, A., Poncin, I., & Hazée, S. (2025). Empathic chatbots: A double-edged sword in customer experiences. *Journal of Business Research, 188*, 115074. https://doi.org/10.1016/j.jbusres.2024.115074

Kaplan, A., & Haenlein, M. (2019). Siri, Siri, in my hand: Who's the fairest in the land? On the interpretations, illustrations, and implications of artificial intelligence. *Business Horizons, 62*(1), 15–25. https://doi.org/10.1016/j.bushor.2018.08.004

Khrais, L. T. (2020). Role of artificial intelligence in shaping consumer demand in e-commerce. *Future Internet, 12*(12), 1–14. https://doi.org/10.3390/fi12120226

Kim, Y. A., & Srivastava, J. (2007). Impact of social influence in e-commerce decision making. *Proceedings of the ninth international conference on electronic commerce*, 293–302. doi:https://doi.org/10.1145/1282100.1282157

Kitchenham, B., & Charters, S. M. (2007). *Guidelines for performing systematic literature reviews in software engineering*. https://www.researchgate.net/publication/302924724

Kumar, V., Ashraf, A. R., & Nadeem, W. (2024). AI-powered marketing: What, where, and how? *International Journal of Information Management, 77*, 102783. https://doi.org/10.1016/j.ijinfomgt.2024.102783

Labib, E. (2024). Artificial intelligence in marketing: Exploring current and future trends. *Cogent Business & Management, 11*(1), 2348728. https://doi.org/10.1080/23311975.2024.2348728

Laradi, S., Alrawad, M., Lutfi, A., & Agag, G. (2024). Understanding factors affecting social commerce purchase behavior: A longitudinal perspective. *Journal of Retailing and Consumer Services, 78*, 103751. https://doi.org/10.1016/j.jretconser.2024.103751

Leong, L. Y., Hew, T. S., Ooi, K. B., Hajli, N., & Tan, G. W. H. (2024). Revisiting the social commerce paradigm: The social commerce (SC) framework and a research agenda. *Internet Research, 34*(4), 1346–1393. https://doi.org/10.1108/INTR-08-2022-0657

Leong, L. Y., Hew, T. S., Ooi, K. B., Metri, B., & Dwivedi, Y. K. (2023). Extending the theory of planned behavior in the social commerce context: A meta-analytic SEM (MASEM) approach. *Information Systems Frontiers, 25*(5), 1847–1879. https://doi.org/10.1007/s10796-022-10337-7

Leung, F. F., Gu, F. F., Li, Y., Zhang, J. Z., & Palmatier, R. W. (2022). Influencer marketing effectiveness. *Journal of Marketing, 86*(6), 93–115. https://doi.org/10.1177/00222429221102889

Liang, T. P., & Turban, E. (2011). Introduction to the special issue social commerce: A research framework for social commerce. *International Journal of Electronic Commerce, 16*(2), 5–14. https://doi.org/10.2753/JEC1086-4415160201

Lin, X., Li, Y., & Wang, X. (2017). Social commerce research: Definition, research themes and the trends. *International Journal of Information Management, 37*(3), 190–201. https://doi.org/10.1016/j.ijinfomgt.2016.06.006

Mariani, M. M., Mura, M., & Di Felice, M. (2018). The determinants of Facebook social engagement for national tourism organizations' Facebook pages: A quantitative approach. *Journal of Destination Marketing & Management, 8*, 312–325. https://doi.org/10.1016/j.jdmm.2017.06.003

Marsden, P., & Chaney, P. (2012). *The social commerce handbook: 20 secrets for turning social media into social sales* (1st ed.). McGraw Hill.

Mpinganjira, M., Dlodlo, N., & Idemudia, E. C. (2024). Perceived experiential value and continued use intention of e-retail chatbots. *International Journal of Retail & Distribution Management, 52*(13), 121–135. https://doi.org/10.1108/IJRDM-04-2023-0237

Muhammad, A. S., Adalier, A., & Adeshola, I. (2025). Digital transformation in youth owned MSMEs: A mixed method exploration on the impact of contemporary social commerce on sustainable performance. *Information Development*. https://doi.org/10.1177/02666669251329908

Nakayama, M., & Wan, Y. (2019). The cultural impact on social commerce: A sentiment analysis on yelp ethnic restaurant reviews. *Information & Management, 56*(2), 271–279. https://doi.org/10.1016/j.im.2018.09.004

Ooi, K. B., Jun-Jie, H., & Binshan, L. (2018). Unfolding the privacy paradox among mobile social commerce users: A multi-mediation approach. *Behaviour & Information Technology, 37*(6), 575–595. https://doi.org/10.1080/0144929X.2018.1465997

Paul, J. (2024). Publishing in premier journals with high impact factor and Q1 journals: Dos and don'ts. *International Journal of Consumer Studies, 48*(3), e13049. https://doi.org/10.1111/ijcs.13049

Paul, J., & Criado, A. R. (2020). The art of writing literature review: What do we know and what do we need to know? *International Business Review, 29*(4), 101717. https://doi.org/10.1016/J.IBUSREV.2020.101717

Peres, R., Schreier, M., Schweidel, D., & Sorescu, A. (2023). On ChatGPT and beyond: How generative artificial intelligence may affect research, teaching, and practice. *International Journal of Research in Marketing, 40*(2), 269–275. https://doi.org/10.1016/j.ijresmar.2023.03.001

Pons Julián, M., & de Luna, I. R. (2024). Exploring live shopping dynamics: Insights from purchase intention using structural equation modelling. *Journal of Marketing Analytics*. https://doi.org/10.1057/s41270-024-00297-z

Pranata, J. A., Riyanto, M. R. P., Hendrawan, S., & Gunadi, W. (2024). The effect of hedonic motivation and IT affordance on impulsive buying decisions in social commerce: TikTok. *International Journal of Electronic Commerce Studies, 15*(2), 63–102. https://doi.org/10.7903/ijecs.2303

Rahman, F. B. A., Hanafiah, M. H., Zahari, M. S. M., & Jipiu, L. B. (2023). Social commerce adoption: A study on consumer's online purchase behaviour of perishable pastry products. *British Food Journal, 125*(1), 318–344. https://doi.org/10.1108/BFJ-07-2021-0796

Rodríguez-Ardura, I., & Meseguer-Artola, A. (2019). Imagine, feel "there", and flow! Immersive experiences on m-Facebook, and their affective and behavioural effects. *Information Technology and People, 32*(4), 921–947. https://doi.org/10.1108/ITP-10-2017-0358

Sadiq, S., Kaiwei, J., Aman, I., & Mansab, M. (2025). Examine the factors influencing the behavioral intention to use social commerce adoption and the role of AI in SC adoption. *European Research on Management and Business Economics, 31*, 100268. https://doi.org/10.1016/j.iedeen.2024.100268

Salvatori, L., & Marcantoni, F. (2015). Social commerce: A literature review. In *Science and information conference (SAI)* (pp. 257–262). IEEE. https://doi.org/10.1109/SAI.2015.7237152

Shanmugasundaram, M., & Tamilarasu, A. (2023). The impact of digital technology, social media, and artificial intelligence on cognitive functions: A review. *Frontiers in Cognition, 2*, 1203077. https://doi.org/10.3389/fcogn.2023.1203077

Sheikh, Z., Yezheng, L., Islam, T., Hameed, Z., & Khan, I. U. (2019). Impact of social commerce constructs and social support on social commerce intentions. *Information Technology & People, 32*(1), 68–93. https://doi.org/10.1108/ITP-04-2018-0195

Shoukat, M. H., Elgammal, I., Selem, K. M., & Shehata, A. E. (2025). Fostering social media user intentions: AI-enabled privacy and intrusiveness concerns. *Spanish Journal of Marketing-ESIC, 29*(2), 253–269. https://doi.org/10.1108/SJME-07-2023-0205

Sidlauskiene, J., Joye, Y., & Auruskeviciene, V. (2023). AI-based chatbots in conversational commerce and their effects on product and price perceptions. *Electronic Markets, 33*(1), 24. https://doi.org/10.1007/s12525-023-00633-8

Stephen, A. T., & Toubia, O. (2009). Deriving value from social commerce networks. *SSRN Electronic Journal*. https://doi.org/10.2139/ssrn.1150995

Wang, Y., Wang, J., Yao, T., Li, M., & Wang, X. (2020). How does social support promote consumers' engagement in the social commerce community? The mediating effect of consumer involvement. *Information Processing & Management, 57*(5), 102272. https://doi.org/10.1016/j.ipm.2020.102272

Webster, J., & Watson, R. T. (2002). Analyzing the past to prepare for the future: Writing a literature review. *MIS Quarterly, 26*(2), xiii–xxiii. https://www.jstor.org/stable/4132319

Wongkitrungrueng, A., & Assarut, N. (2020). The role of live streaming in building consumer trust and engagement with social commerce sellers. *Journal of Business Research, 117*, 543–556. https://doi.org/10.1016/j.jbusres.2018.08.032

Wu, J., Zhang, Y., Cao, R., & Li, Y. (2025). An agent-based emotional persuasion model driven by integrated trust assessment. *Engineering Applications of Artificial Intelligence, 149*, 110567. https://doi.org/10.1016/j.engappai.2025.110567

Xie, C., Wang, Y., & Cheng, Y. (2024). Does artificial intelligence satisfy you? A meta-analysis of user gratification and user satisfaction with AI-powered chatbots. *International Journal of Human–Computer Interaction, 40*(3), 613–623. https://doi.org/10.1080/10447318.2022.2121458

Youn, S., & Jin, S. V. (2021). "In a.I. We trust?" the effects of parasocial interaction and technopian versus luddite ideological views on chatbot-based customer relationship management in the emerging "feeling economy". *Computers in Human Behavior, 119*, 106721. https://doi.org/10.1016/j.chb.2021.106721

Yuan, L., Huang, Z., Zhao, W., & Stakhiyevich, P. (2020). Interpreting and predicting social commerce intention based on knowledge graph analysis. *Electronic Commerce Research, 20*(1), 197–222. https://doi.org/10.1007/s10660-019-09392-1

Zhang, K. Z. K., & Benyoucef, M. (2016). Consumer behavior in social commerce: A literature review. *Decision Support Systems, 86*, 95–108. https://doi.org/10.1016/j.dss.2016.04.001

Zvarikova, K., Machova, V., & Nica, E. (2022). Virtual retail algorithms, behavioral predictive analytics, and geospatial mapping technologies in the decentralized metaverse. *Review of Contemporary Philosophy, 21*(0), 171. https://doi.org/10.22381/RCP21202211

The Rise of Virtual Influencers and the Role of AI in Transforming Influencer Marketing

Maria Amélia Machado Carvalho

Abstract This chapter reviews the literature on how artificial intelligence technologies, particularly machine learning and natural language processing, enable the creation of realistic digital personas. In this context, the chapter explores the emerging domain of virtual influencers (VIs) in digital marketing, analysing their opportunities, challenges, and consumer perceptions and reactions to these AI-generated and programmable digital personas. VIs offer significant advantages, including enhanced brand control, lower reputational risk, and scalability through algorithmic personalization. Their ability to engage users through immersive storytelling and anthropomorphic design fosters parasocial interactions and emotional attachment, positioning them as innovative tools in brand communication. However, VIs face limitations in perceived authenticity, credibility, and experiential authority, especially when endorsing high-involvement products. Their artificiality often leads to scepticism and discomfort. The chapter further examines how AI technologies, such as machine learning and natural language processing, drive narrative construction, engagement strategies, and behavioural personalization, enhancing the strategic effectiveness of VIs. Through a synthesis of current literature, this study identifies key theoretical and practical implications for marketers, emphasizing the need for context-sensitive design and disclosure strategies that align with evolving consumer expectations in the AI-mediated influencer economy.

1 Introduction

The growth of influencer marketing coincides with a parallel advancement in artificial intelligence (AI), which is transforming the ways in which brands identify, engage with, and communicate to consumers (Davlembayeva et al., 2025; Kim et al., 2025). By analysing behavioural and contextual data collected from diverse sources, AI technologies enable hyper-personalized marketing strategies that are more precise, scalable, and efficient than traditional approaches (Sands et al., 2022). Within this

M. A. M. Carvalho (✉)
CEOS.PP, ISCAP, Polytechnic of Porto, Porto, Portugal
e-mail: ameliacarvalho@iscap.ipp.pt

J. D. Santos et al. (eds.), *Artificial Intelligence Transforming Marketing*, Contributions to Management Science, https://doi.org/10.1007/978-3-032-22360-9_19

evolving digital environment, virtual influencers (VIs) have emerged as a new type of influencer.

VIs are computer-generated personas developed through AI and 3D modelling technologies (Yan et al., 2024). Unlike human influencers, they are fully brand-controlled, immune to personal scandals, and can be rapidly adapted to shifting trends (Robinson, 2020). Leveraging big data and machine learning, VIs can personalize content delivery and enhance consumer engagement by aligning communication with individual preferences (Deng & Jiang, 2023). Industry data indicates that VIs currently outperform traditional influencers in terms of engagement (5.9% vs. 1.9%) and return on investment, achieving an average ROI of 13.7% in recent campaigns (Grand View Research, 2023).

However, the rise of VIs also raises important concerns. Scholars and marketers alike question their authenticity, emotional resonance, and potential to erode consumer trust (Influencer Marketing Hub, 2025). Despite their algorithmic precision, VIs may be perceived as "creepy" or emotionally distant due to their lack of human relatability (Arsenyan & Mirowska, 2021). These tensions highlight the importance of gaining a deeper understanding of the trade-offs between technological efficiency and emotional authenticity within the context of influencer marketing.

As AI technologies continue to advance, the adoption of VIs is anticipated to grow, particularly in industries such as fashion, beauty, lifestyle, and entertainment. Market forecasts suggest a compound annual growth rate (CAGR) of nearly 40% in the VI sector between 2025 and 2030 (Grand View Research, 2023). This anticipated growth signifies a fundamental transformation in how brands conceive and execute marketing strategies.

Given the limited understanding of VIs within the broader field of influencer marketing, future research is essential to uncover insights that could significantly shape the evolution of digital marketing. Key questions remain underexplored: What opportunities and challenges do VIs present? How do shifts in power dynamics between influencers, consumers, and brands differ from those observed in traditional, human-centric influencer marketing? In what ways do consumers perceive and engage with VIs and the brands they represent? How can brands ensure alignment between VIs and their core values while maintaining a sense of authenticity? Moreover, is it possible for VIs to foster meaningful and lasting relationships with consumers?

This chapter offers a critical examination of how VIs are transforming the influencer marketing landscape. It delves into the theoretical underpinnings of AI-driven influencer marketing and analyses the emerging dynamics at the intersection of artificial intelligence, digital identity, and strategic brand communication. The chapter is structured to show how virtual influencers (VIs) are transforming influencer marketing. It introduces social media influencer culture (Sect. 1), defines and categorizes VIs (Sect. 2), and examines their role in AI-driven brand communication (Sect. 3). It then synthesizes literature (Sect. 4), addressing AI-driven narratives (4.1), algorithmic personalization (4.2), engagement (4.3), authenticity and persuasion (4.4), and emotional impact (4.5), before concluding with implications for researchers and practitioners.

2 Social Media Influencer Marketing: Foundations and Trends

Influencers first emerged in the early 2000s and have since evolved from a home-based hobby into a lucrative full-time profession (Vrontis et al., 2021). Over time, scholars have provided various definitions to conceptualize social media influencers. Freberg et al. (2011) described them as a new kind of independent, third-party endorser who shapes audience attitudes through platforms such as blogs, tweets, and other social media. Expanding on this, De Veirman et al. (2017) defined influencers as individuals who have built a substantial network of followers and are regarded as trusted tastemakers within one or more niche areas. More recently, Dhanesh and Duthler (2019) emphasized the role of personal branding, describing influencers as individuals who cultivate and maintain close relationships with followers while influencing their thoughts, attitudes, and behaviours.

Building on these definitions, researchers have also explored why people are drawn to influencers in the first place. Lee and Eastin (2020) identified four primary motivations: authenticity, consumerism, creative inspiration, and envy. For influencers to attract and retain followers, they must appear relatable and genuine (Kay et al., 2020). In addition, followers are often drawn to those who display visually appealing content and act as trendsetters, symbolizing sophistication and status (Park et al., 2021). As they engage with such content, followers frequently aspire to emulate influencers, forming strong emotional connections based on shared interests or aspirational ideals (Machado Carvalho, 2024).

These connections are particularly valuable from a marketing standpoint. According to Lou and Yuan (2019), influencer-generated content serves two primary functions: increasing followers' purchase intentions and enhancing their product knowledge and self-perception. To achieve this, influencers often create posts that feature personal testimonials and detailed product information, which increase the perceived informational value (Pelletier et al., 2020). In brand collaborations, influencers assume the role of brand ambassadors by producing sponsored content that aligns with and promotes the brand's image (De Veirman et al., 2017), while also fostering brand engagement and loyalty among their audience (Filieri et al., 2023). As trusted third-party endorsers, they enhance message credibility by sharing their personal experiences with the brand (Lou & Yuan, 2019). Brands therefore rely on influencers not just for their reach, but for the persuasive power they hold due to their authenticity and perceived expertise (Shoenberger & Kim, 2023).

Central to this persuasive power is the strength of the influencer-follower relationship. This bond significantly impacts follower behaviour and is often the most critical factor in an influencer's success (Kay et al., 2020). Influencers are widely viewed as credible, approachable, and highly relatable, largely because of their organic rise to fame and accessible personas (Filieri et al., 2023). Compared to traditional celebrities, they are seen as more trustworthy (Lou & Yuan, 2019) and credible (Sokolova & Kefi, 2020). Platforms like Instagram and YouTube reinforce this image by allowing influencers to share authentic, behind-the-scenes glimpses of their lives, which resonate with audiences on a personal level (Filieri et al., 2023). Consequently, influencer-generated content tends to engage target audiences more effectively than brand-generated messages (Lou & Yuan, 2019).

Additionally, there has been a shift from short-term influencer collaborations to longer-term partnerships, as companies recognize the value of working with influencers who genuinely love their products and can serve as brand ambassadors (Jun & Yi, 2020). This trend aligns with concepts from relationship selling and relationship marketing, which focus on building lasting, trust-based connections with consumers to enhance satisfaction (Okonkwo & Namkoisse, 2023). When influencers promote a brand consistently over an extended period, their endorsements come across as more authentic and credible, which strengthens the overall perception of the brand (Shoenberger & Kim, 2023). Over time, these influencers transition from simple endorsers to brand advocates, deepening trust and fostering stronger emotional bonds with their followers (Okonkwo & Namkoisse, 2023).

Another trend is the increasing importance of nano and micro influencers who are influencers with less than 100,000 followers (De Veirman et al., 2017). Despite having smaller follower counts, they often achieve higher engagement rates due to their perceived authenticity and stronger community ties (Joshi et al., 2023). Kay et al. (2020) found that consumers exposed to micro influencers who clearly disclose sponsorships demonstrate higher purchase intentions than those exposed to macro influencers who do not disclose, suggesting that authenticity, relatability, and openness enhance consumer trust and engagement. Further supporting this, Park et al. (2021) demonstrated that micro influencers are generally more persuasive than mega influencers (over one million followers). Their findings from four experimental studies revealed that endorsements by micro influencers lead to greater perceptions of brand authenticity, which are derived from the influencer's perceived authenticity.

Given this growing effectiveness, many brands are increasingly turning to social media influencers as strategic partners in their marketing campaigns (Joshi et al., 2023). Leveraging their credibility and deep connections with followers, influencers serve as powerful tools to shape consumer perceptions and influence behaviour in desired ways (Shoenberger & Kim, 2023). As influencer marketing continues to evolve, several key trends have begun to shape the industry (Davlembayeva et al., 2025). One significant development is the rise of virtual influencers (VIs).

3 Virtual Influencers (VIs): Definition and Types

In contrast to human influencers (HIs), virtual influencers (VIs) are AI-generated characters with distinctive appearances (Sands et al., 2022) who operate on social media platforms from a first-person perspective (Yan et al., 2024). The categorization of VIs in the literature can be summarized using two key criteria: visual characteristics and creation purpose (Davlembayeva et al., 2025) (Table 1).

The first approach focuses on the appearance and anthropomorphism of VIs. Yan et al. (2024) identified three major types: mimic-human (e.g., @lilmiquela),

Table 1 Types of Virtual Influencers: Pros, Cons, and Best-Fit Use Cases

VI type	Pros	Cons	Best-fit product categories	Examples
Mimic-human VIs (highly realistic, human-like)	Highly realistic and relatable	Risk of uncanny valley effect	Fashion and beauty	@naina_avtr (India's first AI superstar)
	Can simulate real-life scenarios	Potential ethical/ credibility concerns	Luxury goods	@shudu.Gram (the "first digital supermodel")
Animated-human VIs (stylized, cartoon-like humans)	Creative and visually distinctive	Less realism may reduce trust	Entertainment and gaming	@kda_music (virtual K-pop-inspired girl group)
	Lower risk of uncanny valley	Can feel childish or less serious	Youth brands	@knoxfrost (US, youth-focused, stylized)
Non-human VIs—Hyper-realistic (non-human but textured realistically)	Memorable and unique	Limited mainstream appeal	Streetwear & edgy fashion	@fnmeka (AI "robot rapper")
	Blends realism with novelty	May confuse audiences	Experimental art/lifestyle	@imma.Gram (Japanese fashion influencer)
Non-human VIs—Unrealistic (cartoonish/abstract forms)	Strong storytelling potential	Lower trust in serious contexts	Meme culture and casual entertainment	@johnpork (pig-headed VI, meme culture)
	Appeals to niche/ fan communities	Harder to connect with mainstream audiences	Food and beverage	@chefjadesjourney (AI influencer and travelling vegan chef)
Incarnate avatars (brand-created to embody identity)	Full brand control	Risk of being perceived as overly commercial	Corporate brands	Renault's liv (car brand VI)
	Can become iconic brand mascots	Requires sustained investment to remain relevant	Retail and consumer goods	Lu do Magalu (Brazilian retail giant magazine Luiza)

(continued)

Table 1 (continued)

VI type	Pros	Cons	Best-fit product categories	Examples
Innate influential avatars (created independently, lifestyle-driven)	Perceived as more authentic and independent	Less predictable alignment with brand values	Youth culture and fashion	@apoki (K-pop inspired VI)
	Flexible for cross-brand collaborations	Potential conflicts if they promote competitors	Music, art, and creative industries	@guggimon (independent entertainment VI)

Source Author

animated-human (e.g., @anymalu_real), and non-human (e.g., @guggimon). Mimic-human VIs are highly realistic virtual personas that closely resemble real humans in both appearance and behaviour. They often simulate real-life scenarios and can be difficult to distinguish from human influencers (da Silva Oliveira & Chimenti, 2021; Mouritzen et al., 2024; Yan et al., 2024). Animated-human VIs are stylized and human-like, often resembling caricatures or cartoon figures. While they retain some human features, they are clearly animated and less realistic (Moustakas et al., 2020; Yan et al., 2024). Non-human VIs, which represent animals, objects, or fantastical beings, do not conform to human visual norms. This category is further divided into hyper-realistic and unrealistic non-human VIs. Hyper-realistic non-human VIs, such as "John Pork", have realistic textures but low perceived human-likeness. In contrast, unrealistic non-human VIs, like "Good Advice Cupcake", are more cartoonish and abstract in form (Mouritzen et al., 2024).

The second approach, based on creation purpose, focuses on the role and function of VIs in relation to brands (Davlembayeva et al., 2025). Incarnate avatars are created to embody and represent a brand's identity through a consistent digital presence (de Brito Silva et al., 2022; Ju et al., 2024). In contrast, innate influential avatars are developed independently of specific brands, aiming to build personal narratives and engage audiences through lifestyle content, often without overt commercial intent (Mrad et al., 2022).

4 Opportunities, Challenges, and Consumer Perceptions

Influencer marketing has emerged as a dominant strategy in brand communication, evolving beyond traditional celebrity endorsements to include a wide range of social media influencers (Filieri et al., 2023), including virtual influencers (VIs). VIs function much like traditional influencers by endorsing products and serving as brand ambassadors, thereby influencing consumer behaviour (Thomas & Fowler,

2021). However, compared to human influencers (HIs), VIs offer several advantages (Table 2).

One of the main advantages is their reduced susceptibility to reputational risks (Miao et al., 2022). Unlike HIs, who may engage in controversial or inappropriate

Table 2 Virtual Influencers (VIs) versus Human Influencers (HIs)

Aspect	Virtual Influencers (VIs)	Human Influencers (HIs)
Control and risk	Consistent, brand-aligned behaviour	Independent personas
	Lower reputational risks (no scandals, fatigue, emotions)	Risk of scandals/off-brand behaviour
Authenticity and credibility	Lack experiential authenticity (cannot test/use products)	High experiential authenticity (can test/experience products)
	"Authentically fake": Accepted as artificial but engaging-	Stronger credibility and trust in endorsements
Engagement and storytelling	Rich fictional narratives and personalities	Relatable real-life stories
	Strong parasocial interactions (PSIs)	Naturally emotional and spontaneous
Innovation and differentiation	Novelty and tech appeal	Established appeal but less novel
	Immersive storytelling (virtual worlds, CGI)	Limited by human availability and constraints
Cost and efficiency	Cost-efficient over time (no travel, ageing, or physical limits)	Higher ongoing costs (management, contracts, personal needs)
	Scalable with AI (content generation, analytics, personalization)	Limited scalability
Consumer perceptions	Risks of digital dissonance if values clash	Perceived as authentic and relatable
	Ethical concerns (body ideals, stereotypes, cultural issues)	Credibility depends on reputation and behaviour
Technology and AI	Created and managed with AI tools (CGI, NLP, ML)	Not AI-managed
	Adaptive learning from social listening	Limited adaptability beyond personal/agency input
Ethical and social issues	Risks: Unrealistic beauty standards, digital orientalism, stereotyping	Risks: Body image concerns, stereotyping
	Transparency required to avoid backlash	Still subject to personal bias and controversies

Source Author

behaviour, VIs can be programmed to maintain consistent, brand-aligned conduct, as they are unaffected by human limitations such as fatigue, emotional fluctuations, or personal circumstances (Moustakas et al., 2020). The fact that they are created and managed by firms allows brands to exercise greater control over their image, content, and communication style, thereby minimizing the likelihood of public relations crises or off-brand behaviour (Miao et al., 2022).

While HIs have long demonstrated marketing effectiveness (Leung et al., 2022), VIs are gaining popularity due to their adaptability and enhanced storytelling capabilities (Moustakas et al., 2020). Many VIs are given detailed fictional lives, complete with human-like emotions and personalities, which further erode the line between the virtual and the real (Franke and Groeppel-Klein, 2024). Unlike HIs, who manage their personas independently or through agencies, VIs are entirely AI-created and managed with minimal human input (Arsenyan & Mirowska, 2021). Their development involves social listening to tailor their design and persona to target audiences, followed by scriptwriting and digital design (Yan et al., 2024). VIs can be inserted into real-world environments using computer-generated imagery, creating a mixed-reality experience (Ham et al., 2024).

VIs also present advantages for brands seeking innovation and cost-efficiency (Moustakas et al., 2020). Similar to HIs, VIs share content that depicts daily routines, travel experiences, and personal opinions. They maintain ongoing interactions with followers, often responding to comments to foster engagement (Leung et al., 2022). Powered by technologies such as unsupervised machine learning and natural language processing, VIs can analyse consumer behaviour, generate content aligned with brand identities, and continuously refine their communication strategies based on audience feedback (Kietzmann et al., 2021; Thomas & Fowler, 2021). This iterative learning enhances their ability to simulate human-like conversations and cultivate parasocial interactions (PSIs) with followers (Lou et al., 2023).

Moreover, VIs can serve as innovative interfaces in the broader integration of AI into brand communication, fostering novel human-computer interactions (de Brito Silva et al., 2022). Their virtual nature also enables immersive storytelling, such as showcasing fashion items in futuristic virtual settings (Audrezet & Koles, 2023). Another key opportunity is their novelty and technological appeal, which can enhance brand differentiation. VIs like Lil Miquela have successfully engaged audiences through a mix of human-like appearance and bold content on social issues, demonstrating their potential for effective word-of-mouth marketing (Block & Lovegrove, 2021; de Brito Silva et al., 2022).

Additionally, they are fully customizable, continuously available, and immune to ageing unless intentionally designed otherwise (Audrezet & Koles, 2023). Through anthropomorphism, i.e., the attribution of human-like qualities to non-human agents, VIs are perceived as socially present and emotionally engaging, which enhances trust and reduces resistance towards promotional content (Dabiran et al., 2024; Mrad et al., 2022). In some cases, VIs are even considered "authentically fake" (Lou et al., 2023). This concept reflects the consumer acceptance of their artificial nature while still engaging meaningfully with their content (Arsenyan & Mirowska, 2021; Lou et al., 2023). This duality can foster positive consumer outcomes when expectations are properly managed.

Despite their advantages, VIs face serious challenges regarding authenticity, credibility, and emotional resonance (Yan et al., 2024). Unlike HIs, VIs cannot physically test or experience products, which raises questions about the credibility of their endorsements and limits their persuasive power (Lou et al., 2023). This lack of experiential authenticity undermines their effectiveness in product recommendation scenarios, especially in industries like cosmetics, where consumers prefer human testimonials (Franke and Groeppel-Klein, 2024).

Disclosing the artificial nature of a VI can also weaken parasocial relationships and reduce their effectiveness in determining consumer attitudes (Lim & Lee, 2023). VIs are often seen as less human-like, less likeable, and less persuasive than human influencers (Böhndel et al., 2023), leading to concerns about their long-term efficacy in brand communication.

Additionally, consumer criticism can occur when VIs violate audience expectations. For instance, the Lil Miquela x Calvin Klein campaign faced criticism due to its perceived exploitation of identity politics and artificial intimacy (Robinson, 2020). This highlights the risks of digital dissonance, where the synthetic identity of VIs clashes with consumer values.

Perceived autonomy is another critical factor. Digital personalities are managed by agencies or companies, and their appearance and content are tailored to gain popularity among a specific demographic (Yan et al., 2024). As a result, VIs are fully controlled by brands or creators, reducing their perceived independence, which undermines their credibility (Sands et al., 2022).

Aesthetic design also presents challenges, since VIs that closely resemble humans but not perfectly can evoke discomfort and rejection (Arsenyan & Mirowska, 2021). While some followers accept VIs as intentionally staged and stylized, overly realistic designs can lead to consumer scepticism and reduced effectiveness (Lou et al., 2023). The existing literature on AI-based technologies suggests that consumers tend to perceive these technologies as unsettling or "creepy" when they are viewed as being beyond human control, potentially giving rise to ethical concerns (Arsenyan & Mirowska, 2021). Further complications arise from ethical and social considerations. The use of idealized body types and unrealistic digital personas can contribute to body dissatisfaction and distorted beauty standards, exacerbating concerns already present in traditional influencer marketing (Deng & Jiang, 2023). Additionally, cultural representation issues, such as digital orientalism and gender stereotyping, require ongoing scrutiny (Lou et al., 2023).

5 Key Themes in the Literature

5.1 *Artificial Intelligence (AI) in Narrative Construction of Virtual Influencers (VIs)*

The construction of a virtual influencer's identity is a technologically driven process that combines AI with narrative strategies to create engaging and authentic digital personas (Kerley, 2024). At its foundation, identity construction involves defining core characteristics, such as age, gender, interests, values, and communication style, through AI algorithms capable of simulating human behaviour (Tussyadiah et al., 2020). These programmed traits are essential in creating a coherent persona that resonates with audiences. For instance, Lil Miquela has been designed with interests in fashion, music, and social causes, which helps cultivate an authentic connection with followers (Robinson, 2020).

Narrative plays a central role in shaping these virtual identities. A virtual influencer's story, comprising their experiences, relationships, and opinions, is constructed to reflect their personality and maintain consistency across platforms (Kerley, 2024). Teams of scriptwriters and marketers develop and adjust these narratives based on user engagement data, ensuring alignment with audience expectations and maintaining perceived authenticity (Thomas & Fowler, 2021). This consistency is crucial, as audience engagement heavily relies on a believable and relatable storyline (Böhndel et al., 2023).

AI technologies, including machine learning and natural language processing, enhance this narrative construction by enabling real-time adaptation and personalized interaction (Zeng et al., 2024). Natural language processing allows virtual influencers to engage in contextually appropriate dialogue, while machine learning analyses user interactions to adjust content dynamically (Kietzmann et al., 2021). These technologies collectively simulate spontaneity and responsiveness, contributing to the illusion of a lifelike, emotionally intelligent persona (Lim & Lee, 2023).

Content strategies are tailored to reinforce the influencer's narrative and personality, ensuring coherence and authenticity in both visual and textual outputs (Jin et al., 2019). Additionally, digital presence management is vital to sustaining identity consistency across multiple social media platforms, further solidifying the influencer's image and reach (Hudders et al., 2021).

5.2 *Algorithmic Personalization*

The integration of AI technologies into VI systems has significantly transformed audience engagement through algorithmic personalization and automated surveillance mechanisms (Deng & Jiang, 2023). Machine learning and natural language processing are once again central to this transformation, enabling virtual influencers to engage users in highly personalized and adaptive ways (Zeng et al., 2024).

Algorithmic personalization enables VIs to deliver contextually relevant and emotionally resonant communication (da Silva Oliveira & Chimenti, 2021). Natural language processing systems allow them to interpret and respond to user messages in a nuanced manner, while sentiment analysis tools assess the emotional tone of user interactions (Gambino et al., 2020). Based on this feedback, VIs can adjust their communication styles and personas, creating more immersive and human-like experiences (Lim & Lee, 2023). Additionally, behaviour modelling powered by AI enables the simulation and forecasting of user and influencer behaviours, facilitating proactive content adaptation and personality refinement to maintain audience interest and engagement consistency (Looi & Kahlor, 2024).

Alongside personalization, VI systems engage in automated surveillance of user behaviour. AI-driven analytics track engagement metrics such as likes, shares, and comments, offering insights that refine the influencer's content and strategy (Böhndel et al., 2023). This data-driven approach allows brands to segment audiences by demographic and psychographic characteristics, optimizing content delivery and campaign targeting (Deng & Jiang, 2023). As a result, VIs become instruments of continuous feedback loops, constantly evolving to remain aligned with consumer behaviour and market trends (Sands et al., 2022).

However, this hyper-personalized and data-centric approach to audience engagement introduces ethical concerns associated with surveillance capitalism (da Silva Oliveira & Chimenti, 2021). AI-generated personas, while effective in influencing consumer behaviour, raise issues related to transparency and authenticity (Yan et al., 2024). Users may be unaware that they are interacting with AI-driven entities, potentially leading to deceptive marketing practices and erosion of consumer trust (Alboqami, 2023; Kim et al., 2025). Furthermore, these systems can be programmed to exploit emotional and behavioural data, subtly influencing decisions in ways that are not always apparent to users (Lim & Lee, 2023). The lack of disclosure regarding the commercial affiliations and artificial nature of VIs compounds these ethical risks, highlighting the need for regulatory frameworks and industry standards to ensure responsible AI use.

Despite these challenges, the potential of AI to deliver highly personalized and scalable engagement strategies remains a major asset for digital marketing (Deng & Jiang, 2023). By automating content creation and audience interaction, AI enhances the efficiency, consistency, and strategic agility of VI campaigns (Böhndel et al., 2023).

5.3 Engagement and Audience Interaction

Recent studies on VIs (e.g., Arsenyan & Mirowska, 2021; Jiang et al., 2024; Kim & Park, 2023) have explored the behavioural mechanisms and communicative attributes that drive consumer engagement (e.g., likes, shares, and comments), parasocial interaction (users imagined, one-sided relationships with VIs), word-of-mouth (WOM) dissemination, and purchase behaviour or intention.

Davlembayeva et al. (2025) identified eight core attributes for a successful engagement with VIs: warmth, relatedness, interactivity, competence, empathy, uniqueness, fairness, and credibility. These attributes highlight both the human-like qualities of VIs and their perceived professional competencies. Especially, the study finds that behaviour adoption among followers may stem from compliance (social pressure), internalization (value alignment), or identification (psychological closeness), with purchase intention being most influenced by the convergence of all three mechanisms.

Engagement is further influenced by the nature of the VIs. Kim et al. (2025) found that mimic-human VIs foster higher trust and engagement due to their anthropomorphic cues. Highly anthropomorphic VIs tend to be preferred by users, as they are perceived to possess greater warmth (El Hedhli et al., 2023), and an enhanced ability to foster parasocial interactions (Lim & Lee, 2023). According to these studies, increased form realism manifested in distinct personalities, gender cues, three-dimensionality, and visual appeal can elicit more favourable consumer attitudes (Alboqami, 2023; El Hedhli et al., 2023; Lee & Yuan, 2023). Moreover, users tend to engage more with VIs perceived as highly anthropomorphic or intelligent, a pattern especially pronounced among extroverted users (Dabiran et al., 2024). Conversely, less realistic VIs with lower anthropomorphism can sometimes increase engagement by leveraging novelty and stylistic uniqueness (Yang et al., 2024).

However, sponsorship disclosure negatively affects engagement with mimic-human VIs by revealing persuasive intent, which leads to consumer scepticism (Kim et al., 2025). Interestingly, animated VIs (AVIs) respond differently. With this type of VI, disclosure increases novelty and content engagement, as the unexpected combination of cartoon aesthetics with real brand endorsements captures users' attention through schema incongruity (Kim et al., 2025).

Both HIs and VIs can cultivate parasocial interactions, i.e., psychological connections where consumers feel friendships or closeness with influencers (Kim et al., 2024; Lou, 2022). HIs typically do so through personal self-disclosure and tailored content, while VIs build parasocial interaction by responding frequently and creatively to consumers (Yan et al., 2024). The interpersonal communication between VIs, especially mimic-human VIs, and social media users functions as an exchange of perceived benefits and costs (Kim et al., 2024). Influencers provide content, entertainment, and value, while users reciprocate with attention, support, and social status reinforcement (Sands et al., 2022). Engagement is enhanced by language similarity, shared interests, social and physical attractiveness, and attitude homophily (Stein et al., 2024). These factors strengthen interpersonal affinity and connection, because individuals are drawn to influencers who reflect their values and identity, and have physical appeal or social desirability (Kim & Baek, 2024).

The reciprocal exchange of value between VIs and users encourages users to engage socially and spread information, further facilitating WOM (Sands et al., 2022). While VIs can stimulate WOM, they often fall short in influencing purchase intentions (Belanche et al., 2024). This shortcoming is linked to their inability to simulate physical sensations and fully develop parasocial bonds comparable to human influencers (Stein et al., 2024). However, impulsive buying may be triggered when VIs demonstrate congruence with followers' identities (Zhang et al., 2025).

5.4 *Authenticity and Persuasion Power*

Human influencers (HIs) have traditionally derived their persuasive power from high credibility and authenticity, which stem from expertise, trustworthiness, attractiveness, and perceived similarity to their audience (Lou & Yuan, 2019). In contrast, VIs often lack this core credibility dimensions, resulting in lower perceived authenticity and trustworthiness (Arsenyan & Mirowska, 2021; Lou et al., 2023; Moustakas et al., 2020). Instead, VIs' persuasiveness depends largely on their creative storytelling, technological novelty, and entertainment (Lou et al., 2023; Yan et al., 2024). Moreover, consumers respond more positively when VIs openly acknowledge their artificial nature and advocate values aligned with the audience (Lou et al., 2023).

Among VIs, mimic-human VIs tend to evoke more scrutiny due to expectations of human behaviour, especially regarding sponsorship disclosures, which can reduce trust (Kim et al., 2025). Non-human VIs, however, often struggle to evoke positive attitudes, credibility,and purchase intentions, particularly when endorsing high-involvement products (Jiang et al., 2024; Kim & Park, 2023). They tend to be perceived as less authentic and lack the agency and realism necessary for deeper consumer connection (Alboqami, 2023; Mrad et al., 2022; Yan et al., 2024). Followers frequently express scepticism, citing creepiness and robotic traits in comments (Arsenyan & Mirowska, 2021).

Authenticity in consumer perception involves viewing an influencer or brand as original, genuine, and consistent with their own values rather than external expectations (Lee et al., 2025). For social media influencers, authenticity means acting according to intrinsic motivations rather than external pressures like sponsorships (Shoenberger & Kim, 2023). VIs are often perceived as less authentic due to their artificiality and commercial affiliations, weakening their influence on consumer information processing and decision-making. However, VIs that transparently disclose their artificiality and align with social values tend to gain greater acceptance (Lou et al., 2023). This authenticity gap differentiates VIs from HIs, whose genuine self-disclosure and life-sharing foster stronger perceived authenticity and persuasive impact (Lou, 2022).

Disclosure of sponsorship or commercial intent impacts HIs and VIs differently. For mimic-human VIs, sponsorship disclosure invites greater scrutiny and scepticism due to the expectation of human-like authenticity, often resulting in reduced trust (Kim et al., 2025). Conversely, AVIs' overt artificiality means consumers anticipate commercial motives; sponsorship disclosure can actually enhance perceptions of transparency and novelty, positively influencing engagement, particularly for those with larger audiences (Gambino et al., 2020). For AVIs with smaller followings, novelty is inherently high, so disclosure has a diminished effect. These dynamics highlight the need for context-sensitive disclosure strategies tailored to VI type and audience size.

While HIs build credibility through expertise and authenticity, VIs' information quality is often judged through entertainment value and creative content rather than perceived expertise. VIs surpass at engaging consumers via novel storytelling and frequent interaction, but face challenges in conveying information perceived as trustworthy or useful (Lou et al., 2023; Yan et al., 2024).

5.5 *Emotional Attachment and the Affective Impact of Virtual Influencers*

Understanding the affective perspective is crucial, as emotions lie at the core of social media influencers' impact (Engström, 2022). However, much of the existing research on virtual influencers (VIs) has focused predominantly on behavioural and cognitive aspects, often overlooking the important emotional dimension (Kim et al., 2025).

Emotional attachment in consumer behaviour refers to a strong emotional bond with a person, brand, or object, manifesting as feelings of love, passion, connection, and affection (Jun & Yi, 2020). Consumers frequently develop these attachments not only to tangible products or celebrities but also to figures they interact with indirectly, such as musicians, actors, or politicians (Thomson, 2006). Mimic-human VIs, who share personal lives and opinions on topics including products and services, engage with users through comments, likes, shares, and follows, fostering a sense of closeness despite users' awareness that these influencers are AI-based characters (Franke and Groeppel-Klein 2024). This perceived closeness strengthens emotional attachment, leading consumers to feel as though they maintain a genuine and meaningful relationship with the VI (Yan et al., 2024). According to Zhang and Wei (2021), consumers perceive VIs as cool when they possess aesthetic appeal, and are fun and interest. When a VI is regarded as cool, it captivates audiences by projecting a unique, original, and engaging identity.

Yet, this positive emotional relationship is not without its challenges. Compared to animated-human VIs and non-human VIs, human-like VIs sometimes evoke negative emotions, such as anxiety and anger (Arsenyan & Mirowska, 2021). This phenomenon aligns with the Uncanny Valley theory, which describes a nonlinear relationship where consumer affinity increases with anthropomorphism only to decline sharply when a virtual entity appears almost, but not fully, human, triggering discomfort and creepiness (Arsenyan & Mirowska, 2021; Kim & Baek, 2024). A critical factor is the mismatch between a VI's visual realism and behavioural realism. For instance, a highly human-like VI exhibiting unnatural or "zombie-like" behaviours can intensify negative reactions and undermine performance outcomes (Miao et al., 2022). These findings underscore the importance of harmonizing both visual and behavioural realism to optimize consumer responses to VIs (Table 3).

Table 3 Effects of disclosure across virtual influencer types on engagement, trust, and parasocial interaction

VI type	Disclosure outcome	Engagement	Trust	Parasocial interaction / Emotional attachment
Mimic-human VIs	Sponsorship disclosure reduces engagement due to revealed persuasive intent; increases scepticism.	High when not disclosed; declines after disclosure.	Lower trust after disclosure, as users expect "human-like" authenticity	Strong parasocial bonds possible through anthropomorphic cues, but fragile if trust is broken.
Animated VIs (AVIs)	Sponsorship disclosure can enhance novelty and transparency, especially for large audiences.	Engagement increases with disclosure (schema incongruity effect).	Trust may rise with transparent disclosure	Moderate parasocial interaction; closeness grows through interactivity and creativity, less tied to realism.
Non-human/ abstract VIs	Sponsorship disclosure has limited effect (already perceived as artificial).	Engagement often lowers overall, novelty-dependent.	Lower baseline trust due to lack of authenticity/ agency	Weak parasocial interaction, as users see them as less relatable.
Hybrid/ AI-generated personas	Disclosure risks remain underexplored; potential to balance transparency with personalization.	Potentially high engagement if aligned with identity congruence.	Trust depends on AI transparency and data ethics.	Attachment may evolve dynamically through adaptive personalization, but lifecycle unclear.

Source Author

6 Conclusions

Virtual influencers (VIs) represent a significant evolution in the landscape of influencer marketing, offering both opportunities and challenges. Their integration into brand strategy enables enhanced narrative control, scalability, and technological innovation. By simulating human-like personalities through AI and creative storytelling, VIs provide brands with cost-efficient and consistent tools for audience engagement. However, their artificial nature introduces critical concerns regarding authenticity, trust, and emotional resonance.

VIs represent a transformative tool in digital marketing, combining advanced AI technologies with creative storytelling to simulate human-like personalities and behaviours. Their increasing adoption reflects a strategic shift in power dynamics between influencers, consumers, and brands. Unlike traditional human-centric influencer marketing, where influencers often negotiate autonomy and authenticity, brands retain greater control over VIs, allowing for more direct alignment with corporate messaging. However, this centralized control can dilute the sense of authenticity, raising concerns about scripted interactions and manipulated engagement.

Consumers perceive and engage with VIs in complex way. While some are drawn to the novelty, visual storytelling, and AI-driven interactivity, others express scepticism about their artificiality and the lack of lived experience. VIs are capable of sustained interaction, personalize content adaptively, and construct immersive narratives, allowing them to foster parasocial relationships and emotional connections with audiences. Their appeal is particularly strong among consumers attracted to innovation, visual storytelling, and AI-driven content. Nevertheless, engagement often centres on design choices, such as realism, transparency, and ethical framing.

Brands must therefore ensure that VIs are strategically aligned with their core values while maintaining a credible sense of authenticity. This entails ethical design, transparent sponsorship practices, and sensitivity to social issues such as surveillance and body image. While VIs may struggle to match the emotional depth of human influencers, they are capable of fostering meaningful, if mediated, relationships with consumers through sustained interaction and personalized content. Moreover, mimic-human VIs may face greater scrutiny and expectations for human-like authenticity, whereas stylized or animated VIs benefit from being perceived more as creative characters than deceptive simulations.

Ultimately, VIs are not substitutes for human influencers but rather complementary tools that embody a hybrid form of artificiality and relatability. Their growing prominence underscores the need for ongoing research into the emotional, ethical, and narrative dimensions of digital personas. Future studies could usefully examine how generative AI reshapes VI storytelling, the long-term implications of hyper-personalization for trust and privacy, and the boundaries of anthropomorphism in driving engagement. Further research is also needed to develop new measures of authenticity for VIs, to test how disclosure strategies affect different VI types, and to assess how emotional attachment evolves over time, particularly in relation to the Uncanny Valley effect. Cross-cultural, generational, and regulatory perspectives represent additional avenues for inquiry, highlighting the importance of context in shaping audience responses.

As the field continues to evolve, the challenge for marketers and scholars alike will be to navigate the delicate balance between technological affordances and the enduring human desire for genuine connection.

References

Alboqami, H. (2023). Trust me, I'm an influencer!-causal recipes for customer trust in artificial intelligence influencers in the retail industry. *Journal of Retailing and Consumer Services, 72*, 103242. https://doi.org/10.1016/j.jretconser.2022.103242

Arsenyan, J., & Mirowska, A. (2021). Almost human? A comparative case study on the social media presence of virtual influencers. *International Journal of Human-Computer Studies, 155*, 102694. https://doi.org/10.1016/j.ijhcs.2021.102694

Audrezet, A., & Koles, B. (2023). Virtual influencer as a brand avatar in interactive marketing. In C. L. Wang (Ed.), *The Palgrave handbook of interactive marketing* (pp. 319–343). Palgrave Macmillan. https://doi.org/10.1007/978-3-031-14961-0_16

Belanche, D., Belk, R. W., Casaló, L. V., & Flavián, C. (2024). The dark side of artificial intelligence in services. *The Service Industries Journal, 44*(3–4), 149–172. https://doi.org/10.1080/02642069.2024.2305451

Block, E., & Lovegrove, R. (2021). Discordant storytelling,'honest fakery', identity peddling: How uncanny CGI characters are jamming public relations and influencer practices. *Public relations inquiry, 10*(3), 265–293. https://doi.org/10.1177/2046147X211026936

Böhndel, M., Jastorff, M., & Rudeloff, C. (2023). AI-driven influencer marketing: Comparing the effects of virtual and human influencers on consumer perceptions. *Journal of AI, Robotics & Workplace Automation, 2*(2), 165–174.

da Silva Oliveira, A. B., & Chimenti, P. (2021). "Humanized robots": A proposition of categories to understand virtual influencers. *Australasian Journal of Information Systems, 25*. https://doi.org/10.3127/ajis.v25i0.3223

Dabiran, E., Farivar, S., Wang, F., & Grant, G. (2024). Virtually human: Anthropomorphism in virtual influencer marketing. *Journal of Retailing and Consumer Services, 79*, 103797. https://doi.org/10.1016/j.jretconser.2024.103797

Davlembayeva, D., Chari, S., & Papagiannidis, S. (2025). Virtual influencers in consumer behaviour: A social influence theory perspective. *British Journal of Management, 36*(1), 202–222. https://doi.org/10.1111/1467-8551.12839

De Brito Silva, M. J., de Oliveira Ramos Delfino, L., Alves Cerqueira, K., & de Oliveira Campos, P. (2022). Avatar marketing: A study on the engagement and authenticity of virtual influencers on Instagram. *Social Network Analysis and Mining, 12*(1), 130. https://doi.org/10.1007/s13278-022-00966-w

De Veirman, M., Cauberghe, V., & Hudders, L. (2017). Marketing through Instagram influencers: The impact of number of followers and product divergence on brand attitude. *International Journal of Advertising, 36*(5), 798–828. https://doi.org/10.1080/02650487.2017.1348035

Deng, F., & Jiang, X. (2023). Effects of human versus virtual human influencers on the appearance anxiety of social media users. *Journal of Retailing and Consumer Services, 71*, 103233. https://doi.org/10.1016/j.jretconser.2022.103233

Dhanesh, G. S., & Duthler, G. (2019). Relationship management through social media influencers: Effects of followers' awareness of paid endorsement. *Public Relations Review, 45*(3), 101765.

El Hedhli, K., Zourrig, H., Al Khateeb, A., & Alnawas, I. (2023). Stereotyping human-like virtual influencers in retailing: Does warmth prevail over competence? *Journal of Retailing and Consumer Services, 75*, 103459. https://doi.org/10.1016/j.jretconser.2023.103459

Engström, J. (2022). Virtual influencers: Antecedents and typologizing. In *The SAGE handbook of social media marketing* (pp. 276–292). Sage.

Filieri, R., Acikgoz, F., Li, C., & Alguezaui, S. (2023). Influencers' "organic" persuasion through electronic word of mouth: A case of sincerity over brains and beauty. *Psychology & Marketing, 40*(2), 347–364. https://doi.org/10.1002/mar.21760

Franke, C., & Groeppel-Klein, A. (2024). The role of psychological distance and construal level in explaining the effectiveness of human-like vs. cartoon-like virtual influencers. *Journal of Business Research, 185*, 114916. https://doi.org/10.1016/j.jbusres.2024.114916

Freberg, K., Graham, K., McGaughey, K., & Freberg, L. A. (2011). Who are the social media influencers? A study of public perceptions of personality. *Public Relations Review, 37*(1), 90–92. https://doi.org/10.1016/j.pubrev.2010.11.001

Gambino, A., Fox, J., & Ratan, R. A. (2020). Building a stronger CASA: Extending the computers are social actors paradigm. *Human-Machine Communication, 1*, 71–85. https://doi.org/10.30658/hmc.1.5

Grand View Research. (2023). *Virtual influencer market size, share & trends analysis report by application* (fashion, beauty, food, and lifestyle), by region, and segment forecasts, 2023–2030. Grand View Research. https://www.grandviewresearch.com/industry-analysis/virtual-influencer-market-report

Ham, J., Li, S., Looi, J., & Eastin, M. S. (2024). Virtual humans as social actors: Investigating user perceptions of virtual humans' emotional expression on social media. *Computers in Human Behavior, 155*, 108161. https://doi.org/10.1016/j.chb.2024.108161

Hudders, L., De Jans, S., & De Veirman, M. (2021). The commercialization of social media stars: A literature review and conceptual framework on the strategic use of social media influencers. In *Social media influencers in strategic communication* (pp. 24–67).

Influencer Marketing Hub. (2025). *Artificial intelligence (AI) marketing benchmark report: 2025*. Influencer Marketing Hub. https://influencermarketinghub.com/ai-marketing-benchmark-report/

Jiang, K., Zhou, D., Bao, X., & Mo, S. (2024). Self-created or collaborative? The effects of virtual influencers' identity type and post type on purchase intentions. *Asia Pacific Journal of Marketing and Logistics, 37*(3). https://doi.org/10.1108/APJML-07-2024-0980

Jin, S. V., Muqaddam, A., & Ryu, E. (2019). Instafamous and social media influencer marketing. *Marketing Intelligence & Planning, 37*(5), 567–579. https://doi.org/10.1108/MIP-09-2018-0375

Joshi, Y., Lim, W. M., Jagani, K., & Kumar, S. (2023). Social media influencer marketing: Foundations, trends, and ways forward. *Electronic Commerce Research, 25*, 1–55. https://doi.org/10.1007/s10660-023-09719-z

Ju, N., Kim, T., & Im, H. (2024). Fake human but real influencer: The interplay of authenticity and humanlikeness in virtual influencer communication? *Fashion and Textiles, 11*(1), 16. https://doi.org/10.1186/s40691-024-00380-0

Jun, S., & Yi, J. (2020). What makes followers loyal? The role of influencer interactivity in building influencer brand equity. *Journal of Product & Brand Management, 29*(6), 803–814. https://doi.org/10.1108/JPBM-02-2019-2280

Kay, S., Mulcahy, R., & Parkinson, J. (2020). When less is more: The impact of macro and micro social media influencers' disclosure. *Journal of Marketing Management, 36*(3–4), 248–278. https://doi.org/10.1080/0267257X.2020.1718740

Kerley, T. (2024). Digital influencers' visual narratives and algorithmic power: Identity construction and impulsive consumption on social networks. *International Journal of Scientific Management and Tourism, 10*(6), e1196. https://doi.org/10.55905/ijsmtv10n6-012

Kietzmann, J., Mills, A. J., & Plangger, K. (2021). Deepfakes: Perspectives on the future "reality" of advertising and branding. *International Journal of Advertising, 40*(3), 473–485. https://doi.org/10.1080/02650487.2020.1834211

Kim, E., Shoenberger, H., Kim, D., Thorson, E., & Zihang, E. (2025). Novelty vs. trust in virtual influencers: Exploring the effectiveness of human-like virtual influencers and anime-like virtual influencers. *International Journal of Advertising, 44*(3), 453–483. https://doi.org/10.1080/02650487.2024.2386916

Kim, H., & Park, M. (2023). Virtual influencers' attractiveness effect on purchase intention: A moderated mediation model of the product–endorser fit with the brand. *Computers in Human Behavior, 143*, 107703. https://doi.org/10.1016/j.chb.2023.107703

Kim, I., Ki, C. W., Lee, H., & Kim, Y. K. (2024). Virtual influencer marketing: Evaluating the influence of virtual influencers' form realism and behavioral realism on consumer ambivalence and marketing performance. *Journal of Business Research, 176*, 114611. https://doi.org/10.1016/j.jbusres.2024.114611

Kim, M., & Baek, T. H. (2024). Are virtual influencers friends or foes? Uncovering the perceived creepiness and authenticity of virtual influencers in social media marketing in the United States. *International Journal of Human–Computer Interaction, 40*(18), 5042–5055. https://doi.org/10.1080/10447318.2023.2233125

Lee, H., Shin, M., Yang, J., & Chock, T. M. (2025). Virtual influencers vs. human influencers in the context of influencer marketing: The moderating role of machine heuristic on perceived authenticity of influencers. *International Journal of Human–Computer Interaction, 41*(10), 6029–6046. https://doi.org/10.1080/10447318.2024.2374100
Lee, J. A., & Eastin, M. S. (2020). I like what she's# endorsing: The impact of female social media influencers' perceived sincerity, consumer envy, and product type. *Journal of Interactive Advertising, 20*(1), 76–91. https://doi.org/10.1080/15252019.2020.1737849
Lee, Y. H., & Yuan, C. W. T. (2023). I'm not a puppet, I'ma real boy! Gender presentations by virtual influencers and how they are received. *Computers in Human Behavior, 149*, 107927. https://doi.org/10.1016/j.chb.2023.107927
Leung, F. F., Gu, F. F., Li, Y., Zhang, J. Z., & Palmatier, R. W. (2022). Influencer marketing effectiveness. *Journal of Marketing, 86*(6), 93–115. https://doi.org/10.1177/00222429221102889
Lim, R. E., & Lee, S. Y. (2023). "You are a virtual influencer!": Understanding the impact of origin disclosure and emotional narratives on parasocial relationships and virtual influencer credibility. *Computers in Human Behavior, 148*, 107897. https://doi.org/10.1016/j.chb.2023.107897
Looi, J., & Kahlor, L. A. (2024). Artificial intelligence in influencer marketing: A mixed-method comparison of human and virtual influencers on Instagram. *Journal of Interactive Advertising, 24*(2), 107–126. https://doi.org/10.1080/15252019.2024.2313721
Lou, C. (2022). Social media influencers and followers: Theorization of a trans-parasocial relation and explication of its implications for influencer advertising. *Journal of Advertising, 51*(1), 4–21.
Lou, C., Kiew, S. T. J., Chen, T., Lee, T. Y. M., Ong, J. E. C., & Phua, Z. (2023). Authentically fake? How consumers respond to the influence of virtual influencers. *Journal of Advertising, 52*(4), 540–557.
Lou, C., & Yuan, S. (2019). Influencer marketing: How message value and credibility affect consumer trust of branded content on social media. *Journal of Interactive Advertising, 19*(1), 58–73. https://doi.org/10.1080/15252019.2018.1533501
Machado Carvalho, M. A. (2024). Influencing the follower behavior: The role of homophily and perceived usefulness, credibility and enjoyability of travel content. *Journal of Hospitality and Tourism Insights, 7*(2), 1091–1110. https://doi.org/10.1108/JHTI-09-2023-0648
Miao, F., Kozlenkova, I. V., Wang, H., Xie, T., & Palmatier, R. W. (2022). An emerging theory of avatar marketing. *Journal of Marketing, 86*(1), 67–90. https://doi.org/10.1177/0022242921996646
Mouritzen, S. L. T., Penttinen, V., & Pedersen, S. (2024). Virtual influencer marketing: The good, the bad and the unreal. *European Journal of Marketing, 58*(2), 410–440. https://doi.org/10.1108/EJM-12-2022-0915
Moustakas, E., Lamba, N., Mahmoud, D., & Ranganathan, C. (2020). Blurring lines between fiction and reality: Perspectives of experts on marketing effectiveness of virtual influencers. In *2020 international conference on cyber security and protection of digital services (cyber security)* (pp. 1–6). IEEE. https://doi.org/10.1109/CyberSecurity49315.2020.9138861
Mrad, M., Ramadan, Z., & Nasr, L. I. (2022). Computer-generated influencers: The rise of digital personalities. *Marketing Intelligence & Planning, 40*(5), 589–603. https://doi.org/10.1108/MIP-12-2021-0423
Okonkwo, I., & Namkoisse, E. (2023). The role of influencer marketing in building authentic brand relationships online. *Journal of Digital Marketing and Communication, 3*(2), 81–90. https://doi.org/10.53623/jdmc.v3i2.350
Park, J., Lee, J. M., Xiong, V. Y., Septianto, F., & Seo, Y. (2021). David and Goliath: When and why micro-influencers are more persuasive than mega-influencers. *Journal of Advertising, 50*(5), 584–602. https://doi.org/10.1080/00913367.2021.1980470
Pelletier, M. J., Krallman, A., Adams, F. G., & Hancock, T. (2020). One size doesn't fit all: A uses and gratifications analysis of social media platforms. *Journal of Research in Interactive Marketing, 14*(2), 269–284. https://doi.org/10.1108/JRIM-10-2019-0159
Robinson, B. (2020). Towards an ontology and ethics of virtual influencers. *Australasian Journal of Information Systems, 24*. https://doi.org/10.3127/ajis.v24i0.2807

Sands, S., Campbell, C. L., Plangger, K., & Ferraro, C. (2022). Unreal influence: Leveraging AI in influencer marketing. *European Journal of Marketing, 56*(6), 1721–1747. https://doi.org/10.1108/EJM-12-2019-0949

Shoenberger, H., & Kim, E. (2023). Explaining purchase intent via expressed reasons to follow an influencer, perceived homophily, and perceived authenticity. *International Journal of Advertising, 42*(2), 368–383. https://doi.org/10.1080/02650487.2022.2075636

Sokolova, K., & Kefi, H. (2020). Instagram and YouTube bloggers promote it, why should I buy? How credibility and parasocial interaction influence purchase intentions. *Journal of Retailing and Consumer Services, 53*, 101742. https://doi.org/10.1016/j.jretconser.2019.01.011

Stein, J. P., Linda Breves, P., & Anders, N. (2024). Parasocial interactions with real and virtual influencers: The role of perceived similarity and human-likeness. *New Media & Society, 26*(6), 3433–3453. https://doi.org/10.1177/14614448221102

Thomas, V. L., & Fowler, K. (2021). Close encounters of the AI kind: Use of AI influencers as brand endorsers. *Journal of Advertising, 50*(1), 11–25. https://doi.org/10.1080/00913367.2020.1810595

Thomson, M. (2006). Human brands: Investigating antecedents to consumers' strong attachments to celebrities. *Journal of Marketing, 70*(3), 104–119.

Tussyadiah, I. P., Zach, F. J., & Wang, J. (2020). Do travelers trust intelligent service robots? *Annals of Tourism Research, 81*, 102886. https://doi.org/10.1016/j.annals.2020.102886

Vrontis, D., Makrides, A., Christofi, M., & Thrassou, A. (2021). Social media influencer marketing: A systematic review, integrative framework and future research agenda. *International Journal of Consumer Studies, 45*(4), 617–644. https://doi.org/10.1111/ijcs.12647

Yan, J., Xia, S., Jiang, A., & Lin, Z. (2024). The effect of different types of virtual influencers on consumers' emotional attachment. *Journal of Business Research, 177*, 114646. https://doi.org/10.1016/j.jbusres.2024.114646

Yang, D., Zhang, J., Sun, Y., & Huang, Z. (2024). Showing usage behavior or not? The effect of virtual influencers' product usage behavior on consumers. *Journal of Retailing and Consumer Services, 79*, 103859. https://doi.org/10.1016/j.jretconser.2024.103859

Zeng, Y., Pu, G., Liu, J., & Feng, W. (2024). The influence mechanism of narrative strategies used by virtual influencers on consumer product preferences. *Journal of Theoretical and Applied Electronic Commerce Research, 19*(4), 2828–2850. https://doi.org/10.3390/jtaer19040137

Zhang, L., & Wei, W. (2021). Influencer marketing: A comparison of traditional celebrity, social media influencer, and AI influencer. *Boston Hospitality Review*, 1–11.

Zhang, Y., He, J., & Li, J. (2025). The role of flow experience in virtual influencer marketing: Insights into aesthetic, entertainment and parasocial influences on purchase intention. *Journal of Fashion Marketing and Management: An International Journal, 29*(6), 1109–1129. https://doi.org/10.1108/JFMM-05-2024-0201

The Impact of Chatbots Assistance in Customer Experience: A Comparative Analysis of the Hospitality and E-Commerce Sectors

Cláudia Ribau and Ana Torres

Abstract Artificial Intelligence (AI) is revolutionizing the way businesses interact with customers, particularly through the use of chatbots in the service and retail industries. This chapter explores the role of shopping assistance chatbots in enhancing customer experience within two distinct sectors: hospitality and e-commerce. It examines the functionalities, advantages, challenges, and impact of these AI-driven tools, highlighting how they are deployed in each sector to improve customer satisfaction, operational efficiency, and overall business outcomes. The chapter also presents a comparative analysis of these two industries, emphasizing the similarities and differences in chatbot deployment, with a focus on user expectations, sector-specific needs, and technological advancements. By drawing on recent research, industry reports, and real-world case studies, this chapter provides valuable insights into the evolving role of AI chatbots in customer engagement.

1 Introduction

The integration of Artificial Intelligence (AI) in business operations has increasingly reshaped how organizations engage with their customers (Gnewuch et al., 2017). Among the most transformative AI applications are chatbots—software solutions that simulate human conversation through text or voice. Chatbots have become ubiquitous across a variety of sectors, notably in hospitality and e-commerce, where they serve as valuable tools for improving customer service, streamlining operations, and enhancing the overall customer experience.

C. Ribau
GOVCOPP—UID Research Unit on Governance, Competitiveness and Public Policies, Higher Institute of Accounting and Administration of University of Aveiro, Aveiro, Portugal
e-mail: cpr@ua.pt

A. Torres (✉)
INESC TEC, Porto, Portugal; Higher Institute of Accounting and Administration of University of Aveiro, Aveiro, Portugal
e-mail: ana.torres@ua.pt

J. D. Santos et al. (eds.), *Artificial Intelligence Transforming Marketing*, Contributions to Management Science, https://doi.org/10.1007/978-3-032-22360-9_20

Even without being fully aware of it, people incorporate artificial intelligence into their everyday lives in various ways, improving the efficiency and convenience of their routines. Whenever someone uses a digital assistant like Google Assistant, Siri, Amazon's Alexa, or a navigation app, artificial intelligence enhances their interaction and delivers answers to questions.

This phenomenon has prompted enterprises to undergo a transformative transition that has directed their operations towards a more technologically advanced paradigm as opposed to a more conventional and individualized approach.

Internet data reports from 2022 to 2024 show that the number of Internet users who use voice assistances (e.g., Siri from Google or Alexa from Amazon) has increased very rapidly (We are Social, 2025) and experts project that by the end of 2025, 95% of customer engagements will utilize AI-enhanced platforms, and the forthcoming generation of consumers will be supported by chatbot technologies (Anica-Popa et al., 2021).

This is largely because these technologies are accessed on demand through the Internet and offer consumers benefits in terms of convenience, efficiency, and, most notably, enhanced engagement (Torres & Delgado, 2023). As the adoption of artificial intelligence applications expands, users are becoming progressively more dependent on such technological solutions.

AI, nevertheless, is not confined solely to consumer applications. The ramifications of AI across various sectors are notably profound, encompassing areas such as autonomous vehicles and financial consultancy services. Enterprises are incorporating AI frameworks and functionalities into their operational models as an essential element of efficiency (Dwivedi et al., 2021) providing businesses with several increased benefits.

Organizations show that AI enhances revenue generation in sales and marketing while concurrently diminishing expenditures in supply chain management and manufacturing processes. For e-retail enterprises, the implementation of AI technologies presents numerous advantages: enhanced revenue generation, sales reinforcement, strategic price differentiation derived from the customer database, improved customer satisfaction, reduced product return rates, and overall cost efficiency (Syam & Sharma, 2018). Consequently, it is imperative for organizations to move towards the digital transformation of their processes and functionalities through the integration of AI in service automation.

A chatbot is a machine learning-based application designed to simulate human-like interactions, continuously improving its performance through learning algorithms applied to existing data (Moriuchi et al., 2021). As their presence on e-commerce platforms increases, chatbots have become a technological means to enhance customer experience, achieve cost efficiencies, and ensure greater consistency in service quality, thereby supporting decision-making throughout the customer journey.

In the hospitality sector, chatbots are designed to assist guests in navigating their stay, from booking reservations to providing real-time support during their visit (Tussyadiah & Park, 2018). In contrast, the e-commerce sector uses chatbots primarily to facilitate purchasing decisions, offer personalized recommendations, and resolve customer service queries (Chung et al., 2020).

This chapter provides an in-depth exploration of shopping and customer assistance chatbots, focusing on their role in both the hospitality and e-commerce sectors. By comparing these industries, we aim to provide a comprehensive understanding of how AI-driven chatbots enhance customer service, improve operational efficiency, and contribute to customer satisfaction and loyalty. The chapter offers several contributions for organizations to move towards the digital transformation of their processes and functionalities through the integration of AI chatbots in service automation.

This chapter is structured as follows: after this introduction, Section 2 is dedicated to applications of AI chatbots in the hospitality sector; Section 3 depicts the role of applications of AI chatbots in e-commerce sector. Section 4 discusses the similarities and key differences between the two sectors. Section 5 presents the chapter conclusions and finally, in Sect. 6, future research avenues to explore are suggested.

2 AI Chatbots in the Hospitality Sector

The hospitality sector has long been at the forefront of adopting digital solutions to improve customer service and operational efficiency. Chatbots in this context primarily focus on streamlining booking processes, providing instant responses to customer inquiries, and personalizing the guest experience.

The hospitality industry has long been characterized by its reliance on face-to-face customer service. However, the growing demand for instant gratification and the shift towards digital services have prompted hotels, resorts, and other businesses within the sector to explore AI-driven solutions (Kuo et al., 2020). Chatbots in hospitality are now commonplace, supporting everything from initial bookings to in-room assistance.

In line with this trend, Torres and Delgado (2023) find that the category of products and services most frequently acquired online by 50% of respondents utilizing a chatbot pertains to travel-related items (e.g., airline tickets, train fares; taxi or Uber services), followed by accommodation options (such as hotels, hostels, Airbnb, etc.) with a representation of 31%. Conversely, financial services (including insurance, credit, etc.), telecommunication services, and household items exhibiting the least frequency purchased categories (each accounting for 1.1%) assisted by chatbots. These findings suggest that chatbots assistance is more frequent in less complex and risky customers' buying decisions.

2.1 Key Functions of Chatbots in Hospitality

Artificial intelligence (AI) has emerged as a key resource in hotel management, supporting operational effectiveness, enhancing the overall customer experience, and, as a result, fostering revenue growth (Al-Hyari et al., 2023a, 2023b). AI solutions may assume physical forms, such as service robots, as well as non-physical applications, including chatbots (Prentice et al., 2020b). Chatbots enable customers to access real-time information through text-based interactions. Their growing appeal within the hospitality industry stems from their capacity to manage complex customer interactions at scale, provide continuous 24/7 service, and increase customer engagement across multiple technological platforms (Sivaramakrishnan et al., 2007).

The implementation of AI in hotels can occur in various forms (Manyakin, 2023; Kacar, 2023; Tong-On et al., 2021), including:

- AI-based chatbots and virtual assistants, used to respond to customer enquiries, requests, and complaints.
- Revenue management systems, which optimize pricing strategies by analysing data on room occupancy, customer demand, and consumer behaviour, thereby assisting hotels in maximizing their revenue.
- Personalized guest experiences, achieved through the analysis of historical customer data and preferences.
- Tailored marketing recommendations, fostering guest loyalty and enabling the anticipation of market trends within the hospitality sector.
- Predictive maintenance, which helps prevent equipment malfunctions and system failures by forecasting when maintenance is required.
- Security and fraud detection, employing technologies such as surveillance cameras and facial recognition to monitor guest behaviour and identify potential risks.

Additionally, hotels may incorporate service robots, smart rooms, and voice-controlled entertainment systems to offer guests a differentiated experience. Robots can be programmed to perform simple, repetitive tasks—such as vacuuming rooms—without the need for human intervention, thereby increasing employee efficiency (Ivanov et al., 2017). AI technologies also streamline service delivery and contribute positively to the overall guest experience (Prentice et al., 2020a).

Moreover, AI supports hotel staff in organizing guest information, particularly for group bookings, and in making data-informed decisions. It can also provide personalized recommendations based on previous stays, effectively reducing the reliance on human memory (Qiu et al., 2022).

Overall, AI proves particularly valuable in attracting customers and enhancing their experience by offering more convenient and flexible services, which in turn fosters guest loyalty (Prentice et al., 2020b).

Table 1 summarizes the key AI functions identified in the hospitality sector, providing a structured overview of the findings presented in this literature review.

Building on these broader applications of AI in hospitality, one particularly prominent and versatile tool is the AI-powered chatbot. As a form of intangible AI, chatbots play a pivotal role in automating guest interactions while maintaining a personalized touch. They are increasingly integrated into service delivery processes due to their ability to operate around the clock, reduce response times, and improve overall service quality.

Table 1 Key functions of AI in the hospitality sector—business advantages

Function	Description
AI chatbots assistants	Provide instant responses to customer inquiries, requests, and complaints, enhancing responsiveness
Revenue management	Optimize pricing based on demand, occupancy rates, and consumer behaviour to increase revenue
Personalized guest experience	Customize services by analysing guest history and stated preferences to deliver tailored offerings
Predictive maintenance	Forecast when equipment or systems need service to avoid failures and reduce downtime
Security and surveillance	Use facial recognition and smart cameras to monitor guest behaviour and detect threats or fraud
Robots	Perform simple programmed tasks (e.g., cleaning), reducing workload and increasing staff efficiency
Smart rooms	Enable guests to control lighting, temperature, and entertainment through voice-activated systems
Information organization	Assist staff in managing data on guest groups and events, improving planning and communication
Personalized recommendations	Suggest services such as dining, spa, and tours based on guest profiles or past behaviours
Guest engagement	Automate follow-ups and send reminders or promotional messages during the guest's stay

Source Adapted and integrated from Ivanov et al. (2017), Kacar (2023), Manyakin (2023), Meng et al. (2023), Tong-On et al. (2021), Qiu et al. (2022), and Shi et al. (2021)

Chatbots are used for a wide range of functions, each designed to streamline operations and enrich the guest experience:

- *Reservation Management*: AI chatbots help customers book rooms, make inquiries about room availability, and provide instant booking confirmations (Gretzel et al., 2015).
- *Customer Service and Inquiries*: Chatbots respond to common guest questions, such as those related to hotel amenities, check-in/check-out processes, and location-specific information (López et al., 2021).
- *Personalized Recommendations*: Based on past interactions or profile data, chatbots can suggest dining options, spa treatments, and excursions, enhancing the guest's experience (Neuhofer et al., 2015), which potentially triggers cross-sales.
- *Guest Engagement*: Some advanced chatbots provide proactive communication, such as sending reminders about upcoming reservations or offering special promotions during a guest's stay (Cowan et al., 2020).

Table 2 summarizes the functions of AI chatbots, from the user experience advantages.

Table 2 Functions of AI chatbots—user experience advantages

Function	Description
Automated check-in and check-out	These are types of check-in and check-out processes that occur without human interaction
Specific requests	Making requests for food, beverages, or special requirements, which are directed to the relevant department of the hotel, such as housekeeping, room service, or reservations
Guest recommendations	Guests can ask the AI assistant for recommendations on places to visit or dine, and plan an itinerary based on their needs
Inquiries and complaints	It is through the AI assistants that guests can inquire about the hotel and make complaints
Reservations	Through conversations with the AI assistant, customers can make a reservation, receive confirmation, and even modify it if necessary. These functions are usually supervised by a staff member
Smart room	With the AI assistant, guests can control the lights, temperature, and television in their room

Source Adapted and integrated from Al-Hyari et al. (2023a, 2023b), Bhaskar and Sharma (2022a, 2022b), Kacar (2023), Manyakin (2023), Morosan and Bowen (2018), and Tong-On et al. (2021)

2.2 Advantages of Chatbots in Hospitality

Chatbots represent a category of artificial intelligence that has gained widespread adoption in professional customer service contexts, as they are capable of simulating human conversations and progressively enhancing their performance through continuous learning from user interactions (Moriuchi et al., 2021). In recent years, a growing stream of research has emphasized the potential of artificial intelligence within marketing (Wirth, 2018), particularly highlighting the business value of chatbot adoption. These benefits include improvements in customer efficiency and convenience (Faggella, 2018; Waghmare, 2019), as well as stronger customer engagement and more effective marketing outcomes (Ho, 2021; Wirth, 2018). Therefore, the implementation of chatbots in the hospitality sector offers several advantages for both businesses and customers, as follows:

- *Enhanced Efficiency and Availability*: Chatbots are available 24/7, providing guests with instant assistance at any time of day, which is particularly useful in international markets with varying time zones (Buhalis & Law, 2008).
- *Operational Cost Efficiency*: Through the automation of repetitive activities—such as handling frequently asked questions or processing reservations—hotels are able to lessen their reliance on extensive customer service staff, thereby achieving meaningful cost reductions (Chung et al., 2020).
- *Conversations with Users*: Chatbots are software applications developed to engage in natural language communication with users, responding to customer inquiries or inputs in a conversational manner. These systems support a wide range of online functionalities, such as website navigation assistance, virtual support services,

customer service operations, and sales-related activities, among others (Moriuchi et al., 2021).

- *Improved Customer Satisfaction*: Guests appreciate the convenience of receiving quick responses to their inquiries without waiting in long queues or being placed on hold (Tussyadiah & Park, 2018).
- *Personalization at Scale*: Chatbots can process large volumes of data to offer personalized experiences, making guests feel valued and increasing the likelihood of repeat visits (Gretzel et al., 2015).

2.3 Implementation Challenges of Chatbots in Hospitality Services

Despite the clear benefits, the integration of AI chatbots in the hospitality industry presents several challenges:

- *Complex Integration*: Hotels must ensure that their chatbot systems are seamlessly integrated with existing booking engines, customer relationship management (CRM) systems, and other internal platforms (López et al., 2021).
- *Contextual Understanding*: While chatbots excel at providing general information, they often struggle with understanding the nuances of specific guest requests, which can lead to miscommunications (Gnewuch et al., 2017).
- *Customer Expectations*: Overreliance on chatbots may lead to customer dissatisfaction if guests prefer personal, human interaction for certain types of inquiries, especially complex or emotional requests (Tussyadiah & Park, 2018).
- *Privacy and Security*: From the main prevalent AI applications, tools—chatbots, virtual assistants, and recommender systems—show that user's privacy and security issues are among the main challenges and barriers of AI trustworthiness (Faria et al., 2023).

As shown in Table 3, the advantages of adopting an AI assistant surpass the disadvantages, for both customers and companies. However, the primary drawback that causes companies to delay the adoption of this AI technology is customer scepticism regarding its use.

Table 4 provides a summary of the previously discussed themes regarding the functions, advantages, disadvantages, and relationships with both customers and employees of AI chatbots.

It was concluded that the functions and advantages of AI chatbots are universal to any company, serving as an asset for any business aiming to maintain direct contact with customers at any time of the day and from any part of the world.

Regarding the disadvantages, they also become general, with the most significant being the scepticism of both customers and employees concerning new technologies.

Table 3 Advantages and disadvantages of using AI assistants

Advantages	Disadvantages
Available 24/7	System errors
Quick and efficient responses	Maintenance costs
Cost-effective, increasing profits and revenues, reducing labour costs	Failures in customer interaction, as it is not always possible to understand customer requests
Easy installation	Privacy and security concerns
Sustainability	Uncertainty in usage by customers
Customer satisfaction through personalized service	Need for constant human supervision
Simplicity in booking processes	–
Performing simple, repetitive tasks automatically	–

Source Adapted and integrated from Araujo (2018), Al-Hyari et al. (2023a, 2023b), Balakrishnan et al. (2022), Bhaskar and Sharma (2022a, 2022b), Carter and Knol (2019), Dyshkantiuk et al. (2020), Gunawan et al. (2020), Gursoy et al. (2019), Ivanov (2019), Ling et al. (2023), Melián-González et al. (2021), Meng et al. (2023), Prentice et al. (2020a), Rahman et al. (2018), Sam and Jasim (2023a, 2023b), Tussyadiah and Miller (2019), and Um et al. (2020)

These findings align with the relationship between chatbots and both customers and employees. While customers feel the absence of empathy and emotional communication typically provided by humans, employees fear the potential re-placement of their jobs by machines.

Noticeably, it is cautioned that AI-enabled service automation facilitates numerous organizations in refining their operational processes and augmenting employee productivity. Nevertheless, this reliance on AI may engender considerable risks for both institutions and consumers. It could present a potential threat to employment, as it is transforming the labour market by displacing human workers (Frank et al., 2019).

Moreover, it may also affect customers' emotional experiences as human entities. According to Bolton et al. (2018), consumers who experience feelings of detachment, frustration, alienation, or isolation rather than engagement in the customer journey may constrain their willingness to embrace this technology.

Regarding these variations in customer behaviour, organizations face the imperative of reconciling the efficiency and effectiveness of digital technologies while simultaneously enhancing interactions and relationships with their clients, which must remain central to their value proposition (Faria et al., 2023).

Consequently, it is crucial to understand how to alleviate these risks and threats and the context in which they may arise. In this regard, it is vital to ascertain how consumers engage with these applications and what effects they have on their perceptions of trustworthiness, utility, and involvement, as these applications increasingly become integral components of any organization's service framework.

The increasing adoption of virtual assistant agents introduces new challenges for service science, such as the design of smart services. Customer interactions, whether

Table 4 Integrative analysis of chatbots functions, (Dis)advantages, and relationship with customers/employees

Description	References
Functions	
Facilitate access to various hotel functions autonomously	Al-Hyari et al. (2023a, 2023b) Bhaskar and Sharma (2022a, 2022b) Kaçar (2023) Melián-González et al. (2021) Manyakin (2023) Morosan and Bowen (2018) Tong-On et al. (2021)
Allow control over various aspects of the room	
Assist employees with room service, housekeeping, and reservations	
Allow modifications and receipt of reservation confirmations	
Answer guest questions, issues, and frequently asked questions	
Provide audio-guided tours	
Advantages	
Positive cost-benefit ratio	Al-Hyari et al. (2023a, 2023b) Balakrishnan et al. (2022) Dyshkantiuk et al. (2020) Gunawan et al. (2020) Gursoy et al. (2019) Nguyen and Malik (2022) Prentice et al., (2020a) Rahman et al. (2018) Sam and Jasim (2023a, 2023b) Tussyadiah and Miller (2019) Um et al. (2020)
Increase profits and revenues	
Reduce labour costs	
Handle basic and repetitive tasks	
Allow employees to focus on more complex tasks	
Easy installation	
Considered sustainable	
Reduce customer waiting time	
Simplify the booking process	
Available 24/7 and in any language	
Disadvantages	
Negative interactions with customers	Araujo (2018) Bhaskar and Sharma (2022a, 2022b) Carter and Knol (2019) Ling et al. (2023) Melián-González et al. (2021) Prentice and Nguyen (2020) Um et al. (2020)
Algorithms are unable to understand and interpret all words used	
Maintenance costs	
Privacy and security concerns	
Customers find chatbot mimic communication unnatural and question its response capability	
Customer scepticism regarding the use of this technology	
Customer relationship /engagement/ experience / acceptance	
Acceptance depends on age, gender, generation, and frequency of internet use and also, on effective communication and information credibility	Chang et al. (2023) Fan et al. (2023) Holzwarth et al. (2006) Lin et al. (2020) Loureiro et al. (2024) Sam and Jasim (2023a, 2023b) van Esch et al. (2022)
Guests still highly value interactions with staff and accept that AI can handle basic tasks	
Interaction between the guest and AI assistants aims to influence purchasing decisions, save time, and provide product or service advice	

(continued)

Table 4 (continued)

Description	References
Customers hesitate to interact with AI chatbots due to the lack of empathy	
Employee relationship / acceptance	
AI generates significant job insecurity and concerns about changes to their employment	Brougham and Haar (2018) Lie et al. (2019) Nguyen and Malik (2022) Qiu et al. (2022) Xiao and Kumar (2021) Zhang and Jin (2023)
Employees work in teams with AI, and it is important for them that the system is easy to manage	
The use of AI increases job-change intentions, fear of replacement, and feelings of inadequacy	
AI generates significant job insecurity and concerns about changes to their employment	

Source Authors

with service representatives or AI technologies, often drive the development of new services (Cook et al., 1999).

AI-based service automation undeniably enables organizations to enhance operational processes and boost employee productivity, promoting overall efficiency. However, this growing dependence on AI also brings significant risks, including potential employment displacement, as automation reshapes the labour market by substituting human workers (Frank et al., 2019). Moreover, the use of AI can influence customer engagement with brands and service providers. While AI facilitates the delivery of high-quality services and cost optimization, automated interactions may become less personalized, impersonal, or lack of transparency, which can lead to customer dissatisfaction. In particular, deploying AI in sensitive contexts (such as facial recognition or other biometric data captured via sensors, cameras, or audio) can pose potential harm to clients and limit technology adoption (Faria et al., 2023). Such concerns can also erode initial customer trust in chatbots and similar AI solutions (Mostafa & Kasamani, 2022).

In the light of these challenges, companies are responsible for implementing rigorous security protocols to protect sensitive and private information from unauthorized access. Organizations must ensure that entrusted personal data is safeguarded effectively, demonstrating that privacy is both an individual and broader organizational security concern (Heurix et al., 2015).

Therefore, mitigating these risks requires organizations to carefully balance the efficiency and effectiveness of digital technologies with the need to cultivate meaningful interactions and relationships with customers. A central component of this effort involves understanding how customers engage with AI applications and evaluating the impact on trust, perceived usefulness, and engagement, as such technologies are increasingly integral to modern service infrastructures.

3 AI Chatbots in the E-Commerce Sector

The rise of online shopping has driven e-commerce businesses to adopt AI chatbots as part of their digital customer service strategies (Chung et al., 2020). In e-commerce, the primary role of chatbots is to support customers through the purchasing process, offering real-time assistance with product discovery, order tracking, and post-purchase support.

A chatbot is a type of machine learning application designed to emulate human conversations, improving its performance over time by continuously learning from existing data (Moriuchi et al., 2021). In practical terms, chatbots are often used for tasks such as submitting support tickets for refunds or facilitating product exchanges online. Predefined conversational flows enable the chatbot to guide customers to the appropriate department or even process refunds and exchanges automatically.

Similar to chatbots, virtual assistants (or smart assistants) typically consist of three primary components: sensors that monitor environmental and physical conditions, controllers that interpret incoming data, and actuators that execute actions based on those interpretations (Lau et al., 2018). Prominent virtual assistants developed by companies such as Google, Apple, and Amazon offer a range of functionalities, including providing weather forecasts, retrieving information about local restaurants, assisting with scheduling, playing music or podcasts, delivering entertainment, and even telling jokes.

A chatbot constitutes a sophisticated digital application that facilitates a conversational exchange between the consumer and the chatbot itself. The replies provided by the chatbot are meticulously chosen based on keywords discerned within the inquiries posed by the users. In the realms of business and e-commerce, this conversational system has been employed to assist consumers in comparing and acquiring products online, as well as to provide guidance and recommendations to consumers during their online purchasing decision-making processes—ultimately serving to enhance the overall consumer experience (Tuzovic & Paluch, 2018).

The implementation of chatbots within e-commerce platforms also yields advantages concerning the speed of responses, the service quality, and an augmented degree of automation in the management of return procedures, thereby diminishing the resources allocated to the team while simultaneously increasing customer satisfaction and loyalty (Lester et al., 2004).

3.1 Key Functions of Chatbots in E-Commerce

In the e-commerce sector, chatbots are deployed across various customer touchpoints:

- *Product Discovery, Search/Comparison, and Recommendations*: Chatbots guide customers in finding products that meet their needs, leveraging AI to analyse previous interactions and preferences (Liu et al., 2020). Similarly, "Advanced Search/Filters", followed by the features "Price comparisons or product/service" are the most consensual functionalities that customers used regarding online buying support for customer decision-making of product/service (Torres & Delgado, 2023).

- *Order Tracking:* Customers can inquire about the status of their orders, receive updates on shipping progress, and track delivery (Chung et al., 2020).
- *Customer Support*: E-commerce chatbots handle a wide range of queries related to shipping, returns, payment issues, and promotions, helping to reduce customer service workloads (Huang & Rust, 2021).
- *Upselling and Cross-selling:* Through conversational AI, chatbots can suggest complementary products or upgrades, enhancing the customer's overall shopping experience (Liu et al., 2020). Chatbots can further enhance cross-selling and upselling opportunities by providing personalized recommendations for products, services, or communication content. These suggestions are generated through automated data collection, which monitors customer information such as preferences and purchase history (Tuzovic & Paluch, 2018).

3.2 Advantages of Chatbots in E-Commerce

The adoption of AI chatbots in e-commerce offers significant benefits for both customers and businesses:

- *Increased Conversion Rates:* By assisting customers in real time and offering personalized product recommendations, chatbots help reduce friction in the purchasing process, leading to higher conversion rates and lower cart abandonment (Chung et al., 2020).
- *Enhanced Customer Engagement*: Chatbots can interact with customers through personalized messages that consider browsing behaviour and previous purchase history, thereby creating a more engaging and enjoyable shopping experience (Liu et al., 2020). This personalization can boost consumer satisfaction and positively influence purchasing behaviour (Kamei et al., 2010). By delivering tailored responses, chatbots help address one of the primary challenges of online retail: making each customer feel recognized and valued (Lester et al., 2004).
- *Cost Savings:* Chatbots can handle high volumes of customer queries, reducing the need for large customer service teams and enabling businesses to allocate resources more effectively (Huang & Rust, 2021).

3.3 Challenges of Chatbots in E-Commerce

It is consensual that integrating AI in shopping can lead to a better AI-enabled customer experience. While the benefits are clear, there are also challenges associated with deploying AI chatbots in the e-commerce sector:

- *Trust and Security*: E-commerce customers may hesitate to rely on chatbots for sensitive transactions, such as providing payment details, unless the chatbot offers robust security measures (Liu et al., 2020).

From the perspective of end consumers, trust emerges as a pivotal factor in AI-enabled customer experiences. Consumers may encounter significant drawbacks, including reduced human interaction, privacy concerns, diminished control, time demands, and potential feelings of frustration, all of which can negatively impact their experience with AI-based services (Ameen et al., 2021). The study highlights that when companies deliver high-quality, personalized, and convenient AI-driven services, customers are more likely to develop trust in both the brand and its technological solutions.

- *Data Privacy Concerns*: Chatbots gather and analyse substantial volumes of customer data, which raises important questions regarding data usage and protection (Chung et al., 2020). Although these systems are based on machine learning, meaning their algorithms are designed and trained by humans, consumers often express scepticism when interacting with them (Kaczorowska-Spychalska, 2019).

Privacy and security concerns have become increasingly critical in digital environments, as users routinely consent to privacy policies for seemingly minor actions, such as applying a promotion code, making an online purchase, or downloading a mobile application. As a result, external providers are able to track and utilize consumer data in multiple ways, including transactional information from CRM systems, demographic data derived from credit or loyalty cards, survey responses linked to email addresses, and even in-store visitor data. Furthermore, social media data connected to individual activity can significantly enrich customer-level datasets, providing highly detailed insights (Bradlow et al., 2017).

- *Biased Algorithms*: Another critical challenge lies in the risk of algorithmic bias, which can lead to discriminatory practices and poor customer experience. These biases often stem from the data used to train AI systems, which may reflect historical inequalities or unbalanced representations of consumer groups (Raji et al., 2020). In e-commerce, this can result in chatbots providing less accurate, less helpful, or even exclusionary interactions for certain customer profiles, thereby undermining both trust and inclusivity. Moreover, opaque AI models make it difficult for customers to understand how recommendation decisions are made, which may further exacerbate scepticism and reduce perceived fairness in automated service delivery.
- *Lack of Human Interaction*: Some customers may find chatbots impersonal, particularly in cases where they require assistance with complex or high-value products (Huang & Rust, 2021).

Similarly, Torres and Delgado (2023) reported that a substantial proportion of respondents (41.1%) do not consider chatbots their preferred tool when making online purchase decisions. Instead, they favour alternative customer support channels and direct interactions with employees via phone, email, or other means. A smaller segment of users perceives chatbots as not useful (9.5%) or difficult to use (4.3%). These findings suggest that a considerable number of consumers are not yet prepared to fully adopt or engage with AI-enabled technologies during the online shopping process. The study also highlights which traditional assistance tools remain valuable throughout different stages of the consumer buying journey. Overall, the authors indicate that chatbot-based support has yet to be leveraged as a fully effective, win-win strategy for all online consumers, although there is a positive inclination towards its materialization.

Though, human-machine interactions constrain the consumer's decision-making process in several ways. Firstly, chatbots are not multisensory and lack the ability to integrate both real and virtual content in alignment with tangible and digital objects, which limits their capacity to fully simulate a user's actual shopping experience with a product (Faggella, 2018). This limitation positions chatbots primarily as information-gathering tools, similar to personal assistants, that help users access relevant information, enhance awareness of a company and its product offerings, and support decision-making throughout the customer journey. Several studies indicate a general resistance to chatbot technology (Araujo, 2018; Rosenthal, 2017). Consumers tend to have a more engaging and enjoyable experience when interacting with interactive technologies, such as augmented reality applications, compared to chatbots, which can affect both engagement and purchasing intentions (Moriuchi et al., 2021).

Secondly, as virtual mimicry agents, chatbots inherently have limited understanding of real-world contexts and conversational meaning. According to Theory of Constraints (ToC) perspectives, chatbots have never physically interacted with the objects they discuss, which restricts their capacity for comprehension and the negotiation of meaning (Moriuchi et al., 2021). These conversational limitations can generate gaps in interaction with consumers, as chatbots may not fully grasp the nuances of user queries (Moriuchi et al., 2021). A likely explanation is that users approach chatbots with expectations of productivity, seeking direct and accurate answers to their questions. However, most chatbots are unable to provide meaningful feedback or meet user expectations due to unclear purposes, illogical responses, or insufficient usability (Moriuchi et al., 2021). Consequently, technological engagement with chatbots, in comparison to augmented reality, often results in reduced brand engagement, lower satisfaction with the shopping experience, and weaker behavioural intentions, such as repeat purchases (Moriuchi et al., 2021).

Given the uncertainty about consumer reactions to these technologies (Ferrara et al., 2016), chatbots are typically designed to handle straightforward tasks, including offering basic advice on clothing choices or responding to frequently asked questions. Nevertheless, the AI and machine learning capabilities of chatbots allow them to remember previous customer interactions and personalize their responses accordingly, offering opportunities for tailored product recommendations and more efficient service delivery.

On the other hand, companies increasingly employ intelligent assistants, lacking human-like characteristics, as service interfaces. Compared to direct interactions, such as those between a sales representative and a customer, chatbots demonstrate limitations in responsiveness and personalization, which can negatively affect consumer satisfaction. This decline in satisfaction may subsequently influence consumers' intentions to shop with a particular brand or company. Faggella (2018) also notes that chatbots are primarily used as information-gathering tools, functioning similarly to personal assistants. Moreover, transitioning from an established user interface, like a website, to a chatbot platform is not a straightforward process. Moriuchi et al. (2021) observed that consumers reported a more enjoyable experience interacting with augmented reality applications compared to chatbot apps in an e-retail environment. This observation is reinforced by previous research demonstrating the effectiveness of robots in retail settings for product recommendation. For example, small communication robots have successfully guided customers and recommended items in physical stores (Kamei et al., 2010). The study measured customer behaviour, noting that customers spent more time interacting with the robots, and confirmed the effectiveness of the recommendations based on both purchased items and movement trajectories within the store.

Supporting these findings, Torres and Delgado (2023) challenge the assumption that chatbots and other interactive technologies, despite their novelty, automatically foster positive consumer attitudes towards a retail company or increase their willingness to (re)purchase.

4 Comparative Analysis: Hospitality Vs. E-Commerce

While both sectors, hospitality and e-commerce utilize AI chatbots to enhance customer experience, the way these chatbots are deployed and the expectations of customers differ. This section compares the two sectors in terms of the following factors:

4.1 Similarities

- *Customer Engagement*: Chatbots are useful tools to support online purchase decision-making, assisting customers during the (pre)purchase and after-sales support in both sectors. Particularly, perceived usefulness and rewarding interactions are associated with customer engagement with chatbots, which might positively affect re-purchase intentions (O'Brien et al., 2018).
- *24/7 Availability*: Both industries benefit from chatbots' constant availability, ensuring that customers can access assistance at any time (Buhalis & Law, 2008).
- *Personalization:* Chatbots in both sectors provide a degree of personalization, enhancing customer journey by recommending services, products, or offers based on previous interactions and customer preferences (Liu et al., 2020).
- *Efficiency and Cost Reduction*: By automating routine queries and tasks, chatbots reduce operational costs, improve staff efficiency, and help businesses scale (Gnewuch et al., 2017).

4.2 Key Differences

- *Nature of Interaction*: In hospitality, chatbots must offer a more personal, human-like experience, often dealing with nuanced requests related to travel or accommodation. In contrast, e-commerce chatbots focus primarily on product discovery and transactional assistance (Chung et al., 2020).
- *Customer Expectations*: Guests in hospitality may have a greater expectation for emotional intelligence and personalized service, while e-commerce customers generally seek quick, transactional interactions (Liu et al., 2020).
- *Technological Integration*: The integration challenges vary between sectors. In hospitality, chatbots must connect with booking systems, CRM, and operational tools. In e-commerce, chatbots need to interact with inventory systems, payment gateways, and customer databases (Huang & Rust, 2021).
- *Product/Service Category*: Chatbots are particularly well-suited for consumers seeking information about products or services where interactive engagement is not required, such as search-oriented rather than hedonic products. However, researchers emphasize that this finding should not be interpreted as a reason for managers to abandon chatbot deployment. Instead, chatbots should be strategically integrated as communication tools for consumers seeking straightforward, task-oriented responses, such as service support, providing prompt and efficient answers to customer queries (Moriuchi et al., 2021).

5 Conclusions

The deployment of AI-powered shopping assistance chatbots in both the hospitality and e-commerce sectors has revolutionized customer service. Although these sectors have distinct needs, the common thread of enhancing customer experience through automation, personalization, and efficiency is clear. While both industries face challenges in terms of chatbot integration, customer trust, and contextual understanding, the future of AI in customer service looks promising. As AI technologies continue to evolve, we can expect chatbots to become even more sophisticated, bridging the gap between human-like interaction and automated efficiency, ultimately leading to improved customer satisfaction and loyalty.

The use of technology currently influences consumers at various stages of their buying journey, beginning with increased awareness of a company, evaluating available products and services, comparing features and prices across competitors, and ultimately making (re-)purchase decisions. Faggella (2018) notes that companies have adopted chatbots to address challenges such as managing high volumes of customer inquiries and facilitating the purchasing process for consumers. These insights underscore the primary role of chatbots in enabling users to access information in a manner that simulates human-to-consumer interactions throughout the decision-making process (Faggella, 2018). Consequently, chatbots are often employed as information-gathering tools, functioning similarly to personal assistants, assisting customers in obtaining product and service information, as well as comparing prices efficiently.

This chapter provides several contributions for the hospitality and e-commerce organizations to move towards the digital transformation of their processes and functionalities through the integration of AI chatbots in service automation.

A major contribution underscores the larger benefits and advantages of AI chatbots for both organizations and customers, overcoming the disadvantages examined. Advantages and similarities between the hospitality and e-commerce sectors emphasize the role of chatbots in availability and enhanced efficiency, operational cost reduction, conversations with users, personalization at scale, and improved customer satisfaction. However, personalization features and conversations with chatbots entail several concerns and limitations for users.

Another important contribution stresses several challenges and actionable strategies for companies, concerning the different nature of product or service (e.g., hedonic vs. search products) and identified risks and limitations between customers and chatbots of interactions. Chatbots as mimicry agents lack meaningful conversational sequence, negotiation skills, and empathy which limit their full capacity of salespeople replacement, suggesting that chatbots assistance is more frequent in less complex and less risky customers' buying decisions.

This has practical implications for managers or developers. Key challenges include:

- Ensuring data privacy, maintaining security protocols guaranteeing keeping sensitive data and private information safe and protected from unauthorized access.
- Algorithm transparency addressing ethical concerns, AI agents design with human-like characteristics (such as, meaningful conversations and negotiation capabilities).
- Guaranteeing human oversight and decision control over autonomous AI agents and interpreting complex AI technologies for actionable business use.

To address these risks and threats, organizations face the challenge of balancing the efficiency and effectiveness of AI-powered assistance chatbots with the need to strengthen interactions and relationships with customers, which should remain central to their value proposition. Consequently, it is essential to understand how customers engage with these applications and to assess the effects of such interactions on perceptions of trustworthiness, usefulness, and engagement, given that AI-powered assistance chatbots are increasingly integral to the service infrastructure of contemporary organizations.

6 Limitations and Further Research Challenges

Despite the growing integration of AI-powered shopping assistance chatbots in the hospitality and e-commerce sectors, several limitations remain that constrain their full potential and deserve further academic exploration.

One significant limitation is the limited understanding of emotional dynamics in human-chatbot interactions. While much research has focused on functional efficiency and task automation, the emotional engagement and affective responses of users during interactions with AI agents are often overlooked. Yet, the role of emotions is a critical component of consumer experience and decision-making, particularly in service contexts where perceived empathy and trust strongly influence satisfaction and brand attachment (Moriuchi et al., 2021).

Additionally, there is a scarcity of behavioural data on how consumers form attitudes towards and engage with AI-powered chatbots across different cultural and demographic segments. Noticeably, little is known about consumers' behaviour, e.g., attitude and engagement with emerging technologies that incorporate robot technology mimicking human-like communication in a retail ambient intelligence (Kamei et al., 2010; Moriuchi et al., 2021).

Consumer technology readiness, as well, is a pivotal research challenge, as trust and perceived usefulness are not universal and may vary significantly depending on age, digital literacy, and cultural background (Kamei et al., 2010). These variations can affect adoption rates and satisfaction, suggesting a need for comparative cross-cultural studies.

Another research challenge lies in the design of service processes that integrate AI-based interfaces. The increasing use of virtual assistants introduces new paradigms in service design, where interactions between customers and chatbots substitute or complement human frontline staff. This shift raises questions about how such interactions affect perceived service quality, customer satisfaction, and behavioural intentions, including loyalty and re-purchase (Fließ & Kleinaltenkamp, 2004; Wakefield & Blodgett, 2016; Cronin et al., 2000). Furthermore, as chatbot technology evolves, designing adaptive and context-aware AI systems capable of understanding complex or nuanced consumer needs will be essential.

Finally, further research should also examine the ethical and privacy implications of increasingly personalized and data-driven AI applications. As chatbots collect and process large volumes of personal data to offer tailored experiences, concerns about data protection, algorithmic bias, and transparency become more pressing. Studies could explore consumer perceptions of algorithmic decision-making and the balance between personalization and privacy sacrifices.

In conclusion, to fully harness the benefits of AI chatbots in enhancing customer experience, future research must take an interdisciplinary approach that incorporates technological, behavioural, emotional, ethical, and cultural dimensions. This would support the development of more inclusive, trustworthy, and emotionally intelligent AI systems tailored to the diverse expectations of global consumers.

References

Al-Hyari, K., Alnsour, M., Alnazer, M., & Masadeh, R. (2023a). The impact of artificial intelligence on hotel performance: Evidence from Jordanian hotels. *International Journal of Contemporary Hospitality Management, 35*(2), 489–506. https://doi.org/10.1108/IJCHM-10-2022-1234

Al-Hyari, K., Alrawadieh, Z., & Al-Refae, A. (2023b). Exploring the impact of AI-based chatbots on guest satisfaction in the hotel industry. *International Journal of Hospitality Management, 98*, 103034. https://doi.org/10.1016/j.ijhm.2022.103034

Al-Hyari, K., Alshurideh, M., Kurdi, B. A., Al Shboul, M., & Salloum, S. A. (2023). The adoption of AI-based chatbots in marketing: A systematic review. *Journal of Theoretical and Applied Electronic Commerce Research, 18*(1), 1–17. https://doi.org/10.3390/jtaer18010001

Ameen, N., Tarhini, A., Reppel, A., & Anand, A. (2021). Customer experiences in the age of artificial intelligence. *Computers in Human Behaviour, 114*, 106548. https://doi.org/10.1016/j.chb.2020.106548

Anica-Popa, I., Anica-Popa, L., Rădulescu, C., & Vrînceanu, M. (2021). The integration of artificial intelligence in retail: Benefits, challenges and a dedicated conceptual framework. *Amfiteatru Economic, 23*(56), 122–122. https://doi.org/10.24818/EA/2021/56/120

Araujo, T. (2018). Living up to the chatbot hype: The influence of anthropomorphic design cues and communicative agency framing on conversational agent and company perceptions. *Computers in Human Behaviour, 85*, 183–189. https://doi.org/10.1016/j.chb.2018.03.051

Balakrishnan, J., Griffiths, M. D., & Raj, R. (2022). AI in service interactions: Exploring customer engagement, experience, and trust. *Journal of Retailing and Consumer Services, 65*, 102890. https://doi.org/10.1016/j.jretconser.2021.102890

Bhaskar, A., & Sharma, P. (2022a). The role of artificial intelligence in the hospitality industry: A comprehensive review. *Journal of Hospitality and Tourism Technology, 13*(2), 189–208. https://doi.org/10.1108/JHTT-11-2021-0238

Bhaskar, M. U., & Sharma, A. (2022b). AI-powered marketing strategies for consumer engagement. *International Journal of Marketing Studies, 14*(2), 45–56. https://doi.org/10.5539/ijms.v14n2p45

Bolton, R. N., McColl-Kennedy, J. R., Cheung, L., Gallan, A., Orsingher, C., Witell, L., & Zaki, M. (2018). Customer experience challenges: Bringing together digital, physical and social realms. *Journal of Service Management, 29*(5), 776–808. https://doi.org/10.1108/JOSM-04-2018-0113

Bradlow, E. T., Gangwar, M., Kopalle, P., & Voleti, S. (2017). The role of big data and predictive analytics in retailing. *Journal of Retailing, 93*(1), 79–95. https://doi.org/10.1016/J.JRETAI.2016.12.004

Brougham, D., & Haar, J. (2018). Smart technology, artificial intelligence, robotics and algorithms (STARA): Employees' perceptions of our future workplace. *Journal of Management & Organization, 24*(2), 239–257.

Buhalis, D., & Law, R. (2008). Progress in information technology and tourism management: 20 years on and 10 years after the internet–the state of eTourism research. *Tourism Management, 29*(4), 609–623.

Carter, M., & Knol, A. (2019). Chatbots and the future of customer service. *Journal of Information Systems Applied Research, 12*(1), 1–10.

Chang, J. Y. S., Cheah, J. H., Lim, X. J., & Morrison, A. M. (2023). One pie, many recipes: The role of artificial intelligence chatbots in influencing Malaysian solo traveler purchase intentions. *Tourism Management Perspectives, 49*, 101191. https://doi.org/10.1016/j.tmp.2023.101191

Chung, S., Ko, E., & Choi, S. (2020). A study of AI-based chatbot applications in the e-commerce industry. *Journal of Retailing and Consumer Services, 55*, 102081.

Cook, D. P., Goh, C. H., & Chung, C. H. (1999). Service typologies: A state of the art survey. *Production and Operations Management, 8*(3), 318–338. https://doi.org/10.1111/j.1937-5956

Cowan, K. G., Vines, J., & Bennett, K. (2020). Exploring the role of AI chatbots in the hospitality industry: A systematic review. *Journal of Hospitality & Tourism Technology, 11*(1), 89–101.

Cronin, J. J., Jr., Brady, M. K., & Hult, G. T. M. (2000). Assessing the effects of quality, value, and customer satisfaction on consumer behavioural intentions in service environments. *Journal of Retailing, 76*(2), 193–218. https://doi.org/10.1016/S0022-4359(00)00028-2

Dwivedi, Y. K., Hughes, L., Ismagilova, E., Aarts, G., Coombs, C., Crick, T., Duan, Y., Dwivedi, R., Edwards, J., Eirug, A., Galanos, V., Ilavarasan, P. V., Janssen, M., Jones, P., Kar, A. K., Kizgin, H., Kronemann, B., Lal, B., Lucini, B., et al. (2021). Artificial intelligence (AI): Multidisciplinary perspectives on emerging challenges, opportunities, and agenda for research, practice and policy. *International Journal of Information Management, 57*, 101994. https://doi.org/10.1016/j.ijinfomgt.2019.08.002

Dyshkantiuk, S., Shyshkina, M., & Kravchenko, T. (2020). Intelligent chatbots in the digital economy: Tools and perspectives. *CEUR Workshop Proceedings, 2732*, 55–62.

Faggella, D. (2018). How companies are using chatbots for marketing: Use cases and inspirations. *Communications of the ACM*, 209475. https://martechtoday.com/how-companies-are-chatbots-marketing

Fan, H., Han, B., & Wang, W. (2023). Aligning (in) congruent Chatbot–employee empathic responses with service-recovery contexts for customer retention. *Journal of Travel Research, 63*(8), 1870–1893.

Faria, R. M. E. S., Torres, A. I., & Beirão, G. (2023). Trustworthy artificial intelligence and machine learning: Implications on users' security and privacy perceptions. In P. Pires, J. D. Santos, & I. V. Pereira (Eds.), *Confronting security and privacy challenges in digital marketing* (pp. 73–94). IGI Global. https://doi.org/10.4018/978-1-6684-8958-1.ch004

Ferrara, E., Varol, O., Davis, C., Menczer, F., & Flammini, A. (2016). The rise of social bots. *Communications of the ACM, 59* (7), 96–104. https://doi.org/10.1145/2818717

Fließ, S., & Kleinaltenkamp, M. (2004). Blueprinting the service company: Managing service processes efficiently. *Journal of Business Research, 57*(4), 392–404. https://doi.org/10.1016/S0148-2963(02)00273-4

Frank, M. R., Autor, D., Bessen, J. E., Brynjolfsson, E., Cebrian, M., Deming, D. J., Feldman, M., Groh, M., Lobo, J., Moro, E., Wang, D., Youn, H., & Rahwan, I. (2019). Toward understanding the impact of artificial intelligence on labor. *Proceedings of the National Academy of Sciences of the United States of America, 116*(14), 6531–6539. https://doi.org/10.1073/PNAS.1900949116/SUPPL_FILE/PNAS.1900949116.SAPP.PDF

Gnewuch, U., Morana, S., & Maedche, A. (2017). Designing chatbots for customer service: A framework and its application. *Proceedings of the International Conference on Information Systems* (ICIS 2017).

Gretzel, U., Koo, C., & Lee, S. (2015). A case study on the use of social media for customer service in tourism and hospitality. *Journal of Travel Research, 54*(6), 753–762.

Gunawan, H., Purwandari, B., & Setyohadi, D. B. (2020). User satisfaction in chatbot implementation in e-commerce. *Procedia Computer Science, 161*, 1040–1047.

Gursoy, D., Chi, C. G., Lu, L., & Nunkoo, R. (2019). Consumers' acceptance of artificially intelligent (AI) device use in service delivery. *International Journal of Information Management, 49*, 157–169. https://doi.org/10.1016/j.ijinfomgt.2019.03.008

Heurix, J., Zimmermann, P., Neubauer, T., & Fenz, S. (2015). A taxonomy for privacy enhancing technologies. *Computers and Security, 53*, 1–17. https://doi.org/10.1016/J.COSE.2015.05.002

Ho, R. C. (2021). Chatbot for online customer service: Customer engagement in the era of artificial intelligence. In *Impact of globalization and advanced technologies on online business models* (pp. 16–31). IGI Global. https://doi.org/10.4018/978-1-7998-7603-8.ch002

Holzwarth, M., Janiszewski, C., & Neumann, M. M. (2006). The influence of avatars on online consumer shopping behaviour. *Journal of Marketing, 70*(4), 19–36. https://doi.org/10.1509/jmkg.70.4.019

Huang, M.-H., & Rust, R. T. (2021). Artificial intelligence in service. *Journal of Service Research, 24*(1), 3–27. https://doi.org/10.1177/1094670520902266

Ivanov, S. (2019). *Robots, artificial intelligence and service automation in travel, tourism and hospitality*. Emerald Publishing.

Ivanov, S., Webster, C., & Berezina, K. (2017). Adoption of robots and service automation by tourism and hospitality companies. *Revista Turismo & Desenvolvimento, 27*(28), 1501–1517.

Kacar, V. (2023). Artificial intelligence applications in hospitality: Opportunities and challenges. In *proceedings of the international conference on tourism and hospitality research* (pp. 22–33).

Kaczorowska-Spychalska, D. (2019). How chatbots influence marketing. *Management, 23*(1), 251–270. https://doi.org/10.2478/manment-2019-0015

Kamei, K., Shinozawa, K., Ikeda, T., Utsumi, A., Miyashita, T., & Hagita, N. (2010, November). Recommendation from robots in a real-world retail shop. In *International conference on multimodal interfaces and the workshop on machine learning for multimodal interaction* (pp. 1–8). https://doi.org/10.1145/1891903.1891929

Kuo, Y. F., Chen, L. C., & Tseng, H. H. (2020). The application of chatbots in the hospitality industry: A review. *Journal of Hospitality and Tourism Technology, 11*(2), 123–137.

Lau, J., Zimmerman, B., & Schaub, F. (2018). Alexa, are you listening? Privacy perceptions, concerns and privacy-seeking behaviors with smart speakers. *Proceedings of the ACM on Human-Computer Interaction, 2*(CSCW), 1–31. https://doi.org/10.1145/3274371

Lester, J., Branting, K., & Mott, B. (2004). Conversational agents. In *The practical handbook of internet computing* (pp. 220–240). Chapman & Hall.

Lie, W., Beldona, S., & Chi, C. G.-Q. (2019). How AI affects hotel employees' perceptions of job security and work attitudes. *International Journal of Hospitality Management, 78*, 65–73.

Lin, H., Chi, O. H., Zhang, H., & Chen, Y. (2020). Understanding the impact of AI service robots on hotel employees' work: A mixed-method approach. *International Journal of Hospitality Management, 91*, 102664. https://doi.org/10.1016/j.ijhm.2020.102664

Ling, L., Chia, W., & Teo, J. (2023). Chatbots in e-commerce: Enhancing customer experience with AI. *Journal of Retailing and Consumer Services, 74*, 103401.

Liu, S., Li, J., & Zhang, W. (2020). E-commerce chatbot applications in the retail industry. *Computers in Industry, 123*, 103292.

López, D., Romero, M., & González, M. (2021). Chatbots in the tourism industry: A customer service perspective. *Tourism Management Perspectives, 39*, 100808.

Loureiro, S. M. C., Ali, F., & Ali, M. (2024). Symmetric and asymmetric modeling to understand drivers and consequences of hotel chatbot engagement. *International Journal of Human-Computer Interaction, 40*(3), 782–794. https://doi.org/10.1080/10447318.2022.2124346

Manyakin, D. (2023). AI solutions for smart hospitality: From concept to implementation. *Journal of Tourism Futures*. Advance online publication. doi:https://doi.org/10.1108/JTF-05-2023-0067

Melián-González, S., Bulchand-Gidumal, J., & López-Valcárcel, B. G. (2021). Artificial intelligence in hotels: Understanding technology acceptance. *Journal of Hospitality and Tourism Technology, 12*(1), 65–81. https://doi.org/10.1108/JHTT-08-2019-0106

Meng, W., Leung, R., & Law, R. (2023). Chatbots in the hospitality industry: A review and research agenda. *Journal of Hospitality Marketing & Management, 32*(2), 135–156.

Moriuchi, E., Landers, V. M., Colton, D., & Hair, N. (2021). Engagement with chatbots versus augmented reality interactive technology in e-commerce. *Journal of Strategic Marketing, 29*(5), 375–389. https://doi.org/10.1080/0965254X.2020.1740766

Morosan, C., & Bowen, J. T. (2018). Cultural influences on consumer behaviour in the hospitality industry: A review of the literature. *Journal of Hospitality and Tourism Research, 42*(6), 951–973. https://doi.org/10.1177/1096348017711195

Mostafa, R. B., & Kasamani, T. (2022). Antecedents and consequences of chatbot initial trust. *European Journal of Marketing, 56*(6), 1748–1771. https://doi.org/10.1108/EJM-02-2020-0084

Neuhofer, B., Buhalis, D., & Ladkin, A. (2015). Smart hospitality—Interactions between customers and technology. *Journal of Hospitality and Tourism Technology, 6*(1), 38–47.

Nguyen, T. M., & Malik, A. (2022). Impact of knowledge sharing on employees' service quality: The moderating role of artificial intelligence. *International Marketing Review, 39*(3), 482–508.

O'Brien, H. L., Cairns, P., & Hall, M. (2018). A practical approach to measuring user engagement with the refined user engagement scale (UES) and new UES short form. *International Journal of Human-Computer Studies, 112*, 28–39. https://doi.org/10.1016/j.ijhcs.2018.01.004

Prentice, C., Wang, X., & Loureiro, S. M. C. (2020a). The influence of artificial intelligence and employee service on customer experience: A comparative study of luxury and economy hotels. *Journal of Retailing and Consumer Services, 57*, 102304. https://doi.org/10.1016/j.jretconser.2020.102304

Prentice, C., Wang, X., & Loureiro, S. M. C. (2020b). The influence of artificial intelligence and employee service on customer experience: Implications for hospitality service. *International Journal of Hospitality Management, 91*, 102431. https://doi.org/10.1016/j.ijhm.2020.102431

Qiu, H., Li, M., Shu, H., & Bai, B. (2022). Enhancing hotel service experience with AI: Roles of memory assistance and emotional intelligence. *International Journal of Hospitality Management, 102*, 103156. https://doi.org/10.1016/j.ijhm.2022.103156

Rahman, M. M., Al Mamun, A., & Mohiuddin, M. (2018). AI-based service innovation and consumer experience. *Journal of Innovation & Knowledge, 3*(3), 125–130.

Raji, I. D., Binns, R., Shmitchell, M., Gebru, T., Mitchell, M., & Wilson, C. (2020). Saving face: Investigating the ethical concerns of facial recognition auditing. In *Proceedings of the 2020 conference on fairness, accountability, and transparency (FAT20)* (pp. 145–155). https://doi.org/10.1145/3351095.3372873

Rosenthal, V. (2017). *Forbes: Chatbot engagement: 6 tips and tricks for growth.* https://www.forbes.com/sites/vivianrosenthal/2017/07/07/chatbot-engagement-six-tips-and-tricks-for-growth/#26edbce37673

Sam, M. F. M., & Jasim, S. (2023a). The impact of chatbot services on online customer experience. *International Journal of Human–Computer Interaction, 39*(2), 210–223.

Sam, S. J. I., & Jasim, K. M. (2023b). Diving into technology: A systematic literature review on strategic use of chatbots in hospitality service encounters. *Management Review Quarterly, 75*, 1–29.

Shi, S., Gong, Y., & Gursoy, D. (2021). Antecedents of trust and adoption intention toward artificially intelligent recommendation systems in travel planning: A heuristic–systematic model. *Journal of Travel Research, 60*(8), 1714–1734. https://doi.org/10.1177/0047287520966395

Sivaramakrishnan, S., Wan, F., & Tang, Z. (2007). Giving an "e-human touch" to e-tailing: The moderating roles of static information quantity and consumption motive in the effectiveness of an anthropomorphic information agent. *Journal of Interactive Marketing, 21*(1), 60–75. https://doi.org/10.1002/dir.20075

We Are Social. (2025). https://datareportal.com

Syam, N., & Sharma, A. (2018). Waiting for a sales renaissance in the fourth industrial revolution: Machine learning and artificial intelligence in sales research and practice. *Industrial Marketing Management, 69*, 135–146. https://doi.org/10.1016/J.INDMARMAN.2017.12.019

Tong-On, P., Tuntirattanasoontorn, W., & Suanpong, K. (2021). AI adoption in hotel service innovation: A case study in Thailand. *Journal of Tourism, Heritage & Services Marketing, 7*(2), 13–20. https://doi.org/10.5281/zenodo.4739525

Torres, A. I., & Delgado, C. J. (2023). Assessing customer interactions with Chatbots in online shopping experiences: An empirical study. In J. D. Santos & B. Sousa (Eds.), *Promoting organizational performance through 5G and agile marketing* (pp. 203–223). IGI Global Scientific Publishing. https://doi.org/10.4018/978-1-6684-5523-4

Tussyadiah, I. P., & Miller, G. (2019). Incorporating ethics into the adoption of artificial intelligence in hospitality and tourism. *Journal of Hospitality and Tourism Technology, 10*(4), 689–703. https://doi.org/10.1108/JHTT-10-2018-0105

Tussyadiah, I. P., & Park, S. (2018). Online review behaviour and hotel booking: Implications for hospitality and tourism marketing. *Tourism Management, 69*, 244–259.

Tuzovic, S., & Paluch, S. (2018). Conversational commerce—A new era for service business development? In *Service business development* (pp. 81–100). Springer Gabler.

Um, T., Kim, S. J., & Lee, H. (2020). Exploring the role of chatbots in online retail: Value creation and customer engagement. *Journal of Business Research, 116*, 263–274. https://doi.org/10.1016/j.jbusres.2020.05.036

van Esch, P., Cui, Y. G., Das, G., Jain, S. P., & Wirtz, J. (2022). Tourists and AI: A political ideology perspective. *Annals of Tourism Research, 97*, 103471. https://doi.org/10.1016/j.annals.2022.103471

Waghmare, C. (2019). Business benefits of using chatbots. In *Introducing azure bot service* (pp. 147–165). Apress. https://doi.org/10.1007/978-1-4842-4888-1_6

Wakefield, K. L., & Blodgett, J. (2016). Retrospective: The importance of servicescapes in leisure service settings. *Journal of Services Marketing, 30*(7), 686–691. https://doi.org/10.1108/JSM-08-2016-0291

Wirth, N. (2018). Hello marketing, what can artificial intelligence help you with? *International Journal of Market Research, 60*(5), 435–438. https://doi.org/10.1177/1470785318776841

Xiao, L., & Kumar, V. (2021). Robotics for customer service: A useful complement or an ultimate substitute? *Journal of Service Research, 24*(1), 9–29. https://doi.org/10.1177/1094670519878881

Zhang, X., & Jin, H. (2023). How does smart technology, artificial intelligence, automation, robotics, and algorithms (STAARA) awareness affect hotel employees' career perceptions? A disruptive innovation theory perspective. *Journal of Hospitality Marketing & Management, 32*(2), 264–283.

The manufacturer's authorised representative in the EU is Springer Nature Customer Service Centre GmbH, Europaplatz 3, 69115 Heidelberg, Germany. If you have any concerns regarding our products, please contact ProductSafety@springernature.com

Printed and bound by CPI Group (UK) Ltd, Croydon, CR0 4YY
05/10/2026
02228023-0009